Sayyid Qutb

Sayyid Qutb

The Life and Legacy of a Radical Islamic Intellectual

JAMES TOTH

OXFORD
UNIVERSITY PRESS

OXFORD
UNIVERSITY PRESS

Oxford University Press is a department of the University of Oxford.
It furthers the University's objective of excellence in research, scholarship,
and education by publishing worldwide.

Oxford   New York
Auckland   Cape Town   Dar es Salaam   Hong Kong   Karachi
Kuala Lumpur   Madrid   Melbourne   Mexico City   Nairobi
New Delhi   Shanghai   Taipei   Toronto

With offices in
Argentina   Austria   Brazil   Chile   Czech Republic   France   Greece
Guatemala   Hungary   Italy   Japan   Poland   Portugal   Singapore
South Korea   Switzerland   Thailand   Turkey   Ukraine   Vietnam

Oxford is a registered trademark of Oxford University Press in the UK
and certain other countries.

Published in the United States of America by
Oxford University Press
198 Madison Avenue, New York, NY 10016

Library of Congress Cataloging-in-Publication Data
Toth, James.
Sayyid Qutb : the life and legacy of a radical Islamic intellectual / James Toth.
p. cm.
Includes bibliographical references and index.
ISBN 978–0–19–979088–3 (hardcover : alk. paper)
1. Qutb, Sayyid, 1906–1966.   2. Muslim scholars—Egypt—Biography.   I. Title.
BP80.Q86T68 2013
320.55′7092—dc23
2012022797

ISBN 978–0–19–979088–3

1 3 5 7 9 8 6 4 2
Printed in the United States of America
on acid-free paper

The Muslim Brotherhood is a huge structure, but it lacks a deep comprehensive and genuine theoretical basis. Hasan al-Banna realized this, and he always intended to build the theory and leave it to mature. He believed the work should be implemented in phases. But he did not live to fulfill this mission. He was assassinated too soon.

—Gamal al-Banna[1]

1. Sahar al-Bahr. "A Lifetime of Islamic Call"—An Interview with Gamal al-Banna. *Al-Ahram Weekly*. No. 941. 2–9 April 2009.

CONTENTS

ACKNOWLEDGMENTS

This book grew out of the anthropological field work I conducted in the 1990s in southern Egypt, but it has moved several stages beyond just basic ethnography. Following discussions with the late Dr. Richard Antoun who was studying Islamic fundamentalism in Jordan, I decided that it was not enough to represent the ideas and ideology of Egyptian activists grounded in ordinary but incomplete inform-ant statements. A visit to any college library all too easily revealed the large num-ber of shelves with books dedicated solely to this and related topics. Informant statements were not enough, nor were they necessarily accurate. Yet working from their suggestions, I went ahead and began to explore what I was to call "the Grandfathers of Islamism"—Jamal al-Din al-Afghani, Muhammad 'Abduh, Rashid Rida, Hasan al-Banna, and Sayyid Qutb, linking contemporary sensibilities to the work of teachers and thinkers of earlier generations. The small chapter on Sayyid Qutb grew into the present book.

I am grateful to the community in Upper Egypt with whom I lived for sev-eral years in the 1980s and who fostered and sustained my interest in the social roots of Islamic activism throughout the 1990s and up to the present day. Some of the first religious writings I read were those I noticed on their shelves or picked up from references in their conversations. A teaching position at the American University in Cairo allowed me continuous close contact with Egyptian society and its concerns for six years. I thank all my colleagues in the Department of Sociology-Anthropology for their fruitful discussions. More recently, I am grate-ful to the Center for Arabic Studies Abroad (CASA) program which provided a fel-lowship and time to spend reading relevant texts with religious experts in Cairo.

Along the way, numerous people generously and graciously gave me their time, effort, and intellectual acumen. My wife, Virginia Danielson, was foremost among these, tolerating good temperament and bad over a long period of time. I am for-ever grateful and appreciative of her patience and love.

I also want to thank Soraya Altorki, the late Dr. Richard Antoun, Manal Badawy, Asef Bayat, Marilyn Booth, AbdAllah Donald Cole, Juan Cole, Kenneth Cuno, Samer El-Karanshawy, Joel Gordon, William Granara, Nicholas Hopkins,

Peter Machinist, Roger Owen, Ahmad Ramzi, Everett Rowson, Ted Swedenburg, and Asmaa Waguih.

Finally, I wish to thank the people at Oxford University Press, including the three anonymous reviewers who provided insightful feedback and excellent suggestions about the draft manuscripts; my editor, Theo Calderara, for his patience and diligence about my many questions and concerns, Jashnie Jabson who so imperturbably saw this project through to production, and Patterson Lamb who so carefully and painstakingly copy edited the manuscript.

I hope that the results of their advice and counsel will prove rewarding and engaging.

PART ONE

HIS LIFE

1

Introduction

Sayyid Qutb was one of the most radical Islamic thinkers of the 20th century. He endures in the public imagination as the architect of the mind-set that inspired the September 11, 2001, hijackers—or as Paul Berman scathingly called him "The Philosopher of Islamic Terror."[1]

Popular portraits of Sayyid Qutb describe him in dark, negative, and uncomplicated terms. Berman's iconic article in the *New York Times Magazine* is arguably the best known.[2] Berman characterizes Qutb variously as Hitler (his essay reinforced by the portrait on the magazine cover of Qutb wearing his toothbrush mustache); as pathological, paranoid, medieval (or ancient), unreasonable, erratic, misogynistic, offensively anti-Semitic, anti-Christian, anti-secular/modern/Enlightenment; and—perhaps the most profound and complete statement of the enigmatic, occult, delusional, obscure, totalitarian, absolutist, and barbaric—as a believing and practicing Islamic fundamentalist. Berman employs the conventional Orientalist repertoire of tropes and expressions to guide his reader away from not only sympathizing with Qutb but from understanding him at all.[3] Instead, Qutb becomes a token or a flag against whom American forces on both the right and the left can rally. Moreover, Qutb, like other depictions of terrorists, seems completely fixated on those enemies lying outside the gate and totally consumed by hatred for the West. Berman underscores the point that Qutb is obsessed with a medieval loathing of Western secularism, Western freedom, Western women, and Jews. This iron-clad xenophobia and misogyny then makes it easy for Berman and readers alike to cavalierly ignore the chaotic disorder and confusion of complicated domestic politics, of intricate and methodical religious reasoning, and of genuine and historical grievances against imperialism. These complexities, instead, are handled by reduction, simplification, exaggeration, caricature, ad hominem attacks, and judgments of Western superiority, so that any serious, profound, and legitimate ideas are either discounted or dismissed.[4]

Writers like Berman—the late Christopher Hitchens is another journalist who comes to mind—undoubtedly see themselves as liberal, modern, secular, and progressive.[5] But they are also patriotic. For them and other members of the media, the encounter between justice and fairness on the one hand and national sympathy and duty on the other frequently results in a patriotic bias with national interest and allegiance trumping evenhandedness and open-mindedness.[6] But as a scholar, my goals are different. I endeavor to find what is worthwhile in the ideas of a man of Qutb's stature and influence, determine their impact, give him a fair and balanced assessment, regard him like other ideologues who inspire revolutions (however unpopular they may be), and explain what may appear unintelligible so as to correct any scholarly prejudices, particularly those Orientalist-fueled distortions and absurdities so often attributed to Middle Easterners. There is absolutely no other way of coming to grips with Sayyid Qutb's beliefs and biography than to present them as reasoned, credible, and committed. Thus this book aspires to make intellectual, political, and sociological sense of Sayyid Qutb and to comprehend the development of his ideas throughout his lifetime and afterward.

For despite his one-dimensional reputation as the diabolical genius behind terrorism—which I prefer, in any event, to call "Islamic militancy"—Sayyid Qutb was a much more complicated figure than the monochromatic portrayals of so many post-9/11 writers would have us believe. This complexity was built up over the course of years on a journey that paralleled the growth of modern Egypt, a modernity that Qutb grew to despise.

Qutb was alternately a novelist, a poet, and a literary critic. He was a teacher and a school supervisor, but at one point had serious aspirations to become the government minister of education. He was deliberately an independent Islamist and yet eventually became a member of the Muslim Brotherhood, Egypt's premier Islamic organization. He was the director of propaganda for the Brotherhood, yet claimed upon his arrest that he was not involved at all in its militant Secret Apparatus. He was also a gradual reformer, a destructive militant, a liberation theologian, and a social democrat. He counseled caution and education to resolve society's ills, yet he inflamed people's passions with his talk of a violent holy war. He was angry and outspoken against the system, but he was also apologetic and obsequious toward those in power. He was strong-willed but also sickly. He loved his parents and siblings, yet he remained a loner throughout his life. He escaped rural Egypt and "went modern" in Cairo but later recanted and "went Islamist" instead.[7] He saw the roots of Egypt's evil as planted solidly in the influence and imperialism of the West—Europe, Russia, America—but he saved his most toxic hostility and animosity for those of his fellow countrymen who mimicked this foreign lifestyle and culture. He embraced a traditional Islam, but at the same time, he attacked the 'ulama scholars, the keepers of Islamic tradition. He called for a new and fresh interpretation of Islamic law, but one that echoed the very first generation of the faithful.

It is easy to say that Qutb was contradictory and that he did not develop a "self-contained" worldview that scholars such as Nadav Safran once expected and demanded of Egyptian intellectuals.[8] Qutb never authored a single all-encompassing text that precisely defined his entire vision. His books and journal articles reflected his opinions and views at the time and, as the times changed, so, too, did he. It is not that he was contradictory or inconsistent—indeed, no man is completely without paradoxes—it is that he charged full speed ahead and did not seem to worry about incongruities and incompatibilities. Politically, he was active and engaged, starting off in one direction—a modern, secular one— and ending by adopting an Islamist perspective that would rival and ultimately displace his earlier ideas. He was never so renowned or glorified that he had the luxury—or the freedom—of sitting back and writing the definitive tome that would completely lay bare the Islamic world he envisioned.

Ultimately, he was more a thinker than an activist. He was a spiritual guide, but not an amir, an interpreter, but not a commander.[9] His appearance was undeniably that of a writer and an intellectual, and his delicate frame precluded a malevolent temperament or a domineering superiority. He inspired by word not by deed.

Yvonne Haddad once concluded that Qutb's career can be divided into two parts—the early Qutb of poems and novels, and the mature thinker of Qur'anic exegesis. Yet there hardly seems one specific turning point in his life. Rather, Qutb began as a secular and nationalist political writer, turned to a serious study of the Qur'an, and then slowly moved from a position where Islam merely colored his value system (much like Catholicism shaped the values of Liberation Theology) to increasingly seeing Islam not just as a "religion" in the strict Western sense, but as a harmonious, holistic, totalizing institution and civilization, much like modernity dominates the worldview of many Western and non-Western writers. Beginning as a mainstream liberal thinker, Qutb gradually turned his back on what he saw as the religious, cultural, and intellectual imperialism of the West and adopted, instead, an Islamist position without borrowings, without hesitation, and without apologies.[10]

Indeed, he came to define the Islamist movement in book after book, each a masterpiece of reasoning and explanation, of preaching and persuasion. Qutb "advocated a strong socio-political role for Islam" not just in the Muslim world, but as a universally positive and rational system of thought, belief, and practice.[11] His subtle but repeated stress on the universality of Islam made Islamism a viable rival to Western modernity—which some, including Qutb, viewed as essentially Protestant Christianity enforced through imperialism.[12]

It is difficult to decide which of Qutb's major publications is most representative of his thought. Each has its distinctive characteristics that reflect a particular historical time and appeal to a different audience. His social democratic tome *Social Justice in Islam* (1949) is considered a major contribution to the world of Islamic moderation. His next major book, *In the Shade of the Qur'an* (1954–64) was a remarkable project of Qur'anic exegesis that, however, did not follow the standard formats of traditional Islamic scholarship. Many activists refer to it in their efforts to flesh out and fathom Qutb's complex understanding of his religion. In the West, though, it is his next and last text, the fiery, violent, and vehement *Signposts on the Road* (1964) that reserves his foremost place in the rogues' gallery of Islamist enemies. Yet this volume should be contrasted to *Islam and*

Universal Peace (1951b), which juxtaposes an ordinarily peaceful Islamic society with the extraordinary times of warfare, much as philosophers who write about Just War theory do today.[13] Those pundits who wish to ridicule him often cite Qutb's "Sick Singing" article condemning sensuous lyrics. Those who wish to cloak Qutb's modernism in Islamic clothing might well refer to this first two treatises on Islam, *Artistic Imagery in the Qur'an* (1945a) and *Scenes of Resurrection in the Qur'an* (1947), which came close to repeating the heresies committed by 'Ali 'Abd al-Raziq (in his *Islam and the Foundations of Governance*) in 1924 and Taha Husayn (in his *Pre-Islamic Poetry*) in 1925—of undermining the divinity of the Qur'an. Nothing in his writings could pin him down to the one-dimensional caricature so frequently appearing in the West.

Qutb's emergence as a preeminent scholar and ideologue came during a time of turmoil in Egypt, aggravated by the Great Depression, a variety of corrupt government institutions, continued British occupation, a post–World War II recession and political chaos, the republican revolution in 1952, but also the revolutionary government's harsh consolidation of power. Qutb concluded from these experiences that not only was Egypt in trouble—this was obvious—but that the solution was to reject outside influences and rely instead on its own authentic system. This genuine system was Islam. He developed the many facets of this system over a period of 33 years—from 1933 when he graduated from Dar al-'Ulum to 1966 when he was executed for treason.

Qutb emphasized Islam's social, political, economic, cultural, and intellectual functions—as well as, of course, its religious role—which form an over-arching umbrella that covers all of society much like European society had been blanketed by Catholicism before social life was compartmentalized by the Reformation and the Enlightenment.[14] Qutb saw Islam as a harmonious and integrated system that emanates from both God's oneness and God's dominion. Qutb's goals were to repair the ruptures in society that had resulted in apostasy, alienation, and decadence, and to establish a balanced and cohesive system based on the universal principles of Islam.[15]

He repeatedly emphasized the subjective perspective of Islam instead of viewing Islam scientifically or legalistically. His outlook began by stressing the individual's personal engagement with Islam and then generalizing outward to apply this experience to all members of society, so that he never overlooked the emotional and inspirational factors in his religion. Some, like Olivier Carré, called his outlook "mystical" but I would prefer to call it artistic or aesthetic. Qutb believed that it was the beauty of the Qur'an that made it, and Islam more generally, so appealing to so many. The aesthetic of the Qur'an was a force that could integrate Muslims into a cohesive *umma* and inspire a more passionate devotion.[16] This predilection inexorably shaped Qutb's intellectual style, and it greatly widened his appeal to his audience.

Sayyid Qutb's vision of Islam can be effectively characterized, examined, and analyzed as a powerful social movement. Social movements are defined as coordinated, collective efforts aimed at purposely implementing or resisting social change, often in challenge to, or defiance of, constituted authority. Examples of social movements include the civil rights and anti-war movements in the United States, the Solidarity labor movement in Poland, the women's and ecology movements in Western Europe, the anti-nuclear movement in Great Britain, Liberation Theology throughout Latin America, and Fascism in Germany and Italy. The Islamic movement that Qutb helped shape is one that is attempting to transform and restore Egypt and the Muslim world, which are seen as beset by the calamity, decline, and disintegration caused by modernization.

One major advantage in using a social movement framework is that it allows the investigator to examine the perspective of the participants without in any way judging or evaluating the movement and its goals. Social movement analysis can examine feminist movements, anti-abortion movements, emancipatory, or reactionary movements, all with an impartiality and objectivity that transcend personal value judgments. Apart from the actual objectives and goals of the movement as its members and participants articulate them, analysts can explore how the ideas, ideologies, actions, strategies, and tactics are combined to achieve their intended purposes, whatever these might be. It allows us to appreciate the "art and science" of executing campaigns of social change or resisting social transformation, apart from whether we would ever join them or even agree with them.

Thus a social movement framework structures this narrative and situates Qutb's life and legacy in a way that avoids either ethnocentric judgments and condemnation or apologetic praise of his goals and those of his followers. It abstains from belittling or applauding Qutb's own viewpoint so readers can gain for themselves a full appreciation of his genuine experiences and thinking. It enables me to objectively and analytically examine Qutb's subjective anger and personal revulsion; I can explain Qutb's passion without becoming passionate myself. Because this work is presented in the context of *his* movement, and not ours; in the framework of *his* intentions and goals, and not ours, and in the conditions of *his* own life, *his* own country, and *his* own history, not our culture, not our civilization, not our historical experiences—because of this explicit, definite attempt to couch Qutb in his own terms, I feel that the result, while sympathetic or appreciative instead of hostile and antagonistic, is the only fair and proper way to frame Qutb. This narrative is about his fears and hopes, not ours, even though Qutb himself has been so instrumental in shaping such fear and hope in the West, particularly since 9/11.

There are a number of approaches to examining and analyzing social movements. Charles Tilly's 1978 study of collective action remains the most comprehensive analysis of these frameworks. He identified four general theoretical perspectives: (1) the political economy approach of Karl Marx, (2) the theories of relative deprivation and alienation used by Emile Durkheim, (3) the utilitarian and resource mobilization analysis from John Stuart Mill and Mancur Olson, and (4) the ideological and religious methods of Max Weber. One offshoot of the Weberian approach is to see social movements as attempts to revitalize or rejuvenate societies perceived to be suffering from cultural crises and breakdowns. A charismatic leader emerges, transmits his vision of renewal, organizes close collaborators to achieve that vision, and sets about attaining its goals. Revitalization movements were first identified and described by Anthony F. C. Wallace in his 1956 article in the *American Anthropologist*.[17] Wallace used a more psychological or cognitive approach to the development of the revitalizing vision, emerging from a context of stress, disintegration, breakdown, and social anomie. He then examined the communications of the vision (or ideology; what resource mobilization theorists call "framing"), its organization (assembling disciples, followers, and resources), its adaptation and doctrinal modifications, and finally, the cultural transformation of a community "pulling itself up by its bootstraps."

Wallace examined the Religion of Handsome Lake among the Seneca Indians of 19th-century upper New York state. Since his approach was developed specifically in the context of explaining religious movements, it becomes a particularly appropriate analytical tool with which to explore Sayyid Qutb's Islamism. What I find particularly attractive is how Wallace was able to deal with ideas, beliefs, and faith. He combined a Marxist model of breakdown with Durkheimian concepts of relative deprivation and anomie. But his revitalization approach dwelled on emotive and expressive aspects, which perfectly capture the essence of Sayyid Qutb's campaign and his own subjectivism, while staying away from the austere utilitarianism of resource mobilization. This latter approach views movements as the outcome of cold, hard-hearted calculations and rational decision making, rather than heartfelt commitments, beliefs, and outlooks that often display illogical leaps of faith, contradictions, and inconsistencies.

The diagram shown in Figure 1.1 encapsulates the temporal and social phases of a revitalization movement. What I find important are the participants' views of breakdown, blame, and antagonism, the recruitment of fellow believers, and the tactical means of achieving a new and thriving steady state, although perhaps more a utopia than a reality.

More recently, Martin Riesebrodt employed a similar perspective in his analysis of fundamentalist movements in the United States and Iran.[18] What concerned him was identifying the ideology, the carriers (leaders and rank-and-file participants), and the perceived causes of these social movements. I find his ideas about ideology particularly intriguing, for he parsed it out into examining (1) *a social critique* that embraces the movement's grievances, (2) *a salvation history* that places the movement along a historical trajectory that extends from a mythologized past to a crisis-ridden present and into an eschatological future, and (3) *an ideal order* that focuses on what this future might actually look like. What I find useful here is to identify the participant's grievances (real or imaginary), the hostile forces both within and outside the movement and the society at large, and the goals and propositions of the movement, whether or not I agree

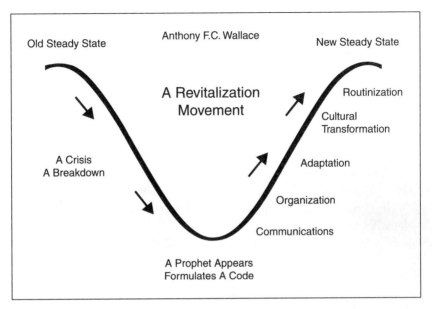

Old Steady State

Anthony F.C. Wallace

New Steady State

A Revitalization
Movement

Routinization

Cultural
Transformation

A Crisis
A Breakdown

Adaptation

Organization

Communications

A Prophet Appears
Formulates A Code

Figure 1.1

with them. These provide three categories that effectively encapsulate the vast majority of the ideas, thoughts, and beliefs in Sayyid Qutb's writings.

Together, these two frameworks for revitalization movements (cultural stress, breakdown, palingenesis, and routinization) and fundamentalist movements (a mythologized past, a crisis-ridden present, and an eschatological future) provide a critical lens through which Sayyid Qutb's ideas and proposals for the Islamist movement can best be examined and understood. Using Qutb's ideas as the framing mechanism for Islam and Islamism—as the leading ideology and guiding principles—helps identify the problem and the solution, the defenders and the villains. This framework describes Sayyid Qutb's notions of where the Muslim world has been, where it should go, and how it ought to get there. It uncovers causes and assigns blame; it fires up the troops to surge ever onward; it basks in its own glow of vain self-righteous piety; it mercilessly destroys its enemies; it stands triumphant as the forces of light overcome the dangers of darkness. It attracts enthusiasts, it trains them, disciplines them, and cheerleads for them in times of doubt. It has its head in a utopian cloud and it has its feet grounded in the muck of mobilizing human and material resources.

The years in and around the middle of the 20th century produced two notable Islamist leaders who had similar visions for revitalizing Egyptian society. Hasan al-Banna was the less prolithic, with his personal skills directed more into organizing the Muslim Brotherhood.[19] Qutb, on the other hand, was the thinker. He became one of the most prominent Islamic intellectuals to carefully construct a social, political, and civilizational understanding of Islam. He was criticized for not following the traditional approach of Islamic exegetes, but his intentions were not passive meanderings in a quiet mosque, but rather, the energetic struggle of a committed campaigner in the midst of battle.

Qutb was personally involved in many of the intellectual, cultural, and political debates of his time, though he is shunned in Western textbooks that review Egyptian intellectual history in favor of a Taha Husayn, Tawfiq al-Hakim, or Muhammad Husayn Haykal because these literati subscribed to a Western perspective while Qutb seriously condemned it.

His intellectual impact was seismic and his legacy was extraordinary. As a key intellectual in the Islamist movement, he and his ideas occupied center stage and became a major target. Earlier activists had appealed to the local elite or else organized religious societies. Qutb's role was the mass diffusion of an Islamist ideology to all parts of society and to many countries well beyond Egypt's borders. He developed a complex and profound model of a true Islamic society, and his writing reflected a number of attempts to systematically flesh out a coherent model from a variety of perspectives—religious, political, economic, historical, cultural, literary, artistic, and philosophical—although he himself would eschew many of these terms for their association with the secular world he came to dislike.

Many examine Sayyid Qutb by reviewing his major publications. Others explore his biography as psychohistory and analyze his ideas over time for clues that can pinpoint just when Qutb "went wrong." Others examine a set of important concepts that Qutb emphasized, such as *jahiliyya*, the antithesis of Islam, *hakimiyya*, or God's total dominion, and *jihad*, the activism or struggle needed to move from the first to the second. This book will use all of these methods in understanding Qutb's critical contribution to the Islamic movement.

However, this is not a biography that just explores personal peculiarities while failing to respect the subject's intellectual achievements. In order to fully appreciate the complexity of both Qutb's life and ideas, this book is divided into two parts. The first part reviews the jagged course of Qutb's life, starting from his boyhood in Musha and then, once in Cairo, going from his modernist years, to his turn toward moderate Islam, and then closing with his radicalization. The second part documents his Islamism and his ideas for revitalizing Egypt and the Muslim world, starting with its current decadence and depravity, and then ending with the utopia of Islam's future political economy and social history.

Qutb is often seen as being more against things than for them. He was against the corruption, depravity, apostasy, and hypocrisy of his fellow Muslims and their government because they senselessly mimicked the inappropriate ways of the West. This sort of ranting and railing is not unusual in a social movement that is attempting to rescue society from collapse and breakdown and move it toward ascendancy and triumph. After all, Qutb's writings must be seen in this social context and not as some dry, ethereal philosophy that is impartial and detached. Qutb was against the international influence and imperialism of the West, its colonialism, its injustice, its physical, cultural, and religious abuse. In this he was and is no different from countless social critics and revolutionaries. Qutb was not necessarily against capitalism, but he did advocate a *softer* or *kinder* capitalism along the lines of social democracy.[20] He was against corrupt government because it had become divided by the plethora of parties gnawing and tearing at each other and at Egypt's delicate social fabric. He was very much against tyranny and injustice, and concluded that any government that does not rule by Islam is ipso facto tyrannical since Islam has built-in safeguards that protect the interests of both the powerful and powerless that non-Islamic governments disregard. He was against gender mingling, public displays of immodesty, and feminism. He was, no question about it, an unabashed adherent of patriarchy. He was also unashamed about promoting Islam as the cure for all of society's ills and as the best doctrine for the entire human race, an arrogant universalism quite analogous to the "White Man's Burden," "Civilizing Mission," and "Manifest Destiny" found in the history of European and American expansion. At the end of his life, in prison, he threw off the apologetics of his earlier years and, indeed, the apologetics of many of his fellow intellectuals, and wrote enthusiastically, sincerely, and unashamedly about the beauty and benefits of Islam, both absolutely and in comparison to any system that humanity had itself designed.

Qutb's profoundly radical ideas have motivated Islamic fundamentalists inside and outside Egypt who have come to dominate the mosques, training camps, and websites that disseminate what those in the West call extremist, anti-modern, and anti-Western Islam but what the fundamentalists (or *salafiyyun*) themselves identify as idealistic, moralistic, emancipatory, revolutionary, and spiritually purifying and rewarding—ironically appearing as Islam's own version of liberation theology.[21] At the same time, Qutb's own personal rebellion aptly illustrates the recurring trajectory of parochial village migrants moving to major metropolitan centers like Cairo who then transform themselves from secularist to moderate to radical Islamist. This makes Islamism a potent ideology for those experiencing the relocation of rural-to-urban migration—not only in Egypt but throughout the Muslim world, and in other regions where rural-to-urban migration takes place, religious fundamentalism more generally emerges as well.[22] Thus, both Qutb's beliefs and biography have made a tremendous impact on the entire Muslim world. This study examines why he has been so significant and why he carries so much weight by seeking to understand the complex meaning of his words and actions, of his ideas and life history.

Qutb's Early and Modern Years

Musha

SAYYID QUTB IBRAHIM HUSAYN SHADHILI was born on October 9, 1906, in the village of Musha in Asyut province of the southern Egyptian Sa'id.[1] Musha was an ordinary farming village, in the shadows of Asyut city, 250 miles (375 km.) south of Cairo, with a not uncommon mix of Muslims and Christians.[2] Qutb's family had five children, but since Sayyid was the oldest, he was pampered for several years. He was also spoiled later by his teachers because of his father's generosity and position in the community. Far from rebelling against his family or community, he experienced a warmth and indulgence that bred two lifelong characteristics: an idealism that underwrote his extensive condemnation of the British and Egyptian governments, and a determination to promote Islamism as an alternative to these secular regimes.[3]

Both Qutb's parents appeared to be modern and secular. But the family fortunes on both sides were slowly ebbing away, dissipated by improvidence and then later by land sales to repay debt obligations. Sayyid's father, who claimed Indian ancestry, was a prominent, but moderate landowner and a member of the 'ayyan, or local village elite. He was politically active in the local branch of Mustafa Kamil's National Party and was a sponsor of the party newspaper al-Liwa (The Standard). Sayyid would later join the successor to Kamil's party, the Wafd (Delegation) Party. During World War I, the family home became a beehive diwan, or salon, for party meetings, and this flurry of excitement always remained with young Sayyid. While his father's influence directed the young Qutb's fervent intellect into political channels, from his mother he developed a highly inquisitive and spirited mind. His mother, Fatima, came from another local but an even more established and respectable family. Her own parents reared two Azhar scholars; later, in Cairo, these uncles provided Qutb with an entrée into the circle of religious and secular scholars.[4] His mother's dominant influence on young Sayyid motivated him throughout his life to excel in order to regain the dwindling family fortunes and reputation. Yet by the time he entered the job market in the 1930s, his goal was more simply to prevent further financial erosion. He sought, therefore, safe and stable employment as a government employee, a sinecure in the Ministry of

Education. He never earned enough through his scholarship and intellectual work to support himself, to retrieve his family's assets, or to restore his family to its former luster. He gained fame, but not financial well-being.[5]

According to Qutb's quasi-autobiographical novel, *Tifl min al-Qarya* (A Child from the Village) published in 1946, a tense, somewhat unsteady balance between modern and traditional schooling seems to have influenced Qutb's later unease over the triumphs of modernity on the one hand, and the defeats of the Islamic challenges to its hegemony on the other. Specifically, his parents debated at length when Sayyid was six years old whether to send their son to the modern, recently established government school, the *madrasa*, or to the traditional (and private) religious *kuttab*, which had a more limited curriculum. The *madrasa* (and his mother) won out. Yet, a short time thereafter, his lessons were briefly interrupted when young Sayyid rejected this choice and attended the *kuttab* instead. However, his repugnance at the *kuttab*'s squalid conditions prompted him to return to public school. Then, in order to show up the *kuttab* students, Qutb organized Qur'an recitation competitions that required participating students to memorize the Holy Book, the chief function, it seemed, of the *kuttab*. Thus, the best of the new *madrasa* and the old *kuttab* were combined. Similarly, once in Cairo, Qutb attended Dar al-'Ulum instead of al-Azhar, again choosing modernity over tradition—the same choice made by Hasan al-Banna, founder of the Muslim Brotherhood, although Qutb began his studies a year after al-Banna had graduated. Qutb graduated in 1933—the same year his father died—and young Sayyid immediately began working at the Ministry of Education.[6]

Qutb's achievements at the village *madrasa* were "highly distinguished."[7] He memorized the entire Qur'an by the age of 10, a commitment that at first had but little effect on him. Yet this mental feat helped him immensely when he began writing on religious subjects. Later, he came to deliberately blend the Qur'an's excitement and beauty he experienced as a boy in Musha with the more complex and difficult scholarly erudition expected of religious thinkers in Cairo. Moreover, his avid dedication to reading, begun in Musha, was nurtured throughout his entire life, clearly evident in his last (1964) and arguably his most influential book, *Ma'alim fi al-Tariq* (Signposts on the Road), in which he deftly quoted from European, Asian, and Arab writers and thinkers. It is no wonder that in choosing his sinecure (which he held for some 15 years), he found a position first as a schoolteacher (six years) and later as a school supervisor. Even when he traveled to the United States, it was ostensibly to study educational curriculum reforms. It was, perhaps, because of this sensitivity to curriculum and schooling in general that Qutb recognized the critical function that education, literacy, and pedagogy played in advancing political programs. His own experiences in schooling (both as a student and later as a teacher and supervisor) also sensitized him to the tension between modernity and tradition, and the need to reconcile modern science and the ageless Qur'an.[8] Qutb's initial appearance on the Cairo intellectual scene as a secular, nationalist poet and his gradual transformation into a major religious-political thinker also reflects this tension. Yet it also indicates that Qutb never completely rejected the modern and the secular for absolute Islamic domination. He was just as frequently discontented with *traditional* Islam and sought a *new* understanding of Islam that could rival modernity.[9]

In *A Child*, the central character, the boy most think is Sayyid Qutb himself, appears to be very idealistic, overly sheltered, and quite innocent, holding broad-minded and humanistic values, and is affronted when those ideals are not realized. If what held true for "the boy from the village" also held true for Qutb himself—which could explain his deep shock as an adult when, repeatedly, people not only fell short of those high expectations but seemed to turn them upside down—then his environment in Musha went far in nurturing this naiveté. Village life also instilled in him an empathy toward the poor and downtrodden, which permeated his political thought, both secular and Islamist. One episode in particular seems striking: his relationship with migrant farm workers—'ummal al-tarahil—whose poverty was so dire that few could understand their perspective on life.[10] Young Sayyid befriended a group of these workers and although the benign assistance he provided was appreciated, it could never really compensate for the exploitation and oppression these workers experienced. Nevertheless, this kindness created a sympathy that remained with the reformer and radical throughout his adult years.

The problems of Musha and other Egyptian villages resulted from their humble position on the ladder of governmental power that unilaterally imposed taxes, injustice, bribery, extortion, and neglect without fulfilling any of its obligations. Qutb's politics, whether secular or Islamist, seldom targeted the affluent, although he often attacked those whose wealth was ill-gotten. Instead, it was the state, not class, that aroused Qutb's discontent and animosity. Political oppression, not economic exploitation, was the key problem—or, as he might argue later, the corrupt and immoral leadership of the state, and the duty of righteous, upstanding Muslims to oppose and disobey such apostate tyrants. The burdens of poverty and deprivation, rural or urban, while lamentable, never received the outrage and indignation that despotic government did.[11] Qutb no doubt realized that the level of power he was concerned with was located in Cairo and that rural Egypt meant little in terms of that power—perhaps as little as *tarahil* workers meant to well-to-do landlords.

After World War I and Egypt's 1919 revolution, beginning in the 1920s, many villagers left the countryside and came to reside in the urban areas. Of these, many turned their backs on the "quaint superstition" of rural Islam and adopted the strident, self-righteous tone permeating urban Islamism. Qutb did not do so. He remained fond of the countryside and proud of its values, to such an extent that he measured those he found in the government and in positions of influence by the notions of honor, dignity, and community that he had encountered in village life.[12]

Qutb's lifelong intellectual engagement began in Musha. His parents and teachers both encouraged him to read books. He was particularly interested in poetry and, under the influence of his maternal uncles who attended al-Azhar and frequently returned home, he became enraptured with classical religious literature. The Sa'id seemed less isolated for young Sayyid as he eagerly read the nationalist writers of the day. His parents also inspired him to read and discuss the popular political ideas of his time, an awareness not commonly shared by boys of his age.[13]

Cairo

In 1921, Qutb left behind the familiarity and intimacy of Musha and moved to cosmopolitan Cairo. The city held all the glamour and confusion for young Sayyid that it still has today. Its unsettling mix of modern and traditional which seems to alienate rural migrants also troubled Qutb, though it was smoothly mediated by the comfort of residing with extended family members. He lived for his first four years with his maternal uncle, Ahmad Husayn 'Uthman in the northeast suburb of Zaytun next to Heliopolis.[14]

From 1925 to 1928, he attended Madrasat al-Mu'allimin al-Awwaliya, a preliminary training school equivalent to an American junior high school, and then matriculated for one year, 1928, in the preparatory high school, Tajhiziyat Dar al-'Ulum. He enrolled the next year in Dar al-'Ulum and became active immediately in student, academic, and literary affairs.[15] He studied logic, philosophy, political history, economics, Arabic, Islamic studies, theology, and foreign languages, including English and Hebrew. He was particularly fascinated by literature and poetry. Qutb also sought to build up the relationships between Egyptian students and their counterparts from non-Western countries. He was in the forefront of efforts to change the curriculum, especially in the area of foreign languages. When the eminent Taha Husayn[16] criticized Dar al-'Ulum's shortcomings in this field, Qutb responded defiantly by replying that students there were not at all satisfied with the status quo but sought fundamental curriculum changes. Qutb then designed a new curriculum and presented it to the dean. It included a number of new directions including foreign languages and expanded Arabic and religious studies.[17]

In 1933, at the age of 27, Qutb graduated from Dar al-'Ulum with a *licence* in Arabic Language and Literature.[18] He joined the Ministry of Education and worked for a little more than six years as a regular teacher. His first teaching assignment was at al-Da'udiyya Preparatory School in Cairo, where he taught from 1933 to 1935. He was then transferred to the primary school at Dumyat, on the Mediterranean coast, for a half year (1935), but soon requested a transfer for health reasons. He taught in the primary school in Bani Swayf, just south of Cairo, for one year (1935–36), and then moved back to Cairo, where he taught in the primary school in Helwan for three years, from 1936 to 1940. Tired of his travels, he took a job first as an inspector in the General Culture Administration, in March 1940, and then quickly moved over to the Translation and Statistics Administration a month later.[19] In July 1944, he was demoted to the post of inspector for primary education because of his political activities, but 10 months later, he was reappointed to the General Culture Administration where he worked from 1945 to 1948.[20] Then, with a scholarship from the Ministry of Education, he began a professional study trip to the United States on November 3, 1948, to become acquainted with the fundamentals of its educational curricula. He returned to Egypt on August 23, 1950, first as an assistant inspector in the education minister's office and then in the Southern Cairo School District in October 1951, and finally, in May 1952, he moved to the Office of Technical Research and Projects. But he resigned his ministerial post just six months later, on October 18, 1952, to protest what he claimed to be the non-Islamic education policies of the new revolutionary government.[21]

When he arrived in Cairo, Qutb soon became swept up into the excitement and spirit of the post-1919 nationalist fervor. At the time, he had no ambition to explore religious politics.[22]

After graduation, he joined the Wafd Party, which had an ironclad hold on the Egyptian nationalist spirit and a monopoly on filling Parliament seats. The Wafd's anti-British policy attracted Qutb, but he was upset by the lack of support from both the Wafd and the Palace for organizing militias to expel the British from the Canal Zone.[23] In 1937, disappointed over the government's lethargy, upset over treaty arrangements with Britain, and tired of domineering Wafd leaders, he joined the Sa'dist Party, which had recently broken away from the Wafd Party and that claimed to more accurately represent the original nationalist ideas and spirit of Sa'd Zaghlul (1859–1927) than the party the Pasha himself had founded.[24]

Before leaving the Sa'id, and during the 1919 revolution, young Sayyid (at the age of 13) had engaged in outright public political activism, composing national-istic poems, delivering patriotic speeches, and marching enthusiastically in dem-onstrations at the village mosque and at public gatherings in Musha, heralding his later political involvement. Almost immediately upon arriving in the capital city, he began publishing poems in local literary magazines. He soon became an "outspoken partisan of the new school of poetry" promoted by the *eminence gris* of Cairo's literary circles, 'Abbas Mahmud al-'Aqqad, leader of the liberal Diwan school of Egyptian writers.[25] The charismatic al-'Aqqad soon became Qutb's mentor.

Qutb's first poem was entitled "al-Hayat al-Jadida" (The New Life) and appeared in 1921 in the Wafd Party's official journal, *al-Balagh* (The Communiqué), when Qutb was just 15 years old.[26] Not surprisingly, it criticized Britain's rule in Egypt and defended Sa'd Zaghlul, the father of Egyptian nationalism.[27] Over the next 40 years, Qutb was extremely prolific, publishing more than 130 poems, 500 articles and essays, and nine books.[28]

Qutb began his literary career as a poet because poetry, he claimed, "served as an intermediary between what is and what ought to be" and was "the highest expression of man's inner feeling and his outside world." It was a way of reconciling his own idealism, slowly being stripped of its naiveté, and the distasteful reality of which he was becoming gradually aware. Qutb saw the poet as a romantic, filled with lofty sensibilities and deep sensitivities, whose superior imagination and outstanding intellect placed him on a higher level than others, a somewhat elitist position that seemingly contradicted his empathy for the poor and powerless—though Qutb himself may not have seen this—but dovetailed closely with his later advocacy for a select vanguard leading the Islamist movement.[29]

Poetry was the avenue through which Qutb searched for meaning. It expressed what he saw as a gap between ideal and real, a reconciliation of contentment and gloom, and an uplifting optimism of his ideals tempered by a restless pessimism concerning the world around him. The synthesis resulted in a "sharp" and "fiery" writing style. Poetry was the highest expression of the connection between humanity's inner feelings and its outside world. It provided an outlet, almost spiritual perhaps, that was later filled by religion and politics. Throughout the 1930s, Qutb remained absorbed by poetry, and literature more generally, but also ventured into philosophy, autobiographical sketches, novels, short stories, and literary criticism. He also criticized those poets and writers around him, motivated less by careerism than by the quest for a comfortable viewpoint that he could accept for himself.[30]

After completing his schooling, Qutb was determined to join the ranks of Cairo's prominent intellectuals, which included such luminaries as al-'Aqqad, 'Abd al-Qadr al-Mazini, Taha Husayn, Muhammad Husayn Haykal, and Ahmad Amin. He was fortunate, then, that within the year, he was asked to join the staff of *al-Ahram* newspaper's literary supplement. At the time, Qutb considered himself an ardent nationalist and modern secularist, promoting such principles as freedom, justice, and equality, and opposing tyranny, oppression, and inhumanity. He was anti-imperialist, meaning against British colonialism, and for complete Egyptian independence, but not yet necessarily against Westernization as a whole. He was particularly inspired by the nationalist poetry of such writers as 'Ali al-Ghayati and his book *Wataniyati* (My Nationality) which had been published in 1910. Qutb wholeheartedly embraced al-Ghayati's program of campaigning for Egyptian independence and opposing British occupation.[31] The liberal nationalist forces that had drawn much of their inspiration from the Western world appeared to have gained the upper hand in the aftermath of the 1919 revolution and the introduction of a constitutional parliamentary system in Egypt in 1923. But Egypt remained largely under British control and millions suffered from poverty and deprivation, even while the concentration of wealth and power in the hands of a few became more pronounced.[32]

Qutb's first book, however, was not a collection of poems. Rather, it was a small volume based on a lecture he delivered in 1932, his last year at Dar al-'Ulum. This lecture was entitled, "Muhimmat al-Sha'ir fi al-Haya wa Shi'r al-Jil al-Hadir"

(The Task of the Poet in Life and the Poetry of the Present Generation) for which his teachers had praised him highly. It then appeared in bookstores with a shorter title, *The Task of the Poet in Life*, a year later. In the book, Qutb challenged Egypt's literary establishment to raise the country from its malaise. This discontent, he concluded, could be seen in Egypt's cheerless and enervated music, literature, and poetry, as well as its ineffectual intellectuals, scholars, and artists. Qutb claimed that the poet was the one redeemer without equal in his ability to describe and understand personal feelings and attitudes that, while perhaps idiosyncratic, still have a more general significance. This gives the poet a privileged position and a responsibility to be the key mediator between the inner domain of the self and the outer domain of public expression.[33]

Two years later, in January 1935, Qutb did publish his first volume of poems entitled *al-Shati al-Majhul* (The Unknown Shore), which reflected his unease, pessimism, and rebellion, what might be called a display of existential angst in his search for meaning, stability, and satisfaction.[34] The volume emphasized Qutb's consideration of human existence and death and, unable to reconcile the two, his flight from the objective, material world into a more subjective and spiritual realm that potentially offered more contentment. It also demonstrated Qutb's independent mind. He wavered between the romanticism, idealism, and optimism of love, and the pessimism, discontent, and despair of death. At this time, his escape from this predicament and from these contradictions was more psychological than political.[35]

Both of these early books reflected the powerful influence of his illustrious mentor, 'Abbas al-'Aqqad (1889–1964) who was a journalist, poet, and literary critic 17 years Qutb's senior.[36] Many opportunities were opened by his close connection with al-'Aqqad, a relationship that was first established through Qutb's uncle, Ahmad Husayn 'Uthman, who knew al-'Aqqad as a fellow journalist and as a member of the Wafd Party, and who personally introduced al-'Aqqad to his nephew. Qutb frequently visited al-'Aqqad in Heliopolis and raided his library, while al-'Aqqad kindheartedly helped Qutb publish his writings. Their discussions created a mutual admiration and a close friendship. Qutb's veneration of the older man soon led to his enthusiastic and outspoken support of al-'Aqqad's fresh and modern approach to poetry. The complexity of al-'Aqqad's intellect challenged Qutb to read much more widely—poetry, novels, and plays, both Western and non-Western sources alike—in order to comprehend his mentor. He stood enthralled by the man's intelligence and soon became his ardent disciple, emulating al-'Aqqad's style in both poetry and literary criticism. Salma Jayyusi even claims that Qutb was al-'Aqqad's "greatest admirer."[37]

The Diwan School

Al-'Aqqad was a member of the previous generation of literary elite and a contemporary of Taha Husayn and his admirers.[38] Al-'Aqqad, together with two of his journalistic colleagues and friends, the rebellious but pessimistic 'Abd al-Rahman Shukri (1886–1958) and the humorous but derivative 'Abd al-Qadr al-Mazini (1890–1949), established a critical and modern anglophile literary circle called al-Diwan, stimulated by such English writers as Samuel Taylor Coleridge, John Stuart Mill, Charles Darwin, Thomas Macaulay, and William Hazlitt.[39] Although the formal movement dated back as early as 1912 or 1913, the name itself came from a famous pamphlet of literary criticism that al-'Aqqad published in 1921 in collaboration with al-Mazini—*Diwan Kitab fi al-Adab wa al-Naqd* (The Collected Volume of Literature and Criticism)—which critically assessed, but also aggressively challenged, the work, language, and style of a host of older, and deeply entrenched, neoclassical poets and writers such as Ahmad Shawqi, Muhammad Hafiz Ibrahim, Mustafa Sadiq al-Rafi'i, Mahmud Sami al-Barudi, and Mustafa Lutfi al-Manfaluti. (Shukri joined later, completing the distinguished triumvirate.)[40]

Back in the years leading up to the First World War, the well-established neoclassical school was proving almost insurmountable for those wishing to modernize Egyptian literature and poetry. But after the war, the 1919 revolution, and the 1923 constitution, Western culture began making inroads among Egypt's literati and educated elite. Prior to this period, Egyptian literary writing had been dominated either by Ottoman neoclassicists or else, more recently, by the Syrian-Lebanese in Egypt and the *mahjar* poetry of Levantine émigrés to the New World. But now, for the first time, it was the Egyptians themselves who were coming to dominate fictional writing. The result was a hybrid of Egyptian nationalism and Western styles and aesthetics. The Diwan school was the first group to attempt to modernize the field and overthrow its stodgy, neoclassical predecessors. Jayyusi states that the school ought to have been called "the English School," since all three founders were "well versed in English literature and were acquainted with the literature of other Western countries" as well.[41]

> The real difference between these [modern] poets and their predecessors in the eyes of the new school lay in the different aims they set for poetry and in their emphasis on the significance of the individuality and the emotional life of the poet for his work.[42]

Al-Diwan was regarded as the beginning of modern poetry and poetic criticism in Egypt. It established the two authors, al-'Aqqad and al-Mazini, as the premier poets and literary critics of the day, along with a third partner, Shukri, who, ironically, was rudely castigated in the school's founding book[43] but who later capitulated and went on to agree with his two colleagues. Al-Diwan's main goal was to "destroy the remaining idols" of contemporary literature[44] by seriously defying the rhythmic and metrical schemes of neoclassical poetry. It sought to abolish the stale and stodgy *qasida*[45] and the *muwashshah*[46] structures that had long dominated the Middle East and to replace them with the irregular, telegraphic style of prose, blank, and free verse that marked modern European poetry.

The Diwan school also sought to challenge the unrivaled position of Ahmad Shawqi (1868–1932) in particular and diminish his preeminence. As a critic, al-'Aqqad could be both magnificent and blistering, not holding back in his disparagement of others, particularly his adversaries and rivals. He was downright destructive in his "bitter and violent" criticism and "willful prejudice." His intense derision helped annihilate both the older neoclassical school and a newer rival, the Apollo group.[47]

Al-Diwan's tone was aggressive and abusive, striving to undermine Shawqi as much personally as aesthetically. Its members launched a vicious attack intended to challenge and emasculate the old master—an attack al-'Aqqad considered his greatest achievement. His attacks were caustic and far too extreme for the rest of Egypt's more traditionally minded literati, filled with "violent ridicule" unbefitting either man. Yet at the same time, al-'Aqqad's deprecations were more often than not politically motivated and intentionally prejudiced.[48]

Al-Diwan attacked other poets as well, including Hafiz, al-Manfaluti and even Shukri himself, a founding member of the Diwan troika, all for their unimaginative skill and styles and for their uninventive embrace of tradition. Their poetry, these critics argued, lacked the individualistic aesthetic that made modern poetry so appealing.

The ad hominem attacks and personal insults were soon aimed at others who merely supported and admired these poets. Al-'Aqqad saw himself as the only imaginable literary reformer, and he did not allow any challengers, no matter how similar their perspective. Those who sought to contest his preeminence, criticize his methods, or offer alternatives were viciously attacked and condemned. Yet rather than engage them on intellectual grounds, he ridiculed them personally. On the other hand, those who openly recognized his preeminence and agreed to suppress their own intellectual accomplishments became valuable and sustaining members of the Diwan school. Qutb and other associates were expected to conform and attack those with whom al-'Aqqad disagreed; otherwise, they, too, became suspect.[49]

The hallmark of the Diwan school was its subjective, emotional, even soulful reflection of personal experiences—a "reflection of the heart and an interpreter of the soul, not merely an outer description of things."[50] The stress on the poet's individual, subjective feelings, and inner states of mind contrasted sharply with the neoclassical focus on public events, patriotic poetry, and nationalistic prose. It demanded that poetry "probe deep into the self and derive its inspiration from human experience."[51] It represented a drive toward modernity that stressed an unwavering individualism, and a move away from what its members saw as the stagnant, civic style of the neoclassicists. Shukri himself sought to turn against what he pithily called "the poetry of daily events, a plague of locusts, a fire, a royal visit, or a party in a sporting club." Instead, he said, poets ought to write about life, the present time, and the expression of feelings. "Life," he proclaimed, "is a beautiful poem."[52]

Shukri also wrote that poets and writers should be set apart from society since they occupy a lofty and transcendent position that enables them to see and comprehend the glories of life that ordinary people are incapable of understanding. Poets are considered prophets, able to "enhance men's souls and move their spirits." The poet, he declared, "does not write for ... one special people but for the human mind and soul everywhere. Moreover, he does not write only for the present day but for every day and every time."[53] Qutb was later to carry these self-righteous qualities into his committed Islamist works.

Al-'Aqqad, like many of his colleagues in the Diwan school, insisted that the poet examine the depths of his own soul, understand his own attitudes and feelings, and appeal to his own personal philosophy. He called for probing into the personal and the subjective, dwelling on the disparity between the inner self and the outer reality.[54]

Yet al-'Aqqad fulfilled this vision more in his literary criticism than in his actual poetry.[55] Al-'Aqqad pioneered an innovative, analytical approach to criticism. Instead of the conventional method of citing a series of confidential anecdotes and personal sketches, al-'Aqqad established a more scientific study of both the literary product and the literary producer. Indeed, he claimed, the two were inextricably bound together. He explained literary compositions by probing the author's personality, which, he thought, contained both explicit and hidden clues to understanding their literary creations. He did not resort to external historical, sociological, or cultural factors as explicatory devices. Instead, he focused almost exclusively on the writer's fundamental disposition and temperament.[56] Nor did he dwell, as Muhammad Mandur did after him (and *because* of him) on the artistic merits of the writers' work, their place in an historical repertoire of traditional techniques, or the contemporary assortment of styles, fashions, and aesthetic conventions. Al-'Aqqad sought explanations extrinsic to the composition itself, relying on psychological aspects instead of objective contextual factors.[57]

The Diwan school constituted the same modernizing thrust as 'Ali 'Abd al-Raziq and Taha Husayn, whose own books shared the West's emphasis on individualism and psychology that the Diwan school reinforced. Both of these writers had become quite controversial when they argued for the secular separation of religion and state,[58] such that the bundling of 'Abd al-Raziq, Husayn, al-'Aqqad, and Qutb together—not incongruous at the time—appears, with hindsight, terribly ironic, given that Qutb came to completely reject the secular position of the first three authors.

At first, Qutb was strongly influenced by many of the Diwan school practices and conventions, intently drawn to its subjective and expressive style and fascinated by its aesthetic. He also adopted its harsh disputational style.[59] As a young man growing up and tearing himself away from the conservative and traditional perspective of the Sa'id, he saw the Diwan approach to poetry as modern, innovative, and stylish. He was, of course, very much captivated by al-'Aqqad's overpowering personality and charm. He did yeoman's duty for his mentor, defending him in numerous publications, perhaps over-extending his loyalty such that it became brittle and easily shattered when the modernization project began to collapse.

Al-'Aqqad's incredible magnetism had a remarkable effect on Qutb's thinking. It was al-'Aqqad who so decisively convinced Qutb to examine poetry, literature, and literary criticism, of Egyptian, Arab, or European origin. He opened the doors to Cairo's literary society for young Sayyid, but exacted a demanding price for his patronage. Qutb was completely enthralled by the older writer, whom he considered "a unique thinker, a first-class poet, and an eminent literary critic of his era."[60] His personality almost completely engulfed the young Qutb's style, substance, and inspiration. He just about overwhelmed Qutb's own maturing viewpoints, persuading him to adopt new ones, such as secularism and individualism, that his student later disputed and rejected.

Yet even later, Qutb continued to focus primarily on the subjective and affective character of the world and to refrain from considering the structural, objective, and legalistic aspects of society.[61] Like al-'Aqqad, he, too, insisted on maintaining the unity of one's creation and overcoming the alienation imposed by modern society and its tendency to separate, divide, and pull apart people, their lives, and their achievements. Later Qutb emphasized the unity of God and His creation, which included humanity and the rules and laws that regulate people's existence. Qutb also continued to view the world from an aloof position when he stressed the creation of a militant vanguard to implement his vision of an Islamic state and society. Although others argued over whether Islamic activism should be populist or elitist, Qutb never quite lost the sense that only a few select advocates really understood the Islamic worldview. Qutb also exhibited the pessimism and alienation of the Diwan school that was, in fact, widespread among his generation. This unease pushed Qutb into considering alternatives to modernization that more genuinely resolved the worries and fears that abounded in a colonized Egypt. Finally, even as Qutb rejected modernization and embraced Islamism, his style of criticism continued to emulate the style of al-'Aqqad— assertive, blistering, and destructive. Especially when Qutb wrote *Signposts on the Road*, he could not, and did not, hold back—stating his feelings and opinions in intense and caustic terms.

Yet it is not clear whether Qutb, when he embraced the modernity and anglophilia of the Diwan school, also accepted the attendant condemnation of any alternative, authentic Egyptian, Arab or Islamic approach. So while al-'Aqqad was firm in his embrace of this intellectual modernism, Qutb slowly became interested in religious issues. Qutb soon worried that he was too closely imitating his mentor. As Qutb began to define his own views and positions, after the middle of the 1930s, tearing himself away from al-'Aqqad was the first sign of real intellectual independence.[62] Qutb's shift into aesthetic and spiritual directions caused him to hesitate and question al-'Aqqad's intellectual influence and personal power. He finally had to sever his intimate and overpowering association with his mentor. As he later came to renounce the modernity, individualism, and temporality of the

Diwan approach, he also thought it necessary to distance himself from al-'Aqqad for fear of gravitating back into his orbit.

4 Disputes with Modernity

Qutb's commitment to the Diwan school was demonstrated in a number of literary debates and intellectual clashes. In three of these disputes, he defended al-'Aqqad and his followers, supporting the Diwan's perspective on modernity. But his was perhaps a pyrrhic victory, as his own reasoning forced him in due course to realize the shortcomings of modernity. In the summer of 1934, a literary battle erupted between the Diwan school and the two-year-old Apollo Society. Four years later, a second debate flared up, between al-'Aqqad and Mustafa Sadiq al-Rafi'i and their respective entourages. In 1939, in a dispute unconnected to the Diwan school—indeed, here Qutb argued instead for the pursuit of an authentic Egyptian culture—he challenged one of the doyens of Arabic literature, Taha Husayn, and his proposals for the wholesale imitation of Europe. Finally, in 1943, Qutb challenged the imported Francophile thinking of yet another literary critic, Muhammad Mandur, a protégé of (and perhaps a proxy for) Taha Husayn.

The Apollo literary society was established in 1932 by Ahmad Zaki Abu Shadi (1892–1955)—a doctor, poet, and critic.[63] Its mouthpiece was the *Apollo* magazine, the first in the Arab world dedicated exclusively to publishing poetry.[64] Abu Shadi, regarded as "a pioneer and an innovator of modern Arab poetry," became the journal's editor. Although the society included a wide array of members and supporters from the younger generation of modern poets, the Apollo ultimately turned into a one-person literary program. The society imported many of its ideas and styles from England. But while it claimed British influence, it also imitated American writers and especially the Syrian émigrés living in New York City renowned for their *mahjar* poetry.[65] It opposed Shawqi, Hafiz, and the neoclassical genre and consciously turned its back on Egypt's poetic traditions by advocating what amounted to an outright and strongly sentimental romanticism. It especially emphasized "the authentic and artistic expression of emotions" and relegated symbolism, philosophical contemplation, and social commitment to secondary importance.[66]

Perhaps because its tone was so sophisticated and supercilious, the Apollo attracted resentment. As a promoter of modern poetry, it, of course, drew criticism from the old guard. But it was also condemned by the Diwan school, which ostensibly shared its views of poetic composition. The differences between al-Diwan and the Apollo ought to have been minuscule.[67] Yet they found themselves fighting to out-modernize the other.

The Apollo Society advocated an unabashed Westernization and attacked al-'Aqqad and the Diwan school for being too old-fashioned. In its view, al-'Aqqad had simply not gone far enough in advocating radical change. Even though the Diwan school had rejected the neoclassicism of the 19th century masters, it continued to use their *qasida* and *muwashshah* poetic styles. The Apollo poets, on the other hand, adopted a stanzaic style and even prose, blank, and free verse formats that allowed for freer composition.[68] These stylistic differences subjected the Diwan school to harsh criticism by a younger generation of writers who accused them of intellectual and prosodic inertia. Yet al-'Aqqad considered himself the leading innovator of modern styles in Arabic literature and poetry; thus, there was no room for a second authority.[69]

Qutb sprang to the defense of his mentor and the Diwan school. His criticism focused on modern poetry, but there was a generational aspect to it as well: young Sayyid deliberately supported and defended the octogenarians of the Diwan camp. It was a case, he argued, of "respecting his elders."

Qutb entered the literary skirmish in the summer of 1934 with an article in *al-Usbu'a* (The Weekly) magazine. He called the Apollo poets "excessively noisy and pretentious but lacking in literary, social and ethical qualities." He labeled them the "Pageant of the Handicapped" since they posed as victims of the older generation but, in the same breath, also claimed an enduring vitality and maturity. He accused them of being opportunists, of lacking any literary, social, or ethical value, and of "knifing each other in the back."[70] Their innovations and attempts at raising their own status were ploys, Qutb wrote, to stand tall by attacking the eminent al-'Aqqad. Qutb personally accused the Apollo members of pressuring him to lighten up his own criticism, of trying to influence his reviews, and then later of blocking his unfavorable assessments altogether.[71]

When Abu Shadi published his harsh critique of al-'Aqqad's poetic volume, *Wahy al-Arba'in* (Revelations at Forty)[72] in his journal in February 1933, the battle turned particularly nasty. The rancor and insult were astounding as "both sides tried to tear to pieces the works of the other group." Ultimately, the Diwan school won the battle when *Apollo* ran out of funds and suspended publication at the end of 1934.[73]

A second literary debate erupted four years later, in the summer of 1938, in the pages of the Cairo monthly journal, *al-Risala* (The Message). This time, the two sides were the respective supporters of al-'Aqqad and Mustafa Sadiq al-Rafi'i. The two had been rivals for years.[74] When al-Rafi'i died in December 1937, his obituary and 40-day eulogy caused the dispute to erupt once again.

An al-Rafi'i supporter, Ahmad al-Ghamrawi, accused al-'Aqqad and his supporters—specifically singling out Qutb—of being (ironically enough) too irreligious and profane. Qutb's response, which appeared a month later, cast the dispute in intellectual terms, as a clash between al-Rafi'i's "old school," which sought to conserve traditional literary styles, and al-'Aqqad's "new school," which wanted to develop newer versions of cultural production. Later, however, in a series of articles that appeared in *al-Risala* from April to November 1938, Qutb launched a torrent of criticism attacking al-Rafi'i and his supporters. Qutb specifically rebutted

al-Ghamrawi's accusations by criticizing him, his mentor, al-Rafi'i, and their colleagues of being overly religious, introducing religion into every discussion, and
of exploiting Islam in order to deceive people by appealing to their sentiments.
He even challenged those "who passed religious judgments on others." Yet Qutb
soon found this position more and more untenable. His devotion to al-'Aqqad was
certainly evident, in the face of the fury and mockery from al-Rafi'i's supporters.
But the strains were also clear, for in 1938, the task of defending his mentor was
more difficult than it had been in 1934.[75]

This particular controversy began with a debate over the literary use of the
Arabic language. Al-Rafi'i and his partisans believed themselves to be more Arab
and Islamic while accusing al-'Aqqad and the Diwan school of being entrenched in
a parochial Egyptianism.[76] They viewed language through a religious lens, arguing
that Arabic and its meanings were permanently fixed by Islam and the Qur'an.
But Qutb argued that this traditional approach had failed to adjust to the need
for social reform and had remained rigid and dogmatic. Arabic, he maintained,
needed to be flexible in its search for an authentic Egyptian identity. It ought to
bend to the goal of finding Egypt's true character instead of the society conform-
ing to fit conventional linguistic practices. Moreover, in line with modernity's disdain for established values and norms, Qutb rejected the past:

> Far from seeing the past as an intellectual burden and an unacceptable
> religious legacy, [Qub] dismisse[d] it totally for the sake of the present
> and contend[ed] that the present and the future are pregnant with pos-
> sibilities that were outside the pale of the past.[77]

Qutb soon began drawing unwanted attention to his employer, the Education
Ministry, which was then under the premiership of Muhammad Mahmud of the
Liberal Constitutionalist Party, which had just defeated the Wafd in the 1938
parliamentary elections.[78] The government wanted Qutb to lower his voice, and
the education minister's consternation resulted in Qutb's reassignment outside
Cairo. Shortly thereafter, he followed his mentor al-'Aqqad and switched from the
Wafd to the new Sa'dist Party.

Qutb's intellectual position here reflected his momentary attraction to
Egyptianism, not an aversion to Islamism. For the time being, he remained a
Muslim secularist, Arab nationalist, and modern humanist. He regarded religion as a set of individual convictions that could benefit society. Yet he wrote
at a time when religion was increasingly seen to transcend individual beliefs
and actions so that instead of people's predilections molding religion, religion
shaped and constrained people's inclinations. Herein lies the kernel of Qutb's
central concept of unity, or *tawhid*. It was the *tawhid* of Islam that integrated
people into their community, but by compelling them to conform to their religion rather than blending together different individual experiences and understandings. Since modernity entails breaking away from the *tawhid* of tradition,

Qutb was beginning to realize that this could have detrimental effects and that social harmony should take precedence instead. This would ensure a just government, unlike the discord of modern, democratic parliaments. Accordingly, while Qutb's personal religion remained lukewarm, his ideas about the social and cultural benefits of religion were beginning to change. Although he won the battle against al-Rafi'i, he soon began to adopt the more religious perspective that al-Rafi'i had embraced.[79]

This emerging perspective can be seen more clearly in the next dispute that Qutb engaged in, when he challenged the preeminent Taha Husayn. Husayn was already notorious for casting doubt on the Qur'an's authenticity.[80] In 1938, Husayn became embroiled in another controversy when, in his new book, *Mustaqbal al-Thaqafa fi Misr* (The Future of Culture in Egypt), he called for Egypt to immerse itself completely in European civilization and to cut its cultural ties to its neighbors in the Middle East. Husayn was certainly not alone in distinguishing the East from the West, but his wholesale approval and acceptance of the West was exceptional. He considered Egypt to be, without question, an essentially European and Western country. Religion, politics, literature—in these matters and more, Egypt should follow Europe's superior example.

> We Egyptians must not assume the existence of intellectual differences, weak or strong, between the Europeans and ourselves or infer that the East mentioned by Kipling in his famous verse "East is East and West is West, and never the twain shall meet" applies to us or our country. [Khedive] Ismail's statement that Egypt is a part of Europe should not be regarded as some kind of boast or exaggeration, since our country has always been a part of Europe as far as intellectual and cultural life is concerned, in all its forms and branches [9].[81]
>
> The dominant and undeniable fact of our times is that day by day we are drawing closer to Europe and becoming an integral part of her, literally and figuratively. This process would be much more difficult than it is if the Egyptian mind were basically different from the European [12].
>
> In order to become equal partners in civilization with the Europeans, we must literally and forthrightly do everything that they do; we must share with them the present civilization, with all its pleasant and unpleasant sides, and not content ourselves with words or mere gestures. Whoever advises any other course of action is either a deceiver or is himself deceived. Strangely enough we imitate the West in our everyday lives, yet hypocritically deny the fact in our words. If we really detest European life, what is to hinder us from rejecting it completely? And if we genuinely respect the Europeans, as we certainly seem to do by our wholesale adoption of their practices, why do we not reconcile our words with our actions? Hypocrisy ill becomes those who are proud and anxious to overcome their defects [15].

Some Egyptians object to Europeanization on the grounds that it threatens our national personality and glorious heritage. I who have long argued that we stoutly protect our independence naturally do not advocate rejection of the past or loss of identity in the Europeans, although occasional bewitched individuals and groups have done this very thing. The only time that we might have been absorbed by Europe was when we were extremely weak, ignorant, and possessed of the notion that the hat was superior to the turban and the fez because it always covered a more distinguished head! [20].

Qutb was greatly disturbed by this. He vigorously rejected the adoption of European culture because of what Husayn mistakenly called "the essential similarities" between Egypt and Europe.[82] Of course, Qutb could not help but recognize that Egyptians emulated the Europeans—he noted that the reverse had been true when the Muslim world had been on top. But it was just this divide between *ibn al-balad* and *ibn al-zawat* that was polarizing the country.[83] He later considered Husayn to be a "pawn in the hands of the colonialists."[84]

More specifically, Husayn called for changes in Egypt's school system that would eliminate all but European subjects. Husayn was faculty dean at Fu'ad I (later Cairo) University at the time and, not surprisingly, held an unfavorable view of its rivals. Dar al-'Ulum, Qutb's alma mater, proved "insignificant and disappointing," incapable of competing with modern schools. He called for the elimination of Arabic instruction at al-Azhar because it undermined the mentality of the educated classes and lead to reactionary politics. Egypt, he continued, could not progress to modernity without adopting the trappings of secular European culture.[85]

To Husayn, language and religion produced division, disarray, and rancor; their study, therefore, should be eliminated. To Qutb, Arabic and Islam were both sources of Egypt's unique identity and indispensable unity: their instruction, however, could be improved.

Qutb's more immediate response appeared in April, 1939, in the journal, *Sahifat* (Pages of) *Dar al-'Ulum*.[86] The controversy was well within his area of expertise—education and school curriculum. But because of Husayn's reputation and influence, Qutb's reply was purposely cautious.[87] Qutb could not or would not be so abrupt as to completely reject Husayn's Occidentalism (or, for that matter, Europe's cultural hegemony) and so maintained that there were some aspects of European culture worth emulating. Here Qutb distinguished between what he called culture and civilization. The first included religion, art, ethics, and traditions. The second included sciences, engineering, and the technical arts. Because the second was so far ahead in Europe, Egypt's adoption of these advancements went unquestioned. But endorsing the first was not advisable.

Qutb also agreed with Husayn's claim that the government, the Education Ministry, and the media were responsible for inconsistent educational policies and practices, and blamed partisan politics for intensifying this predicament. Likewise, he concurred with Husayn's criticism of al-Azhar University and its Arabic language programs, and he declared that al-Azhar as well as Dar al-'Ulum must accept leadership in introducing new ideas. But he rejected Husayn's characterization of the Arabic language by arguing that any language was subjective and contextual, not permanently fixed or definite (still following al-'Aqqad but *not* al-Rafi'i).[88]

Husayn argued that since the time of the Pharaohs, Egypt and Europe had possessed a common intellectual heritage. Because of its ties to ancient Greece and its philosophical traditions and because of early Greek colonization, Egypt was Western and not Eastern.[89] Qutb replied that Egyptians had not really liked the Greeks and instead staked its cultural claims to the Arab East. He defended Egypt's Arabic ties and saw Egypt as a connecting link within the Arab world, between the Arab East (*mashriq*) and the Arab West (*maghrib*).

He also took issue with Husayn's rejection of the intellectual unity between Egypt and the East and his assertion that Egypt was unlike other parts of "The East"—India, China, and Japan. Qutb certainly saw the East as significantly different from Europe, yet he also argued that each country had its own culture, so that variations within "The East" also existed.[90] Instead of clumping the non-West all together, a trait of 19th century Orientalism, Qutb recognized a wide diversity among the countries that made up both East and West.[91]

Qutb went on to argue that Egypt had an extraordinarily autonomous culture despite the repeated introduction of outside influences. What educated Egyptians assimilated, he stated, improved the quality of the country's culture, so that adopting Greek philosophy, for example, supplemented Islam and made the resulting blend better than either component separately. (Qutb would later reject such accretions as weakening Islam and therefore ruining Egypt.) The uneducated masses, by contrast, retained a more unadulterated Islam. The spread of Christianity in Europe, by comparison, created a society notably inferior to Islamic Egypt. It resulted in a very materialistic society that could not compare with Egypt's higher spiritual values.

Qutb strongly embraced this distinction between Western materialism and Eastern spiritualism, which anticipated what Samuel Huntington later called a clash of civilizations. Yet in *The Future of Culture* Husayn belittled this contrast and claimed that neither Christianity nor Islam, as imported religions, had actually affected their adopting societies to any considerable degree. Qutb could not disagree more, and he continued to develop this contrast further when he began his Islamist writing. Europe's mentality was too confrontational, he declared, while Egypt—at least among those unaffected by European culture—was much more harmonious.

Qutb's critique was received enthusiastically by many like-minded Egyptians. Even the Muslim Brotherhood requested permission to reprint Qutb's review in its newspaper, although there had been no previous contact between Qutb and the Brothers.[92] Qutb had staked out a contrary position—perhaps just to oppose Husayn—that eventually steered him away from secularism and modernity.

In 1943, Qutb became involved in yet a fourth literary skirmish. This time, he fiercely attacked Muhammad Mandur (1907–65),[93] a Francophile literary critic and poet who was a protégé of Husayn.[94] Mandur regarded himself exclusively as a literary critic, unlike earlier reviewers whose criticism was tangential to their main writing careers. As such, he sought to drastically "revise the prevailing standards" of literature and literary criticism, an aspiration certain to challenge his rivals, like al-'Aqqad and the Diwan school, who had the same ambition.[95]

There were a number of reasons why Qutb assailed Mandur. Mandur had repeatedly attacked al-'Aqqad, deriding Qutb's patron's poetry, political positions, artistic achievements, intelligence, and knowledge. Mandur also condescendingly belittled rational and intellectual poetry in favor of a more impressionistic, aesthetic, and emotional prosody. Mandur's criticism against a "loud" oratorical tone in written poetry attacked a style that was becoming characteristic of Qutb. The valorization of a whispered poetry over direct and straightforward writing, of opinion over truth, of sentimentality over impartiality, and of subjective particularism over scientific generalization ended up pitting the two intellectuals against one another. The foreign sources of Mandur's prototypes—French, Lebanese, and Arab-American—and the relativism of his values constitute what we might call today Mandur's "secular humanism." Reaching over to Europe instead of delving into Islam resulted in principles, philosophies, and ethics that were not authentic to Egypt and the Arab world. Finally, Mandur's political detachment and disdain for those engaging in political activism while at the same time editing partisan publications drew attention to his apparent double standard.

Mandur was commonly considered a member of the "Taha Husayn school" despite the personal falling-out between the two. Qutb no doubt assumed, as most others did, that Mandur was still Husayn's disciple.[96] After all, Qutb himself was also going in directions that, by the early 1940s, differed from his own mentor. But Mandur's attacks against al-'Aqqad provoked Qutb's instinctive loyalty.[97]

Mandur and Husayn were both committed to a new methodical approach to literary criticism that rejected the "scientific and objective" approach that al-'Aqqad had championed, and advocated, instead, a more intrinsic *"l'explication de texts."* Mandur singled out and condemned al-'Aqqad for the psychological method the Diwan master used to analyze classical poets.[98] Al-'Aqqad's psychoanalytical and eugenic approach contrasted with Mandur's linguistic and semiotic style— not unlike what might be an imaginary contest between Sigmund Freud versus Roland Barthes.

Qutb strongly criticized Mandur for championing the poetry of such diaspora or *mahjar* poets as Mikha'il Na'ima and Nasib 'Arid. Their poetry, Mandur had argued, was an inner-soul poetry, an understated "whispered" poetry.[99] Mandur contrasted this to the harsh rhetoric, often overbearing and excessive, of the previous generations of poets—the neoclassicist, for sure, but also the Diwan school poets who proved, it seems, too dense or dull for such subtle and sensitive approaches. It was only the new generation of Khalil Matran (and by implication, his disciple Ahmad Abu Shadi and those who formed the Apollo school) who could truly express this avant garde art form.

In a fit of patriotic pique, Qutb harshly attacked Mandur for his adulation of émigré poets and his blanket criticism of Egyptian writers, although Qutb mitigated his severity by agreeing with many of Mandur's ideas.[100] Even as Qutb explored the same concepts of "evok[ing] in the reader imaginary pictures, emotional excitement, and artistic feelings," he flatly rejected Mandur's soft, whispering tones that did the same, preferring what he called "the truth." Qutb's own inquiry into the aesthetics of the Qur'an convinced him that these expressive qualities had emerged from Islam's divine book, though few would claim that God quietly whispered them or reduced their expressive intensity. That Mandur recommended the same aspirations for human writing, but instead of emulating the Qur'an, made his conclusions based on a completely secular, French, and even Marxist perspective (read: Godless), may have also angered Qutb.[101]

Mandur also firmly embraced, at least initially, the idea of pursuing "art for art's sake," and rejected any explicit political agenda. He argued that the purpose of poetry was merely to pursue beauty and not to teach or moralize. It was enough to help readers to understand their world, its people, and the place art held in their lives.[102] Yet this political detachment seemed at odds with both Mandur's own journalistic profession and Qutb's fury over Mandur's secular politics. Qutb became exasperated by Mandur's vacillation between claiming to uphold strong secular left-wing ideologies and his aloof and haughty disdain for political engagement.[103]

Of these four debates, three were conducted in defense of Qutb's mentor. They seemed to place Qutb squarely in the modernist camp, underscoring his embrace of secularism, individualism, nationalism, romanticism, and even anti-traditionalism. Yet it may have been loyalty rather than full-hearted support of modernity that motivated Qutb's fervor. By contrast, the debate with Taha Husayn—by no means a linear progression since it was sandwiched between his attacks against al-Rafi'i and Mandur—tapped into Qutb's growing unease with the wholesale imitation of Europe that modernization involved, although it did not yet reflect a Muslim Brotherhood-style Islamism. In fact, there was little indication of the Islamist trends that Qutb would follow and even initiate after World War II. There was a discomfort with wholesale European mimicry, but this was not at all unusual among Egypt's intellectuals in the 1930s. At the time, Qutb's wavering and probing into alternatives to European modernity answered the gnawing malaise brought about by Egypt's failures to grow, develop, and mature as an independent and respectable nation and society, by the worldwide Depression, and by the rise of Fascism in Europe.

Hesitations and Doubts

Yet the encroachment of Western intellectual thought was blunted by other forces in Egypt. Disagreements over modernization could be measured by the proliferation of parties and platforms beginning in the late 1920s. There was, of course, the Muslim Brotherhood of Hasan al-Banna. There was the Young Egypt party (Green Shirts) of Ahmad Husayn, which recruited Egyptian youth into a corporatist party along the lines of Nazism, Fascism, and the Falange in Europe. There were Socialists, Communists,[104] and a number of new secular political parties opposing or breaking away from the Wafd.[105] All attest to the divisiveness that plagued Egypt on the eve of the Great Depression. Above all, this disorder reflected the impact of British colonial rule, its control of the royal palace, and its policies of divide and rule. A unified government, able to momentarily put aside its political squabbles, might have spelled the end of Britain's dominion.

Thus, by the 1930s, scholars and writers started to examine alternatives to unbridled Westernization and failed liberalism, both of which soon became even more discredited because of their inability to solve the country's intractable social ills. Intellectuals sought answers in Arabic and Islamic history and literature that was skeptical of Western hegemony, in general, and liberal nationalism in particular.[106]

Until the late 1930s, Qutb was not at all oriented toward radical Islamism and religious politics. His position, however, was not uncommon at the time. During the Great Depression, he and many of his peers began to question European-style modernity and to see Islam if not in strictly religious terms, then at least as a major influence—for some, *the* major influence—on Egypt's cultural heritage and civilization. This "widespread reaction in Egypt against rampant Westernization and the failure of liberal national establishment" brought many writers and thinkers to question the notions of progress and advancement that so permeated the secular ideas of modernity.[107] This was even more true after the twin disappointments of the Anglo-Egyptian Treaty of 1936 and the Montreux Convention of 1937, which gave greater, but still partial, independence to Egypt.

Alienated by the economic collapse and political bankruptcy of a West they had once admired, reacting against the uncritical acceptance of all things Western, and disheartened over the failure of liberal, national democracy, Egypt's literati began turning instead to what had made Egypt, the East, and the Arab world remarkable, including such traditionalist doctrines as Easternism, Arabism, Pharaonism, and Islamism.[108] These seem to have been adopted in order to essentially cloak modernization in a more palatable and appealing attire. Yet at the same time, this turn away from modernity also reflected a popular discomfort with the outright subordination and even obliteration of local values that the Westernization project demanded. The result for the moment turned out to be a hybrid of Egyptian traditionalism and European modernism.[109]

There were those—like Salama Musa, Isma'il Mazhar and Husayn Fawzi—
who did not budge whatsoever and remained ardent modernist and secularists
throughout their careers. Others, such as Hasan al-Banna, by contrast, rejected
Westernization outright and moved straight away into Islamism. The remainder,
however, reluctant to adopt an unadulterated Westernization or fall back into an
arch-traditionalist Islamism, adopted one of a number of intermediate positions.
This contingent initially included Qutb, who dabbled in Pharaonism, Easternism,
and Arabism.[110]

Pharaonism began in earnest in 1922 after the discovery and publicity of
Tutankhamen's tomb.[111] Writers such as Muhammad Haykal endorsed it as "a
vital source for self-expression."[112] Egypt was understood to possess "an eternal
national spirit that deserved the right to be reborn and the right to express itself;
that Egyptian national identity predated and transcended the religious, class,
and regional differences of modern Egyptians." Years later, in 1944, long after
Pharaonism's popularity had faded, Qutb still called for "a national literature
rooted in the appreciation of Pharaonic civilization, its history, aesthetic styles
and modern relevance."[113] Like many of his colleagues, both Islamist and secular,
Qutb appropriated the legends and stories of ancient Egypt as parables relevant
to the current political and social malaise of the nation.

The early 1930s saw the rise of Easternism, a way of answering Western
Orientalism by proposing a reverse set of binary distinctions such as the crassly
materialist West versus the sublimely spiritual East, or the chauvinist, imperialist
West versus the unfortunate, oppressed East. These ideas provoked a mild opposition to Westernization and a feeble attempt to revitalize Eastern culture. Writers
such as Haykal, Tawfiq al-Hakim, Ahmad Amin, and 'Abd al-Wahhab 'Azzam followed this approach. Qutb adopted this position as well.[114] But Easternism became
so generalized that it appeared vague and ethereal, making it difficult to develop a
concrete program. Nevertheless, it was to reappear again after World War II, this
time in the form of the Third World Non-Aligned movement, which arose out of
the 1955 Bandung conference in Indonesia. Yet by then, and notwithstanding an
occasional reference to the anti-imperialism of the Afro-Asian nations,[115] Qutb
had left Easternism behind and plunged into the more genuine and less derivative arena of Islamic politics. He may well have retained, though, its characteristic
anti-Western outlook.

Finally, Arabism arose in support of Palestine's Great Rebellion of 1936–39.[116]
Many organizations were established to support the Palestinian cause, but also to
create a cultural and even political Arab identity that ultimately morphed into the
pan-Arabism and Arab Nationalism of the 1950s. This effort was in fact a revival of
a pre–World War I movement that sought to create an Arab caliphate even before
the Ottoman Empire had formally collapsed. Qutb's own pan-Arabism subsumed
a number of slight variations. For example, he consistently claimed that while
all Muslims were equal, whatever their nationality, a clear pro-Arab bias seeped
through on occasion, such as when he suggested reviving the Islamic caliphate

with a member of the Prophet's clan uniquely qualified to fill the post. Installing an Arab, Qutb argued, would keep the office uncorrupted. Another Arabist-style proposal appeared in a speech to a pan-Arab conference in Cairo in the middle of February 1947, in which he recommended establishing a coordinating office for organizing Arab nationalist action throughout North Africa. Three months later, Qutb became editor of the monthly magazine, *al-'Alam al-'Arabi* (The Arab World) which was ostensibly a platform for Arab nationalism, although he then began to shrewdly redefine the journal's pan-Arabism into a pan-Islamism confined (for the moment at least) just to the Arab world.[117] Qutb also began to decry the accretions to Islam and the debris that had distorted it. These warped "outside" influences were inevitably foreign—Greek, Persian, Roman, European—not Arab.

These and other, lesser doctrines were all attempts to discover an authentic cultural identity that had been suppressed by the uncritical adoption of Western modernity and also to produce better methods for fixing the social and moral problems that modernity had not solved. By incorporating Egypt's own traditions and culture, writers and intellectuals developed ways of thinking that were less derivative and more legitimate. Yet many of the literati shied away from an outright Islamism for fear it would marginalize Egypt's Copts and overturn the nationalist principles that modernity had ingrained in them. Indeed many rejected Islamism because they had adopted Pharaonism, Easternism, or Arabism by applying the nationalism that Europe had taught them to their own specific circumstances. After all, national and cultural independence together was not considered at all incompatible with modernity.

This frantic search for authenticity and legitimacy in the 1930s ultimately ended at Islam—though, at first, less as a religion and more as a heritage or civilization that provided the values and norms that were more genuine for Egypt than foreign, European customs. In the 1930s, the contemporary understanding of Islam was as a foil, an insignia that symbolized more of what it was against—European culture and modernity—than what it was actually for. In order to find their own cultural heritage, European-influenced writers like Taha Husayn, Ahmad Amin, 'Abbas al-'Aqqad, Muhammad Haykal, and Tawfiq al-Hakim began to write plays, poetry, novels, histories, journal articles, and biographies based on the early years of Islam.[118] Much of the work was apologetic in nature, arguing that Islam was "just as" good, rational, and valid a way of life as the modern lifestyle.[119]

Authors began writing biographies of the first generation of Muslims. Staunch defenders of secular liberalism in the 1920s, such as the journal *al-Siyasa al-Usbu'iyya* (Weekly Politics) edited by Muhammad Haykal, began in the 1930s to publish more articles on religious subjects. Haykal himself wrote a biography of the Prophet Muhammad (*Hayat Muhammad*) in 1935, *Fi Manzil al-Wahi* (The Site of Revelation) in 1937, *al-Siddiq Abu Bakr* (Abu Bakr the Trustworthy, the first caliph) in 1942, *al-Faruq 'Umar ibn al-Kattab* ('Umar the Verifier, the second caliph) in 1945, *al-Imbraturiyya al-Islamiyya* (The Islamic Empire) posthumously in 1964, and, similarly, *Bayn al-Khilafa wa al-Mulk: 'Uthman ibn Affan*, (Between Caliphate and Kingship: 'Uthman the third caliph), issued in 1968. 'Abbas al-'Aqqad, Qutb's mentor, wrote his own biography of the Prophet, *Abqarriyat Muhammad* (The Genius of Muhammad) in 1942, followed by biographical histories of *'Umar* (1942), *Abu Bakr* (1943), *'Aisha*, the Prophet's wife (1943), *'Ali*, the Prophet's son-in-law and fourth caliph (1944), 'Ali's son, *Husayn* (1944) and finally, in 1947, a book simply called *Allah*. Taha Husayn composed *'Ala Hamish al-Sira* (On the Margin of the Prophet's Life) (1933) and *Fitna* (The Great Subversion) (1947), and Ahmad Amin wrote an eight-volume series on early Islamic cultural history that included *Fajr al-Islam* (The Dawn of Islam) (1928), *Duha al-Islam* (The Forenoon of Islam) (1933), and *Zuhr al-Islam* (The Noon of Islam) (1945). Tawfiq al-Hakim published his play *Ahl al-Kahf* (People of the Cave) in 1933, based on the Qur'anic account of the same title. This was followed by *'Awdat al-Ruh* (Return of the Spirit) in 1934, *Muhammad* in 1936, *Taht al-Shams al-Fikr* (Under the Sun of Thought) in 1938 and *al-Rabat al-Muqaddas* (The Sacred Bond) in 1944. The atmosphere in the late 1930s and 1940s was increasingly religious. Even so, the overall intellectual climate in Egypt at the time remained "tumultuous and agitated."[120]

By the middle of the 1930s Qutb's writings had begun to turn away from reflecting on Europe's influence and to move toward emphasizing Egypt and the East, experimenting with Pharaonism, Easternism, and Arab nationalism, all of which were detours on the road to Islamism. Then, on the eve of World War II, Qutb began to explore the Qur'an, initially from a somewhat secular, aesthetic perspective, and to consider more traditional and even nativist topics that embodied the new conservative style.[121]

In Sum

Qutb had arrived on the Cairo literary scene filled with boyhood enthusiasm built out of an uncomplicated nationalism and a rural naïveté. In the 1920s, Cairo was filled with many country boys running around trying to succeed; it is not clear that bumpkins like Sayyid Qutb—or, for that matter, like Hasan al-Banna, Taha Husayn, 'Abbas al-'Aqqad, and Muhammad Mandur—were at a disadvantage when compared to their more cosmopolitan, urban-born compatriots. In fact, the clarity of their vision, gained at an early age in the village and uncluttered with the later complications of city living, earned them a respect and a following that those swallowed up by Cairo's perpetual scramble and compromised by the indifference of its social attachments could not so easily achieve. At this time, Qutb was a modern, secular, liberal scholar. His career of pedagogy, curriculum design, and school supervision—in fact, what became a lifetime vocation dedicated to indoctrination—positioned him well to take advantage of Cairo's intellectual, literary, and journalistic landscape. His contacts were impeccable, his loyalties steadfast, and his motivation to succeed, nurtured by his mother and her memory, drove him to constantly improve.

The histories of Egypt's literary giants fail to include Qutb in their volumes, perhaps because of his later Islamist activism. After all, it is awkward to praise an intellectual who was executed for treason. Instead, these places of prominence are reserved mostly for Egypt's secular writers, those who best approximate Western models and who come the closest to creating art, literature, or poetry as it is defined in London, Paris, or New York. In his time, however, Qutb was greatly esteemed, a respected member of the fashionable Diwan school, and could legitimately stand proud of his accomplishments. Although the road from Musha to Cairo seemed straightforward, he was troubled by his lack of complete success, by his worrisome suspicion that a total victory meant forfeiting his rural values and even his religious beliefs, and by his frustration and despair over Egypt's own stunted advancement and dismal failures. He wanted to do well, but his own definition of success began to change as he started to question modernity and all that it demanded.

Yet his early record was not a straight-line evolution from nationalist to Islamist. Instead, it was checkered and filled with inconsistencies. He began as an ardent nationalist, but repeatedly recognized the value of religion. He leaned in the direction of subscribing to Pharaonism and Easternism, but then returned to embrace European modernization, and then flirted with Arabism even as he began exploring the Qur'an. There was a general trend, however, as he came to recognize the flaws of all these secular doctrines and finally began to focus on championing Islam.

3

Qutb's Transition, From Secularism to Islamism

By 1943, Qutb's reservations about the romantic and personal poetry of the Diwan school had redirected his attention toward social and political issues even while he remained an influential literary critic. He had already begun to recognize the limits of relying solely on personal feelings, experience, and conscience as guides to social, political, and religious conduct. Instead, he turned to the Qur'an. Its revelations portrayed the individual as subordinate, not superior, to the Straight Path that God had set down.

At this time, the rest of Egypt was also rediscovering its religious roots, and writers who heretofore had been modern and secular were likewise exploring Islamic themes. Whether their new orientation merely picked up opportunistically on what was popular or else reflected a sincere inner anxiety and doubt is difficult to answer. For Qutb, though, the end of the 1930s found him beginning to openly question his earlier liberal politics and secular principles.

Although Qutb was turning more toward literary criticism and religious studies, his poems continued to appear in Cairo's main literary journals. In December 1937, a second volume of his poetry appeared, almost three years after the first, entitled *Asda' al-Zaman* (Echoes of Time).[1] One important poem was "Filastin al-Damiyya" (Bloody Palestine), written in October 1938, to condemn the savagery of the West and to proclaim Egypt's support for Palestine's continuing armed struggle for independence.[2]

The year 1939 seemed to be a turning point in Qutb's serious engagement with Islamism, though not necessarily a sharp one.[3] We have seen that when he arrived in Cairo, he eagerly embraced al-'Aqqad, the Diwan school, and its contentious modernization, and turned his back on the Sa'id and religion, except, perhaps, as a civilizational marker. Then, between 1934 (when he defended modernity in his fight on behalf of al-'Aqqad and the Diwan school against the Apollo group) and 1938 (when he attacked al-Rafi'i and his supporters only to score a meaningless victory), he began turning away from his colleagues' embrace of modernity. Qutb came to Islamism after conscious and purposeful reflection. His decision was grounded in an analysis of social and political events in Egypt and an assessment of his own personal position—indeed, it was a rational decision, but one that did not necessarily favor the West's notion that rationality inevitably leads to modernity.

Qutb's shift was a slow but nevertheless calculated move over a two- or three-year period in and around 1939, one that was punctuated by a number of significant social and personal events. Initially, he seized on Egyptianism, Pharaonism, Easternism, and Arabism so as to distance himself further and further from Europe and modernity. Little by little, he came to settle on Islam. At first, he followed the trend set by many of his Egyptian peers that viewed Islam as a heritage or civilizational artifact. But perhaps more sincerely than the others, he began to plunge wholesale into the subject, reviving his childhood fascination, and viewing Islam specifically as a distinct religion, sui generis, that ultimately provides the most appropriate and satisfying way of life. Qutb's perspectives on existential unity, integrity, and comprehensiveness, his stress on inner feelings, commitments, and purification, and the preeminence of the intellectual exploration into metaphysical matters were appropriated from the Diwan school. But his discomfort and unease with modernity and modernization, as goal and process, began to grow.

There was much in Qutb's life and in politics at this time that nudged him down this path. First, the worldwide depression was ending, but the specter of war was rising in Europe, which was bound to affect the Middle East. The rebellion in Palestine (1936–39) and the disappointment and frustration of the Anglo-Egyptian Treaty of 1936 and the Montreux Convention of 1937, which thwarted Egyptian national aspirations, soured many Egyptians on the West. England was the specific agent of domination, but the entire West was complicit.[4] Both the economic and the international events clearly demonstrated the failures of an unbridled Western-oriented modernity.

Qutb's ties to his home community were also changing, particularly as his family situation deteriorated. His ambition to save the family's position was no longer feasible, but even his efforts to forestall financial ruin were stymied by his limited advancement within the Education Ministry.[5] In October 1940, Qutb's mother, Fatima, passed away. His father had died the year he had graduated from Dar al-'Ulum, 1933, and since that time, his mother had been the bedrock of the family. Her death was an emotional shock, and he felt disconnected and lost, still alienated within a somehow familiar terrain. His own emotional life was even more strained since he had not married and therefore had few other sources of affective support. Fatima had, after all, instilled in Sayyid a strong sense of purpose, duty, and inquisitiveness ever since his days in Musha. The melancholy brought on by her death pushed him to reexamine his youth and his mother's strong influence, and his shock alienated him from the Cairene scene, which had been so comforting but now seemed increasingly false and immoral. Images of an untainted Musha and a decadent Cairo both pointed him more and more in the direction of his religion. Qutb's love for and devotion to his mother were channeled into co-writing a book, *al-Atyaf al-Arba'a* (The Four Phantoms), with his younger brother, Muhammad, and his two younger sisters, Hamida and Amina. It was published in 1945. Also in 1940, Qutb transferred within the Education Ministry from teaching classes to working first in the General Culture Administration and then, a month later, in the Translation and Statistics Administration.[6]

Soon thereafter, around 1942 or 1943, Qutb began a romantic relationship with a woman, partly, it has been argued, to fill the vacuum left by his mother's death. This love affair ended for reasons scholars have been unable to discover; many writers see this romance as the basis of Qutb's 1947 novel, *Ashwak* (Thorns).[7] Qutb remained a bachelor for the rest of his life.[8]

As if this were not enough, Qutb's always fragile health took a turn for the worst, deepening his despair and alienation. Few details are known, but his own remarks suggest a deterioration in his physical condition. He mentioned to friends in November 1945, that he had been sick for four months. Other sources report the loss of eyesight, the removal of a lung, stomach problems, acute anxieties, and/or heart ailments, though the evidence remains sketchy.[9]

These personal difficulties, coupled with the political forces that had affected his colleagues—inauthentic identities, inappropriate philosophies, bankrupt government policies, failed reforms, and social and cultural alienation—spurred Qutb's new interest in Qur'anic studies and renewed religiosity. These feelings were supplemented by his own residual religiosity from his childhood, and his dissatisfaction with, and resentment of, the privileged cosmopolitan values of urbane Cairo, which clashed with the more populist and traditional ideals he had learned in the Sa'id. Qutb began finding solace from both these inner needs and national problems by delving deeper into understanding his religion. The Qur'an became a reassuring shelter.[10]

The transition from secularist and modernist to Islamist and radical traditionalist (to use Martin Riesebrodt's phrase) was still not totally surprising.[11] After all, Qutb had memorized the entire Qur'an at the age of 10. He followed the familiar fashion of other middle-class intellectuals, so his move toward Islamism was not so different from that of his colleagues. And his personal life may well have pushed him further, deeper, and quicker along this path. Certainly, by the time he submitted his manuscript, *al-'Adala al-Ijtima'iyya fi al-Islam* (Social Justice in Islam) for publication and left for America in November 1948, his Islamism had hardened, yet it was still moderate and liberal, advocating educational methods for reform, and not yet promoting militant and revolutionary tactics.

As Qutb became a more absorbed student of the Qur'an and a more proficient interpreter of its chapters and verses, he also became a more stern and intolerant moralist. Qutb had always been moralistic, but it took his mother's death and the outbreak of World War II—both in 1939—to bring out his heretofore hidden intolerance. His rural, Sa'idi upbringing had taught him traditional and conservative moral principles, and, unlike Taha Husayn, for example, Qutb had always remained proud of this southern Egyptian background and faithful to his old-fashioned Sa'idi customs and traditions. For almost a decade after he arrived in Cairo, throughout his years at Dar al-'Ulum and after his graduation, and during the 1930s while he was a key player in the midst of Cairo's literary circles, Qutb had demonstrated much greater tolerance and open-mindedness. But his mother's death highlighted his own traditional childhood, and World War II brought British soldiers and their vices to Cairo, living symbols of foreign depravity.[12] Were Qutb determined to condemn moralistic improprieties and express his own rectitude, he might have done so much earlier.[13] But there was no need, since Cairo of the 1930s was peculiarly insular and parochial. The ensuing culture clash between traditional Sa'idi values and unconventional British troop debauchery was more than enough to bring out Qutb's indignation and self-righteousness. By 1940, Qutb had become a deeply conservative moralist.

In September of that year, Qutb published an article in *al-Risala* entitled "al-Ghina' al-Marid" (Sick Singing).[14] He denounced the songs that were broadcast over the radio, in nightclubs, and through record companies, and considered them "dangerous" because they were "a poison running through the essence of the nation" that led to the collapse of morals and virtues in both genders. They "destroyed Egyptian social structure and personal character because they corrupted the virtues of men and women." The music and its lyrics, he claimed, were ruining Egypt's dignity, manhood, and femininity; exciting its base animal instincts; and numbing the body's senses. Such sick singing, therefore, must be censured. He suggested approaching the problem as one might approach drugs, alcohol, or narcotics: as a criminal offense.[15]

At the time, Egypt was just waking up to the power of radio; television had not yet come on the scene. The inhibiting factor was the relatively high cost of radio receivers.[16] At first, these were hardly the playthings of private enjoyment but were bought instead by cafes, merchants, and store owners to blare out on the public streets and attract customers. Thus, the radio was very much a public device and served as the focal point for male gatherings in the late afternoon and evening where men would drink coffee, play cards or dominoes, and discuss politics.[17] Qutb's condemnation was intended to stop such openly available and frivolous decadence.

Yet Qutb was not opposed to all music, just the dissolute and sensual music associated with, or influenced by, the West. He made exceptions for songs of nationalism and social commentary. After all, Qutb himself had engaged in such public political demonstrations as a teenager during the 1919 revolution. Now, he argued that rather than sensuality or immorality, singing ought to contain "dignified humor and biting criticism" or else reflect sophisticated emotional expression that opens the mind to "the thrills of the universe, the secrets of the self, and the beauty of nature." It could also express current important ethical, social, or national issues of interest. He advocated "refined human emotions," not the animal passion so evident on the airwaves.[18]

Similarly, Qutb criticized the quality of the cinema, and especially its romance movies that were starting to flood the Egyptian market.

> In Egypt, movies are shown on the white screen and most of the international movies are based on love. Some of the international movies portray this human desire in a noble and precious image that reflects on human dignity and the goodness of the human soul. We do not mean by human dignity that the image is a spiritual and Platonic image. But we mean that the image is a live image of this human desire, not that of the excited animals or that of the cheap harlotry. Some other movies portray this human desire in a vulgar image. Some of these movies unfortunately are purely Egyptian. The Egyptian movie is known as the lowest of the low of the known movies in the world. The lover becomes effeminate, soft, and flabby, and has nothing more than weeping and grieving. Such movies are disastrous and dangerous to humanity.[19]

Qutb also disapproved of the public bathing scene in Alexandria. He intensely disliked the indecent parade of girls on the beaches that, he believed, undermined their dignity. It was, he said, another slave market for procuring the satisfaction of animal desire. It may have been less the bathing costume—most were fairly conservative and concealing, although he did call some bathers "naked women" akin to "cheap meat"—than the mingling together of men and women. He concluded that this permissiveness was a violation of Egypt's traditional modesty, brought about by people blindly imitating European modernity.[20]

> Undoubtedly, life [based] on the Western style is pleasant, but it is not a pleasant or developed life on the scale of humanity. The life in which both sexes are completely free is a pleasant life, undoubtedly, but this free life is far away from the life of human beings. It is a reactionary life in the development of humanity. Yes, there is freedom, a complete freedom, but not the freedom of spirit. There is freedom of bodily desires, animal freedom, and not the freedom of human beings. He who wants this cheap freedom can find it in the Western style. He who wants human freedom, he can find it in the East, where the freedom of spirit is above the freedom of the body and the freedom of intellect. This life will triumph one day, when those who are swelled by Western modernity have disappeared from the scene.[21]

Qutb aimed his criticism in particular at the young, who seemed to accept modernity mindlessly and to show very little respect for Egypt's traditions and customs. Their lack of moral standards, he concluded, was the result of seeking excitement and pleasure from "sick singing," radio, film, and magazines rather than from serious books.[22] Indeed, Qutb's own prose compositions were aimed at this very generation, recently the beneficiaries of Egypt's expanding school system. His texts were simple and straightforward so that he could appeal to this "lost" cohort.[23]

Qutb's moralism definitely displayed "some affinity" with that of the Wahhabis of Saudi Arabia, a conservative movement promoted by Rashid Rida in the early decades of the 20th century.[24] But it may well have been yet another version of Qutb's anti-Westernism rather than any real displeasure with the various activities themselves. After all, he was not against *all* types of singing—nationalist anthems and refined emotions, such as the substance of his own poetry—were permissible. The "sickness" may not have been so much in the song, or even its lyrics, as much as in the Western decadence which the emotions and passions referred to and embodied. It's hard to imagine that Qutb would disapprove of the adults and *baladi* (traditional) women who (from a Western perspective) remained overdressed on Egypt's north coast. Yet their adoption of modern European styles and gender mingling enraged Qutb.

By the 1940s, Qutb had clearly begun examining the liberal and secular assumptions of his earlier professional career in Cairo. His fascination with poetry began to waver and he started, instead, to explore literary analysis and commentary. This was not an entirely new area of interest, since his 1932 lecture and 1935 booklet on *The Task of the Poet in Life* gave him some authority in this field.[25] Between 1939 and 1947, dozens of Qutb's articles of literary criticism appeared in Cairo's leading journals, such as *al-Risala* and *al-Thaqafa* (Culture).[26] One enthusiast, Muhammad Yusuf Najm, described Qutb's scholarly perspective as "reflecting a fine taste, a deep, original understanding, and a comprehensive Arabic education" and another, Muhammad al-Nuwayhi, while critical of Qutb, nevertheless described Qutb as "a man with pure artistic taste."[27] Both pointed out that Qutb was not knowledgeable about foreign languages and, therefore, understood foreign literature only through Arabic translation. This did not impede his critical approach to non-Arabic literature, however.

His essays and articles of literary criticism were collected together in the 1947 publication of an important textbook, *al-Naqd al-Adabi: Usuluhu wa Manhijuhu* (Literary Criticism: Its Origins and Methods). The book reflected Qutb's deep understanding and appreciation of Arabic culture, yet as a compilation of previously published essays, it still followed, by and large, the approach of al-'Aqqad and the Diwan school.[28]

As an anthology of many different commentaries, *al-Naqd al-Adabi* did not summarize overarching principles which, instead, had to be deduced from its individual chapters. The book generally exhibited Qutb's thinking midway between his national and secular ideas, on the one hand, and his later thoughts about politics and religion, on the other. Qutb did examine spiritual matters, such as the relationship between the Creator and His creations, the universe, and humanity, but his approach remained couched in a philosophical (hence, secular) perspective, with little indication of any actual engagement with Islamic activism. He continued to distinguish between an increasingly pernicious Western influence and a sacrosanct Islamic culture and religion, much as he did in his response to Taha Husayn's *Future of Culture in Egypt*. Now, however, he appeared even more skeptical about how much good could come about from Western influences on Islamic thinking, advocating borrowing in only certain limited domains, such as science and technology, that would have a more narrow impact on Egypt's intellectual pursuits.[29]

Several of his critical reviews analyzed the wave of Islamic writings appearing at this time, especially the biographies of Islamic luminaries. In one article, he contrasted the Diwan approach toward criticism with the method used by such authors as Muhammad Haykal.[30] Al-'Aqqad in his *Abqariyat* (Geniuses) series was more subjective and poetic, Qutb claimed, whereas Haykal, who penned many biographies of the first generations of Muslims, lacked this sensitivity and grace. Al-'Aqqad was reaching out to readers spiritually while Haykal's biographies were relatively strict narratives. Yet in the end, although he considered al-'Aqqad's efforts "the best of his works," Qutb seemed to have rejected the analytical approach used by his mentor.[31] Instead, he opted out for Haykal's "safer" style and a more historical assessment of these personalities, even while stating that Haykal himself lacked a serious appreciation of the actual times and atmosphere in which the early Muslims lived.[32] Qutb became very sensitive to an accurate portrayal of this first generation since he later came to rely heavily on their lives and their social and intellectual atmosphere as models for current social and political conditions.

Qutb also made a major distinction between Islamic and non-Islamic (European) literature and culture, although, he argued, the two could be bridged intellectually. After all, Qutb wrote, at one point, before the Prophet Muhammad's time, Europe and the Arab worlds had had much in common.[33] Since the rise of Islam, however, the two civilizations had diverged, but they could still come together and exchange ideas, although Qutb questioned how harmless such transactions might be to Islamic identity. Even so, Qutb sought to evaluate both civilizations from an Islamic perspective, particularly with regard to biography. For the non-Islamic material, he chose to analyze such European authors as Thomas Hardy, Leo Tolstoy, and Fyodor Dostoevsky, but also writers from the non-Arab East such as 'Umar al-Khayyam (Persian) and Rabindranath Tagore (Indian). For the Islamic examples, Qutb examined such Egyptian authors as Haykal, Taha Husayn, and 'Abd al-Hamid al-Sahhar, all of whom had written recently about Islamic subjects. The amazing feature of Qutb's book, and of his professional career at this time, was his familiarity with non-Arabic material, such as Western critical theory, even though he spoke only Arabic. Qutb's understanding came through translated material, most often from his younger brother, Muhammad. Qutb's book itself examined religious topics, but still reflected a lingering secularism.[34]

By 1943, Qutb came to seriously doubt the purpose of writing poetry.[35] He became particularly apprehensive about his subjective approach, derived from and still shared with al-'Aqqad's Diwan school. Although he continued to see the world from this perspective—sentiment, affect, aesthetics—it became less individual and personal and more a social or political expression—a shift that a social scientist would see as a move from a psychological approach to a more sociological perspective (ironically paralleling a shift from al-'Aqqad to Mandur, his current opponent). It was not that he abandoned poetry altogether—it still represented the highest form of composition in his opinion—but now he saw that it had limits, mostly in its political utility.

With the outbreak of World War II, Qutb, along with the rest of the country, fell into despair and depression. Neither the wartime economy nor the introduction of martial law were conducive to intellectual inquiry or political activism. Qutb's writings during the war years were likewise riddled with restlessness, unhappiness, alienation, and, otherwise, the quest for timeless but unsatisfied ideals. There was also increased emphasis on moral and ethical matters. Qutb's own quest for beauty and truth went more and more in the direction of divinely inspired aesthetics that transcended a more mundane cultural and relativistic definition. "Through beauty," Adnan Musallam notes, Qutb saw "the divinity which inspires worship." In order to fill the void created by his emotional and medical problems, and by the political and military environment, Qutb began to return spiritually to his village years and to revive his earlier interests in the Qur'an and in religion more generally.[36]

By the end of the war, Qutb had risen to become one of the most established literary critics in Cairo. He also continued to write short novelettes. One, entitled *al-Madina al-Mashura* (The Bewitched City, 1946), adopted a Scheherazade-style of storytelling and focused on themes of social justice and class difference. The next year he published a novel called *Thorns* that may have been based on his failed love affair.[37] Yet, more and more, he and his colleagues began addressing political issues. On February 4, 1942, the British ambassador (formerly High Commissioner) Sir Miles Lampson, worried that King Faruq was about to choose the anti-British 'Ali Mahir as prime minister, forced the king to appoint a pro-British cabinet under the premiership of the Wafd Party chief Mustafa al-Nahhas. After this ignoble humiliation, the discredited monarch began diverting his attention into a spasm of indecent and immoral activities. Not surprisingly, Qutb and his colleagues started to address issues of political decadence and social injustice more frequently from an Islamic vantage point. At the same time, as the distant atrocities of World War II in Europe came to light, Qutb and his colleagues became more cynical and more critical of the West. The venues for their political homilies were the various journals that had opened up in Cairo since the start of the war. The imposition of martial law prevented many from publishing anything more than a staid diet of loyal and patriotic oppositional pieces. But with the war's end, and the lifting of martial law in October 1945, the volume began to rise considerably.

By the late 1940s, Qutb "appears to have moved from a Muslim secularist position in the 1930s to a moderate radical Islamism in the late 1940s."[38] This resulted in his moderate Islamist treatise, *Social Justice in Islam,* completed in 1948, immediately before his departure to America, and published in 1949.

When Qutb began to seriously study the Qur'an and Islam more generally, he took a moral and anti-imperialist position. He began writing critical articles and poetry that was highly didactic. He lashed out at government corruption, at the immoral entertainment industry, and the bankruptcy of the official religious establishment, the *'ulama.* He had been critical of the West before, but it had come from a secular and partisan point of view. Now, however, Qutb began to reject partisanship—after 1942, he became very disillusioned with political parties—and to attack the West from a civilizational and religious standpoint. As the scales fell from his eyes, and Europe's barbaric holocaust, concentration camps, and fire bombings were revealed through the media, its respectability likewise fell by the wayside. Moreover, those Egyptians and Arabs from other countries who continued to collude with the West, despite these shocking disclosures, came under fire for their collaboration and betrayal. These politicians and government officials were now blamed for either causing Egypt's social ills or else remaining indifferent to them. Their cooperation with the British was a direct conduit for Europe's barbarism entering Egypt. The antipodes of social justice and tyranny loomed ever larger in Qutb's life and professional career. He sought a religious politics that aimed to change reality in accordance with the basis of the religious and ideological principles of the sacred texts.[39]

Qutb, I believe, may have chosen to examine the Qur'an, and specifically its subjective and aesthetic content, because it was perhaps the only topic left unexplored by his colleagues who were delving into religious subjects.[40] As he probed deeper, he became more convinced that this was the right direction for him. His initial approach was somewhat distant, detached, and reflective, treating the Qur'an as a neutral object and a plain literary text that was subject to a rational, almost scientific, examination. His interest was purely aesthetic and his opinion simply analytical. Qutb's work was so technical at the time that even Hasan al-Banna criticized him for not being sufficiently religious or politically engaged.[41]

As early as 1939, Qutb had re-embraced the "beautiful and beloved Qur'an" of his Musha years. At the beginning, he viewed his study as just another project in literary criticism. He started off with the sincere belief in the separation of religion and literary criticism. For Qutb, the Qur'an was simply a fine piece of literature, a work of beauty, art, charm, and imagination. It was only later that this distance and detachment was worn away by political engagement; that the Qur'an's fires burned into his soul and its beauty inspired political action. What began as an exercise that employed the same critical facilities he had once used in defending the Diwan school was now aimed at explaining his own discomfort with al-'Aqqad, his Diwan colleagues, and even modernity itself. His own study of the Qur'an led him into a deeper understanding of the divine text that went beyond just its aesthetic and expressive qualities and into its social, political, economic, and moral codes. More and more, his writings were laced with quotes from the Qur'an, and his ideas and conclusions grounded in Qur'anic citations.[42]

This project led him to write a number of journal articles between 1939 and 1945 and culminated in the publication of two books, one in 1945 and another in 1947. The first was entitled *al-Taswir al-Fanni fi al-Qur'an* (Artistic Imagery in the Qur'an) and the second was called *Mashahid al-Qiyama fi al-Qur'an* (Scenes of Resurrection in the Qur'an).[43]

Artistic Imagery was a significant and soul-searching volume, one that clearly marked Qutb's first foray into religious studies. It looked to the past by revisiting his boyhood memory (and memorization) of the Qur'an and had a major effect on his future thinking. The book was based on a short, two-part article Qutb published earlier in 1939.[44]

Qutb began his analysis of the Qur'an by "temporarily strip[ping it] of its religious sanctity and set[ting it] aside as a book of legislation and political order."[45]

> It is not the purpose of this book to take up the matter of the message of the Qur'an from the religious point of view, but rather to restrict discussion to the area of expression alone, transcending time and place . . . in order to discover pure aesthetic beauty, originally in its independent essence, everlasting in the Qur'an itself, expressing aesthetic [value] independently of all interest and purpose.[46]

Qutb concentrated on analyzing the Qur'an's artistic elements, such as its images, tales, dialogues, narration, and expressions. How and how well did the Qur'an succeed in transmitting its artful and creative nature to the reader? Qutb tried to bring out the Qur'an's charm, aesthetics, and imagination as well as the elegance of its storytelling, with its deep psychological and philosophical dimensions. He highlighted and analyzed its dialogues, expressions, and representations, describing them as brief but dominant in their precision and beauty. He determined that the Qur'an was the most effective and affective method in conveying its religious ideas and feelings. It was, after all, the seal of perfection that none could improve upon or even imitate. He then related the Qur'an to the Arabic culture in which it had first appeared. He concluded by discussing the Qur'an in the context of the literary traditions of the day such as classicism, symbolism, realism, and romanticism, yet noted its inimitable reflection of Arabic eloquence and culture.[47]

In envisioning how the Qur'an was received or experienced by the first generation of Muslims, Qutb exhibited a style of thinking that continued throughout his lifetime. He extolled the virtues and piety of the *salaf*, or "ancestors," at the time when the Prophet Muhammad began in Mecca, before there was an Islamic state, when there was only religious belief. He shared this strong emphasis on the earliest years of Islam and the first extraordinary generation with the *salafi-yya* movement developed by Jamal al-Din al-Afghani, Muhammad 'Abduh, and

Rashid Rida.[48] It was the ancestors' belief, practice, faith, and action that would become exemplar for all the rest of Muslim society.

In this inaugural study, Qutb intentionally analyzed the Qur'an in a way quite different, almost the opposite, from the traditional, more scholastic, interpretation or exegesis.[49] The words of the Qur'an, Qutb believed, conjured up images, rhythm, and style that had enchanted people well before they understood its precise meaning.

> Imagery is the preferred device in the Qur'anic style. By means of imagined and sensed images, it expresses intellectual meanings and psychological states, tangible events and actually observed scenes, and human exemplars and human natures. Then, it elevates the images it draws and grants them individual life or renewed movement.
>
> So listeners forget that this is speech recited to them and examples given to them. Instead, they imagine that here is a scene being shown to them or an event taking place before their eyes. There are characters coming and going on stage. A range of emotional reactions are on display, arising coherently and appropriately from the situation portrayed. These are living words, words that real tongues form to reveal feelings that have been hidden.[50]

Later scholars, though, forgot this affective quality once they began reading books of exegesis, disputation, and interpretation. Their books and studies never came close to giving Qutb the same thrill and fascination that he had experienced as a child.

Instead of analyzing the usual juridical, dialogical, grammatical, syntactical, and historical substance of the Qur'an, Qutb approached the project by focusing on the artistic beauty and harmony of the book. Qutb was interested in a different view of the Qur'an, one that generalized the subjective understanding of the book and how it then coaxed and shaped the Muslim's own comprehension. This brought the Qur'an down to the level of ordinary people who found it captivating, appealing, and expressive, but were put off by the abstract and erudite reasoning practiced by more conventional scholars and philosophers.[51]

The Qur'an contained, Qutb concluded, two separate aesthetic styles—sensual dramatization and magnification. The first includes many of the anthropomorphisms found in the Qur'an (although many traditionalists have argued otherwise) and the second points to the underlying rhythmic style of the text and the realism of its human imagery. Both, Qutb said, were used to help clarify unclear verses and passages.[52]

> When a person reads the Qur'an or listens to it, he is transported, through its words, to a higher level of reality in which he forgets that he is being exposed to words; he imagines he sees actual scenes as they

unfold, watches real events as they happen, and witnesses existing persons as they act.... He [Qutb] contends that this method or quality of the Qur'an was what impressed the Arabs when they first heard the Prophet Muhammad recite the earliest revealed verses from it.[53]

But Qutb warned, in spite of his own systematic analysis, that the substantive and aesthetic dimensions of the Qur'an could not be separated. For him, the Qur'an expressed "a unified artistic method of expression" and a "charm" that inevitably attracted readers and listeners into accepting God's recitation and His religion, Islam.

> But the teaching of the Qur'an is not merely meant to affect the emotional attitudes of Muslims toward Islam, it is also meant to convince them that external social experience is to be brought into conformity with the aesthetically defined inner experience of truth.[54]

Thus Qutb verified the holistic nature of the Qur'an and of Islam itself, realizing that both were integrated into a single idea. The Qur'an's artistic imagery was an essential means—perhaps the most crucial means—to achieving that end.

At the time, Qutb remained intellectually in the modernist faction. In fact, it was just the purpose of "strip[ping] [the Qur'an] of its religious sanctity and set[ting it] aside as a book of legislation and political order"—no matter how "temporarily"—that had discredited Taha Husayn 20 years earlier in his controversial analysis of pre-Islamic poetry.[55] Although Qutb approached his own Qur'anic analysis with the same scientific detachment—and therefore risked similar condemnation—his results went decisively in the opposite direction: in contrast to reinforcing the separation of religion and politics, Qutb affirmed the absolute unity and integrity of Islam. Qutb never received the opprobrium that Husayn had; perhaps, however, Qutb was consciously aware of the initial secular position he shared with Husayn and sought to distinguish and even contrast himself from his more illustrious colleague by reaching completely different conclusions. Then later, as the full impact of these conclusions penetrated his literary analysis and criticism, he would soon shake loose his acceptance of the modern and the secular altogether.

Qutb's goal was to return the Qur'an "to our hearts" and restore the experiences and sentiments of the first Muslims. Leonard Binder summarizes Qutb's approach:

> Thus, in describing the magic[56] of the Qur'an, he shows how some early converts to Islam were won over by merely hearing a single verse of the Qur'an—much as he was charmed by the Qur'an as a child—and before becoming acquainted with the full teachings of Islam. The Qur'an is a fully integrated theological and artistic unity, but it is not necessary to

know it all before one becomes a believer, nor is that process a voluntary
or rational one. Belief is not based upon the intellectual understanding
of the logical priority of divine creation. The event of belief precedes
the lengthy process of acquiring religious knowledge.[57]

For Qutb, the Qur'an offers the decisive truth about all matters, divine or
mundane, seen or unseen. The Qur'an is the only reliable, indisputable source
and depicts the proper, unexpurgated reality divested of the fables and myths
that had distorted the previous monotheisms. Although history and communities
constantly change, the permanent truth of the Qur'an means that it provides an
enduring and unvarying set of guidelines that regulate the social order no matter how much the society fluctuates. People's devotion and zeal are constantly
shaped and directed by God's Holy Book because it offers a basic, existential statement about the relationships among the universe, God's creation, and human
communities.[58]

In 1947, Qutb published a second study, *Scenes of Resurrection in the Qur'an*.
Here he used the same methods to explore the meaning of Judgment Day, of
ascending to heaven or descending to hell, and the justice embodied in this decision about the afterlife. He argued that this world and the world hereafter are
not at all separate and distant, but instead are united through the mediation of
Judgment Day. The traditional Islamic views of paradise and perdition had been
repeatedly disparaged by pre-modern European observers because these images
appeared far too lenient.[59] Qutb, on the other hand, was anything but indulgent;
instead, he was a strict disciplinarian, not unlike such influential Protestants as
John Calvin or John Wesley.[60] For those truly believing in and correctly worshipping God, paradise is filled with happiness. But for those rejecting faith in God
and regarding His revelation as falsehoods, the punishment is eternal torment
in hell. Then there are people between these two poles who occasionally go astray
and become spiritually weak.[61] Qutb's view at this time was that these people are
obliged to improve their spiritual condition through personal struggle, reorientation, and transformation, exercising a *jihad* of the heart.[62] In later years, though,
Qutb came to realize that such errant worshippers needed more than their own
inner efforts but required outside help in reforming their wavering devotion.

Qutb not only examined Islam but also other religions as well—the ancient
Egyptian religion, Judaism, Christianity, Buddhism, and Hinduism. Yet for Qutb,
the Qur'an presents Judgment Day as a living reality in a very perceptible and
graphic way. It combines and blends these scenes together with the accompanying narratives to create "a calamitous movement which turns everything upside
down, excites the calm, and frightens the secure," leaving the strong and deep
impression that molds the human conscience.[63] It is because of their lurid repre-
sentation of death, life after death, happiness, and suffering that the images and
scenes found in the Qur'an can leave a deep impression on the reader's/listener's
mind and secure a strict discipline and social control.

With this book, Qutb again risked condemnation by engaging in an analysis that could be judged offensive for its secularism. Yet once again, Qutb pursued just the opposite course, reaffirming the glory and beauty of the Qur'an by showing how it contributed to the overall integrity and comprehensive character of Islam and, behind that, of God's strict unity, *tawhid*. Thus for Qutb, the connection between this world and the next points inevitably to the total dominion of God and the overall blending of the divine, the spiritual, and the devotional. To attain paradise one must recognize God's dominion and believe and worship Him according to His revelations. Violating those ways—for example, by not following God's law—brings about punishment in the hereafter. The sense of either contentment or dread, therefore, can be provoked by the scenes and images of Judgment Day in the Qur'an in which rewards or punishments are meted out. For it is the Qur'an, Qutb concluded, that "speaks the truth which deserves to be followed, and those who deviate from the truth are liars and tyrants."[64]

Thus, in *Artistic Imagery* and *Scenes*, Qutb explored the expressive and aesthetic side of the Qur'an. But unlike so many other interpreters, thinkers, and scholars whose approach was more dry, legalistic, and detached, Qutb concluded that it is the subjective quality of the Qur'an that makes Islam a dynamic system such that the Qur'an is not just *about* life, but it *is* life itself.[65] Qutb's perspective was that these two qualities—the subjective and the objective—can only be separated analytically but that, in reality, they are blended together into a unity that combines aesthetics, artistry, imagery, charm, and imagination together and that, as such, it expresses the complete and legitimate knowledge and truth that constitute Islam. The Qur'an is, after all, an eternal, unified, and integrated miracle.[66]

Qutb's interests were definitely shifting toward Islamic liberalism and moderation. Notwithstanding his lingering ties with the Diwan school, Qutb started to question and even dissociate himself from al-'Aqqad. True, both were turning toward Islamic topics, but Qutb seemed much more genuine while al-'Aqqad was simply going along with what was popular. Al-'Aqqad focused on reason and rationality in guiding people's actions whereas Qutb was beginning to put much more stress on revealed faith and practice. Moreover, Qutb was also worried that al-'Aqqad's compelling personality might prove too domineering. Imitating his mentor, he felt, meant weakening his own personality under al-'Aqqad's powerful influence. It was, after all, al-'Aqqad who had pushed the young Qutb into pursuing art, literature, criticism, and poetry. But Qutb now felt he was more and more restrained in his pursuit of spiritual themes. By the middle of the decade, he and al-'Aqqad had parted ways.

Qutb's first formal Islamist composition appeared in the September 14, 1946, edition of *al-Risala*, and was entitled "Madaris li al-Sakht" (Schools for Indignation).[67] Here he expressed his anger at secular politics and politicians who failed to reform the country and simply resigned themselves, instead, to "God's will." Although these ideas appeared as early as the late 1930s, Qutb now began to argue for an outright Islamic activism.

Qutb began to increasingly use Qur'anic verses, slogans, and references in his texts. He continued to criticize and attack foreign imperialism and colonialism; only now, the justification was less Egyptian nationalism or pan-Arab nationalism than Islamism. Perhaps as the degenerate escapades of King Faruq came to light, Qutb (along with many others) responded by plunging into religion and seeking solace in the kind of religious leadership—in stark contrast to what existed in Egypt—that was counseled by the Qur'an. Islam's political science—centered around leadership, tyranny, obedience, social justice—envisioned a highly moral and legitimate ruler.[68] The Prophet Muhammad remained an unblemished example of a spiritual guide, a statesman, and a commander. Islam lost its purpose when it lost its magnificent leadership, when rulers succumbed to earthly pleasures instead of steadfastly guiding their community under God's rule.[69]

Even before he visited the United States Qutb was becoming more and more critical of Western writing and values, and of those Egyptian authors who aligned themselves with the West. Egypt continued to suffer from the presence and perversity of British troops, and Qutb increasingly reproached the crassness, bad taste, and superficiality of Western popular culture. It was, Qutb claimed, an essential part of the West's headlong drive toward oblivion and destruction, of its addiction to throwing out traditions and embracing novelty, and of its move away from religion, God, and God's word. Surely the East, and particularly Islamic Egypt, could do so much better than to imitate the West. In Islam, there was no mimicry but rather a voice of authenticity and decency.[70] Qutb developed a countervailing Occidentalism that reversed the value judgments of Orientalism, such that Europe and America came to represent everything ugly and crass, in contrast to a pure and sincere image of Islam. Yet the power imbalance between the West and Egypt cannot be overlooked, making Qutb's Occidentalism more a form of resistance and opposition, while its antithesis, Orientalism, and its associated prejudices, had become yet another form of obfuscation, propaganda, and intellectual domination.

Politically, Qutb became increasingly disillusioned with parties, elections, parliamentarianism, reform, and the modern liberal process because of pervasive corruption. As mentioned earlier, he had switched from the Wafd to the Sa'dist Party in 1938, but in the 1940s, he gradually stopped any partisan activities. He became increasingly critical of democratic politics, secularism, and "modern morality," perhaps an oxymoron in the first place.

Qutb's denunciation of the West also took more particular forms, responding to the day's current events. Heretofore, he had attacked just France and Britain as colonizers, but now he also came to include the United States and Holland as imperialist powers who were increasingly showing their bankruptcy and corruption—political, economic, and moral. Despite his decade-long infatuation with British authors when he was more involved in the Diwan group, by the 1940s he had turned hostile toward England. He strongly criticized the United Kingdom when it forced the king to install a new Wafd cabinet. He promoted a "48-hour revolt" when the German and Allied troops fought at al-'Alamayn in the summer and fall of 1942, which, he said, might have disrupted and distracted the British just long enough to ensure their defeat. After the Armistice, on February 21, 1946, "Evacuation Day," when strikes and demonstrations erupted throughout the country against the British-backed government, he attacked Britain for mocking its own principles of democracy and freedom. The results of that day—20 dead and 150 wounded—prompted Qutb to write that "blood is the down payment for freedom and that martyrdom is the price of dignity." He harshly condemned the United Kingdom for its continued occupation of both Egypt and Sudan. Qutb perceived this foreign domination and influence were the source of Egypt's corruption, poverty, and injustice.[71]

Just as Britain governed Palestine, Iraq, and Egypt, France ruled North Africa and the Levant. Qutb condemned both for continuing their colonial occupation. After World War II, when Morocco, Syria, Tunisia, and Algeria sought their independence from France, these liberation movements were brutally suppressed. Francophile Egyptians like Taha Husayn were excoriated for glorifying France. The Dutch also came under attack for their colonial occupation in Indonesia (Dutch East Indies) which lasted until 1949.[72] And just as he had supported the Palestinian rebellion of 1936–39, Qutb again called for governmental and private forces to stop Israel's declaration of independence and its expansion beyond its original territory. Qutb criticized US President Harry Truman for his immediate recognition of Israeli independence, for US support of Zionism, and for America's support of immigration to Israel.

In all, Qutb lashed out at those Western governments that opposed the aspirations and liberty of Muslim countries. Just as Jamal al-Din al-Afghani had observed and counseled the Muslim world after his startling experiences in India and the Great Mutiny of 1858, so, too, did Qutb strive to mobilize Egyptians, Arabs, and Muslims more generally to come to the aid of their countrymen in overthrowing the yoke of Western domination. Earlier in his career, his criticism of the West had been cultural. Now, his attacks also targeted the West's political and military domination.[73] He wrote in *al-Risala* in the summer of 1946:

> How I hate and despise this European civilization and eulogize humanity which is being tricked by its luster, noise, and sensual enjoyment in which the soul suffocates and the conscience dies down, while instincts and senses become intoxicated, quarrelsome, and excited.[74]

In the mid-1940s, he called for a *jihad*, but it is not clear what exactly he meant. It may initially have taken the form of resistance or political opposition, but gradually it came to include militancy as well, particularly in response to foreign threats raised outside Egypt—in Palestine, Sudan, North Africa, and the Levant. Inside Egypt, he opposed Western influence but had not yet concluded that those Westernized elements in Egyptian society ought to (also) be the target of militant, *jihad*ist action.

A third major volume of Qutb's appeared in 1946, and was perhaps the last secular work he composed. This was the quasi-autobiographical book, *A Child from the Village*, written to commemorate Qutb's childhood, but also to venerate the culture and communities of rural Egypt and the Sa'id in particular. It has been characterized as "anthropological" for describing Musha (ca. 1920) in dispassionate and unbiased terms.[75] Here, Qutb explored the religious practices of the village, its education and schools, its medical and public health practices, its Robin Hood–like robbers and social bandits, its antagonistic relations with the government, its *tarahil* workers, and the inevitable clash between the village (no matter how cosmopolitan it could be) and the city (no matter how parochial it appeared).

Many biographers and writers see *A Child* as an autobiographical sketch about Qutb's life in Musha. Yet it may not be, and its purpose may not be simply to tell a story about his village days. In fact, the key may well lie in its dedication, where he evokes Taha Husayn's autobiography of his own boyhood life, *al-Ayyam* (The Days).[76] Qutb's *A Child*, while perhaps modeled on Husayn's book, differs significantly from it, and therein lies a good reason Qutb wrote it: not to emulate or praise Husayn (who by the year of *A Child*'s publication had become very prominent), but to subtly criticize him. The populism found in *A Child* contrasts sharply with the haughtiness of *al-Ayyam*. Both intellectuals came from the Sa'idi countryside and both had moved to the city. But Qutb demonstrated a pride in his rural roots whereas Husayn recommended these values be expunged so that Egypt might take its rightful place as a modern, European society.[77] Husayn belittled and disdained the village life of his youth, showing it in an unfavorable light and mocking it. Qutb, on the other hand, seemed proud of the people and the life of the rural Sa'id, and looked upon even the most outrageous activities as fun, entertaining, and comforting, but also as sources of community solidarity. When I lived in southern Egypt, I personally found such populism common in the Sa'id among educated people who were proud, affectionate, and even nostalgic about their rural days, but certainly not haughty or contemptuous as Husayn seemed to be. Husayn evinced the air of a villager who had gone on to the Sorbonne and had never turned back. Qutb, by contrast, demonstrated the populism of someone who had his "bumpkin-ness" thrown back at him, but who was not ashamed of it and, in fact, found pride and honor in his village culture.

Yet Qutb would not, or could not, be so blatant as to criticize Husayn outright. So his approach was to mimic Husayn's *The Days*—using many of Husayn's literary flourishes and style—but departing from his perspective in subtle but significant ways. Where Husayn was sarcastic and ridiculing, Qutb was affectionate and respectful. Where Husayn wholeheartedly embraced France and Europe, Qutb was much less cosmopolitan. Husayn wrote off the village religious schools as vacuous and dishonest, with instructors pretending to teach and students pretending to learn. He would have abolished them completely. Qutb, however, saw them as in need of reform, but he also questioned the benefits of the secular government schools. He sought the best from both institutions. Husayn was intent on freeing Egypt from the backwardness of its tradition in his headlong dash toward mimicking European culture. Qutb, on the other hand, supported a national community that was based on the humor, honesty, and determination of the peasants and petit bourgeois entrepreneurs of the village. Husayn was critical of the lifestyle and folk beliefs of villagers, seeking to eliminate them in modernizing Egypt. These must go, Husayn reasoned, if Egypt was to take its rightful place among modern nations. Qutb, however, did not adopt this modernization project, nor did he see tradition as a shame to be wiped out. His nostalgic view bordered on the romantic, seeing the countryside as the diametric opposite of what he had come to see as the decadent and depraved city. If, in all his years in Cairo, he had seen nothing but a corrupt palace, parliament, and bureaucracy, why then should the city be held up as virtuous? He then went on to represent the countryside as everything the city was not—honest, forthright, sincere, and steadfast.

Qutb was deeply influenced by the traditional rural folk religion woven into the fabric of village life, although not as one might ordinarily expect. In my own research, I found that many rural-to-urban migrants, especially from the middle class, end up scorning the religious practices and beliefs of their old village, as new arrivals to the city self-righteously turn their backs on the more casual style of rural Islam and instead adopt a more legalistic and formal Islam and Islamism that brand village beliefs and practices as "superstition."[78] Yet although Qutb was moving toward Islamism, none of the ordinary ridicule that Islamists so often shower upon their former identities and communities appeared in *A Child*. It was Husayn's *The Days* that emphasized the sneakiness, laziness, and ignorance of rural people. *A Child*, on the other hand, reflected Qutb's pride and appreciation of non-Western Egypt and his recognition of his own country's distorted and deformed character, even at (and perhaps particularly at) the highest levels of society, in the Palace and among the educated elite. If this autobiography is any guide, Qutb saw these rural beliefs as a means of harmonizing village life. Were the village itself appreciated and fondly remembered, then, its religious conventions should be too.[79]

A Child was an important step on Qutb's path to Islamism. Many of the principles drawn from the book would continue to guide Qutb's thinking. These include

- a faith in the ancestors as a source of pride and wisdom that contrasts sharply with today's corrupt and immoral leaders who toss out traditional values;
- a belief in the inherent goodness of his ordinary countrymen who remain oppressed by unjust, tyrannical governments;

- an elitism (albeit not necessarily an arrogant one) that promotes an Islamist vanguard in contrast to (but that assists) the "little people" of Egypt's villages and neighborhoods, and
- a need to anchor one's identity in the authentic traditions of Egyptian society, not in those values imported from the northern shores of the Mediterranean.

After the armistice, Qutb, disillusioned, condemned the existing political system and concluded that corruption and indifference made the government cynical and hardened to the needs of the country and its people. In chapter 9 of *A Child*, Qutb discusses a terrifying episode in which government soldiers intimidated villagers in Musha, ostensibly searching for concealed firearms.[80] Clearly Qutb was on the side of the poor villagers who suffered beatings and coerced confessions. Since the same treatment abounded in the aftermath of World War II with the eruption of public strikes and dislocations, Qutb, without hesitation, condemned the government for its inhuman conduct toward its citizens.[81]

He also criticized the wealthy elite, although class relations never loomed large in his social and political analysis. He attacked the elite as much for their Westernization and libertinism as for their privilege and immoral power. If we refer again to *A Child* for insight into Qutb's postwar thoughts about the upper class, we can see his discussion about migrant farm workers as demonstrating a social-democratic liberalism and predilection toward those less fortunate. There was little, if any, criticism of farmers and farm employers, and since there were no "feudal landlords" in Musha, there was no stage upon which to criticize these unconscionable exploiters. Qutb certainly did not embrace a labor theory of value, but merely expressed sorrow (but not pity) that the little people had such little opportunity and income.[82] But he reserved most of his disapproval for the city-based aristocrats and *bashawat*, those whose wealth far exceeded the moderate incomes and means of the countryside.[83] These people—and their minions (writers, spokesmen, journalists, media personalities, and other apologists) and the politicians they bought and paid for—were repeatedly condemned for their profligacy, dishonesty, and disproportionate influence. At the time, Egypt was experiencing wave after wave of strikes and demonstrations against the government as Egypt suffered a postwar economic collapse. Not only did the elite, politicians, and their henchmen not attempt to implement reforms, some actively provoked these problems. Qutb certainly was not alone in his demand for major transformation in the palace, government, and plutocracy.

Qutb had particularly sharp words for those he considered collaborators and apologists: the media (radio and the press), the *'ulama*, literati, intellectuals, and writers who supported the corrupt and disgraceful national leadership. On several occasions, he called them "opportunists," "hirelings," and "mercenaries." They had sold out, he claimed, attacking them for forfeiting their fight for social justice and liberty and, instead, becoming willing pawns manipulated by partisan politics. Those supporting the Palace and the government, and those fawning over foreign nations, were obvious targets,[84] but so too were political activists of practically any stripe, the liberal and Communist left, and increasingly those advocating any perspective other than Islamic. It was just these denunciations against the elite, the politicians, the media, the Palace, the Parliament, and Western governments that forced Qutb to travel abroad in 1948 in order to avoid arrest.[85]

At the same time, Qutb quickened his disengagement from the influence of 'Abbas al-'Aqqad and the Diwan School. His explorations into the Qur'an had pulled him steadily away from the secular and anglophile positions of what heretofore had been a very influential force in his life. Al-'Aqqad himself reacted to Qutb's estrangement with quiet indifference, which alienated Qutb even further. Qutb became quite resentful about what he saw as al-'Aqqad's unresponsiveness, even though it was Qutb himself, not al-'Aqqad, who was withdrawing. In particular, Qutb began changing his own views about poetry and literature. From 1946 to 1948, Qutb wrote a number of articles clarifying his new perspective that the Diwan school had remained fixated on ideas alone and had failed to engage with the emotions that glued or committed people to these ideas.[86] The Diwan school had "failed to differentiate between ideas and feelings in poetry" and was concerned with the former at the expense of the latter. Qutb had become especially interested in how the faith and beliefs of the early Islamic period in Mecca were accepted and internalized, and that literary analysis ought to similarly consider this as a vital part of poetry, but which the Diwan school had ignored. By 1948, he fully rejected al-'Aqqad's vision of poetry and decided to abandon literature altogether.[87]

4

Qutb's Moderate Islamism

When, at the conclusion of World War II, martial law was lifted, Qutb became much more strident in calling for total independence from a repressive British colonialism and for greater social justice from a morally and politically corrupt Palace. Neither position delighted the government. As the government faced labor strikes, demonstrations, and clashes with the Communists, Muslim Brothers, and those in between, Qutb joined the chorus speaking out against European imperialism more broadly—in Egypt and in other Arab countries—and against Egypt's stagnant economy, especially in the countryside.

As the war wound down, the volume of Qutb's literary criticism increased, but his poetic production declined. His reviews appeared mostly in *al-Risala* and *al-Thaqafa,* and his positive comments and recommendations helped elevate many aspiring Egyptian novelists. In particular, his review of Naguib Mahfouz's 1943 novel *Kifah Tiba* (The Struggle of Thebes) made him "the first literary critic to champion Mahfouz's talents as a novelist," and his assessment of Mahfouz's 1945 book *Khan al-Khalili* helped bring Egypt's future Nobel Prize laureate out "from obscurity... [and] into the limelight."[1]

In addition to writing, reviewing, and his full-time employment at the Education Ministry, Qutb also became chief editor for two major Cairo journals, *al-'Alam al-'Arabi* (The Arab World) and *al-Fikr al-Jadid* (New Thought).[2] Both focused on political, economic, and moral issues in Egypt and in the Middle East more generally.[3]

Qutb used these journals to expound on such issues of the day as poverty, powerlessness, tyranny, colonialism, corruption, social justice, and social, political, and economic reform in general—topics that were extremely relevant in the postwar climate of Egypt, with its economy jolted by the departure of the British military and with its government disgraced by British dominance. Elsewhere in the region, there was the emergence of an independent Israel to the northeast, and the self-determination of French and British colonial possessions. Qutb and other colleagues jumped headlong into these issues.[4]

Qutb saw the real need for reform, and mindful of the rivalry from competing political factions—Socialist, Communist, and nationalist—he developed a moderate Islamic platform to attract those who found these other trends appealing.

He was, not surprisingly, particularly concerned about rural reform. His remedies were not unusually radical nor did they differ greatly from other (secular) proposals. Qutb was outraged at the economic hardships and political marginalization of the countryside. He saw the lack of economic opportunity and upward mobility not only creating economic stagnation but generating moral turpitude as well. He championed agrarian reform, which would involve confiscating and dividing up large "feudal" estates and distributing the parcels of land to those in need. He later made such economic development the centerpiece of his 1951 book, *The Battle of Islam and Capitalism,* which drew the public's attention to the social and economic troubles facing ordinary Egyptians. Qutb was also upset by the fact that so few reformers and planners were actually familiar with the Egyptian countryside, content to remain in Cairo and talk.[5]

More and more, he abandoned the narrow issue of greater independence for Egypt. Nor did he simply stop at supporting a greater Arab national homeland. He rejected nationalism, both Egyptian and Arab alike, and what he viewed as its distorted allegiance and superiority. Instead, he began to gravitate toward calling for the liberation of the entire Muslim world, even veering toward a Third Worldism that would present itself as an alternative to the emerging Cold War superpowers (what would later become the Non-Aligned Movement). For a while, he even advocated the formation of a league of Islamic nations to represent newly minted countries that had to choose between the United States or the Soviet Union. Thus Qutb saw issues increasingly from an Islamic perspective.[6]

Of the two journals, *New Thought* was the more important. Its purpose was to discuss the decline and deterioration of Egyptian society in the postwar years, which ultimately culminated in the 1952 republican revolution. The Communists and left-wing Wafdists were making serious inroads to attract workers and students, and *New Thought* aimed to provide a serious and practical alternative to the Left. Qutb himself felt that Communism encouraged economic justice but not spiritual justice. Islam offered a much more comprehensive vision. One important tenet was to present Islam as a flexible system rather than a rigid and static structure as it was ordinarily portrayed. The topics that *New Thought* dealt with might well have been taken right from the pages of *New Dawn* (*al-Fajr al-Jadid*), the Communist Party organ. These included property ownership, landlord-peasant and employer-employee relations, and the distribution of wealth.[7] The theme of social justice—soon to be addressed separately by Qutb himself—was woven throughout the journal's articles, which focused on the underprivileged and downtrodden and emphasized the practical application of the theories of capital and labor.

However, Qutb's unconventional reputation, harsh words, and belligerent actions—all influences from the Diwan school—soon got him into trouble. He left his position with *The Arab World* because of editorial differences and then left *New Thought* after just 12 issues when the government closed down the journal, ostensibly because of the outbreak of the Palestinian war in May 1948, and the imposition of martial law,[8] but also because of Qutb's denunciation of government corruption and tyranny, foreign domination and imperialism, and the promotion of an Islamic alternative. The campaign for social justice and honest government in the pages of *New Thought* in particular provoked a tremendous uproar from Egypt's elite classes, particularly the Palace. Official pressure to silence him became quite strong.

> Social justice is lost in Egypt.... We are in need of new parties with a constructive mentality that will look to the complete unity of Egyptian society... and prescribe a political renewal and a complete social program for curing Egyptian society of its sickness.[9]

In fact, Qutb became so disliked by the Palace that it issued an arrest warrant for him. The situation was so dire that it required the sympathetic prime minister, Mahmud Fahmi al-Nuqrashi, who knew Qutb from the Wafd and Sa'dist parties, to intervene with Qutb's employer, the Education Ministry, and to quickly arrange to send Qutb on an educational mission to the United States to get him safely out of harm's way.[10]

Yet Qutb's campaign for social justice did not simply end when the *New Thought* journal closed down. Instead, he began writing a major study of the topic since it represented one of the main ideas in Abrahamaic monotheism. Before he departed for America, he gave his brother, Muhammad, his manuscript for *Social Justice in Islam* to submit for publication while he was out of the country. He then set off for the port of Alexandria in November 1948, and from there took a boat to New York, to spend the next two years studying Western educational curricula. He did not return until August 1950.[11]

Between 1945 and 1950, Qutb's rival, Taha Husayn, had begun to move away from his earlier (and controversial) writing on culture and published several works that criticized the established order and focused on social injustice, political corruption, and resistance to oppression and exploitation. *Mir'at al-Damir al-Hadith* (The Mirror of Modern Conscience) and *al-Mu'adhdhabun fi al-Ard* (The Tormented on Earth), both published in 1949, demonstrated that the trust Husayn had once placed in the inevitable success of liberty, parliamentary democracy, and natural evolution was weakening. In particular, in *The Tormented on Earth*, he pointed out that "the government's aim is to increase the luxury of the wealthy and contemplate the misery of the miserable and wretched." He dedicated the book to

> To those who are burning with the yearning for justice
> To those who go sleepless for their fear of justice
> To those who have what they do not spend
> To those who do not have anything to spend

The government immediately confiscated the books.[12] Qutb's *Social Justice in Islam* may well have been intended to counter Husayn's work by showing that Islam, too, contains the same concepts of justice and integrity that Husayn's imported European secularism did.

Immediately after *Social Justice* was published, in April 1949, it was acclaimed as a major landmark volume. Islamic groups and individual intellectuals throughout the Arab world praised the book.[13] It was also well received by ordinary people, perhaps because its erudition was straightforward and not filled with arcane scholastic and legalistic discussions. Unlike his earlier writing, here Qutb was not focused on uncovering the aesthetics of the Qur'an. Instead, his approach was decidedly political, presenting an Islamic program for moral, governmental, and economic reform—a vision of what the Islamic state should stand for. Social justice is one part of the political equation in Islam, with the other parts emphasizing obedience and consultation. Many scholars had already written about the importance of obedience in citizens. Qutb looked at the issue from the opposite direction, examining the obligation of rulers to mete out justice and fairness in dealing with those they govern. The conclusion was obvious, but still necessarily implicit: the governed were clearly correct in opposing, perhaps even overthrowing, a state that ruled without social justice.

In *Social Justice*, Qutb essentially sought to put God back into Machiavelli's *The Prince* so that rulers become circumscribed in their official actions rather than employing whatever means prove necessary to stay in power. In the modern world, Qutb claimed, there are no principles or morals in government, and therefore, no unity. Qutb wanted to change these conditions. What secularization had rendered apart, Qutb eagerly wanted to put back together again. *Social Justice* contains a set of liberal values familiar in the contemporary world and which exist in many societies, secular or religious. But Qutb claimed that a religion-based justice is much more enduring than a secular one, especially where capitalism allows whatever the market can bear. In Islam, what is just and fair is the result of the larger, more comprehensive will of God that governs all social relationships, particularly those between rulers and ruled. It is the opposite of the division, alienation, and antagonism that characterize government relations in the West.[14]

> The nature of Islamic social justice [is] that it must embrace all the aspects of life and all varieties of endeavor; similarly it must include both spiritual and material values. Its political theory in the final resort is concerned with the implementation of the religious law.[15]

Qutb maintained that Islam's theory of social justice consists of three principles: (1) total freedom of conscience, (2) complete human equality, and (3) strong mutual responsibility. "On these three foundations," Qutb wrote, "social justice is built up and human justice is ensured."[16] Although Qutb dissected Islamic justice by analyzing the different principles individually, he recognized that Islam unifies them into an integrated, harmonious totality.

By freedom of conscience, Qutb meant freedom of thought.[17] These two are equivalent and, in turn, require freedom from material want and freedom from servitude (tyranny or coerced obedience). Together, these three constitute the basic elements of Islam's principle of freedom.

Qutb claimed that true liberation is impossible unless people are free from anxiety about their material condition. Although man's freedom is more than just freedom from striving for material necessities, Qutb claimed, this cannot simply be ignored, and so Islam contains the institutions of *zakat* and *sadaqa* (Islamic tithes) as mechanisms for securing material freedom.[18] These allow Muslims to set their eyes on higher goals, such as the worship of God.[19]

Freedom from material want frees people from servitude (*'ubudiyya*, or worship) to anyone but God Himself. Freedom from this sort of mundane bondage, as Qutb called it, also means a freedom from the fear of death, harm, and humiliation, except what God proclaims.[20] It also means eliminating man's enslavement to his senses, to his lusts and desires, to his foibles and bad habits, and to his own nature and egotism.

These three types must all be present to create an overall sense of freedom. Economic security without spiritual and political safeguards simply duplicates what the Communists strive for. Political liberty without a spiritual commitment and economic comfort is nothing more than the secular politics of the West. Finally, spiritual purity without economic stability and political freedom creates an asceticism that glorifies the denial of material and emotional pleasure, or else become an opiate that convinces people they are better off than they really are. Neither has a place in Islam. Islam does not conceal poverty nor deny its cost, but transcends the material plane.

Such freedoms require guidance—they are not simply instinctive—and punishments should people not practice their freedoms responsibly. Freedom of conscience, however, is but one ingredient for social justice in Islam. Islam not only strives for freedom of thought but it also struggles to achieve political freedom (liberty) and social freedom (equality).

When people achieve a freedom of conscience, they have gone partway toward achieving equality, the second principle of social justice in Islam. Equality is a condition brought about by the oneness of humanity's origin and development, and comes close to the West's notion of democratic freedom—the capacity of each person to have an equal impact on government.

Qutb urged people to abandon racial, ethnic, national, and class distinctions, and to renounce other social markers that divide people from one another, so as to integrate themselves together into a unity before God. Qutb argued, as did the *salaf*, the first generation of Muslims, that it is only differences in piety that should distinguish people from one another.[21]

Still, Qutb was not so blind as to ignore social realities nor did he wish to deny differences in talents and aptitudes—"equality" does not mean "identity."

Differences in property and assets, in personal honor and integrity, and in rewards and punishments, are all shaped by individual circumstances. These Islam pledges to protect. However, all social—as opposed to personal—distinctions are inimical to Islam. Qutb strongly objected to the abuse and discrimination that had generated such inequities and strongly criticized Western society for the disparity between its ideals and the reality of its prejudices.[22]

To Qutb, Islam is the great equalizer. If individuals feel inferior, Islam gives them self-respect and confidence. If individuals feel haughty and arrogant, Islam humbles them before God by establishing standards of modesty.[23]

Qutb remarked that a very important test of a society's equality is how, in particular, it treats its powerful and rich. It is insufficient to just alleviate the plight of the downtrodden. If the elite are given special privileges, if their family background, social standing, fame, and affluence help them acquire more wealth and power through no work of their own, then it is up to the people to put Islam into practice and its ideals of freedom and equality.

But it is not only the destitute and the helpless who benefit from Islam's emphasis on equality. It is also the rich and powerful, who can feel contentment in their souls and peace in their hearts because of their *zakat* and *sadaqa* donations. Islam seeks not to eradicate class differences but to alleviate the bad feelings among different strata.[24] The time and place of Islam's origin was one of extremes, with aristocrats claiming noble blood and descent from the gods, and with slaves bearing the brunt of their anger by torture or killing.[25] Social justice in Islam, as Qutb envisioned it, reduces these extremes, for all souls—men, women, leaders, slaves—are the same in God's view.

The final tenet of social justice in Islam is social solidarity (or mutual responsibility[26]), which balances individual and collective needs.

> Islam grants individual freedom in the most perfect form and human equality in the most exacting sense, but it does not leave these two things uncontrolled; society has its interests, human nature has its claims, and a value also attaches to the lofty aims of religion. So Islam sets the principle of individual responsibility over against that of individual freedom; and besides them both it sets the principle of social responsibility which makes demands alike on the individual and on society. This is what we call mutual responsibility in society.[27]

Qutb recognized five sets of mutual responsibilities. In each, there is a balance between duties and benefits. First, there are the responsibilities a man has to himself, to balance his needs and his wants, his desires and his enjoyment. Personal freedom is offset by personal responsibility. Islam asks each person to regulate both themselves and others alike.

Second, there is responsibility between a person and his family, which guarantees shared sustenance, happiness, and cooperation. The family is the main building block of society, especially in the Middle East, and its importance is reflected in concern for the balance among its members individually and collectively.

Third, there is the reciprocity between a person and society. This is the domain of politics, art, literature, the media, and other institutions of civil society, which balances the needs of the individual with the needs of the community. There is a fourth relation, the balance between one community and other communities, which is where Western notions of representative democracy enter, cooperating so as to achieve a consensus or compromise. Finally there is the mutual responsibility between generations, with the young respecting the old, and the old preparing the young for their future. Planning, education, inheritance, and religiosity are crucial here.

It is this area of mutual responsibility and obligation, with its rules about collective needs that trump individual preferences, that can trouble Westerners. Restrictions on individual freedom can become necessary to preserve community morals and values. Qutb went still further and charged community members with the responsibility for encouraging the good and eliminating the evil in order to avoid chaos and conflict. He argued that while Islam certainly values freedom and equality, it clearly recognizes the need to control them for the sake of the entire community.[28]

To Qutb, Islam is much more concerned with the equilibrium between the individual and the community than is the West. Moreover, because of the homogeneity of countries such as Egypt, many more of its restrictions can be enforced by informal custom rather than law. But where this homogeneity breaks down, and where the traditions concerning propriety lack consensus, then formal laws and governments assume the power to enforce this balance.

In sum, social justice in Islam is achieved by combining freedom, equality, and responsibility to create harmony and balance. This concept existed in Christianity and Judaism, but Islam heightened its importance, and Qutb's book emphasized both the importance of the concept in Islam and the need to reestablish its centrality in Egypt.

Qutb probed deep into Islamic history to understand just how Islamic social justice had emerged historically but then declined afterward.[29] He invoked the past not to live in it or to find detailed solutions from it, but to learn broad principles that could then be applied to his own day. Qutb had already started a lengthy examination of history when writing his two books *Artistic Imagery* and *Scenes of Resurrection*. Now, though, he was inspired to learn more about what he called the "greatest spiritual moment" in Islam, the beginning of the Prophet Muhammad's mission, when it was pristine and uncontaminated.

> Is it possible today to renew something similar to that [historical] form
> of Islamic life for the present and for the future? It is not sufficient that
> Islam should have been a living force in the past; it is not enough that it
> should have produced a sound and well-constructed society in the time

of the Prophet and in the age of the caliphate. Since that distant time there have been immense changes in life, intellectual, economic, political, and social; there have even been material changes in the earth, and in its powers relative to man. All these things must be carefully considered before an answer can be given to our question.[30]

The world of early Islam had once been a united and integrated society—belief in a single God mirrored in a cohesive, spiritually homogenous community. How, then, did Islam's noble spirit deteriorate to its current depths of degradation?

Despite the decline of justice, the spirit of Islam has still continued to operate, if not in government, then in the lives of the people and among individuals. Its ideals could be revived once again.

> The period of [Islam's] obscurity and weakness is now at an end, and the tide of Islam has commenced to rise.... I have absolute faith in the possibility of a renewal of Islamic life.... The Western world... is hostile to us, and in particular hostile to our religion. Therefore, it will not permit us to produce a new Islamic system or to renew a truly Islamic form of life, however great the effort we put forth.... The return to the Islamic system is... a great and difficult task, requiring extraordinary effort. Above all, it demands courage to believe in it, boldness to face the inevitable obstacles, patience to endure the hard work demanded, and faith to believe that this is necessary for Islamic society and for mankind as a whole.[31]

At the time he wrote *Social Justice*, Qutb was proposing *da'wa*, or religious education, as the principle technique of reform. It remained for future publications to advocate a more radical approach.

Social Justice was written just before Qutb traveled to America, and it was published while he was abroad, in the spring of 1949. A second, revised edition appeared in 1950. All together, six editions were published, with each slightly updated to reflect Qutb's current views. With the first two editions, Qutb remained independent of any Islamic organization since he did not consider any existing association capable of realizing his reforms. But after his return from the United States, he became more and more radicalized and concerned about achieving an Islamic system, state, spirit, and society. He joined the Muslim Brotherhood about the time the third edition appeared in 1953 because he felt that the society was the best vehicle to achieve his goals, and so the third edition exhibited a greater sympathy toward the Brothers. It was this edition that John Hardie translated into the English version that is known outside the Arabic world. Later, in 1954, when the Brotherhood was charged with the attempted assassination on the life of Egypt's president, Jamal 'Abd al-Nassir, many Brothers and Brotherhood officials, including Qutb, were rounded up, arrested, tried, and imprisoned. In 1958, a number of Brothers were tortured by prison officers, and Qutb was shocked. He became quite angry and bitter, such that the last edition, published in 1964 while he was still confined, reached new levels of outrage, indicating that Qutb's move into militancy was much greater.

William Shepard conducted a brilliant and painstaking study of the changes in all six editions of *Social Justice*. Qutb became more conservative and more radical over time. He turned from a liberal social democrat into a radical Islamist in the 1960s. There was, according to Shepard, more and more reliance on God (as opposed to human agency), a growing emphasis on Islam as a stable and consistent system, and an increasingly moral history of Islam.

The growing trust in God instead of trust in people fits well with Qutb's overall trend from secularism to cultural Islamism to full-fledged Islamist activism based solely on the *salaf*, Qur'an, and *shari'a*, Islamic law. Qutb shifted from seeing people making decisions based on Islamic principles to seeing people as obeying a God Who makes all the decisions, which people are obliged to obey. The shift marks Qutb's growing conservatism.

Qutb also became more of a *salafi*. Increasingly, he came to believe that the Prophet and the ancestors provide strict and well-defined templates of proper behavior, thought, and faith. Qutb's transformation took him from seeing Islam as a religion in the Western sense to seeing it as an entire way of life; from seeing people create their own history to seeing history determined by God, and from seeing the Qur'an as a philosophical statement to seeing it as an instructional guide on how to transform societies.

One major difference between the moderate, even liberal *Social Justice* of 1953 and Qutb's last major book, the far more radical, even extremist, *Signposts on the Road*, is the latter's debt to the Hanbali scholar Ahmad ibn Taymiyya (1263–1328).[32] Ibn Taymiyya is known for his polarized kharijite dogma—intolerant of diversity, hostile to established government, and filled with an overwhelming sense of God's omnipotent authority.[33] *Social Justice* is a major contribution to the Islamist movement; it remained, at its core, a social democratic program (although Qutb would have rejected this secular political term) and not, like *Signposts*, a revolutionary proclamation. Whereas Qutb's attitude in *Social Justice* was accommodating and adaptable, thereafter, and particularly as result of his prison experience after 1954, Qutb adopted more and more Ibn Taymiyya's unyielding kharijite perspective.[34] For the moment, however, this extreme position remained in abeyance, not yet provoked by intense hardship and revulsion. But his visit to America was to radicalize him further.

After Qutb finished writing the manuscript, he handed it over to his brother, Muhammad, and sailed from Alexandria to New York on November 3, 1948, for a two-year visit to study English and school curricula. Qutb's visit to America was his first experience ever in living outside Egypt and his first direct contact with Western civilization.[35] It has produced a surprising number of contradictory accounts, not all of them reliable. Some say he went for a master's degree; others that he just went to observe American education, teaching methods, and curricula. Yet others say he was under no obligation even to take university courses; still others say he officially matriculated. One writer claims that not only did he complete a master's degree in education in Colorado, but that he momentarily considered staying for a doctorate, but gave up this idea and returned to Egypt. His itinerary was also not clear, although Greeley, Colorado, home to what was then the Colorado State Teachers College, now the University of Northern Colorado, seems to be one well-known destination.[36] Wilson College in Washington, D.C., and Stanford University in California were additional and equally important venues for Qutb's study and observation.[37]

The reason behind this intense interest in his American sojourn is that when Qutb left Egypt, he was a moderate Islamist and a social democrat. When he returned, he was an extreme radical. What exactly happened to Qutb on this trip that turned him into a militant? Gilles Kepel has written that a "half-naked" British woman attempted to seduce him on the cruise trip going over.[38] (But here he was not merely an ordinary passenger; he was the temporary imam, or prayer leader, for some of the ship's crew.) Musallam claims that Qutb's radicalization was a response to teachers in the American public schools Qutb visited who encouraged adolescent sexuality.[39] John Calvert, who extensively researched Qutb's visit to Greeley, states that Qutb was scandalized when he observed firsthand the "seductive atmosphere" of a church social where girls and boys danced close together.[40] These incidents and temptations came from letters he wrote his friend, Sayyid Salim.[41] Other determinant reasons are less sensational and prurient. Qutb was deeply affected and disgusted when he heard how triumphant Americans had reacted to Israel's independence six months earlier. He was also amazed at the uncritical acceptance of the Zionist project, with its anti-Arab and anti-Islamic undertones. He was also appalled when he observed how jubilant Americans reacted to the news of Hasan al-Banna's assassination in February 1949. He had discovered numerous books and magazines that regarded Islam and especially the Muslim Brotherhood as threats to American security interests, part and parcel of the insults and abuse of Western Orientalism.[42] He was further critical of US foreign policy such as the Marshall Plan and America's involvement in Korea (the war broke out just as Qutb was about to leave the United States).[43] For all these reasons, and probably more, Qutb came home in 1950 with a largely negative and pessimistic view of the United States and of Western civilization in general.[44]

In America, he visited schools and colleges, hospitals and factories; he read the daily newspapers, watched television, went to the cinema and theater, and attended sporting events such as wrestling, boxing, and football. He went to different church services as well.[45] He met people from different walks of life, of different classes, occupations, and skills.[46] He was thus able to observe and experience America quite broadly. But unlike earlier voyagers outside Egypt who admired and embraced modernity, Qutb righteously rejected much of what he saw in the United States as shallow, materialistic, and shameful.[47]

Qutb's ship arrived in New York City, where he was free to set his own program.[48] While exhausted from the voyage, he traveled forthwith to Washington, DC, where he stayed long enough to learn English at the International Center for Teaching Languages at Wilson College.[49] It was here that Qutb heard his first stories about America's sexual freedom—among youngsters and in public.[50] These accounts shocked him, and he concluded that Americans could not possibly fall in love, except with lucre and lust.

He then journeyed to Denver and Greeley in the early summer of 1949, and later traveled on a West Coast tour to such cities as San Francisco, Palo Alto, and San Diego. His longest visit, though, seems to have been in Greeley, where he stayed six months.[51] He was pleased by Greeley's natural beauty and somewhat sympathetic to the people's social conservatism. But he was also stunned by the amount of care residents bestowed on their lawns and, as a result, the lack of time devoted to social interaction.[52] At Colorado State Teachers College, he audited a course in summer school on English composition and later in the fall semester registered for three courses on American education, secondary education, and oral interpretation. He experienced the fall football season, which he considered "brutal," and listened to American jazz, which he regarded as "unbearable" and "primitive."[53]

He wrote an article for the college's literary magazine, *The Fulcrum*. It demonstrated Qutb's oblique and circuitous style in criticizing those to whom he felt subordinate, such as the majority of American citizens and his host, but also the Egyptian government. This subordination made him much less willing to voice criticism directly. Qutb's article was a parable entitled "The World Is an Undutiful Boy" about ancient Egypt and Greece and the origin of civilization, which had traveled from Egypt, to Greece, to the rest of Europe, and then, by implication, to the United States. It was a statement of Egypt's early superiority but also about the preservation of its moral values, which later declined in other places, finally arriving to the depths of the brutal (football) and animalistic (sexual) character of American civilization. It was, then, an indirect criticism of the West in general, of America more specifically, and of its youth, ingratitude, and disregard for religion and decency.[54]

He wrote to a friend back in Egypt, Anwar al-Ma'adawi, that he found America extremely materialistic and alienated—estranged from itself, from its soul and thought, and its spirit separated from its body. America had become one big factory, monstrously noisy and chaotic, which demonstrated that what had made America rich and successful also made it religiously impoverished and ultimately a failure. Elsewhere, he called it a "fascinating civilization" where "absolute pleasure is free from any form of restriction or custom." Moreover, he met Egyptians and Muslims in America who had come to the country with optimism and high expectations, and then defended and justified to Qutb their resulting shortcomings. These, not ordinary Americans, were the people Qutb criticized for reverting back to such ignorance: crass materialism, unbridled capitalism, sexual animalism, vulgar feminism, public "emancipation," licentiousness, and uninhibited freedom. These were the aspects of Western life that he objected to, and to which many expatriate Arabs and Muslims had long since succumbed.[55]

America, Qutb claimed, had lost its humanity. It came to embody all that Qutb would call *jahiliyya*, or religious ignorance and apathy. Love was animalistic, and life was joyless, sweaty, and noisy. Its goals were purely materialistic and it lacked any spirituality whatsoever. Although admittedly intriguing in parts—particularly its rejection of imported "systems"—America was a civilization based on an absolute freedom unfettered by custom and spirituality.[56] Qutb wrote that the East could benefit from America's science, technology, and invention: "chemistry, physics, biology, astronomy, medicine, industry, agriculture and methods of administration; in both their technical and administrative aspects as well as practical methods of war, fighting and other similar activity."[57] Later, he kept this view, but he also argued that even these systems were tainted and, if adopted, they could hurt the Muslim world.

> During my stay in the United States, there were some people of this kind who used to argue with us—with us few who were considered to be on the side of Islam. Some of them took the position of defense and justification. I, on the other hand, took the position of attacking the Western *jahiliyya*, its shaky religious beliefs, its social and economic modes, and its immoralities: "Look at these concepts of the Trinity, Original Sin, Sacrifice and Redemption, which are agreeable neither to reason nor to conscience. Look at this capitalism with its monopolies, its usury, and whatever else is unjust in it; at this individual freedom, devoid of human sympathy and responsibility for relatives except under the force of law; at this materialistic attitude which deadens the spirit; at this behavior like animals, which you call free mixing of the sexes; at this vulgarity which you call 'emancipation of women;' at these unfair and cumbersome laws of marriage and divorce, which are contrary to the demands of practical life; and at this evil and fanatic racial discrimination. Then look at Islam, with its logic, beauty, humanity, and happiness, which reaches the horizons to which man strives but does not reach. It is a practical way of life and its solution are based on the foundation of the wholesome nature of man."
>
> These were the realities of Western life which we encountered. These facts, when seen in the light of Islam, made the American people blush. Yet there are people—exponents of Islam—who are defeated before this filth in which *jahiliyya* is steeped, even to the extent that they search for resemblances to Islam among this rubbish heap of the West, and also among the evil and dirty materialism of the East.[58]

It seems clear from this that Qutb was much more vehement and critical of the apologists and faux Muslims who practiced these evils, intentionally or otherwise, than the local inhabitants. His diatribes were aimed at his misguided compatriots, not so much at the incurable Americans. He had, of course, written off America as decadent and wicked, but during his visit, he remained merely a bystander and an observer, making his own value judgments privately or in letters back home to friends. He did not seem to entertain any intentions to change America, forcibly or didactically.[59]

Egypt had ignored its own heritage and traditions by importing and adopting foreign systems wholesale—its principles, theories, laws, and solutions. More important, it had marginalized its religious belief and practice, mostly out of sheer laziness and selfishness. Instead, Egyptians had embraced what Qutb called the "soft, perverted, and sick lifestyles" of the West—just those habits forbidden by their own religion and religious texts.[60]

Qutb's view of the United States, some argue, had predated his trip to America, and he was simply inclined to see decadence and decay. Certainly his tour of New York City, Washington, DC, Greeley, Denver, and California convinced him of the dissipation he had come to expect such that even if he had not come predisposed, it would not have taken much to convince him of the religious and moral ignorance of America. Clearly, America's foreign policy, particularly after World War II, was building the country into a global superpower. The growing prevalence of the newly coined label "Third World" and the Cold War between the first two worlds, created a set of power relations that Qutb was keen to condemn. Qutb was well aware before departing Alexandria that the United States was a leading economic and military power—a big, cumbersome machine, as he called it—that used people's hopes and dreams to fuel it to ever greater levels of prominence. Was it just because America presented such a big target? That was at least part of it. But it was also the fact that America, and the West more generally, had been accepted so willingly and uncritically by his countrymen that came to disturb Qutb even more. He might have just outright dismissed America's decadence, but it was when he saw the same ignorance at home, in Egypt among Egyptians, that his strong objections and oppositions burst forth.[61]

Qutb's visit to America certainly reinforced his preconceived pessimism toward Western civilization and strengthened it even more by what he experienced firsthand. He may have gone a moderate and returned a radical, but it required a deepening of Egypt's own crises to turn his potential militancy into a reality. He did not just steadily move toward radicalism nor merely become radicalized suddenly by his American trip. It was both.

His visit underscored his belief that Islam was humanity's only salvation from the chasm of Godless capitalism and modernity.

> His stay in America opened his eyes to the ravages wrought by Godless materialism in the spiritual, social, and economic life of the people, and when he returned he was more than ever convinced that only Islam can save mankind from the abyss of annihilation toward which it is

hurtling at a tremendous speed, propelled by an insatiable greed for material things.[62]

It was during this time that he became convinced that casual, undirected writing was worthless, perhaps even counterproductive. He decided to abandon his literary career and take a more active part in Egyptian politics. Writing, he concluded, was futile unless it had practical applications. He wrote a letter from Colorado Springs to the journal *al-Kitab* arguing that an idea does not live in people's soul unless it becomes a part of their beliefs and convictions. It is only then that this idea becomes convincing, and that the person who believes in it comes to personify this principle. This is why, Qutb wrote, the words of the prophets and saints live on, and the words of [Western] philosophers and thinkers have died.[63]

Qutb was loath to remain in the United States and so, on August 20, 1950, he returned to Egypt, this time arriving at the new Cairo airport. His return was announced in the newspapers and magazines in advance, so that when he stepped off the plane, he was immediately met by a delegation of young Muslim Brothers.[64] Although he had not joined the Brotherhood before or during his travels, he was deeply impressed by this reception and soon established warm relations with the Brotherhood. In the first few days back home, he received visits from friends, colleagues, well-meaning strangers, and also radicals and revolutionaries who were beginning to find his writing inspiring. These sympathetic visits pushed Qutb to devote his life to applying Islamic programs of social reform in his own country. He resumed his earlier position at the Education Ministry—apparently in the clear with those who, before his trip, had wanted him arrested—and continued his work as a supervisor until his resignation in October 1952.[65]

After his return from the United States, and in the course of sharply turning toward a more radical Islamism, Qutb came under the intellectual influence of two major South Asian scholars, Abu al-A'la Mawdudi (1903–79) and Abu al-Hasan 'Ali Nadwi (1913–99).[66] These two, both Muslims surrounded by Hindu majorities, but also immersed in the mundane secularism of post-independence nationalism and modernity, imparted to Qutb important religious concepts that involved rigid sectarian boundaries and resolute religious-political principles that strongly opposed the attenuation of religious differences. Just as these two South Asians felt besieged by British imperialist domination, modernizing Indian compatriots, the "foreign at home," and, therefore, defensive and fearful of total dissolution, so, too, did Qutb face similar constraints imposed by continued British and French hegemony and secular, Westernizing Muslims. While Qutb's opposition to modernity and the West was well advanced, he deepened his antipathy even further by adopting their concepts. Both provided important inspiration to Qutb.[67]

Qutb became personally acquainted with Nadwi after he returned from America, when Qutb performed his first hajj to Mecca and Medina in November, 1950. Qutb's own hostility toward the West was heightened after their discussions and during Nadwi's visit to Qutb's home in Helwan the following February.

Here, Nadwi was the guest of honor at Qutb's weekly seminar. Qutb then wrote the introduction to the second edition of Nadwi's book, *What the World Lost as a Result of the Decline of Muslims*.[68] The two became close friends who stimulated each other's thinking. This was particularly true for *Social Justice in Islam*, and Nadwi's influence shaped Qutb's reworking of later editions of the book.[69]

Nadwi had applied the concept of *jahiliyya*, or the ignorance of Islam reminiscent of pre-Islamic Arabia, in a less literal and more metaphorical manner, and applied it to a much broader range of historical experiences, than previous scholars had intended. For example, Nadwi considered Europe's materialistic civilization to be pagan and *jahili*, not simply secular and lapsed Christian. Nadwi also held the corrupt leadership responsible for Muslim back-sliding, and the "general depravity of humanity." Thereafter, Qutb adopted this extended understanding more frequently in his own writing.[70]

Qutb first encountered the writings of Mawdudi after they were translated into Arabic in the early 1950s.[71] Qutb refined the concepts that Mawdudi had used, particularly the latter's rigorous notions of revolutionary struggle and anti-Orientalism. His own work was strengthened further by citing Mawdudi's anti-modernist considerations of *jahiliyya*, *hakimiyya* (the dominion of God and His laws), and *jihad* (the struggle by Muslims to move from the first to the second). These concepts vary significantly from their classical definitions, but include alternative understandings that arose because of the foreign imperialism and domestic collaboration and duplicity that both writers experienced. The comparable colonial context unsurprisingly produced a convergence in their attitude and approach. Both pointed to despotic rulers and social immorality as examples of the problems wrought by Western modernity.[72]

All three intellectuals, whether independently or under their mutual influence, also demonstrated the strong influence of Ibn Taymiyya, who had long since pointed to the problem of true and pious Muslims living in the context of a pagan society, either foreign, colonial, or indigenous. His rigidity and intolerance were adopted by Qutb, Mawdudi, and Nadwi: true Muslims should believe and act according to a narrowly defined orthodoxy and orthopraxy; otherwise, they are unbelievers (*kuffar*) and therefore eligible for punishment. *Jihad* then becomes the means for such retribution. It is somewhat useless to argue whence this kharijism came; the routes are circuitous, but numerous.[73] Yet it is just this legacy that arguably represents the greatest impact of these scholars, especially Sayyid Qutb.

> Thou shall not find a people who believe in God and the Last Day befriending those who oppose God and His messenger, even though they be their fathers or their sons or their brothers or their kinfolk. As for such, He has impressed faith upon their hearts and hath strengthened them with His Spirit. He will bring them into gardens beneath which rivers flow [paradise], wherein they will abide. God is

well-pleased with them and they are well-pleased with Him. They are God's party. Now surely the party of God are the successful ones.[74]

Qutb increasingly exhibited this stark kharijite thinking and its intolerant, Manichean approach to defining good and evil. More and more, it meant a heavy stress on obedience to God, and no one else except those who govern by the Qur'an, as verse 5:44 declares—"Whoever does not judge by what God has revealed is an unbeliever." This growing kharijism gradually became a much more dogmatic set of principles. Qutb began insisting that there is either an Islamic world or a *jahili* world, a pious and upright community or one steeped in immorality, blasphemy, and wickedness. No place existed for the conciliatory middle position found in the more liberal, Mu'tazilite distinction of good Muslim, bad Muslim—but still Muslim—and *kafir*.[75] Moreover, the characterization of what defines a "good Muslim" became increasingly narrow so that those falling outside these restricted limits were not even to be considered Muslim at all. This sliver of acceptability gradually became limited to Qutb's own narrow point of view and its stiff, uncompromising message: those who commit wrongs or sins without repentance can be excommunicated or even executed.

Unlike any of his Egyptian predecessors—al-Afghani, 'Abduh, Rida, and al-Banna—Qutb adopted this kharijite perspective and rejected their moderate Mu'tazilite approach.[76] Qutb came to divide the world into two, and only two, parts: Those who are true believers and those who are guilty of unbelief. There is no room for "lapsed Muslims."

> Two situations alternate in human life at all times and in all places: guidance and misguidance, whatever form misguidance may assume; truth and falsehood, whatever form falsehood may assume; light and darkness, whatever form darkness may assume; divine law and human whim, whatever form whim may assume; Islam and *jahiliyya*, whatever form *jahiliyya* may assume; belief and unbelief, whatever form unbelief may assume. In short, [there is] either commitment to Islam as a religion, as a way of life and a social order, or unbelief, *jahiliyya*, ignorant desires, darkness, falsehood, and misguidance.[77]

By identifying Egyptian society on the wrong side of these polarities and accusing nonconforming Muslims of apostasy, Qutb was able to justify the militancy and violence that, he finally concluded, was the only way to solve the ills of Egypt and the Muslim world.

5

Qutb's Radical Islamism

The Egypt to which Sayyid Qutb returned in 1950 was a country that was falling apart, afflicted with poverty, disaffection, and unrest. Since the end of World War II, Egypt had witnessed rising prices, unemployment, labor strikes, little investment, political assassinations, royal profligacy, government corruption, partisan scuffles in and out of office, a massive and growing gap between rich and poor, and a widespread, uneasy sense of disorder and chaos.[1] The official political parties, the Muslim Brotherhood, and the leftist, Communist organizations were all demanding reform and many were suggesting concrete solutions, some of which involved violence. The secondary ranks of officers in the national army were grumbling after its abysmal and embarrassing performance in the 1948 war for Israeli independence. Qutb wrote a doomsday scenario in *Signposts on the Road* while he was in prison after 1954, not only because of the newly discovered atomic bomb, but because of the West's loathsome inhumanity. It seems equally appropriate to Egypt at mid-century:

> Mankind today is on the brink of a precipice, not because of its ability to annihilate itself which is hanging over its head—this being just a symptom and not the real disease—but because humanity is devoid of those vital values which are necessary not only for its healthy development but also for its real progress. Even the Western world realizes that Western civilization is unable to present any healthy values for the guidance of mankind. It knows that it does not possess anything which will satisfy its own conscience and justify its existence. Democracy in the West has become sterile...[and] Marxism is defeated [because] this theory conflicts with man's nature and its needs.[2]

Qutb maintained that Egypt had lost its moral anchor and had been inundated with perverse corruption and domestic conflict, which were causing discord and destroying the country. He blamed this devastation on immorality, imitation of the West, modernization (or Western cultural imperialism), and political and military colonialism.[3]

Oh Cairo! Your reality is ugly and deformed, cheerless and miserable, poor and tortured, ignorant and backward. From you emanate the deformity and your sorrow is clearly seen. Your cries of sorrow resonate in your quarters. Your whines of pain are residing in between your ribs. Your gloomy and sick appearance, your bleeding and ailing body, all are seen by he who is searching within and around you, he who unveiled the outer layer of your overlaid garment.[4]

Qutb concluded that Muslims were in a malaise, succumbing to nationalism and secularism—loyalties to those other than God. In order to remedy this "sick world," Islam must "free the Muslims from a mountain of wrong notions, man-made values and traditions, false laws and constitutions, and the ocean of modern ignorance."[5]

Qutb laid the primary blame on a spiritual weakness, not on political, economic, or international forces. The disorder that Egypt was experiencing was derived from its Westernization.[6] The problems he had encountered in America were coming to afflict Egypt but now in their own peculiar way: vulgar movies, music, and clothing; corrupt aristocrats, officials, and political parties; vastly unequal incomes and property ownership, high unemployment and consumer costs, and chaotic factories and workshops.

Qutb pointed to the decades-long decline of spiritual vitality since the 1870s. The answer was not just economic—to think so was the mistake of the Communists. Nor was the answer merely political, for the government's cooperation and collaboration with the West was due to the spiritual decline of each and every Egyptian. Instead, lying at the center of the economic and political dilemma was a religious emptiness. Egypt urgently needed a virtuous leader to apply the spirit of Islam.

It is not difficult for a scholar to restore what has been lost from our civilization and to overcome the corruption and divisions which are happening at the expense of the country. It is not difficult to overcome the political disputes that degraded the spiritual energy in this country. The accumulated spiritual energy and its resources were never renewed since the time of Jamal al-Din. Similar to him, we can correct much of what we see of this moral degradation on the level of the individual and society. We can restore the sacred flame in the face of the waves of the corrupt Europe which become a machine without heart....However, political awareness cannot continue or live by itself, nor can its level be elevated without the breath and support of spiritual energy. Where is the spiritual leadership of this generation? The leadership which creates great personalities similar to those who were created by al-Afghani. The leadership which elevates the individuals and groups from the transitory requirements to the higher horizons. Will this condition of degradation result in a great spiritual leadership, as we have learned from the spirit of Islam over centuries? We hope that there is a leap in the near future during our time.[7]

This affliction affected the entire Arab and Muslim world, but it required a steadfast and vigorous leadership from Egypt to guide people along the Straight Path of Islam.[8] Qutb reckoned, however, that Egypt's current leadership was similar to the morally bankrupt leadership of the past. Its spiritual weakness had afflicted the entire country, especially the youth. Qutb's focus became both political and religious: real political change and transformation could not take place until Egypt was firmly guided by virtuous, spiritual rulers.[9]

None of Egypt's leaders escaped Qutb's blistering criticism. Anticipating the fury that burned down parts of Cairo on January 25, 1952, Qutb wrote a number of articles two months earlier that harshly criticized the government for being in league with feudalists, capitalists, and the commercial bourgeoisie, whose interests were all diametrically opposed to those of the people.[10] He wrote scathing attacks on government corruption and the hopeless political party system. He published outraged fulminations against moral decay and the extensive breakdown of public order. He was particularly incensed over Israel's war for independence, Egypt's incompetent response against the Zionists, Parliament's failure to abrogate the existing Anglo-Egyptian treaties, and the continued presence of the British in the region.

Even the country's spiritual elite came under fire. In fact, the 'ulama, or Islamic scholars and officials, were an especially common target for Qutb's denunciations. He referred to them as "professional men of religion who sold themselves, not to God or the homeland, but to Satan."[11] Their weakness, passivity, and compliance earned them Qutb's scorn, and their inexcusable compromise with power made them corrupt and ineffectual.

Initially, he may well have even included the leadership of the Muslim Brotherhood, particularly those who succeeded Hasan al-Banna after the Supreme Guide's assassination. Before he had left for America, Qutb had known of the Muslim Brotherhood, but remained uninvolved. After his return from the United States, his writing began to exhibit a greater urgency for social reform, and this attracted greater attention from both the Muslim Brotherhood, under the temporary leadership of Salih al-'Ashmawi, and the Free Officers movement inside the army under the leadership of Jamal 'Abd al-Nassir. Qutb was at the intersection where the two groups met. He was well aware of the reasons for the Free Officers revolution and was similarly sympathetic to the Brotherhood battalions operating in the Canal Zone.[12]

On January 25, 1952, 50 Egyptian policemen died in a shoot-out with British troops stationed in Isma'iliyya in the Canal Zone, and 100 were wounded. Shortly thereafter, angry riots broke out in Cairo in which protestors burned down a number of foreign establishments in the central downtown area. Ordinary Egyptians were angry, not just with the British, but also with their own Wafd Party government for its ineffectiveness and incompetence. Prime Minister Mustafa al-Nahhas declared martial law and the king dismissed the government. Over the next six months, he appointed four different, but still inept, administrations. Soon after the Cairo burnings, on the eve of the republican revolution, Qutb joined forces with the Brotherhood as a contributing writer and propagandist, although he did not officially join the organization until early 1953.[13] He was appointed to the executive Guidance Bureau and placed in charge of its *da'wa* (missionary or propaganda) division.[14]

It is significant and somewhat incongruous that Qutb had remained an independent Islamist thinker for so many years before officially joining the Muslim Brotherhood. Perhaps it was because he had begun his Cairo career as a secularist and only belatedly came to realize that his own ideas matched those of the Brotherhood. The total commitment demanded by the Brothers would appeal much more to those already devoted to its program. In this regard, Qutb's trip to the United States rapidly pushed him into sympathizing with the Brotherhood. The elation and arrogance of Americans over al-Banna's assassination, and later, the subsequent shut-down of the Brotherhood's legitimate activities in Egypt, changed his perspective and loyalties.

Still, Qutb chose to remain relatively independent even while attacking the government and the West and calling for economic and political reforms. But joining the Brotherhood was perhaps inevitable. He continued to publish in *al-Risala*, yet as he moved more in the direction of Islamism, he began to submit articles to al-'Ashmawi's Brotherhood-backed journal, *al-Da'wa* (The Mission or The Call), and to another Brotherhood-sponsored magazine, Sa'id Ramadan's *al-Muslimun* (The Muslims). Still, even as of September 1951, Qutb insisted that the Brotherhood did not hold an exclusive monopoly on Islamic missionizing and reform, even though he sympathized with their position. The following spring, however, Qutb adopted the Brotherhood's positions on the Wafd and the Communists and on training guerilla fighters to attack the British in the Canal Zone.[15] And both Qutb and the Brotherhood were fully behind the July 23rd revolution, at least initially.

Nevertheless, Qutb hesitated, perhaps, because the Brotherhood itself was rent by the conflicts over al-Banna's succession between the radicals under al-'Ashmawi and the moderates under Hasan al-Hudaybi. Al-'Ashmawi had been the director of the Brotherhood's Secret Apparatus and became the new Supreme Guide immediately after al-Banna's assassination until shortly before the Brotherhood was legalized.[16] Al-Hudaybi became the new Supreme Guide of the Muslim Brotherhood in October 1951 because it was hoped that as a judge and an outsider with no prior connection to the Brotherhood, he would help moderate government relations and put the society back on good terms with the royal palace. Al-'Ashmawi and Qutb had been good friends ever since Qutb had returned from the United States.

Yet it was al-Hudaybi who finally recruited Qutb with his promise that Qutb would be directing the powerful Brotherhood's Propaganda Section. At the time, al-Hudaybi was reshuffling the top ranks of the Brotherhood and certainly wanted newcomers who were politically new, candid, and pliable. It appears that when Qutb did formally and officially join the Brotherhood—sometime in February 1953, perhaps after his hopes for a ministerial appointment in the new government cabinet were finally dashed—he sided with al-Hudaybi and the Supreme Guide's more moderate camp against the criticism emanating from al-'Ashmawi, Muhammad al-Ghazali, Ahmad Jalal, and other radicals.[17]

For the moment, the Free Officers' revolt and the Muslim Brotherhood's *jihad* coincided, and there seemed to be a camaraderie never seen before or since. The Officers greatly appreciated the public support the Brothers provided, and the Brothers were hopeful that the revolution would usher in an Islamic state. The Revolutionary Command Council (RCC) re-opened the investigation into Hasan al-Banna's assassination, closed down the secret police of the Interior Ministry, and even arrested Interior Minister Muhammad al-Jazzar, who was hated by the Brothers for his harassment, arrests, and torture. The RCC also released many imprisoned Brothers. For its part, the Brotherhood established a liaison with the RCC through Rashad Muhanna, a close associate of the Brotherhood who was appointed a member of the government's Regency Council.[18]

Qutb himself fully supported the Free Officers' revolution of July 23. He even wrote to General Muhammad Naguib, the titular head of the Free Officers, to demand an end to political corruption and the creation of a new constitution that would implement Islamic law and form an Islamic state. Qutb firmly believed that after July 23 he and other Brothers would play a very critical role in the new and popular government.[19]

At the time, Qutb was regarded as one of Egypt's major intellectuals and was considered an important voice for students, workers, and peasants. He considered himself a very loyal supporter of 'Abd al-Nassir. Mahmud al-A'zab, who was both an RCC officer and a Brotherhood member, even went so far as to call Qutb "the father of the revolution." Another called him the "Mirabeau of the July 23rd" events.[20]

Qutb and 'Abd al-Nassir were close neighbors in the Helwan suburb south of Cairo, and Qutb participated in a number of private, informal meetings held between the Free Officers and the Muslim Brothers in preparation for the July events. The Brothers were asked to rally support and popular acceptance for the revolution, to maintain public order alongside the police, and to provide the Free Officers a safe haven should the revolution fail.[21]

In the month immediately following the revolution, Qutb was invited to lecture at the Officers' Club in Zamalik on the intellectual and spiritual liberation of Islam, and his talk was very well received by the attending officers. Qutb even had an office in the RCC leadership building in Zamalik and was assigned the task of helping to write new education curricula. Qutb resigned from the Education

Ministry shortly thereafter, on October 18, 1952, expecting, perhaps, a senior appointment in the Ministry, but he did not get one. His supervisor in the Ministry, Isma'il al-Qabbani, tried to persuade Qutb not to resign, and even when he did, al-Qabbani attempted to post-date the resignation by one year in order for Qutb to receive a better pension. This did not work out, and so Qutb left the Ministry after 34 years of service.

In January 1953, the RCC abolished all political parties in order to extirpate corruption. Qutb, who did not support multiple political parties anyway, approved this move. The Muslim Brotherhood was defined as "merely" a religious organization and conspicuously circumvented this closure. Then, on January 23, 1953, Qutb was appointed secretary-general of the government's new mass mobilization and indoctrination party, the Liberation Rally. Qutb hoped that he might build the Rally into the Islamic party many had called for. But he resigned less than a month later, in February, saying that the Rally was not the mass party he had initially envisioned.[22]

Another reason that Qutb might have resigned was that 'Abd al-Nassir's plan to appoint him as the new minister of education had collapsed and, in spite of their close relationship, Qutb became angry with the new government. His alienation mirrored the evolving position of the Brotherhood, with whom he was becoming more involved, as both he and the Brothers began to distance themselves from the nationalist revolutionary government. It was possible that Qutb was moving closer to al-Hudaybi and away from al-Hudaybi's rival, the radical al-'Ashmawi. After the republican revolution, al-Hudaybi began to side with Muhammad Naguib, and both might have appeared to 'Abd al-Nassir as threatening elements of opposition in league with the former king and the royal family. The Brotherhood insisted on a return to civilian rule, a position the officers might have perceived as part of a counterrevolution. Qutb's support of al-Hudaybi may well have alienated 'Abd al-Nassir, who then squelched Qutb's appointment as the new education minister. Thus Qutb and 'Abd al-Nassir parted company, and their friendship soon turned sour—not for personal reasons but because of strategic differences.[23]

Other disagreements soon arose between the RCC and the Muslim Brotherhood. It was clear that the RCC intended the revolution to remain nationalist and secular, while the Brotherhood wanted it based on Islamic principles. When the Brotherhood's Guidance Bureau insisted on veto authority over new laws, the RCC refused outright. Then, when the Brotherhood demanded the wholesale implementation of *shari'a* law, this, too, was rejected by the government. Other demands, such as the abolition of alcoholic beverages, were similarly ignored.

Their dispute finally came to a head when the government concluded a new treaty with the British in July 1954. The 1936 Anglo-Egyptian treaty had been abrogated in October 1951; the new agreement, though, still allowed the United Kingdom to station soldiers in the Canal Zone. Both Qutb and the Brothers had been highly critical of the royal government for acquiescing to British interests, and now the new republican government was taking the same route. The

Brotherhood demanded that the treaty be ratified by public acclamation through a referendum, but the RCC declined the call.[24]

Shortly after the July 23 revolution, Qutb had demanded that the new government release all political prisoners, even Communists. Yet, when the government clamped down on the "Communist-inspired" labor unrest in the spinning and weaving factories in Kafr al-Dawwar on August 12, 1952, Qutb not only stopped defending the Communists but, in an abrupt reversal, insisted instead that the government should act strongly against such "counterrevolutionaries." This led to court trials, guilty verdicts, and executions. In justifying his response, Qutb argued that an authoritarian administration was needed to purge Egypt of corrupt politicians, even within the military itself. He went on to demand the formation of a "just dictatorship" or a "refined dictatorship" to tighten up on illegal or immoral political activity.[25] The dictator he was referring to was not 'Abd al-Nassir, but Muhammad Naguib. Qutb argued that this was a justified Islamic response to tyranny, but he did not say exactly when or how such a "just dictator" could turn unjust, or tyrannical. The international press adopted the phrase, "just dictator" and its application to Naguib, but more as a term of derision.[26]

More seriously, Qutb believed that Egypt would never solve its problems of chronic poverty, misery, and political unrest unless there was a strong hand steering the country. Qutb was not a democrat, nor did he see democracy as a goal. Instead he saw it now as a danger, for it gave power to individuals who lacked the proper training and education. The liberation of Egypt from its economic, political, and spiritual woes—and from its international (i.e., British) bondage—required, in his opinion, a strongman, not a parliamentarian.[27] Unfortunately, he endorsed Naguib as the designated autocrat, not 'Abd al-Nassir who, later that spring, deposed Naguib and assumed the presidency.

At this point, Qutb advocated only targeting *foreign* enemies, although we can see in his demand for a "just dictator" the call to clamp down strongly on *domestic* enemies as well. Thus, when the new government signed the unpopular treaty with the United Kingdom. Qutb advocated outright attacks against the British but only leveled verbal assaults against the RCC, now firmly under the control of 'Abd al-Nassir. Still, it is no wonder that 'Abd al-Nassir began to see Qutb (as well as al-Hudaybi) as a possible source of counterrevolution.

Soon Qutb was accused of writing secret pamphlets that condemned the government, and of coordinating Friday sermons attacking it for its moderation and meekness.[28] This may well have happened, for Qutb had been appointed as the director for propaganda, or *da'wa*—what is called "public relations" today—and his job description required him to organize the Brotherhood's public information, the selection and assignment of public speakers and lecturers, the composition and placement of accommodating articles published by in-house journals and those sympathetic to the Brotherhood's program, and the design and development of a unified curriculum for Brotherhood and independent Islamic schools. Thus Qutb was squarely in charge of presenting the Brotherhood's doctrine and ideology.[29]

The split between Qutb and the new revolutionary government became irreversible when, on January 12, 1954, Qutb and al-Hudaybi were arrested and detained for three months for publicly speaking out against the government's foreign policy in the Canal Zone at a student rally at Cairo University. Qutb was also apprehended for his role as editor of the Brotherhood's flagship journal, the *Muslim Brotherhood,* whose publication 'Abd al-Nassir himself had actually authorized the previous December. The Brotherhood was now officially declared a political organization and closed down. Muhammad Naguib, however, acted on March 28 to free Qutb and al-Hudaybi and to repeal the closure. 'Abd al-Nassir was not so powerful yet and so Naguib's actions proved successful. However, this only added to the power struggle between 'Abd al-Nassir and Naguib, clearly placing the Brotherhood, or at least the al-Hudaybi-Qutb faction, on the Naguib side. Qutb resumed his position as editor-in-chief once he was released, and the *Muslim Brotherhood* resumed publishing, appearing on the newsstands starting May 20, 1954. Yet it published only 12 more issues before it was closed down again in August. From May to August, Qutb published strong anti-government articles and severely criticized 'Abd al-Nassir and his foreign policy, especially the new Anglo-Egyptian treaty. He may well have made himself ripe to become one of 'Abd al-Nassir's political targets, liable for arrest when the right circumstance arose.[30]

On October 26, 1954, an attempt was made on 'Abd al-Nassir's life in Manshiyya Square in Alexandria, and the government accused the Muslim Brotherhood. The Brotherhood still found itself torn by the radical-moderate split, which may have allowed either an actual assassination attempt to surface (perhaps even as real counterrevolution) or else drove one faction within the Brotherhood to attempt to eliminate the other. Each side may well have tried to set the other up and implicate it in the plot. Alternatively, the assassination may have been bogus from the start, a pretext to move against the Brotherhood.

The government acted promptly and severely to arrest the assassins and to quell any potential revolt. The Muslim Brotherhood was closed permanently, and its officers and thousands of its members rounded up and jailed. Public trials took place rather quickly and the Brothers were convicted of conspiracy to assassinate the president. Naguib was implicated in the hearings, quietly removed from office, and placed under house arrest. Seven men accused of the actual crime were found guilty and sentenced to death. Al-Hudaybi was one of the seven, but his sentence was commuted, because of his age and health, to life imprisonment and then later, after 1961, to house arrest. The remaining six were executed on December 4, 1954.[31]

A few Brothers, like Sayyid Qutb, remained free at first. But on November 18, 1954, Qutb was arrested at his home in Helwan.[32] Then on November 22, he was forced to testify against al-Hudaybi and Naguib about their alleged plans to overthrow the government. Qutb himself was not immediately placed on trial, for he did not play a direct role in the assassination attempt nor was he a member of the Secret Apparatus of the Brothers, which was believed to be behind the scheme.

Instead, he was tried in January 1955, essentially for his membership, leadership, strong criticism, and agitation against the government. He was found guilty and sentenced on July 13, 1955, to 15 years at hard labor in Liman Tura prison. He did not begin serving his sentence until November 1955 because in May he was hospitalized for six months with serious lung and heart complications.[33]

In his first three years in prison, it is believed that Qutb was beaten and tortured, because his health declined quite sharply, though he was in ill health even before his arrest.[34] This prior condition prevented the worst cruelty, but the trauma and torment wore him down considerably. From 1955 to 1964, Qutb repeatedly entered the prison hospital. His fellow prisoners, however, endured even worse torture—and occasionally death—for their actions in prison. In particular, on June 1, 1957, prison guards killed 21 Muslim Brothers and wounded many more for refusing to turn up at their daily assignments at hard labor or for supporting those who were absent. This shocking episode made Qutb extremely bitter and cynical, outraged over torture and other acts of barbarism perpetrated against Muslims by fellow Muslims. The horrible treatment, screams, and prisoner accounts convinced him that violent and aggressive opposition was the only solution to these abominable acts. Social justice was no longer the primary issue; rather, it was the very validity of the state itself that was in question. However much 'Abd al-Nassir appeared as a national hero to the Egyptian public, his government's refusal to follow Islam made it vulnerable to assault. Egypt had indeed returned to the tyranny and injustice characteristic of a *jahiliyya* society.[35]

Yet even as a political prisoner, Qutb was still permitted to write. Before imprisonment, he had begun a major project of Qur'anic exegesis, which was serialized in the monthly journal *al-Muslimun* from January to July 1952.[36] The series was so popular that the publishing house Dar Ihya' al-Kutub al-'Arabiyya contracted with him to continue writing his commentaries and to publish them all together. Once in prison, he decided to continue his efforts and to turn the articles into a monumental work to be called *Fi Zilal al-Qur'an* (In the Shade of the Qur'an). When prison officials prevented Qutb from writing, his publisher successfully sued the government for a breach of contract that allowed Qutb to continue writing, but under the confining gaze of prison censors.[37] One can only imagine how much more radical and militant Qutb's compositions might have been had the censors not been scrutinizing his texts. This project was an enormous undertaking, and that he was able to complete it successfully under such horrible conditions was a major accomplishment.

It seems a foregone conclusion, then, that Qutb's time in prison was one of the traumatizing events that would help explain his turn to extreme radicalism. The torture and carnage so tormented him that he could only conclude how little weight Islam and the Qur'an carried in the lives of most Egyptians, especially those who were prison guards and security officers. These outrageous acts prompted him to shift from the moderate pacifism he had exhibited before his court trial to an angry, militant approach to reforming Muslim society. Before his arrest, he had advocated violent tactics, but only against the British and other foreign imperialists. Now, however, he encouraged much more militant methods and their use against domestic enemies. Even so, it was not until his last major book, *Ma'alim fi al-Tariq* (Signposts on the Road), which itself was an abridged version of *In the Shade of the Qur'an*, that he explicitly proposed outright violence: a *jihad* of the sword. But even then, it was done quickly and discreetly. Yet it would take another activist, 'Abd al-Salam Faraj and his organization, Tanzim al-Jihad, organized in the late 1980s, to mold Qutb's proposal into a definite plan for organized militant action.

In the Shade of the Qur'an remains Qutb's magnum opus, a 30-part, six-volume commentary on the Qur'an, his most impressive intellectual undertaking and one carried out under the brutal conditions of the Liman Tura prison. It is what Olivier Carré called an "icon-text," which is to say it appears at the very top of the canon of commentaries and interpretations studied by faithful and learned Islamists from the Philippines to Morocco, from Africa to Europe, and on to the Muslim diaspora in both North and South America.[38] If *Social Justice* and *Signposts on the Road* represent Qutb's two most often read books in the non-Muslim West, it is *In the Shade of the Qur'an* that is most studied by the devout.

The installments stopped after only seven articles (covering the first *sura* [or Qur'anic chapter] and some of the second) issued before the July revolution. Under the contract from Dar Ihya' al-Kutub al-'Arabiyya, Qutb published 16 parts before his first arrest, in January 1954. During the following two-month prison sentence, he issued two more. He finished and published the remaining 12 parts in 1959, but then went back to revise the first 13 for a new, second edition published in 1961. After Qutb's execution in 1966, his brother, Muhammad, revised the entire commentary to produce the final, authorized 1978 version. Khatab maintains that the original edition showed a transformation similar to the one Shepard uncovered for *Social Justice*,[39] with Qutb becoming more conservative, radical, and militant as time went on. In the 1961 revised edition, Qutb had rewritten the first 13 parts to match the ferocity of the last volumes. All this was done under the close watch of prison censors.[40]

Over the course of his career, Qutb gradually moved away from depending on well-known but secular writers, scholars, and philosophers, both Egyptian and European. During the years when he wrote *In the Shade*, he no longer used Western or Westernized sources but relied totally on the Qur'an and the first Muslim communities in Arabia. His mistrust of secular sources was clear. Nor did he rely any longer on the Qur'an just for inspiration, beauty, and refined taste; it was also the political, social, and religious perspectives in the Qur'an that began to shape his thinking. That is, he no longer concentrated just on subjectivity, sentiment, and aesthetics. Now he was motivated to action by the objective and impartial dimensions of the Qur'an—its critique of the corrupt present and what could be a glorious future; what was wrong with today's Muslim and non-Muslim societies, and how to go about correcting these problems. The Qur'an became a guidebook for militant action against the enemies of Islam. Qutb interrogated the Qur'an in order to develop an Islamic movement, not just a passive and intellectual casuistry, but an action-oriented plan for reform and victory. Qutb relied on the Qur'an for what we would call theory; what he called the Islamic method. He relied on the *salaf*, the original community of Islamic believers, but he avoided any dependence on non-Islamic history or philosophy. He evaluated and judged today's society by Islam and Islam's early principles, not by the mistaken thoughts of nonbelievers which he considered contaminated by colonialist, imperialist, Zionist, and Crusader influence. Qutb was also critical of traditional Islamic thinkers who themselves had relied on Western scholarship, for they were indirectly tainted as well. This made him conservative, in the true sense of the word—preserving the past—but also in the political sense as well. He relied on Ibn Taymiyya and his Manichean perspective on the good and the forbidden. There is also a Shi'ite influence as well.[41]

Many writers point out that *In the Shade* does not follow ordinary Qur'anic commentaries, which are usually legalistic, scholastic, and pedantic. Perhaps one major reason for his unconventional approach is that Qutb wanted to be as effective and successful as possible in persuading ordinary Egyptians, particular those from the middle- and lower-classes uninitiated into the mysteries and arcane details of traditional Qur'anic exegesis. Because of the displays of emotion in the text, Musallam calls *In the Shade* a "commentary of the heart."[42] Throughout, it clearly exhibits the anger and anguish that Qutb felt about his barbaric prison experiences and the forces that put him there. These flashes of rage and torment were intended to convince those who had similar experiences and outlooks. John Calvert characterizes Qutb's innovative approach this way:

> He designed his commentary as a vehicle for his personal ruminations on the meaning and implications of the Qur'an for Muslims living in the current period. It would speak to the existential and practical concerns of modernizing Muslims.... Qutb aimed at a thematic approach that would be conversational in tone. He would provide summaries of the suras and break them into topical units, drawing the reader's attention to pertinent points. He would discuss the Qur'an's ethical teachings but also draw attention to the political implications of the divine message.... He would attempt to understand the Qur'an principally though its own expression, using the Qur'anic text as the primary reference point for every single matter. His goal was to approach the "unadorned but complete Islamic idea" without the encumbrance and complications of the layers of received tradition.[43]

Qutb's commentaries, explanations, and clarification of the Qur'an provided him with numerous opportunities to remark on specific issues of the day as they emerged from each of the sacred book's chapters and verses. He interpreted the Qur'an in terms of his own specific times, like many other commentators, and referred as much to Egypt's current conditions as to the context of the Prophet and the *salaf* in Arabia. The past offered lessons to the present, but the present also served as a lens through which to interrogate the past. *Fi Zilal* is "profoundly allegorical" in that it sought practical examples that provide solutions to the present dilemmas of Egypt and the Muslim world.[44]

Qutb explored such questions as the nature of God, the function of man as God's vice-regent, the ability of the Islamic system to offer comprehensive guidance, and the establishment of a just and equitable society. He examined such concerns as faith/belief and worship/practice; reason and revelation; government, laws, nationalism, and Islamic unity; secularism, knowledge, and epistemology; wealth, poverty and Islamic economic principles, using such concepts as religious ignorance (*jahiliyya*), struggle and activism (*jihad*), and God's universal dominion, or *hakimiyya*. (These topics are discussed in the second half of this volume.) Qutb attempted to not only provide definitive answers to the problems of Islam's dramatic decline and Muslims' disappointing powerlessness in the contemporary period, but more significantly, to also provide the methods and tactics to solve these dilemmas. In other words, Qutb argued that people should not just debate these issues in isolation but *apply* them to all matters of actual life and lifestyles in the current period.

Qutb used his exegesis of Qur'anic chapters and verses in *In the Shade* to demonstrate the following:

- Islam (with its unity) and *jahiliyya* (with its secularism) are complete opposites.
- The Muslim world is currently steeped in *jahiliyya*.
- Islamic unity will solve economic, political, and moral problems universally.
- For this reason, the Islamic system and its solutions are superior to other systems.
- The goal of the Islamic movement, then, is to install an Islamic system.[45]

Sayyid Qutb's next and last book, *Signposts on the Road*, is certainly his most famous and without doubt his most incendiary. Published in January 1964, it consists of four chapters excerpted from *In the Shade of the Qur'an* and from letters written in prison.[46] But it is no mere repetition of Qutb's Qur'anic commentaries. Rather, these were edited to express his fiery outrage and indignation over his own imprisonment, that of his companions and collaborators, and the general corruption and decadence of *jahili* Egypt. *Signposts* contains convictions that crystallized many of Qutb's earlier ideas. Qutb revised the standard triptych of *jihad*—jihad of heart, tongue, and hand—by adding a fourth type: that "of the sword." Now in theory as well as in practice, there was an authoritative, militant version of *jihad*. *Signposts* was not necessarily an official decree for the Muslim Brotherhood, for the Brothers were ambivalent (and still are) over whether to use violence or to participate in the electoral process. *Signposts* exhibits Qutb's horror at a world that was disintegrating into disasters and crises. It displays his rage and resentment over the bankruptcy of modernity and secularism, both in the West and among those in Egypt who had been indoctrinated by the West. It has become the radical manifesto of the Islamist movement.

Qutb's Manichean perspective and kharijite beliefs are more clearly in view than ever before. He was against those who lorded over others in place of the dominion of God. He was against man-made laws instead of *shari'a* law. He was against immorality and all the signs of Western decadence. He was against all those—Muslim and non-Muslim alike—who do not adhere to his program of militancy and revolution. He was against the secular and nationalist state. He was against corrupt societies. He was against ineffective and bickering officials and their political parties. He rejected those who elevated themselves to the level of God by creating personality cults and contrived charisma. Clearly, Qutb was very intent on achieving God's plan and dominion on this earth, and did not tolerate any deviation from this path.

Signposts was not as subtle as *In the Shade*, nor was it supposed to be, notwithstanding the prison censors. Nor was it abstract, scholastic, or hypothetical. *Signposts* clearly was not intended for the general public. Instead, it was dedicated primarily to the Islamic vanguard, to those devout, pious, and active Muslims who become united by their faith, who reject all their previous relationships in order to embrace true Islam, and who can be depended upon to be true spirits, forthright and steadfast, to lead the way and fight to overthrow and destroy *jahiliyya* and to establish a new and genuine *Islamic* community, not just a *Muslim* one.

> Our foremost objective is to change the practices of this society. Our aim is to change the *jahili* system at its very roots—this system which is fundamentally at variance with Islam and which, with the help of force and oppression, is keeping us from living the sort of life which is demanded by our Creator.[47]

Signposts was intended as their practical handbook for overthrowing the government and establishing an Islamic state and society. Its purpose was to convince the vanguard of the evils and horrors of *jahiliyya*, how to recognize this apostasy, what to do about it, and how to prepare and train to overthrow it. What are the signposts of triumph or failure as men move from defeating *jahiliyya* to achieving victory for *shari'a*, unity, and God's dominion? For the answers, *Signposts* looked to the *salaf* of Mecca.

> At one time this Message created a generation—the generation of the Companions of the Prophet—without comparison in the history of Islam, even in the entire history of man. After this, no other generation of this caliber was ever again to be found.... Never again did a great number of such people exist in one region as was the case during the first period of Islam.[48]

Qutb was particularly preoccupied with early Mecca because of its clear-cut resemblance to the contemporary world. Then, too, the Arabian community was steeped in *jahiliyya* and it was from within this corrupt and immoral majority that arose the first Islamic vanguard.

Just like in the days before the Prophet Muhammad, today's society is entirely secular, immoral, corrupt, and tyrannical. The crucial, litmus-paper test for Qutb was that Islamic societies had to be ruled by God's laws, not by men and man-made laws. *Signposts* taught the vanguard how to distinguish a true Islamic community from false *jahiliyya* societies, the unity under God versus polytheism, and *Dar al-Islam* versus *Dar al-Harb* (the Homeland of Islam versus the Homeland of War).[49] This final book became their set of guiding principles.

The vanguard first fosters its faith and beliefs, and only when these are strong and secure does it regulate its practices and actions. Only after their convictions are assured can organized groups then become separate and distinct from *jahiliyya* and therefore, become a true vanguard, one that is active, harmonious, cooperative, viable, and dynamic.

> When people recognized their Sustainer and worshipped Him alone, when they became independent not only of other human beings but also of their own desires...then God, though this faith and through the Believers, provided everything which was needed....The society was freed from all oppression, and the Islamic system was established in which justice was God's justice and in which weighing was by God's balance. The banner of social justice was raised in the name of One God, and the name of the banner was Islam.[50]

But it is not the custom of *jahili* communities to simply let the true word of the Qur'an go unchallenged. Thus the vanguard is forced not only to defend itself, but to actively and aggressively spread Islam, by force, if necessary.

> Only those whose hearts are so purified will come together to make a group, and only such a group of people, whose beliefs and concepts, whose devotional acts and laws, are completely free of servitude to anyone other than God can start a Muslim community.... [A] new community is born, emerging from within the old *jahili* society, which immediately confronts it with a new belief and a new way of life....The old *jahili* society may become submerged into the new Islamic society or it may not, and it may make peace with the Muslim society or may fight it. However, history tells us that the *jahili* society chooses to fight and not to make peace, attacking the vanguard of Islam at its very inception....[51]

For the first time, Qutb discussed the idea of an actual Islamic movement when the word "movement" became a euphemism for "militant revolution." He abandoned nonviolent forms of struggle and instead emphasized a militant *jihad*, one meant to utterly destroy *jahili* society and raise the banner of true Islam to fly over an Islamic state. His list of enemies no longer contained vague categories— atheists, idolaters, hypocrites, or infidels—but instead focused specifically on Jews, Christians, Communists, and apostates.

Qutb's book is, in general, a call to battle—a summons to fashion a dedicated vanguard which in turn will create the true Islamic community. Much of *Signposts* is cheerleading and inspirational writing from Qutb to motivate this vanguard into achieving ever greater heights of glory and to keep their heads held high when encountering failure, defeat, or the overwhelming power of the surrounding *jahili* majority. Don't be defeatist. Don't be apologetic. Don't feel defensive. Don't be impatient. Challenge your enemies with love and kindness. Never lose your faith. Islamic morals and values are higher, Qutb asserted, than any other society known to history, and Islamic civilization is the only real civilization, notwithstanding the claims of dominant but *jahili* nations.

Qutb demonstrated how the Prophet Muhammad and his followers frequently encountered oppression, pain, and fear, yet still held their heads up high and remained strong in their hearts and their faith. Even while the enemy might seem victorious, and the vanguard defeated, these are only momentary events. The injustice of punishing the good and rewarding the evil will be reversed on the Day of Judgment when the good go to paradise and the bad burn in hell. Even in defeat, true believers are superior and can look down spiritually on the filth and decay of the *jahiliyya* surrounding them. After all, the true believer is better no matter what.

> "Do not be dejected nor grieved. You shall be the uppermost if you are Believers" (Qur'an 3:139)...describes that eternal state of mind which ought to inspire the Believer's consciousness, his thoughts, his estimates of things, events, values and persons. It describes a triumphant state which should remain fixed in the Believer's heart in the face of everything, every condition, every standard and every person; the superiority of the Faith and its value above all values which are derived from a source other than the source of the Faith.[52]
>
> Conditions change, the Muslim loses his physical power and is conquered; yet the consciousness does not depart from him that he is the most superior. If he remains a Believer, he looks upon his conqueror from a superior position. He remains certain that this is a temporary condition which will pass away and that faith will turn the tide from which there is no escape. Even if death is his portion, he will never bow his head....
>
> The society may be dominated by beliefs, concepts, values, and customs which are entirely opposite to his belief, his concept, his value, and his standards. Yet the consciousness does not depart from him

that he is the most superior and that the rest are all in an inferior position. From his height he looks at them with dignity and honor, and with compassion and sympathy for their condition and with a desire to guide them to the good which he has and to lift them up to the horizon where he lives.[53]

Qutb reflected on the dismal defeat of death itself, when believers are martyred in fighting for their faith in God and His religion.

All men die, and of various causes; but not all gain such victory, nor reach such heights, nor taste such freedom, nor soar to such limits of the horizon. It is God's choosing and honoring a group of people who share death with the rest of mankind but who are singled out from other people for honor.[54]

Martyrdom becomes the ultimate result of Qutb's zealotry, where faith proves more important than life itself. Death is no longer a punishment, but a reward, though one attained in the afterlife. Martyrdom is proof that the believer truly does value faith more than he values life, family, friends, neighbors, (nominal) co-religionists, and all other previous interests and identities. Martyrdom, then, is the ultimate act of conviction, of applying unity, justice, obedience, and *jihad* in a final act of self-annihilation. It is, after all, God Who decides the time of death. Indeed, the fighter merely becomes an instrument of God's overpowering will. Martyrdom demonstrates, then, the extent of his own true faith.[55]

Humiliation, dishonor, and torture are difficult to withstand *unless* the partisan remains true to his faith and steadfast in his beliefs. Perhaps Qutb foresaw his own death, seeing himself a martyr to the tyranny of Egypt's government and the 'Abd al-Nassir administration.

Signposts was a how-to-fix-it book that identified the problem, the solution, and the method to achieve the right results. No longer, as in *In the Shade* did Qutb expound on theoretical or intellectual ideas. Nor did he examine the subtle details or obscure reasoning of a larger Islamic concept. Now he directed his troops to go out and smite evil and propagate the good. Qutb raised the banner of the *salaf* to show how once it was done and how it should be done again.

More than ever, in *Signposts on the Road*, Qutb reversed his earlier ideas. His secularism and Westernization or modernization were stripped away and discarded. He turned his back thoroughly on his previous notions and on the people he knew—quite easy to do in an isolated prison cell. But it was also his prison experiences that fueled an anger and hostility toward Western-based modernity as the source of Egypt's corruption, immorality, barbarity, and depravity. In America, Qutb saw and heard much that disgusted him. Now, he saw those very things in his own society and came to detest it.

Here Qutb's anti-Westernism, anti-secularism, and anti-nationalism came to a climax. Contemporary secular societies—both outside and inside the Muslim world—had to be obliterated, he argued, and replaced by true Islam. In order to move societies from the present *jahiliyya* to the future *hakimiyya*, or God's dominion, there is *jihad*—certainly by the heart, tongue, and hand, but now also by the sword. Militancy as a tactic has its rightful place—a place subsequently widened by his followers—that not only does not contradict Islamic principles but actually fulfills them. Qutb felt that the strength of *jahiliyya* was so unyielding that it requires violence to overthrow and destroy it. The tiny vanguard that forms out of its shared faith grows from within *jahiliyya* society. It must, therefore, use its own concentrated power if it is to overcome the obstacles that thwart the call to Islam and its endorsement by free-thinking people. The tyranny and oppression that prevents this freedom must be eradicated, and therefore, militant combat becomes crucial.

This angry manifesto was the principal source of evidence presented at Qutb's Military Court trial in 1966. He had been arrested for participating in an insurrectionary organization and charged with treason; his position as spiritual guide indicted him as surely as if he had engaged in outright violence. Yet his membership, his duties, and his assignments were much less important than the incriminating text of *Signposts,* which single-handedly convicted him for crimes, real or imagined.

Sometime in the first half of 1964, Qutb suffered a heart attack, and his already fragile condition deteriorated even further. Iraq's nationalist president 'Abd al-Salam 'Arif, who was close to 'Abd al-Nassir, yet also sympathetic to the Muslim Brotherhood in Iraq, intervened on Qutb's behalf while visiting Egypt, and Qutb was released from prison for health reasons in May 1964. But just six months later, he was re-arrested, imprisoned, and indicted for treason. *Signposts on the Road* was published before his May release and went through five printings in its first six months. It and its author inspired a tremendous following in Egypt, particularly from existing Islamist vanguard groups, including those members of the still-illegal Muslim Brotherhood.[56]

In his 10 years under incarceration, Qutb had organized a close-knit Islamic study group and reading circle inside Liman Tura prison. This coterie included Muhammad Yusuf Hawwash, a Muslim Brother and Qutb's "in-house" editor, who later became Qutb's designated political and religious successor. Together, these two thinkers concluded that the Islamic movement in Egypt was still at a stage of weakness and deficiency. So, based on the model of the *salaf,* they decided that a program of ideas, not action, was called for, one that involved reading the classics and developing an Islamic program based on a vanguard of dedicated Islamists.[57]

Not all Muslim Brothers stayed in prison for life. Some had evaded arrest, others had exiled themselves to a more sympathetic Saudi Arabia, and yet others simply went underground. In 1962, one former Brother, 'Ali 'Abd al-Fattah Isma'il, who had been released from prison in 1956, and Zainab al-Ghazali, from the affiliated Muslim Sisters, formed an Islamic study group with the consent of Hasan al-Hudaybi, still the Brotherhood's Supreme Guide. Through Qutb's sister, Hamida, they asked Sayyid to supply the course of readings he was using in his own circle. These included Qutb's own publications, as well as those of his brother Muhammad Qutb, Mawdudi, Ibn Taymiyya, Muhammad ibn 'Abd al-Wahhab, Isma'il ibn Kathir, and other intellectuals.[58]

After Qutb was released in May 1964, he wanted to avoid outright political entanglement and instead to promote Islamic teaching. So when Isma'il asked him to serve as his study group's spiritual guide, he consented. But when Qutb met personally with the circle 10 months after his release, he learned that, like the Muslim Brotherhood itself, this group also had a Secret Apparatus intent on a more militant approach to establishing an Islamic state. The study group had already begun designing plans to attack the government. Two hundred fighters were training in clandestine camps and weapons had been purchased with funds from exiled sympathizers.[59]

Qutb hesitated. He was certainly impressed with the enthusiasm of his quixotic companions. Yet he was also practical and warned them against precipitate action, worried that rash adventures would bring more disaster and government repression. And all acknowledged that the probability of successfully executing their plans was nil.[60] Instead, Qutb pushed for a 13-year instructional program, 13 years being the first years in Mecca before the Prophet's migration to Medina, and the syllabus was based on the Meccan chapters of the Qur'an. Thus, this program would educate Egyptians to the proper beliefs of their religion as Qutb said it was originally conceived, including economic, political, and, of course, spiritual guidelines. Every 13 years, the group would actually survey the country to measure its degree of readiness. When 75 percent of the population became convinced of the need for an Islamic system, then the demand for such a structure would go out. Until then, there would be more instruction for another 13 years, and the same steps would be repeated.[61]

Not receiving much support, Qutb compromised and advised the group that their plans for militant action could continue but only if they were seen as defensive acts against government aggression. This concession essentially allowed the training and armament to continue but shifted the battle plans from provoking government attacks to simply reacting to them. But as John Calvert describes their plans:

> They discussed the possibility of going for the state's jugular vein: assassinating 'Abd al-Nasser [sic], Prime Minister 'Ali Sabri, and the directors of the General Intelligence (*Mabahith 'Amma*) and military security services (*Mukhabarat 'Askariyva*). The organization floated various scenarios: rake the president's motorcade with machinegun fire, blow up the train carrying his party from Cairo to Alexandria, or dynamite the grandstand from which he addressed a political rally in

Alexandria. They also talked about destroying the Nile Barrage, the bridges that spanned the Nile at Cairo and the electricity generating station at Alexandria. These attacks, they reckoned, would sow confusion and hinder the efforts of the security forces to search out and destroy the organization, thus allowing its members to escape and regroup. The attacks would also send a message to the regime that any effort to destroy it would come at a high price.[62]

Qutb again hesitated. Another compromise was reached by permitting the assassinations but rejecting the destruction of public utilities. Preparation continued. Yet when the weapons were set to arrive, Qutb realized that these were not hypothetical plans anymore, and he attempted to cancel the entire project.

On July 30, 1965, Qutb's brother, Muhammad, was arbitrarily detained without charge. Sayyid strongly protested, and he, too, was arrested 10 days later, along with 'Abd al-Fattah Isma'il and Muhammad Yusuf Hawwash. Thus began an intense government crackdown on Islamist groups, particularly those that included former Muslim Brothers. Hasan al-Hudaybi was also arrested, and two weeks later, Qutb's two sisters, Amina and Hamida, were detained along with Zainab al-Ghazali. One of the leaders of Qutb's group, 'Ali al-'Ashmawi, was severely tortured, confessed the names of all the members, including the Qutb brothers, and revealed the entire plan to overthrow the government. These arrests were publicly announced in *al-Ahram* on September 7. They were indicted on charges of subversion (for plotting armed insurrection), sedition (citing *Signposts* as evidence), and for conspiring to assassinate President 'Abd al-Nassir and other government officials. At the same time, thousands of others—members of reconstituted cells of the Muslim Brotherhood scattered throughout the country—were arrested as well.[63]

The existence of the two radical study groups, one in prison and one outside, came to serve as the main basis for the government's indictment against Qutb, for it claimed these circles were linked to a resurrected Muslim Brotherhood Secret Apparatus that was plotting to overthrow the ruling order. The government prosecutors later accused Qutb, under orders from al-Hudaybi in 1959, of organizing Islamist political prisoners into "vanguard families" (AKA "study groups"), not only in Liman Tura but in other Egyptian prisons as well.[64]

It remains unclear the degree to which Qutb actually advocated and advanced concrete militant action against the state. Qutb was of two minds, one acceding to ongoing battle plans to attack the government and another counseling caution and realism for fear of repression. He did not enjoy a monopoly over authority, and others vetoed his ideas as much as he rejected theirs. Both Calvert and Hamid Algar report that on two occasions, Qutb had attempted to stop militant activity and had stressed education first and foremost.[65] Kepel cites Qutb's brother, Muhammad, who stated in defense of his brother, that he had "heard him [Sayyid] say more than once

'We are preachers and not judges. Our objective is not to legislate against people, but to teach them this truth: that there is no god but God. The problem is that people do not understand what this formula requires of them.'"[66]

The only documentary evidence that was submitted at his trial was *Signposts* itself, with its telegraphic but enigmatic passages advocating violence. Qutb was clearly condemned and convicted for what he had written.[67]

Once Qutb's arrest and indictment were announced, his book *Signposts* received special attention in the press and in the prosecuting attorney's office. Quotations from the book were excerpted out of context in his two trial appearances, one on December 21, 1965, and the second on April 12, 1966, in military court. Qutb's defense argued that the accused had just promoted an educational approach; state prosecutors insisted, instead, that he had planned subversive acts of terrorism and bloodshed. On the one hand, Qutb was placed among the ranks of such luminaries as Che Guevara, Mao Tse Dong, Ho Chi Min, and a long line of revolutionaries. On the other hand, Qutb was demeaned and humiliated, and his movement tarnished and discredited. The government became the primary perpetrator of misrepresenting the Islamic movement. Indeed, Qutb joined the gallery of al-Afghani, 'Abduh, Rida and al-Banna as major champions of the Islamic movement, but now the entire movement was disparaged and maligned.[68]

On August 21, 1966, Qutb was sentenced by a military court to death by hanging. Six other Brothers, including Isma'il, Hawwash, 'Ali al-'Ashmawi, and al-Hudaybi, were also convicted, although four of the guilty verdicts were commuted, including those of al-'Ashmawi and al-Hudaybi. Despite attempts to reduce the verdict in exchange for recanting his doctrine and confessing his errors, Qutb held fast and did not repent. In the early hours of Monday, August 29, 1966, Qutb was executed, together with Isma'il and Hawwash, making Qutb the first major Islamist ever officially put to death by the state. His martyrdom was thus assured. Instead of halting the dissemination of Qutb's ideas, it guaranteed it, notwithstanding (or perhaps because of) the government official ban on his books that had begun back in October 1965.[69]

PART TWO

HIS LEGACY: IDEAS AND ISSUES

6

Sayyid Qutb's Islamic Concept

Sayyid Qutb called his own understanding of Islam "the Islamic concept." In this personal statement, he examined the nature of humanity; its position in the cosmic order and its relationship to its Creator; the purpose, meaning, and value of life; and the functions of men and women in society. This Islamic concept is, in essence, the rules and regulations that should govern the relationship among humanity, nature, the universe, and God; it is what gives this relationship value. It seeks to provide Muslims with a comprehensive understanding of these topics, as well as the concepts of unity, obedience, struggle, worship, social justice, and universalism. It helps Muslims to understand the purpose of their own existence and gives them all the necessary information to live a good life. Qutb's concept also teaches Muslims about their distinctive character and instructs them in the fundamentals of their religion, all of which are necessary to generate concerted political action within the community.[1]

This kind of comprehensive description can be found in the Qur'an. But the Qur'an cannot be understood simply in a scholastic manner. Instead, one's understanding must be shaped through a kind of praxis, through struggle—the effort to reestablish a true Islamic life—and by applying the Qur'an to this struggle in a critical fashion.

> Our aim is not some frigid knowledge that deals only with men's minds and adds to the accumulation of "culture." Such an aim does not deserve pain and effort, for it is a cheap and foolish aim. We seek "movement" as a stage beyond "knowledge." We want knowledge to transform itself into a motivating power for realizing its meaning in the real world. We seek to enlist the conscience of man to achieve the purpose of his existence, as traced out by this divine concept. We seek to return humanity to its Lord, to the plan He had drawn up for it, and the noble and elevated life that conforms to the nobility that God prescribes for mankind.[2]

Qutb once wrote that there are three types or degrees of knowledge. There is ordinary human knowledge, which is fairly limited; there is God's divine knowledge, which is absolute; and then there is prophetic knowledge, which is privileged human knowledge inspired, transmitted, or revealed by God. Qutb did not claim any special consideration for himself, though he placed a great deal of value on his own personal beliefs.[3]

Qutb did not necessarily intend his Islamic concept to harden into dogma since it was just his own individual and educated understanding of his religion. Yet it attracted countless numbers of adherents because of Qutb's personal authority and character and because it was constructed in the forge of fire and persecution. His idealism and rage became contagious.

Qutb believed that people had drifted away from Islam and the Qur'an, sliding back into *jahiliyya*, or religious ignorance. It became necessary, therefore, to provide them with a true understanding of Islam, which would equip them to wage a *jihad* against their own wicked tendencies, against errant and deviant Muslims, and against those who attack Islam or prevent others from understanding the religion.[4]

Qutb's Islamic concept is similar, in purpose, to philosophy. But Qutb did not, and would not, use the term "philosophy" because that particular field of inquiry, he concluded, had removed God from its explanations, by addressing questions about man's existence in the universe without any reference to God whatsoever. Qutb felt that since his own words about the Islamic concept came directly from the Qur'an, they had God's authority behind them.[5]

Qutb also shunned the term "philosophy" for its association with what he called deviations from Islam that included Islamic dialectic theology, *kalam* (the Mu'tazila, Murji'a, and Khawarij lines of thinking),[6] and those who were influenced by the Greek philosophers (al-Kindi, al-Farabi, Ibn Sina, and Ibn Rushd).[7] Their arguments centered on eschatology, the nature of God, the Qur'an, sin, and God's will versus human will. Qutb found these topics divisive and disruptive, like the different schools of *fiqh,* or Islamic law.[8] Such convictions had been contaminated by Greek, Persian, and Western thought, thereby distorting people's understanding of Islam. Just as Qutb wished to abolish the different schools of *fiqh*, he also wanted to eliminate these various schools of *kalam* and purge Islamic thinking of Aristotle, Plato, and Plotinus.[9] He wanted to return instead to the basics in the Qur'an. The Qur'an contains both *shari'a* law and *'aqida* beliefs, and Qutb's proposal to return to them meant returning to a pure, unadulterated knowledge of Islam as the Prophet and the first generation of Muslims had originally understood it.

Qutb also shied away from calling the Islamic concept "theology," for it did not deal with many of the topics conventionally considered the domain of theology, such as the nature of sin, the attributes and nature of God, and the proofs of God's unity and dominion, nor did Qutb himself have the training and background to command authority in these fields. Qutb's exegesis of the Qur'an in the volumes of *In the Shade of the Qur'an* also differed from traditional *tafasir* (sing: *tafsir),* or explanations, of religious topics, since it failed to cite references and authorities and discuss precedence.[10] This is perhaps why Qutb's writings were so well received in a population just recently introduced to mass public education. His style was direct and uncomplicated, unlike the texts of most Islamic scholars and intellectuals.[11] He did discuss some standard ideas, such as God's unity, which he kept in the forefront throughout all his writings, but the focus was practical, not contemplative. Many theological topics were considered because of their political and social consequences. Qutb's role was to translate Islam into an active and dynamic political movement.

Qutb believed that his Islamic concept was pure and simple, an enduring characterization that could attract millions of converts to embrace Islam and to submit to a single God. Thus Qutb hoped that this concept would become a motivating force behind the actions of men and women attracted to a true Islam, to its message, and to God's dominion.

In 1962, while he was still detained in Liman Tura prison, Qutb's final, complete account of the Islamic concept was published under the title *Khasa'is al-Tasawwur al-Islami wa Muqawwamatihi* (Characteristics and Fundamentals of the Islamic Concept).[12] Yet many of these ideas had been developed over the years since the mid-1940s, and many elements of his all-embracing vision of Islam appeared in such works as *Social Justice, In the Shade of the Qur'an,* and *Signposts on the Road.* He listed seven characteristics that defined his personal conceptualization of Islam: (1) divinity (*al-rabbaniyya*), (2) stability (or permanence) (*al-thabat*), (3) unity (*al-tawhid*), (4) comprehensiveness (*al-shamul*), (5) faith (*al-iman*) and practice (*al-'amal*), (6) balance (or moderation) (*al-tawazun*), (7) positive orientation (or optimism) (*al-ijabiyya*), and (8) realism (or truth) (*al-waqi'iyya*). I added an additional category not in Qutb's original list: faith (*al-iman*) and practice (*al-'amal*), because many of his ideas fall under this rubric, and I placed it fifth in the list in order to maintain a certain flow of logic.

Divinity (*al-rabbaniyya*)

Divinity is the central focus of Qutb's Islamic concept. It clearly places God at the very epicenter of Islam. It is a whole, complete, and primordial concept, not dependent on any other to define itself. All things emerge or emanate from divinity, making it the one characteristic that includes not only the other seven but, in fact, all else beyond the other seven, such as values and norms, morals and deeds. It endows them with a divine quality. God's divinity is, of course, permanent and constant, and all of human life revolves, or should revolve, around it. Because it is everlasting and unvarying, men and women cannot add to it, subtract from it, or modify it in any way. Other religions have decentered themselves and moved away from God. Even in Islam, the arguments and debates among various schools of *fiqh* and *kalam* move the religion away from God and thereby change the nature of Islam itself.

The divine reality of God's existence and the absolute quality of His will is everlasting and immutable. This is not to deny human will, for Qutb believed that people are certainly free, even free to refuse God and God's will. But God determines the universe, nature, and humanity and the direction these should take. If they do what God wills, they benefit. If people do otherwise, they pay the penalty.

One of the debates in Islamic philosophy concerns the attributes of God. Are these attributes distinct entities? Or do they merely imply separate characteristics of one single, divine Being? Qutb avoided the intricacies of this debate, but argued in such a way as to ensure that the second position prevailed. Qutb embraced the second position because it reinforces the unity of God and the centrality of that unity for the superiority of Islam in solving difficult dilemmas.[13]

Stability (or Permanence) (*al-thabat*)

Qutb maintained that there are certain values and beliefs that do not change. These are the fundamentals of the Islamic concept. While many things *do* change or evolve, they are, as Qutb wrote, "motion within a fixed framework, around a fixed pivot" of unvarying truths.[14] Stability on the other hand is what preserves Islamic thought and society from the contamination and pollution from other societies. Islam not only has values and beliefs that never change but they actually offer guidance to subsequent transformations.

Qutb took a fairly dim and conservative view of social change. The flexibility offered by the well-used legal concepts of "*'ibadat*" (permanent ritual obligations) and "*mu'amalat*" (nondivine social relations and ideas) to sanction social change became extremely restricted because Qutb reduced *mu'amalat* to *'ibadat*, and the two together further reduced to *'ubudiyya*, worship, or permanent servitude, whereby even the most marginal embellishments of Islam should remain or become immutable parts of obedience and devotion to God.[15]

In particular, Qutb considered human nature, or the "humanity of man," to be stable and constant, with people's impulses and desires remaining fixed even as values and norms change from place to place and time to time. Human nature also contains a permanent sense of reasonableness that is not eroded, though it is often hidden by passion or outside influences. Religious fundamentals provide a constant scale against which emotions, thoughts, ideas, situations, and relationships can be measured.

Qutb claimed that it is absolutely necessary for the continuation of life that human existence should operate within this stable and permanent framework. In his day, he argued, there was no stability, and change was encouraged, often merely for the sake of change, with nothing enduring or remaining sacred. Everything had become relativistic, and life had no anchor of values, truths, and beliefs from which to evaluate the world. Qutb used the analogy of a planet unattached to a sun, tumbling through space, knocked from its orbit, and colliding with other planets.

Qutb portrayed the West as just that sort of society where there are ever-changing values and truths, all relative to a person's social position and cultural understanding. Nothing is bad, and the individual does whatever feels good. The West, therefore, has no stable basis of values to depend on. This has resulted in violent eruptions, confusion, alienation, exhaustion, mental health problems, pervasive corruption, and empty lives. Europe and America were now imposing this fluctuating relativism on others, Qutb claimed, and calling it modernization. Instead, it has cut societies loose from any permanent moorings, stable principles, and constant truths, and this instability is now afflicting all of humanity.

Stability, therefore, offers Muslims a set of fixed principles. They are not free of restraint, as in the West, to do whatever they want. There is not a right to practice tyranny, injustice, immorality, disunity, or irresponsibility; these are not norms nor should the community willingly suffer them. Yet, at the same time, the existence of this stability means that Muslims have the freedom and the duty to pursue new and different ideas and relationships. Stagnation is *not* an element of Islam, any more than absolute freedom. It is just the permanent presence, or existence, of these core values and truths that has given the Islamic community a coherence over the centuries and today allows it to resist modernization if that seems to go against its values.

Unity (*al-tawhid*)

Qutb, like his predecessors Jamal al-Din al-Afghani, Muhammad 'Abduh, Rashid Rida, and Hasan al-Banna, emphasized the concept of the unity of God, or *tawhid*, and a strict understanding of monotheism. *Tawhid* became a staple in Qutb's understanding of Islam especially because it unites belief and practice. Qutb and these forebears all stressed the significance and centrality of unity as the defining characteristic of the Islamic system, in contrast to the West, where secularism separates religion from other elements of social life.[16] It marks off the true monotheism of Islam from other religions where the unity of God has fallen by the wayside. The Islamic Testimony bears witness to this unity—"There is no god but God..."—and this is reflected in everyday life in the integration of all the various aspects of human existence. There is just one Creator, and this means that the unity of the Creator permeates all of God's creations—nature, the universe, humanity, and the relationships with God and among people.[17] Assigning these elements, instead, to diverse and distinct functional domains, with each domain nearly isolated conceptually and disconnected from the others, is viewed as the archetypal hallmark of Western secular society since the Renaissance.

Qutb's notion of *tawhid*, what he called "the great universal unity," is a theme he carried over from even his earlier, secular days of the 1930s and early 1940s.[18] It includes the relationship between the Creator and His creation, between humanity, nature, and the universe. It also denotes the relationship between matter and spirit, and the mediation by the human mind or intellect. These are always integrated, despite attempts to separate them. Thus the mind-body distinction employed so frequently in Western philosophy is transcended and fused together, instead, as a mind-spirit-body unity that reflects the unity of the Creator. Human beings need both spiritual guidance and material sustenance. The unity of spirituality and materialism, not their separation or distinction, is what makes people human. People need a certain level of material stability before they can direct their energies toward worship and submitting to God. Conversely, there is no asceticism in Islam. Islam is of this world and in this world, combining faith and practice together into acts of worship and submission to God. Thus the domination of one over the other—of materialism over spiritualism, as in Communist societies, or spiritualism over materialism, as in monastic communities—is foreign to Qutb's vision of Islam. When the two are separated—and usually the materialist desires trump the spiritual needs—men and women are unable to tell right from wrong. Unlike either Communism or Western capitalism, Qutb maintained, Islam incorporates all the elements of human life, not just the material or economic, but also the spiritual. Islamic unity offers a balance and a moderation such that no one single aspect of life can assume too large a function. Life must be balanced between the material and the spiritual in order to properly fulfill God's plan and creation.[19]

The unity of God implies an integrity and a wholeness in all that God created, including humanity, nature, and the universe. It regulates humanity's inner character and public associations, it unites its spiritualism and activism, and focuses these on realizing God's dominion through *jihad*, or struggle. This unity of God creates in human society a social system that encompasses all human activity and religion, and blends these together. This organic, functional system or society then goes on to create the harmony, peace, and freedom that allow men and women to strive to their fullest—spiritually, intellectually, physically, politically, and economically. The person who does not know or acknowledge this unity is unable to fulfill his functions and obligations. Because of this balance and harmony *shari'a*, prophecy, and Judgment Day are able to moderate and regulate individual and community life so as to command the good and forbid the evil.

Qutb also used "the great unity" to stand for government authority, the people, and God's law and religion. So united, these three together ensure social justice, the worship of God, and the submission to His laws.[20]

Tawhid is activated by God's dominion as the unifying force in the universe. A practical result of this unity is a natural consensus among people and between them and those who govern by God's law. Obedience is expected and not enforced by coercion since the laws and beliefs of the community and the character of its members are in agreement with one another. Belief in God and the unity of God maintains the justice and harmony required to preserve a viable community. There should be no discord between God and humanity, between people and nature, and among people themselves, as these relations are based on God's revelations, the

Qur'an, and on His laws, the *shari'a*. When this does not hold, or when people's man-made rules and laws are followed instead, then disharmony and injustice follow, along with oppression and tyranny. Muslims must decide—Islam or secularism—and once they do, the path to follow flows logically. One of the main messages of *Social Justice* and *In the Shade* is the necessity of following, practicing, and applying *shari'a* law. Those communities that do not are (1) not Muslim, (2) steeped in *jahiliyya*, (3) tyrannical and unjust, and (4) in need of subjugation to God's law and doctrine.

The concept of unity is intended not only for Muslims, but for *all* people. Islam is the most recent version of "hanifiyyism" or a universal monotheism that also once included Judaism and Christianity. These two earlier religions, however, became distorted by their loss of this unity and the deterioration of cohesiveness in their societies. Qutb reviewed the beliefs of early prophets, even those predating Judaism, as well as those since that time, and concluded that they all believed in monotheism. He then criticized both Jews and Christians for doing away with this monotheism when Jews incorrectly deified Ezra and Christians incorrectly deified Jesus, as revealed in Qur'an 9:30.[21] Such a polytheistic society abolished divine unity as other power centers rivaled God in summoning worshipers, demanding submission, and executing their own legal codes. He concluded that those who do not believe in God's unity are therefore atheists.[22]

Muslims, Qutb argued, have followed the same misguided path as Jews and Christians, having lost the sense of divine unity and, therefore, destroying the integrity of religion, politics, economics, morals, education, family, gender, and relations with nature and other parts of God's creation. The result has been polytheism or paganism, the worshipping of false or alternative gods. This, in Qutb's views, is the core of religious ignorance, or *jahiliyya*, and the primary reason for the decline of Islam.

Faith and practice, concepts and laws, theory and action—all these lack the autonomy so frequently conceptualized in the West. Instead, they combine together and act as one, creating a permanent unity. The West, with its long tradition of secularism, tends to label some acts as religious and others as not religious. In Qutb's mind, since society should *not* be secular, then all acts have a religious function whether or not that function is explicitly acknowledged. The lives of true, devout Muslims are devoted to worshipping God; every act is an act of worship, and all these acts are infused with belief and faith. Without the concept of the secular, there is no special mosque service on Friday (except for reasons of socializing and governing) that makes some Muslims "Friday Muslims" like there are "Sunday Christians." Without the concept of secular, there are no specifically religious acts and beliefs that are not in themselves also social, economic, political, and cultural. Qutb's understanding is that Islam becomes a magnifying glass that concentrates and converges all the light into one sharp focal point—the worship of God.

Qutb criticized those faux Muslims who go through empty ritual gestures without any faith in their hearts because, otherwise, practice and faith prove inseparable. God's dominion requires the worship of and submission to God, he argued. These help constitute the unity of social life, which is willed by God. Those who argue against this unity, or practice secularism as "natural," are in violation of God's dominion and thus embody *jahiliyya*.

Qutb repeatedly asserted that the notion of *tawhid* contrasts sharply with the West, and with the modern elements within Egypt, the Middle East, and the Muslim world. Here he was concerned about *dis-integration* rather than integration and unity. Thus his emphasis on injustice, slavery, tyranny, man-made laws, the lordship of people over people served to remind readers about *jahiliyya* and what would happen should the unity of God break down as in Europe, America, and among those Middle East communities heavily influenced by modern secularism. Thus, Qutb dwelled overwhelmingly on *jahiliyya*, which contrasted with Islam in general, with God's dominion, or *hakimiyya*, with worship and submission to God, *'ubudiyya*, and with God's unity, *tawhid*. When *jahiliyya* is overthrown and destroyed, the world can once again experience these good elements, as society will be re-integrated, glued back together, with its various and distinct elements woven together with the threads of *shari'a*, faith, and Islam, and with God as the absolute and supreme ruler, law-maker, and judge. All humanity will be subordinate to His will and power; those who think otherwise will remain apostates, blasphemers, and unbelievers.

Qutb's stress on *tawhid* represents a serious critique leveled at secularism. He maintained that religion ought to permeate all aspects of life, all the major and minor affairs of humanity. This view, so unlike Western society's individualism, narcissism, and radical autonomy, became increasingly important to Qutb, particularly as he became more aware of the current barbarities of real political and social life.

> A person who does not believe in the unity of God does not worship God alone....Anyone who performs devotional acts before someone other than God—in addition to Him or exclusively—does not worship God alone....Anyone who derives laws from a source other than God, in a way other than what He taught us through the Prophet—does not worship God alone. In this society, the beliefs and ideas of individuals, their devotional acts and religious observances, and their social system and their laws, are all based on submission to God alone. If this attitude is eliminated from any of these aspects, the whole of Islam is eliminated.[23]

Once this unity is reasserted and reestablished, then peace can come to what then will be a truly Islamic community.

One of the biggest challenges in Islamic life, then, is withstanding and even reversing the growing secular tendencies in the world. Other elements of life are also affected by secularism, and it is the duty of the Islamic vanguard to point out the pitfalls of this *jahiliyya* and set people straight. It is Islam's duty to reform and improve community life, and the vanguard should not be hesitant or timid in furthering Islam's message to all corners of the world.

One interesting example of the social unity derived from divine *tawhid* contradicts the labor theory of value articulated by Karl Marx. In capitalist societies, the product of labor's efforts is alienated and appropriated by the owners of capital. This creates two *antagonistic* classes. Class conflict, to Marx, is the motor force of history. Qutb, on the other hand, rejected the division of opposing classes as detracting from the notion of the unity of God and the unity of His creation. The labor unions created by the Muslim Brotherhood, therefore, advocated cooperative relations between management and workers. On the other hand, socialist unions (Marxist, Social Democrat) recognized, instead, a tension if not an outright hostility between the two. These two principles competed after World War II for the hearts and minds of Egypt's working classes, often colliding with each other and working at cross purposes. Strikes were often undermined by Brotherhood unions because of territorial turf wars and their views on economic relations.[24]

Party politics are another domain in which *tawhid* influenced Qutb's views strongly. Since multi-party systems create and exhibit divisiveness and conflict, and thus violate the notion of *tawhid*, Qutb proposed alternatives, such as a single mass-mobilization party, in order to eliminate these unseemly acts and replace them with a system that realizes social and political integration.

The unity of the various parts of the universe, nature, and society ought to produce an integrated, harmonious, and balanced existence that lacks the tensions, dialectics, and conflicts ordinarily expected in a complex society. Qutb clearly subscribed to a functionalist, organic model of harmony while Marx preferred a conflict model. For Qutb, there is no antagonism between nature, science, religion, and society. He argued that in the West, with the division of labor between God and Caesar (and elevating Caesar to a level associated with God), conflicts and enmities emerge that then are spread worldwide through modernization. Islam, he claimed, can resolve these differences by once again applying the harmony and balance derived from *tawhid*.

The only acceptable antagonism Qutb envisioned is the one between Islam and *jahiliyya*, a struggle to the finish, presumably with Islam the victor. Islam, and Islam alone, can correct irregularity and dissonance and save humanity from its own *jahiliyya*. Islam is able to unify all forces and powers, to integrate together desires, inclinations, and compassions, and to harmonize all predispositions, thus restoring the unity and balance of the universe, nature, and people.[25]

This seems to be one of the bases for Qutb's kharijite thinking, whereby if even one element of society is non-Islamic, then the entire community is *jahiliyya*.[26] Qutb's position is that there is no compromise between Islam and *jahiliyya*, no middle ground or intermediate position. This came to be understood by many of Qutb's followers as supporting the doctrine of *takfir*, or declaring

Muslims unbelievers if they think differently from the accuser. Such an intolerant, Manichean outlook colored Qutb's whole perspective, but it derives from the idea of God's unity and the integration of His creation.

Socially and historically, *tawhid* also means the inclusion of various national, ethnic, and racial groups. Despite different languages, the language of the Qur'an supplies a lingua franca, but various linguistic groups are treated the same. There is not an "Arab civilization"; rather, there is an "Islamic civilization" with its unique set of customs, values, and habits. *Tawhid* also means equality between men and women, at least in theory. It means the unity of classes. Communities are held together by belief in God and His unity, not through common language, color, class, or nationality. They share the common bond of faith, and come together on an equal footing in the worship of and submission to God.

Those who deviate from this system and want some other system, whether it be based on nationalism, race, class struggle, or similar corrupt theories, are truly enemies of humanity. They do not want man to develop those noble characteristics which have been given to him by his Creator, nor do they wish to see a human society benefit from the harmonious blending of all these capabilities, experiences, and characteristics which have been developed among the various races of mankind.[27]

Shari'a law, Judgment Day, and God's will ensure that this unity can continue; their absence means prolonging *jahiliyya*.

> This obedience to the *shari'a* of God is necessary for the sake of this harmony, even more necessary than the establishment of the Islamic belief, as no individual or group of individuals can be truly Muslim until they wholly submit to God alone in the manner taught by the Messenger of God.... Total harmony between human life and the law of the universe is entirely beneficial for mankind, as this is the only guarantee against any kind of discord in life. Only in this state will they be at peace with themselves and at peace with the universe, living in accord with its laws and its movements. In the same way, they will have peace of mind, as their actions will agree with their true natural demands, with no conflict between the two. Indeed, the *shari'a* of God harmonizes the external behavior of man with his internal nature in an easy way.[28]

Disrupting this harmony and balance, not obeying or even acknowledging God's legal codes, and, in fact, elevating man-made law to the level of obedience and submission leads to humanity's disintegration and decline. People will be judged on Judgment Day, but God also intended that social life be shaped in this world and not just in paradise or hell.

The unity of Islam means that Islam is applied at all levels of human existence—spiritual, legal, political, economic, financial, cultural, personal, and social. Qutb called Islam "a great emancipatory revolution" that seeks breakthroughs and advances at all these levels. Its goals, therefore, include freeing humanity from economic exploitation, political privilege, and social mistreatment (as do most contemporary revolutions) but it also seeks to confront and free people from atheism, religious fanaticism, racial and ethnic discrimination, adverse and oppressive conditions, and, of course, injustice.[29] For Qutb, Islam is Egypt's liberation theology. None of Qutb's stated goals for Islam appears reactionary, notwithstanding his reaching back in time for principles from the original Muslim community.[30]

Comprehensiveness (*al-shamul*)

Closely tied to Qutb's ideas of divinity and unity is the concept of comprehensiveness, which attributes everything in the universe to one single, comprehensive will, the will of God. It is more than the idea that God essentially integrates all that He creates and that all He creates is unified under Him. It also goes on to conclude that His will determines all aspects of life and that, therefore, His will, as embodied in the Qur'an, makes Islam a comprehensive or total way of life. It is the way in which Muslims view themselves, the universe, and the position of men and women in that creation. It is a characteristic that regulates every aspect of human life—"the hidden and the visible, the small and the great, the petty and the significant, ritual and law, belief and faith, the individual and the society, this worldliness and the other worldliness."[31] What seem to be opposites are joined together and merged. It includes all the different aspects of God's creation.

Comprehensiveness is a concept that brings together into the worship of God all aspects of life, no matter how small or trivial or no matter how seemingly distant from the domain of religion in the narrow (or Western) sense.

> One result of the integration of man's life is that the entirety of human activity becomes a single movement, directed toward realizing the purpose of human existence—the worship of God alone, manifested in all the aspects of man's viceregency.
>
> This characteristic [of comprehensiveness] makes Islam suitable as a complete way of life, embracing individual belief and social order; not only do these two not contradict each other, they are interconnected with each other, indeed inseparable from each other. They are like a single indivisible package; to tear it apart would ruin the religion of Islam.
>
> According to the Islamic concept, there is no activity in human life to which the concept of worship does not apply or in which its realization may not be sought. The entirety of the Islamic way of life has as its aim the attainment of this aim, first and last. Human activity does not attain its true purpose, as clearly defined by the Qur'an, unless and until it is in conformity with the divine plan in all its aspects. It is only

then that God will truly be worshipped in exclusivity; otherwise, man will have deserted true worship and servitude to God and abandoned the purpose that God has willed for human existence. In a word, he will have abandoned religion.[32]

If God's unity becomes the die that casts human society, then all existence can be attributed back to God Himself, a single comprehensive will, internally consistent, and in harmony with all the parts of that existence. Since *tawhid* means integrating the different elements of God's creation, then *shamul* is the result of that unification. It contains all knowledge of God, the universe, nature, and humanity combined together in a unified system, with God as its unifying force. Thus the problems of humanity and the imbalances and discord of society are solved by reintegrating society's various institutions. The social justice that Qutb wrote about, for example, rebalances and reconnects various aspects of social life that were previously and comprehensively integrated. Tyranny arises when this social unity falls apart because people ignore God's message in the Qur'an. Thus while the concept of unity stipulates an organic society, well integrated and harmonious, the notion of comprehensiveness reinforces the necessary outcome and the moral imperative of that integration.

Although the characteristic of comprehensiveness is built on the notion of unity, it is more than just unity, which is a static condition. It is unity-in-the-making. It is not motionless; it implies an action and a direction. Thus the whole of existence derives from a divine source, God, and is stable and permanent. But furthermore, it actively brings that existence together, integrates it together in a oneness that is of God. God could have made the world permanently centrifugal, flung out in all sorts of different directions. Instead, Qutb argued, that existence is comprehensive since it includes everything and encompasses everything into it.

Since Muslims are so often and so much beset by centrifugal forces, separation, division, and alienation, they are in serious need of this message of comprehensiveness. Thus, supplementing unity, which just "is," comprehensiveness is an active unity-in-the-making, a "becoming." Since it is a cure to solve the problems of their communities, humanity therefore is responsible for establishing comprehensive social systems that reflect God's unity.

The Qur'an serves as a complete and comprehensive guide to the world. God revealed this message in order to instill unity, for it includes all matters of concern for men and women: politics, economics, civilization, morality, and more. In so many ways, humanity is unaware of God's unity, and it is up to thinkers like Qutb to alert people to His purpose and plan. The actions needed to maintain God's unity or the methods required to recapture it—representing the remedies for personal and social ills—are all part of the *shamul* found in the Qur'an. God informed humanity of values, truths, and morals that enable it to live an integrated life. This is God's gift, and for this, He becomes the object of humanity's worship and obedience. Violations of this unity, inadvertent or otherwise, should be and must be corrected. The notion of comprehensiveness presents unity as a goal to strive toward, in worship and in social life.

Qutb used this notion to examine other cultures and civilizations. Because he intended Islam to be a worldwide system, the application of comprehensiveness, of evaluating other societies by the Qur'an, results basically in an ethnocentrism, not so much different in function, really, from the ethnocentrism found in modernization. Other societies, regardless of their particular history and values, can be labeled *jahiliyya* as long as they fail to integrate along the lines of Qutb's Islamic comprehensiveness. Clearly Qutb intended for the unity and the comprehensiveness of Islam to be universal, to create a worldwide harmony and balance that delivers justice, freedom, and equality.[33]

Faith/Belief and Practice (*al-iman* and *al-'amal*)[34]

Many scholars have written about the equilibrium between belief and practice in religion. The focus on correct practice, or orthopraxy, derives from the emphasis on the Islamic pillars (or obligations), *shari'a*, and *jihad*. This is the dry and legalistic side of Islam that many consider to be the minimum requirements in order to be a Muslim.[35] Yet Qutb, for his part, leaned in quite the opposite direction, emphasizing correct belief, or orthodoxy. It is for this reason that Qutb so intensely analyzed the Meccan chapters of the Qur'an, for it was in Mecca—before the migration to Medina and the establishment of the first Islamic state based on *shari'a*—that the first Muslims had to concentrate on belief to maintain their commitment and steadfastness in an otherwise *jahili* community.

This emphasis on faith and belief represents a continuity of Qutb's thinking even from his secular days in the 1930s. Even as Qutb turned toward examining religious issues, he never completely dropped his concern for the subjective, the aesthetic, and the expressive. He maintained the same approach and concerns to the extent that Carré calls him a fideist, where knowledge depends on faith or revelation instead of on reason or the intellect.[36] For Qutb, belief and conviction are paramount in importance and are the sine qua non for the success of an Islamic system. Without faith, all will fail. Still, Qutb was far from being an Islamic Martin Luther, with the latter's motto of *in solo fide*, "in faith alone." Qutb also placed considerable emphasis on establishing an Islamic state and an Islamic legal system.

For Qutb, there was no separation of belief and practice; the two are necessarily woven together and indissoluble. Separating faith and practice disrupts the unity of God that lies at the heart of Qutb's conceptualization of Islam. He saw practice simply as the application and realization of faith (rather than what Carré calls a "knowing and rational faith").[37] Whatever is done without this faith cannot achieve any benefit. Faith, Qutb said, comes from the heart, from sentiment, and from "an inner experience"—not necessarily intellectual reasoning. In fact, Qutb was quite suspicious of intellectualism, for it rarely produced action, only deliberation. On the other hand, he was not against reason as such, and felt that faith itself is rational—to believe in God is itself an act of reason. Faith is utilitarian, he argued, and is helpful in inspiring commitment, but the arid and distant faith that prevails among most traditional scholars, an intellectualism that is confined to just mosques and libraries, appeared to him to be quite useless.

In his book *In the Shade*, faith is not passive and inert, but is practical and active. All good work and good deeds come from having faith in God in one's heart. Returning to an earlier theme found in *Social Justice*, Qutb then argued that the only system of justice that is based on faith and not just on utility is the one found in Islam. Those who judge or act otherwise are apostates, atheists, or polytheists, representing religious ignorance, *jahiliyya*, and are enemies of Islam. Those, on the other hand, who *do* have complete faith, are those who recognize the complete dominion of God.

Applied faith results in a strong, unwavering commitment to God. However, Muslims, and others as well, continue to maintain allegiance to others beside God, such as to the "primordial affiliations" of ethnicity, nationality, and even family and tribe. These ties must all be ruptured without compromise, Qutb argued, so that a person's complete attention is focused on God. Of course, Qutb realized he could not encourage people to break entirely from family responsibilities— after all, these were the bedrock of Muslim society. But, he concluded, the heart must show faith to God before building ties with others. The persons who can do this become superior to others in their piety and devotion. To Qutb, faith is engagement and action rather than passive knowledge and reflection. It demands a zeal—enough so that the zealous Muslim is one who breaks all ties except those with God.[38]

Thus merely going through the actions of proper worship—the Five Pillars, for example,[39]—without faith, makes them empty gestures. This unity is reproduced in the twofold structure of the first pillar, reciting the *shahada*: the belief in a single all-mighty God and a belief and commitment to follow the Revelations recited by the Prophet Muhammad, God's messenger. Both parts are necessary for each part to make sense. Qutb was one to turn the Testimony into a radical, even revolutionary statement: reject as polytheism all authority that is elevated to the level of God, and reject as unbelief all faith and practice not stated in God's message, the Qur'an and its *shari'a*.

Balance (or Moderation) (*al-tawazun*)

Qutb's characteristic of balance advocates moderation and the golden mean. It safeguards against extremes, both excesses and deficiencies. It forbids exaggeration or deviation from statements of religious truth. Much of Qutb's exposition on this characteristic focused on actually mediating between binary opposites.

Divine Will and Human Will

A major issue that requires balance is the relationship between the limitless nature of divine will and the limited quality of human will:

> In the Islamic concept, man deals with an existing God, a Creator possessed of will, dominion, and power, One Who acts as He wills, to Whom all things revert. The creation of the universe and its further unfolding, and every motion, change, and development that take place within it—all are dependent on Him. Nothing happens in the universe except by His will and His knowledge, His power and His wise disposition of affairs. He is directly involved, by means of all of these attributes, with all of His servants, and with all of their states and conditions.[40]

Yet although Qutb was politically conservative and increasingly so, he did not advocate surrendering completely to God's will, a recipe for either authoritarianism and tyranny or for passivity and fatalism. Religious thinkers, Muslim and otherwise, who conclude that all is willed by God tend to be morose and conservative, their followers fatalistic. Qutb avoided such morbid determinism by arguing that the world is still contingent. The fact that all matters are the product of God's absolute will does not invalidate human will, he maintained. God is the ultimate odds-maker (my term) Who shapes the context in which humanity decides. Such decisions are not always correct—were it so, then humanity would be flawless. But God did send down guidance, most recently in the Qur'an. God has set up the correct path, the Straight Path, but humanity is still free to choose His way or other ways, to select good or bad. Qutb claimed that the Qur'an actually says that people's decisions are part of God's decisions. Even though God created a plan that includes the best for humanity, individuals have the ability to counter that plan. Qutb suggested that even this rejection itself is a part of God's creation, which then subsumes human will under or within God's will. But, by contrast, Qutb did not agree with predestination, either, and so despite God's absolute and omnipotent power and creativity, humanity is considered capable of doing otherwise.

To Qutb, God is omnipotent and determines how the world operates. Yet humanity plays an active role in its achievements or failures. Its actions have a moral quality that are rewarded or punished in the next world. Qutb explained this by writing that God's plan, decisions, and actions take place beyond the ability of people to comprehend. That is, God moves in mysterious ways, and we know not the reasons. Yet even with their limited knowledge and understanding, men and women still have the option of pursuing justice, freedom, and truth. And if they have the option to do good, they also have the possibility of doing wrong. God could have created humanity with a nature that made them obey without reflection, criticism, or awareness. But He did not do so, and He willed humanity with a nature to ask, question, probe, and criticize. No one is entitled to ask why

God does the things He does, because no one is endowed with His knowledge and comprehension. Yet people do. The choice to worship and submit to God can only be achieved by having freedom, options, and alternatives. As much as God has shaped the direction humanity should take, the freedom that God gave humanity also permits them to go in other directions.

Qutb followed, to some extent, the dominant Ash'arite perspective of occasionalism that explains all effects as caused by God, not by other divinely created but merely material causes.[41] Yet he also asserted that his position fell between those of the Ash'arites and the Mu'tazilites who, by contrast, believe in absolute human will. He did not completely adopt the fatalism like many Ash'arites, but nevertheless appeared less liberal than his Mu'tazilite predecessor, Muhammad 'Abduh.[42] Nor was he altogether deterministic, for he believed that human beings must act and consider their actions important, whether or not they are part of God's mysterious and unknown plan, but though people are free to choose their actions, these actions only come to fruition, or are realized, by the direct will of God.[43] His position seemed necessary if Qutb wanted to retrieve the idea of an activism or struggle, *jihad,* to alter the abysmal conditions in which Muslims found themselves.

Qutb understood that human behavior is not totally "free" despite our own false impressions. However, nothing is completely deterministic, and contingencies do exist. Human acts are contextually determined and connected to other events, in the past or at the precise moment of occurence. Action is conditional because God created people with minds to think, even if, eventually, they think in the direction that God created and intended. Men and women can think logically and rationally, Qutb argued, but it is God Who, after all, created logic and reason.

Qutb thus rejected both the unadulterated Ash'arite argument of complete God's will but also denied its opposite, the Mu'tazilites contention that it is all human will instead.[44] People resolve to do what they want, and feel God upon their hand. Yet at the same time, they should not be surprised if what happens turns out different from God's plan.

Just as there is no opposition between God's will and human will, so, too, is there no opposition between reason and revelation and between science and religion. Qutb believed that insofar as humanity does what it wants, it is doing what God wills. This returns us to the argument that (1) people are duped to think they have individual "free" will, and (2) that in doing otherwise and still doing God's plan means that God works in mysterious ways humanity cannot totally comprehend.

Humanity cannot change God's plan by its own efforts, and yet if these efforts were not made, then humanity is no different from the animals, which is not what God intended. God clearly sees that total devotion and worship to Him can only come out of freedom and not out of an unavoidable enslavement. Consequently, although Qutb envisioned a balance between God's will and human will, it was not an exact balance, but rather one that leaned in the direction of God's absolute and overpowering will.

Another type of balance that must be considered, Qutb wrote, is the balance between the absoluteness of God's will—He does whatsoever He wishes—and the stability or permanence of the values, norms, and rules that govern existence. This is the condition under which miracles take place: God's own suspension of the principles He created, including those discovered by science. Even though God created the permanent laws that regulate human life, which people use to control their lives and interact with other elements of God's creation, God Himself can contradict and violate these rules. To humanity, these rules and norms are invariant and absolute, the product of God's creation. They provide people with a firm foundation from which to think and act. They can construct theories and scientific explanations about how the natural world and universe operate. Yet at the same time, since God is all-powerful, He is not necessarily bound by the very rules He once created. The Qur'an is such a miracle, for it was not revealed in a "natural" or "scientific" manner. Another example is virgin birth. Qutb did not deny the virgin birth of Jesus, which he claimed is supported in the Qur'an as well, and he agreed that Jesus was a prophet. He only disagreed that this means Jesus was the son of God. Still, God can create these "miracles" while human beings cannot, thus demonstrating the superior power and will of God.

Good and Evil

Human free will is necessary to make sense of the idea that humans will earn rewards or punishments, paradise or perdition, on Judgment Day.

Qutb discussed the notions of this, the visible world and the invisible world that consists of paradise and hell, and of Judgment Day when the sins and achievements of this world are evaluated, and the divine rewards or punishments in the next are conferred. It is Judgment Day, after all, that motivates people to achieve their best and avoid their worst. People are well aware of these two worlds, Qutb suggested, and the mix of delight and fear, of pleasure and suffering, inspires people to follow the Straight Path. One of Qutb's objectives was to convince Islamic activists that while they suffer on earth, the pleasures of paradise await them if they do good.

There is a recurrent theme in Qutb's writings that not all that seems bad is intended that way. Suffering and tribulations may in fact be God's tests to determine people's commitment and religiosity. Men and women can be tested with both good and evil to see which way they choose, particularly since they have the ability to decide. God may assist those who wish to attain His satisfaction, but in the end, it is their choice. God has revealed to Muslims specific obligations and prohibitions; evil comes in the form of temptation.

This consideration is particularly important in understanding why those who have chosen the right way, the Islamist way, are nevertheless tortured and killed. Present-day martyrs realize, correctly, that there is no contradiction here, for the reward for being righteous and pursuing the Straight Path comes on Judgment Day and in the next or invisible world. Similarly, those who do evil and "get away with it" in fact, do not, for their punishment is decided on Judgment Day as well. Qutb discussed God and Satan, but said little more than that Satan is merely part of God's divine plan, possibly playing no greater role than man's own free choice in following the ways of God, or not.

In chronicling this debate on divine justice, Norman Daniel once remarked that before the modern period, Christians condemned Muslims for applying lax punishments and offering rather lusty rewards, evidently in contrast to Europe's harsh punishments and very faint, if any, incentives.[45] Qutb himself advocated punishments in this world, and considered those prescribed in the Qur'an appropriate and acceptable. Yet if the crimes and sins are so great as to escape punishment on earth, then, Qutb argued, the sufferings and miseries in hell will certainly compensate.[46]

Qutb went on to consider the issue of death: who or what determines the end of life? And is it good or evil? Qutb reasoned that God is the time-keeper and sets the hour of our death (as well as our birth). Despite our attachment to this world and our sadness in leaving it, death becomes positive if, indeed, we have chosen the correct path to follow. If not, then the Judgment will go against us.

Qutb firmly believed that death is not in people's hands, but is only in God's power to determine. A refusal to go into battle for fear of dying is absurd, because it is up to God, not the soldier nor the enemy. Qutb accepted the idea that a death or murder is not the fault of the perpetrator because that person is only the instrument of God's will. The Ash'arite position which Qutb adopted states that the one who kills another is not the actual murderer but is merely an accomplice.[47] If a person has followed God's laws and His doctrines, then he has nothing to fear from death.

Qutb also explored questions about theodicy and the problems of evil and suffering. What explains the existence of evil in this world? If humanity does have agency, and can choose alternatives beside the ones God intends, then certainly this may lead to evil and suffering. But why has humanity been created with such a capacity for evil? To this, Qutb replied defensively that this question can only arise out of ignorance. For God created humanity in this way, and to ask for an explanation is irreverent and blasphemous. This reverts back to a "God works in mysterious ways" answer, and ultimately folds human will back into the notion of God's will and His intentions in creating humanity the way He did.

Aware of the close parallels with his own life, Qutb wrote much to explain the virtuous believer who strives to follow God's path and to implement God's dominion but who then suffers pain and misery. The question of why good people fail and bad people succeed is answered by referring to divine wisdom that can ensure punishments for the evil and rewards for the good in the afterworld. What happens on this earth is not the end and what appears horrific can result in rewards in the next world. A true believer will be compensated with satisfaction and even contentment in this world. These inner rewards come from the person's recognition that they are pleasing God and following His way. On Judgment Day, these events are all weighed in the decision to punish or reward.

Qutb did not subscribe to the notion that human nature contains elements of good and elements of evil in equal proportion and that the evil is the material or physical, bodily needs and that the good is the spiritual or civilizational needs. This particular perspective sees people's natural desires for food, drink, and sex as evil while their ascetic and even monastic spiritualism is good. This asymmetrical tension between the material and the spiritual, common in Western Christianity, is not found in Qutb's writing. Nor did Qutb agree with the distinction that people's spirituality is God's spirit inside them, a soul, and that people's materialism is evil, marking the presence of Satan.

Instead, Qutb argued for a balance and a moderation between the material and the spiritual and, indeed (not surprising) a unity, not a dialectic, between the two. Qutb's notion of unity meant that there can be no separation between the material and the spiritual. Human nature includes both, not in juxtaposition, but blended and intertwined, only to be distinguished analytically. The physical is not possible without the spiritual, and the intellectual must have support from the material in order to operate. Humanity's material life is infused with the spiritual, that these and other practices cannot take place apart from the spirituality of God's will and authority.[48]

This balance and harmony within human nature must be revived and restored through Islam and an Islamic society. If humanity's physical world marginalizes its spiritual life, or if its intellectual pursuits lack a concrete and practical material base, then this imbalance will generate alienation or anarchy. But once this balance is achieved, men and women can avoid the extremes and function in ways that reflect God's laws.

Humanity, therefore, must establish a coherent system of guidance that balances action and thought. This system must take into account both material requirements and psychological ambitions. Qutb concluded that Islam is just that system that establishes a balance such that deviating from the Islamic concept generates extremism, radicalism, and fanaticism. Other, man-made systems—either Communism or free-market capitalism—do not ensure such balance and harmony. The equilibrium and concord of the Islamic system are the very forces that create the social justice Qutb claimed emerged from the Qur'an and which has been forgotten in times of tyranny and *jahiliyya*. Upsetting this balance, as has happened in the West, constitutes injustice. Instead, humanity should follow the Qur'an, God's message, and the rules and regulations therein.[49]

Revelation and Reason

Qutb also proposed that the characteristic of moderation in the Islamic concept includes a balance between revelation and reason, although Qutb himself leaned in the direction of revelation. Similar to his approach with divine and human will—that human will can go only so far—Qutb believed that reasoning can go some distance in providing explanations and meanings, but not all the way. Islam, he wrote, considers revelation the ultimate source of true knowledge, unassailable by falsehoods and immune to error. But, he wrote, this does not diminish reasoning, nor does it invalidate knowledge obtained by reasoning, for God's revealed word is, by definition, reasonable since God Himself created both. There is no contradiction between the two since both reason and revelation derive from the same Divine Being. Yet there are limits to human reasoning, and when that limit is reached, revelation supplies the missing ideas, values, norms, and beliefs. Qutb criticized Europe and America for not only placing reason above revelation but in fact for abolishing revelation all together. This was the basis for its secularism, atheism, and decay.

Like other Islamic commentators, Qutb insisted that not only is there no tension or inconsistency between reason and revelation, but that there is no contradiction between their more concrete manifestations, science and religion, because there is divine unity and the worship of one God. Qutb pointed out that Islam, as the seal of all religions—the most mature—did not engage, or need to engage, in the miracles and "tricks" that he said Christianity had resorted to in order to attract followers. Presenting reason/science and revelation/religion as being in conflict or in tension may be more appropriate to Christianity, Qutb argued, since Christianity is based on miracles that suspend the laws and logic of physics and biology. Then, as nature and science came to increasingly challenge Christianity's lack of rationality, intelligent Europeans were unable to accept these unnatural actions, these "miracles," and so distanced themselves from church doctrine. In Islam, there are no miracles but the Qur'an itself.[50] Thus, there is no break with the laws of science and, therefore, no need to see reason and revelation as conflicting polarities. Science and religion in Islam do not conflict; one agrees with the other. Therefore, there is no ground on which to contrast the two since Islam is inherently rational.[51]

As an argument about the power of reason and revelation, Qutb discussed the idea of Darwinian evolution in his book, *In the Shade*, replicating many of the arguments known in the United States as creationist theory or the theory of intelligent design. For Qutb, revelation always trumped reason, creation trumped evolution. But he also rejected the idea that there should be any tension between the two, for God created both and evolution is part of divine creation. Unity means that there can be no discord between God and humanity, between people and nature, and among the people themselves. However, Qutb went on to note that in an evolutionary approach, man and animal are the same; in creationism, man is above the animals. God made humanity His vice-regent on earth and gave people superiority over nature, which it can thus control, by giving humans a soul. Darwinian evolution, he argued, suggests a demotion of humanity. But at the same time, people also inflate their importance even higher, and elevate themselves up to the level of God (the associates of God or the rivals of God). Instead, they should humble themselves before God and remain modest. For mankind can dominate, but God has dominion over all. Qutb was quite concerned about those who become arrogant and show superiority because their own narcissism destroys the unity of mankind and society, a major ingredient for the downfall of Islam.[52]

In the same way, Qutb also referred to the equilibrium between accepting and probing. He focused on humanity's ability to observe or understand, and either accept unquestionably and submit, or else probe and inquire, seeking evidence and proof. Both dispositions are fundamental aspects of the human nature created by God-satisfaction with the known, visible, and comprehensible, and dissatisfaction with the unknown or the unseen. Both are realized in the political acts of obedience and resistance.

A religion that has no mysteries to explain, no transcendent truths that seem unclear, is not, Qutb claimed, a religion at all. But a religion that contains "nothing but incomprehensible riddles" is not a religion, either. A complete religion is one that solves concrete problems and answers people's needs but also addresses humanity's aspirations and capacities for higher understanding and reflection. It provides answers, like science does, and it asks more existential questions about humanity's nature and God and His creations.

> Thus one finds in the Islamic concept everything that responds to the aspirations of human nature: the known and the unknown; the realm of the unseen that can be comprehended neither by the mind nor by the eye, and the realm of the manifest, where the mind and the heart may find what they desire; a realm broader than man's perception that induces in him a sense of the majesty of the Creator, and another in which his perception may freely operate, inducing in him a sense of man's value in the cosmos and his nobility in the eyes of God.[53]

The unseen and the unknown are matters, Qutb said, which Muslims are expected to explore for they must learn what is to be encouraged and prohibited. But beyond this, they must refrain from searching into incomprehensible matters. Thus Qutb's view is that humanity should probe to an extent, up to a certain limit, and then back off and accept the results without further questioning. He sought the middle ground.

God—Humanity—Nature

God created the world and the larger universe; between Him and all that He created lies humanity, which serves as God's vice-regents on earth. It is humanity that mediates between nature and God since it lords itself over the rest of nature, but dutifully submits to the authority of the Divine Creator.[54] Nature is not just parks or woodlands; it involves God's entire creation in the universe, including people, society, and the physical environment. Qutb did not envision a tension or even a conflict existing between nature and humanity; "subduing" or "dominating" nature are not necessary since God created humanity to be inherently superior. Qutb pointed to *jahiliyya* societies as ones that wage battles against nature, violate it, and despoil it. Surely, as God's vice-regent, humanity can benefit from nature, and nature is at humans' disposal. But because both are creations of God, there is no adversarial relationship or survival of the fittest.[55]

The wisdom that God gave humanity allows people to make use of the physical and material universe, not for its conquest, but for their mutual benefit. God anticipated that humanity is to be physically small and weak, and so gave them the intelligence—spiritual, physical, scientific, political, economic, and cultural—to adapt resourcefully to the world and universe around them.[56] Qutb thus saw humanity's adaptation as a combination of both its physical and mental capabilities.

Qutb therefore pictured a harmony between Islam and nature since both are creations of God. In the West, technological advances are detached from humanity and nature. Machines give people the power to subjugate and exploit nature for people's unlimited material demands. Science has become commercialized rather than a method to realize and acknowledge God's material creations. In the West, science is portrayed as ethically neutral and thereby emptied of any spirituality or morality. This is irresponsible, Qutb concluded, and advances an immorality, secularism, and unbridled tyranny.[57] It is not in the character of Islam to be isolated from nature.

God thus created humanity's position to be above nature, but to be subordinate to Him. Moreover, it is this one blanket subjugation that allows men and women to be free of domination from other people. Since all people are dominated by God, how is it possible for one of them to attempt to dominate their peers? Men and women bow their heads to just One—to God—and to no other. This protects people from arrogance, tyranny, and corruption. It leads to equality before God. Qutb added that since all of this is true, then the issue of one person being both divine and human, that accordingly assumes a divinity reserved only for God, is polytheism and is therefore prohibited. Similarly, elevating ordinary people and imparting to them a divine status in order to give them power over others is also a sacrilege. There is no contradiction between humanity's elevated and dominant status in the universe, its dignity and its honor, and yet its obligation to submit to His will and authority. Anyone assuming a position akin to God is blasphemous.

In order for humanity to dedicate itself to worshipping God and God alone, and to avoid some people dominating others, it requires a religious system—Islam—that includes the values, divine laws, and other principles and values prescribed by God. Humanity thus must reject other, man-made social systems that create their own laws, morality, values, and standards. Accepting Islam and rejecting man-made systems is thus pleasing to God.

> Throughout every period of human history, the call toward God has had one nature. Its purpose is ... to bring human beings into submission to God, to free them from servitude to other human beings so that they may devote themselves to the One True God, to deliver them from the clutches of human lordship and man-made laws, value systems and traditions so that they will acknowledge the sovereignty and authority of the One True God and follow His law in all spheres of life.[58]

Although God demands that there be no allegiance to lesser, primordial relations—family, tribe, community, and the like—He also recognizes that these social relations require attention. Since all these relations are benefits from God, then earnestly taking care of them is also doing work for God. Thus, people's commitment to God and God's path should absorb the greatest amount of effort, but not all. Here Qutb was careful to note that denial or asceticism is not part of Islam. These social responsibilities constituted Qutb's notion of vice-regency—of administrating the material possessions and social relationships that are God's gifts. Vice-regency means taking proper care, and not rejecting them (as in asceticism) but nonetheless still focusing principally on God and His revelations.

Qutb encouraged a moderate relationship between God and humanity that simultaneously inspires in people fear, awe, and apprehension as well as tranquillity, intimacy, security, and contentment. Thus the balance is a mental one, between fright and serenity. Men and women embrace Islam and the path to God with open eyes, minds, hearts, and hope. At the same time, their inspiration, vigilance, and perseverance are motivated by the trepidation and worry over sliding backward. They are diligent, but not frivolous; they are mindful and not negligent.

Max Weber once referred to an Old Testament God who was fearful, vengeful, and wrathful and a New Testament God of love, kindness, and serenity. Qutb's version of Islam, not at all unique, combines the two sets of qualities, and adds a third of God as reasonable, sensible, and judicious. The characteristic of balance and moderation here means that all three sets of traits merge and blend together.

Positive Orientation (*al-ijabiyya*)

The seventh characteristic of the Islamic concept Qutb called a "positive orientation" or a positive, optimistic worldview. Islam is not inherently gloomy or ominous. God's attributes are the best of good qualities—the most wise, the most merciful, the most just—in contrast to a view of God as the worst of bad qualities—the most vengeful or the most wrathful.

Qutb distinguished between a God who is distant, harsh, and uncaring, and a God who is close, sustaining, and forgiving. Islam's sense of God, in Qutb's mind, is more the second. In Islam, God is just, generous, and merciful. He dislikes abomination, but he is pleased with those who try to do good. He accepts those who are repentant and faithful. There are still wisps of God's wrath and punishment, but the emphasis is on the positive.[59]

Islam's goals are also positive—ones like achieving freedom, equality, and truth—and not ones that merely prevent disaster like avoiding or redeeming sin, seeking repentance or salvation, eluding hell-and-damnation, and so on. Sociologically, it refers to societies that are thought to be coherent, harmonious, and functional, as opposed to societies that are considered to be in crisis, breakdown, cultural stress, and dysfunction.

Qutb conceived of God as omnipotent, yet he still understood humanity's role as a positive one because of its agency as an active and effective force. It is these dynamic actions and beliefs, found especially within the vanguard, for example, that will actually (re)establish the Islamic state, although this takes place within the environment designed by God.[60] Qutb felt that God's omnipotence inspires and activates men and women and thus His positive orientation provides for ultimate success and victory.

The first generation of Muslims epitomized that good and righteous community. They were living under God's immediate protection and He intervened daily in their lives and affairs. He guided their steps and scrutinized all that they did. This closeness enabled them to develop confidence, alertness, and tranquillity. Their trust in God was based on action and belief. They feared God, but hoped to achieve His salvation. They realized their humanity through Him, by submitting to Him, and by obeying His laws. This glory contrasted greatly with the decline and decay launched by the Umayyads as they led the Muslim community back into *jahiliyya*. The positives turned negative, and notwithstanding moments of brightness and splendor, the Muslim community has declined in terms of this positive orientation.[61]

There is a high degree of irony here in Qutb's view of Islam as positive at a time when he also painted it in negative terms. Qutb clearly saw the Muslim world in decline and decay, and, like many so-called fundamentalists (such as the 18th-century New Englander, Jonathan Edwards), preached in negative tones and terms against a sinful world.[62] Qutb himself was particularly overtaken with the evil in the world and not the beauty, not surprising given his experiences in prison. His negativism increased and displayed its full pessimism and hopelessness in *Signposts on the Road*. It is not clear whether he realized his own departure from the way he characterized Islam. In general, Islam *is* positive and optimistic, but those, like Qutb, who are committed to changing the world of *jahiliyya*, often see more the negative side than the positive. There are, after all, numerous examples of true revolutionaries who could not make the transition from the negative, necessary to mobilize the troops, to the positive, needed to calm and administer the population after victory.

"Positive orientation" also points to another of Islam's characteristics—the notion of purity and clarity in the Islamic conceptualization of God. When Islam emerged, the world was full of what Qutb called "debris," erroneous beliefs, concepts, philosophies, myths, superstitions, customs, and traditions. "Truth was mixed with falsehood," he wrote.[63] What Qutb sought then, was a purification of Islam, freed from the pollution and contamination of this accumulated debris, the accretions amassed from over the centuries that have distorted Islam and caused Muslims to deviate from the right path. Here he included Greek (Aristotle, Plato), Persian (Zoroastrian), Roman (Plotinus), Jewish (the Old Testament God), and Christian (the deification of Jesus) ideas.

The tendency of these accretions was to introduce, and then over-rely on, human "free" will to offset God's will. These additions also introduced other and lesser gods (apparent or hidden), which turned the Muslim community back to polytheism. In both cases, God's positive essence was diluted and corrupted. His attributes had been responsible for Islam's positive orientation; their distortion meant a weaker conceptualization of God. By sweeping away the debris and returning to this original understanding of God, the Muslim community once again could achieve freedom, equality, and truth.

Realism (or Truth) (*al-waqi'iyya*)

Another characteristic of Qutb's Islamic concept is realism, or perhaps "truth" is a better term, since Qutb wrote that this characteristic deals primarily with objective truths, real and verifiable existence, and precise measures of actual impact. By contrast, this characteristic does not deal with what might be considered theological or philosophical issues, abstractions, and ideals that are without substantiation in the real world. Islam, Qutb wrote, is a realistic, active, and practical guide for human existence and social life. It is a practical, everyday religion, one that very much shuns the notion of contemplation, mysticism, or secularism. He would choose Weber's "this-worldliness" over "other-worldliness."

Qutb's idea of God's positive attributes having a positive impact on the Muslim community, is also an aspect of realism. That is, God's attributes are real, pragmatic, and effective. His revealed word, the Qur'an, is just, merciful, and wise. The guidelines and regulations therein are equally so, and their regulation of social life is real and significant for the Muslim community. Qutb very much wanted to distinguish Islam from other religions, notably Christianity, that merely provide abstract ideals that, he thought, are rarely achieved.

For Qutb, Islam operates in this world, and not the next. Even though Muslims are punished or rewarded in the next world, that is not their motivating factor. Instead, it is the impact in this world that prompts and inspires people. The Qur'an itself is very practical, and notwithstanding Qutb's earlier examination of Qur'anic aesthetics, he was convinced in his later career that the practical experiences of the first Muslim community, using just the Qur'an itself and no other documents, were the most glorious and successful.

The more we delve into the Qur'anic texts that define the precepts and duties of the Islamic life, the more we are impressed with the realism of this system, its congruence with the actuality of human nature and the limits of human powers and capacities; it neither suppresses any capacity man has or dissuades him from using it, nor does it impose on him anything beyond his capacities or alien to his nature.

Islam is a religion of realism, a religion for life and movement. It is a religion for work, production, and development, a religion whose imperatives conform to human nature, enabling all man's capacities to function for the purpose for which they were created. At the same time, man is able to reach his highest levels of perfection through movement and effort, through responding to his aspirations and longings and not by subduing or suppressing them.[64]

Qutb once again inveighed against the debris accumulated over centuries that has distorted the Islamic concept. He condemned those influences for their lack of concreteness and pragmatism. They remain abstract, he claimed, and discuss obscure subjects. They depict God as distant and uninvolved. Their understanding of God comes through scholarly debate, not active engagement. God, then, becomes the outcome of an idealism and abstract reasoning, not the result of practical and concrete experience.[65] Such a perspective lends itself to secularism, but Islam is not a religion that can be easily secularized, at least not without violence.

Islam then is a real religion with an immediate and intimate God Who deals with real, down-to-earth matters. Qutb was, of course, well aware of the diversity and alienated character of the world, and Islam's desire to unify these far-flung ends into a comprehensive whole or unity. His argument for realism not only conflicted with other religions, like Christianity, but also with other interpretations or understandings of Islam, such as those of the 'ulama, the Muslim scholars of al-Azhar, and religiously trained officials in the government. Qutb's Islam was an action-based method that would guide activists in their attempts to establish an Islamic state and society.

Similarly, the humanity which is the agent of Islam is a familiar one, with strengths and weaknesses; aspirations and desires; hunger and thirst; minds, hearts, and souls. This is a major reason that Qutb insisted on an understanding of Islam through action, through praxis, for by this way alone could the Qur'an be adapted to the vanguard as it is actually constituted, not to an ideal model in someone's mind or on paper. Qutb remained a very realistic revolutionary.

Qutb thus concluded that the Islamic concept as he conceived it is a very truthful approach to existence and to God. He advocated having an open mind that does not idealize the world but engages with it as it actually is. Because of this realism, Qutb was convinced that Islam can raise humanity to higher levels any other system. Islam seems here to be both realistic and idealistic, dealing with humanity and the world the way it actually appears, and then summoning humanity to achieve lofty and honorable goals. Thus, Islam and the Islamic vanguard can achieve practical and effective results that Qutb believed would surpass those of any other religion, past or present. The combination and integration of ideas and actions, spiritualism and pragmatism, morality and freedom, provide the best system for humanity.

Implications

The Islamic concept could also have been called Islamic philosophy or even Islamic theology. But it wasn't. It was Qutb's concept concerning what constituted Islam's basic and fundamental ideas, beliefs, and values. Together it constitutes a system, a model, and an ideal prototype for human belief, practice, and civilization. The emphasis on unity, inclusivity, moderation, optimism, and pragmatism were important to Qutb and his perspective on Islam as a movement, of going from *jahiliyya* to *hakimiyya* by means of *jihad*. The Islamic concept is the unifying theme for what Qutb saw as the aspiration and achievement of Islamic activism.

Qutb was resolute that the Islamic concept be the pure essence of Islam, devoid of accretions and accumulated debris. Qutb concluded that no Islamic community existed in the world, that all was *jahiliyya*, since many Muslims held a distorted and deviant view of their own religion because they believed in the power and the dominance of the West.[66] Thus, Qutb repeatedly returned to the first generation of Muslims, the *salaf*, for insight into Islamic politics, economics, civilization, and more—going back to what he envisioned as the pure essence and fundamentals of the religion, which he called the Islamic concept. In both social and intellectual terms, this return to the basics would allow true and pious Muslims to achieve a better life and a better world.

The effects of the Islamic concept include freedom, equality, and truth:

- freedom from outside pressure in order to decide one's own religious beliefs and practice
- equality of all believers who submit to God's authority and acknowledge His dominion, and
- truth of God's message delivered by the Prophet Muhammad as the last and final handbook for practical life.

Qutb's Islamic concept reinforced the central notion of unity and monotheism in Islam. This unity is derived from God and provides a template for social, political, economic, and civilizational integration among people. This unity is tied together, in turn, by submission to God and His dominion. This "great universal unity" is absent today from all existing concepts and systems of thought and social organization. Its uniqueness, however, directs humanity toward noble and honorable aspirations that can advance civilization and, Qutb maintained, lead to the liberation and emancipation of humanity and to a genuine peace on earth. This concept can do this because it presents humanity with a complete and comprehensive way of life based on humanity's capacity to freely choose.

Islamism as a Revitalization Movement

Jahiliyya, Hakimiyya, and Jihad

Sayyid Qutb's Islamic concept proved to be more than mere words. Egypt was in turmoil, and its words had to be applied boldly to solve the country's problems. Qutb repeatedly counseled that a solid understanding of Islam could only be forged in fire—where ideas are applied, tried, analyzed, evaluated, revised, and rechanneled. He certainly was not the traditional, contemplative *'alim*, or religious scholar. Instead, he was immersed in the maelstrom of political activism. He sought to renew Egypt and regain not only its former glory but also the earlier brilliance of the entire Muslim world.

Qutb envisioned an Islamist revival that would transform Egypt from a crisis-ridden, corrupt society into a magnificent and unified community modeled on earlier exemplars of moral decency and spiritual well-being. His program embraced three important concepts that he used repeatedly in his political writing: *jahiliyya*, or ignorance ("what's wrong with society"), *hakimiyya*, or God's dominion ("the glorious future"), and *jihad*, or activism and struggle, the means or method of moving from one to the other. These concepts correspond closely to the trajectory outlined by Anthony Wallace: cultural breakdown and crisis, the formulation of a revitalizing vision, the organization and adaptation of this vision to transform society, and finally, a social palingenesis and renewal. These notions also conform to the categories highlighted by Martin Riesebrodt, which include a social critique (the movement's grievances), a salvation history (the mythologized past, the crisis-ridden present, and the eschatological future), and an ideal order (the future in detail).[1]

Qutb's ideal Islamc movement came to include personal epiphanies and intellectual reorientation, the emergence of a vanguard, *da'wa* and missionary work, and finally, the use of force for defense, for "clearing the path," and for destroying *jahiliyya*. The movement is led by a special, dedicated vanguard that rises up and establishes an Islamic society. It has its victories and defeats, its internal debates and public relations dilemmas. To Qutb, the Islamist movement becomes the natural outgrowth of the Islamic concept.[2] It is the same movement that the Prophet

Muhammad created and advanced in the 7th century and it is this movement that can liberate humanity today.

Qutb strongly advocated and promoted the establishment of an Islamic state and society. The first is ruled by *shari'a* law; the second is populated by righteous and devout Muslims whose faith and practice follow Islamic standards. Together, the state and society constitute the Islamic system, composed of Islamic government, politics, economics, and moral values. They are held together pragmatically by an Islamic spirit; intellectually by an Islamic concept.

What permeates this Islamic system is the singular recognition of God's total and absolute dominion, or *hakimiyya*. But this is not found at all in today's societies, which are Muslim in name only. Instead, these communities are steeped in ignorance of the true way and immersed in contemporary *jahiliyya* akin to what the Prophet Muhammad and his followers fought against in the first years of Islam. In order to move from this wasted, decadent society to the freedom and truth of *hakimiyya*, a multi-faceted *jihad* must be raised, a *jihad* that can include, but cannot be limited to, militant action. Moreover, since Islam is universal, the aim of *jihad* is to Islamize the entire global community, an expansion analogous to, and competing with, Western modernization.

The *shahada* mandates that no others should be raised to the level associated with God (polytheism) nor should other messages or paths, such as man-made laws, be followed. Taken to its extreme, Qutb used the *shahada* to raise the cry for revolution: overthrow those who do not believe in God and His dominion, or follow His path. Qutb's subversive goal, then, was to overcome *jahiliyya* and declare one's loyalty, or worship, *hakimiyya*, to God alone.

At the same time that all good Muslims, or good people, are expected to obey God, they can also expect justice according to the *shari'a*. The absence of *shari'a* means the dearth of justice. Injustice is the result of disobedience to God, to His revelations, and to correct practice and belief. If people do not worship and obey God, then there is little they can expect in the way of justice. Those rulers and governments that fail to rule by *shari'a* are considered tyrannical. Whether it is people who should first reorient themselves and purify their hearts and souls, or whether the government must begin by implementing and honoring *shari'a*, was a major topic of debate among Qutb's followers.

The model for establishing an Islamic system is the first generation of Muslims, those who followed the Prophet Muhammad in the early years in Mecca, before moving, or migrating, to Medina. In that 13 years, Muhammad and those he converted faced challenges similar to those of Qutb's Egypt. They, too, encountered *jahiliyya*, along with conflict and contempt, and they, too, had to fortify their faith to gain strength for the spiritual battles that followed. A militant *jihad* was neither advisable nor acceptable at this time, but other types of *jihad*, of personal orientation and oral persuasion, could be employed. Faith became the quintessential element that gave them the courage and commitment to spread Islam. Qutb repeatedly returned to the *salaf* for lessons that could be applied today. Because they relied solely on the Qur'an, their story became the handbook for current strategizing, for the measures used to evaluate current conditions and leaders, which sorely lack the stature and honor of early Islam.[3] Today's Muslims had forsaken Islam and its message in their hurry to adopt Western ways. Qutb wanted to solve this problem, which lay at the root of Egypt's ills.

Social Critique and Salvation History: *Jahiliyya*

Jahiliyya is the vile, detestable world that includes both Western secularism and the local Muslim community permeated by Western influence. Social injustice, immorality, the lack of social solidarity, unity, and harmony; the dominance of man-made laws over divine laws—all of these and more are what Qutb labeled as "jahiliyya." *Jahiliyya* stands for everything barbaric and evil: secularism, narcissism, charismatic personality cults, democratic legislatures, knowledge (epistemology), tyranny, injustice, free (unrestricted) capitalist markets, usury, family disintegration, immorality (mixed gender practices, erotic popular culture, and what Michel Foucault called "bio-power"), and the disunity and division within and among communities (racism, nationalism, classism, but not necessarily sexism). It is hard to avoid the conclusion, though somewhat exaggerated, that almost everything modern, Western, and secular—with its decadence, hubris, wickedness and Godlessness—defines *jahiliyya*. Similarly, everything in the Muslim world that is tainted by Westernization or modernization is also *jahiliyya* and must be purified. Those who are not Muslims include other monotheists, unbelievers, pagans, and polytheists; those who *are* Muslims but nevertheless mimic the ways of the *jahili* West are even worse: apostates and hypocrites.[4] Both groups have to be fought and destroyed in order to arrive at a the new Islamic system of government and society. *Jahili* society and Islamic society can never meet, never mix, never compromise.

Jahiliyya is, of course, the term that most commonly refers to the religious conditions of west central Arabia, the Hijaz, in the time before the Prophet Muhammad and God's revelations. The term is used at present to refer to a similar ignorance. Yet the *jahiliyya* exhibited by today's lapsed Muslim communities, as well as by nonbelievers and non-Muslims outside this community, is qualitatively different from the one found before the Prophet Muhammad began to recite in 610. In the prophet's days, there had not yet been any revelations. Therefore, ignorance was to be expected.

> When Islam came, the world was full of accumulated debris: beliefs, concepts, philosophies, myths, thoughts, doubts, superstitions, customs, and traditions. Truth was mixed with falsehood, right with wrong, religion with superstition, and philosophy with mythology. The human mind, buried beneath this debris, was flailing around in darkness and doubt, unable to find certitude. Human life was drifting into

corruption and dissolution, into tyranny and humiliation, hardship and misery, a life unfit even for animals![5]

Today's ignorance is compounded by the fact that Muslims *should* know better, but either do not know, or else do know but do not care to practice and believe correctly, hypocrisy. So while the term originally had been anchored to the time before the early 7th century, it now became used to refer to any group or any society in any time period that does not heed the ways of God. *Jahiliyya* in the 20th century is not just sloth or forgetfulness. It is Islam's *replacement*, of practicing non-Islamic acts and believing in non-Islamic convictions, that dooms today's society—with no exception—to the degradation of *jahiliyya*. There is, in today's world, no excuse for not following God's way, Qutb reasoned, because the information is out there. Most know it, but wish to imitate European and American lifestyles and behaviors rather than follow the right path.

> We are also surrounded by *jahiliyya* today, which is of the same nature as it was during the first period of Islam, perhaps a little deeper. Our whole environment, people's beliefs and ideas, habits and art, rules and laws—is *jahiliyya*, even to the extent that what we consider to be Islamic culture, Islamic sources, Islamic philosophy, and Islamic thought are also constructs of *jahiliyya*.[6]

Qutb even claimed that since it is no longer just innocent unawareness, today's *jahiliyya* actually constitutes an *aggression* against God, His ways, and His dominion on earth. It is not simply the *opposite* of Islam; it is an active *attack* on Islam.[7] Before the Prophet's time, *jahili* polytheists at least respected and honored *all* their gods, including Allah. Today, everyone presumably recognizes the one true God, but then either erroneously or else in determined fashion, elevates others, deifying them, to the level associated with God Himself. The two polytheisms, therefore, are somewhat different, one showing deference and admiration for all, the other demonstrating disdain and contempt for the One.

At first, Qutb used the term *jahiliyya* to refer simply to religious ignorance and unawareness. In the late 1940s, his use of the concept became more precise—those who do not follow God's path—but it remained vague, a metaphor referring to those who are simply not serious Muslims. But by the time Qutb entered prison in 1954, his understanding of the term had been honed to a very sharp edge, hurled as an epithet at the enemies of Islam, external and internal, in a much more intense and targeted way.[8]

The use of the term *jahiliyya* for both the past and the present is not just a figure of speech that superficially compares the 20th century to the 7th. It means that the malady that afflicted pre-Islamic Arabia is now afflicting Muslim (and other, non-Muslim) communities worldwide. This illness has the same root cause: the lack of belief in, and disregard for, God and His message.

Qutb's writings recount story after story of disbelief, of people and communities veering off in the direction where men are ruled by men and where laws are humanly legislated, changed, revoked, and reestablished. He harangued readers and listeners to realize that there is a chasm—with Islam on one side, and *jahiliyya* on the other. There is no middle ground. Salvation means joining Islam and renouncing *jahiliyya*. This is the only way.

There are many characteristics of *jahiliyya* societies, but the principal one is not governing, judging, or ruling by what God revealed to the Prophet Muhammad in the Qur'an. Thus, Qur'an 5:44 says,

Whoever does not judge by what God has revealed is an unbeliever

which leaves no doubt whatsoever about the absolute and total application of *shari'a* law.

According to the *shahada,* Muslims must obey one indivisible God and His message as revealed in the pages of the Qur'an, which means obeying the *shari'a.* It also means recognizing the unity of God and God's dominion. *Shari'a* should integrate all aspects of social life, for all these different aspects—politics, economics, family life, marriage, culture, leisure activities—fall under the same overarching regulatory umbrella of Islam. Secularism, the separation of social life from religious regulation, is the sine qua non of a *jahiliyya* community. There is no reason to separate the two since Islam combines all elements of social life together, integrating them into one harmonious whole. Those societies that separate all these are *jahiliyya* societies.

Jahiliyya becomes the antithesis of Islam and the Islamic spirit. It includes everything that violates Islam and Islamic rules and convictions. It is an abyss in which humanity is wallowing in its own depravity and animal desires. Islam is under siege from *jahiliyya*, Qutb proclaimed, and true Muslims must do whatever it takes to eradicate it.

What is a *jahili* society and how does Islam confront it? [It] is any society other than the Muslim society...which does not dedicate itself to submission to God alone, in its beliefs and ideas, in its observances of worship, and in its legal regulation.[9]

Jahiliyya is a world of disbelief, nonbelief, and idolatry, which has to be completely rooted out, eliminated, and replaced by the *umma*, the Islamic state, *shari'a,* and the divine unity commanded by God. Until then, paganism, polytheism, apostasy, and hypocrisy prevail. The transgressions consist of modern capitalism and materialism; the greed of usury, monopoly, and unrestricted markets; the injustice of courts and governors marginalizing and disobeying divine law; the selfish individualism and animal sexuality, the mixing of the genders, the slave market of liberated women, and racial and ethnic discrimination. Individually, there are mind-numbing drugs, drunkenness, sexual obsession, infidelity, suicide, betrayal, family disorder, constant anxiety, and alienation. At the social and cultural levels, there are injustice, war, crass materialism, secularism, atheism, false loyalties such as nationalism; poverty, greed, oppression and exploitation, monopoly, licentious music, and frivolous entertainment.

Economic Jahiliyya

The existence of usury, of earning money beyond one's own labor or through the sweat of another's brow, proves that a society is *jahili*.[10] In such a society, *zakat*, the obligation to pay religious tithes, is ignored and even what is collected is not redistributed correctly on behalf of the poor. The massive gap between the rich, with all their luxuries, and the poor, who are starving, is inimical to Islam. Islam does not despise the private ownership of property, but since its original owner is God, then man serves merely as His vice-regent. *Jahiliyya* societies abuse that privilege of ownership, making individuals accountable to themselves alone, not to the community nor to God.

Political Jahiliyya

Where tyranny exists—and that means where one person lords it over other people, thus denying God's dominion, disobeying His law, discarding His principles of social justice, and subjecting the community to oppression and exploitation—then so, too, does *jahili* government. Qutb argued that where people worship and obey people and not God, when people have authority over other people, making some superior and others subordinate, then *jahiliyya* dominates. Even where people presumably obey God but argue endlessly over the different schools of religious law, and thus divert attention away from "real and earnest work," then *jahiliyya* has made serious inroads.[11]

Social Jahiliyya

People's dignity, honor, and pride originate in the worship of, and obedience, to God and God alone. In *jahiliyya* society, people are thwarted by social relationships and identities based on race, class, and nationality. These are chains that hold them back from realizing the truth and freedom that only Islam can provide. *Jahiliyya* means that people scurry around, concerned with material and sensual cravings that blind them to the worship of God.

The patriarchal family is the bedrock of the Islamic community, and immorality has deprived it of its wholeness and inviolability.[12] Promiscuity, homosexuality, pornography, adultery, pre-marital sex, women's liberation, and other illegitimate sexual relationships are not even considered immoral in *jahiliyya* society. They are regarded as merely matters of individual choice, the product, Qutb observed, of excessive individualism and misguided freedom.

Jahiliyya is also characterized by sexuality and animal desires controlling men and women, rather than the other way around. People knowingly allow "sexual disorders" and "personal freedoms" to destroy the moral barriers that enhance social life. In the 7th century, Islam had improved women's lives drastically, eliminating their roles as instruments of pleasure and sensuality, and transforming them into community members valued as mothers and wives who could own and inherit property, insist on support and maintenance, and demand the same human rights as men.

Yet, in recent decades, families have declined and women have been forced to seek employment, and too often they are valued only for their pampered bodies and perverse sensuality. Once again, without religion, these societies witness adultery, fornication, homosexuality, male-female uniformity, permissiveness, and shamelessness. *Jahili* societies merely pay lip service to women's rights, but actually deny them by permitting free sexual relationships, pornography and eroticism, promiscuity and illegitimate children, relationships based solely on "lust, passion, and impulse" and the woman's liberty to show herself off while mixing with men.[13]

Cultural Jahiliyya

Islamic culture, what Qutb called civilization, means following the laws that forbid adultery, licentiousness, and promiscuity. The elevation of the self and one's clique to a level commensurate with God Himself is considered blasphemous and polytheistic. Islam requires true existential freedom to worship and obey God alone. In *jahili* culture, freedom is limited by emphasizing lesser identities and channeling a person's energy into materialist and sensual concerns. Here, individualism takes precedence over collectivism, and both belittle the worship of, and obedience, to God.

Freedom is limited in *jahiliyya*, purposely so, to deny people the independence to freely choose how to follow God's path. As God's vice-regents, people have responsibilities to care for His domain but they also have the ability to choose their destiny—to be rewarded or punished on Judgment Day—as long as they are free to do so. *Jahiliyya* restricts that freedom so humanity will choose in ways contrary to God's dominion. Righteous Muslims are responsible for removing obstacles to that freedom so that mankind can attain its independence and free choice.

Jahiliyya society is riddled with deception, the accumulation of erroneous beliefs, concepts, philosophies, myths, superstitions, customs, and traditions. Left without direction from the Qur'an, people wander aimlessly through the fields of falsehoods disguised as truths. The human mind is simply not capable, by itself, of distinguishing verity from error. God's messengers, His prophets, have revealed this truth to humanity since time immemorial. But up to the time of the Qur'an and the Prophet Muhammad, these truths had become distorted and falsified, succumbing to *jahili* rulers and human desires. Such human frailties purposely mask these truths in order to subordinate humanity under their power. People are surrounded by the debris of *jahiliyya*'s aberrations that lead them into darkness. Discarding this debris requires a new effort to restore the authority of what God revealed.

Religion has to be faith applied through action. In *jahili* society, however, it remains detached from the rest of existence, a museum exhibit brought out during religious holidays. In Islam, religion is a lived experience practiced daily. Secularism is abhorrent, a rejection of religion and God's way. In Islam, faith heals the moral predicament, economic despair, political weakness and defeat, and cultural depravity. But in *jahili* society, since religion is sidelined, these ills continue unabated. To destroy *jahiliyya* gives people new hope, new lives, more freedom, and self-respect that are unattainable when *jahiliyya* exists.

* * *

In short, *jahiliyya* is a world that is sick.[14] All that is bad is *jahiliyya*, and all that is good is Islam.

Qutb described *jahiliyya* as both darkness—including the wickedness of superstition and incorrect beliefs, the iniquity of uncontrolled passion and cruelty, the anguish of instability, insecurity, and alienation, and the confusion of disoriented values and immorality—and backwardness—as in the primitiveness of uncivilized, animalistic society, notwithstanding its material and scientific advancement. In fact, it became the very term in Islam for "backwardness"[15] turning upside down the polar opposites, modern versus traditional. By contrast, Qutb understood "Islam" to represent an enlightened, humane, and transcendent society that rises above petty, primordial identities such as race, ethnicity, and class, and reaches higher levels of love, dignity, and true freedom.

Qutb claimed that there are several types of *jahili* communities, some predictable, some surprising, but all opposing true Islam by denying the dominion of God and His laws.

Communist societies, of course, are *jahili* because they officially embrace atheism and deny God altogether. These communities are entirely materialistic because they assume that all that motivates humanity is material gain or loss. In addition, these societies deprive people of their freedom for the sake of production and deny people their choice to believe as they wish.

Other societies are perhaps just as atheistic, but more subtly. Idolatrous societies believe in more than one god. They derive their laws from a source other than God. These societies include polytheistic religions such as those in India, Japan, and Africa. But they also include secular societies that have elevated others, even other prophets, to the level of God and, therefore, engage in paganism. Here, the other sources for laws are magicians, priests, astrologers, but also more recently, legislators, national elders or statesmen, or just political parties and national parliaments. Laws are man-made, not divine.

Ideally, Jews and Christians should be Muslims and follow the *hanifi* religion of Abraham, the generic monotheism of which Islam is essentially the last manifestation. But Jews and Christians, however much related, went astray, distorting their original beliefs and now embracing false faiths and polytheistic institutions. Jews incorrectly deified Ezra, falsified their scriptures, and were wrong to contaminate their religion with pagan ideas, myths, and fables; to resume idol worship despite their deliverance by Moses; and to subscribe to a racial arrogance where offenses against non-Jews go unpunished. Christians incorrectly deified Jesus, falsified their scriptures, and were wrong to believe in a trinity that separates God into three parts, to interpret Jesus's virgin birth as proof of his divine nature, and to duplicate the original sin of Adam as a reborn guilt for all.[16]

Neither religion follows God's law and, therefore, both are guilty of undermining God's dominion by supplanting it with their own sovereignty. They no longer follow the Torah or the Gospels, because these, too, have been warped over the centuries so that God's original message, as it was delivered to and through the Jewish and Christian prophets, became lost or misshapen. Jews and Christians now engage in *jahili* belief.[17]

Qutb repeatedly chastised Christians and Jews for obeying their priests and rabbis instead of God, and, in so doing, worshipping them. In Islam, there is no human mediation between humanity and God; the relationship is a direct and immediate one.

In Sunni Islam there is no clergy or religious hierarchy. The imam leads the congregation in prayer and gives the Friday sermon, but this is optional. Every Muslim can directly call to God without intercession. This also parallels the character of governmental authority under God's dominion. There is no person, institution, or power that exists between God and His creation. Where this happens, there is the lordship of one person over other persons, the submission to others that denies submission to God. An Islamic leader is only a first among equals.

But even so-called Muslim communities are also *jahili* societies, not because they believe in or worship other gods, but because their lifestyles are not based on *shari'a*. They may believe in God's unity, and even say they believe in *tawhid*. But in practice, they dissect their own communities and parcel the various functions out to different secular and colonial institutions. They all have parliaments and legal codes mimicking Europe's. Many are out-and-out secularists, declaring a nationalist program that clashes profoundly with Islamic loyalties and commitments. Others pray five times a day, and even go on pilgrimages and fast during Ramadan. But their ordinary, day-to-day lives ignore God and His laws, and their minds are filled by unbelievers with sciences and secular subjects, which slowly nibble away at their faith. Science and nation take precedent over Islam and God which are then relegated to Friday services. There are even those Muslim countries that claim their laws agree with *shari'a*, even though these laws come out from the mouths and pens of mere people and their parliamentary committees, and not from the Qur'an. All together, these so-called Muslim societies are not based on a complete submission to God, but cut this short in favor of pursuing their own power, dominion, and laws.

Qutb (and others) divided the world into two starkly contrasting domains: Dar al-Islam and Dar al-Harb, identifying them synonymously with (plain, unmarked) Islam and *jahiliyya*. Dar al-Islam, or the homeland of Islam, is defined as the territory where the Islamic state exists and where Islamic law is applied. Where there is no Islamic state and no Islamic law, there is Dar al-Harb, homeland of war.

The relationship between Dar al-Islam and Dar al-Harb need not be one of combat and perpetual *jihad*. There can also be momentary peaceful relations as well, based on treaties and contractual agreements that, however, can be extended to such a degree that it makes the "momentary" phase practically an unending period of amity. Yet Qutb's growing kharijite perspective offered no such middle ground, not even one that allowed for righteous Muslims living in a non-Islamic state.[18]

To Qutb, Dar al-Islam and Dar al-Harb were as much spiritual states as they were geographic locations. A true Muslim has no real home other than Dar al-Islam. If the country is not ruled by *shari'a* law, then it is not an Islamic state and is not part of Dar al-Islam and the person is not a true Muslim. The only alternative is that the country is then Dar al-Harb, or *jahiliyya*. Thus, Dar al-Harb is where true Islamic institutions are absent, despite the fact that the people are Muslims and that they firmly and piously practice and believe in the *shari'a*.

> Islam knows only two kinds of societies, the Islamic and the *jahili*. The Islamic society is that which follows Islam in belief and ways of worship, in law and organization, in morals and manners. The *jahili* society is that which does not follow Islam and in which neither the Islamic belief and concepts, nor Islamic values and standards, Islamic laws and regulations, or Islamic morals and manners are cared for.
>
> The Islamic society is not one in which people call themselves "Muslims" but in which the Islamic law has no status, even though prayer, fasting and Hajj are regularly observed; and the Islamic society is not one in which people invent their own version of Islam, other than what God and His Messenger have prescribed and explained, and call it, for example, 'progressive Islam.'...
>
> There is only one place on earth which can be called the home of Islam (Dar al-Islam), and it is that place where the Islamic state is established and the *shari'a* is the authority and God's limits are observed, and where all the Muslims administer their affairs of the state with mutual consultation. The rest of the world is the home of hostility (Dar al-Harb).[19]

For Qutb, the new *jahiliyya* meant that no community or society in his day was Islamic, for none governed by what God revealed. A few claimed to do so, but in truth, it is men and women who wrote the laws. Even those societies calling themselves Muslim were in fact *not* Muslim at all. Instead, the Muslim world was dominated by Europe and America. Countries like Egypt ceased to rule by Islamic law, or what was called Islamic law, in the 19th century, notwithstanding superficial attempts since then to reinstate it. Islam's leadership had collapsed over the previous 100 years, with the final blows coming in 1924 with the full abolition of the caliphate, no matter how weak and ineffectual that office had become. As early as 1948 Qutb wrote in *Social Justice*:

> Islamic society today is not Islamic in any sense of the word. We have already quoted a verse from the Qur'an that cannot in any way be honestly applied today: "Whoever does not judge by what Allah has revealed is an unbeliever" [5:44].[20]

Thus for the most part—in most places, among most people—Islam has simply disappeared. It no longer existed, even among those who would like to think of themselves as Muslims.

This means that *jahiliyya* is not limited to any particular age, to any particular place, or to a particular group of people. It is a condition afflicting all those who deviate from the ways of Islam, past, present, or future.[21] It is an individual condition, but summed up over a community or a society, it also means, or leads to, political disorder, misguided leaders, economic inequities, cultural abnormalities, and civilizational stagnation, even decline.

Qutb blamed this condition on the devotion and submission to human desires rather than the worship and obedience to God. Such cravings include animalistic, sexual desires, but also individualism, egotism, and narcissism. This means focusing on one's own self-importance and wishes instead of heeding God's requirements.

> *Jahiliyya* is evil and corrupt, whether it be of the ancient or modern variety. Its outward manifestations may be different during different epochs, yet its roots are the same. Its roots are in human desires, which do not let people come out of their ignorance and self-importance, desires, which are used in the interest of some persons or some classes or some nations or some races, whose interests prevail over the demand for justice, truth and goodness. But the pure law of God cuts through these roots and provides a system of laws, which has no human interference, and it is not influenced by human ignorance or human desire or the interests of a particular group of people.[22]

One of *jahiliyya*'s meanings is the lack of moral character or moral integrity, and it is sometimes used to counter the term *hilm*—"humility" or "gentleness"— coming close to meaning arrogance.[23] The two meanings—the antithesis of Islam and God's dominion on the one hand, and the opposite of humility and gentleness on the other—converge when ruthless, tyrannical, and egotistical rulers become so enamored with their own power that they elevate themselves to God's level, and then insist that their subjects do the same, giving rise to personality cults, saints, holy men, and the like. Ironically, this turns Weber's charismatic leader upside down, for rather than being that "something extra" that makes men follow them, charisma, to Qutb, became a hubris that deifies, even if only partially, some men to lord over others. Islam, then, expects all men to humble themselves before God, and so humbled, there is no man who is superior to another in God's view.

Individuals can and do go astray; it is the responsibility of the domestic social, political, and religious establishment to steer them back to the Straight Path. Here, however, the institutions of national guidance prove acutely defective. Qutb placed more blame on Islam's leadership, especially the 'ulama, but also on government officials. (Others coming after Qutb faulted the society at large.)[24] This leadership, Qutb argued, had collapsed over the last century, powerless against, or mindless of, the effort to implant jahiliyya as the Islamic spirit declined and as the colonial project advanced. Moreover, if the main problem is failure to rule by God's law, then it is the country's rulers who are to blame. Their surrender to personal narcissism, luxury, wealth, and their own weakness have brought about the degeneration of the societies they govern.

> I am aware that between the attempt at revival and the attainment of leadership there is a great distance. The Muslim community has long ago vanished from existence and from observation, and the leadership of mankind has long since passed to other ideologies and other nations, other concepts and other systems.[25]

Qutb also blamed jahiliyya on European imperialism. European domination is applied according to the ideas and philosophies of Western Christianity and secularism. Europe became materialistic when it jettisoned the church, and before that, when it abandoned religious regulation, and even before that, when it denied the true meaning of the Gospels (and the Torah, for that matter). It deviated from Christianity's original monotheistic message, a distortion that goes back to the Council of Nicaea in 324.[26] Europe could have continued such wickedness in isolation, but unfortunately, its colonialism forced Muslim countries to follow its example.

Yet although Islam has been beaten down, it is not entirely defeated. The halt is only temporary, and Islam can be revived now if a vanguard of renewers can emerge once again. If sincere and righteous people reorient their perspective, they can re-ignite the Islamic spirit and lead the world.

> It is necessary to revive that Muslim community which is buried under the debris of the man-made traditions of several generations, and which is crushed under the weight of those false laws and customs which are

not even remotely related to the Islamic teachings, and which, in spirit of all this, calls itself the "world of Islam."[27]

As a small number of people come to realize that they are living in the midst of *jahiliyya* despite the superiority of Islam, and even more, come to recognize the huge chasm that exists between the true way and the way of *jahiliyya*, they can acknowledge their obligation to overcome that gap by first purifying and removing themselves from *jahiliyya*'s stranglehold.

> We must also free ourselves from the clutches of *jahili* society, *jahili* concepts, *jahili* traditions and *jahili* leadership. Our mission is not to compromise with the practices of *jahili* society, nor can we be loyal to it. *Jahili* society, because of its *jahili* characteristics, is not worthy to be compromised with. Our aim is first to change ourselves so that we may later change the society, ... to raise ourselves above the *jahili* society and all its values and concepts. We will not change our own values and concepts either more or less to make a bargain with this *jahili* society. Never! We and it are on different roads, and if we take even one step in its company, we will lose our goal entirely and lose our way as well.[28]

The emerging Islamic vanguard, then, is obligated to abolish the existing system of *jahiliyya* and replace it with a new Islamic system. Such a replacement requires concentrated effort and action, a form of personal, community, and militant struggle, or *jihad*, to cleanse the world of *jahiliyya* and establish God's dominion, *hakimiyya*, over all.

What Has Been Lost—What Must Be Gained: The Islamic Spirit

Qutb often explained the decline of Islam after the usurpation of the caliphate by the Umayyad dynasty by using a construct he called the Islamic spirit (*al-ruh al-Islami*).[29] When Qutb claimed that Islam had stopped, he meant that *shari'a* had been tossed out as the dominant code of law. But he also meant the extinction of the Islamic spirit.

This spirit, or fortitude, means a zeal, a passion, or an enthusiasm individuals possess that goes beyond the ordinary levels of commitment, action, and faith. Sometimes Qutb called it a "keen moral sense" of right and wrong, a zealous self-righteousness clearly visible at Muslim Brotherhood rallies, for example, when the highly disciplined Brothers line up and defiantly wave their Qur'ans in unison. This spirit is a flame that Islam kindles in a person's soul, an ardor that committed activists display in their daily lives and in their Islamist campaigns. Elsewhere, Qutb used this elusive quality to capture the aesthetics of Islam, which he examined in the 1930s. Later, he wrote about a spirit of equality and a spirit of social justice—those enthusiasms that go well above and beyond the common-place approach, even in Islamist activism.

Qutb wrote in *Social Justice in Islam* about this Islamic spirit as it developed historically, even as Islam declined. However tenuous, it remained embodied in the deeds of heroism and awakened genius that kept the flame of true Islam alive through the centuries. From time to time, it even changed the course of human history.

> It is this spirit that dictates the very high standard required by Islam as the objective to which its adherents must strive and seek; not merely by the observance of obligations and rites, but even more by that inward obedience that is greater than any obligation or rite. This standard is difficult of achievement and still more difficult of permanent retention. For, the tendencies of human life and the tyranny of human necessity do not permit most people to achieve such a high standard, or, if in a moment of high ambition and aspiration they do reach it, to remain long on it. For such a standard involves difficult responsibilities, duties of life and property, of beliefs and conduct. But perhaps the heaviest of these duties is the constant watchfulness which Islam enjoins on the individual conscience and the keen moral sense which it evokes in a man; it gives him a clear view of his rights and his responsibilities to himself and to the community in which he lives, to the human race to which he is related, and to the Creator Who watches over him in small things and great, and Who knows his most secret and inner thoughts.[30]

This spirit seems quite similar to the "spirit" in Weber's Spirit of Capitalism or the "courage" in Weber's sense of charisma. Likewise, it may be comparable to Hegel's notion of spirit, of ethics and idealism. But, of course, the Islamic spirit is pure, and not contaminated by such European thinking. Still, for Qutb, it came to include faith and personal exertion, knowledge, and reason, but it also went beyond these to focus on expressing a fiery attitude and passionate dedication.

Qutb's Islamic spirit appears when people are true Muslims, and disappears when they lapse.[31] It contains optimism and hope for the future, but it also includes resistance against oppression and exploitation. The spirit of Islam is especially intensified and whipped up to oppose Europe's Crusades, Reconquista, and Orientalism. The Islamic spirit is what permeates the vanguard and what is reserved for them, since the common, ordinary Muslim, however devout and pious, is not expected or obligated to exhibit such intensity. If it could be said that the Islamic tide is rising, it meant, in Qutb's mind, the rise of the Islamic spirit, but not without obstacles that have to be surmounted. To overcome *jahiliyya* and achieve *hakimiyya* through *jihad* requires the Islamic spirit to carry and drive the vanguard through to its final victory.

Qutb analyzed the rise and decline of the Islamic spirit and saw history moved by men infused with this attitude. These individuals are not just abstract individuals preaching moral directives or fanciful dreams that prove empty. Instead, they are real people who rise above the crowd and lead them, however momentarily, to a better understanding of Islam. They inspire others to join them, to transmit and infect them with the spirit of Islam, and together to go on and pass the spirit on to yet others, again, in an ever-upward spiral. People become inspired by their genius and heroism.

Carriers of the spirit, the vanguard, exist outside of government, for it is in the halls of government and national leaders where the spirit of Islam died the earliest. In Qutb's reading of history, the Islamic spirit fell with 'Uthman, the third caliph, although it did reappear from time to time, such as in the caliphate of 'Umar ibn 'Abd al-'Aziz, or 'Umar II (r:717–20), and continued to rise (less) and fall (more), reaching a low point in the 19th century with the marginalization of *shari'a* law. But it never died completely. At the worst moments, when Islam was squeezed of all meaning and stood as an empty shell, the spirit of Islam, though weak, was not extinguished, not so long as just one lone individual continued carrying the torch. Such people then became the kernel of Islam's renewal. Yet it is in the current age that Islamic renewers are once again attempting to spread the Islamic spirit and establish an Islamic system.[32]

This Islamic spirit appears in the day-to-day preaching that appeals to a person's mind, conscience, and heart. It avoids any kind of coercion, but simply persuades and convinces others of the rationality and spirituality of the true Islamic message. It infuses its recipients with just that extra surge of effort and energy, that extra piety and passion, to effect an Islamic triumph. Without this zeal and sense of righteousness, without this Islamic spirit, Islamists cannot transcend the momentary defeats to fight new battles in order to achieve their final goal.

The renewal of the Islamic spirit, in Qutb's thinking, was to start from the bottom up, at the grassroots level, and only then, at the end, to overthrow the *jahili* government. This requires a strengthening and clarification of the Islamic spirit such that those affected by this intensification strive to fortify and expand it even more, in an exponential fashion. This accelerated growth is not easy, and the vanguard therefore requires intense spiritual and physical training. The obstacles to this intensity are many, and it is up to the vanguard, immersed in the Islamic spirit, to overcome them completely. Thus the zeal, passion, and self-righteousness of Islamic militants, so obvious to the outside observer, is the very spirit Islamic activists should have. The Islamic spirit imposes heavy obligations and responsibilities on members of the vanguard—to be constantly alert, keenly sensitive, aroused, and anxious to complete their duties. [33]

The Ideal Order: *Hakimiyya*

For Sayyid Qutb and for many other Islamic thinkers, the primary purpose and final outcome of the Islamic movement is to overthrow *jahiliyya* and establish *hakimiyya*, God's dominion on earth and, specifically, the rule of Islamic law.[34] Until this goal is achieved, communities remain steeped in *jahiliyya*, and activists (*mujahidun*)[35] will continue to oppose it and strive to establish the Islamic system. It is only when societies govern by what God has revealed can they escape *jahiliyya* and, through struggle, achieve a good and righteous community, a true Islamic civilization. *Hakimiyya* and *jahiliyya*—God's dominion and human barbarism— are diametric opposites. God alone has ultimate authority over people's affairs, Qutb reasoned, and it is when a community acknowledges His authority, and no other, that it can leave *jahiliyya* behind and embrace God's way. The concrete demonstration of that authority is obedience to His laws and to His laws alone. In Egypt, God's authority was abandoned when Egyptians began importing and following French law which replaced *shari'a* in the 19th century. That deviation, Qutb concluded, must be corrected, and God's dominion reasserted.

Many writers translate *hakimiyya* as God's "sovereignty." But because "sovereignty" also means "integrity" or "autonomy"—such as when we discuss a personal "sover- eignty" or personal independence that cannot be sullied or violated—I prefer instead to translate *hakimiyya* as "dominion." Yet one useful idea in translating the term as "sovereignty" is that it underlines the fact that the "sovereignty" of God directly con- flicts with national sovereignty. Insofar as both require "loyalty," then loyalty to God becomes greater than (or even opposed to) loyalty to the nation, while in the case of contemporary secular nationalism, this is reversed.[36] To Qutb, the source of *hakimiyya* is God and only God—"There is no god but God"—and loyalty to any other authority is polytheism and paganism. In the United States, and in most secular, democratic Western nations, it is the citizen who is the source of sovereignty or legitimacy, for it is all of them, in theory, who must decide on the destiny of their nation. Qutb strongly disagreed with this position, for the sovereignty of God means that only God is the final source of authority. Anything else means acquiescing to *jahiliyya*.

Qutb considered obedience, worship, and service to God to be the ultimate goals of human existence.[37] In an Islamic system, Qutb explained, there is room for all kinds of people to follow their own particular beliefs while still acknowl- edging the dominion of God and following His laws. But it is those Muslims who go through all the correct motions but fail to recognize God's complete authority and, instead, obey the man-made rule of other men who have gone astray and have descended into *jahiliyya*.

> In the sight of Islam, real servitude [actual bondage slavery] is follow- ing laws devised by someone, and this is that servitude [worship] which in Islam is reserved for God alone. Anyone who serves someone other than God in this sense is outside God's religion, although he may claim to profess this religion.[38]

Qutb also argued that God's dominion does not just mean strictly obeying *shari'a* law. It also means worshipping God in all the ways ordered in the Qur'an, with additional guidance from the *sunna* of the Prophet (Muhammad's words and actions). This has come to include not just legal codes in the strict sense, but all the social, political, economic, and cultural institutions—what Qutb called Islamic "civilization"— that regulate human existence. It involves establishing an Islamic state, society, spirit, and system in which the lessons about comprehensiveness from the Qur'an and Sunna can be applied. It consists of habits, morals, and values. It embraces, in practical terms, a community's art, music, entertainment, family life, and social relations. It means God and God alone is the divine arbiter in *all* matters of life. In other words, the entire society, not just its laws, must be shaped by what God has revealed.

> Islam constructs its foundation of belief and action on the principle of total submission to God alone. Its beliefs, forms of worship, and rules of life are uniformly an expression of this submission and are a practical interpretation of the declaration that there is no deity except God.[39]

God's dominion means, over the long term, His overpowering will and determination. In the short term, there is the guidance provided by *shari'a* law, which creates social order, human rights, and mutual obligation. Despite Judgment Day, when God rewards or punishes people for their deeds, there is still need to enforce *shari'a* law to ensure God's dominion, since men and women are theoretically free to violate God's rules, regulations, and social order. Qutb saw the task of the Islamic movement and the vanguard to be an altruistic chore of bringing back those who deviate—by force, if necessary. Death becomes insignificant in comparison to the punishment that can take place on Judgment Day. Thus the Islamic movement is doing humanity a great kindness by applying *shari'a* law.[40] Qutb envisioned Islam as a universal religion. Therefore, God's dominion must also be worldwide. This means that all people everywhere must recognize and submit to God's authority. Where His dominion is not acknowledged, there is, by definition, tyranny and slavery, which must be destroyed.

In Liman Tura prison, the concept of the proper and exclusive worship of God, *'ubudiyya*, loomed larger and larger in Qutb's mind as he experienced the torture and barbarity of prison guards, officials, and government administrators. The growth of a charismatic personality cult surrounding Jamal 'Abd al-Nassir incited Qutb to condemn the worship of idols and gods other than the true God. This condition, he argued, was imported from Europe. Qutb criticized the Renaissance in Europe as the moment when Europeans ceased to guide their lives by scripture but, instead, by reason, thus elevating the latter over the former. It was the Renaissance when Europeans began worshipping those other than God—their materialist and animal desires, other men, and themselves. It was out of this setting that the sciences and arts emerged, signifying to Qutb their Godless or *jahili* quality. Qutb warned true and devout Muslims not to imitate this.

'Ubudiyya, what I call "worship," is often translated as servitude. Perhaps one might even call it "slavery," as in a "slave of God" ('Abd Allah, a common Muslim

name), but certainly to no one else. I feel uncomfortable with that translation, but Qutb clearly meant for humanity to submit to God as slaves of God and to obey no one whatsoever but Him—total, absolute, unconditional obedience. Indeed, Charles Lindholm points out that there is, in fact, a fierce and robust independence among the tribal groups he studied—the Pathans and Moroccans—and I would claim that this stern autonomy also exists in many other Middle East tribal and post-tribal cultures as well.[41] This means that while Muslims submit totally and absolutely to God, with others—especially including governments—there are always, figuratively speaking, negotiations and bargaining before people agree to comply and allow governments to rule them. Ironically, the stereotype of Oriental Despotism—whereby the Sultan snaps his fingers and everyone instantly and automatically bows down—takes this unmediated relationship between the Creator and His creation and projects it as the actual relationship between the ruler and the ruled. Qutb argued that this subservient relationship is reserved for God alone.[42]

Qutb combined the two concepts of dominion and worship. Men and women must acknowledge God's dominion, *hakimiyya*, and do so by submitting absolutely to His will, obeying His laws, and worshipping God alone, *'ubudiyya*.

Qutb maintained that the worship of and submission to God, *'ubudiyya*, on the one hand, and tyranny, *taghut*, on the other, are antithetical to one another. *'Ubudiyya* means the complete worship, submission, and obedience to God and His laws; *taghut* is the result of governing by other than God's laws. Qutb's idea was that the worship of any other but God gives power and authority to a self-styled ruler instead of acknowledging God's dominion. Such tyrants are to be overthrown and replaced by an authentic Islamic authority.[43]

Hakimiyya and *'ubudiyya* mark key elements in Qutb's thought. He went well beyond one's simple loyalty and commitment to God, and demanded, instead total worship and obedience. There is a suspicion of, even a resistance to, any human authority, but true believers ought to submit without hesitation to God. This "trust no one but God" doctrine can then imply an Islamic justification for revolution, when rulers do *not* rule by what God has revealed, and thus turn into tyrants.

> When God tried them and they proved steadfast, relinquishing their own personal desires, and when God knew that they were not waiting for any reward in this world, now were they desirous to see the victory of this message and the establishment of this religion on earth by their hands, when their hearts became free of pride of lineage, of nationality, of country, of tribe, of household—in short, when God saw them to be morally pure—then He granted them the great trust, the conscious assumption of the viceregency of the earth.[44]

A Muslim's obedience is stated in the oath of allegiance, *bay'a*, he or she takes and which is stated publicly at the Friday communal service. But this allegiance is ordinarily to the earthly ruler, not the heavenly one. Qutb wrote that this mundane type of allegiance is essentially temporary, tentative, and contingent, unlike the real oath that is placed with God and His prophet—and then with Muhammad only insofar as he was God's messenger.

If submission to political rulers is provisional, based on the leader's implementation of *shari'a* law, then people are free to withdraw their *bay'a*. Submission and obedience to unIslamic rulers and to man-made laws are the opposite of God's intentions and the antithesis of Islam. True Muslims bow their head to no one but God. All people's acts, from the trivial to the sublime, become acts of worship, *'ubudiyya*, that are infused with faith in God's power. Thus human existence, in Qutb's view, becomes synonymous with *hakimiyya*. God created humanity; therefore, the act of worshipping and obeying their Creator is of the highest value.

As long as men and women worship God, He will reward them with righteousness and evenhandedness. Should an unjust, tyrannical leader prevent that, then the people must mount a *jihad* in order to follow God's way.

The Path from *Jahiliyya* to *Hakimiyya*: The General Manner of the Islamic Method

The Islamic method is the manner in which Qutb intended to bring about an Islamic society. It is more general and strategic than the issue of *jihad*, which is more about tactics. The Islamic method provides the general contours in which *jihad* takes place.

Qutb's method aimed to change people's beliefs and actions, and turn them into Islamic practices and values. Moreover, this method is an inherent part of Islam, derived from God's message, the Qur'an; His prophet, Muhammad; and *shari'a*. It is a divine creation, not merely a collection of vague theories or abstract principles. Instead, it is a *practical* method to be applied to real life and to the struggle for establishing an Islamic society.

> It is not possible to establish this religion without following its particular method.
>
> One should also understand that this religion has come to change not only the beliefs and practices of people but also the method of bringing about these changes in beliefs and practices. This religion constructs beliefs together with forming a community; it also develops its system of thought while it spends its energy in enforcing its practical aspects.
>
> This religion has a particular method of action. Now we ought to know that this method is eternal.
>
> Islam's function is to change people's beliefs and actions, as well as their outlook and way of thinking. Its method is divinely-ordained and

is entirely different from all the valueless methods of short-sighted human beings.

[If] we remove the divine method and divine outlook from its character...we reduce it to the level of a man-made system of thought. [45]

The method used to expand Islam targets people's hearts before anything else. Unlike man-made methods that address people's material or biological needs, God's method targets their spiritual requirements first and transforms these into a unified set of religious actions that shapes all aspects of human life. When these become rock-solid, then it continues hardening the resolve of the vanguard to expand its worship and submission to God. It ultimately aims to create a new condition for humanity.[46]

The first stage strengthens the heart's faith and disciplines the conscience. People come to accept with all their hearts that they must submit to God and to no one else. When this faith is stamped on people hearts and minds, then together, as a vanguard, they can begin the next stage of gaining practical control of their society, administering Islamic law, and similarly implanting God's faith in the hearts of other people. Then people's needs can be addressed in a practical fashion. This is the best and most assured way of establishing God's dominion, authority, and laws on earth.[47]

By emphasizing faith over all other needs and desires, God is able to cleanse people of their *jahili* ways and their ignorance of His dominion. In the place of secularism, immorality, arrogance, and man-made political systems, this method provides a way of thinking of and understanding God's creations so that all attempts to rival God are defeated and God's Straight Path is realized. Thus, people are simultaneously infused with religious faith and are freed from the evil of *jahiliyya*. The first group of cleansed souls must band together and form a vanguard and then separate and distance themselves from their old habits and beliefs under the *jahili* system.

Instilling faith into people's hearts is not a classroom exercise nor is it a lecture or even a debate. It takes place through an active application of the principles found in the Qur'an to real struggles. This method cannot simply lie dormant in the hearts of humanity. It must be sharpened to a fine edge by creating a vanguard of active, harmonious, and cooperative members.

When the vanguard finds a new community and introduces faith into their hearts, and they, too, submit themselves to God, then the process is repeated, community after community. The ultimate aim is to develop humanity's spiritual capacities and to make the Qur'an their guidebook. Then people's material and spiritual needs will both be satisfied. Education, not force; persuasion, not coercion, are the keys to establishing God's dominion on earth.

Reading the divine scriptures with potential recruits and forming them into a radical reform movement are the principal means of expanding the Islamic method. But Islam is not just a religion of classrooms, lecture halls, or mosques. It has to be applied and understood in the heat of struggle in order that the practical points come out loud and clear. Yet any effort that fails to emphasize faith first is doomed to fail.

The Path from *Jahiliyya* to *Hakimiyya*: The Specific Tactics of *Jihad*

The word "*jihad*" means exertion, striving, or struggle in pursuit of God's way, to spread belief in the One God, and to further or promote God's kingdom on earth. But how is this to be established when *true* Islam is an island surrounded by a sea of *jahiliyya*? The aim of *jihad*, according to Sayyid Qutb, is to uproot this *jahiliyya* way of life, replace it with God's dominion, and establish *shari'a*. *Jihad* seeks to free humanity from its obedience to tyrannical rulers, from its own brutish desires and selfish lifestyles, and from its overweening narcissism, and instead to reorient it toward service to God. *Jihad* is intended to free men from every authority but that of God. According to Qutb, this is to be done by way of a vanguard of committed and righteous Muslims who share, at the least, both their faith in God and their convictions in establishing an Islamic state and society.[48] In terms of a revitalization movement, *jihad* is the means for moving from the cultural breakdown that *jahiliyya* represents to the new steady-state, goal society that *hakimiyya* embodies.

Qutb wrote in *Signposts*:

> If they [the *mujahidun*] had been asked the question, "Why are you fighting?" ... They would have answered...
>
> "God has sent us to bring anyone who wishes from servitude [worship] to men into the service of God alone, from the narrowness of this world into the vastness of this world and the Hereafter, and from the tyranny of religions into the justice of Islam. God raised a Messenger for this purpose to teach His creatures His way. If anyone accepts this way of life, we turn back and give his country back to him, and we fight with those who rebel until we are martyred or become victorious."[49]

Yet Qutb was at pains to argue that Islam is essentially a religion of peace. It is a peace that is derived from the unity of God with His creations that establishes a social harmony, consensus, cooperation, and homogeneity. All living things on earth constitute one big family that has the same origin. Even though people are different, there should be no disputes, but rather familiarity and mutual aid. According to Islam, there are no grounds for discord because there is only one religion which calls for absolute submission to God in both material and spiritual matters.

> In Islam, peace is the rule, war is the exception. Peace means harmony in the universe, the laws of life, and the origin of man, while war is

the result of violations of harmony [such] as injustice, despotism and corruption.[50]

Moreover, Islam eliminates most of the reasons that in secular societies inevitably lead to outbreaks of war. Qutb's own form of "Just War theory"[51] condemns the kinds of wars that arise because of

- unjust gain and oppression
- ostentation, pride, and pomp
- racialism
- looting and booty
- ambition and exploitation
- forceful conversion to Islam
- capturing markets, acquiring material, or exploiting human labor and resources.[52]

Qutb argued that Islam preaches peace and lawfulness, but he also warned:

> Peace must imply freedom, justice, and security for all people. Following the Islamic criterion, peace cannot be established by abstaining from war when there is oppression, corruption, despotism, and denial of God's supremacy.[53]

Thus, Islam permits *jihad* so that the word of God prevails, and so as to

- establish justice in its widest sense
- eliminate oppression, chaos, ill-treatment, tyranny, despotism, extortion, injustice, and to do so by administering *shari'a* law
- insure justice, order, dignity, and respect
- spread good and forbid evil
- secure people against terror, coercion, and injury
- fight for the cause of God
- abolish polytheism, idolatry, and disbelief
- ensure the submission of all people to God
- propagate the oneness and the dominion of God on earth
- overturn obstacles restricting the free propagation of Islam
- oppose those who prevent others from converting to Islam
- let freedom prevail
- assist others who are too weak in all these tasks

Thus the declaration of *jihad* is . . .

1. not just for the *defense* of Islam—the standard reason given for *jihad*—as a legitimate response against those enemies who are clearly on the offensive; and

2. not just for *overturning obstacles* or "clearing the way" for the propagation of Islam, *da'wa* (although taken to its logical extent, and with an organic, functionalist model of society, this "clearing the way" could produce a social nihilism),

3. but also for actually *imposing shari'a* as a caring and compassionate duty since Islam is good and beneficial for all humanity—both absolutely, and relative to any alternative.[54]

It is well recognized that the methods of struggle and *jihad* include self-reorientation, preaching and proselytizing, teaching and education, community welfare and social development, partisan politics, and, when necessary, militancy and violence. Many Islamists employ the following triptych, based on a *hadith* (or report) concerning the Prophet Muhammad who said:

> Whoever among you sees any evildoing, let him change it with his hand; if he cannot do that, let him change it with his tongue; and if he cannot do that, let him change it with his heart; and that is the minimum faith requires.[55]

From this, three types of *jihad* can be derived:

- *jihad bi al-qalb*, a struggle of the heart and soul;
- *jihad bi al-lisan* or *al-kilma*, a struggle of the tongue and words; and
- *jihad bi al-yad* or *al-haraka*, a struggle of the hand or action, of proper deeds and achievements.[56]

Ordinarily, then, there are these three types of *jihad*, not just the violent kind that most Westerners know. The *jihad* of the heart requires personal reorientation and a renewal of personal faith, piety, and devotion. The *jihad* of the tongue means preaching and proselytizing Islam, or *da'wa*, to convince others to follow the Straight Path. The third type of *jihad*, by the hand, is the *jihad* of action. But it does not necessarily mean militancy or violence. Instead, it can involve Islamic charity and development, political and partisan participation, and organizing associations to practice the first two types of *jihad*.

To these, however, Qutb added a fourth type, a *jihad bi al-sayf*, or struggle by the sword, that explicitly promotes militancy and holy combat, following the conservative interpretation of Ibn Qayyim al-Jawziyya (1292–1350).[57]

These types—or even stages—of *jihad* reflect the path of the Prophet Muhammad and the early Islamic *salaf* who started in Mecca, then fled to Medina, where they regrouped and fortified their mission, and then finally returned triumphant to a repentant Mecca.[58]

Many Muslims also believe that the Prophet Muhammad regarded the inner struggle for faith a *greater jihad*, more important than the external and violent struggle for God, the *lesser jihad*. Ahmad ibn al-Husayn al-Bayhaqi (d. 1066) wrote in his famous *al-Zuhd al-Kabir* (Grand Asceticism):

> A number of fighters came [from the battle of Tabuk] to the Messenger of God and he said: "You have done well in coming from the 'lesser *jihad*' to the 'greater *jihad*.'" They said: "What is the 'greater *jihad*'?" He said: "For the servant of God to fight his passions."[59]

It is ironic, given the worldwide identification of *jihad* as holy war, to recognize that there are not only different types of *jihad*, but that the *jihad* of the heart is the greater and the *jihad* of action is the lesser. Popular perception, however, might have changed after al-Bayhaqi's lifetime, during the Crusades of the 11th and 12th centuries, when *jihad* became understood as a war against the attacking Christians.[60]

Qutb did not disagree with this greater-lesser distinction, and he argued that the progression from the first to the second constitutes a set of training stages whereby the strengthening of one's personal faith is the most important and necessary phase before true believers can advance to more collective or militant forms of *jihad*.

There are four "scourges" pitted against the Islamic community today, Qutb explained, and the different types of *jihad* also correspond to different kinds of enemies. First there are the atheists. Next, there are the secularists, nationalists, and modernists who, in relegating God and His dominion to a small, private corner of social life, essentially declare that God is dead. Then there are the People of the Book, Jews and Christians, but far from respecting them, Qutb declared a *jihad* because they distorted God's word and deviated from God's path.[61] In addition to these three external sources of *jahiliyya*, there is also—and perhaps more insidious—the internal *jahiliyya* of lapsed Muslims. More than just ignoring God's dominion, these so-called Muslims immerse themselves in the *jahiliyya* of the colonialists, crusaders, Communists, and Zionists. They show their idolatry and their faithlessness through their daily conduct, their dress, parties and dancing, egotism and greed, and, in general, their adoption of Western values and culture.[62]

Qutb's revulsion toward errant Muslims—he called them hypocrites—became much greater than his loathing of "Zionists" and "Crusaders," a characteristic of his emerging kharijism.[63] He spent much time and ink admonishing so-called Muslims who had modernized, secularized, and had stopped acknowledging the dominion of God and His laws. This was where *jihad* was really important. Muslims who seem sincere, who practice the five obligations, but who do not engage in the sixth, *jihad*, or follow *shari'a* law, became frequent targets of Qutb's invective. Yet at the same time, he reserved the *jihad* of the tongue for apostates while designating the *jihad* of the sword for non-Muslims.[64]

Jihad *of the Heart*

Qutb characterized this first type of *jihad* as an internal struggle of purification, fighting with one's inner self against idolatry, immorality, false beliefs, and man-made laws and customs. It is a personal, moral, and spiritual battle, a reorienting of one's mind and heart to God's true path. It is not done in isolation, but by applying beliefs in real-life situations.

> Before a Muslim steps into the battlefield, he has already fought a great battle within himself against Satan—against his own desires and ambitions, his personal interests and inclinations, the interests of his family and of his nation; against anything which is not from Islam; against every obstacle which comes in the way of worshipping God and the implementation of the divine authority on earth, returning this authority to God and taking it away from the rebellious usurpers.[65]

Yet an Islamic society cannot come into existence simply because of the righteousness and firm beliefs filling the hearts of all true Muslims, however numerous they may be. Because of the deep-rooted and penetrating malevolence of *jahiliyya*, there must first be a vanguard of dedicated and dynamic believers, trained systematically to develop their spiritual and physical capacities.

This vanguard begins as a small group that arises from within *jahili* society and gradually establishes the faith and trust in God in the hearts of its members. Then it separates itself from modern, secular society, from its relationships and loyalties, its beliefs and customs, its norms and values, and its theories and knowledge, to become free and distinct from the surrounding decadence, and turn instead to the Qur'an for guidance and "to quench its thirst for knowledge."[66]

It is this vanguard that God inspires and that becomes completely absorbed in their faith, and who later set forth to enlighten others, Muslims and non-Muslims alike, about God and His message. It is this small, exclusive coterie of pioneers that establishes the Islamic society, for Qutb did not trust those Muslims currently in power, for their abject failure spoke clearly of their dismally poor abilities.

Qutb displayed a resolute elitism. Qutb thought *jahiliyya* had such great power and complexity that ordinary individuals were simply not up to the task. The vanguard, however, could read the Qur'an, study and discuss it, and brush away the confusion of competing philosophies and doctrines in order to look deeply into Islam for God's true message. Their training would consist of a personal and political revolution, a reaching into their own hearts before reaching into the hearts of others. It required absolute unshakable faith with no room for doubt, hesitation, compromise, or fear of defeat.

This dedicated vanguard has to exhibit a keen moral zeal, virtuosity, and heroism unmatched in ordinary Muslims. They must demonstrate an inner harmony and a genuine cooperation that can intensify their strength and commitment. The ultimate aim of this vanguard is to "awaken the humanity of man" in others and to "develop it and make it powerful and strong and make it the most dominant factor among all the elements of a person's being."[67] It is this vanguard that is responsible for establishing a true Islamic system. There can be, Qutb argued, no other way.

The isolation that Qutb advocated requires the vanguard to cut itself off from its ties and interactions with all of *jahiliyya* society. This means wrenching oneself away from one's family, neighborhood, occupation, and property, while encounter-ing the hostility of nonbelievers. It means renouncing one's racial, class, national, and ethnic identities, coalescing with others in the vanguard on the basis of faith alone, and calling the misguided and unlearned to Islam. A member of the van-guard must see himself as a hero, and yet forget his own ego, origin, background, and personal desires. The fact that members of the vanguard shun their earlier identities of flesh, blood, color, and pride, and instead focus on faith in one single, all-powerful God gives them a power and strength far superior to their enemies. Contact, however, with *jahiliyya* society before their training is complete could result in contamination and failure. The vanguard has to show patience because the task of changing people's hearts, overthrowing *jahiliyya*, and establishing the Islamic system requires years of perseverance, just like the Prophet Muhammad when he preached early on in Mecca.

> When a person embraced Islam during the time of the Prophet...he would immediately cut himself off from *jahiliyya*. When he stepped in the circle of Islam, he would start a new life, separating himself off completely from his past life.... He would turn toward Islam for new guidance....
>
> Thus there would be a break between the Muslim's present Islam and his past *jahiliyya*....
>
> Their [the Emigrants from Mecca] relations with the Helpers of Medina became strengthened on the basis of a common faith. They became like brothers, even more than blood relatives. This relation-ship established a new brotherhood of Muslims.... The pride of lineage was ended, the voice of nationalism was silenced, and the Messenger of God addressed them: "Get rid of these partisanships; these are foul things."[68]

The vanguard steadily and relentlessly trains itself, persevering in the pursuit of divine understanding and ever cautious about the dangers of the surrounding *jahili* community. Their training has to be practical and concrete above all else, not abstract or hypothetical. Nor can its training be based on spontaneous bursts of undirected passion. It is through the real and constant application of the Qur'an in everyday life that the vanguard comes to understand its own faith. The Qur'an did not come down at once, Qutb maintained, but was revealed gradually in order to lay the foundations of the community and the movement on a solid basis and to build faith and practice simultaneously as the movement grew. Just as the Prophet Muhammad started Islam this way, by instilling strong faith in the hearts of his followers, so, too, must the vanguard today start its training by ensuring its own faith before it can begin to change the faith of others.[69]

As the vanguard learns to conduct *jihad*, the Qur'an becomes its guidebook for inner purification and preparation and its training manual for military plans and victories.[70] Combat and triumph require preparation at both the level of faith and the level of dexterity since *jihad* is spiritual and military combat combined. The Qur'an teaches patience, courage, common sense, and the ability to distinguish good from evil, justice from tyranny, worshipping God from the arrogance of despots.

> The Qur'an on the one hand constructs the faith in the hearts of the Muslim community and on the other attacks the surrounding *jahiliyya* through this community, while struggling to remove all the *jahili* influences which are found in the ideas, practices and morals of the Muslim community.[71]

The vanguard needs to know the landmarks and milestones toward this goal. It needs to understand where the pitfalls might lie, and how to survive defeat. It is this vanguard that was the intended audience for Qutb's *Signposts*. The vanguard needs to recognize the signs that mark the progress and advancement on the correct path to establishing a true Islamic society. It needs to understand when to coalesce and when to disperse; what is true Islam and what is true *jahiliyya*, who are on their side and who are against them; what topics to address and what problems need solving, and how to find more answers, all derived from the Qur'an.[72]

Once the hearts of the vanguard are filled with faith—filled through praxis and not just discussion—then it can return and re-engage with the surrounding *jahiliyya*. Islam does not operate in a vacuum, in isolation from the surrounding *jahiliyya*. It is an active and practical religion, not a contemplative one; this-worldly, not abstract. For these reasons, the vanguard's birth, revival, and reappearance occur in what Qutb identified as "stormy conditions."[73] *Jahili* society is not ready to simply allow this return, for Islam's very existence undermines jahiliyya.[74]

Once the Islamic movement has developed to a certain maturity and attained sufficient power, it must attempt to abolish and demolish the *jahiliyya* from which it was born. Such force requires training, superb moral character, organization, a sustained community, and firm solidarity. The leader of a vanguard group—the first actually being the Prophet Muhammad himself—must be the best, the most virtuous, and the most dedicated of this small assembly. Until *jahiliyya* is overcome and a genuine Islamic state and society established, these true and righteous Muslims are obligated to confront *jahiliyya* at every moment and point of its existence.

Once so trained, this vanguard can go on to use such tactics as (1) preaching and persuasion, for reforming the system, but also (2) militancy and combat, for abolishing the prevailing and surrounding *jahili* society which prevents people from understanding the truth about Islam. Thus a *jihad* of the tongue, of education and proselytizing, is employed to advance the cause, but a *jihad* of the hand and sword is used to beat down those who attempt to hold it back.[75]

Jihad *of the Tongue*

Preaching is the second type of *jihad*, used when people are free to listen and make up their minds. The Prophet Muhammad spent 13 years in Mecca calling its residents to Islam. Thus the call, or *da'wa*, is to bring people and faith together, to teach people the nature of Islam—the obligations it imposes on them and the benefits they can receive. The true believer is motivated by knowing he is "paying his debt to God for the blessing of Islam," by his "love for others in that he wishes to guide them to the good that he has been granted," and by his heavy "responsibility for their going astray unless he has conveyed the message to them."[76] Even erstwhile Muslims need to hear the call, for very often, they remain knowingly or inadvertently steeped in their own *jahili* corruption and apostasy.

Qutb advocated educating people and persuading them to start with the fundamentals and build up to an Islamic society. Faith and belief cannot be imposed upon people—for this is the way of *jahiliyya*—but have to develop from within, when people feel free to make the right choices.

> The bearers of the Islamic message should keep in mind this dynamic method of Islam...[and] ought to know that the stage of the construction of belief, which spread over the long period of Meccan life in this fashion, was not separate from the stage of practical organization, under which an Islamic community came into existence.[77]

Should there be no obstacles to preaching, then no combat is necessary. The preaching and proclaiming of *da'wa* is the ideal *jihad*, although it is rarely possible because of the belligerent and obstinate nature of *jahiliyya*. In Mecca and early Medina, the Prophet did not need to use combat because his freedom to speak freely was guaranteed by his Quraysh kinsmen in Mecca and by the conditions of his position and function in Medina, where all warring factions had agreed to a *pax Muhammadana*. After all, it is only when there are obstacles to the free flow of information about Islam that a combative *jihad* becomes necessary. Until then, *da'wa* remains the preferred method.

Qutb initially considered that God's dominion on earth could be established just through Islamic education, and that holy combat was unnecessary.[78] Unlike many of his followers and successors, Qutb advocated a gradualism that emphasized learning, training, and dedication. The Prophet Muhammad, Qutb stressed, had taken 13 years to instill the elements of faith and belief in people's hearts. The reason for such a lengthy incubation was the issue of praxis—of learning the faith through its lived reality. Even then, when the road became too bumpy and the antagonists too threatening, Muhammad and his followers moved to Medina—retreating to regroup and struggle yet another day. Migration, then, became yet another tactic in the tool kit of Muslim *mujahidin*. Faced with overwhelming odds, it is not dishonorable to fall back and withdraw so that one's energies, resources, and spirits can be replenished and rededicated to spreading Islam. Thus Qutb's notion of gradualism emphasized *da'wa* over holy combat. But Qutb also foresaw the possibility that *da'wa* could not be freely exercised without interference, which would make a *jihad* of the sword necessary.

> Thus the stage of constructing the faith should be long, and it should be gradual. Every step should be taken with firmness. This stage should not be spent in teaching the theory of beliefs but in translating the belief into a living reality. First it should be implanted in the hearts of men; it should materialize in a dynamic social system whose internal and external growth reflects the evolution of the belief. It ought to be a dynamic movement which challenges *jahiliyya* both in theory and in practice, so that it becomes a living faith which grows struggling against the surrounding forces. . . .
>
> The Qur'an did not come down at once but took 13 years to construct and strengthen the structure of faith. Had God wanted, He would have revealed the entire Qur'an at once and then left the Companions to learn it for a period of approximately 13 years. . . .
>
> But God did not choose this method; He wanted something else. He wanted to lay the foundations of a community, a movement, and a belief simultaneously. He wanted the community and the movement to be founded on belief, while with the dynamic progress of the community the faith also grew. He wanted faith to grow with the progress of the community, which the practical life of the community was at the same time a mirror of the faith.[79]

Jihad *of the Hand*

The third type of jihad is a *jihad* of the hand or action. But it need not imply militancy alone. It can mean engaging in partisan political activities, organizing peaceful, nonviolent campaigns, or even planning and implementing community development programs. The last has been particularly important among Islamist organizations in Egypt. Even the Muslim Brotherhood spent its early years (1928–36) organizing charitable welfare agencies that alleviated the problems of ordinary Egyptians, most of whom were poor and powerless. Hamas—the Muslim Brotherhood in Gaza and Palestine[80]—does the same thing today. Some of these development activities include providing schools, clinics, tutorials, college dormitories, employment, youth clubs, Boy Scouts (Rovers), tax advice, government assistance, hospital rooms, housing, and emergency relief. The Brotherhood itself considers its activities in the domain of national politics a form of *jihad*—not at all violent, but certainly not quiescent, either; often with speeches and sermons, delivered with enthusiasm and spirit. In the 1980s, it was the very success of these popular activities that caught the eye and ear of the Egyptian government and created strong resentment over their success at winning the hearts and minds of ordinary Egyptian citizens.[81]

Qutb's thoughts in the late 1940s and 1950s centered on the notion of the educational *jihad* of the tongue and the legitimate activities of the *jihad* of the hand. In *In the Shade of the Qur'an*, he advocated *da'wa* and educating people to properly understand Islam, led by those in the vanguard who acquired a very clear understanding in their minds and in their hearts, and who could keep focused on traveling the Straight Path and not deviate back into ignorance. Qutb argued that it takes a while for these beliefs to solidify and strengthen in people's hearts so that militant struggle is needed only sparingly. Instead, time and effort should be spent on (1) education and training the vanguard, and (2) teaching and preaching to those still steeped in *jahiliyya*.

Spreading Islam requires patience in shaping minds, creating active organizations, building a viable community, and forming new kinds of government even all the while fighting and struggling against *jahiliyya*. Qutb further concluded that political and social changes should come from the grass roots. This overall incrementalism, Qutb argued strongly, is the only way to solidly establish the Islamic path. God had ordained this method in Mecca, and now humanity would succeed if it is followed again.

Yet because of the brutal and barbaric actions of the Egyptian government, particularly in Liman Tura prison, Qutb ceased to be optimistic and came to realize that the fourth kind of *jihad*, the *jihad* of the sword, was especially necessary. It was in his most renowned book, *Signposts on the Road*, that Qutb proposed *jihad* by the sword. It was mentioned quietly—not surprising since there were prison censors looking over his manuscripts—but his followers read it with great alacrity. Thereafter, Qutb did not shy away from advocating the use of violence and justifying it as a means of defeating *jahiliyya*.[82]

Jihad bi al-sayf remains the most controversial position Qutb endorsed—that *jihad* must aggressively wipe out *jahiliyya* instead of assuming the more traditional position that *jihad* either defends Islam against outside attack or else, more proactively, eliminates the obstacles to the free understanding of the religion.[83]

But why would one even need to use force, Qutb once asked rhetorically, if Islam is so very beneficial for everyone and Islamizing the world through *jihad* is good for people?[84] He replied,

> It is in the very nature of Islam to take initiative for freeing the human beings throughout the earth from servitude to anyone other than God;

and so it cannot be restricted within any geographic or racial limits, leaving all mankind on the whole earth in evil, in chaos, and in servitude to lords other than God. . . .

This struggle is not a temporary phase but an eternal state—an eternal state, as truth and falsehood cannot co-exist on this earth. Whenever Islam stood up with the universal declaration that God's Lordship should be established over the entire earth and that men should become free from servitude to other men, the usurpers of God's authority on earth have struck out against it fiercely and have never tolerated it. It became incumbent upon Islam to strike back and release man throughout the earth from the grip of these usurpers. The eternal struggle for the freedom of man will continue until the religion is purified for God.[85]

Qutb was seldom apologetic about using violence, always intending it for the sake of reforming the Islamic community, for eradicating *jahiliyya*, and for raising up the true spirit of Islam. His goal was to revitalize Muslim society and re-install God as the only One deserving of worship. All means could be employed; certainly the *jihad* of the heart and the tongue are important. But if the intransigence of *jahiliyya* requires militant action, then for the greater glory of God it has to be carried out.

To Qutb, *jihad* was an important obligation for all Muslims.[86] It becomes incumbent upon all true Muslims to strike out against *jahiliyya*, destroy it, and release humanity universally from the grip of the tyrant and usurper, the ruler who does not govern by what God has revealed.[87] Since Qutb realized that *jahiliyya* exists inside and outside the Muslim community, and must be fought no matter where it appears, he advocated a permanent, universal *jihad* to counter a pervasive, worldwide ignorance. *Jihad* by the sword is, therefore, eternal until humanity is free and until religion is purified for God.[88]

Jihad *of the Sword*

Jihad bi al sayf is seen as a means to clear the way for achieving the greater types of *jihad*. Islam seeks the universal freedom for humanity, to allow it the independence to make up its mind about religion. However, obstacles exist that include all the tyranny that opposes Islam and the general *jahiliyya* that prevents it from expanding. Thus a *jihad* of the sword seeks to destroy all that stands between people and Islam. Qutb argued that the assertion that *jihad* can only be defensive is defeatist and apologetic.[89] Since Islam is good for all humanity and since it is meant to save the world from *jahiliyya*, then a violent and aggressive campaign, a *jihad* of the sword, is rightly necessary to defeat its enemies, to remove impediments, and to spread Islam worldwide.

Islam cannot freely expand throughout the world if it faces the obstacles of *jahiliyya*. "It is in the very nature of Islam to take the initiative for freeing human beings throughout the earth from servitude to anyone other than God." *Jahiliyya* must be destroyed so as to give humanity the opportunity to freely accept Islam. Those who wish to reject Islam can do so, so long as there has been ample opportunity to consider Islam's message.

> How could the message of Islam have spread throughout the world when it faced such material obstacles as the political system of the state, the socio-economic system based on races and classes, and behind all these, the military power of the government?
>
> It would be naive to assume that [when] a call is raised to free the whole of humankind throughout the earth, [that] it is confined to just preaching and exposition. It strives through preaching and exposition when there is freedom of communication and when people are free from all these influences.... But when the above mentioned obstacles and practical difficulties are put in its way, it has no recourse but to remove them by force so that when it is addressed to people's hearts and minds, they are free to accept it or reject it with an open mind.[90]

Qutb never claimed that Islam is nonviolent. To some extent, he took pride in his honesty. The Islamic movement, he claimed, intends to wipe out tyranny, introduce true freedom, and proclaim Islam universally. There is no embarrassment over these goals. Qutb disagreed with those—he called them "Orientalists," and he included both Western scholars as well as secular Muslim thinkers—who either apologetically argue that Islam is peaceful just like Christianity, or else cynically paint a misguided picture of Islam as completely violent.

Those who define Islam as pacifist, he rebutted, do not understand that the goal is not *jihad* for its own sake. Rather, *jihad* has to be seen as a means to achieve God's dominion on earth, and that the different types of *jihad* correspond to different times, stages, contexts, and conditions. To deny any of the types of *jihad* is to weaken Islam by depriving it of the necessary tools to accomplish its goals.

Those who depict Islam as essentially terroristic then go on to argue that, as a solution to such bloodshed, true *jihad* can only justifiably mean defensive action. But if, in fact, *jihad* were merely defensive, then it still must be waged in order to protect humanity from all the *jahili* institutions that turn humanity away from Islam. However, Qutb argued for something more: for a pro-active Islamic movement that promotes God's dominion and defeats man's self-rule.

Thus, he concluded, those who either interpret Islam as pacifist or else reserve *jihad* just as a defensive response are both wrong; *jihad* is both defensive *and* aggressive.[91] Islam protects itself from attack by *jahili* societies, but it also initiates action and struggles to free people and open them to God's divine message. To argue that Islam is nonviolent or merely defends the homeland ignores the benefits that Islam will bring to all people. It is a defeatist and inferior mentality, Qutb asserted, promoted by the colonial powers that, through Orientalism, relegate Islam to the lower levels of religion. Islam has a right to remove all those obstacles which are in its path so that it may address the human predicament without interference and opposition from others.[92]

Qutb no longer felt it necessary to stake out the inferior position that basically reinforces the judgments and outcome of European imperialism. He was unwilling to assume a second- or third-class status in the ranking of world religions, and so argued that Islam, being more perfect than its predecessors, should instead be brought to all humanity for their edification and enlightenment. Thus, there must be a worldwide *jihad* determined to Islamize the world.[93]

Qutb argued that holy combat is not preordained; nor is personal purification so private, or preaching and proselytizing simply innocuous. These all constitute tactics that can be used or not according to the circumstances Islamic activists encounter. Qutb understood the different types of *jihad* as a progression from an inner spiritualism to persuasion and education, to more activist methods, and then finally to militant combat. These stages also match the development of Islam in the 7th century—conditions that have reappeared today. Such parallels offer lessons: steady advancement, persistence, and patience were important ingredients in the first campaign to spread Islam, and Qutb counseled the same approach now.

The Prophet Muhammad initially avoided combat because the very people he fought would later become fellow Muslims and comrades. God commanded the Prophet to restrain himself, to be patient and to conquer his pride so that despite verbal and physical attacks, he managed to maintain control, not lose his temper, and remain dignified and disciplined. But he also took a firm hand, knowing that the outcome of his battle against *jahiliyya* was observed by those around him. His victory demonstrated God's blessing on his campaign. So what emerged in those 13 years in Mecca was a strong vanguard of true believers. As Qutb admitted, the Prophet Muhammad might have built this vanguard sooner by relying on kinship, tribalism, and even nationalism. Instead he took a more cautious route, substantiating and hardening their faith first. Without this firm base, any further ambitions would have had little results.

Justification for Jihad

Qutb went to great lengths to demonstrate not only that violent struggle may be necessary, but that it is prescribed in the Qur'an. To support his views, he cited the fiery justifications authored by Ibn Qayyim al-Jawziyya.[94] According to al-Jawziyya, the Prophet was first told to recite, then to preach, then to warn. He was commanded to restrain himself, then migrate, then fight, and then to fight just those who fought him, and then finally to fight the polytheists in general. With this in mind, Qutb looked to the *salaf* for guidance on when, how, and why *jihad* could be employed. He argued that God commanded the Prophet Muhammad to first use a *jihad* of the heart and of the tongue in Mecca because these were acceptable and temperate. This was especially crucial in the beginning because the community of true believers was small and surrounded by *jahiliyya*. Muhammad called people to God through preaching and proselytizing, restraining himself from fighting, and practicing patience and forbearance. This personal reorientation was required at first so that the faith in the one true God would grow in men's hearts and minds. But, when the conditions in Mecca became intolerable, God commanded Muhammad to move to Medina rather than stay, fight, and be defeated by the overwhelming power of *jahiliyya*. Even in Medina, there was no need to fight as Muhammad had come with a ready-made peace. After the migration, and as *shari'a* and orthopraxy appeared, the Prophet Muhammad established the first Islamic state. That in itself was a *jihad* of the hand, setting up the Islamic system and establishing the first Islamic community. Then, when that state and community were attacked by discontented tribes, Arab and Jewish, God instructed Muhammad to fight those who fought him—that is, a defensive engagement. Next, in order to expand and bring peace, truth, and freedom to humanity, a pro-active *jihad* was organized to eliminate the obstacles to the free flow of Islamic information. It was only when this failed, when the *salaf* were confronted with the overwhelming power of *jahili* society, that an aggressive *jihad* was raised to attack and destroy *jahiliyya*. Finally upon his return to Mecca, Muhammad was ordered to fight the polytheists until he entered the gates of Mecca in victory and God's religion was fully established. Thus the different types of *jihads* represent tactics, used at particular moments, under certain conditions, and with certain purposes in mind.[95]

Qutb, like all other Muslim thinkers, stated emphatically that Islam forbids the imposition of faith through compulsion. But if requiring correct belief is wrong, compelling correct action may not be. Orthopraxy can be enforced because in God's laws is that quality that prevents the rise of tyranny, injustice, slavery, and servitude by those who would block the dissemination of Islam. Destroying *jahiliyya* and establishing the Islamic system means that humanity must be freed from the tyranny and injustice that prevent it from making correct, independent choices. Thus, going on the offensive and creating an Islamic state not only does *not* violate the Qur'anic injunction, it actually promotes it by giving men and women true freedom and liberty.

> It is not the intention of Islam to force its beliefs on people, but Islam is not merely "belief." As we have pointed out, Islam is a declaration of the freedom of man from servitude to other men. Thus it strives from the beginning to abolish all those systems and governments which are based on the rule of man over men and the servitude of one human being to another. When Islam releases people from this political pressure and presents to them its spiritual message, appealing to their

reason, it gives them complete freedom to accept or not to accept its beliefs. However, this freedom does not mean that they can make their desires their gods, or that they can choose to remain in the servitude of other human beings, making some men lords over others. Whatever system is to be established in the world ought to be on the authority of God, deriving its laws from Him alone. Then every individual is free, under the protection of this universal system, to adopt any belief he wishes to adopt.[96]

Conclusions

There are several approaches to the propagation of Islam through *jihad*, only one of which is actually militant. The impact of Sayyid Qutb's ideas about the different kinds of *jihad* has proven far-ranging and the subsequent debates have been especially heated. Who declares *jihad*, who joins, under what conditions, and with what consequences are all questions very much open for discussion. If only a true Muslim ruler can declare a *jihad*—and here Ibn Taymiyya's caveat that a true Muslim ruler is he who rules by *shari'a* and *shari'a* alone—then what happens when the ruler is an alleged apostate? Can others then declare a *jihad*? If so, who? If *jihad* can only be defensive, then what constitutes the first attack, aside from the obvious? Need it take place inside a Muslim country? Need it be violent itself, or merely the threat of violence? Do European imperialism and colonialism constitute "first attacks?" If *jihad* is to eliminate the obstacles to the free flow of information, what exactly constitutes these barriers? Are they the immediate, obvious roadblocks or are they all the subtle bigotries of Orientalism that cloud people's understanding of Islam? Or are they the entire range of social institutions—society and culture at their very core—that, interconnected, impede the appreciation of Islam? Need these obstacles only be domestic obstructions, inside Dar al-Islam? Or are they just those impediments that exist where Islam does not dominate, in Dar al-Harb? Hasan al-Banna's 1978 treatise on *jihad* (written in the late 1930s) states that women and children cannot be harmed and that combatants cannot engage in *jihad* with hatred in their hearts. Some scholars might restrict a militant *jihad* to such a degree (as did al-Banna's proclamation) that, for all intents and purposes, it is off limits.[97] Others, like Qutb, have been much more aggressive, and reject these fine distinctions in favor of raising the concepts of counterattack, eliminating obstacles, and spreading Islam universally so as to require a continuous, militant *jihad*. Killing women and children is regrettable collateral damage that can be overlooked if the target is valuable. And it should be dedication and zeal, not hatred and loathing, that lie in a combatant's heart, but then, who can tell?

Others have argued about which type of *jihad* should take precedence, under what conditions, under whose authority, and against which enemy. Should *jihad* take the slow, gradual path, the one Qutb identified as the way of the Prophet? Or should there be more immediate results that only violent militancy can achieve? Should the movement target just government officials? Or is the entire community "to blame" for its slide back into *jahiliyya*? Some activists have taken Qutb's lesson on the *hijra* and migration to heart, advocating a lengthy isolation during which preparation and training can take place. Yet others argue that Islam is a practical, this-worldly religion that eschews separation and encourages social interaction. Thus the vanguard can be a detached organization, operating on the margins of society, or else intermingled among the unbelievers in disguise. Should the movement be controlled top-down, like Salih Sirriya and his Islamic Liberation Army that attempted to take over Egypt's military academy in April 1974? Or should it be managed from the bottom up, like the *tabligh* ("missionary") and *da'wa* movements that preach the correct Islamic path throughout the Muslim world? Should the movement follow al-Jama'a al-Islamiyya that argued for complete community reform? Or should it support Tanzim al-Jihad that proposed to target only government officials?[98]

Those who came after Qutb have argued that history demonstrated that the first three types of *jihad* have failed, and that resorting to a militant *jihad* is now necessary. Many Islamic activists had become satisfied and complacent with *da'wa* and missionary associations. But if these activities are in any way impeded—and Qutb argued that secular, modern, and colonial societies, with their governments based on man-made laws and its lordship of one person over others, are just those obstacles that obstruct the free expansion of Islam— then these impediments need to be eliminated and destroyed. If governments do not rule by *shari'a* law, then these *jahili* governments become obstructions that must be eliminated. If people engage in secular activities, disregard their religion, and follow immoral habits, then these behaviors become barriers to the true understanding of Islam. Muddled minds and bankrupt officials, then, need to be purged in order to propagate God's religion. Qutb reserved *da'wa* for lapsed Muslims gone astray. But he marked *jihad* of the sword for governments that "get in the way."

Qutb's position was unequivocal. He did not say one thing but mean another. He was direct and to the point. Militant combat in the name of God and in the name of advancing His religion was not only justifiable, but obligatory and honorable.

Qutb saw Egyptian society and the greater Muslim world as being consumed by overwhelming crisis and breakdown. He astutely diagnosed the country's problems in his portrait of *jahiliyya* as social critique, and meticulously outlined Egypt's glorious Islamic future in his description of *hakimiyya* as salvation history. He offered the various types of *jihad* as major tactics to be used in moving from the old steady state to a new one. But he did not stop there. Instead, he went on to elaborate what he saw as Islam's ideal order and what constitutes an Islamic society, state, and economy, all based on his reading of Islamic history. Perhaps Qutb reserved his most fiery and bitter remarks for *jahiliyya*, and his most spirited and inspirational words for *jihad*. But his idealism and exuberance became most notable when he discussed what Islamism actually stood for, and not just what it was against. His own interpretation of Islam's political economy and social history, as I would call them, demonstrates the full power and range of his intellectual abilities created in the midst of battle.

The Islamic Society and Islamic System

Sayyid Qutb wrote frequently about an Islamic society and the Islamic system. He derived the first from the array of historic and functioning societies experienced by actual Muslims, both true believers and otherwise. He defined the second as a set of hypothetical relationships woven together by Islamic principles. The first is real, or determined from real experiences, and measured against Islamic practices and beliefs; the second is theoretical, derived from Islamic tenets, and is more prescriptive than descriptive. This distinction is comparable to the contrast between "Muslim" and "Islamic": the former is based on self-perceived identities, the second is based on religious doctrine. A country can be Muslim if the majority of its citizens are now or were historically Muslim, but not necessarily Islamic since it does not operate on Islamic principles.

An Islamic Society

An Islamic society is a community that is integrated through Islam and its practices and beliefs. It consists of devout and righteous Muslims who use the Qur'an and the Sunna as guidelines to their daily lives. These members are neither too materialistic, groveling for sustenance, nor do they have their heads in a cloud, in some sort of mystical ether. They engage in both, in moderation. They have freedom, but it is not absolute. Their leaders administer *shari'a* law and consult with the community about paths forward. This society maintains stability by subscribing to a set of permanent values, yet still develops and grows in constructive ways. It includes all types of people who are nevertheless equal because of their shared beliefs, faith, and practice. In sum, it may be a utopian community, but it does provide Qutb's Islamic movement with a goal it wishes to achieve.

Another term for an Islamic society that is often used, both by Qutb and other Islamic writers, is the Arabic term for community, "*umma*." But the boundaries for an Islamic society and the *umma* are not necessarily congruent. The borders of a society are ordinarily maintained by a single state government. The Islamic *umma*, however, is more varied; it can consist of many states, sometimes including all Muslim countries, or it can refer just to a common village or neighborhood.

Qutb's use of the term *umma* was more precise, referring to an Islamic society based specifically on Islamic principles. It is often stated that the goal of the Islamic movement is to establish the *umma*, although Qutb also considered the existence of God's dominion, *hakimiyya*, as its major aspiration. Both are correct, in a sense, since the Islamic *umma*—as opposed to just a Muslim community— exists only when it acknowledges God's dominion, authority, and law.[1]

"*Umma*" can also be translated as "nation." This is a bit awkward, though, when examining a religious movement attempting to overthrow existing national and nationalist governments and to establish Islamic ones. The word "nation" ordinarily refers to a group of people who share a common culture, language, history (however contrived), and a central government. In a nation-state, all citizens are equal, in principle, regardless of race, religion, or gender. But the Islamic "*umma*" marginalizes such secondary identities as ethnicity and class by emphasizing the chief principal identity established by worshipping and obeying God and His message. In the *umma*, moreover, not all religions are equal. *Dhimmis*, or People of the Book, for example, are not equal to Muslims. Were they to embrace an undistorted monotheism, they would reasonably be expected to then become Muslims and achieve true equality.

Qutb also used the term "*umma*," perhaps in a more metaphorical sense, to refer to a much larger community of monotheism than just the Islamic one. This is the *umma* established by the Prophet Abraham, sometimes called the "*millet* of Abraham"—*millet* being the Arabic word used by the Ottomans to refer to its confessional communities. It thus includes the other related monotheisms, Judaism and Christianity, no matter how "distorted" they have become.[2] When Qutb discussed hanifiyyism, or the generic monotheism that Abraham initiated, then the community, or *umma*, stretched to include many more than just those who embrace Islam. (Although, of course, true Muslims would continue to be the only correct element in this wider public.)

An Islamic society is possible only when its members dedicate themselves to God's dominion and no other, establish an Islamic state and reject all others, recognize *shari'a* as the only legal code, subscribe to the values and morals that please God, develop their economy and productive capacity in a moderate and harmonious fashion, and combine spiritual, moral, and material advancement. Only then will society reach the apex of progress and become truly civilized.[3] Qutb was correct when he said that, in fact, no *umma* exists today, in Egypt or anywhere else, although he pointed out that individuals can still exhibit the Islamic spirit even if their government remains in a *jahili* state. Yet without the state and *shari'a*, no Islamic community can actually exist except as unorganized fragments.

This led Qutb to conclude that there can be just three categories of Muslims: (1) Muslims who think they are Islamic, but are not; (2) true Muslims who, however, do not live in an Islamic society; and (3) true Muslims living in a proper Islamic society. The first category is equivalent to *jahiliyya*, and the third category abides by *hakimiyya*. But it is the second category that fluctuates and it is this group that Qutb specifically targeted.[4]

They must be part of the struggle to achieve an Islamic community, worldwide. "People cannot be Muslims if they do not put it [Islam] into effect," Qutb wrote in *Social Justice*. Those who do not make this effort and struggle cannot be considered true Muslims no matter what else they believe, think, or practice. Islam cannot be divided into parts, with some of it practiced and believed, while other aspects of it are neglected.[5]

> A Muslim community can come into existence only when individuals and groups of people reject the worship of anyone except God...and come into submission to God, Who has no associates [equivalents], and decide that they will organize their scheme of life on the basis of this submission. From this a new community is born, emerging from within the old *jahili* society, which immediately confronts it with a new belief and a new way of life based on this belief, presenting a concrete embodiment of the Testimony "There is no god but God and Muhammad is the messenger of God."[6]
>
> What makes this path distinctive is that this religion is an indivisible whole: its worship and its social relations, its laws and its moral guidance. Its devotional rituals are not separated in their nature or their goals from its provisions for government and social affairs....[It] means one complete program for life, based on the absolute liberation of both inward emotion and action from all worship to anything other than God.[7]

Thus the Islamic society, as Qutb often envisioned it, becomes as much a moral space as it is an actual society since it is based on a set of values that should infuse and permeate every institution. Qutb noted that there can be a great variety of actual historical instances of Islamic societies, but all of them share the permanent values of the ideal Islamic society, or the Islamic system. These values come from God and can be found in the Qur'an.[8]

If Islam emerges under other conditions, it can, in Qutb's view, still develop Islamic values. There are, he claimed, immutable values derived from the Qur'an that do not change, regardless of transformations in the environment and the economy. Qutb did not embrace a cultural relativism where values change according to the stage of economic development. Those societies in which values *do* change this way, are examples of *jahiliyya*. Such societies validate their values as true or false not according to God's guidance but based on positivistic proofs that exist outside of God's will. They are man-made standards, while Islamic values are divinely created, permanent, and absolute. Only Islamic societies can rightly be called civilized, Qutb concluded.[9]

Islamic values must be the *core* values of a society, for, after all, Qutb did realize that societies differ over time and space, and that they differ precisely in their values.

But those values that remain permanent must be the set of divinely established core values, whereas the peripheral or secondary values are the ones that vary according to other factors. Qutb's own conceptualization of evolution was that in the West, growth is materialistic, but it could be, as in Islamic societies, spiritual as well. Moreover, the spiritual element plays a more vital role in social change than the material factor.

The Islamic System

The Islamic system is a system in the same sense that other doctrines or ideologies such as secularism, capitalism, socialism, and nationalism are systems.[10] Qutb intended the Islamic system to signify a model society, similar to Max Weber's ideal type.

> Islam is a perfectly practicable social system in itself; it has beliefs, laws, and a social and economic system that is under the control of both conscience and law and which is open to growth through development and application.
>
> It offers to mankind a perfectly comprehensive theory of the universe, life, and mankind, as we have shown, a theory that satisfies man's intellectual needs. It offers to men a clear, broad, and deep faith which satisfies the conscience. It offers to society legal and economic bases that have been proved both practical and systematic.
>
> Islam bases its social system on the foundation of a spiritual theory of life that rejects all materialistic interpretations; it bases its morals on the foundation of the spiritual and moral element, and it rejects the philosophy of immediate advantage. Thus it is very strongly opposed to the materialistic theories that obtain in both the Eastern and the Western camp.[11]

The Islamic system, as Qutb defined it, constitutes a complete and integrated set of social relationships, built upon Islamic principles, and covers all areas of a unified community—economic, political, cultural, moral, and civilizational. What distinguishes the Islamic system from all existing systems, Qutb claimed, is that while all others are simply materialist, driven by economic factors, the Islamic system is both material *and* spiritual. It is not a system that grovels to maintain physical sustenance nor is it a supernatural system of emotions and rituals. Instead, it combines and integrates both, creating a social unity, derived from the *tawhid* of God, that brings all people together into a single harmonious and cooperative society. Not surprising, Qutb favored the spiritual side, for he felt that this element made the Islamic system unique.

Qutb maintained that an Islamic system is sufficiently flexible that it will not remain stagnant but will, with a stable core of values, grow and develop to adequately respond to people's religious and economic needs. He foresaw a diversity of people, with a multiplicity of nationalities, ethnicities, and races, existing side by side. This is possible because the Islamic system only recognizes faith and piety, without heeding color or language.[12]

Qutb used the concept of the Islamic system primarily as an analytical and didactic device to contrast it with man-made ideological systems. He consistently praised its merits and condemned the shortcomings of other ideologies such as secularism, nationalism, capitalism, socialism, communism, and democracy.

Islam versus Other Doctrines

versus Secularism and Modernity

The entire set of practices embodied in secularism and its more general condition, modernity, represented for Qutb gross violations of God's unity, *tawhid*. Modernity became Qutb's black beast, criticized and condemned over and over again, in order to convince his readers and followers of the intrinsic evils of modern secularism, individualism, and liberalism.[13] Qutb totally rejected secularism, for in Islam, belief and practice combine together to contribute to a divine unity, and similarly, religion and worldly affairs remain intertwined, unlike in the West where there is (supposedly) a separation of church (or religion more generally) and state.[14]

Qutb strongly believed that Islam is a religion and a way of life intended for all of humanity—for Egypt, for the Arab and Muslim worlds, and beyond. He was thus not only aiming to revive Islam and retrieve its former greatness, but to extend that glory beyond the present-day Muslim community to the far reaches of the planet. Qutb sought to universalize Islam much as Europe and the United States had globalized modernity. It was an idea unique to Qutb, which is not found in his predecessors: al-Afghani, 'Abduh, Rida, or al-Banna.[15]

By establishing freedom, justice, and equality for all people, Qutb sought to bring a universalistic, open-minded spirit to Muslims and non-Muslims alike. His mission seemed to him no less humanistic and progressive than those lighting all the dark corners of the world for the sake of progress and advancement; that is, for the sake of modernity. This meant creating a worldwide reform or revitalization movement that could solve many, if not all, today's current problems.

> This religion is not merely a declaration of the freedom of Arabs, nor is its message confined to the Arabs. It addresses itself to the whole of mankind, and its sphere of work is the whole earth....
>
> This religion is really a universal declaration of the freedom of man from servitude to other men and from servitude to his own desires which is also a form of human servitude; it is a declaration that the sovereignty belongs to God alone and that He is the Lord of all the worlds. It means a challenge to all kinds and forms of systems which

are based on the concept of the sovereignty of man; in other words, where man has usurped the divine attribute. Any system in which the final decisions are referred to human beings, and in which the sources of all authority are human, deifies human beings by designating others than God as lords over men. This declaration means that the usurped authority of God be returned to Him and the usurpers be thrown out— those who by themselves devise laws for others to follow, thus elevating themselves to the status of lords and reducing others to the status of slaves. In short, to proclaim the authority and sovereignty of God means to eliminate all human kingship and to announce the rule of the Sustainer of the universe over the entire earth....

Islam has the right to take the initiative. Islam is not a heritage of any particular race or country; this is God's religion and it is for the whole world. It has the right to destroy all obstacles in the form of institutions and traditions which limit man's freedom of choice. It does not attack individuals nor does it force them to accept its beliefs; it attacks institutions and traditions to release human beings from their poisonous influences, which distort human nature and which curtail human freedom.

It is the right of Islam to release mankind from servitude to human beings so that they may serve God alone.... God's rule on earth can be established only through the Islamic system, as it is the only system ordained by God for all human beings, whether they be rulers or ruled, black or white, poor or rich, ignorant or learned....

Islam is not merely a belief so that it is enough merely to preach it. Islam, which is a way of life, takes practical steps to organize a movement for freeing man. Other societies do not give it any opportunity to organize its followers according to its own method, and hence it is the duty of Islam to annihilate all such systems, as they are obstacles in the way of universal freedom. Only in this manner can the way of life be wholly dedicated to God, so that neither any human authority nor the question of servitude [worship] remains....[16]

In advocating this universal or universalized Islam, Qutb was offering the religion as not only an equivalent to modernity but also as an *alternative* modernity.[17] Qutb's vision of a united, unified, and integrated society, unspoiled by social divisions, was no more utopian than Marx's classless, stateless society.

Moreover, Qutb's anti-modernity was not some sort of vague or general indictment. Instead, he pointed to specific aspects of modernity and supported his opposition with well thought-out arguments. He and his followers quarreled and debated contemporary scholars who advocated a modern Islam constructed along the same lines as Christianity in England or the United States. These Islamic secularists included 'Ali 'Abd al-Raziq, Taha Husayn, and Khalid Muhammad Khalid,[18] among others. These writers argued for a separation of religion and government, for the compartmentalization of different elements of social life that mimicked European society, and for greater unlimited and unrestrained economic, political, and moral activity.

Before colonialism, there had been no opposition to secularism, for it had remained in Europe, and countries like Egypt could easily maintain the illusion that they were ruled by Islamic law. With the intrusion of colonialism, however, that fiction became much more difficult to maintain. With the victories of secular Egyptian nationalism in 1919, 1936, and 1952, any pretense that *shari'a* law ruled the land disappeared.

Qutb felt that Europe's secular society had originated in the lack of divine legal codes in Christianity, and even before Christianity had become officially adopted, from pagan Rome and Greece. The absence of divine revelation gave Europe a materialist streak that became, according to Qutb, morally repugnant. Unmoored from the divine, law could turn any which way it wanted—in support of the good, but also in support of the wicked. It could follow blindly, and comply with the primacy of human instincts and desires, instead of molding those instincts and desires to conform to divine precepts.

Qutb concluded that, far from being universal, secularism was a unique product of specific conditions. Europe became secular, but the Muslim world need not turn out this way. There seemed no good reason for Muslims to imitate Western Christians, to separate religion and society, unless it was to worship the superior power that Europeans exhibited. Were this the case, Qutb argued, then Muslims would be raising Europeans to the level associated with God and would slide into polytheism.

This particular secularism had dramatic effects. It was in Europe that the separation of church and state led to the emergence of science—although, Qutb claimed, science really had its roots in the Islamic society of Andalucía.[19] Yet, far from being neutral, science and positivism negated established authority (especially divine authority) and left the material world to exclusively define social, economic, and political relations. In the Islamic world, science did not initially contradict religion. But when scientific studies reached their intellectual and moral limits, the larger political and economic conditions began to deteriorate, and further inquiry was discouraged in ways that did not happen in the West. Islamic society did not allow whatever the market could bear, but instead restricted moral action by divine law.

In discussing the abstract realm of epistemology, Qutb sought to distinguish which lessons can be learned from either European or Muslim scholars and which have to be learned from Muslim educators alone. At first, Qutb stated that pure science was neutral and could be borrowed by devout Muslims without fear that it would contaminate their values. Muslims could learn chemistry, physics, biology, and the like from either Muslims or non-Muslims. It was only in the humanities that a non-Islamic understanding had become tainted and incorrect.[20] He argued that these subjects must be learned in the proper climate, one cleansed of *jahili* thinking.[21]

Later, however, he came to realize that no knowledge can ever be neutral. If modern science was born out of secularism, then Muslims needed to worry that it could corrupt their lives. "The entire scientific movement in Europe started with Godlessness," he wrote in *Signposts,* and this pernicious influence went beyond science to include an enmity toward *all* religions, including Islam.[22] Qutb advised true believers not to be fooled by the false neutrality of Western ideas.[23]

There was one exception, however, that allowed devout Muslims to study modern, secular, *jahili* thinkers, and this was in order to "know thy enemy." In fact, Qutb himself claimed that he had spent 40 years doing just this, and had come away with an appreciation of the limitations of *jahili* perspectives—and a better ability to rebut them.[24]

Qutb would have nodded in agreement with the complaints against "secular humanism" raised by American evangelicals. And, just like many evangelicals, Qutb, rejected Darwinian biology and evolution. He did not necessarily evoke a creationist perspective gleaned from Genesis, but he criticized Darwinism for taking God out of creation and for assuming that there is no need for a divine power outside the physical world.[25]

Many secularists think about Islam in the same way they do Christianity—or at least Protestant Christianity—as possessing a set of sacred beliefs, but not containing any truly holy practices or divine laws enforced by a sovereign state. This architecture follows the historical division of labor between God and Caesar: God created the sacred faith, Caesar created the temporal law. If Islam can be similarly understood as just a set of beliefs, then the secularization of the Muslim world is easily possible. That is, were Islam essentially constructed like Christianity, then none of this would be happening. But this is not the case.[26] When the fact of God-given and God-sanctioned laws is taken into account—and firm, rock-solid belief in the divine nature of these laws—then secularism (separating government from religion), and parliamentarianism (voting laws in and out), become not only difficult but constitute the very denial of God.

Yet notwithstanding this secularism, law and government in Europe were, if not divinely created, then at least divinely inspired, and kings and popes often invoked God and Christ to support their authority. Before the advent of modernity, religion did color European society in general, if not specifically its laws and government. What Protestant societies in England and northern Europe experienced in and after the 16th century was a gradual 200-year *de-linking* of religion and social life. This did not happen without a struggle, however, and the bloody wars of Europe testify to the difficult and violent birth of secularism and modernity.[27]

Secularism is happening today in Islam, and also not without a fight. Its appearance in Islam did not happen so much officially as it did through the unauthorized agency of European imperialism, making the opposition to secularism the same struggle as the conflict against colonialism. Sayyid Qutb was and is an essential part of this battle. He argued constantly against adopting the model of religion that Christianity provided and the role that Christianity played in Europe. His arguments went as far back as the Enlightenment, Reformation, and Renaissance to illustrate that secularization in Europe should not be repeated in the Muslim world. Qutb concluded that Islam's situation is different from Europe's, that what transpired to the north of the Mediterranean should not be heeded and emulated on its southern shores. What he wanted was a *re-linking* of the religious with other social elements. His antagonism to secularism and modernity can also be viewed as anti-colonialism and even a liberation movement. He subscribed to a social contract in which people obey an authority that rules by social justice. But it was a social contract constrained by God's dominion, not a utilitarianism that says that the individual limits underlying government constitute the greatest good for the greatest number of people, although Qutb's approach might have worked out the same way.

versus Nationalism

Qutb's Islamic system faced two principal adversaries: nationalism and capitalism. They were opponents because his audience in Egypt was primarily affected by these two doctrines and because he wanted to persuade them that Islam was superior. Qutb considered nationalism, with its loyalty to a territorially based ethnic group instead of to God, to be blasphemy and therefore, *jahiliyya*.[28]

However, sometimes he used nationalism as a metaphor for loyalty (like 'Abduh and Rida did), as when he claimed that a Muslim's nationality is Islam. He compared nationalism to the *umma*, the Islamic community, or to Dar al-Islam, the Islamic homeland, recognizing the importance of territoriality in the construction of nationalism. Here, people band together within defined borders but decidedly *not* because of ethnicity, nationality, language, or culture, but because of their common belief in God and their submission to and acknowledgment of God's supreme authority. Qutb's idea of an Islamic nationalism is actually an Islamic supra-nationalism.[29]

Nationalism divides people, Qutb maintained, which undermines the unity of God and His creations. Nationalism, in contrast to *tawhid*, emphasizes asymmetrical distinctions such as race and color whereby certain ethnic groups become dominant over others, not only politically, but also culturally. It is this tendency to divide that Qutb rejected, and he responded by noting that Islam, on the other hand, unites people and brings them together on the basis of practice, belief, and submission to God's authority. Qutb was particularly outraged at the national zealotry and ethnic extermination that was taking place in Europe toward Jews and the hatred and malice that European imperialism had brought to his own country. He noted that such unseemly contempt was unfortunately taking place among other Arab nations as well. Nationalism, he concluded, generates a competition among nations, with each claiming superiority over the next.[30]

Nationalism is misdirected loyalty toward something other than God. It is an unnatural, man-made loyalty, created artificially. All people are really Muslim at birth, Qutb suggested, since religion and Islam are more "natural" identities, and since it is human nature to identify just through one's religion. It is only later that men and women are erroneously taught their tribal or national identities. Qutb frequently cited examples from European history of the violent bloodshed that was exacted for the sake of the emerging nations. The Reformation in particular was full of wars pitting those (the emerging bourgeoisie most often) who increasingly wanted a unified nation-state and were willing to commit violence in order to achieve it, against the traditionally minded who looked to religion as a source of strength, identity, and stability.[31]

In the Muslim world, nationalism was the artificial outcome of European colonialism. Some countries, such as Egypt, were already "natural" nations since their territory had been well defined for centuries. Others, like Lebanon or Iraq, however, were quite contrived. Even so, nationalism began to orient people in many ways to look outward, and up, to Europe instead of looking to their own neighborhoods, villages, and communities, and building up from below.

In a country like Egypt, European intervention and the creation of an Egyptian nationalism divided the country between the moderns, who support it but who also identify with Europe, and the traditionalists, who remain focused on their face-to-face associations and their identity as part of the larger *umma*. Egypt had been religious up until the 1870s. The last non-European government was part of the Ottoman millet system, which recognized the different monotheisms under the aegis of the Islamic caliph in Istanbul. The fact that Islamism first appeared with Jamal al-Din al-Afghani in the late 1870s attests to the fact that before the British and the French, the reliance of Egyptians on religious identity had worked well. There had been no need for Islamic revivalism until the Europeans arrived.[32]

Qutb tended to focus more on specific examples of Egyptian and Arab nationalism. Since he was concerned with a large youthful population who had been taught to identify with the Arab and Egyptian fatherland, Qutb's challenge was to reorient their eyes so that they see themselves first as Muslims, and only later as Egyptians or even Arabs.

Islamism, he reasoned, preaches the equality of brotherhood. There are no races, no superior nationalities, no ethnic fanaticism. Islam is blind and does not see these artificial social borders and geographic boundaries. There is only one homeland, the universal motherland of Islam. Qutb claimed that no other system has as good a record in reconciling or uniting the different races and nationalities.[33]

Qutb's thinking was strongly shaped by this frequently-cited verse:

> O mankind! We have created you male and female and have made you peoples and tribes that you may know one another. The noblest of you in the sight of God is the most pious. (Qur'an 49:13)

People and tribes were not created to compete, fight, and hate one another, but instead to learn from one another and to live in peace. In other words, God created difference in order to reflect the diversity of cultures in a variety of environments and conditions, not as a divide-and-rule strategy of European racialist colonialism. This promotes egalitarianism, not a hierarchy of superior and inferior—except with regard to religion itself.

Qutb discussed how the Prophet Muhammad might have formed an Arab national movement to solve the problems of the disunity he observed in Arabia. But, Qutb concluded, such a superficial organization would instead have simply divided and subdivided into warring factions, and Islam would never have reached the vast extent it did by simply being a synonym for Arab nationalism. It would have lasted a few decades or even centuries, but then disappeared. The weakness of Islam had always been to tie it to national aspirations introduced by the Greeks, Persians, Turks, and the Europeans. God's method, however, through His messenger, created a campaign that had much more solid roots and much more long-term effective results.[34]

Any other relationship among the Prophet's followers, that first generation of Muslims in Mecca, would have produced an inferior product. The *salaf* were able to discard their national identities, their family and tribal identities, and their racial, regional, ethnic, and class character, and form the first *umma* by uniting through their faith and belief in the one single God. This unity gave them the incentive and inspiration to expand Islam to the limits of the known world. Today, Qutb concluded, a renewed and reestablished Islam has the same capacity to become truly global.

Qutb maintained that the Prophet Muhammad asked his followers to forget all their other ties but the one connection through their faith to God. Forget, he said, ties of nationality or ethnicity, and of tribe, clan, and even family, all in favor of the divine system of Islam. Muhammad did concede the need to maintain family ties, yet he also foresaw that religion could unfortunately divide the family, pitting believer against unbeliever. Higher affiliations, however, should be entirely discarded, although this was easier to say than to achieve.[35]

Qutb pointed out that the Prophet Muhammad fought against these *jahili* affiliations in Mecca in the name of the new religion, even though Mecca was his birthplace and the home of his extended family and relatives. Likewise, his followers had property and family there, and the Prophet asked them to battle the city. This could only happen, Qutb concluded, because of the superior faith that had grown and developed in their hearts.[36]

Notwithstanding the metaphorical references to a territorial *umma* or a Dar al-Islam, Qutb believed that these are not the same thing as a nation, only organized differently. Nor are there individual Islamic countries with their own different governments. Instead, they are merely Muslim states. Nor is there an official "national" language, although God did recite the Qur'an in Arabic. Islam is unlike a nation. It is not a country with a flag and other national symbols. It is not a country where one is a citizen by birth. Here, one is a Muslim by choice. It is a moral space where Islam is the accepted religion, where the Islamic faith and way of life prevail, and where God's dominion and *shari'a* rule.

In general, Qutb offered the Islamic system as a sharp contrast to nationalism. Nationalism is *jahiliyya* because it worships itself instead of God, because its ethnic and national loyalties are more important than loyalty to God, and because loyalty is based on the accident of birth or language. Nationalism, Qutb concluded, divides, while Islam unites. Although Qutb clearly recognized the reality of a number of national Islams existing in different countries,[37] his goal of universality meant that there will eventually be only one *umma* with one government administering God's unified law, recognized by all Muslims.

versus Capitalism

Qutb believed capitalism was a force that could create progress, but only at the expense of ordinary individuals and the community. Capitalism did liberate humanity from the inhuman treatment of the feudal period, help raise humanity's creativity, and further the utilization of its natural resources through science and engineering. But it did so through the use of bank interest and crass consumerism. Because bank interest is one of the major prohibitions in *shari'a*, societies that rely fundamentally on it are condemned.[38]

Qutb saw capitalism as essentially a European construct that appeared in the Muslim world as a result of 19th century imperialism. For the preceding 10 centuries, Islamic societies had dominated the region and created a quite different dynamic from that of capitalism.[39]

Qutb maintained that Islam has no complaint against capitalism's right to private property and has always been a staunch supporter of this principle by permitting the free distribution of wealth and assets, however imbalanced.[40] In both capitalism and Islam, the state has the obligation to protect the owners and their properties from theft, robbery, looting, or fraud. Islam's resolute protection of property ownership can also be seen in its severe punishment for theft.[41] Islam defends the right of free disposal of property by any recognized means—sale, rental, gift, or inheritance—as another hallmark of private ownership. As in all contemporary states, Islam gives the government the right of eminent domain, which allows it to appropriate land for public need in exchange for sufficient compensation.

Yet private property in the modern world constitutes a major means of producing wealth for some and denying it to others. Islam, therefore, allows income and wealth from property ownership but in moderation. The right to property cannot be abused. Owners are not permitted to make use of their property in contradiction to the community norms and values that Islam supports. Nor can property be accumulated to the extent that it can force others to do things against their wishes.[42] Differences in accumulating property are permitted, but not if they are gained illegally or immorally. Natural class differences can appear in principle, but not if the basis of their disparity is illegal, forced, or improperly leveraged, as in the case of monopolies, for example.

Even so, the division into classes found in modern capitalism exhibits just the discord and hostility that Qutb warned the Muslim community about. The very few rich and the large number of poor, all regulated by parliaments that favor the wealthy and the privileged, is just the sort of society that Qutb called *jahili*. Qutb was adamantly against class struggle and conflict since Islam seeks a balance and a harmony between the bourgeoisie and the proletariat. Islamic labor unions and syndicates, for example, should be organized on the basis of a cooperative relationship between management and labor, not an antagonistic one.

Islam permits individuals to earn income in ways that benefit themselves privately as long as they do not cheat others, hoard goods, manipulate prices, exploit and deceive others, or commit fraud. It can be said that capitalist societies do not allow these offenses, either, but Qutb argued that in the Islamic system, the limits on acceptable behavior are stricter and determined not by the idiosyncratic laws written by people but by the permanent laws revealed by God. Owners are restricted to only the religiously sanctioned ways of earning incomes, absolutely prohibiting gambling, prostitution, liquor, usury, and, of course, theft. Both Islam and capitalism permit competition, but Islam prohibits cut-throat rivalry if it creates permanent and irreconcilable divisions that violate the unity created by God's dominion.[43]

Unlike modern capitalism, with its unrestricted private rights to use and abuse property, Islam limits owner's rights as an expansion of the eminent domain concept whereby the community retains not just the right to confiscate property for public use, but also the right to limit how that property is used altogether. It can be used to earn a legitimate income and a livelihood, but it also must be used for the general commonwealth. Owners must make their property useful to the entire community and not just for their own benefit. If the community's welfare is violated, then the community has a right to limit the owner's use of the property. Owners are expected to demonstrate sound judgment and proficiency in using their property. Should they be unfit in these regards, the community can step in.[44]

Qutb considered the unrestricted accumulation of property to be without religious value and to be tolerated only insofar as it contributes to the work and income needed to sustain the family, thus enabling its members to serve God.[45] The enthrallment with materialism ought, instead, to be redirected toward worshipping God. Wealth is a gift from God, but to gloat over one's riches instead of exhibiting gratitude and humility goes against God's law. Qutb again used the example of the early Meccan community. Those who hesitated to follow the Prophet often did so for fear of losing their property and business. Those few who did have property, but still followed, might well have lost their possessions, but in their place, gained an inner wealth—faith and peace of mind—which proved far more valuable.[46]

Qutb also criticized the capitalist system because it has no fair means of redistributing incomes. Although there is the welfare state, in capitalism the single most important objective is to maximize production, profits, and wealth, which reduces ordinary incomes and thereby leaves large numbers of people to live in destitution and misery. Despite the occasional moment of care and concern, by and large capitalist societies foster a decline in labor's earnings, a high level of unemployment and poverty, and the accompanying social problems of crime and immorality.[47] In capitalism, general welfare is a temporary and expedient means to ward off social disorder, while in Islam, it is an intrinsic part of the religion.

Qutb also disapproved of the excessive individualism and narcissism of Western capitalist society. In Islam, people are free, at liberty to make economic choices and religious decisions, but not free to violate community values, norms, and morals, or to violate God's laws. The *shari'a* provides a framework to ensure good relations among people. In capitalism, choice is regulated only by the market. Western capitalist societies have moved in the direction of anarchy and disorder by putting the individual first, while Islamic societies should remain stable by putting the community first.

At the same time, Qutb claimed that despite the self-centeredness of the individual, capitalism nevertheless attempts to "annihilate" the individual's uniqueness as a human being.[48] He realized that individuals need the acceptance and the affiliation that Islam's community-focus provides, but that capitalism does not. As a result, individuals in capitalist society desperately need to acquire traits and characteristics that can attach them to particular groups, but capitalism constantly insists on disconnecting and isolating them.[49] In the Islamic system, individuals are required to conform to community standards, but this gives them a fellowship in which their own individual needs can still be met.

Qutb also argued that although capitalism did correct the injustice found in feudalism, it still has not provided the degree of universal justice and equality that is found in Islam. Instead, capitalism seeks to exploit people and oppress them when they resist. In the process, capitalism dehumanizes people, and although people organize and oppose this dehumanization, the government cooperates in repressing them. To Qutb, capitalism is the product of bourgeois commercial and industrial society, which reduces the rest of humanity to "a trivial and undignified status," surprisingly echoing Marx's own theory of alienation.[50]

The unlimited acquisition of wealth, the unbridled individualism, the disregard of the community and morality, and the capricious legal system that is bent here or twisted there to serve private economic interests—all are characteristics of Western capitalism that Qutb abhorred. Certainly it is not a society that acknowledges God's dominion and submits to God's authority and law. Nor is it a society that exhibits the social justice and equality that are part and parcel of the Islamic system.

Thus, Qutb concluded that in capitalism, the interests of society are secondary to those of the individual, and this makes social ethics or morality simply a product of consumerism and competition. This, in turn, creates divisions and antagonisms rather than the unity and harmony that Qutb considered hallmarks of Islam.

versus Socialism

Qutb also criticized the main alternatives to capitalism, Socialism and Communism. All three are, in Qutb's view, crassly materialistic and secular, and completely devoid of religion, spirituality, and faith. None of the three—or, for that matter, any other system at all—recognizes God's dominion and submits to His authority and laws. The secularism and materialism inherent in Socialism, Communism, and capitalism separate religion from the rest of social life, thereby marginalizing it. Muslims living in such a society may go through the motions, but, without the faith and the freedom to apply it, their actions are merely empty gestures. In Qutb's view, they are nonbelievers and just as much a part of *jahiliyya* as non-Muslims.[51]

Qutb did not see much difference between capitalism and Socialism because both permit usury and maintain class distinctions. He noted that the second differs from the first by requiring central state ownership of major production facilities.[52] Socialism emerged to correct the problems generated by capitalism, glitches in the market that make the gap between the rich and the poor untenable. Unlike capitalism, but in some ways, similar to Islamism, Socialism advocates reducing this gap by income redistribution, primarily through heavy taxation. Socialism also controls the markets and the economy to help the poor, but not in same way that Islamism does, and not for the same reason. For Socialism, helping the poor creates political stability for the ruling class, but in Islam, this help is a heart-felt element of a larger package that intends to enhance unity, harmony, and stability without antagonizing any particular group within society.[53]

Qutb pointed out that in Egypt under Jamal 'Abd al-Nassir, the very rich were taxed quite heavily and the government spent this revenue on the poor. Unfortunately, military expenses and debt repayments ate up much of the income before it was even allocated. Moreover, the hostility generated by the graduated tax policy—left to fester because there was no faith or divine guidance behind the policy—created a recalcitrance in the upper classes that led to attempts to overthrow the government.

In the end, Qutb concluded that 'Abd al-Nassir's Socialism was no better at solving Egypt's problems than the governments that had come before. Socialism became just as materialistic and anti-religious as capitalism. Both, in fact, are nationalistic, and substitute "the people" for God, "vox populi" for "vox deus." In Egypt, Socialism went so far as to create a state religion and to call it "Islam." Politics dominated religion instead of the two forming a partnership. In 1961, while Qutb was still in prison, 'Abd al-Nassir reformed al-Azhar—Egypt's 1,000-year old university and center of Islamic literature and learning—but as a result, it became even more of a tool of the state than it had been before.[54] The *'ulama* scholars of al-Azhar even went so far as to legitimate the secularism and Socialism of the administration in stark opposition to the real meaning of Islam.

One similarity between 'Abd al-Nassir's Arab Socialism and Qutb's Islamism was the reliance on mass-mobilization political parties. 'Abd al-Nassir saw this as a way to regiment Egyptians and dictate his policies to them. For Qutb, however, such a party should erase the divisions among the members of society and offer an undivided single path forward. 'Abd al-Nassir's Arab Socialist Union (ASU), the heir to the Liberation Rally of 1953, brought together workers, farmers, soldiers, intellectuals, and owners of "national" capital. Class differences were not eradicated but simply attenuated. The ASU did not solve the problems of secularism and man-made legislation but in fact intensified them. Thus Socialism became just a centralized form of capitalism, so that the basic materialist and secularist principles remain the same.[55]

versus Communism

Communism, to Qutb, was just another man-made system like nationalism, capitalism, and Socialism in that it is also secular and materialist. But Communism goes further and abolishes the individual's right to the private ownership of property and makes the state the supreme owner, ruler, and arbiter. Clearly, it remains at odds with the Islamic system.

Communism is not so very different from Socialism, and so the same criticisms hold true. To some, Socialism is supposed to be merely a transitional society on the road from capitalism to Communism. Communism then would eradicate class differences and destroy the bourgeois state, though neither goal was ever achieved successfully. Instead of rich and poor classes, Communism produced managers and workers and, far from withering away, the state in Communism became gigantic and monolithic, taking the collective place of capitalism's fragmented bourgeoisie. If Socialism is just Communism-in-the-making, then Communism, at least historically, is just state (or centralized) capitalism.

Insofar as Communism and Islamism seek a classless society, both are similar. Qutb, though, pointed out that classlessness in Islam is merely a means of uniting and harmonizing the community in order to worship and submit to God. It emerges, he argued, from the common faith and spiritualism that Muslims share and the marginalization of secondary identities. Communism, by contrast, sees this classlessness coming out of struggle and revolution.

Communism advocates a social justice that Qutb found similar to the justice of Islam. But since justice in Communism is not based on faith, it is slippery, irregular, and apt to change. It does not have the permanence and stability that Islam offers. Both systems seek to abolish egotism and selfishness, especially the individualism found in capitalism. Both advocate the collective, to the benefit of the community. In Communism, the state imposes its sparse consumption and meager lifestyle onto the workers and middle class. Islam advocates a larger free-dom, only so long as this does not violate God's prohibitions.

However, the principal problem with Communism is, of course, its atheism. The mere mention of the label implies to so many not only a lack of faith, but an active antagonism to religion altogether. Marx's view that religion is an opiate of the people could apply to Islam under certain conditions, Qutb believed, espe-cially when Islam is interpreted and presented by the government 'ulama who serve the state and not the people. But Qutb's version of Islam was, not unlike Catholic Liberation Theology in Latin America, more revolutionary and decidedly against the status quo.

Communism makes the economy dominant over all. In Islam, it is God who is dominant, and His dominion is the key element. It is the spiritual and reli-gious, not the material and economic, that makes Islam work. Humanity is not the result of productive forces and productive relations; it is the product of God's will. In Communism, humanity is free only to produce and, perhaps, to consume. In Islam, however, humanity is free to create, to enjoy, and to worship God, lim-ited only by the restrictions on its behavior and morality imposed by the shari'a. Communism has separated humanity from its own mind and from its own spir-itualism. Islam reunites all of these together into a comprehensive, integrated whole, and makes humanity the vice-regents of God on earth. In Communism, by contrast, people become cogs in a machine that manufactures widgets.[56]

versus Democracy

Qutb was no kinder toward democracy. To Qutb, democracy is no more than just another man-made system, with its own rules and regulations, its own ideas of justice and freedom. By contrast, Islamism is a permanent system created by God. Were people to change or vote out shari'a and shift dominion away from God to themselves, this would be blasphemous. Islam's sense of justice, freedom, equal-ity, and truth emerge from the Qur'an. They cannot be reshaped to reflect human desires, weaknesses, and self-interest. Those systems that do shift values accord-ing to whim, no matter how high-minded, are merely jahili systems. Islamism's val-ues, by contrast, are divine and eternal. When God revealed His laws, he intended them for all humanity, not just for particular economic or political interests and not just to benefit certain national or ethnic groups.[57]

Shari'a, God's dominion, and God's authority are all permanent and stable, combining together to serve as an anchor for humanity's social development. Democracy, on the other hand, is transient and irregular, with no permanent leg-islation whatsoever. Not even its secular constitution (in the case of the United States) is permanent, although it is difficult to amend, but certainly nowhere near as eternal as the Qur'an, the Islamic "constitution."[58] When people author their own laws, they can be rewritten at any time. When God reveals His own laws, they do not change but through His will.

In democracies, the highest authority is humanity itself, mediated by elected officials. Thus, in Qutb's view, humanity obeys and worships itself. When these officials seize power, they appropriate as much power as they want and turn themselves into tyrants. Islam not only opposes tyranny and prohibits rulers from taking any more power than is necessary to apply *shari'a*, it even encourages people to withhold their obedience from such despots. Tyranny disrupts the Islamic social contract between rulers who expect obedience and the ruled who expect justice.

Parliaments and congresses also reflect disunity, division, and conflict among various interests that go against the grain of Islam and its *tawhid*. Arguing and debating opposing interests reinforces the different and fragmented interests of a society. Islam's goal, by contrast, is to unite these various interests by downplaying material concerns and building upon the shared spirituality of the community.[59]

Yet on the other hand, Islam does have a notion of consultation, *shura*, in which leaders and representatives of the people, if not the people themselves, confer with one another over important issues, policies, and understandings of God's message and law. It does not legislate, but it can interpret. People can then discuss or debate various interpretations, ranging from conservative to liberal, and although all interpretations are derived from the Qur'an, the different supporters of an issue can determine which interpretation is the most desirable, a type of public opinion or consensus-building to arrive at formal legal decisions and policies.

Democracies allow people to devise their own laws as provisional regulations to administer a community's current affairs, its momentary interests, and to advance its material development. Western societies publicize the flexibility of this legal system to readily adapt and adjust to a changing world, even calling it "rational."[60] Qutb felt that *shari'a* can function the same way, through consultation and interpretation, which were strongly encouraged by the Prophet himself. Far from becoming backward or stagnant, the Islamic system has the true capacity to transform itself and change society as well as the ability to adapt to new circumstances.

What makes Islam particularly different from democratic societies is the source of authority and power. God remains the sole and unique authority. Rulers have power, but only enough to implement God's law. The Qur'an and the *shari'a* can be interpreted and adapted to new conditions, but their original declaration cannot be amended or tampered with. In Islam, people are not sovereign, it is, instead, God Who has dominion over all that He created. The earthly authority of Islamic rulers derives from applying God's law, but nothing more than that. Should they become tyrants, it is up to the people to defy them.

In General

Qutb considered all these other doctrines sterile and defeated. Islam is the only true system, he concluded, that reflects both God's will and the human nature

He Himself created. No other system recognizes both the spiritual and the material side of social life. Islam does so because it combines both, as God intended. All other ideologies are imported from outside the Islamic community and have harmed the *umma*. They distort Islam, weakening it and making it susceptible to the forces of *jahiliyya* that then tear it apart. The failure of these Western systems in countries like Egypt attests to the fact that they do not find fertile ground or an atmosphere conducive to their acceptance. Egypt and other Arab and Muslim societies would do better, Qutb concluded, to adopt the Islamic system, which is more natural and authentic to their history and civilization. Currently, these foreign imports are tearing Egyptian society apart. This disorder may benefit part of the society, but the largest majority is floundering in the chaos of an inappropriate system and an unsupportive society. Qutb held the Egyptian government responsible for the flourishing of *jahiliyya* and the weakening, perhaps even the disappearance, of Islam. Were the people to turn back to Islam, reawaken and revitalize the spirit of Islam and rekindle its passion, enthusiasm, dynamism, and struggle, Egypt and the Arab and Muslim world would quickly overthrow their leaders and once again achieve greatness.

When people act as if their right to property is absolute or when people use immoral methods to obtain their wealth, then social and divine unity is disrupted, and *jahiliyya* is the result, just as the modern secular world has demonstrated. Vice-regency, or stewardship, on the other hand, means people are responsible for controlling their property or their wealth in ways that benefit themselves, their family, and their community, and which maintains social integrity. Qutb's operating principle was to demonstrate how Islam generates unity, not division; harmony, not discord. Those who believe otherwise—the secularists, philosophers, pagans, apostates, and unbelievers—are those steeped in *jahiliyya,* who must be defeated.

Qutb based his vision of an Islamic economy on two effective axioms stated in the Qur'an, one positive—the use of *zakat* as an income distribution mechanism—and the other negative—prohibiting usury on which modern society so vitally depends. Both fulfill the Islamic precept of justice and unity by reducing the gap between rich and poor and diminishing the antagonism of class opposition. Both hearken back to a time before European modernity had overtaken Egypt. As in other elements of the Islamic system, Qutb employed a model of earlier times on which to base his ideal society, not unlike other visionaries for social change.

The Islamic Economy

Sayyid Qutb's vision of an Islamic economy is one based on the Islamic principles of social justice and the harmony derived from the unity of God. Together, these establish two major economic principles that are found in the Qur'an, were implemented at the time of the Prophet, and have operated in theory ever since. The first is the obligation to give *zakat* alms. This moderates the large gap between the rich and the poor by redistributing the bounty of the first to alleviate the misery of the second, and by making the wealthy humble and the indigent noble. The second outlaws usury, or the charging of interest, *riba*, which prevents the creation of wealth from anything but useful economic activity such as labor, management, or trade.[1] In addition, the Qur'an emphasizes a collective economic role for both the state and the local community.

Armed with these principles, Qutb felt that Islam could limit the heights of wealth and the depths of poverty that in secular, free-market capitalism are given free rein. In essence, Qutb took the Hidden Hand of Adam Smith's *Wealth of Nations* and claimed that, instead, it is the hand of God that regulates the economy. Smith's Hidden Hand places no restrictions on what is bought and sold or on how extreme wealth and poverty can become. The hand of God, by contrast, constitutes a set of moral principles stated in the Qur'an and in those guidelines derived from the Qur'an that are embodied in the *shari'a*. Instead of allowing whatever the market will bear, Islam provides what I call a social democracy whereby the excesses and glitches of the marketplace are resolved within the confines of a collective, God-given moral economy.[2]

Rich and Poor

Qutb was greatly concerned with the plight of the poor. Some say this came from his childhood; the chapter in his autobiographical sketch of Musha that describes *tarahil* workers demonstrates an early, albeit naive, concern for the needy. At the same time, Qutb's gradual shift into Islamism in the 1940s took place as major turmoil swept Egypt. The Communists, the Wafd, and the Muslim Brothers were all competing for the hearts and minds of ordinary Egyptians, and strikes, assassinations, and political chicanery were afflicting Egypt as its post-war economy went into a tailspin, investments were sluggish, and prices rose dramatically. A platform that not only supported the poor but attracted workers and ex-peasants to Qutb's way of thinking is not surprising. It was both genuine and opportunistic.

There are some understandings of Islam, just as in other religions, that reinforce the socioeconomic status quo, citing chapter and verse from sacred texts that buttress the notion of allowing the rich to remain so, and of asking the poor to stay content with their lot in life. Qutb did not agree with this understanding, and he blamed the official *'ulama* scholars and other professional men of religion for supporting Egypt's polarized condition.[3] Instead, Qutb provided a different understanding, one that re-interpreted religion along the lines of a mild social democracy. The rich should not be too wealthy, and the poor should not be too wretched. This position harkens back to an earlier social climate in which rich and poor were linked together by a "many-stranded" patron-client relationship, where personal familiarity moderated the distance between the two strata.[4] In Islam, responsibility for the poor becomes a community obligation, and society has a collective duty to ensure that no one goes hungry or homeless.[5]

Of course, as Western societies became more impersonal and bureaucratic, this many-stranded relationship broke down into class hostility. Qutb, it seems, wanted to bring back the more convivial, paternalistic class relationships of yesteryear. On the other hand, the radical individualism of the West helped promote, first, an antagonism between the two classes and then, later, merely a galaxy of unrelated individualistic "stars." Nicos Poulantzas once discussed the function of capitalist democracy as ideologically separating everyone out into a pattern much like a far-flung solar system, and then re-uniting them, but only under the exclusive control of a Leviathan state.[6] Without saying as much, Qutb was pushing against this excessive individualization and the manipulative role of Western governments. In a society like Egypt, which still valorized community and collective identity independent of the state, this position resonated loudly among his readers and followers.

Qutb argued that the accumulation of wealth and the corresponding lack of it among the poor generates community divisions and creates the forces for corruption, resentment, and hatred.[7] These are certainly the antagonisms of Marx's class conflict. Qutb argued, against Marx, that this conflict is not inevitable, but that a return to the *shari'a* and to God's dominion can once again reinstate harmony and moderation between the rich and the poor.[8]

Great wealth and extravagant luxury, Qutb concluded, lead inevitably to wickedness. The wealth of the elite and the Palace in Egypt outraged him tremendously. When confronted by their corruption and decadence, he raved against the usury, monopoly, corruption, wastefulness, and dishonesty that created dire poverty and contaminated the entire community.[9]

The passages of the Qur'an and the Hadith [reports about the Prophet Muhammad] that disapprove and forbid luxury are frequent and numerous....

Lovers of luxury must have their easy, perverse, and sickly life; they must gratify their desires and have their pleasures; they must have around them followers and courtiers who are submissive....

Many times in history, mention is made of the lovers of luxury as always impeding not only themselves but also their followers in pursuing the way of truth; for so long as there are such, there will also be weaklings who will flatter their pride; minister to their desires, and lose their personality like insects. 'We have never sent anyone as a warner to a town, but that the men of luxury have said, 'We do not believe in your message' (Qur'an 34:34).[10]

Qutb went on to say that the Prophet Muhammad described houses of luxury as temples of Satan because of the corruption and temptation found in them.

Undoubtedly, luxury is the cause of destruction in the course of history, as it is the cause of insolence. "How many towns have We destroyed which were insolent because of their prosperity?" (Qur'an 28:58). And equally, certainly, luxury is a reason for punishment in the world to come, because it results in grave sin....

The community will be held responsible for this evil that exists in its midst; for luxury must inevitably lead to evil by reason of its very existence in the community.[11]

As elsewhere, those in Egypt with wealth also possess power; the two reinforce one another. Should there be no morals or ethics involved in making wealth, then it is quite probable that there will be no principles whatsoever in wielding power. Moreover, those in power operate to increase their wealth, and the wealth of their family and friends, even further, thus creating more concentrated oligopolies and monopolies, and, hence, a tighter rein on power. This works to initiate and sustain tyranny and social injustice. Qutb often noted the nefarious connections between those who are wealthy and those who are in power, and loathed such despotism since it goes against the unity of God, His social justice, and His dominion. His view was that escalating wealth and luxury on the one hand and increasing misery and suffering on the other are rejected by Islam, and the protection of these extremes by the modern state easily translates into injustice and corruption that has to be overthrown through *jihad* and replaced by an Islamic state grounded in God's authority.[12]

The moderation and balance that Qutb claimed as the hallmarks of Islamic economics are no different from the same values found in so many formal religions before the advent of modernity. Western Christianity, too, once discouraged extreme wealth and poverty such that a reasonable gap between the two was acceptable, but not more than this, in order to demonstrate righteous Christian behavior. Such moderation is also evident in other major religions—Hinduism, Buddhism, Confucianism, and Judaism. It was the novelty of John Calvin and other like-minded thinkers in 16th-century Europe to argue in favor of wealth as a sign of God's grace: the more wealth, the more grace. The Reformation did manage to turn the world upside down,[13] or at least upset its values, and church-men as well as secularists were found on both sides, debating whether extreme wealth was grace or disgrace. Max Weber maintained that this new Protestant ethic served as the ideological midwife for the ethos of capitalism and that its this-worldly asceticism and predetermination together encouraged those who successfully made profits. Richard Tawney, however, notes that Catholics and early Protestants—even Calvin himself at times, along with other churchmen—actually formed a *bulwark* against the emerging free (and secular) marketeers whose goal was to rid society of any religious restrictions whatsoever. The Islam that Qutb preached thus harkens back to a time when extremes were discouraged worldwide. Islam continues to advocate moderation. Christianity did, too, for a while, but the Enlightenment formally separated church and economics, so that afterward, any religious limitations that might have been imposed were seen as altogether quaint or backward. There has been no Enlightenment in the Islamic world, though some say that colonialism introduced it through the back door, so to speak. The Islam that Qutb promoted seeks to close that back door, to rid itself of colonial influence, and to reassert Islam's traditional moderation of wealth and poverty, seen as valuable and ethical, not peculiar and atavistic.[14]

Qutb maintained that in challenging excessive wealth and indigence, Islam aims for a golden mean. Opulence and destitution are equally proscribed. Both profligate waste and miserly stinginess are admonished. Avarice and abstinence are similarly rebuked, since greed is seen as a self-indulgent moral transgression while abnegation is rejected as unduly harsh and unwarranted. Cupidity is espe-cially viewed as an animal desire that Islam wants eliminated, for love of wealth detracts from concentrating on worshipping God.

Calvin's asceticism seemed to Qutb a misuse of income; austerity is discour-aged if available resources permit more and better consumption. Islam expects men and women to concern themselves with both material and spiritual well-being. Calvin believed that the material *is* the spiritual; in Islam, the two remain somewhat antithetical, though still interconnected. If, in Islam, an extreme increase of material wealth violates God's unity, then an emphasis on spirituality alone—what Qutb identified as asceticism—is also not acceptable. The Calvinist or Puritan ethic was not well received, it seemed. Qutb drew many examples from the *hadith* about individuals who went one way or the other as illustrations of incorrect emphasis, calling them both "misguided idolaters."

> Abu Ahwas al-Jashimi reported from his father, "The Prophet saw me dressed in rags and said, 'Do you have any property?' I said, 'Yes!' He

said, 'What property?' I said, 'All the sheep and camels that God has given me.' He said, 'If God has given you property, then let Him see the signs of His blessings and generosity upon you.'"[15]

Instead, Qutb argues for a balanced blend of these two concerns.

Qutb stated that Islam recognizes many legitimate means of earning incomes, but other methods that go well beyond ordinary, customary relationships are unlawful and off limits. No occupation is allowed if it disrupts community integrity and unity. No means of increasing wealth or income are permitted but those that involve actual work. Islam does promote private property, but views people merely as fair-minded stewards or vice-regents for God, the ultimate proprietor. Islam's moral economy also prohibits corruption, fraud, dishonesty, exploitation, and other economic practices that unbalance the playing field and cause undue misery for all but a few. The rich are not allowed to form monopolies, to swindle their competitors, to cheat workers of their wages, or to charge interest. Exploiting tenants, rack-renting, and establishing monopsonies that drive up costs and prices, as well as other excesses, are seen as unethical. Wealth restricted to a very small circle of the rich and monopolies created to unilaterally control the market and fix prices are forbidden by Islam. Monopolies over the necessities of life are particularly disliked, because they place undue power into the hands of a few. Criminal methods to increase wealth, such as harsh exploitation or cut-throat competition, are not allowed. Islam places great importance on honesty in commercial and financial transactions; the development of extreme wealth and monopoly means, therefore, that this principle has most likely been violated. In all cases, the welfare of the community is at risk and those who seek wealth and monopoly threaten to harm its collective interests.[16]

In addition, if the rich are restricted to lawful endeavors, so, too, are the poor, so that theft and begging, for example, are strongly discouraged. Qutb repeatedly stated that the faith and passion required to establish an Islamic state and society also call for material stability and comfort before true Muslims can address social and religious problems. Islam hates poverty and seeks to set people free of material want so that they can give their full attention to honoring and worshipping God. Qutb noted that the Qur'an affirmed that poverty was the work of Satan, a way to weaken people's resolve and trust in God. God did not intend the poor to be weak and humiliated, and therefore prescribed *zakat* as a means of not only providing them with a decent living but also of giving them dignity. Trust in God allows the poor to confront those with wealth and in power in order to negotiate better opportunities for themselves.[17]

> When men have only the bare necessities of life, they cannot gain any respite from labor in which to satisfy these spiritual yearnings or these intellectual capacities; then they have been robbed of their nobility and are reduced to the level of animals. . . .

Man can never achieve any of this so long as his whole life must be spent in the pursuit of his daily bread.[18]

Qutb's ethics for the rich and the poor required placing qualitative, moral restrictions on the gap between the two strata such that it could never grow so wide as to breed class division and discontent. To this end, Islam contains important institutional mechanisms for income redistribution—*zakat*, *sadaqa*, and inheritance—that become crucial for limiting the divide between the rich and the poor that could otherwise lead to strife. All three practices function to ensure social solidarity and unity and to exhibit the social justice that, all together, infuse Islam.

Zakat

The Islamic system carefully provides for the general prosperity of the community as a basic obligation. Members are obligated to give *zakat*, religious tithes, as a means to limit the gap between rich and poor, to provide additional, voluntary tithes, *sadaqa*, and to offer fast-breaking meals during Ramadan. No individual is excused from contributing. Qutb concluded that under Islam, the poor have the right to a reasonable standard of living and to a share of the wealth of those who are more fortunate. The principle of *zakat* establishes the religious justification for these entitlements. What Qutb's Islamic system also provides is a compassionate charity to the poor that does not reek of the condescension and disdain he found in the West.

Zakat is the most essential element of the economic principles of Islam with regard to wealth and poverty. Even modern or secular Muslims see this as the basis for an Islamic socialism;[19] certainly it constitutes a major means of income distribution and social democracy. As one of five mandatory duties of Islam, it obliges donors to give in charity for the poor roughly 2½ percent of their income and assets annually, including monetary profits, crops, livestock, real estate, mining, and petroleum.[20] *Zakat* is assessed on all possessions and is to be given in a generous spirit. There is also *sadaqa*, which is an additional, but voluntary and therefore variable, contribution. Qutb called both "social taxes" to be levied by the Islamic state. Those who are eligible for *zakat* include the poor, but especially the super-poor, or destitute. It is given to recent converts, freed slaves, debtors, errant Muslims, travelers, the sick, and the *mujahidin*. It includes anyone who has exhausted his own provisions. Ordinarily, it is handed over to government mosques, or collected by private mosque committees and then distributed to the poor, or else dispensed directly to known beneficiaries by well-meaning Muslims.

People should feel obliged to give *zakat* just from their faith and conscience. After all, Qutb reasoned, compassion and kindness in Islam are signs of faith and piety that underline all religious actions, and charity leads to paradise.[21] This assistance becomes the responsibility of the entire community. Setting up tables for the poor for fast-breaking meals (*iftar*) during the month of Ramadan represents another example of community charity. Legal trusts, hospitals, orphanages, and public conveniences (such as water dispensers) are also established for communal use.

But some people feel they should or can voluntarily give additional amounts. Qutb strongly emphasized the concept of *sadaqa*, for he saw it not just as a donation to the poor, but as a contribution to God. Qutb likened *sadaqa* to a loan made to God whose repayment is assured in paradise. It is a means of purifying one's soul, an expenditure that credits the donor on Judgment Day. *Zakat* and *sadaqa* should be given in private, according to the Qur'an, in order to "preserve the honor" of the recipient, and to "prevent conceit and boasting" by the donor.[22] Qutb considered tithing both a social duty and an act of worship, for all these donations are given in the name of God.

Charity and welfare for the poor also demonstrate, according to Qutb, that the community is more important than the individual. His grievance about Muslim societies during his lifetime was that *zakat* was being neglected, either withheld or else given resentfully. Or else the government withheld so much that very little remained to be redistributed to those in true need. Instead, the free market of unrestricted wealth and poverty operated with abandon. The spirit of *zakat*, of giving without a return, was no longer alive. *Zakat*, Qutb argued, is a state of mind, and this way of thinking was disappearing under the tide of the "survival of the fittest" and the unbridled competition for material increases.

Qutb was annoyed that the idea of *zakat* had weakened to the point of being an empty ritual, much like the idea of Christmas gift-giving in the West had turned into mere financial transactions. In a Muslim society like Egypt, where Western influence was strong, *zakat* tended to fall by the wayside. Wretchedness and stinginess were both increasing. The destitute were made to feel humiliated and marginal, even though they surely constituted the largest portion of Egyptian society. But this reflected the more general problem of the community disintegrating and breaking down under the influence of modernization. As Westernization increased, the sense of community was weakening, and along with it, the sense of obligation to those without sufficient income and property. *Zakat* should be collected more strenuously, charity recognized as a mutual obligation, and community solidarity strengthened. If people do not have the faith, they should be shamed into giving. And those who still refuse to give should be forced to do so under the authority of *shari'a*. The ruler can also exact additional amounts for the poor if necessary.

Even so, I have found that charitable giving in general, and of whatever kind, is done in the Muslim world with much less of the miserly attitude seen in England and the United States. This kind of stinginess comes in part from the Calvinist teachings where poverty is the absence of God's blessings and, therefore, represents the Unsaved who are then treated with contempt. In this Protestant way of thinking, the cause of poverty is the victim himself. Receiving welfare and public charity can become humiliating and lead to resentment or resignation. During the

Reformation, Protestantism distanced itself from the earlier Catholic perspective that viewed charity as what good Christians gave with a full heart, and moved toward the Calvinist approach that denied charity so as not to interfere with God's predestined path that made poverty an opportunity to demonstrate either God's blessing—by extracting oneself from penury—or else His damnation—by confirming sloth and indifference.[23] Qutb would claim that *zakat* is more the "full hearted" variety—common, I would argue, in many pre-modern societies—and not the stingy, reluctant kind that puts down recipients.

In the Muslim communities that I have observed over the last 20 years, the poor do not feel demeaned in accepting *zakat*, *iftar* meals, or other acts of charity. Nor are these given unwillingly or grudgingly but rather they are offered kindly and piously as part of people's religious conviction and obligation to God. This has especially increased since September 11, 2001, as religiosity itself has returned and intensified. To be sure, there are Muslims who are stingy and do not wish to part with their income, and, in Egypt, they simply withhold their *zakat* donations. In other countries, especially where *zakat* is required by law, there are always those who refuse to give merely as a gesture of opposing the state and its taxes.

Still, Qutb argued, *zakat* is more than taxes or alms; it is also more than income redistribution and social democracy. Qutb saw *zakat* as a state of mind based on mutual assistance and solidarity in which all participants, donors, beneficiaries, and the rest of the community are inspired and faithful. Here, *zakat* reflects the much broader Islamic principle of social justice. It strives to instill a social harmony and integrity by reducing the gap between rich and poor that once again reflects the central principle of *tawhid*.

> The true image of *zakat* has faded from our consciousness and from the consciousness of the wretched generations that have not seen the system of Islam applied in the real world. It [the Islamic system] could make *zakat* the basis of this [economic] system, in contrast to the *jahili* system based on usury. It could cause life to grow and the economy to progress by means of individual effort or by means of cooperation free from usury.
>
> This picture of charity has faded from the consciousness of those wretched and ill-starred generations that have never actually seen that lofty form of humanity but were born and have lived completely under the influence of the materialistic system based on usury. They have seen the stinginess and miserliness, the brawling, the wrangling, and the selfish individualism which rule of the souls of men and make it so that money passes to those who need it only in the despicable form of usury![24]

Qutb stressed that *zakat* and *sadaqa* are not gifts but are duties, willed by God, and definitely not acts of patronizing handouts. Every person should live by his own labor and effort, but if this is not possible, then the community is responsible for his economic support. But instead of provoking hatred as a response to the patron's condescension—self-evident in societies where such social taxes are begrudgingly granted—in Islam, no one feels degraded since all assets ultimately belong to God and people are merely caretakers or stewards of His creations on earth.

Usury

Arguably one of the most discussed and condemned institution of Western economies found in Islamic discourse is the charging of interest on loans, or usury. If *zakat*, *sadaqa*, and inheritance reflect the righteousness of Islam, then usury or *riba* reflects the ruthlessness and decay of *jahiliyya* society. The prohibition on usury is derived from the concept of vice-regency and the idea that all possessions come from God. To improperly extract wealth from others violates these principles since this wealth is obtained without one's own work and at the expense of people in the community. Usury has been controversial for most, if not all, formal religions. Prior to the modern era, it was commonly condemned and proscribed. Nevertheless, it was not unusual to find usury operating in fact despite religious punishments.

Qutb viewed usury as just the opposite of *zakat*. While *zakat* diminishes the disparity between the rich and the poor, usury makes creditors richer and borrowers poorer. Qutb frequently wrote about "*ribawi*" or usurious societies; true Islamic communities were, by contrast, those that readily and kindly donated their *zakat*. In contrast to *zakat*, *riba* reflects an individuated, scattered, and alienated society where everyone is on his own, united at best only by the state or the market. Charging interest divides people, creditor against borrower, rich against poor. Collecting and distributing *zakat*, on the other hand, integrates and harmonizes society, as long as the intentions are honorable and genuine.[25]

It is well known that usury in Islam is forbidden. But it is not entirely clear whether this means prohibiting *all* interest whatsoever, or merely when it readily exceeds market-determined rates. Even before the modern period, there were often various "tricks" (*hiyal*) used to evade the prohibition, and, in a pinch, non-Muslim minority groups could be relied upon to supply needed capital.[26] Muhammad 'Abduh was able to justify usury in 1904 by saying it was vital for national competition and survival; for reasons, we might say today, of "national security." Today, of course, interest-charging banks thrive throughout the Islamic world; indeed, their very existence constitutes a major part of *jahiliyya* that Qutb and others wished to defeat.

By criticizing the earning of profits that are not based on actual work, Qutb came quite close to condemning capitalism altogether. Prohibiting such activity, he maintained, would go far in eliminating the idleness, flabbiness, and luxury that arise from basically holding legal ownership papers and nothing else. Such a parasitic class of people, Qutb said, is not tolerable in an Islamic society.[27]

He was quite indignant about the moral corruption that usury generates, was concerned about the larger damage it creates by dehumanizing economic transactions, and feared that such methods might substantially increase the gap between rich and poor. He was hardly unique in demanding the abolition of any kind of interest whatsoever, claiming, like other Egyptians, that it was the French who brought the concept of interest to Egypt.

> When a man borrows money and then falls on evil circumstances, "Then let there be indulgence until better times" (Qur'an 2:280).... Forbearance in collecting a debt preserves the self-esteem of the borrower and encourages in his heart an affection for the lender; it gives him an incentive to work hard in order to repay his loan as far as he can.[28]

Qutb argued that the use of usury valorizes greed and corruption as the highest goals of human existence and encourages people to obtain wealth by any means possible and to consume it wantonly. This places wealth above human social relationships and causes people to put more effort into earning profits than into worshipping God. "This creates a system," he wrote, "that crushes humanity completely." Those who engaged in usury put money and profits on par with, or even ahead of, God. In Qutb's mind, that made them the lowest and most despised of God's creatures.[29]

Qutb declared that there are two types of interest. First, there is *riba al-nasi'a*, traditional compound interest. Second is *riba al-fadl* which is the profit made by buying low and selling high.[30] Many Islamists permit the second, but prohibit the first. Qutb was much more inflexible and rejected both, seeing the second as gradually leading to the first. Qutb discussed the hazy difference between commercial profit (which is permissible) and *riba al-fadl* (which is not) but did not reach a definite conclusion.[31]

Money should be lent, Qutb maintained, particularly to the poor, but loans should be interest-free and repayment should be just for the full principal. This is the obligation of the wealthy and powerful, and is a sign of generosity and Islamic charity. Money can be lent for production or consumption purposes, Qutb wrote, as long as repayments are not atrocious, meaning, perhaps—he was never quite clear—that interest remains at market levels.[32] Qutb himself recommended that where loans are for productive purposes, then repayment should be based on the profit or loss of the enterprise. Such arrangements maintain harmony between the creditor and the borrower.

"*Ribawi*" societies are those communities where bank interest not only thrives but where it has so infected the economic system that the freedom to grow, acquire, and consume is absolute, without moral or religious restrictions. Those who seek unlimited wealth, or else are condemned to unlimited poverty, live in a *jahili* society. Such unbridled individualism risks disrupting and even destroying communities.[33] For Qutb, usury was a way of man exploiting man, of creating divisions and conflict, and moving away from a harmony and integrity that reflects Islamic *tawhid*.

Qutb's own stress on the productive use of capital prefigured the rise of non-interest banking. The most common Islamic instrument is the *mudaraba* contract, a type of commenda or limited-partnership agreement, whereby both the creditor and the debtor together share either the profit or the loss, thus sharing the risks and sharing the income. Here, loans turn into either mutually beneficial or mutually detrimental transactions, rather than holding steady or even compounding. The idea behind *mudaraba* has also been extended to non-interest-bearing bank accounts as well.[34] But Qutb did not live long enough to appreciate the pioneering efforts by Islamic scholars in Pakistan and elsewhere who have been developing legitimate ways of banking without interest. The Islamic banking sector flourishes today in the Muslim world as well as the West, demonstrating that economic development *can* take place *without* unIslamic interest.

Property

Qutb believed that people who own property are merely stewards entrusted with both rights and responsibilities, yet the property ultimately belongs to the community and to God.[35] God granted humanity control over nature so that all might benefit from it, but also protect it. It is this vice-regency that restricts owners because *shari'a* prohibits owners from violating community well-being and morals. As trustees, owners can still utilize and profit from the property. But they are not at liberty to use their property any which way they choose. They are limited by God's authority and the welfare of the community. People's submission to God and the superiority of His dominion trumps any individual right that owners might have.

Islam thus advocates a socialized form of ownership, where owners can benefit individually, but are not allowed to misuse or abuse their commission. Ownership is not the unconditional control of a material thing, but rather it is a set of social relationships, and these relationships are regulated by God's law. Accordingly, there is a moral dimension to these relations.

> The fundamental principle is that property belongs to the community in general; individual possession is a stewardship which carries with it conditions and limitations. Some property is held in common, and this no individual has any right to possess. A proportion of all property is a due that must be paid to the community, in order that the latter may disburse it to specified individuals of its own number; these constitute

cases of need that may thereby be remedied so that the community may preserve its health.

I have not emphasized this principle in order to teach any communistic doctrine of property, for the right of personal ownership is firmly established in Islam.... [But] the individual must realize that he is no more than the steward of this property, which is fundamentally the possession of society; this must make him accept the restrictions that the system lays upon his liberty, and the bounds that limit his rights of disposal.[36]

In assuming divine ownership and human stewardship, usufruct, Qutb either considered that the Islamic ruler was just the *symbolic* owner or caretaker, or he regarded all land as a *waqf* (*waqf*, sing.; *awqaf*, plural, for the endowment of land) that is a perpetual trust from God.[37] In pre-modern Egypt, the temporal ownership of most ordinary land (*raqaba*) was vested in the state or ruler—with such exceptions as freehold land (*milk*), and incorporated religious and family endowments—but where true ownership belonged to God. The peasant-farmer who tilled the land just enjoyed usufructuary rights (*tasarruf*).[38]

In many traditional Islamic systems, it was considered that the state (or the ruler), as the representative of the Islamic community, was the ultimate owner of the land. This right was predicated on conquest. While the state or the ruler held absolute ownership (*raqaba*), the actual farmers held usufruct rights (*tasarruf*).[39]

Qutb's idea of Islamic property, as discussed earlier,[40] contrasts sharply with capitalist patterns of absolute private ownership, but it closely parallels Egypt's earlier, pre-modern pattern. The Islamic system of property fosters, in theory, a cooperative relationship among owners, and encourages them to preserve the land as temporal stewards of God's trust.

Islam also advocates the system of partible inheritance, whereby each child receives a portion of his parents' property, although sons and daughters do not receive equal shares.[41] Qutb maintained that inheritance constitutes a very important social aspect of property since the right to own property means the right to bequeath it to heirs. It motivates men to work hard in order to provide for their children so that the effort invested into property yields rewards beyond the lifetime of the owner. It contributes to mutual aid within the family, unites the family, ensures harmony between the generations, and enhances community solidarity. It reduces extreme wealth by redistributing it upon death of the owner. Inheritance is an adhesive that links generations and insures justice. Qutb defended this arrangement despite what some argued are imbalances, because, he said, they are divinely ordained. In the case of poverty or orphancy, where there is no property, then the community or government should intervene. In both cases, the community benefits because its members remain mutually committed to one another.

Islam's system of partible inheritance bestows land to all siblings. It contrasts with Europe's traditional system of impartible intestate inheritance where only one heir inherits and his siblings are disinherited.[42] Impartible inheritance can undermine the solidarity and love within a family by setting one brother against another. Partible inheritance, on the other hand, confirms and strengthens the unity of the family and of Islamic society—both of which, Qutb would argue, are derived from *tawhid*. Whereas the Islamic system prioritizes the unity of the family, the European system prioritizes the unity of the property. Qutb would have argued that this confirms his conclusion that Europe's materialism is one reason for its lack of moral principles and religion, a condition he warned fellow Muslims about time after time.[43]

Capitalism

Qutb was not against capitalism as such, despite his vehement disapproval of usury, which, however, was not so clear as to forbid all bank interest whatsoever. He found a middle ground by permitting capitalism but opposing *unrestrained* accumulation, *unlimited* profits, and *unreasonable* monopolies and monopsonies—and the extreme poverty and misery that went along with these. He argued for a productive use of capital and for a compassionate constraint on capitalist operations. The social democracy model he proposed (although he never used this specific term) places limits and restrictions on the free market, which reflect the unified relationship between God and His creations.

This can be seen in the borderline case of *riba al-fadl*—commercial profit—which, if too extreme, can disguise illegal and immoral usury. Still, just what constitutes comfortable profit and what constitutes greed and exploitation is relative. Qutb concluded that the outcomes that really matter are those that maintain community solidarity and divine harmony, not individual profits and material wealth.

In contrast to modern economists and political scientists who disaggregate the economy into its constituent parts, Qutb closely followed Islamic thinking and argued for the integrity of the economy and for re-embedding it into its social relations. Qutb believed that the economy is not separate from the rest of social life but is integrated and regulated by *shari'a* and the Qur'an. Spiritual and economic values are not located in two different and disconnected domains, as they are in the West. Instead, they mutually influence one another.

The Islamic State

The Islamic state is based exclusively on the supreme authority of God, *hakimiyya*, and His message as revealed in the Qur'an. It is imbued with *tawhid*—the unity of God with His creations and the integrity of the Islamic community—which demands equality among all Muslims, without any distinction or discrimination based on color, race, class, ethnicity, or nationality.[1] The first Islamic state in Medina is the model upon which Sayyid Qutb based his vision of an Islamic government, acknowledging, of course, the much greater complexity and diversity found in today's societies.

The leader of the Islamic state must be a true believer in God and in His law. In Medina, Muhammad was the sole earthly authority—administrator and executor, revealer and interpreter of law, and judge and arbitrator resolving conflicts within the community—and the Qur'an was his constitution. The role of such an authority in a modern Islamic state is just to administer Islamic law. He has no independent power to legislate—God is the supreme legislator. He is also not a priest or any mediator between people and God. Indeed, he is only the first among equals.

The Islamic state is often dismissed as a theocracy, a supposed relic of the pre-Enlightenment era. A theocracy is ruled by divine or saintly persons raised above the level of the ordinary public. In the West, this means being ruled by a priesthood, a body of clerics who mediate between worshippers and God and who derive power and authority from the Divine.

Qutb defended the Islamic state from such accusations by arguing that since the Islamic ruler is merely a conduit for religious law, he has no added authority, nor does his position sanctify him. The notion that priests and popes are consecrated or even anointed ("elected") is foreign to Islam.[2] Since Islam does not have a priesthood, it cannot be a theocracy.

"Holy men" can be found among Sufi mystics, but Sufism is denounced by most Islamic activists. In strict Islam, the highest ruler is not divine, partly divine, or divinely chosen. Authority derives from enforcing God's law and consulting with popular representatives, not from the religion itself.[3] Once that enforcement weakens, or another legal system is imposed, then the ruler loses his authority, becoming a tyrant subject to dissent or defiance.

If Islam combines politics and religion, which, in the West, are separated, and if Islam, unlike Christianity (but similar to templar Judaism), has divine laws, then, as one might expect, Islamic politicians and officials are those steeped in religion.[4] The separation of Islam from the government—mimicking the separation of church and state in the West—is considered a sacrilege. There is no theoretical distinction between the ruler, the head of state, and the religious leader, the caliph or the *imam*. The state's legal codes are based on the *shari'a* as represented by its schools of law (*fiqh*). The state allows for consultation, *shura*, between its rulers and the people's representatives and adjudication through judicial courts. But there is no legislative branch that can overturn or vote out sacred laws since their divine origin means they cannot be changed or deleted, though they can be interpreted and adapted to contemporary life.[5]

There is no tripartite system of government—executive, legislative, and judiciary—derived from Montesquieu's separation of powers. The checks-and-balances that the West has come to expect from this system are provided for within the Qur'an itself, which imposes the obligations and constraints otherwise compelled by a formal constitution.[6] The Qur'an and *shari'a* "provide a protective shield in defense of the rights and liberties of citizens against arbitrary power" or tyranny.[7]

Thus, Qutb noted that the Islamic state is based on unity, not division. There are, then, merely governmental relationships:

> Political theory in Islam rests on the basis of justice on the part of the rulers, obedience on the part of the ruled, and consultation between ruler and ruled. These are the great fundamental features from which all the other features take their rise.[8]

Instead, the government has, in theory, a much more limited function, merely carrying out God's will and administering His laws. Qutb and others consider the Islamic government to be tightly restricted by its Qur'anic constitution, not unlike constitutional regulation in the United States and elsewhere. It is just this Islamic constitution that prevents the state from becoming authoritarian or autocratic. Unlike a man-made constitution, however, the constitution in Islam cannot be amended, although it can be understood in a different way according to new circumstances.[9]

The Ruler

If humanity is the vice-regent of God on earth—positioned above all of God's other creations, but humbled before God Almighty Himself—then the principal vice-regent should be the *imam* or caliph. Qutb claimed that the caliph is God's deputy or the head vice-regent only to the extent that he carries out divine law. He has no other special status or privileges that rank him above others. This successor to the Prophet Muhammad is owed obedience only insofar as this submission is like submitting to the Prophet himself and that the caliph applies, and only applies, *shari'a* law.

The caliph is executor, administrator, judge, and general. His prime function, though, is to command what is right and forbid what is wrong according to God's law. He is obligated to preserve the unity of the Islamic community, to ensure internal peace and solidarity, to guard the *umma* from strife, and to protect it from outside aggression. He is responsible for improving the people's welfare and working for their benefit.

If the ruler successfully executes his duties, this should mitigate against the rise of any dictator, despot, or tyrant. In turn, the people ought to receive a just resolution of their disagreements. Those rulers who do carry out *shari'a*, benefit from its regulatory function, from its unifying function, and from the utility, decency, and righteousness of following God's law. Those rulers unable or unwilling to carry out the precepts of *shari'a* are subject to punishment or removal.[10]

Qutb maintained that there is a definite social contract in the Islamic state, not unlike the one famously proposed by Jean Jacques Rousseau. In Islam, people have the right to expect social justice from their ruler as long as they obey Islamic law, presumably administered and executed properly by their leader. In turn, a ruler has the right to expect obedience from those ordinary people below him, which is true as long as *shari'a* law, and only *shari'a* law, is applied.[11] Thus the people have the right to select their ruler; the ruler has the duty to enforce the law. The ruler is obligated to consult with popular representatives, and, Qutb added, the people have the right to impeach or depose the ruler (although Qutb also envisioned more militant action) should he stray from executing divine regulations.

The caliph, while exercising little extraordinary power, nevertheless should be charismatic, since his leadership in managing the affairs of his compatriots often requires the personal appeal that persuades rather than coerces them to hear and obey. Part of this charisma also involves (as it does in the West) education and schooling: the right religious knowledge that makes his decisions and policies better than any rival.

Qutb called Abraham, father of Isma'il and Isaac, the first *imam* for all humanity, the leader of Friday prayers, and the ultimate source of knowledge of divine law.[12] Interestingly (and ironically), Qutb's model for this lofty position was David, the founder of Jerusalem and the First Temple in Judaism in approximately 1000 BC. David, of course, is one of the prophets recognized in Islam. He wisely combined judge, general, and ruler into one position, which he attained by his own efforts. But Qutb rejected the fact that the office turned into an inherited kingship when David bequeathed the throne to his son, Solomon, notwithstanding the latter's wisdom. The caliph, despite his high position, cannot hand down his position. Qutb argued that the Prophet Muhammad purposely did not designate a successor for fear that this person and his family would acquire additional benefits by virtue of their appointment by the Messenger of God. Qutb left it to the community, instead, to pick the successor—in contrast to both the 'Alids and the Umayyads (Shi'ites and Sunnis), but in accord with the minority Kharijite perspective.

The ruler of the Islamic state should assume his office by virtue of the free choice of Muslims. However, Qutb was never really clear whether this selection should involve universal popular suffrage, indirect voting by an elite 'ulama, or election by another, yet unknown arrangement. But he plainly rejected European styles of selection.[13] Qutb stated that an Islamic society should emerge before the actual founding of the Islamic state, and only after that could a precise selection procedure be put into place.

Many Islamic thinkers, including Qutb, reject the notion of a multi-party political system. Instead, Qutb advocated a single mobilization party, similar to the Liberation Rally that was established in Egypt in 1954. He criticized the idea of separate political parties with competing interests because they become a source of division and thus violate the concept of *tawhid*. They promote competition, rivalry, and conflict, not unity, harmony, and cooperation. What parties that do exist in his Islamic state demonstrate Qutb's polarized thinking since there are only two—the party of God (*hizb Allah*) and the party of Satan (*hizb al-shaytan*); the party of Islam and the party of *jahiliyya*.

Yet within the party of God, as in any other corporatist mobilization party, internal factions representing farmers, workers, businessmen, bureaucrats, and the like can exist to articulate the interests of their constituents and to formulate sympathetic interpretations of Islam. These factions could also nominate candidates for consultative councils and other offices that mediate between the ruler and the general public.

Once chosen, the ruler is inaugurated by receiving the pledge of allegiance, or *bay'a*. The *bay'a* confirms his position and represents a mutual consent or social contract between the ruler and the rest of the Muslim community. The abrogation by either side of their responsibilities produces discord, or *fitna*.

The *bay'a* is ultimately an unconditional oath to God, but since He is unseen, the oath has been physically redirected toward obeying the just ruler. In the beginning, the first generation of Muslims pledged their personal allegiance to the Prophet Muhammad, placing their hands in his hand, and promising their loyalty, not so much to him as to God.[14] They pledged to obey the Prophet, his successor, and, ultimately, God Himself in Whose name the first two spoke. After the death of the Prophet, the oath was redirected to God and became attached to the caliphs only on the condition that they continue to be true and pious Muslims. However, agreeing to obey the ruler is not identical to the submission of devout Muslims to God's dominion because compliance can be withdrawn should the ruler stop governing according to *shari'a*. To pledge allegiance to an unjust ruler—that is, to one who is not implementing *shari'a* law—is to lose altogether God's protection (or grace), according to Qutb.[15]

When Ibn Taymiyya, the conservative, Hanbali scholar, was asked in 1312 about obedience to the invading Mongols who were only nominal Muslims—having converted to Islam merely to avoid military attacks from "fellow" Muslims—he reportedly said that true Muslims were those who thoroughly follow and execute *shari'a* law. That is, if the ruler fails to apply Islamic law, he is no longer a Muslim, notwithstanding his own claims and testimonies of faith.[16] Qutb extended Ibn Taymiyya's argument by writing that those who give their allegiance to such rulers—deemed unbelievers—lose God's protection and risk failure. To the customary Sunni adage that it is better to obey a bad ruler than to have no ruler at all—if by "bad" it is meant that the ruler is a tyrant because he does not administer *shari'a* law—Qutb would counsel true Muslims to withdraw their *bay'a* even if it results in disaster.

The ruler in an Islamic government essentially applies *shari'a* law as stated in the various schools of *fiqh*. He is more a primus inter pares, a coordinator or organizer, than a superior power; he possesses no power but what is necessary to administer the law. In practice, though, with the rise of the Umayyad dynasty in the 7th century, the executive, the caliph, came to monopolize much more power than the Islamic system would otherwise have entitled him.

Qutb believed that the caliphate itself had been usurped by the Umayyads who, beginning with the first ruler, Mu'awiyya (r: 661–680) and his son Yazid (r: 680–683), had turned the caliphate into an inherited kingship and had thus moved away from selecting the best, most devout person to lead the community. Qutb claimed that, as a result, the caliph ceased to be just and legitimate, thereby ushering in an unconstitutional tyranny. The position has been in decline ever since.

In Muslim states, while there should be no theoretical distinction between the government ruler and the religious ruler, there had been, for some time, an implicit and unofficial separation between the caliph and the sultan—a major part of the problem that Qutb identified. Some argue that the very position of sultan recognized an unofficial secularism by separating a more temporal leadership from its religious foundations.[17] It was the establishment of the sultan, Qutb would protest, that constitutes a sacrilege. More recently, imperialism, colonialism, and neo-colonialism aggravated this long-simmering problem.

The caliphate was officially abolished by the new secular government of Turkey in 1922 and 1924.[18] By this time, though, it was no longer a truly authentic office. Even so, as weak as the caliphate had become, it was a bad mistake, Qutb claimed, for Kemal Ataturk to eliminate it. Qutb considered the caliphate a soiled concept since it had allowed *shari'a* law to slip away. It had to be purified after centuries of contamination, but could still be revived to reestablish Islamic law and acknowledge God's dominion.

Qutb argued that the best replacement should come from the Arab Quraysh, the Prophet's descendants.[19] He maintained, however, that the Quraysh would have no status above ordinary Muslims, no authority for their blood relationship to the Prophet, because Islam does not recognize identities based on race, color, ethnicity, or nationality. Even if the progeny of the Prophet do offer the best candidates for the office, they still have to demonstrate their superior knowledge and piety. Their charisma, however, could be useful in legitimizing their rule.[20]

Qutb and many other Islamic thinkers have argued that reestablishing the caliphate is necessary to administer Islamic law. But he did not dwell on reconstituting the caliphate. His criteria of rule by *shari'a* law was paramount. The uniting of all Muslim countries under one caliphate seemed too utopian, too distant, and too large a task. On the other hand, establishing (or reestablishing) Islamic law, even within one country, or country by country, was more realistic.[21]

Shari'a Law

When Qutb and other committed writers discuss *hakimiyya*, God's dominion, as the main goal of the Islamic movement's *jihad*, they mean first and foremost the establishment of Islamic law. Derived from the *shari'a*, the Straight Path that is found in the Qur'an, this set of religious regulations is by far the most important element in the Islamic state and, indeed, the entire Islamic movement. Muslims are expected to submit completely to *shari'a*, to express a pure faith in God, and to acknowledge God's authority. Since Islam is a total way of life, all issues can be resolved through *shari'a*.

Qutb's emphasis always tilted to the moral side: that the ills of society could be laid at the feet of abolishing *shari'a*, adopting Western legal codes, and perhaps as important, adopting the legislative mechanisms to change laws through debates and votes. It was Qutb's strong conviction that restoring *shari'a* law would solve all the problems of *jahili* society.[22]

Shari'a law protects and defends the public. It guarantees security, livelihood, and social equilibrium.[23] According to Qutb, *shari'a* guarantees

- *Legal Justice* by applying and abiding by an impartial Islamic law where both sides have rights and duties.
- *Security* by meting out just punishment for violations, which allows the state to guarantee life (by the penalty for killing and the regulation of retaliation), honor (by the penalties for adultery, fornication, false accusation, perjury, and slander), and property (by the penalties for theft, violation of the home, spying, and subversion).
- *Material sustenance* by ensuring people's physical and spiritual well-being, employment, livelihood, and income; by protecting people against poverty, destitution, vagrancy, indebtedness, and by securing community liability, compensation, and mutual responsibility.
- *Social Equilibrium* by ensuring an adequate standard of living according to the principle "to each according to his efforts and his needs" [sic] and by including the poor in the circulation of wealth; regulating the private ownership of property; executing the state's eminent domain based on public interest;

taking precautionary measures that promote public welfare and prevent evil and corruption; prohibiting usury, monopolies, bribery, hoarding, and concessions; controlling public resources, public property, and utilities as trusts for its people ("nationalization"); prohibiting extravagance and dissipation, and condemning luxury, yet without prohibiting pleasures and enjoyments, and levying *zakat* as a tax on capital and assets.[24]

It practically amounts to an Islamic Bill of Rights! In order for these guarantees to be accepted willingly and not imposed by force, they address both material and spiritual matters. Each Muslim can expect an adequate standard of living and consumption so as to ensure social harmony, and each Muslim can expect justice and honor that exemplify God's way. Thus, there is both social security and spiritual safety.[25]

Once, I had a discussion about Islamism with a quite knowledgeable and cosmopolitan Islamic scholar, and I casually commented that I thought Islamists simply wanted to apply *shari'a* law. His response was much more serious: "Which *shari'a* law do you mean?" he asked. He meant not just which one of the four traditional schools of Sunni *fiqh*—Hanafi, Maliki, Shafi'i, or Hanbali,—or the Shi'ite Jafari school, but also, perhaps, a new school of *fiqh* based on different principles, possibly even liberal and progressive ones. He was also implying an eclecticism of many schools, the practical outcome of decades of legal and judicial practice. In other words, it is very easy to simply say "apply *shari'a* law;" but it is a different matter altogether to decide just *which shari'a* law to apply. Qutb warned that there cannot be a smorgasbord of laws, taking some from *shari'a* and others from man-made laws. Otherwise, he noted, there would be legal schizophrenia. No mixing or compromising is allowed. Nor did he advocate a medley of legal sources from within *shari'a*, either.

Egypt's legal system was once based on the *shari'a* of the liberal Hanafi school of *fiqh*.[26] In the 1840s, the government began to adopt French commercial law in order to facilitate trade with Europe. In 1854–55, it also adopted the Ottoman *tanzimat* reform codes, themselves embodying a strong European influence.[27] From 1879 to 1882, Qadri Pasha, Egypt's Justice Minister, codified existing *shari'a* law and produced the *Murshid al-Hayran* (Guide of the Confused),[28] but his work was interrupted by the 1882 'Urabi revolt and Britain's subsequent invasion and colonization. In 1875–76, Egypt established national Mixed Courts to put both Europeans and Egyptians on trial, thereby adopting even more European law, although later in 1883, it separated out National courts just for Egyptians. *Shari'a* courts existed, but their mandate shrank gradually until they operated only in the domain of personal status law—marriage, divorce, and inheritance, a very small segment of the much larger *shari'a* law that also covers criminal, commercial, civil, international, and contract law. Throughout the 19th century, French law was increasingly used, with the exception of property laws that were adopted from the British. Also, many national laws were passed by the Egyptian parliament, going back as far as the first Assembly of Deputies under Khedive (Viceroy) Isma'il in 1866.

When the caliphate was abolished in 1924, was Egyptian law pure Hanafi law? At the time, how much of Egypt's legal code was derived from European law and how much was originally *shari'a*? Just where is it that Islamists wish to go back to?

The Montreux Treaty of 1937 abolished the Mixed Courts, but implementation was slow. From 1936 to 1948, 'Abd al-Raziq al-Sanhuri (1895–1971), a lawyer trained in the modernist tradition of Muhammad 'Abduh, was authorized to revise the Egyptian civil code. He stated he wanted to make Egypt's laws more Islamic, yet have the laws apply to all Egyptians—Muslims, Christians, and Jews—and updated. Yet despite his sincere intentions, much depended on al-Sanhuri's own personal interpretations, and his revision more firmly relegated *shari'a* to just the domain of personal status law, effectively secularizing the legal system. When al-Sanhuri's efforts were finally concluded, he was both castigated and commended by the religious establishment. Not surprisingly, the debate turned political, and not all of al-Sanhuri's changes were adopted.

Later, there were attempts to improve al-Sanhuri's monumental opus, often evaluating European-derived laws simply by whether they disagreed with *shari'a*. If they did not, they were kept, although this did not necessarily mean they were genuine Islamic statutes. In addition to these efforts, there were customary tribal laws ('urf) to contend with, as well as codifications from other Muslim countries, Arab and non-Arab. Needless to say, Egypt's legal system can be messy and very confusing. Nor is Egypt alone in this situation; other Muslim countries also suffer from a hodge-podge of laws based on *shari'a*, British case law, French Napoleonic Code, customary law, and expediency.

Qutb never examined this disorder in detail. Nor did he specifically answer the question: "Which *shari'a*?" Rather, he indicated his strong support for *shari'a* in general.[29] He pointed out that *shari'a* is not the rigid code of law that detractors and critics make it out to be. It is firm and stable, but not unyielding. *Shari'a* can be applied to all aspects of life because it is based on a permanent human nature. This nature makes men and women social beings, and *shari'a* law regulates their relationships with each other as well as with God. God intends that humanity receive continuous guidance and care, and *shari'a* is the manifestation of that concern.

In Islam, *shari'a* is generally adaptable through the process of interpretation, or *ijtihad*. But Qutb was distrustful of *ijtihad*, fearing that it could further introduce falsehoods and disbelief, which had afflicted Islam ever since the rise of the Umayyads. He did concede that within certain boundaries defined by divine law, people could interpret *shari'a* to meet their contemporary needs. Yet at the same time, Qutb also asserted that the Qur'an is the only indisputably reliable source of truth,[30] and he failed to acknowledge that this truth is necessarily a *mediated* or conditional truth, which is why there are a number of different legal schools, ranging from liberal to conservative. On the one hand, Qutb claimed that the

Qur'an is an enduring reality that cannot be voted out or ruled against and that it cannot be proven scientifically or judged right or wrong. It is the "decisive truth for each generation of Muslims." But he also denied that the Holy Book is static and fixed since, as a *mediated* truth, it is adjusted and applied to new and novel circumstances. It is this concept of interpretation that allows the Qur'an, along with other Islamic documents such as the Sunna, to be used in a flexible, adaptive manner. In a critique of the Pakistani thinker Muhammad Iqbal,[31] Qutb explicitly rejected any sort of "dialectical" thinking as a distortion of Islam. Yet his own deliberation about *ijtihad* might well be described in just this way.[32]

In discussing *ijtihad*, Qutb leaned more in the direction of relying just on the Qur'an, which existed at the time of the Prophet and his followers, rather than on the Sunna, which was compiled later, making the Qur'an practically his sole source of legal authority.[33] Thus Qutb appears (surprisingly) more in line with the liberal approach of Hanafi *fiqh* rather than the micro-management style of the conservative Hanbali school, which heavily relies on *hadith* from the Sunna to fill in the empty spaces left open by the Qur'an.[34] For Qutb, those empty spaces left room for *ijtihad*.

Qutb jettisoned many of the standard rules and methods for formulating new interpretations from old material that, in addition to the Qur'an and Sunna, rely on consensus (*ijma'*), analogy (*qiyas*), reasoning (*ra'y*), tradition (*taqlid*), and public interest or utility (*maslaha*). Instead, he arrived at explanations that were both contradictory and personally politicized.[35] Qutb did this to create a more dynamic and pragmatic *fiqh*; it also demonstrated his disdain for the traditional, hide-bound *'ulama*, whom he accused of being responsible for Islam's stagnation. Qutb was much more populist in his interpretation and did not agree that such exegesis was the sole province of these religious scholars.

If it is the hallmark of modernist Islam to call for the re-opening of the doors of *ijtihad*, then, paradoxically, Qutb should be considered a modernist thinker.[36] Qutb did, indeed, call for new interpretations without regard to the previous 1,400 years of traditional understanding and explanation. While many modernists— appearing more as updated traditionalists, but otherwise not deviating greatly from traditional understandings—were slow to change Islam's adaptation to current situations, Qutb charged full-speed ahead, advocating changes that made *shari'a* and *fiqh* much more dynamic.

Yet what really made Qutb different from many of his contemporaries and modernists was his vigorous rejection of any compromise with non-Islamic regulations. Instead, he was in this regard an arch-traditionalist, returning to the *salaf* and the very basic principles of *shari'a* and Islam, condemning and discarding the intervening centuries when *shari'a* had become compromised, diluted, and distorted by foreign accretions and contamination, and demanding an original, unadulterated *fiqh* based on a pure *shari'a* as it was stated in the Qur'an and understood by the first generation. In this way, he felt he was able to ensure purity, authenticity, and validity.[37]

He revisited the days of the *salaf* for answers to contemporary questions not because he sought a return to yesteryear, or a reliance on a backward and rigid understanding of Islam, but because it was only the very basics, embodied in the *shari'a*, and not in any of its subsequent interpretations, that needed to be recalled, reasserted, and emphasized. And if Qutb strongly rejected the centuries-long distortions from within the Muslim community, he was even more adamant about disallowing foreign laws and European influence. Shedding all this accumulated buildup requires diligence and enthusiasm from the vanguard. The vanguard's members, already zealous about conducting a *jihad* to overthrow *jahili* society and establish God's dominion, are responsible for creating a genuine *fiqh* from the original *shari'a*.[38] In this way, Qutb felt assured that the changes in the application of *shari'a* necessary to sustain a true Islamic state could indeed come about.

The most basic requirement, in Qutb's mind, for a new approach to interpreting *shari'a*—he refrained from calling it a new school of *fiqh*—was to make it very pragmatic. Yet in order for this to happen, *shari'a* has to rule the land, and the people have to recognize that there is no god but God and that the Qur'an offers all the necessary guidelines and moral principles necessary for social life. This pragmatism also requires an internal conviction among believers that the answers provided by the Qur'an can, indeed, be applied to them, their community, and their world, and will result in more freedom, equality, and justice.[39]

Without an Islamic state, the development of a new, pragmatic *fiqh* remains many years in the future. There is no benefit, Qutb concluded, in discussing a new approach in a vacuum since it would only distract from the movement and from the worship of God.

> Only when such a society comes into being, faces various practical problems, and needs a system of law, then Islam [can] initiate the constitution of law and injunctions, rules and regulations. It addresses only those people who in principle have already submitted themselves to its authority and have repudiated all other rules and regulations.
>
> Later when an autonomous state came into existence in Medina, general laws were revealed and that system came into existence which satisfies the needs of a Muslim community and the power of the state was behind its enforcement.
>
> Thus when such a society actually comes into being and the basic teachings of Islam are its guide, it will proceed to formulate laws and regulations for the existing practical needs according to the general teachings of Islam.[40]

First of all, there is a key distinction between *shari'a* and *fiqh*: *shari'a* is divine; *fiqh* is not. *Shari'a* is derived from the Qur'an and Sunna, and is the realization of God's will. It is the Straight Path of Islam, consisting of correct, divinely ordained action and laws as well as sacred beliefs, morals, and epistemology. *Fiqh* is human, and is more detailed than *shari'a*. While it is based on and derived from *shari'a*, it is supplemented by nondivine methodological resources (consensus, analogy, reasoning, tradition, and utility) and the accumulation of case law. It has been developed by individual, eponymic scholars who are widely accepted because of their intellectual acumen and personal beliefs. The results are the four schools of fiqh named earlier—Hanafi, Maliki, Shafi'i, and Hanbali—or five, if the Jafari school in Shi'ite Islam is included.[41]

Qutb deliberately stressed the establishment of *shari'a* as the basis of the Islamic government's legal code. Its human distillation into particular schools, on the other hand, occurred historically, but can also be nullified and rebuilt. *Shari'a* itself is sacrosanct and cannot depend on scholarly deductions or inferences that are, by definition, subjective. But the scholars who established the four standard schools of law are not infallible.[42] For his part, Qutb did not hesitate to offer his own interpretations that adapted *shari'a* to the present times.

Once Qutb separated provisional *fiqh* from the permanent and more general *shari'a*, he was able to focus on those changes that were necessary in order to adjust Islamic law to the contemporary world. He was also able to answer the secularists who constantly complained that an Islamic state would be inflexible, permanent, and atavistic and would merely repeat answers to problems that were both centuries old. In fact, Qutb argued, these secularists were actually referring to the permanence of divine *shari'a*, not its temporal interpretation, the schools of *fiqh*. These schools, he argued, are instead analytical: derived through meticulous scholarship and applied to many contemporary problems. Combined with their founders' own personal beliefs and their existing social environments, these schools find a wide range of acceptance along a full spectrum of political positions that vary from liberal (Hanafi) to conservative (Hanbali), with Shafi'i and Maliki in between, and with each carving out a territorial dominance. Hanafi dominates Turkey, Egypt, and South and Central Asia; Maliki governs North and West Africa and the Arab Gulf; Shafi'i rules South and Southeast Asia and the Aden Gulf, and Hanbali (including its offshoot, Wahhabi) reigns over the Arabian peninsula. The fifth school, Jafari, is followed by Shi'ites in Iran and Lebanon.

Qutb was reluctant to call for a new school of *fiqh* because he saw the profusion of rival schools, the mixture of legal systems, and the conflict of legal opinions as detrimental to the unity of Islam and the Islamic state. Debates over which school or schools to apply in which circumstances resulted in a hodge-podge that detracts from the supremacy of God. The schools are in danger of being seen as replacements for, not interpretations of, *shari'a*, and therefore becoming part of *jahiliyya*.

Qutb came to realize that these traditional schools of *fiqh* were obedient not so much to God as to blind traditionalism. Faith had become blind faith, not active and pragmatic faith. *Shari'a* and its interpretations had turned stilted and stagnate. Lawyers, judges, and *'ulama* often proved to be unbelievers, apostates, heretics, and even polytheists, even though all the while, they called themselves

Muslim. Worshipping traditionalism has to be replaced by returning to the true worshipping of God. Opening the door to *ijtihad* helps, but what is more necessary is to rid Islamic law of its unnecessary influences and centuries-long accretions. Since these schools had become so divisive, Qutb maintained, they ought to be abolished altogether. Instead, true Muslims need to return to one, immutable divine law. Basing new interpretation on the fundamentals of Islam, as seen in the days of the Prophet and his followers, is the best formula for reviving *fiqh*. It is this necessary revitalization that will lead the way in overthrowing disbelief.[43]

And yet, although Qutb rejected the different schools of *fiqh* for confusing and cluttering people's understanding of Islamic law, he still went on to propose just that: establishing yet another school of law. (Similarly, he denounced the various schools of *kalam*[44] for relying too heavily on non-Islamic beliefs, such as those from Greek philosophy, but then went on to fashion his own concept of Islamic thinking, albeit one that he claimed referred back to the first generation of Muslims.) Qutb believed that this new legal school would combine and even supersede the standard four in Sunni Islam.

In his own *ijtihad*, he first considered the well-used concepts of "*'ibadat*" (permanent ritual duties) and "*mu'amalat*" (transitory social relations and convictions). These two standards are conventional exegetical devices for capturing the notion of stability and change and for adapting to transformations in the contemporary world by incorporating these changes into *fiqh*. These concepts were explored by early Islamic thinkers and by Qutb's predecessors—al-Afghani, 'Abduh, Rida, and al-Banna—to distinguish what human actions and beliefs are permanent and fixed and which are transitory and subject to alteration.[45] *'Ibadat* (sing., *'ibada*) include the absolutely essential elements of Islam, such as ritual practices, fixed religious observances, and permanent acts of worship, such as the five pillars that Muslims are obligated to perform. *Mu'amalat* (sing., *mu'amala*) are alterable conceptualizations subject to personal interpretation and understandings, including ephemeral social relations, contingent transactions, and changeable religious concepts, as found in criminal, family, inheritance, and commercial regulations.

Qutb's use of these methods, however, proved fairly conservative, and he frequently argued against recognizing any distinction between these two whatsoever. He felt that all acts and beliefs mean the worship of God and the acknowledgment of His dominion. Every act a Muslim performs must be an act of worship to God. Every *mu'amala* becomes an *'ibada*, every *'ibada* requires a *mu'amala*, and every act of worship requires faith and conviction. Therefore, the two must be united. Were they separated, he wrote, they would be unIslamic. Empty ritual gestures—*'ibadat* without *mu'amalat*—are *not* acts of worship, but are acts of blasphemy or *jahiliyya*. Turning every *mu'amala* into an *'ibada* means bringing every human act and relationships under *shari'a* law. He further argued that over the centuries, this very distinction between *'ibadat* and *mu'amalat* had led to secularism and the separation of practice and faith. This had resulted in many so-called modern Muslim communities that were not really Islamic at all.

Qutb made much of the similarity between 'ibadat, ritual worship, and 'ubudiyya, the worship, obedience, and submission to God. (Both are derived linguisti-
cally from the same trilateral Arabic root ayn-b-d.) The second term, 'ubudiyya,
is the broader of the two, incorporating most, if not all, human activity. Qutb
reasoned that since all rituals, 'ibadat, are essentially acts of worship, 'ubudiyya,
the first can be subsumed by the second. For to otherwise distinguish 'ibadat
from 'ubudiyya is to suggest that rituals are just shallow, and not reflective, acts of
worship. He then expanded the term 'ubudiyya to such an extent that it came to
include all acts of worship, human relations, and religious beliefs. Qutb concluded
that 'ubudiyya incorporates 'ibadat which then requires mu'amalat in order to work
correctly. None of these can change without falling into the pit of jahiliyya.

For Qutb, the larger notion of worship and submission, of 'ubudiyya, came
to combine both faith and practice, mu'amalat and 'ibadat. Obeying Islamic law
and following Islamic belief in God's supreme authority, both absolutely necessary in Islam, actually make this distinction insignificant. Both become 'ubudiyya.
Secularism renders these separate; the Islamic movement strives to unite them
together again.

Qutb's examination of the salaf led him to conclude that, in the beginning,
'ibadat was, indeed, 'ubudiyya—the two were synonyms, notwithstanding the
larger meaning of the second relative to the first. At the time, acts of worship
also included human relations, convictions, and social organization, which could
change, of course, but only within the prescribed guidelines revealed by God. This
did not thwart or reverse change, but it guided and eased these transformations.
Certain changes were simply off limits, but others were valued and encouraged.

Qutb ultimately concluded that mu'amalat were really as permanent as 'ibadat. Far from being transitory, the social and political relationships that make up
an Islamic society and state are infused with enduring Islamic principles and are
therefore immutable. Yet Qutb's position was uneasily one-sided and rigid, and he
warily recognized that people could more easily be persuaded to change by modi-
fying their faith than by altering their ritual practice.

In the end, Qutb did not find the distinction between the permanent and the
transitory very helpful for changing Islamic law. Instead, he sought a new understanding of shari'a by resorting to the original principles of the Qur'an, and uti-
lizing them to establish the new Islamic state. It would be the struggle of state
formation that would generate Qutb's new interpretation. Instead of calling it
"ijtihad" (so as to avoid controversy), he called it simply "dynamic law" (fiqh haraki),
which would emerge out from jihad and would be based not on theory but on practical experiences. Here he explicitly sought to counter the criticism that shari'a is
inflexible and stagnant by arguing that through "dynamic law," change and vitality can be incorporated into God's law and that it can be adapted to new circumstances. Fiqh has to be dynamic in the sense of changing through the dialectics
of struggle to create the Islamic state and system. This continuous interpretation
would guide true Muslims and assist them in creating a new Islamic society.

Qutb maintained that there are two stages to dynamic law. First, a temporary stage that grows out of the sea of *jahiliyya* that surrounds the struggle, one that can quickly adjust activists to new needs and demands. Then, a second stage can commence as the Islamic state is built. This new approach is based on two principles. The first relies on public interest or utility (*al-masalih al-mursala*) and the second is called "blocking of the means" (*sadd al-dhari'a*). The first can lead directly to an unbridled capitalism as its European cousin, utilitarianism, had once done before in the West. Therefore, it is necessary to couple the first with the second, the blocking of the means that can lead to bad ends.[46]

The government in Islam is authorized to promote good and forbid evil. Obviously, Qutb thought the second function was more important than the first. Yet the notion of "blocking" goes even further. It requires eliminating anything that might lead to forbidden outcomes. One example that Qutb provided in *Social Justice* is the case of a businessman cutting his prices—itself not an illegal act—in order to undercut and bankrupt his competition. The injury of insolvency is wrong, and the means to achieve it—price-cutting—is therefore wrong as well. Thus, price cuts, under certain circumstances, ought to be blocked. A second example is forbidding monopolies, which of themselves are not wrong. But the *effect* of monopolies *is* wrong, so they must be forbidden, even though this is not stated specifically in the Qur'an or Sunna.

Combining public utility with the principle of enjoining the good and prohibiting the evil curbs the excesses of utilitarianism by blocking their undesirable effects. This emphasizes not the motives of people—these remain private intentions, hidden and unknowable but to God and rewarded or punished in the next world—but instead, and more important, the observable social consequences of their actions. In this way, the law seeks to secure the common welfare of the community.[47]

This "dynamic law" could prove highly adaptable to current situations and conditions and, all the while, avoid atavism and stagnation. A sincere and dynamic law would reject the shallow traditionalism that developed over the centuries after the rise of the Umayyad dynasty and return instead to the very origins of Islam. Basing a new interpretation on one or more of the existing schools would merely add insult to injury, compounding accumulated problems without going to the root of the dilemma. Qutb aimed to remove this influence, these accretions, and this empty traditionalism, and instead revitalize Islam with what stood triumphant at the gates of Mecca when the Prophet Muhammad returned from Medina.

Qutb often compared his "dynamic law" and, more generally, the *shari'a*, with Western law, which he condemned as blasphemy. Indeed, he wrote that there was a definite need to create a new, more dynamic *fiqh* in order to counter *jahiliyya*, which was making steady inroads into Muslim society. He frequently commented on international law and legislation, looking down on Western systems with contempt and looking up at Islamic systems with admiration.

From the time of his return from the United States to his last years in prison, Qutb increasingly refused any moderation in his interpretation, rejecting the decadence and depravity of *jahiliyya*, and embracing the unique freedom and equality of Islam and *shari'a*. Qutb realized early on that the door of *ijtihad* required re-opening. But it was the specific results of this renewed interpretation that concerned him, not the mere exercise itself. Clearly, he agreed that Islam had stagnated from the lack of adaptation, but he also recognized that it had stagnated for the very reason that it had adopted non-Islamic influences. *Shari'a* needed, therefore, to return to its original, pristine character, not simply re-awakened as if nothing had happened to it over the centuries.

> God's religion is not a maze nor is its way of life a fluid thing, as the second part of the declaration of faith—"Muhammad is the messenger of God"—clearly limits it.[48] It is bounded by those principles which have come from the Messenger of God. If there is a clear text available from the Qur'an or from him [Muhammad], then that will be decisive and there will be no room for *ijtihad*. If no such clear judgment is available, then the time comes for *ijtihad*—and that according to well-defined principles which are consistent with God's religion and not merely following opinions or desires.
>
> The principles of *ijtihad* and deduction are well known, and there is no vagueness or looseness in them. No one is allowed to devise a law and say that it is according to the *Shari'a* of God unless it is declared that God is the legislator, and that the source of authority is God Himself and not some nation or party or individual, and a sincere attempt is made to find out the will of God through reference to His Book and the Sunna of His Messenger. But this right cannot be delegated to a person or persons who want to establish authority by taking the name of God, as was the case in Europe under the guise of "the Church." There is no "church" in Islam; no one can speak in the name of God except His Messenger. There are clear injunctions which define the limits of the divine law, the *shari'a*.[49]

Law-Breaking and Punishment

Islam uses two methods to ensure compliance to government authority: persuasion and coercion. The first is a matter of faith and spirituality, of the sentiment in people's hearts. The second uses the law and the promise of Judgment Day to ensure the maintenance of a secure community in accordance with God's will. Qutb's repeated stress on faith indicates his greater concern for the first, since in his mind, obedience comes from the heart instead of the lash. People obey the law administered by their rulers because it is divine, and therefore true. Their faith in God and His dominion convinces them of the suitability of abiding by *shari'a* law. After all, the law's real objective is to elevate humanity to the standard that God has set for it.

Even so, Qutb regularly wrote about Islamic punishments since they involve the protection and welfare of the Islamic community and the prohibition of illicit and immoral acts—most of which he felt had been imported from the West. Because these penalties—especially the *hudud* punishments, which involve bodily injury—are so constantly maligned by non-Muslims and the West, and particularly because they come directly from the Qur'an, Qutb strongly defended them. His efforts to explain how deeply embedded social justice can be in *shari'a* law turned into an apologetic justification. The more fiercely they were assailed, the stronger was Qutb's defense.

Most Westerners condemn these punishments—cutting off of hands, stoning, whip lashing—even though most punishment and criminal systems essentially reflect the basic values and priorities of particular societies. These values are then written into their penal laws. No society, of course, condones murder and rape, treason and dishonesty. American society, for example, considers treason against the nation a capital crime, notwithstanding the absence of a corpse or an actual murder.

Islamic punishments demonstrably show the emphasis Islam places on *family* (disrupted by improper sexualities), *property and security* (disrupted by theft in commercial communities), *religious obligations* (disrupted by blurred thinking arising from alcohol and drug consumption), and *honesty* (disrupted if people are falsely accused of crimes). These four institutions are cornerstones of Islamic society, and so its system of criminal justice reflects these values. Defending and protecting the interests of the community (more often paramount over the interests or even freedom of its individual members), caring for the welfare and material well-being of its poorer and weaker members, and placing restrictions on the most powerful and wealthy members—all point to a social balance, harmony, and moderation that Qutb repeatedly emphasized. He also pointed out that *shari'a* procedural law is based on the testimony of honest witnesses, with their dishonesty itself a crime to be dealt with. And even though the Qur'an stipulates strict *hudud* penalties, these punishments are not rigid, for the Qur'an also recognizes the need for regret, repentance, and leniency.[50]

After all, punishments are established for those not convinced to obey God's law following their inner submission and faith. However horrible the punishments might be, they intend to correct misbehavior *before* Judgment Day, when the final punishment of eternal hell would be even more horrific. All Muslims should follow God's law and acknowledge His dominion because of their inner devotion. Those who do not follow faithfully have the law and its justice system to redirect them back onto the right path. In other words, social life depends, by and large, on the human conscience, which has been trained to comply. Those who don't get the message the first time find they are notified again and again until they get it right, except for the last time, when it is up to God.

Shura

A major principle of Islamic government is *shura,* or consultation between the ruler and the ruled. *Shura* involves guidance counseling and consensus building, and it is effective because it is flexible and accommodating. Its purpose is to ensure that the ruler continues to seek guidance from the Qur'an and Sunna and that he operates within the restrictions laid down by these sources. At the time of the Prophet, *shura* was used at moments of crisis, similar to war councils. It is at just those times that charismatic leadership can prevail independently, but the idea of *shura* is to arrive at a consensus. It is then up to the leader to implement the decision. Citing the Qur'an and Sunna, Qutb claimed the *shura* council members are temporary; and their advice, therefore, is intermittent. Thereafter, the ruler is on his own without need for furthering consultation.[51]

The delegates of the *shura* council are to be selected by neighborhoods and small communities. The exact mechanism for selecting them still remained to be worked out, although Qutb did point out that unlike the very formal and anonymous relations in European parliamentary democracy, *shura* should begin at a very local level. Even so, Qutb argued that hypotheticals are useless; the actual selection method would be devised in a practical fashion once the Islamic state was established. He did emphasize the need to consider the moral caliber of candidates. In the past, these delegates were often the *'ulama* scholars of the community. But Qutb rejected the idea that *shura* could be performed only by those from al-Azhar University and other schools who staffed the government offices and mosques. He branded these modernists as collaborators for preaching that Islam should conform with Europe.

Some Muslim thinkers claim that *shura* is roughly analogous to representative government; a few, in fact, actually assert that this institution appeared long before the notion of democratic parliamentarianism ever emerged in the West, thus making Islam superior. Qutb did not deny that the Islamic state should include *shura,* but he intensely disliked any comparison to Western governments. He detested apologizing for a different system of government (although he did so himself from time to time) because it emphasizes the inferiority of one system. Qutb insisted that *shura* does not have a legislative function but is merely a means of advice and consent, an intermediary between the state and the people.[52]

Despite some superficial similarities, consultation is different, Qutb maintained, from European parliamentary democracy—with its political parties, partisan squabbles, disunity, and the possibility of voting out God's law—and he warned against imitating Europe, where religion and government are separate. Without faith in God and acknowledgment of His dominion, Qutb warned, *shura* could turn into European parliamentarianism, which is merely a means of protecting wealthy interests. True *shura*, on the other hand, always acts under the auspices of God's supreme authority and, therefore, embodies a social justice that stresses social equality.

Political Culture and Values

Equality

Two of the lofty, liberal, and divinely inspired values that Qutb stressed most often in his writings were the principles of equality and justice. Although he did not always say why he gave these two values such emphasis, I believe that it was in part a result of the racial inequality Qutb had seen in America. Qutb considered equality and justice to be the cornerstones of any Islamic society.[53] We have seen in Chapter 4 that social justice was the key theme of Qutb's major volume, *Social Justice in Islam*. Here, we examine Qutb's view of equality.

Qutb felt that all humanity is equal before God. Since God's unity only emphasizes faith and belief rather than social or physical traits, then all people are equal in the Islamic state. He rejected unequal relationships: master and slave, bourgeoisie and proletariat, landlord and peasant. He also criticized identities based on wealth, color, race, nationality, class, tribe, or lineage. What unites humanity and makes all its members equal, he concluded, is their intense devotion to and worship of God, and the acknowledgment of God's dominion and laws. When these have the highest of priorities, other identities make no difference.[54]

Societies that are torn by inequalities and divisions—Europe and the United States being prominent examples—are *jahiliyya* societies. Qutb went all the way back to the Crusades to explain how Europe's separation of religion and social life resulted in Godlessness and materialism, which in turn produced social inequality, discrimination, and injustice. These characteristics were essentially compounded by the rise of capitalism. But these superficial social identities ought not to distinguish one believer from the next since all people originate from the same source and since all people ought to submit to God. Praying and bowing down before the *qibla*, or prayer niche, demonstrates Islam's inherent equality.[55]

Islamic society also has secondary values—love, kindness, morality, charity—at its core, but Qutb placed less emphasis on these.[56]

Freedom

Qutb believed that obedience to and the worship of God create for humanity a true freedom from the servitude and subjugation to others. This liberty defines proper human civilization. It is only when God's dominion is actually operational that such a civilization can emerge, and with it, full autonomy and dignity for all its members. Those who remain in *jahili* society, however, and who remain enslaved in their obedience to earthly authority instead of God lack this freedom.[57]

Jihad becomes necessary to clear the obstacles that deny humanity the freedom it needs to choose to submit to God's dominion. Only when people are free to decide can the Islamic movement be successful, and Qutb sincerely believed that so liberated, people would naturally choose Islam.[58]

Yet despite the freedom that Qutb considered the uncontestable prerogative of each individual, he nevertheless also argued that society often trumps the rights of the individual, and that society may curtail individual freedoms if it so warrants. Men and women are susceptible to getting carried away by their instincts, desires, and pleasures to the point of damaging themselves and others. In these cases, people must be protected from unqualified personal freedom.[59]

Any emphasis on individual freedom of belief and thought contrasts with a notion of God's overwhelming authority. After he wrote *Social Justice*, Qutb's slide deeper and deeper into conservatism was such that humanity's own freedom gradually became eclipsed in his mind by God's overpowering will. Nevertheless, this contradiction can be resolved by the notion that God provides humanity with the correct path and direction, but people still remain free to choose either good or evil. Since Islam itself is rational and the logical outcome of God's message, then it is only natural that people choose Islam. Yet Qutb could not deny people the freedom to choose evil, else the idea of Judgment Day would fall apart.[60]

Social Order

In addition to equality, social justice, and freedom, Qutb also emphasized the value of social order or stability. He did not intend that societies should be stagnant and never change, nor did he mean that society ought to jettison all restraints. Instead, social transformation is to be constrained and guided by the Qur'an and God's laws. Qutb's view of change and stability was unlike that of most modern thinkers, who valorize social progress over steadfastness. Qutb attempted to balance the opposing forces of change and stability by maintaining the coherence of the Islamic community in the face of the shocks that challenge its existence. While retaining the core beliefs and values dictated by God's dominion, there is room for a reasonable, though conservative, growth. Qutb also argued that since modernity was simply a disguise for Western Christianity, he rejected it and proposed to replace it with a universal Islam. Islam, he asserted, seeks a stable authenticity that embraces long-term local values and customs over those insidiously imported from Europe.

Morality

Once an Islamic civilization is established, the morals of that community are of the highest caliber, rising above the level of animals that are controlled by their bodily needs, the very characteristic of *jahiliyya* society. These morals are not transient or relative; they are fixed and unchanged by their environment. People's moral universe is derived from the Qur'an and God's dominion.

> If a society is based on "human values" and "human morals" and if these remain dominant in it, then that society will be civilized. Human values and human morals are not something mysterious and undefinable, nor are they "progressive" and changeable, having no roots and stability... They are the values and the morals which develop those characteristics in a human being which distinguish him from the animals and which emphasize those aspects of his personality which raise him above the animals....
>
> According to this view, moral standards are not determined by the environment and changing conditions; rather, they are fixed criteria above and beyond the differences in environments. One cannot say that some moral values are "agricultural" and others are "industrial," some are "capitalistic" and some others "socialistic," some are "bourgeois" and others "proletarian." Here, the standards of morality are independent of the environment, the economic status, and the stage of development of a society; these are nothing but superficial variations. Beyond all these, we arrive at human values and morals and at "animalistic" values and morals, this being the correct separation, or, in Islamic terminology, "Islamic" values and morals and "*jahili*" values and morals.[61]

Qutb's harsh and strict moralism—a stern discipline not unlike the Wahhabi restrictions of Saudi Arabia—was aimed at the younger generation, whose promiscuous and permissive conduct was promoted, Qutb claimed, by the mass media. He continued to exhort Egyptian youth against giving in to the dark forces and the sway of the West and its *jahiliyya* decadence and depravity. Qutb called for the restoration of the Islamic *umma* and a decontamination of people's understanding of Islamic morality, which had been infected by foreign influence.[62]

Qutb's moral conservatism was more than just the product of his visit to America in 1948. It may have begun appearing as early as 1939, following his mother's death. It was also inherent in Qutb's background in the rural Sa'id and his upbringing in a protected environment. Throughout the 1930s, Qutb's experiences in Cairo were upbeat and liberal, and it was only in the dark days of the 1940s, with the war, martial law, and his own turn toward Islam, that he recalled his more wholesome days in Upper Egypt.[63]

In sum

At times, Qutb seemed more interested in the spirit of Islam that holds the government together in its unity than in its actual structure. He appeared more interested in pan-Islamic sentiment than in the formal law itself. He emphasized faith and orthodoxy more than practice and orthopraxy. He insisted, time after time, on God as the sole sovereign. He was against a multi-party system for its lack of harmony and cooperation. He minimized the role of interpretation, since he felt that all schools of *fiqh*, present, past, or future, are divisive. Instead, they ought to be combined and consolidated into one school of *fiqh* and one brand of *shari'a*.

Qutb believed that establishing an Islamic state would solve all the problems caused by the *jahiliyya* of present-day Muslim society. Although he argued against apologetic perspectives in his writings, he often fell into this trap by the sheer necessity of trying to convince those who admire Western systems to reexamine Islam, and the state and society that could be established in its name. The Egyptian nation, of course, was reconstructed after the British invasion of 1882 on the basis of European experience, not its own. Therefore, Qutb felt constantly motivated to do battle against Europe and its political system, ever vigilant that this system from the north was the cause of Egypt's secularism and distance from God. Overthrowing *jahiliyya* and establishing *hakimiyya* is the goal of *jihad*. Therefore, the Islamic movement was to first establish such a state and then to resurrect Islamic law and revive the caliphate. Qutb deeply believed that the troubles and difficulties afflicting Egypt and the larger Muslim world could be resolved once that government, its legal systems, and political authority was restored.

Islamic History

As long as Muslims sincerely follow Islam and obey its principles, Qutb asserted, there will be no *jahiliyya*, no social, political, economic, or moral dissipation, and their obedience to God and His law will be rewarded in this life and the next. As long as the Islamic ruler acknowledges God's dominion and strives to administer *shari'a* law and no other, then Muslims can expect social justice and harmony to prevail. When rulers and subjects deviate from *shari'a*, tyranny and social injustice appear, and the Islamic community declines in morals, respectability, and honor.

What exactly constitutes this Straight Path can be learned from the first generation of Muslims led by the Prophet Muhammad. Studying how they understood the Qur'an and how they acted can give contemporary Muslims a more complete grasp of Islam. For Qutb, the Qur'an remained the most reliable source of historical information and how that information can be understood. The Torah and the Gospels are also historical documents, he maintained, but because Judaism and Christianity became distorted, their holy books are no longer trustworthy.[1] The only reliable source, then, for the history of God and His relationship to humanity is the Qur'an.

> It is absolutely necessary to read the Qur'an within the framework of the actual circumstances of the primitive community, for the Qur'an adheres to that reality in a precise way, and that is where its inimitable character resides: both very concrete and universally true.[2]

The story of how Islam rose and how it declined contains lessons that good Muslims should study and benefit from, so as to overcome the current crisis and renew their faith and the convictions of their community. And even though Muslims deviated from true Islam, the spirit of Islam, however weakened, was never completely extinguished. Even in its most frail condition, it continued for more than a thousand years to oppose and fight deviation, and to suffer and resist attacks. The flame never died, although it sputtered. And at other moments, it flared up brilliantly, only to fade once more. The lessons for again reaching the Straight Path can be found in the pages of its history.[3]

Qutb's historical method is noteworthy. Take, for example, his discussion of the *hijra*, or migration from Mecca to Medina in 622. For Qutb, the *hijra* is an obligation for all believers, in order to escape from the sedition (*fitna*) that appears from outside their faith. He said that it was for a specific situation that the *hijra* was prescribed, and for a particular group of believers. Yet now the obligation holds true at any time and at any place, and for all believers as soon as they are threatened with "*fitna* in their religion" by means of their wealth, kinship ties, friendships, or weakness. Like the Prophet Muhammad and his followers, every believer is required to migrate to "a homeland (*dar*) of Islam" as soon as one exists somewhere, where the faith is safe, the message is proclaimed, the rituals are practiced, and life is regulated by the laws of God. Qutb conceded that the elderly, women, and young children are exempt from *hijra*, and there are those who are physically constrained to stay behind, however sincere they remain in their beliefs. They can even deny their faith and feign idolatry when confronted by force, but this "dissimulation" (*taqiyya*), Qutb wrote, is only legitimate in the absence of an Islamic state.[4] The lesson for today is that, steeped in *jahiliyya*, true Muslims must move away from such unbelief and segregate themselves until they are able to confront the larger community of unbelievers and bring them over to their side.

Thus Qutb's primary method was to take the events of the Qur'an and Sunna and apply their lessons to the present. *Ijtihad* would then suggest that a minority of true believers—as Qutb saw himself and very few others after mid-century—should follow a similar approach, since the circumstances so closely resemble those at the time of the first *hijra*. Thus, the truths that are found in the Qur'an are indeed true universally. But they become interpreted and adapted more specifically according to current, concrete circumstances. In this way, the Qur'an becomes the critical index that measures the righteousness or the decadence of Muslims. Even things not mentioned explicitly in the Qur'an or the Sunna can be measured as to whether, in the abstract, they conform to Islamic principles.

The historiography displayed in the Qur'an is not the same method used in the modern world, although the purposes of both are similar. History is not a neutral narrative—not in Islam, nor anywhere else. Until quite recently, it has tended to extol the virtues of modernity, explicitly or otherwise, and demonstrate its rationality and inevitability.[5] Correspondingly, Qutb explained many historical events by their prefiguration of Islam, by their prediction in the Qur'an itself, their conformity with the Qur'an, or else simply their attesting to the fundamental superiority of Islam.

Inasmuch as academic historians today apply the past to the present, so, too, do Islamic historians draw lessons from the Qur'an for their contemporary guidance. But Islamic history does not excavate an exact scientific certainty out of older times, but instead, discovers moral implications in both domains of orthodoxy and orthopraxy.[6] Qutb ominously warned against using Western science to evaluate the historical accuracy of the Qur'an, much like 19th-century evangelical Protestants opposed European biblical criticism for its rational explanation and, hence, its elimination, of biblical miracles.[7] The truth of the Qur'an is not a factual or objective truth, Qutb maintained, but rather, a moral, prophetic, and social one. The Qur'an contains religious truths, and it is the only dependable source for them. The Islamic method takes these principles from the early Muslim community and then applies them to the complexities of the 20th century.

If history does contain lessons, then the history of Islam, written by non-Muslims—Orientalists in Europe and America—also involves lessons, more often ones about the Western writers themselves and their own culture than about the Islamic world. Qutb warned readers to be wary of these Orientalist histories, not to trust their conclusions, and to take their endeavors with a grain of salt. Instead of viewing their own world through the eyes of unbelievers and those steeped in *jahiliyya*, they must see to it that they learn from true Muslims. Muslims must rewrite Islamic history in order to revitalize Islam and renew the Islamic state, relying on Arabic texts and not on the "flights of fancy" dreamed up by Orientalists with ulterior motives. The new Islamic historian has to be one who is spiritually and intellectually sympathetic to Islam.[8] Historians, too, Qutb concluded, can be *mujtahidin*, or interpreters of texts.

Europeans in the Old and New Worlds have written histories extolling the virtues of their own "progressive" civilization and debasing the "traditional" civilizations they encountered and usually conquered. Steeped in Western philosophy and religion that have reinforced imperialism and colonialism, they have blamed Muslims for their societies' deterioration and have credited Europeans with Muslims' salvation. The Islamic world, according to these Orientalists, was floundering in stagnation and backwardness until the arrival of Europeans, who nudged them onto the secular path toward what the Europeans called enlightenment and advancement. Failure to modernize, a sin in their eyes, could only be overcome by Europeans or their European-trained collaborators. This colonialist history, Qutb concluded, has to be replaced by an authentic Islamic history.[9]

This new history must be a history of the religion before, during, and after the life of the Prophet. Qutb advocated a social history because this method is most often infused with the preferences of the author. It can therefore be sympathetic to the religious beliefs and practices of west central Arabia before the advent of Islam and then concerned with the magnificent transformations God created through His messenger. Documenting military conquests is important, but clearly these actions were not entirely responsible for Islam's expansion and victory, and so the intellectual and civilizational contributions must be analyzed as well. What is most important is to uncover the reasons for Islam's rise and decline, for here is where the lessons for contemporary Muslims are most crucial.[10]

Islamic history is full of setbacks and declines. The only true golden period was in the beginning, with that first generation of Muslims. This period has lessons for all humanity. But then decline set in, and the causes of this decline become important case studies to examine in order to know what to avoid in the contemporary world and how to evade it. Thus, an Islamic history must document and analyze exemplary moments in the movement from the pre-Islamic *jahiliyya* to the heights of Islamic grandeur—a period that was unfortunately quite short—and then, sadly, record Islam's decline, all in order to discover the ingredients of both its greatness and its deterioration.[11]

In examining pre-Islamic Arabia, Qutb reviewed the genealogy of the Arabs in order to demonstrate their distinctiveness, their ancient bloodline, and their patrilineal descent from earlier prophets. There are two branches, issuing from Qahtan and 'Adnan. Qahtan is the ancestor of northern Arabs and is descended from Eber, Shem, and Noah. 'Adnan is the ancestor of southern Arabs and is descended from Isma'il and his father Ibrahim (Abraham), the grandfather of the prophets, and his wife's handmaiden, Hajar.[12] (Ibrahim's other son, by his wife Sara, is Isaac who, through his own son Jacob, established the 12 tribes of Israel, thus making Jews and Arabs cousins.)

Why did God choose the Hijaz in the 7th century for His final message to the world? Qutb's answer emphasized the complete autonomy that existed in the Hijaz, equidistant from the political and economic power of the Byzantines, Sassanids, Abyssinians, and their neighboring Arab clients. Qutb believed in a primordial monotheism, hanifiyyism, that includes Jews and Christians. Yet Islam appeared in a place far from the homeland of the earlier monotheistic prophets, distant from their immediate influence, and removed from their earlier attempts, which had gone astray under the influence of vast and impious empires. But yet, Islam, too, emerged out of the *hanif* tradition that had affected the entire Semitic world. This made the Hijaz the ideal place for God to deliver His message. The Arabs had been monotheists, but apparently had gone astray and reverted back to polytheism. They needed an Arab prophet to bring a message in the Arabic language to this corner of the world. Nevertheless, it was, Qutb claimed, a message for all of humanity. What restored monotheism to these descendants of Ibrahim was a worldwide calling to submit to God's will and dominion. Clearly, it was the Prophet Muhammad who reintroduced monotheism to the Hijaz, and scattered and eliminated all but the One God.[13]

Qutb provided the evidence for his claim that in the early 7th century, Arabs in the Hijaz were steeped in polytheism and ignorance of God. Before the Prophet Muhammad, they worshiped lifeless objects, pagan shrines, and divine idols. Qutb's detailed description appears to me to refer both to a tribal religion, with its various personal deities and sub-deities paralleling the tribal structure, and to an Olympic-style religion, with functionally specialized, anthropomorphic gods. One of these gods was God, Allah, but He was not considered unique. This abundance of gods and their sanctuary in Mecca created a lively commerce that greatly profited the local elite, supplementing the long-distance trade traveling along the Red Sea coast.

The Hijaz was in the process of evolving from a tribal or chiefdom society to a city-state when the commercial collapse sparked by the Byzantine-Sassanid wars (and those of their proxies) severely disrupted and undermined its economy and political relations. Qutb wrote that the Arabs were located next to failing commercial states, and that only the Hijaz, Tihama, and the Najd remained independent, a few scattered oases surrounded by desert and caravan trails, all in economic and moral decline. Accompanying this collapse was social injustice, tyranny, immorality, and social disintegration as a result of ignorance of God and His ways. Islam thus appeared at a very opportune moment. Qutb called it a revolution that radically transformed nomadic and commercial Arabs, with their primitive "tribal" religion, into a major global civilization grounded in Islam.[14]

Nevertheless, Qutb's main emphasis was not on this original *jahiliyya* period but on the 13-year period of Islam's birth and growth in Mecca, before the *hijra* to Medina, the establishment of the Islamic state, the triumphant return to Mecca, and the righteous succession after the Prophet's death. It was the cohort of early Muslims in Mecca that became Qutb's principal focus, serving as the prototype of what an effective Islamic spirit and system could really be. Over and over again, Qutb was able to demonstrate just how Islam was able to change society for the good, to develop it, and to overcome the problems from its earlier *jahiliyya* disorder.[15]

The chapters in the Qur'an are formally organized according to length, not temporal sequence. Yet Qutb understood the early Meccan chapters of the Qur'an, with their emphasis on subjective faith, belief, God's will, and orthodoxy, to be quite different from the later Medinan chapters, with their focus on objective laws, practice, nation-building, and orthopraxy. Furthermore, it is generally acknowledged that the current version of the Qur'an, compiled under the first two caliphs and finalized under the third, 'Uthman, had placed verses together because of their thematic similarity that were not necessarily in the same chronological order. Qutb therefore conducted painstaking scholarship to examine each chapter and to evaluate it as to whether it was Meccan or Medinan. Then he scrutinized each chapter's verses because some, even though they were in Medinan chapters, still had a Meccan quality to them (or the converse). He used two analytical methods generally found in *fiqh* studies. To establish the chronology of the revelations, he resorted to identifying the reasons for revelation (*asbab al-nuzul*), or the occasions or circumstances of their appearance. He then assumed that the latest verse abrogates, or supersedes, the earlier verses, according to the priority based on *al-nasikh* and *al-mansukh*, the abrogating verse and the abrogated verses. With these methods, Qutb was able to explore the subjective ideas and beliefs of the entire corpus of Meccan material, especially the earliest revelations. This reflected his lifelong pursuit of the more expressive side of Islam.[16]

These Meccan texts announced that there is but one God, that humanity must worship Him and Him alone, and that other social relationships and identities are much less significant. These were essentially matters of the heart and mind, groundwork for the more concrete matters that followed. All the problems that might emerge in a society begin with problems of belief. If these remain unsolved, then any solution of more practical problems will fail. For example, those Muslims

who do not have faith, yet who practice their religious obligations while emptied
of conviction, rightly deserve a tyrant as a ruler. If these faux Muslims themselves
do not believe in one God, how can they expect their ruler to abide by *shari'a*?
Thus the *jahiliyya* of Mecca is repeated today. Those who first feel the spirit are
then able to practice the religion's obligations, spread that faith to others, and
overthrow this religious ignorance.

The Prophet Muhammad and the first generation were exceptionally successful
in making the Qur'an their guide for all life's questions, both abstract and concrete. It became the only source they needed—the Sunna came later, of course—
for God deliberately intended that they absorb their lessons from this Book alone,
to "drink solely from this spring."

> The Holy Qur'an was the only source from which they quenched their
> thirst, and this was the only mold in which they molded their lives. This
> was the only guidance for them.[17]

The Qur'an became an encyclopedia that taught its readers all they needed to
know about the universe, the world, their place in it, and their relations with one
another. All these were creations of the One Creator, and thus, the *salaf* came
to understand the secrets and ways of these creations, and of God Himself.
Belief and understanding were the only focus at this time. More practical matters would come later. As Qutb said so often, it was all about the first phrase of
the Testimony—"There is no god but God"—leaving the second portion—"and
Muhammad is the messenger of God," which focuses on practice—for later. The
first part was solely to establish God's dominion and to ensure that no others—
priests, tribal leaders, the rich, the rulers—would try to usurp this authority.

Qutb was able to derive from the Qur'an not simply stories and images, but
actual, lived examples of inspiration and devotion. In other words, these were not
just allegories, but authentic and genuine truths. Yet more than just words from
the past, these Qur'anic chapters also contained shared experiences that needed
to be revived and implemented today. What those early Muslims did, but more
important, what they believed and how they so fervently embraced these convictions was what mattered to Qutb. The Meccan chapters were not scholarly and
obscure interpretations created in musty mosques and analyzed in secluded classrooms, but were the dynamic lived experiences of an exemplar generation, a set of
pragmatic guidelines to be applied in real life.[18]

This first generation could not afford to treat religion as mere erudition. Instead,
it embraced the beliefs as guidelines for survival. In its enormous battles against
the forces of *jahiliyya*, the early Muslim community had to unite in a brotherhood
and sisterhood of faith. So unified, they could face these much larger forces and
overcome them. But without the strength that came from strong internal faith,
the *salaf* would have failed and vanished. The ideas and doctrines of religion, by
themselves and separated from the rest of social life, would have mattered very

little. It was the real-life application of those beliefs, strengthened in the fires of battle, that made this first generation exemplary.

> Those of the first generation did not approach the Qur'an for the purpose of acquiring culture and information, nor for the purpose of taste or enjoyment. None of them came to the Qur'an to increase his sum total of knowledge for the sake of knowledge itself or to solve some scientific or legal problem, or to remove some defect in his understanding. Rather he turned to the Qur'an to find out what the Almighty Creator had prescribed for him and for the group in which he lived, for his life and for the life of the group.[19]

This gave the *salaf* a unique quality in contrast to later generations, a purity that made them righteous examples "without comparison in the history of Islam, even in the entire history of man." This noble generation had the highest character even as they lost their personalities and old identities in their new orientation toward God.[20]

The Prophet Muhammad was a social transformer who appeared at a very propitious moment. During his Meccan years, he emphasized belief and faith in God, for he had only preaching and persuasion at his disposal to convert his fellow Meccans to Islam. God did not reveal the entire religion all at once as a ready-made system that could be applied instantly. Instead, He revealed it gradually, to let it sink in and be absorbed by the community.[21] This required patience and confidence. That it was God's system and no other system ensured the community's survival and growth.

Had Muhammad formed his revolution on any basis other than that of faith, then the beliefs would merely be a curious sideline, the frosting to a materialist cake. Yet he did not create a movement based on tribalism, or Arabism, or what Qutb called nationalism (although the last was a distinct doctrine that was still many centuries away). Muhammad could have kindled these fires of Arab loyalty to quickly unite the tribes and eliminate warfare and feuds. So organized, they could have pushed against the Byzantines and the Persians and freed Arab lands from foreign domination. The Prophet could have done this, and Arabia might have united behind him. But such a temporary unity would have fallen apart had it not reflected the unity of God. The wars of apostasy after Muhammad's death attest to this centrifugal force; it might have been worse had not God's message brought them back together.

Yet instead of emphasizing these tribal and national identities that might have united Arabs internally against their external enemies, the Prophet Muhammad sought to unite all these ethnicities—Arabs, Persians, Greeks, Romans, and more—and to bring both allies, collaborators, *and* enemies together under the much larger unity of Islam. He chose to begin by instilling faith and trust in God into the hearts of new converts. This was not the easiest way of creating a revitalization movement, but it was the most certain, because once strong in belief, this first generation was able to overcome other problems.

At the time in Meccan society a wide gap existed between a very few rich and the much more numerous poor. In order to maintain this hierarchical status quo, injustice and tyranny were rampant. The first converts to Islam came from among the poor, and the Prophet's revolutionary ideas tremendously upset the wealthy. The poor lacked dignity and honor, and so faith in Islam and God restored their pride.

But the Prophet was not a proto-Marxist. He could have created a social movement that pitted rich against poor. And had the Prophet emphasized this and created a polarized community, his social movement might have risen faster. This was the easy way, but not the best way. God intended that *shari'a* law regulate the lives of both the rich *and* the poor, that both acknowledge God's dominion, and that both work to maintain social unity. Thus instead of class conflict, God, through His messenger, sought a harmonious and cooperative society. Class was not abolished, but the means of regulating and moderating class relations were created. By placing God's seal of approval on this new system of income redistribution, social justice, and class amity, a more prosperous and peaceful society would emerge.[22]

In the years before Muhammad and during the first years of his prophecy in Mecca, the community had descended into debauchery. There was drinking, gambling, cheating, fornication, and illicit marriage. In response, Muhammad could well have started a movement of moral transformation and purification. He could have found those morally upright members of the community and cast them against their immoral, degenerate neighbors. But the movement would have been hollow, creating a moral righteousness that leaves the good feeling smug, but the wicked digging deeper into their depravity. The prophet said, however, that true reform must be based first on faith, which, unlike morals, cannot be imposed, but has to grow from within. A movement of moral reform without such faith would prove empty, while a movement of faith creates, among other things, a moral rejuvenation that is authentic. Only when the community recognizes God's dominion, and worships Him and obeys His laws—when, as Qutb said, "There is no god but God" is imprinted on their hearts—then there will be improvement, not only in morality, but in politics, economics, family life, and civilization more generally.[23]

"If the call of Islam had not started in this manner...then it would not have been possible to establish this blessed system with this high standard," Qutb wrote. Had it been simply a nationalist campaign, or a class movement, or a drive to reform morality, then its greater and long-term victory would not have happened. Muhammad was offered wealth, power, position (a kingship), and worldly possessions if only he would give up the struggle. Had he done so, the movement soon would have been dust, not a lively and dynamic system of freedom and truth. Had it been a movement about anything but faith, it would have ultimately led to the victory of the unbelievers.[24]

The lifelong struggle of the Prophet himself was a major and significant lesson to those in the vanguard who wished to learn how to establish an Islamic society and state. It was a struggle against himself, and then a struggle within his own neighborhood and community, among friends and family. These efforts finally forced him to move to Medina, and his return to Mecca was yet another struggle. Likewise, his companions and helpers themselves strived, in ways similar to the Prophet, but also in ways unique to themselves, coming as they did in Muhammad's shadow. Their struggles were an effort to emotionally and intellectually understand God and His dominion, and then to take that knowledge and apply it to everyday life. It was this *jihad* that transformed them into the rightly guided, wise, learned, and experienced leaders of the whole of humanity.[25]

Muhammad's followers were not only struggling to appreciate God, but they were also fighting to overcome *jahiliyya* and to defend themselves against attacks from unbelievers. Their personal and collective efforts were difficult enough, but the external assaults from those steeped in, and profiting from, *jahiliyya*, made the overall process even more arduous. At the time, it was a matter of believing Muslims persevering against nonbelieving Meccans, of a small but growing minority against the status quo. Those who were unbelievers were neighbors, friends, even family and kinfolk; thus, the *salaf's* communal activities and their proselytizing were among very familiar people. Qutb saw a similarity with his own times, for it was also neighbors, friends, even family and kinfolk who had lost their true religion and slid back into *jahiliyya*. The situation in Mecca was a world that is mirrored in today's society, with Qutb's vanguard as the emerging believers against the vast majority who remain steeped in religious ignorance.

This first generation was both an experiment and a trial. God entrusted the Prophet Muhammad to gather this following and to teach and work with them to instill a steadfastness, to relinquish their own personal desires, and to work on behalf of God and His dominion. When this first generation thus proved that they were not desirous of personal reward nor impatient to achieve quick victory, that their hearts were free of pride of lineage, tribe, and country, then God, seeing them as morally pure, delegated them to be His vice-regents on earth.[26]

It was the *salaf* who recognized God's sole authority and that there can be no intermediaries between them and God. Although later generations did elevate others, consciously or otherwise, to the loftiness associated with God, this first group of Muslims was true and sincere, and concentrated on God alone, to the detriment of their personal and familial well-being.

> In this regard, there is no difference between our present condition and the condition of Arabia during the time of the Prophet. Some people think that the call for liberation of the people from the obedience to the lords is nonsense today: No! The worship of the sundry lords today is not less than the worship of the sundry lords in the *jahiliyya*. What has been changed is only the type of the lords, not the worship of the lords.[27]

It thus became the duty of subsequent generations of Muslims to imitate this unique cohort, to transcend the divisions of race, nationality, and class, and to come together as one community to acknowledge God's dominion and His law and to wage *jihad* to overcome *jahiliyya* and to establish a true Islamic state.

It was the simplicity and beauty of this period that served as a model for Islam's future. In the 20th century, Muslim communities became Egyptian or Iraqi, a rich gated community, a poor slum, a theater district, or a soccer team, but that which can unite them and make them invincible, their genuine belief in God and His religion, was no longer there. In order to become a true Islamic community, the vanguard must replicate the trajectory of the early Islamic community in Mecca.

This new community exhibited the highest level of harmony, unity, and probity, and its rulers were the most faithful in following the Qur'an. This high ideal continued until the reign of 'Uthman, the third righteous caliph, who, old and susceptible to corruption, capitulated to the Umayyads, which began a downward decline in Islamic government, if not also in the Islamic spirit. Islam continued to endure more assaults from the Mongols, the Crusaders, and European colonialism. Through all this, the Islamic spirit continued resisting this downhill slide, wavering at times, bursting forth at others, even while the government itself increased its decadence and corruption.[28]

The migration, or *hijra*, of 622 has been discussed and interpreted in numerous ways. Qutb understood the migration to be not the end of a journey, but the beginning of one. It was a tactic used to escape overwhelming force and still maintain one's spirit and faith. It is a regrouping and a renewing of the soul that is necessary before the final battle and victory. Otherwise, the long-term battle might be lost. The *hijra* is a temporary and tactical move, away from the tidal wave of *jahiliyya* where Muslims are vulnerable, to a place where they can establish an Islamic home. Once their strength is replenished and reinforced, the Islamic community can return, overthrow *jahiliyya*, and finally establish an Islamic society.

The word "retreat" sometimes implies cowardice. Here, however, migration becomes a tactic that avoids an inevitable defeat. Qutb argued that any Muslim community that is confronted by disorder or destruction should retreat from such overwhelming force, regroup, and re-attack. If the battle is continued unabated, and if one does not leave, community life and social relations can become completely corrupted, ground into dust by the forces of immorality, secularism, and tyranny. Worshipping God and obeying His laws can take energy and effort away from defense; until faith is renewed, it is better to retreat to a safe haven, strengthen one's resolve, and return to the battle refreshed. Where physical separation and removal is impossible, then a mental *hijra*, a peace of mind, is recommended.[29]

The *hijra*, then, was a different kind of *jihad*, a momentary one, until the main *jihad* could continue. Once the Prophet found himself and his followers in the safe environs of Medina, the *jihad* came to include organization, government, and laws. The climate was safe to strengthen faith and conviction, but now a new stage of development could take place. This made Islam not just a religion of orthodoxy but a religion of sacred practices as well. If the Meccan years were marked by an emphasis on faith, the Medinan years were marked by an emphasis on state building and legislation by God. Faith and law, both found in the Qur'an, came to be applied to the lives of true Muslims.

The *jihad* in Mecca had targeted unbelievers and was conducted through the gentler means of persuasion and proselytizing. Once in Medina, there was no need to mount new *jihad*s, since the residents of the city and environs were quite willing to accept the new religion, notwithstanding a few errant tribes, such as the Jewish ones, that refused peace treaties and cooperation and who felt superior to those without a scripture. There was nothing in people's hearts that thwarted the spread of Islam. But in planning for the future, a new *jihad* was developed, one to eliminate obstacles to the spread of Islam, and to overthrow and to destroy the *jahiliyya* communities that refused to recognize God's dominion. In Medina, the new Muslim community had the freedom and the time it needed to spread God's message. But as the eyes of the community began to once again look back toward Mecca, training for a forceful and militant *jihad* became necessary.[30]

In the small Muslim community in Mecca and later in the larger one in Medina, members were held together by shared love and affection, mutual responsibility and solidarity.[31] Islam was thus in its highest and purest form, not needing coercion but relying just on persuasion ("soft" power over "hard" power). This was not to last. But while it did, Muslims ceaselessly explored more deeply the ways of worshipping and obeying God. They asked questions in a lively and vital fashion, and accepted answers with an open mind. They understood the monumental project they were engaged in, as they trained their hearts and their bodies for better acknowledging God's dominion. They created a true leadership that asked nothing for itself but to serve and worship God, to administer His laws and only His edicts, and to acknowledge His authority. Even in losing specific battles in their quest to return to Mecca, these leaders learned to turn defeat into victory and return again to the battlefield. This method was the approach that the vanguard should adopt in the 20th century as well.[32]

Most histories of Islam discuss the Prophet Muhammad and the four righteous caliphs. Qutb also critically examined the rule of the early caliphs but reduced their magnificence, however, to just the first two. He argued that as long as Muslims continued to worship God and obey His laws in a righteous and faithful manner, and as long as they continued to follow *shari'a*, then no weakness or crisis would take place, no harm would come to the community. This persisted throughout the lifetime of the Prophet and his first two successors, Abu Bakr al-Siddiq (r. 632–34) and 'Umar ibn al-Khattab (r. 634–44). Indications of decline appeared, though, during the reign of the third caliph and, during the fourth, civil war erupted. Thus it was when the spirit of Islam and social justice no longer filled the Muslim community that it began to fall apart. Qutb argued that the new Islamic community was simply too young to withstand the forces of *jahiliyya* erupting from the Umayyads. It was the third caliph, 'Uthman ibn Affan (r. 644–56), who began to deviate from the Straight Path. 'Ali ibn Abi Talib (r. 656–61), the fourth caliph, attempted to resume what Abu Bakr and 'Umar had initially established, but which 'Uthman had undone. By this time, the forces of *jahiliyya* had overwhelmed an unsuspecting Islam, and it began to decline. Corruption and tyranny among its leadership were responsible for Islam's dishonor. It was their deviation, not that of the population in general, that caused Islam to fall.

Qutb concluded that if 'Uthman had become caliph later, then 'Ali could have succeeded Abu Bakr and 'Umar, or if 'Uthman had become the caliph earlier, then he would have been stronger to resist the pressure of the Umayyads, and Islamic history would have been considerably different. "The real tragedy," he wrote, "is that 'Ali was not the third caliph."[33] Thus, the critical errors came during the reign of the third caliph, 'Uthman, and Qutb examined his administration with extreme care and detail in order to understand what exactly went wrong, and what lessons today's Muslims might learn from it.

Both Abu Bakr and 'Umar had exemplified the best of the Islamic principles of government. They had been freely chosen by the Muslim community, they had refused to create special power or to expect special treatment for their position, and they had dispensed social justice and sought consultation from the community. In so doing, they could expect, and did receive, obedience from those they ruled. Qutb cited a number of stories and anecdotes that demonstrate the righteousness of their administration. For example, when his own son was caught drinking wine, 'Umar handled the case just like any other crime, notwithstanding the familial relationship.[34]

The main question that arose in Abu Bakr's time was how government funds should be collected and distributed, especially in support of the military. The public treasury belonged to the entire community and was used for community service. Abu Bakr sought to tax both rich and poor at the same rate and distribute equal stipends to both the earliest converts to Islam and those who converted later. 'Umar disagreed, however, and stated that he would discriminate between early and later converts, and that earlier believers were to have precedence and privileges over later ones. "I will not treat one who fought against God's messenger the same as one who fought along with him."[35] 'Umar also distinguished the Prophet's family and those closer to his affections from others.

Yet those who had first submitted to Islam in the Meccan years were primarily from the lower strata of society. Then, after the *hijra*, and later, as the Islamic army returned to fight and subdue Mecca, the last to convert were the wealthy and powerful of the city. Thus the most religious Muslims had originally been the poorest Meccans; the richest Meccans had been the last to submit.

The Prophet Muhammad himself had said that the only factor that makes one person greater than another in the eyes of God is their degree of piety and righteousness. In the 7th century, this meant that the longer one was a Muslim, the more that person demonstrated true devotion. 'Umar attempted to counterbalance social inequalities by compensating the early converts more than the later ones, the poor more than the rich. His technique essentially took money from the rich and gave it to the poor. This method emphasized class distinctions that seriously disrupted the new community. On the other hand, Abu Bakr's approach reinforced the unity of Islam, for he sought true equality.[36]

Abu Bakr argued that no one had more rights and privileges than another. 'Umar countered by saying that some had more privileges than others, because of their piety. Both had legitimate reasons to support their position. Yet Abu Bakr's understanding was closer to the true spirit of Islam and its concept of equality. Discrimination, no matter what the basis, Qutb claimed, leads to wickedness. 'Umar, at the end of his administration, came to realize the truth of Abu Bakr's perspective after seeing the results of his own discriminatory policy. He renounced his own approach and attempted to revert to the earlier policy of Abu Bakr.[37]

However, once the principle of discrimination had been established, it was much easier to keep the policy of official favoritism, but then go ahead and actually reverse the criteria, than to undo it completely and return to equal taxes and stipends. When 'Uthman became caliph, he continued 'Umar's policy, yet now in favor of the upper class rather than against it. His new policy, in fact, favored tax cuts for the wealthy (thereby affecting the public funds from which came military stipends), and allowed the rich to keep their wealth, and even to increase it by gifts of landed estates in the newly conquered territories, establishing what Qutb called "a malevolent feudalism." Both Abu Bakr and 'Umar had initially ordered the elite, the Quraysh, not to join the wars of expansion so as to avoid any unnecessary claims to conquered property. 'Uthman, on the other hand, reversed this policy, even though it had been for the good of the community, and instead passed out land grants to this former elite.

When 'Ali became the fourth caliph, he concurred with Abu Bakr's approach, but by then, the forces of inequality were such that 'Ali was powerless to change direction and return to the true spirit of Islam.[38] By then, the Quraysh, and particularly the Umayyad clan, had profited from the differential treatment and refused to revert back to the earlier and better policies.

This issue of government budgets gave rise to the social inequities that Abu Bakr had anticipated and that 'Umar eventually foresaw as well. The vast economic differences created a nonworking aristocracy and an exploited peasantry—Qutb's feudalism—despite the original intentions of uniting both rich and poor in their submission to God and His dominion.[39]

When 'Uthman became caliph, he was already old and weak. He delegated the management of affairs to his secretary, Marwan ibn al-Hakam, himself an Umayyad. Marwan distributed government funds in ways that favored his kinsmen. 'Uthman was too disengaged and not able to counter Marwan, and the Umayyads who supported the secretary, in turn, benefited from his misrule. 'Uthman defended Marwan by claiming that as caliph, he, 'Uthman, had rights unlike those of other Muslims, rights adhering to his office that allowed him to distribute gifts and stipends in ways he felt fit. It was his right, he claimed to honor those who protected and advanced Islamic society. Qutb claimed, however, that the acknowledgment and worship of God as the supreme authority meant that the caliph or any Islamic ruler has no special rights. His duty is merely to administer God's laws. 'Uthman's deviation, however, created a corrupt and tyrannical leadership.[40]

'Uthman's caliphate was unfortunate, for Islam was yet still young and its principles, spirit, and institutions had not yet penetrated every soul and permeated the entire society. His unIslamic and corrupt practices benefited the elite, particularly Marwan, Mu'awiyya ibn Abi Sufyan, and their Umayyad clan. Qutb increasingly viewed the Umayyads—the Umayyad "gang" with 'Amr ibn al-'As, the conqueror of Egypt, as its head[41]—as a source of evil, and pinpointed the beginning of Islam's decline to the actions of Marwan ibn al-Hakam in service to a toothless and faithless ruler.

The companions and helpers of the Prophet were still alive, and they noticed this departure from Islam's true spirit. They gathered in Medina to discuss solutions and attempted to "rescue" 'Uthman from disaster. But 'Uthman was unable to distance or protect himself from Marwan. When he tried, he was murdered.[42]

Despite whatever true spirit may have existed in his heart, 'Uthman's weakness and frailty allowed excesses that, once out, could not be easily taken back. These included (1) the creation of a hereditary kingship for the caliphate instead of its selection by the Islamic community; (2) the plunder of public funds as the personal property of the king and his family; (3) the pillaging of conquered territories and the distribution of this booty in ways that reinforce wealth and power rather than counterbalance it, and (4) the emphasis of division and difference that weaken the spirit of solidarity within the Islamic community. These problems ultimately led to the breakup of the Islamic community as its leadership shifted to the Umayyads and away from legitimate aspirants who demonstrated piety, faithfulness, and knowledge of Islam. This led to a period of dissension, *fitna*, and even civil war. One side displayed the spirit of Islam and disapproved of these deviations; the other side pretended to be Islamic—"who wore Islam as a cloak." One side was spiritual and faithful while the other side was "swept up by worldly desires." This set up an inevitable conflict between the next caliph, 'Ali, and those who had profited from 'Uthman's flaws, the Umayyads.[43]

'Ali was more in line with the first two caliphs. But the conditions now were entirely different. Abu Bakr and 'Umar rode the crest of a wave of true Islamic achievement. 'Ali, however, rode an avalanche tumbling downward, and he was near powerless to stop it. 'Ali reverted to the policies and principles of the first two caliphs, but it was too late. The Umayyads were now back again as the wealthy elite, and they would soon translate this return into political power, except that 'Ali and the followers of a true Islam stood in their way. 'Ali tried to return to a more egalitarian, spartan approach, Qutb claimed, and this stirred the Umayyad to rebel.

'Ali's problem, according to Qutb, was that he took his spartan lifestyle far too seriously. Like the Prophet Muhammad, 'Ali had been born into a poor branch of a powerful clan. But when he became caliph, he continued to live a self-imposed asceticism, and to experience unnecessary hardships that were not really true aspects of Islam. He rejected his rightful share and stipend from the state treasury and was stingy in using state funds for performing the public services expected of the caliph. In other words, in returning to the policies of Abu Bakr and 'Umar, 'Ali adopted an extreme approach in hopes that his example could correct the excesses of his predecessor, 'Uthman. He wanted to set an example whereby public funds were not wasted and squandered, but were spent properly and frugally. He wanted to restore the dignity and honesty of the caliphate that had been seriously interrupted before his administration. Qutb quoted him saying: "Oh, people. I am only a man like yourselves, with the same rights and obligations. I will lead you in the path of your Prophet and will enforce upon you what has been enjoined upon me."[44]

Those, like the Umayyads, who thirsted after wealth, were hardly satisfied with a ruler who exemplified prudence and thriftiness. Having, under 'Uthman, become accustomed once again to a luxurious lifestyle that had been denied them by Abu Bakr and 'Umar, the Umayyads became extremely displeased, and therefore rebelled against 'Ali. 'Ali had tried to restore the "vitality" of the caliphate, Qutb wrote, but the decadent and depraved Umayyads wanted nothing to do with it.[45]

The confrontation between Mu'awiyya and 'Ali is well known. Qutb recognized in 'Ali a naiveté that made him weak. His followers hesitated when confronted with his asceticism, fearing that even this moderation would come under attack as soon as the extremism of the elite was eradicated. 'Ali lost to Mu'awiyya because he lacked the political sophistication and magnetism that his adversary displayed and because, all-too-readily, 'Ali delegated his responsibilities to Mu'awiyya rather than hold his ground and fight. Qutb seems to have sided with the Kharijites in supporting "none of the above"—neither Mu'awiyya nor 'Ali—in selecting the next successor, although Qutb argued that the Kharijites were still not justified in killing 'Ali.[46]

The Umayyads returned the community to the ways of *jahiliyya* that existed before the Prophet Muhammad, motivated by their own desires and ambitions and by selfishness and greed. Qutb did not see any good qualities in them whatsoever and considered them worse than criminals, particularly for the policies they set for future Muslim rulers. They and those who followed them in office became tyrants, plundering the public treasury, arbitrary in their so-called justice, surrounded by sycophants, and rising to new heights of arrogance and self-importance. What victories Islam and righteous Muslims had achieved under the Prophet and the first two caliphs, which had wavered under 'Uthman and 'Ali, finally fell and turned to dust under the Umayyads. The spirit of Islam was clearly lost among the community leaders and only endured among ordinary people.[47]

'Uthman was too old and weak. 'Ali was too young and naive. Neither was up to the task of ensuring that the leadership in the new Islamic community was able to withstand the pressure of the corruption and tyranny of so-called Muslims who sought to glorify their own authority, not the authority of God. They sought to establish a kingship rather than select the best candidate to succeed the caliph. The wealthy and powerful remained in service to themselves, and the poor were not able to oppose them, notwithstanding their larger numbers. The very disunity that the Prophet, Abu Bakr, and 'Umar sought to eliminate, took an even stronger hold over the faith and beliefs of the new community. Under 'Uthman, 'Ali, and Mu'awiyya, Islam began to expand into North Africa and Spain to the west, and into Persia and central Asia to the east. But, Qutb concluded, the Islamic spirit retreated all the while.

With the succession of the Umayyads, the spirit of Islam flickered and sputtered. It occasionally reemerged, as with 'Umar II, who, during his administration, momentarily reinstated many of the policies of the first two caliphs. The next dynasty, the 'Abbasids, was no different; it continued treating the caliphate like a hereditary kingship and plundering the public treasury. Later caliphates increased their wealth and that of their families and friends while at the same time keeping those who were poor in misery. Those who failed to agree and comply were bought off. The rulers turned into tyrants, and swept aside the real spirit of Islam.[48]

On the other hand, Qutb argued, this spirit did remain "more or less strong" within the society at large.[49] There were those who still retained this passion and zeal, and they became "righteously angry" when they witnessed the *jahiliyya* of their leaders. Islam was to encounter more shocks—the Crusader and Mongol invasions, the loss of Andalucía, and finally the colonialism of the Europeans. In all of this, the leadership capitulated and saved their own lives even as the "life" of Islam declined and their subjects were mistreated.

Muhammad began his prophecy in 610. 'Ali served from 656 to 661. Thus the golden years of Islam were from 610 to 661, a period of some 50 years. In little more than a generation, Islam rose and declined. Qutb argued that 50 years was simply not long enough for the roots of the Islamic spirit, concept, and institutions to dig deep and anchor themselves against the onslaught of *jahiliyya*. There had not been enough time to grow strong and resilient and to develop the necessary safeguards against corruption and tyranny. Islam had not been in existence long enough to overcome the desires and arrogance of human nature and to expand and persuade enough hearts and souls of God's dominion and the righteousness of His laws. It could have been otherwise, but for the unfortunate accident of history and the "evil coincidence" of 'Uthman and Mu'awiyya. The times might not have been advantageous or auspicious. But clearly Qutb thought that the spirit of pure Islam still continued even if it remained extremely weak within the Islamic leadership.[50]

Once Mu'awiyya established a dynasty in Damascus, and then later when the 'Abbasids created a new one in Baghdad, and even later yet when the Turks set up their capital in Istanbul, Islam never completely recovered, although there were moments, even years, when the Islamic spirit shone through and captured the hearts and minds of lapsed Muslims and returned them to their religion. Elsewhere and at other times, Muslims reverted to *jahiliyya* and henceforth forgot about *jihad*; their fighting became mere wars of conquest. They surrendered to animal desires and wasteful luxury while their intellectuals designed different interpretations of *shari'a* and then fought among themselves as to which was the correct one. Muslim society became divided and their rulers became tyrants. Islam became influenced by the Greeks, Persians, Romans, Turks, Mongols, and Europeans, and deviated from submitting and worshipping God and from obeying His authority and His laws. As the Muslim empire spread to all corners of the known world, and it interacted with foreign cultures, it absorbed the values of these cultures rather than impart its true religious concept and method to the new converts. This created debates among various philosophical schools which became hopelessly entangled in insignificant arguments and lost the larger, complete picture of Islam.[51] Islam became polluted and contaminated by these foreign influences, and the coherence of Islam was lost.

True Islam was chipped away invasion by invasion, conquest by conquest. The revolt that brought the 'Abbasids to power and made them victorious over the decadence of the Umayyads was fueled by the growing inequalities that Muslims were experiencing and suffering through. The 'Abbasids initially treated all those in the Islamic community as equals, but this was only momentary, and soon, the egalitarianism passed. Instead, the caliphate was afflicted by "foreign communities"—here Qutb meant the Persians—whose recent submission and true motives were "not yet purified" in Qutb's view. Tribalism and national loyalty conflicted with the demand for an unmitigated devotion to God and His dominion. Yet as the Persians became integrated into Islam, the caliphate had to turn to yet other outside communities (Qutb called them "races") such as the Turks and Circassians to provide the military force necessary to support their tyranny.[52]

The Islamic community was slow to absorb and assimilate these new communities, and its ability to continue intact became weaker with each new group. Legions from the East were followed by the destructive invasion of the Mongols, who became nominal Muslims but who essentially remained outside Islam. The community's capacity was stretched to the limit; indeed, it was torn by the Mongols whose embrace of Islam proved very suspect.

Further shocks hit the over-extended Islamic community from the West. It was invaded by the wild and unruly Christian army of the Crusaders, and it lost Andalucía in the Iberian peninsula to a resurgent and xenophobic Catholicism. Both demonstrated that Islam continued to suffer hostile attacks but could still maintain an inner vitality that allowed it to rise above this brutality and remain independent. The animosity directed toward Islam took centuries to build, but its roots grew deep and strong. Europe treated Islam like a disease, ferreting it out from inside Europe and holding it at a distance—with arms and weapons, if at all possible.[53]

The last invasion of the vast Islamic community, Qutb wrote, brought about Islam's final overthrow, for in its imperialist and colonialist conquest, Europe sought to unequivocally change Islam by "modernizing" it. This extended the shadow of the Crusades and the Reconquista over the entire Islamic world, from Morocco to the Philippines.[54] It expanded the hostility of those in Europe who attempted to extinguish the Islamic spirit and completely subject Muslims to a renewed *jahiliyya*. Secularism, atheism, and polytheism have all attempted to supplant Islam. It is up to the new Islamic movement, Qutb wrote, led by an Islamic vanguard, to eliminate this *jahiliyya* and reestablish a true Islamic society and state.

To Qutb, all three episodes—the Crusades, the Reconquista, colonialism— were efforts to invade and conquer, physically and spiritually, to force Muslims to submit to European rulers instead of worshipping God. He warned readers to not be fooled by Europe's pretense to respect religious freedom or by Europe's claims that it had shed its Christianity and missionary fanaticism during the Enlightenment.[55]

Qutb explained European animosity toward Islam by saying that Europe's objective is not only military but cultural. The difference between Christianity and Islam is the primary cause, he argued, as Europe had long since separated the material and spiritual worlds, which, in Islam, remained closely inter-twined. The Enlightenment was but the most recent stage in this development. Christianity dwelt on the spiritual and disregarded God's dominion and His laws while Islam, of course, combines both belief and practice. Christianity had always been uneasy or perplexed about worshipping the Trinity while Islam represents a pure, unadulterated monotheism. Peaking in the modern period, Europe continued to slander Islam with accusations of sensualism and violence. Qutb believed that Europe is constantly at arms, and its immorality has been raised to a high level—part and parcel of *jahiliyya* society. He viewed Europe's antagonism as the outcome of anti-Islamic propaganda that had started long ago with the Crusades, reappeared in Andalucía, and became particularly viru-lent when the French invaded Egypt. He also admitted that the Turk's conquest of Constantinople, renaming it Istanbul, and crossing the Bosporus and threat-ening Europe at Vienna, added to Europe's fear of Islam and the eruption of Islamophobic disinformation.[56]

Qutb concluded that Europe profited from its Islamophobia and Orientalism.[57] By this, I take him to mean that Europe, particularly its leaders and intellectuals, could stand tall by standing atop a prostrate, defeated Islam, belittling and derid-ing its customs and people in order to call attention to its own presumed superi-ority. It is as if European identity depended on distancing itself from the terrible Other, and turning Islam into a hated Menace, which it finally had to conquer and subdue. Europe had refused to acknowledge its debt to the Islamic world: the many inventions and ideas it made use of but for which it repeatedly failed to acknowledge authorship.[58] And Qutb also maintained, though perhaps not in these exact words, that even the very immorality that Europe accused Muslims of indulging in was simply a reflection of its own lack of principles and ethics.

Qutb analyzed the writings of Voltaire (whom he claimed was an enthusiastic enemy of both Christianity and Islam) and the French Enlightenment more generally. He argued that the separation of religion and state was a logical outcome, since Christianity was based on so many unscientific myths, but was then redefined as "natural" and imposed on the rest of the world as a "universal good." Even so, he wondered why, when religion in Europe was finally marginalized and its religious feelings had vanished, it continued to spew hatred against Islam. (This assumes, of course, that the hostility toward Islam is simply a matter of different religious beliefs and ideas.)

Qutb also examined the notions of cultural relativity, although he did not use this exact phrase. But he did question just how Europe could change into a society that welcomes foreign cultures and studies them earnestly, even with some degree of sympathy. Yet, when it comes to the Islamic world, he noted, relativism and sympathy disappear. No matter how close Europe comes to understanding other cultures, when it comes to Islamic civilization, the gap between the two remains unbridged. Contempt for Islam, he concluded, was deep in the European *zeitgeist*. Europe's invasions and conquests, and now its Westernization in the guise of modernity, are enemies that justify the various *jihads* that Qutb discussed.[59]

In the end, Qutb updated his enemies list by adding Zionism and Communism. Qutb discussed his experiences in America, and emphasized the Jewish financial influence he found there. He also noted the class conflict and massive social, political, and technical machinery found among the Communists. He determined that these new ideologies were merely extensions of the Crusader mentality established 800 years earlier. This is what led him to conclude that Europe's Islamophobia is embedded in its soul. He saw all these ideologies united through their centuries-long hatred of Islam.[60]

The shining light in all of this was that the spirit of Islam, long dead among the leadership of Muslim nations and even weak among ordinary people, is still alive, and still powerful enough to spark a revitalization of Islam that in turn can ignite a revival in humanity itself. Islam is too great and its principles too powerful, Qutb concluded. History will validate Islam's revitalization.

In Sum

Qutb's history was a scholarly effort to position his brand of Islam in a temporal context that enabled him to explain Islam's rise and fall, its appeal and its deterioration, over the centuries. History explains where society has been, why it turned out the way it did, and what lessons can be learned to change it if necessary. Qutb used his history to justify the rise of the Islamic movement in the 20th century.

It seems strange that Islam's glory years were so brief. Qutb, however, did not let this bother him. Instead he sought to recast this fall from glory as evidence that Islam suffered from poor leadership and needed a revolution. He examined the conditions that existed before Islam as a way of explaining why it was so critically needed, and he explored the reasons that Islam's initial light was so exceptionally bright and how it dimmed so quickly. He also drew boundaries between true Islam and its enemies, both inside and outside the community, and explained that what made Islam unique was its resistance to its enemies' attempts at secularization and modernization. But his historiography was not abstract or academic. It was intended to coax, convert, and inspire his readers into adopting his Islamism—which he called simply "Islam"—as their guiding authority.

Qutb tailored and textured his studies for the purpose of changing hearts and minds and for convincing his readers of the righteousness of his cause. His history, then, became the background for his efforts to define the Islamic system, society, economy, and state that would, through struggle, replace the ignorance of Islam with God's authority.

Epilogue

On August 9, 1966, Sayyid Qutb was arrested on charges of sedition and treason. On August 21, he was sentenced by a military court to death by hanging. Eight days later, he was executed.

Some thirty years later, Qutb-inspired violence seemed finally to be coming to an end. On July 5, 1997, during the prosecution of Military Court Case 235 against members of al-Jama'a al-Islamiyya (The Islamic Association), one defendant stood up in the courtroom and read out a proclamation, signed by the Association leaders, calling on its members to stop all violence and bloodshed.[1] A year and a half later, in October 1998, the same leadership responded favorably to an appeal from the Association's former spiritual leader, Shaykh 'Umar 'Abd al-Rahman—the "blind shaykh" convicted in the United States for inciting the 1993 bombing of the New York City World Trade Center—who called for the Association to pursue its goals by nonviolent means.[2] In March 1999, the Association's Shura (Consultative) Council moved forward on this new policy and initiated a reevaluation that resulted in a four-volume treatise called *Taslih al-Mafahim* (Revised Concepts) that was issued in January 2002. These books covered four major errors in Islamist thinking: (1) practices of violence, (2) accusations of unbelief and apostasy, *takfir*, (3) theories of combat, *jihad*, and (4) policies of *hisba*, or the practice of "enjoining the good and forbidding the evil." These errors were attributed to the teachings of Sayyid Qutb.[3]

Leaders from Tanzim al-Jihad (the Jihad Organization) soon followed suit. At the time when the Islamic Association declared its end to violence, in 1997, many of the Jihad leaders were also in prison, and they promptly signed on to the initiative. They were joined by other Jihad leaders exiled in Europe. However, unlike al-Jama'a, which had fostered a more centralized, coordinated leadership, Jihad's leadership was scattered and autonomous. Some of its exiled leaders outside Europe did not agree to the Association's proposal. In particular, the exiles in Afghanistan under Ayman al-Zawahiri dissented and, therefore, were abandoned without any further support from Egypt or elsewhere. As a result, they were driven to ally themselves more closely with the Saudi businessman, Usama bin Ladin, for financial and organizational support.[4] This splintered the Jihad organization, with some of its leaders endorsing nonviolence and others leaving the organization.[5]

Although these two Egypt-based organizations differed on tactics—Tanzim al-Jihad was more elitist and clandestine, primarily recruiting military officers and only targeting government officials, while al-Jama'a al-Islamiyya was more populist and open, generally recruiting ordinary Egyptians and extending their targets to include civilian sites—they both acknowledged the same mistaken thinking. Militant members, as well as many devout and pious Egyptians, had begun using a number of concepts drawn from Qutb's writings, accredited to Qutb himself (or blamed on him), and expanded in the years since his death. These were now repudiated.

- The act of *takfir* charges erring Muslims with disbelief, *kufr*, and then excommunicates them, declaring them non-Muslims. This has created confusion, chaos, and often, fatalities. Self-appointed arbiters of what constitutes "true belief" often lack education, experience, and authority, and youthful critics in particular often become intolerant zealots in their eagerness to become more Islamic than anyone else. This rigid and narrow-minded kharijite perspective has troubled Egypt for some years.[6]
- In a similar manner, the practice of *hisba* allows community members, independent of the government, to define what is good or evil in order to protect the community's general welfare and morals.[7] Carried to extremes, young men and women began declaring a wide range of activities as *haram*—forbidden—and therefore susceptible to Islamic punishment. This includes playing soccer, watching TV, or going to movies. Music was completely proscribed.
- Restricting the definition of *jihad* to just holy combat exempts many from pursuing the greater *jihad* of spiritual cleansing and preaching. Correcting this narrow thinking became the primary focus of the *Revised Concepts* project. Elsewhere, rehabilitation programs in Saudi Arabia and Yemen educated recanting jihadists to the larger, more nuanced meaning of the concept. The goal in Egypt and abroad was to turn militants into pacifists.

Many members of the incarcerated leadership had received prison sentences of 20 years or more. The *Revised Concepts* initiative emerged just as many prisoners faced still further detention time even as their statutory terms expired, a not uncommon government practice. Many, therefore, changed their perspective on violence, either sincerely or else to curry favor.[8] They confessed to the excess of their earlier violence, acknowledging that this would not end the tyranny they had sought to overthrow. They professed epiphanies in which they realized how much damage they had caused to the community and to their religion. Now they wished, instead, to promote community welfare in more peaceful ways. They were particularly concerned about the effects of the older concepts on Egypt's youth and on the image of their religion in the West. Consequently, they developed new interpretations that revised their earlier thinking, and the four-volume set of "new ideas" was the result.

With these revised concepts, domestic Islamist militancy, carried out in order to overthrow *jahiliyya* and achieve *hakimiyya*, was thought to have come to a halt by the end of the decade.

The militant Islamist organizations that applied Sayyid Qutb's concepts and ideas had begun to appear in the late 1960s and early 1970s, shortly after his execution.[9] Their members were impatient with the moderation and pacifism of the Muslim Brotherhood and with the lack of change in government policies. They called for a campaign to destroy an Egypt corrupted by Westernization and to build an Egypt revitalized by the true Islam, God's unity, and God's laws. Many had started as small independent and nonviolent efforts in small towns and city neighborhoods initiated by Qur'anic study groups and charitable development associations connected to local mosques.[10] Only a few ever elevated themselves to a national level of intense combat. Two of the most important precursors that later shifted to Islamic militancy were the Society of Muslims and the Islamic Liberation Party.

The Society of Muslims, or Jama'at al-Muslimin, was more often labeled in the press at the time as Takfir wa al-Hijra—Excommunication and Migration. It was established originally by 'Ali 'Abduh Isma'il but became better known after 1969 under the leadership of Shukri Mustafa, an agricultural engineer from Abu Khurus, Asyut. The group was founded in prison; in 1971, President Anwar al-Sadat released a number of imprisoned Muslim Brothers and Islamists, including Mustafa, as part of his May 15 "Corrective Revolution," and the Society was reconstituted outside.[11] The Society took to heart many of Qutb's lessons about *jahiliyya* and Egypt's current corrupt and pagan society, the elite vanguard of believers, the 13-year Meccan period of learning the faith, and the subsequent *hijra* to Medina to find strength before returning and conquering the infidels in Mecca. However, it went further than Qutb by advocating that individual Muslims could declare others to be unbelievers and apostates. Its program required two stages. The first was recognizing the organization's spiritual and military weakness, and withdrawing to fortify its resolve. The second was to reenter society and to attack *jahiliyya*. In the early 1970s, it found itself in the first stage, and therefore chose to isolate its members while they intensified their belief and determination. A number of them actually retreated to the desert beyond the Nile Valley while others remained living in ordinary urban apartments, but prayed at their own separate mosques and isolated themselves spiritually and socially from the rest of the community. This enabled many to continue working in the Society's businesses, which helped finance its activities.

At first Jama'at al-Muslimin appeared more intent on retreat than on militant action. But it also earned a reputation as a cult because of the more visible segregation of its urban members. In 1974, Mustafa began recruiting members from other organizations, and a feud erupted between the Society and the Shabab Muhammad (Muhammad's Youth). Each association accused the other of "raiding" its membership. Two years later, in the fall of 1976, local newspapers began publishing derisive articles that, Mustafa argued, insulted his organization's honor. The impetus for such defamation may have actually come from rival Islamist organizations. But to stop this media slander, on July 3, 1977, the Society kidnapped Muhammad al-Dhahabi, a former government minister of religious foundations (*awqaf*) who was seen as a representative of the pro-government *'ulama*. The Society demanded a halt to the ridicule, the release of arrested members, and the publication of explicatory Society documents. Shortly after his abduction, government forces stormed the Society's hideout and, amid the commotion, al-Dhahabi was killed. Five Jama'at al-Muslimin members, including Mustafa, were arrested, tried, and executed, and many more received prison terms. The organization ceased operation, although the practice of *takfir* continued informally among ordinary people.[12]

On April 18, 1974, a militant Islamic organization attacked Egypt's Military Academy in Heliopolis, northwest of Cairo. Its goal was to assassinate President al-Sadat who was scheduled to speak there. Fortunately for al-Sadat, Cairo's classic traffic jams delayed his arrival, but the shoot-out killed 11 people and wounded 27. The militants had adopted the name Hizb al-Tahrir al-Islami (Islamic Liberation Party) and were led by Salih Sirriya, a Palestinian educator and administrator living in Egypt and employed at the Arab League headquarters in Cairo. The Hizb was an offshoot of the Jerusalem branch of the Muslim Brotherhood, which had been founded in 1953 by Taqi al-Din Nabhani, a *shari'a* court judge. The organization was also known as the Shabab Muhammad, the same name as the organization that had broken away from the Muslim Brotherhood in 1939–40 and the same name as the Muslim Brotherhood organization in Syria.[13] Whereas Mustafa's Society of Muslims had accused all of society of being ignorant of Islam, Sirriya's Islamic Liberation Party faulted the government more specifically, with the larger society viewed merely as victims deceived by corrupt state officials. Consequently, the Party targeted government installations, such as the Military Academy, and did not seek to withdraw or retreat in order to reenergize itself. It scorned Qutb's instructional route and focused on mounting immediate attacks, specializing in quick operations preceded by training its cadres, infiltrating the army and police, tracking its prey, mapping their activities, and then, afterward, seizing media outlets and setting up shadow governments. By contrast, the Society of Muslims sought the slower route that Qutb had counseled, of spiritual and intellectual education before undertaking its battles. The Society condemned the larger populace, choosing to attack the religious establishment as representative of the larger, society-wide *jahiliyya* (which explains its hostage victim).[14] It advocated more long-term planning and placed more emphasis on education. Its kidnapping al-Dhahabi was undertaken more out of desperation than with any strategic forethought.

Thus Hizb al-Tahrir al-Islami sought sudden, top-down action against government personnel whereas Jama'at al-Muslimin emphasized gradual, long-term, bottom-up community organizing. The two organizations also differed in their leadership styles, with the Party more democratically discussing its issues while the Society exhibited a more autocratic approach. Yet both "demanded total commitment and ironclad discipline from their members."[15] The Hizb recruited its members mostly at mosques where it could observe their piety and faith, while the Jama'a sought new members from the network of existing affiliates, very often from among kinfolk and close friends. There was also a regional distribution to their recruitment and activities. The Party operated primarily in Cairo and Alexandria, while the Society was more rural, with its roots in the Egyptian countryside, particularly in the south, but also among recent urban migrants.[16]

On October 6, 1981, another assassination operation took place. This time it succeeded in killing President al-Sadat during a military parade in Heliopolis marking the eighth anniversary of Egypt's 1973 Ramadan war against Israel. A group of four soldiers, led by Lt. Khalid al-Islambuli, was riding in an army jeep that seemed to have "broken down" directly in front of the presidential reviewing stands. The soldiers stopped, opened the jeep's hood, and it appeared that they were beginning to repair it. Instead, the soldiers took out their army-issued weapons, and began tossing hand grenades and spraying machine-gun fire at the official platform. At first, the president thought the soldiers were coming forward to honor him and so he arose instinctively to greet them. Instead, the soldiers killed him and a number of government officials. Al-Islambuli shouted out, "I have killed the Pharaoh!" In coordination with this attack, another group of soldiers attempted to spark an insurrection by taking over the police headquarters in Asyut in southern Egypt. The rebel soldiers fought off army loyalists for four days before succumbing.

As it turned out, al-Islambuli was a member of the Jihad Organization, whose members included Lt. Col. 'Abbud al-Zumar, Karam Zuhdi, Muhammad 'Abd al-Salam Faraj, and Ayman al-Zawahiri. Faraj, an engineering graduate of Cairo University, was the author of *al-Farida al-Ghayiba* (The Neglected Duty), the doctrinal justification for the assassination. Al-Islambuli led the Cairo operations in order to avenge his brother's incarceration a month earlier during al-Sadat's famous police dragnet. Tanzim al-Jihad was new on the scene; earlier the same year, it had emerged as Jama'at al-Jihad—an amalgam of a number of small, independent *jihadi* groups. The two most prominent constituents were (1) the remnants of Hizb al-Tahrir al-Islami that had scattered to Alexandria and Cairo after its debacle in Heliopolis five years earlier, and (2) al-Jama'a al-Islamiyya, a local Islamic society that had formed in Asyut in 1978. Hizb al-Tahrir al-Islami had continued to dominate Cairo and the Delta while al-Jama'a had come to lead in southern Egypt and those parts of Cairo "colonized" by incoming southern migrants. But their alliance was not to last; the two split in 1984 shortly after the end of the government trials of those arrested for al-Sadat's assassination.

Tanzim al-Jihad did not differ significantly from its predecessor, Hizb al-Tahrir al-Islami. It focused on infiltrating the Egyptian military, as it had done for the al-Sadat killing, and on targeting government officials. Al-Jama'a al-Islamiyya, on the other hand, adopted many of the practices of Jama'at al-Muslimin, although it no longer advocated retreat, isolation, and gradualism. Instead it endorsed the immediate violent overthrow of Egyptian *jahiliyya*, but its target was Egypt's society and not just the government. Al-Jama'a continued its recruitment through personal networks and worked primarily among the poor and dispossessed in places like Imbaba, an impoverished informal neighborhood on the west side of Giza, across the Nile River from downtown Cairo. Although the two organizations had merged and become indistinguishable in early 1981, it seems clear that Jihad was responsible for the al-Sadat assassination while al-Jama'a was accountable for the short-lived Asyut uprising.

Al-Jama'a al-Islamiyya, the Islamic Association, had begun as a charitable, mosque-based organization providing hospital beds for the poor, low-cost health clinics, affordable housing, after-school tutoring, free textbooks, clothing exchanges, veterinarian services, small-scale business assistance and low-cost credit, and guidance through the labyrinthine state bureaucracy for permits, licenses, and tax abatements.[17] It was organized by professional doctors, engineers, lawyers, and teachers who had graduated from the University of Asyut and the newer college at al-Minya, who then worked abroad in the Gulf and Arabian Peninsula, remitted their substantial salaries back home, and sought to realize *hakimiyya* in their local communities by financing and performing charitable activities and good deeds among impoverished Egyptians. As many indigent Egyptians moved north to Cairo to find employment, creating informal neighborhoods and businesses, al-Jama'a followed and initiated projects to provide education, utilities, and medical services that the government was unwilling or unable to supply.[18] Government raids on these stalwart activists, however, began to stoke the fires of radicalism. The organizers of these charitable projects were arrested and their activities were closed down. In response, many al-Jama'a members turned to militant acts to combat government repression. Many applied the lessons learned from Sayyid Qutb.

After the split in 1984, the two *jihadi* organizations began to develop different priorities and tactics. Many members, of course, were simply arrested and imprisoned without trial. Those who escaped these manhunts often reconsidered their ideas and returned quietly to ordinary jobs and family life. Others, however, and especially those who were particularly zealous, moved abroad where Egypt's police were unable to reach them. Even so, a sizable number of members who fell outside these three camps remained active militants and continued to plan the overthrow of *jahiliyya* and to build an Islamic society and state in Egypt.

More and more, however, Jihad members, in particular, became involved in foreign operations, particularly as the state's repression became more successful. Its local cadres thinned out and even disappeared. After the mid-1980s, Jihad mounted fewer militant operations that targeted Egypt. There was a failed plot to assassinate former Egyptian Interior Minister Hasan al-Alfi in August 1993, and then, that November, an unsuccessful assassination attempt on former prime minister 'Atif Sidqi. In 1996, Jihad was held responsible for attacking the Egyptian embassy in Islamabad, Pakistan, with a truck bomb.

In 1984, Jihad's new *amir*, or leader, 'Abd al-Qadir ibn 'Abd al-'Aziz, was acquitted of all charges related to the al-Sadat assassination.[19] Two years later, he left Egypt and began moving between Afghanistan and Pakistan where he directed Jihad operations until he was succeeded by Ayman al-Zawahiri in 1993. Al-Zawahiri had visited Afghanistan once in 1980 and then again in the months right before the al-Sadat assassination. He was arrested in connection with the October 6 presidential assassination and served three years in prison. Two years after his release, in 1986, al-Zawahiri returned to Afghanistan to stay.

In late 1992, the Egyptian government uncovered a clandestine network of Jihad leaders who had organized Tali'a al-Fath (Vanguard of the Conquest) as its new military wing. The government arrested and imprisoned over 1,000 members. The subsequent fallout over this leadership crisis forced Ibn 'Abd al-'Aziz to resign and be replaced by al-Zawahiri. As the new expatriate leader of Jihad, al-Zawahiri (and others) signed the statement that established the World Front for Combat against Jews and Crusaders—later to be called al-Qa'ida—in February 1998.[20] Yet just the year before, Jihad's prison leadership had signed on to the nonviolent initiative from al-Jama'a al-Islamiyya. For all practical purposes, Jihad in Egypt was now finished.[21]

For its part, al-Jama'a continued to work quietly in Egypt's urban slums and informal neighborhoods. Even as Jihad became absorbed into the World Islamic Front, the Islamic Association quietly kept on operating in poor, unserviced communities like Imbaba in Giza.

Yet on December 8, 1992, the government mounted a full-scale military attack against Imbaba in an attempt to root out the Islamists, particularly al-Jama'a al-Islamiyya. State security had deemed Imbaba a "state within a state" for privately offering many government services otherwise unavailable to local residents from official line ministries. Unable to shut down the Association in southern Egypt, the government was more capable of eliminating it when it was closer to the actual seat of power. It ordered 15,000 troops to "invade" this Islamist semi-state, declaring war against the Islamic Association, which, according to officials, had "seized control of the district." The government intended to "take it back."[22]

One reporter, Geneive Abdo, described "the Battle of Imbaba" in these words:

> The police broke into the houses of suspected militants, destroying the possessions inside. Dozens of Imbaba residents were arrested off the streets merely because their beards and Islamic dress looked suspicious. The wives, mothers, and sisters of wanted militants were arrested and detained for up to a month at a time. They complained of being tortured at the Imbaba police station and ordered to strip naked before giving forced confessions for crimes they had never committed.

Children between eight and fifteen years old were beaten by security police aiming to coerce information from them about their wanted relatives.[23]

Elsewhere, Mary Anne Weaver's informant reported similar atrocities.

Women were tortured with electroshocks and beaten in the streets— dragged by their hair, after their *hijabs* were savagely torn off their heads.

Police arrested no fewer than 5,000 people, 4,500 of whom were released over the next year. Of the remaining 500, only 100 were ever brought to trial.[24]

Shortly after the Battle of Imbaba, on February 26, 1993, followers of Shaykh 'Umar 'Abd al-Rahman—the former spiritual guide of the al-Jama'a who had clandestinely fled Egypt to Jersey City, New Jersey—attempted to blow up the World Trade Center. Two years later, on June 26, 1995, al-Jama'a attempted to assassinate President Husni Mubarak in Addis Ababa, Ethiopia.[25]

Only once more did al-Jama'a raise its bloody sword. On November 17, 1997— just three months after its arrested leaders had begun to recant by reading their July 5 statement against violence—six al-Jama'a militants attacked and killed 58 tourists and four Egyptian guards at the Pharaonic sites in Luxor.

The violence seemed to seriously contradict al-Jama'a's courtroom drama. It was also the first time that any militant group had targeted tourists. The action appears to have resulted from a colossal mix-up and miscommunication among the foreign-based, prison-based, and locally based leadership of the group. After Luxor—and perhaps as a result of it—concerted Islamist attacks ceased altogether and Qutb-inspired religious violence in Egypt appeared to end. There were still a few new incidents, but these were blamed not on local jihadists but on franchise operations initiated from outside by al-Qa'ida based in Afghanistan and Pakistan.

Yet, despite a lengthy respite, on January 16, 2010, some 13 years after militant violence had stopped, Dr. Muhammad Badi'a, a 64-year-old associate professor of pathology at Bani Swayf University's Faculty of Veterinary Medicine, was chosen as the eighth Supreme Guide of the Muslim Brotherhood. Badi'a, from the Delta town of al-Mahalla al-Kubra, had been recruited into the reconstituted Muslim Brotherhood in 1961 and had been arrested along with Qutb in 1965 on charges of treason. He spent nine years in prison. His election by the Brotherhood's *Shura* Council represented a stunning victory for the radical, Qutbist branch of the Brotherhood over its more moderate, reformist wing.[26]

The rivalry between radicals and moderates had been brewing for months. The previous Supreme Guide, Mahdi Akif, himself a moderate, threatened to resign in October 2009, when he was pressured by the radicals into appointing new members to the 16-member Guidance Bureau that administers the organization. Moderate reformists advocated a modernization of the Brotherhood with innovations such as democratic elections, policy debates, procedural transparency, public media campaigns, national partisan participation, and greater tolerance toward women, Christians, and the West. Hard-line Qutbists, by contrast, wanted to maintain the Brotherhood's historic position on these issues—exclusive Guidance Bureau appointments, confidentiality, media blackouts, nondivisive politics, and ideological firmness. Not wishing to split the organization, Akif announced that he would step down in January 2010, when his term ended—the first voluntary resignation in Brotherhood history (his six predecessors had all died in office). This set up an intense political campaign for his successor in the larger 100-person Shura Council. The Council's vote in December to select a new Guidance Bureau assured the radicals a solid majority; the election of Badi'a as Supreme Guide a few weeks later became a foregone conclusion.[27]

Within days of Badi'a's victory, the Egyptian government began arresting and incarcerating Brotherhood leaders, both radicals and moderates. Octogenarians were aroused from their sleep in police raids at dawn, in front of their grandchildren, and dragged off to the Interior Ministry's headquarters. Over 25 leaders were immediately detained on security violations and held indefinitely without trial. Almost one-third of the Guidance Bureau ended up behind bars. Over the course of the next two months, between 350 and 400 Brothers were imprisoned. The official charges included not only the customary "belonging to an illegal organization" but now, much more significantly, "belonging to an organization based on the ideas of Sayyid Qutb." The Brotherhood had been illegal since 1954. But it had long been tolerated by the government and even allowed to participate in the 2005 Parliament election, in which it won 20 percent of the seats, 88 members. Now, however, the government accused those it arrested of belonging to the Brotherhood's resurrected Secret Apparatus, alleging that they sought to pursue militancy instead of following its official policy of nonviolence. A number of those detained were also charged with possessing copies of *In the Shade of the Qur'an*.[28] It appeared as if Qutb-inspired radicalism had not gone away at all.

About a year later, on January 25, 2011, two virtual reality protest groups, both organized through the social media of Facebook and Twitter, staged a textbook-example demonstration that began in several neighborhoods throughout Cairo and ended up converging on Tahrir (Liberation) Square.[29] One group was called the April 6th Movement, a Facebook group with almost 70,000 members organized by Ahmed Maher and Waleed Rashed.[30] It was named for its coordination with a major labor strike staged by textile workers in the industrial Delta town of al-Mahalla al-Kubra on that date in 2008. This strike was called principally for economic grievances, but protestors also demanded political justice.[31]

The other group was the "We're All Khalid Sa'id" Facebook group administered by the "obsessively anonymous" Wael Ghonim, which brought together nearly 160,000 sympathizers in solidarity with Khalid Sa'id.[32] Sa'id was a 28-year-old man in Alexandria arrested and then beaten to death by state security police in the summer of 2010. Photographs of his brutalized body were quickly posted on Facebook and galvanized an angry public into a political protest movement.[33]

Both groups, then, appeared because of the same economic despair and political corruption and repression that had enraged Sayyid Qutb and were continuing to plague Qutb's followers, moderate Muslim Brothers, and even secular, nationalist-minded activists.

Initially, the Muslim Brotherhood remained aloof, refraining from contributing to or participating in the January 25 demonstrations. But two days later, while still not officially endorsing the protest, the Guidance Bureau permitted individual Brotherhood members to take part, especially those from its Youth wing. Then, as the Egyptian government shut down the Internet and social media, the revolution grew in size and strength because of the contribution of Brotherhood members in Tahrir Square. Eventually, over 100,000 Brothers participated in the uprising; as many as 40 died in the police attacks on the demonstrators.[34]

It took a long and anxious 18 days to bring down the government of President Mubarak. No one in his wildest imagination ever thought the government could be overthrown simply with civil disobedience instead of the massive militant operations envisioned by Tanzim al-Jihad or al-Jama'a al-Islamiyya. No one ever saw the government as so fragile that nonviolent people power, in an 18-day whirlwind of wild, dangerous, and exhilarating tumult, could bring down the Pharaoh.

Yet, even before Mubarak finally stepped down, as the top leadership shifted to 'Umar Suliman, former director of General Intelligence Services (Jihaz al-Mukhabarat al-'Amma) and more recently appointed vice-president, the Muslim Brotherhood saw a new and exciting opportunity. The government proposed high-level talks and meetings with the political opposition, perhaps as a bulwark against further decline and final defeat. But now, strangely, this opposition came to include, with hardly any discussion, the Muslim Brotherhood, whose existence was thus unexpectedly acknowledged and approved after so many decades of arrests and persecution. When the secular and nationalist opposition hesitated to meet Suliman without Mubarak first resigning, an opportunity opened up on February 5 for Muhammad Badi'a, the radical Supreme Guide, to hold "direct, preliminary talks" with the vice-president, which received substantial media coverage. All of a sudden, the Muslim Brotherhood stood transformed as a legitimate—and powerful—player on the Egyptian political scene.[35]

Almost immediately, fierce debates erupted, both within and outside the Brotherhood, about the extent of the Brothers' participation in the new democracy. The media in the United States presented the new Oriental danger as an ominous choice between stability and chaos, with the Brotherhood clearly belonging to the latter and the ancien regime representing the former. Inside the Brotherhood, there was anxiety over whether its newfound legitimacy and authority would soil the Brotherhood or raise new expectations about its organizational prowess and domination. Brotherhood moderates demanded the creation of a new political party, which meant endorsing a platform of religious and gender equality along with the possibility of rejecting God's laws. The radicals, instead, wanted to keep the Brotherhood a "social movement" which requires steadfastness and ideological fidelity.

Shortly after Mubarak resigned on February 11, the Wasat (Center) Party, created in 1996 by former Brothers Abu al-A'la Madi, Salah 'Abd al-Karim, and 'Issam Sultan, but repeatedly denied legal recognition, was finally approved by a judicial court. It was one of the first Brotherhood-related parties to emerge from the revolution, although it was not officially endorsed by the Guidance Bureau. It promoted a moderate, even a liberal, interpretation of Islam, admitted Copts and women to its membership, advocated an Islam "consistent with the values of a liberal, democratic system," and maintained a view of *shari'a* that was flexible and compatible with pluralism and national citizenship.[36]

Then, on April 30, the Brotherhood's Guidance Bureau announced the formation of its new officially sponsored party, the Freedom and Justice Party (FJP), modeled on the Justice and Development Party of Turkey.[37] Muhammad Mursi became its president, 'Issam al-Arian its vice-president, and Sa'ad al-Katatni its secretary general.[38] All three were among the last remaining moderates on the otherwise radical Guidance Bureau; after they assumed their party offices, they all resigned from the Muslim Brotherhood.

The FJP's platform emphasized social justice, a well-managed economy, job creation, and freedom of speech and assembly. Unlike the Brotherhood's clumsy attempt, in 2007, to offer a party agenda that subordinated gender and religion, this time the platform proclaimed women and Copts eligible for political office (but not the office of president). It then went on to promote tourism as a principal source of national income, free market capitalism (but no monopolies), and Islamic law (in a very broad sense). Its outlook, according to Mursi, would be "a civil one with an Islamic frame of reference." Since Islam in its widest sense provides guarantees for civil society, the Party claimed, its Islamic platform belongs to all people regardless of religion.[39]

But the formation of an official Brotherhood party drew critical attention to the moderate-radical split within the Brotherhood. The Guidance Bureau became concerned that the appearance of Brotherhood dominance could spark a reaction against it, leading to more arrests and prison sentences, in spite of the new democratic principles of the revolution. This worry was heightened by the sectarian clashes that broke out between Copts and Islamists during March and April of 2011. The Guidance Bureau was fearful that there might be a backlash against the Brotherhood. The Bureau was not opposed to the formation of a political party as such, but its members were worried about remaining dedicated and untainted by secular politics. The old guard wanted to stick to its stricter version of Islamism and adhere closely to the outlook of Sayyid Qutb. It was concerned that there could be too much overlap (and contamination) between the Brotherhood and the FJP.

To distance itself from the Brotherhood, the FJP decided that only 80 percent of its founders could actually be Brothers, with the remaining 20 percent to include Copts and secularists. The FJP announced that it would campaign for only half of the 454 seats in Parliament and would not field its own candidate for president. When the liberal, reformist Brother, 'Abd al-Mun'im Abu al-Fatuh, publicly announced his candidacy for the highest office, he was quickly expelled. Yet the FJP soon broke both promises; it fielded more than 230 Parliament candidates and nominated a candidate for president. Initially this was Khairat al-Shatir who, when disqualified, gave way to Muhammad Mursi, who then won the presidential election.[40]

Shortly after the FJP inaugural announcement, a group of discontents from the Youth wing broke away from the parent organization and announced the formation of yet another political party, the Current Party, which advocated a "more centrist and liberal version of Islamist politics." Its platform promoted individual freedoms and Islamic morals and culture, but it rejected the adoption of Islamic law and the mixing of religion and politics.[41]

Clearly the Brotherhood was splintering under the stress of its newfound recognition. This worried the radicals, who prized unity. At the same time, however, it served a cleansing function by pushing out the moderates and consolidating the remaining radical members into a more ideologically pure Islamist organization. The Qutbist branch of the Brotherhood was now free to take over.[42]

As Egypt's authoritarian leadership literally dissolved under the detergent action of the vast thousands of protesters, a dormant wing of quiescent Islamic activists unexpectedly began to emerge and mount a counterrevolution. These were the Salafis, members of the *salafiyya* movement. They rejected the *jihad* and political involvement promoted so strongly by Qutb, the militants, and the Brotherhood, but they continued to advocate the pure Islam first practiced at the time of the Prophet and now followed by many clerics, scholars, and ordinary Muslims influenced by the Wahhabi Islam of Saudi Arabia.

Although Salafis and jihadis are both Islamists and share the same conservative outlook, they differ quite drastically in the distinction between political quiescence and political opposition. One is Sunni—who strictly follow any Muslim ruler—and the other is Kharijite—who oppose all but the most legitimate authority. One is accommodating to the prevailing government while the other is hostile to it. There is seldom any competition for recruitment or overlapping membership.

The *salafiyya* movement goes back to the 1882 publication of *al-'Urwa al-Wuthqa* (The Firmest Bond) by Muhammad 'Abduh and Jamal al-Din al-Afghani. The influence of Wahhabi thinking in Egypt's Islamic movement dates back to the writings of Rashid Rida and his journal, *al-Manar* (The Beacon) in the first half of the 20th century. Sayyid Qutb himself subscribed to both the fundamentalism of the Salafis and the conservatism of the Wahhabis. Yet what distinguishes the Salafis from the Qutbists in the 21st century is their doctrine of quiescence over activism, of conformity over radicalism. Today's Salafis are not so much direct doctrinal descendants of Qutb as they are his ideological cousins, originating instead from 'Abduh and Rida and constituting a movement that parallels, but does not derive directly from, the *jihadi* militancy of Hasan al-Banna, Sayyid Qutb, 'Abd al-Salam Faraj, Tanzim al-Jihad, and al-Jama'a al-Islamiyya.[43]

The shrinking moderate wing of the Brotherhood falls between these two poles, starting with the second Supreme Guide, Hasan al-Hudaybi, and proceeding down to and stopping at Muhammad Badi'a. This wing occupies an unsteady middle ground that advocates political action and challenge authority but remains within the system rather than moving outside it and attempting to radically transform it, if not outright destroy it. Yet, in the 1980s and 1990s, the Mubarak government frequently used its Salafi allies to confront and counter the Brotherhood, pushing it even farther in the direction of Sayyid Qutb.[44] The Salafis, while conservative, represent instead a revivalist strain, *sahwa*, and a missionary zeal, *da'wa* or *tabligh*, that shrewdly avoids arrest, torture, and imprisonment by completely disavowing any political engagement. For reasons of ideology, interpretation, or perhaps mere survival, the Salafis chose to support the Mubarak administration from the start.[45]

Far from defying the state, many Salafis actually embraced Egypt's authoritarian leadership. They follow the Sunni adage that "it is better to have a bad or corrupt ruler than no ruler at all." Many Salafis had become apolitical back in the late 1970s, along with those who had joined Jama'at al-Muslimin (Takfir wa al-Hijra) before it turned violent. Others joined more recently, as remnant members of Tanzim al-Jihad or al-Jama'a al-Islamiyya, after their leaders had revised their conceptualization of Islam and had renounced their violent *jihad* of the sword. In the past, young, alienated middle-class men and women might have joined these *jihadi* organizations, but the government's campaigns to suppress these associations and to depoliticize university students succeeded in channeling them, instead, to small, mosque-based *salafi* congregations. More recently, other members have joined networks of Salafis because of their penchant for intolerance and declaring the unorthodox and the unorthoprax to be unbelievers, the self-righteous practice of *takfir*.[46]

The Salafis do not have a single leader or a specific organization. Instead, they are scattered, attracted to particular mosques located mostly in Alexandria and in the Cairo neighborhood of Shubra, but also, and perhaps more important, drawn to preachers broadcasting on the new, independent satellite TV channels. The Salafis of Alexandria are considered more radical, or severe, than those in Shubra; the TV preachers appear the closest of all to the old regime. Some of the Cairo Salafis also belong to the more formal organization, the Ansar al-Sunna (Followers of the Faith), headed by Mohammad Hassan, a preacher who appeals as well to an even broader range of followers through his television programs.[47]

Many, if not most, of these charismatic clerics have been influenced by the strict Wahhabism of Saudi Arabia and the Gulf where they worked during the height of the worldwide oil boom of 1974 to 1985.[48] Their repatriation to Egypt paralleled the rise of the militant associations and complemented their conservative beliefs, though without the violence. Then, as militancy lost its appeal—or else lost its membership due to arrest, exile, or death—many former Islamists adopted this nonconfrontational Wahhabi approach. They became even more inspired as the technology of satellite television, broadcast independence, and funding from the Arabian Gulf propelled the television preachers to even greater heights.

The Salafis strongly opposed the January 25 revolution, but the TV clerics were even more hostile to the protesters. The funding and influence from Saudi Arabia and the broadcast opportunities provided by Egyptian TV effectively shaped their sermons and speeches. They remained close to the Mubarak government until (and even after) the bitter end. In 2005, they had condemned as heretics those who stood against Mubarak in the presidential elections. In 2010, when Mubarak's government closed down the satellite TV stations due to sensitive sectarian tensions, these TV preachers simply went to other agencies within the government and continued broadcasting on regular state channels instead. After January 25, they condemned the protest as a foreign plot, even calling the demonstrators Zionists, a position similar to that of Wahhabi clerics in Saudi Arabia at the time.[49]

As the government ceded victory to secularist and Brotherhood demonstrators alike, the Salafis took advantage of the lawless atmosphere to revile those they had come to define as "the enemy," by attacking Coptic churches and Sufi shrines, both of which, they believed, were signs of wickedness and blasphemy. Coptic pressure had forced the Mubarak government to permit additional church building, and Sufis preached a mysticism that violated the tenets of the Qur'an and the principle of strict Islamic monotheism. Yet both controversies were much more salient in Saudi Arabia and not so significant in the ideas of Sayyid Qutb, Hasan al-Banna, or even 'Abd al-Salam Faraj. Their appearance in Egypt seemed unusual.

Yet, at the same time, the loyalty of the Salafis to the Mubarak government suggests their attacks on Christian churches and Sufi shrines represent less an ideological position and more a strong counterrevolutionary force that remnants of the old regime were exploiting to discredit the uprising.[50] The Salafis, while devout and conservative, proved no match for those who had pursued the *jihadi* path promoted by Qutb and his acolytes. Instead, they appeared more as supporters of tyranny than followers of justice. Their emergence, though, underscored the essential difference between these two approaches to Islam.

The Arab Spring of 2011 not only overthrew entrenched despots; it overthrew archaic notions of powerlessness that had prevailed for centuries. Egypt's collective imagination could now take flight. Egypt's future had been bleak and barren pretty much since the 1880s and the time of Isma'il, the British invasion, a thwarted nationalism, and a dispirited Islamism that repeatedly produced the crisis and breakdown that Qutb himself was trying to remedy. Now hope could open wide, at full throttle.

As the seeds of real democracy began to sprout, so the Islamic movement received a tremendous jolt of legitimacy that it had lacked for decades. As much as modernity seemed to be on the rise, with Facebook, Twitter, and a new generation of computer-savvy activists, so, too, was the Islamist imagination allowed to bloom. Of course, the dire but false choice between stability and chaos can be dismissed, for this is more an Orientalist fantasy than a historical reality. The move to Islam, even while demonized in the West as an excuse to support dictatorship, is not the reprehensible alternative portrayed in the media. The advance toward Qutb's Islamic state and society, with *shari'a*, *tawhid*, and *hakimiyya*, need not spell mayhem. It represents, instead, a viable alternative to a Western-derived modernity. Its authentic character may well prove to be the correct antidote for the corruption, ill-will, depravity, and hedonism that have plagued Egypt. The January 25 revolution threw off the mantle of tyranny and has allowed a true and free Egypt to come forward. There's no telling at this point exactly which way the country will go. The hope is that it will be better than the dismal excesses of the past.

The awesome irony, of course, is that with brave steadfastness and faith that nonviolence could topple tyrants—a wonderful replay of David and Goliath—the January 25 revolution realized what so many, including Sayyid Qutb, thought could only be achieved through force of arms. But putting aside the different tactics, the Islamic movement (Qutbist or otherwise), the April 6 Movement, and the "We're All Khalid Sa'id" Facebook group all struggled to achieve the same goals: a change of government and the end to arbitrary arrest, police torture, unjust incarceration, fraudulent elections, despotism, oligarchy, opportunism, and distorted, inhuman values. Yet while militancy and a *jihad* of the sword may no longer be necessary to realize Sayyid Qutb's goals—if, indeed, they ever were—both a *jihad* of the hand, of political involvement and activism, and *da'wa*, of debate and dissent, in determining the country's policies, policy makers, and officials, still seem necessary.

The January 25 revolution polarized Egypt's political landscape. The succession of Muhammad Badi'a to the office of Supreme Guide of the Muslim Brotherhood symbolizes the continuing appeal of Sayyid Qutb. The internal schisms in the Brotherhood divest it of those moderates chafing at the ideological blinders imposed by the radical wing of the Society. The public appearance of Salafis highlights the difference between a quiescent Islamism that supports despotism and an activist movement that opposes it. The Brotherhood now stands more doctrinaire and more united as it moves into the political arena. It does so with an unwavering focus on achieving a genuine and authentic Islamic community.

The legacy of Sayyid Qutb endures despite (or perhaps even because of) the advance of modernity. For it was Qutb who realized, crystallized, and substantiated many of the ideas that constitute the foundation of the contemporary Islamic movement. He became the magnifying lens that focused all the intense light on just one spot, bringing together streams of thought and action, and concentrating them together. He articulated the anger and rage toward the West and he compiled all the inaccuracies and mistakes of Islam. He demanded that true Muslims must overcome both—imitation of the West and ignorance of Islam—and return to what made Islam remarkable, distinctive, and proud. He was convinced that after all his years of trial-and-error, of experimenting with various doctrines, that Islam—the very first ideology he had ever learned, as a child—was, in fact, the best, the most authentic, and the most true. Now, nearly 50 years after his death, Sayyid Qutb's heirs are attempting to bring his vision of a truly Islamic Egypt to life.

APPENDIX

I. Dramatis Personae

(in alphabetical order)

Muhammad 'Abduh (1849–1905)

Muhammad 'Abduh was both the father of modern, secular Islam and a major contributor to *salafi* Islam and the Islamist movement. He accomplished these contradictory undertakings by claiming that modern Egyptians could be devout Muslims and that devout Muslims could also be modern. He was a student of Jamal al-Din al-Afghani and was swept up into al-Afghani's maelstrom of religion and politics. While he was in exile for two years, he and al-Afghani published the very influential journal, *al-'Urwa al-Wuthqa* (The Firmest Bond) in which the *salafiyya* movement was born. It sought to revive Islam by referring to the precedents established by the first generation of Muslims, the *salaf*. Yet when 'Abduh returned to Egypt, he turned conservative once he was appointed the chief mufti of Egypt. His students continued his contradictory approach, including both Rashid Rida, the famous Islamist, and Sa'd Zaghlul, the father of Egypt's secular nationalism. 'Abduh attempted to reform the al-Azhar by making it a better nationalist university, yet he also wrote about *tawhid* and *ijtihad*, unity and interpretation, as ways of revitalizing Islam.

'Abduh was born in 1849 in Shanra, a village near Tanta, Gharbiyya province, in the central Delta, although he and his family soon moved to Mahallat al-Nasr in neighboring Bahaira province where they owned property. In 1862, 'Abduh enrolled in the Ahmadi mosque school in Tanta, second in prestige only to al-Azhar. In 1869, he attended al-Azhar where he studied Sufism and philosophy, although his uncle discouraged him from continuing with mysticism.[1]

When al-Afghani arrived in Cairo in 1871, 'Abduh was still a student. He soon joined the growing circle of enthusiasts captivated by al-Afghani's magnetism. He finished his al-Azhar studies in 1877. Afterward, as al-Afghani plunged into local politics, 'Abduh became associated with the intrigues of his teacher. Al-Afghani joined a number of local Masonic lodges, stood accused of conspiring to assassinate Khedive (Viceroy) Isma'il, participated in the successional rivalries for Egypt's throne, and endorsed a constitutional republic. When al-Afghani was arrested and deported in August, 1879, 'Abduh was banished back to Mahallat al-Nasr for a year.[2]

Within the year, he returned to Cairo now as editor of the official government gazette, *al-Waqa'i al-Misriyya*, director of government publications, and member of the Council of Higher Education.[3] 'Abduh was soon caught up in the tumult of the nationalist movement under Colonel Ahmad 'Urabi and became one of its ardent civilian leaders, although he claimed later he was but a "reluctant" participant.[4] Echoing popular sentiment, he, too, was angered by the imperiousness of the "Joint Note" of January 1882 in which the British and the French sought to restrain the khedive's authority and he joined ranks with the Chamber of Deputies and other intellectuals to oppose foreign intervention in Egypt's domestic affairs. When an ad hoc national assembly, al-Jam'iyya al-Umumiyya, met for the second time in July, 1882 as the British navy bombarded Alexandria, 'Abduh was its secretary in a meeting that denounced Tawfiq as a traitor, supported 'Urabi's insurrection, and called for a war against England. With the British victory, 'Urabi surrendered and was tried by a military tribunal. As secretary, editor, and conspirator, 'Abduh was exiled, this time out of the country.

'Abduh first traveled to Beirut, but by the end of 1883, he moved to Paris where he joined his old teacher, al-Afghani. Together the two collaborated in publishing *al-'Urwa al-Wuthqa* from March to October 1884. Despite its short lifespan, its 18 issues were widely distributed throughout the Arab and Muslim worlds and had an immense impact on numerous Islamic intellectuals and scholars.

Until 1879, 'Abduh's politics were pan-Islamist under al-Afghani's influence. Then between 1879 and 1882, 'Abduh became a devoted nationalist while the editor of *al-Waqa'i al-Misriyya* during the 'Urabi revolt. After 1882, he reverted back to pan-Islamism under the renewed influence of al-Afghani and exile in Paris, until the end of his foreign sojourn in 1888. When he returned to Egypt, not only did he become a nationalist once again, but he also became a collaborator in support of British tutelage and a dignified member of Egypt's colonial and religious establishment.

Coming on the heels of France's occupation of Tunisia and England's victory in Egypt, *al-'Urwa al-Wuthqa* championed al-Afghani's earlier themes of Islamic solidarity in defense against Europe's hegemony. But whereas before the two writers defined unity more in terms of a unified civilizational focus, now it involved a much more concrete political alliance. Pan-Islamism became the solution to the failures of Muslim nations and their individual nationalisms. Political and military defeats were explained as the consequence of incorrigible rulers, their absolute despotism, and weak religious devotion. A revitalized Islamic *umma*, with a unified outlook, rejuvenated Islamic law, and a heightened sense of justice could restrain the tyranny of its rulers. The journal proved to be strongly anti-authoritarian and critical of Muslim rulers for not being Islamic.[5]

In the end, al-Afghani's personal commitment remained much greater than 'Abduh's, and the two parted company. 'Abduh followed strong leadership and adapted himself to the prevailing winds. Once he distanced himself from al-Afghani's charisma, his political ardor cooled. He left Paris and never saw al-Afghani again. He moved to Beirut where he taught for three years at the newly established al-Madrasa al-Sultaniyya (The Sultan's School) which became a liberal center for Muslims and non-Muslims to discuss Arab nationalism.[6]

It is not clear what negotiations took place that allowed Muhammad 'Abduh to return to Cairo. What is obvious, though, was that his political intensity had diminished. He preferred mild educational and judicial reforms over defiant subversion. Gone were the radical intrigues, the polemical journal articles, and the bold plans for regicide. Disenchanted, he abandoned al-Afghani's strident provocation and adopted a conciliatory approach toward the British based on gradual reforms. Evelyn Baring, Lord Cromer, the chief British administrator in Egypt from 1883 to 1907, urged Khedive Tawfiq to pardon 'Abduh and to appoint him to a prestigious position. 'Abduh returned in 1889 and became a *qadi*, or judge, in the religious courts and later an appeals judge in the national courts. Very soon, he became one of the most popular Islamic reformers, along with 'Abd Allah al-Nadim and 'Ali Yusuf. However, unlike the other two, 'Abduh was much more conformist.[7]

'Abduh and his supporters became the center of the new Umma (People's) Party and its publication, *al-Jarida* (The Newspaper). They considered themselves to be the representatives of those with real interest in their country, best served, they concluded, by cooperating with the British. The *Umma*'s main rival was the anti-British Watani (National) Party of Mustafa Kamil.

In his later years, 'Abduh became convinced that religious and educational reform represented the true solution for Egypt's malaise. This required a revitalization of the true spirit of Islam. Salafiyyism's return to a pure Islam was seen as the only way to face Europe's domination because it had been the accretions and innovations over the centuries that had made Islam weak. Islam did not contain the knowledge needed to compete equally with the West. Thus 'Abduh recommended an overhaul of traditional education by introducing modern disciplines and modernizing the *shari'a*. This meant reforming al-Azhar, the mosques, and the *shari'a* courts. This moderate approach would avoid confrontations with the Palace. Yet Khedive 'Abbas Hilmi II still saw 'Abduh in league with Lord Cromer seeking to undermine his authority. Thus the khedive rejected many of 'Abduh's proposals, as mild as these were, and attempted to discredit 'Abduh's reputation.[8]

In 1895, 'Abduh was appointed to an administrative council for reforming al-Azhar. He remained the chief advocate for reform until shortly before his death in 1905, when he resigned in frustration and began to campaign for a secular university. In 1899, he was appointed Mufti of Egypt and a member of the national Legislative Council, established in 1883 as the smaller successor to Egypt's Chamber of Delegates. These appointments came with the full support of Lord Cromer, and for the rest of his career, 'Abduh remained obligated to the English. The progressive politics he had nurtured, inspired by al-Afghani, were replaced by a much more moderate position that advocated gradual changes through educational and legal reforms.[9]

He died on July 11, 1905.

Ahmad Zaki Abu Shadi (1892–1955)

Ahmad Zaki Abu Shadi was born on February 9, 1892, the son of a well-to-do lawyer. His first volume of poems appeared in 1908 when he was just 16, and he may have even established his own journal, *Hada'iq al-Zahir* (Gardens of Flowers) the same year. Others claim his first volume of poetry was called *'And al-Fajr* (With the Dawn) and was published in 1910. Two years later, in 1912, he attended medical school in Egypt, but a shattered love affair pushed him to leave and travel first to Istanbul and later to London where he resumed his medical studies. There, he received a diploma in bacteriology and married an Englishwoman. He remained in England for 10 years, even during the outbreak of the 1919 revolution. Nationalist admirers may have exaggerated his patriotism, emphasizing the poems he composed at the time, such as "Bilad al-Nil" (Homeland of the Nile) and the suspicions these verses engendered with Scotland Yard, as signs that he had not completely succumbed to the English.

When his father's health declined in 1922, Abu Shadi returned to Egypt. He sought employment as a bacteriologist and jumped immediately into the swirl of Egypt's literary societies. He set up the Rabitat al-Adab al-Jadid (New Literature League) in Alexandria in 1927 before founding the Apollo Society in Cairo in 1932. He published 15 books of poems, and his most famous collection was *al-Shafaq al-Baki* (The Sad Twilight) published in 1927.[10]

Abu Shadi had already irritated the literary world well before he founded the Apollo Society. In March 1917, while still in England, he published a letter in *al-Muqtataf* (Selections) chastising two of the founders of the Diwan school, 'Abd al-Rahman Shukri and 'Abd al-Qadr al-Mazini, for the literary debate they were engaged in before they joined together with al-'Aqqad in 1921 to publish *Diwan Kitab fi al-Adab wa al-Naqd* (The Collected Volume of Literature and Criticism) that established the new school.[11]

Abu Shadi was influenced by the literary society, the Writers' League (al-Rabita al-Qalamiyya), founded in New York City in 1922 by three early Arab American literati of Christian Lebanese Syrian background: Jibran Khalil Jibran (1883–1931), Amin al-Rihani (1876–1940), and Mikha'il Na'ima (1889–1988). He was also inspired by the Poetry Society that had formed in England in 1909.[12]

Abu Shadi insisted that there had to be a new, modern style of poetry in Egypt and an end to the neoclassical approach. Poetry, he wrote, is the means of discovering "the secrets of existence. It is the expression of the spirit of the universe, whose greatness and beauty it reveals."[13] He promoted himself as the single most important innovator in Egypt's poetic scene, an egotism that engendered much resentment. Since he was heavily influenced by British poets and English literature in general, he became a major conduit of Anglo-European ideas and style.[14]

Echoing ideas found in the Diwan school, Abu Shadi claimed that poetry should be restricted to feelings and imagination. He agreed with that school's founder, 'Abbas al-'Aqqad, on the central idea that poetry requires a unity; its beauty and truth are to be based on this unity and not on its separate components. He advocated a free flow of ideas, even if they conflict with traditional themes and conventions. Personal emotional expression means a flexible style, language use, and rhythm.[15]

Abu Shadi took sides in a literary battle between al-'Aqqad and the neoclassical poet, Mustafa al-Rafi'i (1880–1937) that had begun back in 1930 and that continued to fester until it erupted later in 1938.[16] Abu Shadi's Apollo Society came to al-Rafi'i's defense despite its intentions to remain neutral. This earned Abu Shadi the intense acrimony of al-'Aqqad and his supporters, including Sayyid Qutb. In September 1932, al-'Aqqad wrote an article in the *Apollo's* first issue strongly disparaging the journal's name, whose Greek origin, he argued, symbolized its complete Westernization. Six months later, after al-'Aqqad had published a collection of poetry, *Wahy al-Arba'in* (Revelations at Forty), the journal published two blistering critiques by Abu Shadi and Isma'il Mazhar.

Al-'Aqqad accused the Apollo Society of harboring political motives and cooperating with the Palace and the Sidqi government. The Diwan members were avowed Wafdists while the Apollo members were associated—"collaborated," Qutb was to write—with the more authoritarian administration of Isma'il Sidqi, his Sha'ab Party, and the royal palace. The Apollo Society was also accused of seeking government funds for its publications. Such fights soon alienated financial contributors, and the journal ran out of money, forcing Abu Shadi to close it down in 1934.[17]

The following year, Abu Shadi moved to Alexandria where he established a similar literary society, although this may have simply been the continuation of his 1927 activities in the same city. There, he published one new journal, *Adabi* (My Literature), and revived a second, *al-Imam* (The Minister). But since he was far removed from the center of literary activity in Cairo, he failed to maintain the same influence, and his literary efforts were marginal.

The brief two years of vigorous composition, publication, and debate in Cairo earned Abu Shadi much acclaim for inspiring poets inside and outside of Egypt and for providing a new channel in which poets could express their modern romanticism and nostalgia. The Apollo Society and its journal supported young poets and helped introduce them to Western poetic styles in ways that contrasted with the Diwan school with its more parochial and limited influence just inside Egypt.[18]

In 1942, he was appointed the chair of bacteriology and deputy dean of faculty at the Medical School at the newly established Alexandria University. But after his wife died in 1946, Abu Shadi moved permanently to the United States where he worked for the Saudi Arabian delegation at the United Nations and for Voice of America.

He died in New York City on April 12, 1955.

Jamal al-Din al-Afghani (1838–97)

Jamal al-Din al-Afghani was the first Islamist and, until Sayyid Qutb, the only major Islamist to target the West (primarily Europe) and not just focus on criticizing and attacking national governments in the Muslim world. This international focus involves what the Islamic movement came to call "The Far Enemy," in contrast to "The Near Enemy" of local regimes.[19] Between al-Afghani and Qutb came a series of domestic-oriented radicals—Muhammad 'Abduh, Rashid Rida, and Hasan al-Banna. Al-Afghani operated within the global imperium of Britain and Qutb acted under the global hegemony of the United States. Both perspectives reflected a globalism that was absent in the interim period characterized by heightened nationalism and a strong state corporatism.[20]

Al-Afghani was the first major pan-Islamic intellectual in Egypt, warning of the dangers of European imperialism. He was the first to see that the emerging social breakdown required a new understanding of Islam. He considered the relationship between Europe and Islam to be an antagonistic one that threatened the Muslim world with its very existence. Earlier Egyptian thinkers, such as Rifa'a al-Tahtawi (1801–73), had envisioned Europe as an attractive, but distant, partner, with bodies of knowledge (science) and ways of thinking (philosophy) that could be learned and adopted without harming Egypt.[21] Al-Afghani, however, saw in Europe's intense materialism and lack of strong morals a peril that could dominate not just Egypt but the entire Islamic community. He was a man very much ahead of his times. At a time when Egyptian intellectuals were still fascinated with Europe, al-Afghani was preaching caution.[22]

Al-Afghani, together with his student, Muhammad 'Abduh, was also the first major intellectual to define the *salafiyya* movement. This doctrine meant returning to the pure Islam of the first generation of Muslims, or *salaf*.

Al-Afghani was born in October–November 1838 in the town of Asadabad in Qazvin province in northwest Iran. His *nisba* name of origin, the Afghan, shrewdly disguised his true sectarian identity—Persian Shi'ite—that would have limited his activities and travels in the Sunni world of the Middle East and India. Shi'ite Islam still permitted Islamic interpretation, which had declined after the 9th century among Sunni Muslims. Al-Afghani advocated the Shi'ite perspective, but in the Sunni world, this was considered heresy.[23]

As a boy, al-Afghani moved to the provincial capital for further schooling and then on to Tehran before attending higher education in Iraq in the 1850s. There he was introduced to the near-heretical, liberal Shaykhi doctrines that undermined the elite position of Shi'ite clergy by arguing, instead, that any layperson could interpret *shari'a*. From 1856 to 1858, al-Afghani was traveling through India when in May 1857, the Indian Mutiny erupted, a ferocious rebellion against British colonial rule. This experience strongly impressed upon him the dangers of Western domination. He continued his travels, stopping briefly in Cairo in 1869, and then on to Istanbul where he stayed until 1871. His intellect and personality quickly brought him into elite circles. Yet al-Afghani moved back to Cairo two years later after a dispute over modernizing Islam, of bringing religion, science, and rational philosophy together. He stayed on after the Egyptian government awarded him a stipend to teach at al-Azhar.[24]

Al-Afghani lived in Egypt from 1871 to 1879. He exerted a major influence on the political activists and reformers attempting to raise Egypt out of the economic, social, and political malaise caused by the cotton market collapse of the late 1860s. His stay occurred at the same time as Europe's heightened intrigue and energetic efforts to gain territory so as to resolve the "Eastern Question" of what to do with—or how to conquer—the "sick man of Europe," the Ottoman Empire.[25]

From 1871 to1877, al-Afghani avoided political activism and worked just as a teacher, although he was very charismatic and greatly admired by a growing circle of students, officials, and intellectuals. They were inspired by his sharp intellect and dynamic lessons in philosophy, logic, theology, jurisprudence, mysticism, and current events. His followers became the leaders of Egypt's new political and intellectual scene, including Muhammad 'Abduh, 'Abd Allah al-Nadim, and Sa'd Zaghlul. He lectured on the dangers of European intervention, called for a national unity to resist it, and promoted the broader solidarity of all Muslims everywhere.[26]

Although initially he was on good terms with Egypt's Khedive Isma'il, their relationship soon soured. In 1879, al-Afghani called for a national constitutional party and he delivered fiery public speeches denouncing Egypt's ruler. When the British contrived to depose Isma'il, al-Afghani supported the wrong side of the successional struggle, favoring Isma'il's uncle Halim over his son, Tawfiq. Although al-Afghani appeared to be on positive terms with Tawfiq, his public position against the Europeans who installed the new ruler raised suspicions that his support for the throne was insincere. The new khedive believed that al-Afghani was working for a constitutional republic and so in August 1879 arrested him and deported him to Jeddah in the Hijaz.[27]

Al-Afghani traveled to India, where he wrote a number of important books, including his most famous, *al-Radd 'ala al-Dahriyyin* ('Ihe Refutation of the Materialists) in which he challenged the Islamic modernizer and secularist Sayyid Ahmad Khan of India (1817–98). When the 'Urabi officers revolt took place in Egypt in 1882, al-Afghani left India and joined Muhammad 'Abduh in Paris where the two published the influential, mass circulation newspaper, *al-'Urwa al-Wuthqa* (The Firmest Bond) which targeted the relations between the Islamic and the European worlds and demanded reforms in Islam.[28]

Writing for *al-'Urwa al-Wuthqa* crystallized al-Afghani's ideas about a practical pan-Islamic response to the European threat that bordered on subversion if not outright militancy. He began to see himself as a Muslim Martin Luther, reforming Islam as a religion but also shaping an entire civilization. He wanted to transform Islam but not necessarily secularize it. For unlike Christianity which had to jettison either religion or modernity, Islam, he felt, could reconcile the two. Modernizers like Khan had essentially relegated religion to secondary importance. But Muslims could be modern *within* Islam and had no need to reject religious doctrines.[29]

Al-'Urwa al-Wuthqa lasted only seven months, but it had a very significant impact on the region's intellectuals. It introduced Arabs to such new ideas as freedom, independence, and the rights of the ruled. It focused on reforming governments, overthrowing tyranny, resisting imperialism, and inspiring Islamic unity. It diagnosed the reasons for Islam's decline—ignorance, fatalism, disunity, and despotic, corrupt, and incompetent rulers—and it explained the reasons for the West's high achievements—its science, rational philosophy, and political doctrines. If Muslims were to retain parity, they had to learn these new ideas. But their rulers had betrayed them. Steeped in greed and ignorance, and repeatedly capitulating to Europeans, they had to be tightly restrained through constitutions and parliaments.[30]

In 1885, al-Afghani continued his travels to England (to convince the British to end their rule in Egypt), Russia (to stir up opposition against the British), and Persia (to conspire to overthrow the Shah) before being invited to Istanbul in 1892 by the Ottoman sultan, 'Abd al-Hamid II. Their relationship soon deteriorated, however, and al-Afghani was placed under house arrest, which limited his ability to publish and speak. There, he died from cancer in 1897.[31]

Al-Afghani did not write profusely, and his ideas were often disorganized. But he popularized a number of intellectual trends in Islamic thought, and his impact, either directly or through his students, was substantial. His main theme was the idea of solidarity in the face of Western encroachment. Real unity in a Muslim nation rests on common religious conviction. If that dissipates, society itself dissolves, and this is what al-Afghani believed to be taking place in the Muslim world. Only by a return to a true Islam could the strength and civilization of Muslims be restored. Had Muslims been strong and united, Britain could never have conquered India, first, and later Egypt. Europe was successful because of its advanced material state and technology. Although these had developed in Europe due to the separation of religion from education and government, this division did not have to happen—and should not happen—in Muslim countries. Islam itself is already rational, he argued. It does not require secularization to thrive.[32]

'Abbas Mahmud al-'Aqqad (1889–1964)

'Abbas Mahmud al-'Aqqad was born on June 28, 1889, in the southern provincial capital of Aswan. His early life very much paralleled the trajectory of Sayyid Qutb, his disciple. As a young boy, al-'Aqqad was immersed in both nationalist and Islamic discourse, from his father, elementary school, and his own curiosity. At the age of 16, he began his career as a government clerk, but left public service three years later and moved into journalism as the editor for the Cairo newspaper, *al-Dustur* (The Constitution). This move coincided with the beginning of Mustafa Kamil's National Party in 1907, and *al-Dustur* and al-ʿAqqad quickly aligned themselves with both Kamil's nationalism and a pan-Islamic rhetoric. Al-ʿAqqad soon broke with *al-Dustur*'s pan-Islamism, bending more and more in the direction defined by Muhammad ʿAbduh and Saʿd Zaghlul. In 1909, he became unemployed when *al-Dustur* ceased publication, and afterward alternated between Cairo and Aswan, between government and journalistic employment, and between mental acuity and mental breakdown. He worked on the editorial staff of a number of important newspapers and magazines and met many influential men of letters. He taught himself literature and poetry.[33]

Throughout the 1920s, al-ʿAqqad was an active member of the Egyptian Parliament. He spoke out strongly against the rising authoritarianism of Prime Minister Ismaʿil Sidqi who suspended the Egyptian constitution on October 22, 1930. His speech against Sidqi and King Fuʾad earned him nine months in prison. Upon his release in 1931, his fame skyrocketed. However, in 1935, he was expelled from the Wafd Party because of personal conflicts with the party leadership, and in 1937, joined the splinter group, the Saʿdist Party, under Ahmad Mahir and Mahmud Fahmi al-Nuqrashi, and was once again elected to Parliament.

Al-ʿAqqad wrote more than 100 books on such topics as philosophy, religion, biography, and poetry. He was ordinarily somber and aloof, but he reacted viciously to personal criticism. He demanded firm, undying loyalty from his supporters, and cruelly attacked those who turned treacherous toward him. The sum total of his seriousness, egotism, and haughtiness was an arrogant and patronizing demeanor, buttressed by a lurking insecurity due to his lack of formal schooling. Al-ʿAqqad was a polarizing figure, charismatically attracting both friends and enemies, but seldom leaving those he met unmoved. His acerbic style, clarity, and precision won him admiration. But he earned the enmity of many who suffered from his sharp pen, his biting vitriol, and his stinging attacks.

Al-ʿAqqad was a staunch proponent of Romantic poetry in Egypt, and he published eight major collections. His poems were strongly influenced by the English Romantic poets, but they also reflected classical styles as well. Yet his fame was based primarily on such scholarly works as his *Abqariyyat* (Geniuses) series and his 1937 novel, *Sarah*. His most controversial religious book was published in 1942 and was simply called *Allah*.

Of the three co-founders of the Diwan school—al-ʿAqqad, ʿAbd al-Rahman Shukri, and ʿAbd al-Qadr al-Mazini—al-ʿAqqad became the most iconoclastic. His lifelong mission turned into a campaign to tear down the old literary tradition and erect a totally new one as the exclusive and unassailable reformer of contemporary Arabic literature in Egypt. He approached his studies of literature and his criticism of the literati with a crusading zeal and displayed an extensive range of knowledge and interests, particularly notable for an autodidact. His mind constantly probed the motives and character of those he reviewed.[34] He introduced new standards of writing and composition, and a new perspective in evaluating the efforts of others. He was convinced that "his ideas would open a new chapter in the history of Arabic literature" as he called for "modernism, truth, greater depth and portrayal of the poet's self" and sought to initiate a "revolution" in poetry and literary criticism, while independently assuming the entire burden of modernizing these two genres for himself.[35]

Although al-'Aqqad modestly called Shukri the school's leader—he was, after all, the oldest member—it was really al-'Aqqad who was the most established and foremost poet of his times. He was the most outspoken of the three and presented his own compositions in grandiose terms. Ironically, the other co-founders of the Diwan school ended up fighting each other and pretty much stopped writing poetry, leaving al-'Aqqad the group's leading lyricist by default.[36]

The school had a very influential role in Egyptian literary circles, sponsoring and publishing modern writers, and entering the fray in literary battles in 1934, 1938, and 1943.[37] Even without the further contributions from al-Mazini and Shukri, the Diwan school continued to promote an anglophile, romantic and individualistic style of poetry.

Al-'Aqqad's criticism and arguments are classic examples of modernizing apologetics.[38] The superior qualities of the works he reviewed and critiqued were repeatedly attributed to European influence and the inferior traits were always excused by their Arabic or Semitic origin (following the intellectual fashion of the late 19th century of bundling these two together). Al-'Aqqad's ideas were quite similar to those of the French Orientalists, Ernest Renan and Gustave Le Bon. At the beginning of his career, al-'Aqqad also employed the well-known theories of the famous 19th-century English essayist and critic William Hazlitt (1778–1830) who had concluded that the formative elements in intellectual production can be predicted from knowing the thinker's personal temperament and inherited physical and racial characteristics. This temperament, Hazlitt determined, is inborn. Al-'Aqqad adopted Hazlitt's ideas that a poet's disposition, once known and understood, is the primary predictor of the author's writings, and that this temperament is established at birth. Thus al-'Aqqad wrote about "the Arab manner of thinking" and "the Egyptian natural disposition"—all familiar expressions of national character studies derived from late 19th-century eugenics theory.

Jayyusi comments,

> He was able to create in the minds of a generation thirsty for change and modernization but hazy in vision and perception, a mental impression of his importance as a poet. This may have been the result of the abundance of his poetic output on the one hand, and his well-informed and authoritarian critical writings on the other. Consequently, a good number of critics and writers on poetry in Egypt accepted his poetry (together with the poetry of al-Mazini and Shukri) as an example of

what modernized poetry should be in Arabic, with the inevitable lower-
ing of the standards of aesthetic appreciation in Egypt.[39]

During World War II, al-'Aqqad supported the Allied side. It was during the wartime that al-'Aqqad and Qutb began parting company. In 1952, al-'Aqqad similarly
supported the Revolution under Jamal 'Abd al-Nassir. In 1959 he was awarded the
State Prize for literature.

On March 12, 1964, he died quietly in his home in the suburb of Heliopolis
located northeast of Cairo.

Hasan al-Banna (1906–49)

Hasan al-Banna was the founder, at the age of 21, of *Jama'at al-Ikhwan al-Muslimin*
(The Society of Muslim Brothers or the Muslim Brotherhood) in Isma'iliyya in
1928. (It relocated to Cairo in 1932.) Al-Banna subscribed to the *salafiyya* doctrines and concepts of social and political unity, *tawhid*, adopted by his intellectual forebears, Jamal al-Din al-Afghani, Muhammad 'Abduh, and Rashid Rida. Yet
more than these earlier three, who for the most part remained writers, he set
about organizing a permanent organization to realize these principles through
concrete action. The Brotherhood established charitable activities, newspapers
and journals, and paramilitary battalions. When the Palestinian revolt erupted in
1936, al-Banna shifted from concentrating on social justice and welfare to emphasizing anti-colonialism and armed combat. It was never absolutely clear whether
the Brotherhood promoted participatory democracy and elections or advocated
military force and violence. Twice al-Banna announced his intentions to run for
parliamentary elections. Yet at the same time, the Brotherhood also established
the Secret Apparatus to wage war against the Zionists in Palestine but which could
also be turned against adversaries inside Egypt. Just as his lifelong institution
building was remarkable, he also met his death in a dramatic fashion, assassinated
by an assailant suspected of working for the security forces attached to the prime
minister, Ibrahim 'Abd al-Hadi.

Al-Banna was born on October 17, 1906, in the town of Mahmudiyya in the
Delta province of Bahira, the oldest of Shaykh Ahmad 'Abd al-Rahman al-Banna's
five sons. He was influenced by his father who was the local imam, a watchmaker,
and an independent Islamic scholar; by his teacher, Shaykh Muhammad Zahran,
editor of an Islamic journal and head of the local Hasafiyya Sufi branch; and by
the nationalist revolution of 1919. He studied with Shaykh Muhammad until the
age of 12 when he enrolled in the Primary Teachers' Training School in nearby
Damanhur, where he studied until 1923 when he moved to Cairo to attend Dar
al-'Ulum.

At the age of 12, he joined his first Islamic organization, the Society for
Moral Behavior, and founded a second, the Society for Prohibiting Evil. He also

established the Hasafiyya Benevolence Society (HBS). In school, he was elected president of the school's literary society, and along with other students, founded the Society for the Prevention of Sin. Later, in Cairo, he joined the Society for Islamic Ethics and the Association of Muslim Youth (YMMA). Such societies were active in organizing efforts to reform Islam and to prevent the backsliding that their members considered prevalent throughout Egypt. Both the HBS and the YMMA served as prototypes for the Muslim Brotherhood.[40]

Al-Banna graduated in May 1927; the following September, he was assigned his first teaching post in Isma'iliyya, a city midway along the British-controlled Suez Canal. In March 1928, al-Banna founded the Society of Muslim Brothers in order to help six workmen employed by the British army who had come to him complaining of discrimination and exploitation.[41]

Soon, new branches appeared in towns and cities throughout Egypt. By June 1933, the Brotherhood had opened 15 branches, 100 by March 1936, and over 300 by June 1938. In 1936, it had registered more than 20,000 members. Eight years later, the number ranged between 100,000 and 200,000, and by 1948, after al-Banna's assassination, the number peaked to well over a million members.[42]

In October, 1932, the Education Ministry transferred al-Banna to Cairo. He immediately began to propagate the Brotherhood message through the mass media of newspapers and journals as well as providing weekly programs of lectures, sermons, and public readings in coffeehouses, mosques, and branch offices.

The Brotherhood's primary goals included teaching Islamic morals, strengthening Islamic unity, reviving religious activism, and modernizing Islam. It established programs for private Islamic schools, adult literacy programs, clinics and hospitals, ambulance services, pharmacies, mosque construction, carpet and embroidery workshops, sports teams and athletic activities, Boy Scouts (or Rovers), model farms, Ramadan *iftar* tables, subsidized burials and cemeteries, village electrification, and welfare payment channeled through Brotherhood-operated *zakat* committees attached to neighborhood mosques.[43]

In 1936, the Brotherhood took up the cause of Palestinians rebelling against the British and Zionists by organizing programs of fund-raising and material support. It staged rallies, scheduled special "Palestine Days," convened mass meetings, dedicated public prayers, wrote and published incendiary pamphlets, mounted posters, and published special editions of the Society's newspaper. The Palestine campaign had a major impact on the Brotherhood. It changed from being simply a benevolent society that had emphasized charity, preaching, and education to an organization that stressed political activism and displayed hostile attitudes toward the government and imperialist powers. By 1939, the Muslim Brotherhood became a major player in Egypt's national politics. The British and the Palace were both wary that its anti-Zionism was essentially a pretext for promoting anti-Palace and anti-colonialist policies.[44]

In order to protect the organization and appease the authorities, al-Banna sought patrons from the Palace, al-Azhar, and Parliament, although this contravened the policy of avoiding elite ties that might compromise Brotherhood policies and actions. Yet even as al-Banna warned against violent confrontations, the Brotherhood soon came under increasing pressure to adopt more radical tactics.

In October 1937, at a mass demonstration of several thousand protesters in Cairo, the police were called in, and, for the first time, Brothers were arrested for their political activities. In September 1938, in response to calls for defending al-Aqsa Mosque in Jerusalem, the Brotherhood initiated programs training its Boy Scouts (or Rovers) in paramilitary techniques and organizing them into battalions. When in February 1940, the radical Society of Our Master Muhammad's Youth (Shabab Muhammad) broke away from the Brotherhood, al-Banna still advocated nonviolence. But he also went about creating the Secret Apparatus the following April as a new internal structure to carry out a more subversive approach to domestic and regional politics.[45]

After February 4, 1942, when the British imposed a Wafd cabinet on the government, new elections were called for that March and the Brothers decided to contest the elections. Al-Banna himself ran for Parliament from Isma'iliyya. Worried that the Brotherhood would pull votes away from the Wafd, Prime Minister Mustafa al-Nahhas demanded that al-Banna stand down. Al-Banna agreed, but only on condition that the Brotherhood resume its publications closed down under martial law and that the government forbid prostitution and the sale of alcoholic beverages. When new elections were scheduled again in 1944, al-Banna and members of the Muslim Brotherhood again promised to field candidates. This time they did not withdraw, even under strong pressure from the British. Nevertheless, they were defeated, even in districts considered Brotherhood strongholds.[46]

The war's end lifted martial law but did not diminish British control. When the 1936 Anglo-Egyptian treaty came up for renegotiation, the Brotherhood rose up four-square against any infringement of Egyptian sovereignty. Student demonstrations in early February 1946 protested Britain's continued domination. Demonstrators from all fronts—Wafd, Muslim Brothers, and Communists—came together in the National Committee of Students and Workers and called for a general strike at the end of February. But the Brotherhood refused to participate—it viewed such alliances and united fronts with suspicion—even while its members unofficially joined the rally.

After November 1947, when the issue of Palestine came up before the United Nations and Britain absolved itself of the matter, many groups, including the Muslim Brotherhood, prepared for Israeli independence by training their paramilitaries for action. Government indifference simply angered and provoked ordinary Egyptians.

In October 1948, a Brotherhood ammunition depot was discovered on the estate of one of its members. An even more incriminating incident occurred in November when a policeman stopped a jeep that turned out to carry documents pointing to armed violence by the Secret Apparatus. Al-Banna was arrested two weeks later but was released almost immediately. Yet when Cairo's police chief was killed by a bomb in early December, the government banned the Brotherhood again. Three weeks later, Prime Minister Mahmud al-Nuqrashi was shot in the back as he entered the Interior Ministry. In response, the new prime minister, Ibrahim 'Abd al-Hadi, arrested and persecuted Muslim Brothers with a vengeance.[47]

On Saturday evening, February 12, 1949, as al-Banna left a meeting at the central offices of the Muslim Youth (YMMA), a lone stalking gunman emerged from the shadows and shot him in his chest seven times before stepping into a waiting taxi. Al-Banna stumbled back into the YMMA offices to call the police but passed out. He was whisked away to the closest medical center and eventually transferred to Qasr al-'Aini Hospital where he was admitted to intensive care. Shot at 8:25 in the evening, he died just before 2 o'clock in the morning of the 13th. Four months later, the expected assassination attempt on 'Abd al-Hadi failed. By the time he left office in July 1949, though, close to 4,000 Muslim Brothers had been arrested and imprisoned.[48]

Taha Husayn (1889–1973)

Taha Husayn, one of the leading writers in the 20th century, was known as "the dean of Arab Letters."[49] He was born on November 14, 1889, in the village of Izbit al-Kilu, outside the town of Maghagha, in the southern Egyptian province of al-Minya. His family was a middle-class family with some land. When he was two years old, he suffered a mistreated eye ailment and as a result was blind for the rest of his life. In al-Minya, he attended the local Qur'anic school, the *kuttab*, and memorized the Qur'an.[50] At the age of 13, he was sent to Cairo to live with an older brother and attend al-Azhar University. But he did not perform well, failed his final exams, and dropped out before completing his studies. Then in 1908, he enrolled in the newly established—and secular—Egyptian (later Fu'ad I, and later Cairo) University as one of its first students. At the time, the university was staffed with European faculty, and Husayn gravitated toward such Orientalists as the Italian Carlo Nallino and the German Enno Littmann with their focus on the ancient world and its early civilizations. In 1914, he was the first Egyptian to receive his doctorate from the university, with a dissertation on Abu al-'Ala al-Ma'arri, a blind 10th-century Syrian philosopher and writer who attacked religious dogma and supported rationalism.[51]

Husayn became a protégé of Lutfi al-Sayyid, one of the most prominent Egyptian nationalists of the early 20th century and the first president of the national Egyptian University. Al-Sayyid helped Husayn at key moments in his life—receiving a coveted scholarship to study in France, achieving prestigious faculty and dean appointments at the national university, and obtaining career-saving pardons from political storms. At the time of World War I, Husayn received his scholarship to France, first to the University of Montpellier and then later to the

Sorbonne. He attended classes taught by Emile Durkheim, Gustave Lanson, and Lucien Levy-Bruhl. His 1919 dissertation was written about Ibn Khaldun's social philosophy. He also obtained a *diplome superieur* in ancient history, Latin, and Greek based on a thesis about crimes of treason in ancient Rome. In 1917 he married a French woman, his loyal reader. After completing his studies, he returned to Egypt in 1921 and was appointed to the faculty at his alma mater as a professor of ancient Greek and Roman history. Since he was an Azhar dropout, his selection generated an outcry of protest.[52]

In 1925, Husayn switched his faculty affiliation from ancient history to Arabic literature. Then in 1926, he published his highly controversial book, *Fi al-Shi'r al-Jahili* (Pre-Islamic Poetry) which denied the divine authenticity of the Qur'an.[53] This case brought him public outrage, investigations by the national parliament and al-Azhar, and near-expulsion from the faculty but for his ties to al-Sayyid. Despite the book's republication the following year in a toned-down version, he remained controversial throughout his career, especially among religiously minded scholars and politicians.

In 1930 he was appointed dean of the Literature Faculty, but was subsequently dismissed under the Sidqi administration in 1932. Nevertheless, he was reappointed in 1936. This second appointment failed, however, and Husayn moved from the university faculty to the position of inspector with the Ministry of Education where Sayyid Qutb worked. Here Husayn published another divisive book, *The Future of Culture in Egypt*, which, while ostensibly dealing with the immediate problems of schools and education, advocated a complete imitation of all things European. Despite this wholesale Westernization, Husayn also wrote about Islamic themes, indicating, perhaps, more an opportunism than a genuine curiosity about religious subjects. J. Brugman called him a "free thinker" and a "radical liberal."[54]

In 1942 he benefited from the British-imposed Wafd administration and became first a consultant to the education minister and then later president of the new Alexandria University. He further capitalized on his Wafd connections when, in 1950, he became the minister of education. After the 1952 revolution, Husayn lost his position, along with other Wafdist officials. He tepidly supported 'Abd al-Nassir and Egypt's newfound nationalism. He was the first to be awarded the State Prize in Literature, in 1952.

He passed away on October 28, 1973, in Cairo.

Muhammad Mandur (1907–65)

Muhammad Mandur was born in 1907 in the village of Kafr Abu Mandur—named for his elite family—in northern Gharbiyya (now Kafr al-Shaykh) Province. He was a student at Egypt's national university from 1925 to 1929 where he doubled majored in law and literature. He attended courses taught by Taha Husayn, who persuaded Mandur to study in both disciplines and later played a key role in obtaining a scholarship for him to study in France. Mandur did not receive a study-abroad scholarship at first because of his poor eyesight, but soon, with sympathetic assistance from Husayn, who himself was blind, Mandur went on to France where he attended the Sorbonne from 1930 to 1939. Although he earned several diplomas in economics and legislation and in experimental phonetics, as well as a *licence* in both French and African literature, he failed to earn a doctoral degree.[55]

He returned to Egypt when the war broke out in Europe and secured a lecturer appointment at Fu'ad I (later Cairo) University that was arranged by Ahmad Amin who had just succeeded Taha Husayn as the new dean of the university's Faculty of Literature. Then, in 1942, when Mandur began attending the new Alexandria University to earn his doctorate, he startled his professors by choosing Amin as his supervisor instead of Taha Husayn, his undergraduate mentor, who, by then, had become president of the new university. Subsequently, when Mandur graduated in 1943, he was deliberately passed over for further promotion at the university. Mandur resigned, left university teaching completely, and began a career in journalism. This episode might have implied a falling out between Mandur and Husayn, but Brugman declares that "an ideological difference of opinion between Taha Husayn and Mandur can hardly have been the cause of this delay [Brugman actually means "rupture"] in Mandur's career, for nothing in their writing of the period points in this direction."[56]

Moreover, despite this disagreement, the two remained philosophically alike. Both had studied with, and were strongly influenced by, the same teacher, Gustave Lanson (1857–1934), the well-known historian and critic of French literature who had emphasized the study of artistic and textual characteristics instead of extrinsic contextual and subjective factors. Brugman claims, however, that since Lanson had died in 1934 at the age of 77, he was probably too old during the 1930–39 period Mandur studied in Paris to teach any classes for Mandur to attend. Yet Lanson's influence remains clear. Mandur translated one of the French scholar's celebrated articles that appeared in Arabic as "Manhaj al-Bahth fi al-Lugha wa al-Adab" (Research Program in Language and Literature), he relied on Lanson for his intellectual foundations, and he assumed Lanson's pioneering perspective that criticism should not be an exact science.[57]

Mandur sought to revolutionize literary criticism by advancing the methods followed in France. He urged his colleagues to adopt the French romantic style of expression that evoked aesthetic values such as beauty and that aroused the feelings and the imagination of the reader.[58] He argued that whereas science investigates the general, literary criticism should analyze the particular. His imaginative and groundbreaking articles appeared in *al-Thaqafa* (Culture) which had been launched in 1939 by Ahmad Amin, his mentor and dean at Fu'ad I University.[59] His most famous book was his first, *Fi al-Mizan al-Jadid* (New Balance).

Mandur chafed against "all restrictions against liberty" which extended to adopting a distinct libertine outlook, and it was Mandur who translated Gustave Flaubert's *Madame Bovary*, then considered as "an outrage against public morality" even by Parisian standards.[60]

Mandur argued that all those who considered literary criticism an exact science were doomed to failure. He rejected any method that employed external factors, such as culture and history, and he also eschewed explanations based on the personality of the writer, the approached promoted by 'Abbas al-'Aqqad, founder of the rival Diwan school of poetry. None of these, Mandur argued, gives agency to a writer's creativity and imagination or allows for artistic originality.[61] (For al-'Aqqad's methodology, see his biographic sketch in this Appendix.)

He repeatedly attacked critics like al-'Aqqad who believed literary criticism contained general deductive rules and causal explanations—what might appear today as a structuralism determinism: "If we adopt only the rind and the skeleton of things," Mandur wrote, "and leave out the essence and hidden meanings, we will lose our authenticity without achieving a [new] and genuine [sensibility]."[62]

Mandur condemned positivist science altogether and rejected material causality. In their place, Mandur offered studies that concentrate just on the texts themselves, the "*l'explication de texts*" method that alone can unlock the secrets of aesthetic and expressive creativity. Juxtaposed to the failed scientific technique employed by his rivals was the true and successful artistic and impressionistic styles adopted from France.[63]

Mandur assumed a political aloofness and feigned partisan neutrality. This position was particularly emphasized in his 1949 book, *Fi al-Adab wa al-Naqd* (Literature and Criticism). Written at the height of both left-wing demonstrations and political action against the Palace and the Egyptian government, as well as during his own professional career editing liberal and socialist publications, the book described Mandur's attitude toward politics:

> The free mind does not submit to coercion, whatever its motives may be. Just as mankind is in need of emancipation from tyranny and ignorance, it also needs to be emancipated from suffering and bad taste. Art for art's sake can let man escape from himself, thus making him oblivious of his agony. It also polishes his feeling and smoothes the rough edges of his taste. These are indubitable services to mankind and, probably, have more influence on the human personality than we think.[64]

Yet gradually Mandur began to claim that although he advocated a politically impartial literature, he was unable to deny that literature had a "social function"— what he called "battle literature." In his later years, he promoted a more socially engaged literature despite his earlier, apolitical theories of literary criticism.[65]

After leaving teaching in 1943, Mandur began his journalism career as the editor of the Wafdist journal, *al-Misri* (The Egyptian). Three months later, he moved on to edit the party newspaper, *al-Wafd al-Misri* (The Egyptian Wafd). Under Mandur, the party organ acquired a notorious reputation as a Communist publication. He went on to work at *Sawt al-Umma* (Voice of the Nation), another Wafdist newspaper, and, in 1950, he was elected to Parliament. A year after the 1952 revolution, which he supported, the Wafd and its publications were shut down. He was then appointed to the faculty in Arabic literature at the Institute of Higher Arabic Studies associated with the Arab League. He later traveled to Romania and the Soviet Union, which reinforced his strong socialist politics, and, afterward, turned to theater and drama. He secured a teaching appointment to the Institute of Theater and became its director in 1959.[66]

He died in Cairo in 1965.

Abu al-A'la Mawdudi (1903–79)

Abu al-A'la Mawdudi was born on September 25, 1903, in Aurangabad, in the state of Maharashtra in central India. He came from an aristocratic family that generations earlier had served in the Mughal government of India before the British takeover. Mawdudi's father was particularly religious and he sought to provide his son a classical education that did not involve English schooling. This elite but traditional education was cut short, however, when his father died and Mawdudi dropped out of school. He began to work as a journalist and soon became an ardent nationalist. In 1919, he joined the Khilafat movement, a pan-Islamic effort to strengthen the Ottoman caliphate from 1919 to 1924. The Khilafat movement also had ties to the Hindu Congress Party; together they sought to end British rule in India. Mawdudi moved to Delhi and became acquainted with many of India's Islamic scholars. For three years, he edited their official newspaper, *Muslim*. This gave his writing a distinct Islamic tone. When Mustafa Kemal Ataturk abolished the caliphate in 1924, Mawdudi renounced his nationalist perspective, worried that nationalists in the Congress Party were more Hindu than Indian. In 1926, he received a certificate in religious training in the Deobandi (or Hanafi) legal tradition.[67]

In response to the assassination of a Hindu revivalist in 1925 and the subsequent anti-Islamic backlash, Mawdudi called on all Muslims to defend their faith. His sermons were published in a groundbreaking treatise called *al-Jihad fi al-Islam* (Jihad in Islam). This elevated Mawdudi to the upper ranks of religious scholars and proved to be the final step in his transition from secular nationalist to Islamist.[68] He began writing intensely on Islam, particularly addressing its minority status in South Asia. Like Sayyid Qutb in Egypt, Mawdudi blamed the decline of the Muslim community in India on corruption and foreign accretions that had distorted the religion. The solution, in his mind, involved returning to Islam's original practices and beliefs. When the government refused to respond, he attacked it for its fecklessness and corruption.

Mawdudi soon shifted from passive writing to committed political action. In 1938 he joined with Muhammad Iqbal to create an ideal Muslim commune in the Punjab called Dar al-Islam. In 1942, he began writing a series of Qur'anic interpretations, *Tafhim al-Qur'an* (Understanding the Qur'an) that, like Qutb's *In the Shade of the Qur'an*, appealed to readers in a simple, popular style. Nevertheless, his Islamism remained elitist and tied to parliamentary democracy by working through the existing constitutional system, much like Egypt's current Muslim Brotherhood, rather than violently overthrowing the government like Egypt's more radical Islamist associations.

Mawdudi established the Jama'at Islami, or Islamic Party, in 1941. But the organization soon weakened so that the events of the 1947 partition between India and Pakistan caught it unprepared. Mawdudi relocated to Lahore, launched a new party branch, and began campaigning for an Islamic state instead of a secular, nationalist one. Even though Pakistan had anchored its national identity firmly to religion, Mawdudi demanded an even greater role for Islam. He was arrested repeatedly from 1948 to 1950 for his agitation, again in 1954–55 when he barely avoided capital punishment, again in 1964, and finally in 1967, for challenging the legitimacy of Pakistan's secular government. His final political campaign occurred in 1970 but the Jama'at Islami lost in national elections to the leftist Awami League and the centrist Pakistan People's Party. Mawdudi then resigned and returned to writing.[69]

He died on September 22, 1979, and his funeral in Lahore attracted over a million admirers.

Abu al-Hasan 'Ali Nadwi (1913–99)

Abu al-Hasan 'Ali Nadwi was born on December 5, 1913, in Rai Bareli, in the state of Uttar Pradesh in northern India. He was born into an aristocratic family with genealogical ties to the Prophet's family and which earlier in the mid-19th century had organized a religious movement based on a Wahhabi-style Islamism. His family was strongly associated with the Nadwat al-'Ulama (Scholars Circle) of Lucknow, a scholastic and reformist movement that started in 1894, and with the seminary associated with the Nadwa, called Dar al-'Ulum, which Nadwi's father directed. Both institutions were connected to the Deoband movement that started earlier in 1866 to promote Islamic missionary work (*da'wa* or *tabligh*) and to the Khilafat movement for reinvigorating the caliphate. Young Abu al-Hasan received a thorough education at his father's school, but one that was anchored more to the Arab world than to India.[70]

In response to the growing Hindu nationalism and British secularism of the 20th century, Nadwi attempted to distinguish a pan-Islamic identity in India through *Arabization*. He hoped to revitalize Islamic scholarship and to expand its intellectual horizons by emphasizing Arabic and the Arab world. Islamic studies would cease to be archaic, medieval, and classical, he concluded, but become, instead, a lively discussion held throughout the Muslim world. In essence, Nadwi sought to further strengthen the ties of Indian Muslims with the Arab world as a way of carving out a distinct but historical minority status and identity. This meant dining and dressing like Middle Easterners, and reading the Arabic language press from Egypt, Syria, and Saudi Arabia. Many of the ideas Nadwi shared with Muhammad 'Abduh, Rashid Rida, and Sayyid Qutb were learned from the pages of Rida's Islamic journal, *al-Manar*, and other Cairo magazines such as *al-Risala* and *al-Thaqafa*. These gave Nadwi a thorough introduction to contemporary intellectual trends in the Arab world and strongly influenced the political programs of the Scholars' Circle in the 1930s.[71]

Nadwi and the seminary encouraged educational reform. It adopted textbooks from Egypt that taught modern standard Arabic instead of the classical language, although there was criticism that these were too secular.[72] For this reason, Nadwi began writing his own textbook based on Egyptian prototypes but stressing Islamic and Indian content. He wrote children's books in Arabic and edited an anthology of Arabic prose for advanced students. In 1984 Nadwi helped establish the League of Islamic Literature, based in Riyadh, Saudi Arabia, and became its first president.

Nadwi was essentially an Arabophile—he wrote his books in Arabic instead of English or Urdu—and an Easternist, by contrasting the spiritual East, with its moral superiority, and the materialist West and its secular decadence. He viewed nationalism as a European ruse to divide the Islamic world and to undermine its collective strength. Arab nationalism in particular proved to be a destructive doctrine constituting a new *jahiliyya*—a term he adopted from Abu al-A'la Mawdudi and used in a kharijite fashion. Arabs could once again overcome *jahiliyya*, he argued, and restore their lost leadership by reducing their Arab identity and expanding their Islamic character. This anti-nationalist perspective corresponded with the anti-Nassirist Islamists in Egypt and Nadwi's pan-Islamist supporters in Saudi Arabia. It also fit well with his own attempt to strengthen the Islamic connections between Arab and non-Arab Muslims. What made the Arabs great— Islam—was also what made non-Arabs great as well.

Nadwi's 1950 book, *Madha Khasira al-'Alam bi Inhitat al-Muslims* (What the World Lost as a Result of the Decline of Muslims), analyzed the history of Islam, with its early glory, the loss of pious leadership, and its gradual decline into the abyss, much like Qutb concluded in the final chapter of *Social Justice*. Similarly, the spirit of Islamic revival, lost among its rulers but still flickering among ordinary Muslims, could spark Islam's resurgence. This awakening required an intellectual elite and a reformist *'ulama* to first rewrite Islamic history—"correctly" this time—and then overcome the Western-derived *jahiliyya* and revitalize an authentic Islam. For Nadwi, this also meant reviving Islam in India by emphasizing its affinities to his Muslim confreres in the Middle East. Thus he rejected both the colonial facade of English and the hybrid veneer of mixing Persian, Hindu, and Urdu, and sought, instead, an authenticity based on Islam's original medium, Arabic.

Nadwi served as the rector of the Nadwa in Lucknow. He received the King Faisal Award from Saudi Arabia and the Sultan Hassan al-Bolkhaih International Prize from Brunei and Oxford University for his publications and service on behalf of Islam.

He died on December 31, 1999, and more than 200,000 followers attended his funeral.

Muhammad Rashid Rida (1865–1935)

Muhammad Rashid Rida was a student of Muhammad 'Abduh and Jamal al-Din al-Afghani, but took their radical ideas in a more conservative direction, discussing such ideas as *tawhid* (unity) and the *salaf*, the first generation of Muslims, for example, in a less figurative and more concrete fashion. He criticized and rejected Sufism as the distorted outcome when Islam is reduced to mere orthodoxy without orthopraxy, faith without *shari'a* law. He gravitated first toward a Hanbali interpretation of Islam, the most conservative of the four codifications of Islamic law, and the one most commonly found in his native Syria. Later, however, Rida inclined in the direction of the even more conservative Wahhabi branch of Hanbali law practiced in Arabia (later to become Saudi Arabia). This led him to appreciate both a stricter interpretation of Islam and the danger of rival, but false, theologies. More rigid and disciplined than his two mentors, Rida condemned the Europeans for achieving their hegemony by abandoning their religion. He therefore encouraged a return to Islamic law and a strict orthopraxy. Rida's ideas and proposals appeared on the pages of his famous Cairo journal, *al-Manar* (The Beacon), which began publishing in 1897 and continued for the rest of his life. His conservative views were also documented in such books as *al-Wahhabiyun wa al-Hijaz* (The Wahhabis and the Hijaz [the west coast of Saudi Arabia, the site of Mecca and Medina]), *al-Manar wa al-Azhar* (Manar and the Azhar), and *al-Sunna wa al-Shi'a* (The Sunnis and the Shi'ites).

Rida was born on September 25, 1865, in al-Qalamun, a seacoast town just south of Tripoli, Syria (later in Lebanon). His family was well known for its piety and scholarship, an elite *sayyid*, descended from the Prophet Muhammad, which gave it considerable standing in local religious and political affairs. Young Rashid received a traditional education in the town's Qur'anic school. He then attended an Ottoman government school in Tripoli for one year before enrolling in the new National Islamic school established by the distinguished Shaykh Husayn al-Jisr (1845–1909) who synthesized traditional religion together with modern science. Rida's teachers introduced him to journalism, and he wrote for several journals and gained a respectable reputation as an intellectual. He graduated in 1892.[73]

An early aversion to Sufism turned him in the direction of Ibn al-Hanbal, Ibn Taymiyya, and Ibn 'Abd al-Wahhab.[74] Rida's embrace of their arch-conservative interpretations of Islam branded the Islamic movement with a rigid, reactionary character. Whereas his predecessors had attempted to modernize Islam, Rida and his successors sought to Islamize modernity instead.[75]

After reading *al-'Urwa al-Wuthqa*, the famous publication of Jamal al-Din al-Afghani and Muhammad 'Abduh, Rida became fascinated with their ideas and the *salafiyya* movement they initiated, the return to an original, unadulterated version of Islam purged of innovation, superstition, mindless traditionalism, and passive fatalism. He had hoped to study with al-Afghani, but loathed living in Istanbul. Instead he moved to Cairo in 1897 to collaborate with 'Abduh.[76]

A year after his arrival, Rida began publishing the *salafi* journal *al-Manar*, closely modeled on *al-'Urwa al-Wuthqa*. 'Abduh warned Rida to avoid politics and to focus instead on reform through education. Rida complied until 'Abduh's death in 1905, but thereafter published more explicitly doctrinaire articles. Over its 37 years, *al-Manar* proved to be one of the most influential journals on Islamic reform. It published articles on religious, social, political, and scientific issues. It criticized the *'ulama*, the Westernized elite, and cosmopolitan notables. It serialized 'Abduh's explanations (*tafsir*) of the Qur'an, reviewed books that discussed educational and religious reform, and disseminated legal opinions (*fatwa* or *fatawi*).[77]

Rida saw himself squeezed between the secular nationalists who blindly imitated Europe and al-Azhar *'ulama* who blindly imitated tradition. He was one of the earliest Islamic thinkers to see danger in the emerging doctrine of modern nationalism, but he also castigated Islamic clerics for their doctrinal errors, their abuse of power, their support of tyranny, and their unworthy leadership and apathy.[78]

Like earlier reformers, Rida advocated reviving interpretation, but he wanted this to be less lenient than his predecessors. Too flexible a scope for *ijtihad*, he argued, allowed for Westernization. He relied heavily on hadith, a characteristic of the conservative Hanbalis, and exhibited a more literal understanding of religion, as opposed to a symbolic interpretation.[79]

Rida sought an enlightened *'ulama* who had a genuine ability to interpret the Qur'an, exercise electoral judgment, and consult with the leaders and the community. To this end, he established a seminary, the Institute of Preaching and Guidance. He tried first to set the academy up in Istanbul, but the Sultan refused. He turned to Cairo, and received approval and financial support from Khedive 'Abbas in 1912. However, the school closed two years later when World War I began.[80]

Initially Rida embraced al-Afghani's radical repudiation of the West and its imperialism. However, once in Cairo and under the moderating influence of 'Abduh, and seeing the benefit from appeasing the British, Rida assumed a more conciliatory tone. He embraced pan-Islamism and at first considered the Ottoman Empire as its embodiment, as the only way to protect Muslims from external attack. Yet in due course, Rida began to question this accommodation. In 1912, when Italy invaded Libya, he became alarmed by the weakness of the Ottoman Empire and by the ferocity of the Europeans. He blamed Istanbul for the decline of the Muslim world and proposed major religious and political changes to strengthen the government and to prevent disintegration.[81]

Religiously, he called for a renewed unity of all Muslims to improve their abject conditions and confront European aggression by eliminating differences among the various schools of Islamic law and smoothing over the sectarian differences between Sunnis and Shi'ites. Politically, he called for constitutionalism and consultation (*shura*) as mechanisms for restraining authoritarian rulers, and for the renovation of *shari'a* law by either creating a new legal school or else merging existing schools together. He worked relentlessly to establish political associations, parties, and conferences to advance these reforms.

When Husayn ibn 'Ali, Sharif (governor) of Mecca, declared war against the Ottoman Empire and sparked the Arab Revolt of 1916, Rida enthusiastically embraced the idea of an Arab to replace the incumbent Turkish caliph. However, when he learned of Husayn's reliance on British funding, his enthusiasm cooled, and he turned and embraced Husayn's rival from the central Arabian Nadj, 'Abd al-'Aziz ibn Sa'ud. Then, as the Young Turk radicals in Istanbul moved more in the direction of a narrow Turkish nationalism, Rida began promoting a pan-Arab sovereignty and a more authentic Arab caliphate headquartered in Mecca.[82]

World War I dismantled the Ottoman Empire, which was allied with Germany. The caliphate soon came under attack. On November 1, 1922, the imperial sultanate was abolished, leaving the caliph as a symbolic figure without power. Then Turkey was recognized as a republic on July 24, 1923, and the caliphate was abolished altogether on March 3, 1924.

In 1923, after the caliphate had been weakened but before it was completely abolished, Rida published his book *al-Khilafa aw al-Imama al-'Uzma* (The Caliph or the Great Imamate), a passionate plea for its restoration in order to defend Islam, maintain order, and enforce *shari'a*. Yet when the office was finally eliminated a year later, two controversial books appeared—'Ali 'Abd al-Raziq's *al-Islam wa Usul al-Hukm* and Taha Husayn's *Fi al-Shi'r al-Jahili*—and Rida was at the forefront of those condemning their publications. He called 'Abd al-Raziq an enemy of Islam and accused Husayn of apostasy.[83]

In response, Rida decided that he would devise a complex and detailed program that called for a new caliphate, a revival of *shari'a* law, and a return to the *salaf*. What he designed was no less than a systematic Islamic political science. Although the plan lacked specific details that could have made the program operational, it went much further than previous proposals toward conceptualizing the actual steps of Islamic revival.

After World War I, Rida rejected the policy of cooperating with colonial rulers. Realizing that 'Abduh's advice of appeasement merely led to disappointment, he returned to the radical perspective of al-Afghani. He became disillusioned by

British treachery with the Arab Revolt and with Zionist colonization in Palestine. He concluded that British reforms were an illusion intended to further its imperialism, to divide and rule Egyptian society, and to insert enemies in their midst by moving European Jewish settlers to Palestine.

Throughout the 1920s, Rida and *al-Manar* became enthusiastic champions for the most conservative interpretation of Islam, that of the Wahhabis who, together with Ibn Sa'ud, were uniting much of Arabia.[84] It was after a trip to Suez to meet Ibn Sa'ud that Rida died on August 22, 1935, in Cairo.[85]

II. Sayyid Qutb on Women and the Family

Sayyid Qutb maintained that the family is the foundation of Islamic society. It is a natural order "which arises from the basic way in which humans are created" and is decreed by God and regulated by the Qur'an.[1] There is, he claimed, a division of labor between husband, wife, and the children, producing what might be called a "mild" patriarchy where men officiate but where women's rights are not denied. The family serves a variety of functions: the upbringing of children (including moral and religious education); the regulation of sexuality (including wedlock, birthright, and inheritance, and governing passion and desire); the realization of income and consumption (the former constituting the husband's realm and the latter being the wife's domain), and the guidance of each gender based on its "natural gifts."

> The family system and the relationship between the sexes determine the whole character of a society and whether it is backward or civilized, *jahili* or Islamic. Those societies which give ascendance to physical desires and animalistic morals cannot be considered civilized, no matter how much progress they may make in industry or science.[2]

Marriage and family are the most effective way of joining together the contrasting needs of men and women that extend outward to create communities and ensure the cooperation between the sexes and between the generations.

Qutb rejected early schooling and institutionalizing child socialization—"industrial childcare centers," he called them—and insisted that the natural family is the best atmosphere for child development. This requires the mother's attention primarily—"without sharing or competition"—and the father only secondarily.

Qutb had modernized sufficiently to encourage free choice among marrying couples rather than marriage arranged by their parents, although parents should be involved ex post facto in order to maintain harmony and family solidarity. Qutb opposed religiously mixed marriages, rejecting outright the marriage between monotheists and polytheists. He begrudgingly approved of marriage among

Jews, Christians, and Muslims as long as the husband is Muslim but forbade it otherwise. Qutb considered divorce a formality of the family, not the state, and regarded judicial involvement, as in the West, humiliating and demeaning. It represents the last resort when there are irreconcilable differences between spouses. Similarly, Qutb claimed that adoption is deplorable; orphaned children are best raised by relatives or the government.[3]

Qutb unequivocally supported monogamy, claiming that it is the best way of begetting children and avoiding confusion. Moreover, it facilitates the love and care that lies at the core of the family and best achieves the socialization of the children. He acknowledged the wisdom of polygamy at the time of the Prophet Muhammad for the practical reasons of protecting and caring for widows. But as the circumstances changed, so, too, did the need for polygamy. Qutb denounced multiple wives were this merely the satisfying of carnal desire. Qutb disagreed with Muhammad 'Abduh who argued that the Qur'anic verse of fair treatment abrogated the permission to marry more than one wife. Qutb considered this a sign of Western influence and an attack on Islamic authenticity, which he denounced. But he did not, in turn, unconditionally embrace polygamy. At best, polygamy is necessary for protection, when divorced or abused women require care, and for procreation, when the first wife is in menopause or is sterile, but, in both cases, only if the wives are compatible.[4]

Qutb believed that in gender relations, Islam guarantees men and women the same human rights. In terms of religious and spiritual issues, and in terms of economic and financial matters, the two are equal. Qutb argued that a woman has absolute personal rights, such as her own dowry going into marriage, and not as a "sale price"; her own choice in marriage, and not as a commodified exchange; and her own personal share of her father's estate, notwithstanding her brother's appropriation of it in exchange for her life-time security. At the same time, she is expected to give "voluntary and loving obedience" to her father, brother, or husband. In order to uphold family honor and reputation—and thus reinforce the family's central place as the cornerstone of the Islamic community—both men and women are expected to behave in a modest fashion, according to the morals and standards established by the Qur'an. Islam oversees the virtuous behavior of both genders. An unemployed man is just as much a disgrace as a flirtatious woman.[5]

Yet at the same time, the two genders are not assumed to be identical.[6] The two have their unique and distinctive natures, and this makes their legal and moral positions different. The primacy of one sex over the other is based on their complementary temperaments. Anthropologist Larry Rosen points out, based on his fieldwork in Morocco, that women are seen to have more desire, *nafs*, and men are considered to have more reason, *'aql*, although both have some of each. Thus, because of their different makeup, women display more emotion and less sound judgment; men, on the other hand, demonstrate a greater capacity for sensible composure and decisions. This, then, generates two human temperaments—Rosen's informants even believed in two different creatures, almost bordering on two different but interbreeding subspecies—but not just one human nature as is commonly accepted in the West. His fieldwork revealed that Moroccan women primarily concern themselves with social and community relations while Moroccan men principally deal with political and technical relations. And while men can remain autonomous, women require men to control them (notwithstanding their own policing). Men and women, Rosen concludes, occupy two different socialized spaces, remain separate, and otherwise ignore the other gender they regard "as intrinsically worthless." When women do enter the man's space, the so-called public sphere, she requires male guidance or proper covering. When he enters her space, the household, or particular parts of the household, he is teased and ridiculed.[7]

The equanimity of men's character and the histrionics of women's disposition mean, for example, that twice as many women as men must serve as witnesses in an Islamic judicial proceedings so as to ensure accuracy. Again, the difference in treatment, Qutb explained, is a result of the genders' different temperaments. What appears in the West as discrimination instead basically recognizes the divergent natures of the two genders.

Qutb upheld the traditional patriarchy of his society that pressed women to be modest in the face of their ability to distract men by their beauty.[8] He also gave greater emphasis to women's behavior instead of men's because of his experiences in America and the Westernization he witnessed in Egypt, which had a greater impact on women's conduct. Qutb agreed that the Qur'an prescribed seclusion for women because of their ability to disrupt the lives of men, increasingly important as women leave the confines of the family domicile and emerge in a mixed public setting. Although men and women are both strongly obligated to uphold family prestige and status—each in their own way—Qutb argued that women are under more intense pressure to conform and heed public morality. It is the woman who bears the greater burden of preserving family dignity and its reputation. Working and employed outside the family, women are in a particularly delicate situation that can wreak havoc on social life. Released from their child-rearing duties, and free from immediate male control, women in public must be more vigilant.

In the 1920s, gender inequality came under attack. Egypt's Parliament legislated judicial divorce for women if they suffered from their husbands' desertion, imprisonment, or death, and official restrictions on their husbands' free, threefold pronouncement of divorce. The parliament did decline, nevertheless, to limit polygamous marriages.[9] With the onset of the Great Depression and later with the outbreak of World War II, female employment greatly expanded in urban Egypt, especially as it became increasingly impossible for families to live on one income alone. Qutb noted that the necessity for women to forsake the house and work outside actually indicated the failure and the dishonor of men to properly fulfill their duty as the exclusive breadwinner of the household.

It is well to remember that the West brought women out of the home
to work only because their menfolk shrank from the responsibility of
keeping them and caring for them; and that too, although the price
was the chastity and honor of woman. Thus and only thus were women
compelled to work.

It is to be remembered also that when women did emerge to work,
the material West seized upon the opportunity offered by this event,
and paid them lower wages; thus employers were able to dispense with
men in favor of women, who were cheaper to pay, because the men were
beginning to raise their heads and demand their true value.[10]

Clearly Qutb did not seem to recognize that employment might also have a
creative, imaginative, or even self-fulfilling character, as much for women as for
men.[11]

Qutb used gender issues less to criticize Egyptian women than to berate
Western women for their looseness and liberation, and for their focus on beauty
and sexuality. This served as a warning, presumably, of what could occur with
further modernization.

If, on the other hand, free sexual relationships and illegitimate children
become the basis of a society, and if the relationship between man and
woman is based on lust, passion, and impulse, and the division of work
is not based on family responsibility and natural gifts; if [the] woman's
role is merely to be attractive, sexy, and flirtatious, and if [the] woman
is freed from her basic responsibility of bringing up children; and if,
on her own or under social demand, she prefers to become a hostess
or a stewardess in a hotel or ship or air company, thus using her ability for material productivity rather than the training of human beings,
because material production is considered to be more important, more
valuable and more honorable than the development of human character, then such a civilization is "backward" from the human point of
view, or "*jahili*" in Islamic terminology.[12]

Qutb was very critical of the free mixing of the sexes, as well as women's liberation, for it involved, in his perspective, pushing women out into a slave market to
be displayed and procured. He went on to declare that expressive pastimes should
be forbidden, whether male or female. Music and singing, dancing and theater,
beaches and baths, and overall public displays go against the intentions of Islam.
Not surprisingly, he also opposed what he called the "sexual communism" of free
love, common-law marriage, adultery, sexual pleasure without family or family
responsibilities, recurrent divorce, and the obstruction of procreation, either
through birth control, abstinence, or abortion.[13]

III. Sayyid Qutb on "People of the Book," Dhimmis

People of the Book, or *dhimmis*, are the Jews and Christians found inside Muslim societies where they are minorities. Their relationship to the larger Islamic community should involve either (1) paying the *jizya*, or *dhimmi* tax (but barred from serving in the military or paying *zakat*), (2) participating in a formal but temporary treaty, or (3) engaging in a state of hostility, which could result either in their final defeat or continued combat. Qutb firmly felt that Jews and Christians ought to become Muslims and that to retain their original religion was just plain *jahili* folly. But still, he grudgingly recognized that a stable, though hierarchical, relationship could allow them to retain their religion. But when they turned into external or foreign Crusaders and Zionists, these scripturaries became adversaries, no longer honoring the 7th-century "Pact of 'Umar" but instead battling Islam for supremacy. Muslims therefore have to wage a *jihad* against them.

This early pact or treaty, attributed to the second caliph, 'Umar ibn al-Khattab (r: 634–44) detailed the duties, but also the rights, of Christian and Jewish minorities in Dar al-Islam, the Islamic homeland. Scholars are skeptical of the actual provenance of this treaty since no actual copies have been found from before the 10th or 11th century but also because such policies toward minorities had been applied earlier to Jews living in the Christian Byzantine empire, embodied in its Justinianic and the Theodosius Codes. But the Pact of 'Umar remained permanent and relatively incontrovertible, unlike Western Christianity, where statutory conventions such as the Fourth Lateran Council of 1215 became susceptible to repeated modification. The Pact of 'Umar was not considered divine, but any deviation from it quickly brought demands for restoring its original intent, and thus served to preserve stable majority-minority relations. Meanwhile, in Europe, the conventions regulating minority religions—Judaism was the only one—weakened and deteriorated over time, subject to the whims and vagaries of competing rulers (secular and ecclesiastical), their subjects, their commercial and financial conditions, and their desire to scapegoat. Over the centuries, such laws turned against Jewish civil rights and became a major source of anti-Semitism.[1]

Ironically, the animosity European Crusaders began directing toward Middle East Muslims in 1095 also targeted European Jews, continuing for over 800 years and finally culminating in the Holocaust of the 1930s and 1940s. Yet as Edward Said points out, Ashkenazi Jews began to assimilate into Europe in the post-Enlightenment secularism of the 19th century.[2] Part of this integration included adopting the same hostility toward those in the "Oriental" category that had once included themselves as well. Many European Jews came to exhibit the same Islamophobia as their Christian neighbors, and this was retained when they established the state of Israel. The predominantly easygoing relationship between Middle East Jews (Sephardic and Mizrahi) and Muslims did not change until 1948 when Israel became independent.[3] Thus both the Crusaderism and Zionism that Qutb denounced came out of the same European cauldron. Local People of the Book—domestic Christians and Jews—were one thing; but their co-religionists in Europe became something else entirely different.

Qutb published one article exclusively on the subject of Jews, although he also made scattered references to them in his Qur'anic commentary *In the Shade of the Qur'an*. In this article, published in the early 1950s, he wrote in ordinary, almost formulaic, terms about Jewish "wickedness and double-dealing" that took place in early Medina when three Jewish tribes refused to submit to the *pax Muhammadana* negotiated with local tribes and disparaged the rise of Islam. Such past antagonisms were then projected onto the present relationship between Muslims and Jews, for the same "deception and plotting" were occurring now as well. The Jews, he argued, had become the worst enemies of Muslims in the days of the Prophet, and they remained so today. The reason for their intense enmity, what Qutb called their "black fury," was their jealousy over the Prophet Muhammad who had been chosen by God instead of them to carry forth his mission and to receive God's most mature revelations—an indication of a significant shift in God's generosity, the bestowal of His divine choice. Qutb warned against Jewish deception and their attempts to undermine Islamic belief either directly or else through Orientalism, secularism, and modernity. He also commented on several Qur'anic verses, 3:69–71, 4:51–54, 5:82, 17:5–8, that discuss God's warnings about the deviations, idolatry, hostility, and evil-doing of the Jews. However, Qutb did not care to repeat the standard accusations of the Jew's deification of Ezra, their distortion of the Torah, and their deviation from monotheism that he mentioned elsewhere (see note 21 in Chapter 6). It was also clear, from his repeated references to Israel, that his remarks were directed at Jews outside the Middle East (i.e., those who are not *dhimmis*).[4]

Qutb's animosity toward Zionists and Jews—the two were the same in his mind—became particularly strong from the time of the Palestinian revolt of 1936–39; then when he was in America and heard the news about Israeli independence in 1948; and later, in 1954, before he went to prison, when he learned about the Lavon Affair.[5] Like many, he saw Israel as colonizing the Muslim world in ways that earned them the same enmity as the Christian colonizers of the 19th century: Britain, France, Holland, and Belgium.

Yet Mark Cohen discusses what he calls the so-called myth of interfaith utopia that went uncontested for the most part until 1948.

> The "myth of the interfaith utopia" went largely unchallenged until its adoption by Arabs as a weapon in their propaganda war against Zionism. According to this view, for centuries Jews and Arabs lived together in peace and harmony under Islamic rule—precisely at a time when the Jews were being relentlessly persecuted by Christianity [in Europe]. Modern antipathy toward Israel began only when the Jews destroyed the old harmony by pressing the Zionist claim against Muslim-Arab rights to Palestine. Accordingly, Arab hatred and antisemitism would end, and the ancient harmony would be restored, when Zionism abandoned both its "colonialist" and its "neo-crusader" quest.[6]

Cohen hesitates, of course, because the reality was not so rosy and cordial; there were a number of pogroms in the Arab world when Jews were killed, and Jews were never co-equal subjects in the pre-modern Muslim world. Still, Qutb would wholeheartedly agree and affirm that his anger was directed at the imperialism perpetrated by foreign Jews and Christians but not at those living peacefully as neighbors.

IV. Sayyid Qutb on Apologetics

Writers who argue in an apologetic fashion do so to defend their religion against real or imagined attacks from followers and supporters of other religions.[1] Apologetics assumes a power imbalance in which the defending side is lowermost and is attempting to prevents its members from flocking to the presumably superior side. In the battle against modernity, Islam is perceived to be the less powerful and the inferior, and intellectuals like Sayyid Qutb often wrote in an apologetic style to prevent Muslims from becoming enthusiasts of Western modernity. This often resulted in extreme claims of reverse preeminence and in an awkward outpouring of defensive discourse.

Thus, other Egyptians or Muslims who draw hypothetical associations or claim vague resemblances between Islamic institutions and those found in Europe, either now or in the past, do so, Qutb argued, from a position of perceived weakness. It shows an inferiority complex, he concluded, not a sense of pride and firm conviction of Islam's inherent superiority.

> Some Muslim writers, discussing the Islamic political system, labor to trace connections and similarities between it and the other systems known to the ancient or the modern world, in the ages before and after Islam. And some of them believe that they find a strong support for Islam when they can trace such a connection between it and one of the other ancient or modern systems. In reality this attempt represents nothing but an inner conviction that the Islamic system is inferior to those of the Western world. But Islam does not take pride in any similarities between it and these other systems, nor is it harmed by their absence. For Islam altogether presents to mankind an example of a complete political system, the like of which has never been found in any of the other systems known to the world either before or after the coming of Islam. Islam does not seek, and never has sought, to imitate any other system, or to find connections or similarities between itself and others. On the contrary, it has chosen its own characteristic path and has presented humanity with a complete cure for all of its problems.

It sometimes happens in the development of man-made political systems that they agree with Islam in some respects and differ from it in others. But Islam is in itself a completely independent system that has no connection with these others, either when they agree with it or when they differ from it. Such divergence or agreement is purely accidental and occurs in scattered points of detail; in such coincidence or in such divergence there can be no significance. The truly significant thing is the underlying theory or the philosophy peculiar to the system; Islam has both of these, and it is from these that the details of the system take their rise. These details may either agree with or differ from similar details in other systems, but Islam continues on its own unique way, irrespective of such agreement or divergence.

Thus it is not the task of the Islamic enquirer who embarks on a study of the Muslim political system to look for similarities to, or agreements with, any other system, ancient or modern. Nor do such similarities and agreements add anything to the strength of the Islamic position, as some Muslims believe—especially since they are superficial and in matters of detail only; they arise from chance in merely particular matters and not from any general philosophy or underlying theory. The true method is to turn to the fundamentals of the religion itself in the firm belief that in them lie the complete bases of the system. It makes no difference whether all other political systems agree or disagree entirely. The sole reason for seeking to strengthen Islam through its similarities and agreements with other systems is the conviction of inferiority, as we have said; no Muslim scholar should venture on such a course, but rather should know his own faith with a true knowledge and study it with a true zeal.[2]

Qutb criticized many modern Egyptian writers, such as Taha Husayn, Muhammad Husayn Haykal, and several contemporary religious 'ulama for being apologists who attempted to fit the round pegs of Islam into the square holes of Europe. Questions about Islamic imperialism, democracy, freedom, and equality were repeatedly measured against Europe and, in the process, reaffirmed Europe's superiority and the weak position of the Muslim world. Qutb condemned this attitude. He felt the Islamic system is one that stands by itself, independent of other systems, and is unique. In fact, if there is any influence, it is to the disadvantage of Islam, not to its benefit. So not only did he condemn those who spoke or wrote admirably about the West and implicitly apologized for Islam's alleged inferiority, but he used their position as a way of denouncing the West for its own inferior qualities of secularism, paganism, immorality, inequality, and injustice.[3]

Ironically, Qutb himself was not without his own apologetic moments. Much of his defensiveness took place in his attempt to prevent his readers, mostly the young, from giving into the "dark forces" of *jahiliyya* that emphasize animal desires and narcissism. Instead, he encouraged them to stay with a righteous and principled Islam that focuses on values, faith, and discipline. In the course of his career, he increasingly eliminated this mild, apologetic posture and became more aggressively anti-Western. He assumed more pride in the uniqueness and preeminence of Islam, and showed much less goodwill toward the West.[4]

When Qutb cited examples from the *salaf*, he did so unabashedly without any reference whatsoever to other practices and institutions at that time or later. Since their faith and righteousness made them unique, he reasoned, there is no point in examining Greek, Jewish, Roman, Persian, or European societies. There is nothing these civilizations exhibit that can be considered similar or related to Islam. Instead, their influence is seen as harmful, embodying the accretions, influences, and debris that Qutb wanted removed.[5]

Qutb accused those who apologize for the supposed inferior qualities of Islam of being so defeatist that there can be no hope for them at all. They are not real Muslims, he claimed, notwithstanding their praying, fasting, and pilgrimage, nor do they understand the real meaning of their own religion. As long as these modern Muslims continue to look for resemblances between Islam and modernity and can not understand why these two are antagonistic, then they are part of *jahiliyya*. Qutb condemned this apologetic discourse as defeatist, and he placed those who apologized for Islam in the same category as Orientalists, Crusaders, and Zionists.[6]

> There is nothing in our Islam of which we are ashamed or anxious about defending; there is nothing in it to be smuggled to the people with deception, or do we muffle the loud truth which it proclaims. This is the defeated mentality, defeated before the West and before the East and before this and that mode of *jahiliyya*.[7]

NOTES

Chapter 1

1. This was the title of Berman's well-known article, "The Philosopher of Islamic Terror," *New York Times Magazine*, March 23, 2003.

2. Paul Berman, "The Philosopher of Islamic Terror," 2003. Also see Dale C. Eikmeier, "Qutbism: An Ideology of Islamic-Fascism," *Parameters* (Spring 2007): 85–98; Marc Erikson, "Islamism, Fascism and Terrorism," *Asia Times Online*, Part 1, November 5, 2002; Part 2, November 8, 2002; Jeffrey Herf, *Nazi Propaganda for the Arab World* (New Haven: Yale University Press, 2009).

3. Orientalism is identified as the subtle, negative stereotyping of Muslims, Islam, and the Middle East. It is best defined in Edward Said's renowned 1979 book *Orientalism*. Qutb labeled modern Orientalists as those scholars who continue Europe's traditional hostile relationship and malevolent attitude toward Islam. He considered them to be merely the most recent version of Christian missionaries, but ones supposedly based on science, not religion. John Calvert concurs when he writes:

   > Qutb argued that Western studies of Islam facilitated the imperialist project. Orientalists constructed a false identity for Muslims through a series of libels and negations, and then attempted to impose that identity on Muslims, who then internalized it, believed it, and lived it to the point that the falsehoods became reality.

   John Calvert, *Sayyid Qutb and the Origins of Radical Islamism* (New York: Columbia University Press, 2010), 166–167.

4. Another example is a not atypical editorial column written by the well-known journalist, Thomas Friedman, published in the *New York Times* for November 28, 2009. Friedman is discussing the angry and lethal shootings by Major Nidal Hasan at Fort Hood, Texas, three weeks earlier.

   > Major Hasan was just another angry jihadist spurred to action by "The Narrative."

   The narrative is Friedman's euphemism for Islamist ideology and beliefs.

   > The Narrative is the cocktail of half-truths, propaganda and outright lies about America that have taken hold in the Arab-Muslim world since 9/11. Propagated by jihadist Web sites, mosque preachers, Arab intellectuals, satellite news stations and books – and tacitly endorsed by some Arab regimes – this narrative posits that America has declared war on Islam, as part of a grand "American-Crusader-Zionist conspiracy" to keep Muslims down.
   >
   > But for every Abu Ghraib [the US war prison in Iraq], our soldiers and diplomats perpetrated a million acts of kindness aimed at giving Arabs and Muslims a better chance to succeed with modernity and to elect their own leaders.
   >
   > The Narrative was concocted by jihadists to obscure that.

www.nytimes.com/2009/11/29/opinion/29friedman.html?_r=1&scp=12&sq=thomas%20
friedman&st=cse.

    I offer this book as a response to Friedman's cavalier and frankly deficient manner of
understanding Islamic militancy.

5. See, for example, Christopher Hitchens, *God Is Not Great: How Religion Poisons Everything*
(New York: Twelve, 2007); his "Minority Report" columns in *The Nation* magazine for October
8, 2001; December 17, 2001; and May 13, 2002; "Where the Twain Should Have Met" in the
Atlantic Monthly, September, 2003; "Holy Writ" in the *Atlantic Monthly*, April, 2003; "Stranger
in a Strange Land" in the *Atlantic Monthly*, April, 2003; "Londistan Calling" in *Vanity Fair*,
June, 2007.

6. Edward Said, *Covering Islam: How the Media and the Experts Determine How We See the Rest of
the World* (New York: Vintage Books, 1997), ch. 1.

7. Islamism is a Western term for political Islam, although Qutb would argue that this latter
phrase is redundant, or even blasphemous, since Islam inherently combines politics and religion, similar to classical Judaism but unlike Christianity, which lacks divine law, and unlike
contemporary Western society which separates religion and politics ("church and state").
Islam includes politics—along with economics, culture, morality, and all other facets of social
life—unless they are separated as non-Islamic secularists might do. I use the term in this book
to refer to that doctrine or those activists who are particularly zealous or passionate about
establishing Islam as the dominant system. See note 26 in Chapter 8.

8. Nadav Safran, *Egypt in Search of Political Community: An Analysis of the Intellectual and Political
Evolution of Egypt, 1804–1952* (Cambridge, MA: Harvard University Press, 1961), 39.

9. Yet spiritual guidance is not without its hazards. 'Umar 'Abd al-Rahman, "the blind shaykh"
who counseled the perpetrators of the 1993 World Trade Center bombing from a store-front
mosque in Jersey City, New Jersey, is today serving a life sentence in prison for his "spiritual
guidance." Similarly, Sayyid Qutb was released from prison in 1965 and, because he had earlier suggested a "great books" list for an Islamist study group, was asked to be its spiritual
guide. He was arrested for sedition and treason in 1965 and executed at the gallows in 1966
for his role in "guiding" their conspiracy.

10. Yvonne Haddad, "The Qur'anic Justification of an Islamic Revolution: The View of Sayyid
Qutb," *Middle East Journal* 2, no. 37 (1983): 17; Sayed Khatab, *The Power of Sovereignty: The
Political and Ideological Philosophy of Sayyid Qutb* (London: Routledge, 2006), 1.

11. Sayed Khatab, *The Political Thought of Sayyid Qutb: The Theory of Jahiliyyah* (London: Routledge,
2006), 5.

12. For more on this relationship between modernity and Protestantism, see note 15 in
Chapter 8.

13. For more on Just War theory, see note 51 in Chapter 7.

14. Richard H. Tawney, *Religion and the Rise of Capitalism* (London: Penguin Books, 1926, reprint
1990), 27–48.

15. Khatab, *The Power of Sovereignty*, 1.

16. Olivier Carré, *Mysticism and Politics: A Critical Reading of Fi Zilal al-Qur'an by Sayyid Qutb
(1906–1966)* (Leiden: Brill, 2003), 73, 95, 195, 249, 252, 268; Leonard Binder, *Islamic
Liberalism: A Critique of Development Ideologies* (Chicago: University of Chicago Press,
1988), 193.

17. Anthony F. C. Wallace, "Revitalization Movements," *American Anthropologist* 58:2 (1956):
268–270.

18. Martin Riesebrodt, *Pious Passion: The Emergence of Modern Fundamentalism in the United States
and Iran*, Don Reneau, trans. (Berkeley: University of California Press, 1993; originally published in 1990), 24.

19. A biographic sketch of Hasan al-Banna can be found in the Appendix, Part I, "Dramatis
Personae."

20. Social democracy is a term originally appearing in 19th century-Europe to refer to liberal and
left-wing political parties. Although it originally included socialist and revolutionary parties, by
the 20th century it had come to emphasize reform over revolution. I am using the term to stand

for those who advocate government regulation of the economy and government welfare pro-grams to redistribute incomes. The stress is on Keynesian redistributive policies and economic justice, not so much on democracy in the strict sense of suffrage and parliamentarism. For a discussion about using secular labels in religious political movements, see note 38 in Chapter 3.

21. It is, of course, problematic to use a word like fundamentalism that was developed in one context, American Protestantism of the 19th century, but now used in another, the Islamic world of the 20th and 21st centuries. This question occurs over and over again in the enor-mous scholarly undertaking by Martin E. Marty and R. Scott Appleby in their monumental Fundamentalism Project published by the University of Chicago Press in five volumes. Many scholars question the application of the concept to the Islamic world.

If the defining characteristic of Protestant fundamentalism is the followers' earnest belief in the divine authorship of the Bible—and not all Protestants agree—then using this same definition for Muslims means that *all* Muslims are fundamentalists since they all believe that the Qur'an is the actual word of God. Yet if we want to retain this term to differentiate among Muslims, because it implies a political conservatism based on religion, then we should per-haps use it as it was originally intended by A. C. Dixon who edited the 12 volumes of essays between 1905 and 1915 called *The Fundamentals* (of Protestantism). That is, to be "fundamen-talist," Muslims need to return to the basics or fundamentals of Islam as articulated by the Prophet Muhammad and his followers and helpers in the original communities of Mecca and Medina in the 7th century. This, in fact, is the intention of those called Salafis, followers of the *salafiyya* movement, which, ironically, arose at the same time that Protestant fundamentalism first appeared in the United States, in the late 19th century. Salafiyyism refers to a purifica-tion movement started by Jamal al-Din al-Afghani and Muhammad 'Abduh to expunge Islam of centuries of accretions and wrongful interpretations and return to the uncontaminated practices and beliefs of the original Muslim community. Thus I use the word "fundamental-ism" to refer to the *salafiyya* movement.

22. Riesebrodt, *Pious Passion*, 186.

Chapter 2

1. Sayed Khatab, *The Political Thought of Sayyid Qutb: The Theory of* Jahiliyyah (London: Routledge, 2006), 44.

2. In the 1976 census, Musha had a population of 16,442, people—a little less than twice its 1907 population of 9,510. In the 1976 census, Christians constituted 11.4 percent of Musha's population; in 1907 they represented 10.9 percent of the populace. In 1925, as much as 80 percent of Egypt's Christian population resided in the Sa'id alone; today, only half of the Copts live in southern Egypt. In the 1986 census, Christians constituted 16.5 percent of the urban population in the Sa'id, 9.2 percent of the rural population, and 11 percent overall. Thus Musha appears quite typical. In all of Egypt, Christians represent 6 to 10 percent of the total population. Nicholas S. Hopkins, *Agrarian Transformation in Egypt* (Boulder: Westview Press, 1987), 37 and 53; Cornelis Hulsman, "Christian Life," in *Upper Egypt: Life along the Nile* (Hojbjerg, Denmark: Moesgard Museum, 2003), 121.

3. Hamid Algar, "Introduction," *Social Justice in Islam by Sayyid Qutb*, (Oneonta, NY: Islamic Publications International, 2000), 1; Adnan A. Musallam, *From Secularism to Jihad: Sayyid Qutb and the Foundations of Radical Islam*, (Westport, CT: Praeger, 2005), 32–33; Sayed Khatab, *The Political Thought of Sayyid Qutb: The Theory of* Jahiliyyah (London: Routledge, 2006), 46.

4. Al-Azhar is the world renowned Islamic university in Cairo. It was established in 970, shortly after the founding of Cairo itself in the Fatimid period. Ever since, it has been a major cen-ter of religious scholarship. In 1961, the university was reorganized under Egypt's president, Jamal 'Abd al-Nassir, and came to include other disciplines such as medicine and engineering. Its graduates—Azharites—have staffed mosques through the Muslim world.

5. Musallam, *From Secularism to Jihad*, 30–31; Khatab, *Political Thought*, 45.

6. Musallam, *From Secularism to Jihad*, 41.

7. Ibid., 32.

8. Although Qutb initially embraced modernity, he did not, as many Islamists do, to turn his back completely on the countryside. After all, he wrote *A Child from the Village* in the mid-1940s more as a nostalgic memoir than as a trenchant critique of the Egyptian village. And although he went on to promote a very radical, self-righteous interpretation of Islam, he never directly condemned rural Egypt, its lack of sophisticated education, or its other-worldly religious style.

9. Ibid., 31; William E. Shepard, *Sayyid Qutb and Islamic Activism: A Translation and Critical Analysis of Social Justice in Islam* (Leiden: E. J. Brill, 1996), xv; Khatab, *Political Thought*, 45.

10. In the book, the *tarahil* workers turned down the meat that the boy's father provided as a noncash part of their income, in order to receive higher wages instead. This shocked the entire family, revealing a plebian lifestyle that seemed incredible to an ordinary middle-class rural family.

11. Qutb described Robin Hood-like thieves in *A Child* but they appeared as much a part of the local community fabric as other occupations. He seemed much more critical of the government for forcing people to work in dishonest ways.

12. Virginia Danielson's classic biography on Umm Kalthum discusses the rise of the Egyptian diva in the 1920s when, by coincidence, phonographs were just coming on the market. Cairenes could now hear music mechanically, and they chose to listen to the music that reminded them of their village. This matches much more the fondness of the countryside that Qutb expressed in his memoir and far less the low-brow absurdity that Qutb's rival, Taha Husayn, showed in his own autobiography, *al-Ayyam* (The Days). Umm Kalthum wisely capitalized on her village roots and background from Daqahliyya province in the northern Delta. Clearly, records and phonographs were not cheap, and the large market and Umm Kalthum's meteoric rise indicate both the ex-rural character of the consumers and their ample wealth. See Virginia Danielson, *The Voice of Egypt: Umm Kulthum, Arabic Song, and Egyptian Society in the Twentieth Century* (Chicago: University of Chicago Press, 1997), ch. 2. For more on Taha Husayn and his autobiography, see Chapter 3.

A distinctly new social stratum was beginning to emerge, called "the new effendiyya" by Israel Gershoni and James P. Jankowski, *Redefining the Egyptian Nation, 1930–1945* (Cambridge: Cambridge University Press, 1995) and Israel Gershoni, "The Reader—'Another Production': The Reception of Haykal's Biography of Muhammad and the Shift of Egyptian Intellectual to Islamic Subjects in the 1930s" (*Poetics Today* 15, no. 2 [Summer 1994]: 241–277). These *effendis* were the middle-class Egyptians situated structurally between the elite (*bashawat*) above them and the workers ('*ummal*) and peasants (*fallahin*) below them, who came of age after the 1919 revolution. They evinced a Western lifestyle, attended Western-style secondary schools and universities, but also remained traditional and conservative in their outlook. They were the principal vectors of Egypt's newfound nationalism. Sayyid Qutb was part of this new effendiyya class.

"The *effendi* cohort was the embodiment of modern Egypt" (Gershoni and Jankowski, *Redefining the Egyptian Nation*, 11) but was not necessarily homogenous. Gershoni ("The Reader," 253–269), distinguished six different (though not mutually exclusive) subgroups: (1) the intellectuals, such as the editors and writers of the important cultural journals of the period; (2) the Islamist *salafiyya* movement; (3) right-wing nationalist forces; (4) reformist Islamic orthodoxy; (5) conservative Islamic orthodoxy, and (6) the modernist, secular opposition. He originally reduced the six subgroups to four groups by merging 2 and 3, and 4 and 5 together, but I have kept them separate. In the 1930s, this generation began to lean in the direction of renewing their Islamic identity, and writers sensitive to the tastes of their readers soon followed suit.

It is not clear what were the *effendiyya*'s social origins or how these origins influenced their political affiliation. I found in my own fieldwork that the political membership of the urban-born educated differs significantly from middle-class ex-villagers. The former join nationalist parties while the latter become members of religious associations such as the Muslim Brotherhood. Thus not all effendi shifted toward Islamism; many remained dedicated to secular, nationalist political organizations.

13. Musallam, *From Secularism to Jihad*, 32; John Calvert and William Shepard, "Translators' Introduction," Sayyid Qutb, *A Child from the Village*, trans. John Calvert and William Shepard (Syracuse: Syracuse University Press, 2004 [originally published 1946]), xxvii.

14. The circumstances of Qutb's move to Cairo are not entirely clear. Based on Qutb's 1946 memoir *A Child from the Village*, young Sayyid may have left for Cairo in 1921 after a two-year delay caused by the outbreak of the 1919 revolution, to live four years with his uncle, Ahmad Husayn 'Uthman. The account of his emotional departure from his family and Musha appears in the book. See Musallam, *From Secularism to Jihad*, 35, and Qutb, *A Child from the Village*, ch. 12. On the other hand, Qutb's entire family may have moved to Helwan, a suburb south of Cairo, when Qutb was just 13 years old, the year of Egypt's revolution. Were this the case, he would not have lived with his maternal uncle in Zaytun. See Hamid Algar, "Introduction," Sayyid Qutb, *Social Justice in Islam* (Oneonta, NY: Islamic Publications International, 2000), 1, and Mohammed Moinuddin Siddiqui, "An Outline of Sayyed [sic] Qutb's Life," in Sayyid Qutb, *Islam and Universal Peace* (Plainfield, IN: American Trust Publications, 1993), ix, who, however, omits a specific departure date. John Calvert claims that that Qutb's family joined him in Helwan after his father had died in 1933 and after the Education Ministry assigned him a position there in 1936. See John Calvert, *Sayyid Qutb and the Origins of Radical Islamism* (New York: Columbia University Press, 2010), 62.

15. Dar al-'Ulum was established in 1872 by Khedive Isma'il and the educational reformer 'Ali Mubarak, who intended it to be a school of higher education that provided teachers for Egypt's new government schools. This was the same year that al-Azhar University was reorganized into a more modern religious institution. The two schools were closely linked—Dar al-'Ulum students graduated entirely from al-Azhar—except for a nine-year window in the 1920s when Dar al-'Ulum assumed a more modern contrast to al-Azhar, when it saw itself in the forefront of fashioning the new effendiyya (see note 12 in this chapter).

    Initially, Dar al-'Ulum intended to be a post-graduate school for al-Azhar alumni, training them to teach Arabic but also expecting them to teach in other subject areas as well. This made foreign language training a very controversial issue: whether to retain its initial, but narrow national mandate or else yield to the practical and competitive demands for better jobs and careers for its graduates.

    In 1908, Dar al-'Ulum began requiring more preparation than al-Azhar provided and in 1920, it established its own preparatory (*tahjiziya*) section as a remedial program for qualified candidates, a move that relinquished its association with al-Azhar and declared itself a secular, professional teacher training school. By 1923, however, the government sought to restore the connection, curtailing Dar al-'Ulum's independence and strengthening al-Azhar's curriculum. In 1925, Dar al-'Ulum was placed under the authority of al-Azhar (though the curriculum remained under the Education Ministry's supervision) and in 1929, the preparatory section was dissolved. This limited the education offered at Dar al-'Ulum, which was not restored until 1945 when it was incorporated as a college into Fu'ad I (later Cairo) University. Lois A. Aroian, *The Nationalization of Arabic and Islamic Education in Egypt: Dar al-'Ulum and al-Azhar.* Cairo Papers in the Social Sciences, vol. 6, no. 4 (Cairo: American University in Cairo Press, 1983), 1, 15, 41, and 62.

16. A biographic sketch of Taha Husayn can be found in the Appendix, Part I, "Dramatis Personae."

17. It is not clear what results Qutb's proposal achieved. But his boldness in addressing the dean was duly noted by the school authorities. See Musallam, *From Secularism to Jihad*, 35, 36; Adnan A. Musallam, *Sayyid Qutb: The Emergence of the Islamicist, 1939–1950* (Jerusalem: Palestinian Academic Society for the Study of International Affairs, 1990), 113; Siddiqui "An Outline," xi; Khatab, *Political Thought*, 49.

18. This was the equivalent of a bachelor of arts degree. Qutb also received a diploma in education. Musallam, *From Secularism to Jihad*, 43.

19. Musallam, *From Secularism to Jihad*, 43. According to Khatab (*Political Thought*, 49–50), Qutb's first post after graduation was not as a teacher but instead as a *mu'id* (a *repetiteur*, or teaching assistant) at Dar al-'Ulum for three years. It was only then that he was employed

in the Education Ministry's General Culture Administration. This resume, however, omits Qutb's interim appointments as a teacher and it is not clear how it corresponds with the vita Musallam provides, unless the position of *muʿid* was concurrent with his Cairo teaching assignments.

I wish to thank William Granara for clarifying this position of teaching assistant.

Calvert claims (*Sayyid Qutb*, 61) that it was Taha Husayn, then supervisor of elementary education for the Ministry of Education, who gave Qutb his first job. This seems improbable since routine entry-level teaching posts seldom require patronage (although actual community assignments might). Husayn, a friend of ʿAbbas al-ʿAqqad, had been dismissed in 1932 after three years as university dean, had been transferred briefly to the Ministry, but remained in disfavor, and was dismissed from government service soon thereafter. Husayn became editor of *Kawkab al-Sharq* (Star of the East) in the spring of 1933 at the same time Qutb graduated. Husayn did not return to university teaching until late 1934 and university administration until 1936. He was dismissed once again in 1938 and then assumed the position of *muraqib*, or inspector, at the Ministry. J. Brugman, *An Introduction to the History of Modern Arabic Literature in Egypt* (Leiden: E. J. Brill, 1984), 363–364; Pierre Cachia, *Taha Husayn: His Place in the Egyptian Literary Renaissance* (Piscataway, NJ: Gorgias Press, 2005 [originally published London: Luzac, 1956]), 61–62.

20. This demotion was punishment for his cultural, literary, and political activities in opposition to the Wafd Party. Calvert, *Sayyid Qutb*, 105; Salah ʿAbd al-Fattah al-Khalidi, *Sayid Qutb min al-Milad ila al-Istishhad* (Sayid Qutb from His Birth to His Martyrdom) (Damascus: Dar al-Qalam, 1994), 87.

21. Al-Khalidi, *Sayid Qutb*, 86–87.

22. Khatab, *Political Thought*, 47; Musallam, *From Secularism to Jihad*, 200.

23. Khatab, *Political Thought*, 50.

24. Calvert, *Sayyid Qutb*, 78; Olivier Carré, *Mysticism and Politics: A Critical Reading of Fi Zilal al-Qur'an by Sayyid Qutb (1906–1966)* (Leiden: Brill, 2003), 2.

25. Musallam, *From Secularism to Jihad*, 36; Khatab, *Political Thought*, 46.

26. In 1924, Qutb was elected to the editorial committee of *al-Balagh* whose chief editor after 1921 had been ʿAbbas al-ʿAqqad, young Qutb's future mentor. Khatab, *Political Thought*, 55. Musallam, citing ʿAbd al-Baqi Husayn, states that Qutb's first poem appeared in 1925 when Qutb was 19 years old. Musallam, *From Secularism to Jihad*, 35, ʿAbd al-Baqi Muhammad Husayn, *Sayyid Qutb: Hayatuh wa Adabuh* (Sayyid Qutb: His Life and His Literature) (Al-Mansura, Daqahiliyya, Egypt: Dar al-Wafa', 1986), 122.

27. Calvert and Shepard, "Translators' Introduction," xvii.

28. ʿAbd al-Baqi Husayn claims (*Sayyid Qutb: Hayatuh*, 41) to have collected 455 articles written by Qutb from the time of his first poem in 1921 up to when he was arrested with the Muslim Brotherhood roundup in 1954.

29. Musallam, *From Secularism to Jihad*, 37–38; Ibrahim M. Abu-Rabiʿ, *Intellectual Origins of Islamic Resurgence in the Modern Arab World* (Albany: State University of New York Press, 1996), 98.

30. Musallam, *From Secularism to Jihad*, 37–38 and 47; Abu-Rabiʿ, *Intellectual Origins*, 98; Algar, "Introduction," 1–2; ʿAdil Hammuda, *Sayyid Qutb min al-Qarya ila al-Mashnaqa: Sirat al-Ab al-Ruhi li Jamaʿat al-ʿUnf* (Sayyid Qutb from the Village to the Gallows: The Biography of the Spiritual Father of Violent Associations) (Cairo: Dar al-Khayyal, 1996), 45.

31. Musallam, *From Secularism to Jihad*, 43; Khatab, *Political Thought*, 47 and 62. Al-Ghayati's poems were considered so inflammatory at the time of their publication, 1910, that two of the authors who wrote its three introductions were arrested at the request of the British: Muhammad Farid, successor to Mustafa Kamil as head of the National Party (receiving a sentence of six months in prison) and ʿAbd al-ʿAziz al-Shawish, editor of the party's journal, *al-Liwa* (sentenced to three months in prison). In her memoirs, Ghayati's daughter's claims that the poet was "prosecuted and jailed by a British judge" but Mounah ʿAbdallah Khouri states that although al-Ghayati was accused of insulting the authorities and inciting the public to political crimes, and sentenced to 12 months in prison at hard labor; since the poet was in Istanbul at the time, his trial and sentence were in absentia. Khatab, *Political Thought*,

47 and 184; Mounah Abdallah Khouri, *Poetry and the Making of Modern Egypt (1882–1922)* (Leiden: E. J. Brill, 1971), 88–89.

32. Musallam, *From Secularism to Jihad*, 1.

33. William Shepard, a well-known and experienced analyst of Qutb's work and ideas, describes *The Task of the Poet* as "a significant work of criticism." William E. Shepard, *Sayyid Qutb and Islamic Activism: A Translation and Critical Analysis of* Social Justice in Islam (Leiden: E. J. Brill, 1996), xv. See also Khatab, *Political Thought*, 49; Calvert, *Sayyid Qutb*, 78; Musallam, *From Secularism to Jihad*, 53.

34. Qutb published only three collections of poetry. The first was *al-Shati al-Majhul*. The second book was *Asda' al-Zaman* (The Echoes of Time) and appeared in December 1937. A third volume was published posthumously in 1989 with the title *Diwan Sayyid Qutb* (The Works of Sayyid Qutb); Khatab, *Political Thought*, 56.

35. Musallam, *From Secularism to Jihad*, 38–39.

36. A biographic sketch of 'Abbas al-'Aqqad can be found in the Appendix, Part I, "Dramatis Personae.".

37. Salma Khadra Jayyusi, *Trends and Movements in Modern Arabic Poetry*, 2 vols. (Leiden: E. J. Brill, 1977), 524; Khatab, *Political Thought*, 54; Calvert and Shepard, "Translators' Introduction," xvii.

38. All three, incidentally, were distinguished "country bumpkins" from the Sa'id: Qutb from Musha, Asyut; Husayn from Maghagha, al-Minya, and al-'Aqqad from Aswan.

39. For Shukri, see Brugman, *An Introduction*, 112–121, and Jayyusi, *Trends and Movements*, 157–160. For al-Mazini, see Brugman, *An Introduction*, 138–147, and Jayyusi, *Trends and Movements*, 161–163.

40. Musallam, *From Secularism to Jihad*, 5 and 36; Brugman, *An Introduction*, 94 and 114.

41. Jayyusi, *Trends and Movements*, 152. This English inspiration derived from the literature of the Romantic Lake Poets from northwest England—Wordsworth, Coleridge, Keats, and Shelley—who, together with Byron, all wrote at the beginning of the 19th century. In Egypt of the early 20th century, however, there was very little interest on the part of the British imperium to promote English literary culture, as Lord Cromer plainly pointed out in his classic 1908 book, *Modern Egypt*. The English influence, therefore, came inadvertently from the attempts to educate the bilingual administrators necessary for London's colonial bureaucracy. The Teachers' College was established in Cairo in 1889 for this purpose, and both Shukri and al-Mazini attended the school—considered the best school in Egypt at the time—and cut their teeth there on English poetry and literature. There was also a significant influence from the Syrian-Lebanese or *mahjar* poets writing in the United States, although this seemed to have affected more the Apollo group that arose later in the 1930s under Ahmad Zaki Abu Shadi and Khalil Matran that was then to clash with the members of the Diwan school. (See the discussion in the section "4 Disputes with Modernity" later in this chapter.) Both the Diwan school and the Apollo group exhibited a romanticism and an individualism that undoubtedly benefited (or suffered, depending on one's viewpoint) from the literary creations of such expatriates as Amin al-Rihani, Jibran Khalil Jibran, Mikha'il Rustum, Farah Antun, Jirji Zaydan, and Mikha'il Na'ima. Jayyusi, *Trends and Movements*, 144; Brugman, *An Introduction*, 96–99, 107–110, and 113.

42. Brugman, *An Introduction*, 95.

43. Al-Mazini maliciously attacked Shukri in *al-Diwan* for his reliance on neoclassical styles, but there may have been much truth to the fact that al-Mazini was simply settling scores for Shukri's earlier accusation that al-Mazini had plagiarized his own compositions. Al-'Aqqad's attempt to restrain al-Mazini was half-hearted. David Semah, *Four Egyptian Literary Critics* (Leiden: E. J. Brill, 1974), 24.

44. Ibid., 21.

45. The *qasida* is a form of polythematic love and panegyric poetry developed in pre-Islamic Arabia—the earliest odes dating to the end of the fifth century—and continued to be used throughout Islamic literary history up to the present time. It has always been respected as the highest form of poetic art and as the main area of expertise of the pre-Islamic poets. The

classic *qasida* has a strict structure that is considered among the most elaborate in the world. It is an ode of 30 to 100 verses, each consisting of two complete hemistiches, a single meter, and a single end-rhyme that runs through the entire piece. The same rhyme also occurs at the end of the first hemistich of the first verse. The *qasida* typically begins with the amatory verses of the *nasib* and ends with verses of praise, *fakhr*, passing through themes of eulogy, *madih*, satire, *hija'*, or morals, *hikam*. There is a middle portion that "travels a journey," *rahil*, from the sadness and melancholy of a past love affair to realizing the patron's grace and generosity that "turns [the poet's] frustration and grief into happiness and bliss." At first, the *qasida* reinforced the transcendence of tribal or community values over individual emotions, but after the emergence of Islam, it focused more on praising and eulogizing religion and the sponsoring patron, such as the caliph or, conversely, condemning and criticizing an unpopular ruler elsewhere through satire. Adapted from Julie Scott Meisami and Paul Starkey, eds., *Encyclopedia of Arabic Literature* (London: Routledge, 1998), 630–633.

46. The *muwashshah* is an Arabic lyric poem written in a strophic form. It is frequently sung and at times accompanied by musical instruments. It is usually written in classical Arabic and covers such themes as "hopeless love, unrequited love, separation, and the cruelty of the beloved." It first developed in Andalucían Spain in the 11th and 12th centuries and thereafter spread east (as well as into Europe). In Baghdad, it offered a new format for the wine poetry and songs made famous earlier by the 8th-century Baghdadi poet, Abu Nuwas. The *muwashshah* frequently has five stanzas, each numbering four, five, or six lines, with a complex rhyming scheme. Typically, rhymes distinctive to the stanza constitute the opening *ghusn* and the rhymes repeated throughout the poem form the final *simt*. The repeated rhyme is usually introduced before the stanzas in a preliminary section called the *matla* which then turns the *simt* into a refrain. In the very last stanza, or *kharja*, the first part of its *ghusn* introduces a kind of personal declaration leading to the last *simt* aimed at the audience and stated in contrasting colloquial Arabic. It is in the *kharja* that poets express their own personal emotion, longing, and sadness. The *matla*, *simt*, and *kharja* lines often contain internal rhyming segments in limerick-like fashion. This is also common with the *ghusn* as well. Adapted from Julie Scott Meisami and Paul Starkey, eds., *Encyclopedia of Arabic Literature* (London: Routledge, 1998), 563–566.

47. Jayyusi, *Trends and Movements*, 167. Shawqi's main artistic transgressions that the two critics denounced included the disunity of his poems, his "wholesale" but unsuccessful imitation (perhaps even plagiarism) of the classical style, absurdities, artificiality, and superficiality of form over substance and essence. Al-'Aqqad contended that Shawqi wrote in such a disjointed and incoherent fashion that he lacked any harmonizing theme. His poems were "more like interrupted glimmers of light" than a "constant star that shines steadily and illuminates everything around it." He also used "incompatible expressions." When al-'Aqqad criticized Shawqi's poetry as absurd, according to Jayyusi, it meant that his poems exhibited absurd meanings, unlimited exaggerations, untruths, contradictions in meanings, a lack of logic, and "other defects." Semah, *Four Egyptian Literary Critics*, 19 and 21; Jayyusi, *Trends and Movements*, 167 and 169.

48. Jayyusi, *Trends and Movements*, 168; Muhammad Zaghlul Sallam, *al-Naqd al-'Arabi al-Hadith: Usuluhu, Qadayahu, Manhijuhu* (Modern Arabic Criticism: Its Origins, Issues, and Methods) (Cairo: Maktabat al-Anjlu al-Misriyah [Anglo-Egyptian Bookstore], 1964), 235.

49. Semah, *Four Egyptian Literary Critics*, 21.

50. Musallam, *From Secularism to Jihad*, 36.

51. Jayyusi, *Trends and Movements*, 142 and 156–157.

52. Brugman, *An Introduction*, 95.

53. Jayyusi, *Trends and Movements*, 158 and 160.

54. Ibid., 170–171.

55. Al-'Aqqad's *cri de cour* for a revolutionary style may have been less a broad inspiration to modernize but more just a part of his "unrelenting" attacks against Shawqi. Jayyusi, *Trends and Movements*, 30.

56. For more on al-'Aqqad's use of eugenics theory, see his biographic sketch in the Appendix, Part I, "Dramatis Personae."

57. If, as al-'Aqqad believed, "what really matters in all art is the motive that exists independently of the tool" and that critics should explore the inner workings of the author's mind, then Mandur was more concerned with the tools and outward forms. Semah, *Four Egyptian Literary Critics*, 14; 'Abbas Mahmud al-'Aqqad, *Shu'ara Misr wa Bi'atuhum fi al-Jil al-Madi'* (Poets of Egypt and Their Milieu in the Past Generation) (Cairo: Maktabit Higazi, 1937), 48.

58. On March 3, 1924, the nearly 1,300-year-old Islamic caliphate came to an end under orders from the president of the new Republic of Turkey, Mustafa Kemal Ataturk. Angry opponents in Egypt considered a number of possible alternatives. A year later, 'Ali 'Abd al-Raziq, the scion of a well-known Azhar family, offered his own response—that Islam had never actually advocated the institution of the caliphate, and so, no replacement was necessary—in his famous book *al-Islam wa Usul al-Hukm: Bahth fi al-Khilafa wa al-Hukuma fi al-Islam* (Islam and the Foundations of Governance: Research into the Caliphate and Government in Islam). This provoked yet another outburst of outrage since many Egyptians felt that religion and government went hand in hand, making them different from Christian Europe, which had separated God and Caesar. 'Abd al-Raziq argued that not only was secularism a natural condition in Islam, but that it had been so from the beginning. His selection of Qur'anic verses and hadith was egregious, guaranteed to antagonize the pious. Many denounced his opportunism and Westernization, and 'Abd al-Raziq was a pen stroke away from arrest and imprisonment but for sympathetic supporters in the Palace and the Interior Ministry. This protection pointed, perhaps, to another response—that King Fu'ad himself should be nominated to become the new caliph. Many who heard this second scenario thought 'Abd al-Raziq was in league with the Palace to promote Fu'ad's candidacy. This, too, received much opposition.

    In 1926, Taha Husayn published an equally shocking book, *Fi al-Shi'r al-Jahili* (Pre-Islamic Poetry). Husayn questioned the validity of the Qur'an by "scientifically proving" that early Muslims had forged pre-Islamic poetry, that the story of Ibrahim, Isma'il, and the Ka'ba was a Jewish fabrication adopted in order to emphasize a illusory kinship with other monotheisms, and that the Qur'an was merely a product of its immediate environment and not divinely authored. Because of the uproar, his book was quickly withdrawn from the bookstores and reissued a year later with a new title, *Fi al-Adab al-Jahili* (Pre-Islamic Literature), with some, but not all, of the obnoxious theories removed. Husayn was subsequently dismissed as the dean of the Faculty of Arts at the national Egyptian (later Cairo) University and, but for the intervention of the prime minister, would have lost his teaching post as well. Husayn's secularism may have sown the seeds of acrimony between himself and Qutb, even though Qutb was hardly a religious scholar at the time. Qutb later criticized two of Husayn's books *The Future of Culture in Egypt* and the autobiographical *Days* because of Husayn's haughty, cavalier, and cosmopolitan dismissal of traditional Egyptian culture. Cachia, *Taha Husayn*, 95; Charles C. Adams, *Islam and Modernism in Egypt* (Oxford: Oxford University Press, 1933), 253–256; Afaf Lutfi al-Sayyid Marsot, *Egypt's Liberal Experiment: 1922–1936* (Berkeley: University of California Press, 1972), 75.

59. Musallam, *From Secularism to Jihad*, 5; R. C. Ostle, "Iliya Abu Madi and Arabic Poetry in the Inter-war Period," in *Studies in Modern Arabic Literature*, R. C. Ostle, ed. (London: Aris and Phllips, 1975), 40–41. Calvert remarks (*Sayyid Qutb*, 70) that "Qutb's style in these debates was hostile. He called opponents 'flies' and 'worms.' On one occasion, he [even] questioned a literary rival's humanity."

60. Khatab, *Political Thought*, 54; Sayyid Qutb, "Bayna al-'Aqqad wa al-Rafi'i" (Between al-'Aqqad and al-Rafi'i), *al-Risala* 6, no. 201 (April 25, 1938): 694.

61. John Calvert (*Sayyid Qutb*, 9, 10, 83, 107, 201, and 206) frequently asserts that Qutb's focus on the subjective and affective characteristics of Islam reflects a "mystical temper" and a "Sufi-like disposition." Rather than anchor these introspective interests in religion, I am claiming that this lifelong emphasis derives from Qutb's early immersion in and fascination with the Romantic poetry of the Diwan school, itself imported from Europe. That is, the genealogy here derives from the northwest England of Wordsworth, Coleridge, Keats, and Shelley, not from the Sufi orders of the Rifa'iyya, Qadiriyya, Ahmadiyya, Burhamiyya, or Shadhiliyya (Hoffman-Ladd 1992: 632). Qutb never joined a Sufi order (Calvert, *Sayyid Qutb*, 9) and

despite the fact that his last name is the same word as the title given the founders of major Sufi orders (*qutb, aqtab,* axis/axes or pole/poles, the "overall spiritual master of the age"), this coincidence should in no way be mistaken for a familiarity or involvement with Sufism.

Similarly, Olivier Carré (*Mysticism and Politics,* 31, 48, 51, and 171) even describes Qutb as a "fideist," a term more commonly reserved for Martin Luther, the father of Protestantism, and his concept "sola fida," by faith alone, that implies a singular stress on belief over action. While it is true that Qutb was much more fascinated by the Meccan years of the Prophet Muhammad that emphasized faith and its propagation over the later Medinan years of laws and state building, this was not generated by a whimsical, other-worldly spirituality but by a reasonable, this-worldly pursuit of the personal and introspective that derived from the years he was involved with the Diwan school.

62. Musallam, *From Secularism to Jihad,* 40.

63. A biographic sketch of Ahmad Zaki Abu Shadi can be found in the Appendix, Part I, "Dramatis Personae."

64. The *Apollo* magazine appeared between September 1932 and December 1934, for only 25 issues. It discontinued its publication primarily because of the damaging and fatal attacks from al-'Aqqad and his Diwan school. Brugman, *An Introduction,* 151; Jayyusi, *Trends and Movements,* 386.

65. Apollo's second president, Khalil Matran, was of Christian Lebanese-Syrian origins. This fostered a close connection to the Writers' League of émigré poets in New York City, which may have pulled *Apollo* away from England and more toward America. Brugman, *An Introduction,* 57.

66. Brugman, *An Introduction,* 153–155, 170–171; Jayyusi, *Trends and Movements,* 370; Kenneth S. Mayers, "Apollo: Arab-language literary magazine, 1932–1934," *Encyclopedia of the Modern Middle East,* Vol. 1, Reeva S. Simon, Philip Mattar, Richard W. Bulliet, eds. (New York: Macmillan Reference; Simon & Schuster Macmillan, 1996), 164.

67. Brugman, *An Introduction,* 155.

68. Jayyusi, *Trends and Movements,* 190; Brugman, *An Introduction,* 190–191. Apollo's promotion of unmitigated modernization was contradicted by the fact that Abu Shadi had asked the neoclassicist poet Shawqi to be the Society's first president even while Abu Shadi denied being a devotee of the man. Although Shawqi composed a poem in honor of the Society, it was the neoclassicist's connections to the Palace that made his selection all but inevitable, sustaining Qutb's criticism about the Society's improper political associations. Brugman, *An Introduction,* 152; Mayer, "Apollo," 164.

69. Al-'Aqqad had dabbled in free verse as early as 1913 and advocated this style in his introduction to al-Mazini's first published collection. It was only later, in 1943, that he renounced this and similar innovations, well after the debate with Abu Shadi. Brugman, *An Introduction,* 194.

70. An ironic claim since the founding of the Diwan school had involved al-'Aqqad and al-Mazini attacking Shukri in the 1921 volume that had named the group. Shukri later joined his two "friends" in establishing the school.

71. Musallam, *From Secularism to Jihad,* 44–45.

72. The title refers to the Prophet Muhammad who began his mission at the age of 40, in 610.

73. Jayyusi, *Trends and Movements,* 157 and 387.

74. Musallam, *From Secularism to Jihad,* 45–46; Brugman, *An Introduction,* 89–90.

75. Sayyid Qutb, "al-Dalala al-Nafsiyya li al-Alfaz wa al-Tarakib al-'Arabiyya" (The Psychological Indication of Arabic Expressions and Structures), *Sahifat Dar al-'Ulum* 4, no. 3 (January 1938a): 23; Musallam, *From Secularism to Jihad,* 45–48, 51; Calvert, *Sayyid Qutb,* 71–72.

76. Musallam, *From Secularism to Jihad,* 46–47.

77. Abu-Rabi', *Intellectual Origins,* 97.

78. Musallam, *From Secularism to Jihad,* 46–47.

79. Shepard, *Sayyid Qutb and Islamic Activism,* xv; Abu-Rabi', *Intellectual Origins,* 96–97; Khatab, *Political Thought,* 97 and 99; Musallam, *From Secularism to Jihad,* 52.

80. For more about this controversy, see note 58 in this chapter. Qutb and Husayn had both memorized the Qur'an as part of their traditional education. Yet Qutb came to embrace the wisdom of the Qur'an while Husayn went on to undermine it.

81. The bracketed numbers refer to the pages in Sidney Glazer's translation of *The Future of Culture in Egypt* published by the American Council of Learned Societies in 1954.

82. Taha Husayn, *The Future of Culture in Egypt*, 20.

83. *Ibn al-balad* (sons of the country) refers to "authentic" Egyptians. *Ibn al-zawat* (or *dhawat*, sons of importance) refers to "elite" or "Westernized" Egyptians. Sawsan el-Messiri, *Ibn al-Balad: A Concept of Egyptian Identity* (Leiden: E. J. Brill, 1978); Laila Shukry El-Hamamsy, "The Assertion of Egyptian Identity," in *Ethnic Identity: Cultural Continuities and Change*, George DeVos and Lola Romanucci-Ross, eds. (Palo Alto, CA: Mayfield, 1975), 276–306.

84. Abu-Rabi', *Intellectual Origins*, 101–103; Sayyid Qutb, *Ma'rakat al-Islam wa al-Ra'smaliyya* (The Battle of Islam and Capitalism) (Cairo: Dar al-Shuruq, 1974 [originally published in Cairo in 1951]), 100–101.

85. Musallam, *From Secularism to Jihad*, 78; Calvert, *Sayyid Qutb*, 94.

86. Qutb and two friends from Dar al-'Ulum established this journal in 1934, a year after Qutb graduated. It published articles on curriculum, schools, and education, in Arabic and foreign commentary in translation in order to raise the intellectual quality and reputation of students and graduates. Lois A. Aroian, *The Nationalization of Arabic and Islamic Education in Egypt: Dar al-'Ulum and al-Azhar*. Cairo Papers in the Social Sciences, vol. 6, no. 4 (Cairo: American University in Cairo Press, 1983), 60–67.

87. Husayn had been removed as dean of the Faculty of Arts at the Egyptian (later Cairo) University because of his 1926 book *Pre-Islamic Poetry* but had been reappointed in 1936 when, two years later, he published *The Future of Culture in Egypt*. Qutb was hard-pressed to criticize outright a person with such an illustrious academic position (Khatab, *Political Thought*, 50).
    Sometime between May 1942, and October 1944, Qutb got into trouble once again with his employer, the Education Ministry. (The first time took place after his debate with Mustafa Sadiq al-Rafi'i's supporters mentioned earlier in this chapter.) The minister himself had wanted to dismiss Qutb after General Security informed him of Qutb's political writings for the opposition Sa'dist Party. Taha Husayn, who was just a consultant to the Ministry at the time, nevertheless called Qutb into his office at the Ministry to discuss the matter. Khatab reports the actual conversation (*Political Thought*, 50–51). Qutb was more than ready to resign rather than submit to government pressure. Husayn reminded him, however, of his financial and family difficulties—astonishing that this was so well known to Husayn—but also, in the process, reinforced Qutb's subordinate status. Husayn actually threatened Qutb with house arrest should he quit, although it was attributed formally to the martial law in effect at the time. Qutb remained obstinate, not caring whether he remained or left. Husayn closed the conversation by saying he would intervene on Qutb's behalf. The result, however, was hardly satisfying: Qutb remained with the Ministry but received a two-month reassignment—an exile—back to the Sa'id to examine Arabic language pedagogy, the very pedagogy that Husayn proposed in *The Future* to eliminate. Khatab presents this dialogue to demonstrate Husayn's "generosity," the actual expression that Qutb also used. To me, however, it indicates Husayn's condescending effort to belittle and dominate Qutb. Such unpleasant conversations could only have alienated Qutb to Husayn's position and perspective. It was hardly the kind of relationship that could be called "collegial."

88. Musallam, *From Secularism to Jihad*, 78. Qutb had declared earlier, in January 1938, that "we should not feel guilty to declare openly that this language is not our native language. Rather it is the language of another people who differ from us in many traditions, customs, ideas, environment and economic and political factors....All that ties us to these people [the Arabs] are religious connections and the literary heritage." Yet how quickly did Qutb turn around! Now, a year and a half later, he unambiguously rebutted Husayn's veneration of Egypt's European roots and underscored, instead, the country's Arabic traditions, along with its religious and literary conventions. Qutb, "al-Dalala al-Nafsiyya," 27, cited in ibid., 52.

89. Because of the scholarship of those like Martin Bernal, it is now well recognized that before Greece's very recent Europeanization, it had much more in common culturally with the southern and eastern Mediterranean than earlier suspected. However, both Husayn and Qutb assumed that Europe was homogenous throughout its current boundaries and that these borders contained a historical Greece that was invariably the same as northern and

western Europe. Martin Bernal, *Black Athena: The Afro-Asiatic Roots of Classical Civilization* (New Brunswick: Rutgers University Press, 1987).

90. Qutb actually used words like "mentality" and "civilization" to signify what I am calling "culture" here.

91. Edward Said, *Orientalism* (New York: Vintage Books, 1979), 52; Musallam, *From Secularism to Jihad*, 80.

92. It appeared in the Brotherhood's weekly newspaper, *al-Nadhir* (The Harbinger) on June 9, 1939. It was also published as a booklet, *Naqd Kitab Mustaqbal al-Thaqafa* (Criticism of the book *The Future of Culture*) later the same year.

93. A biographic sketch of Muhammad Mandur can be found in the Appendix, Part I, "Dramatis Personae."

94. Before Mandur, both the Diwan school and Apollo Society had exhibited a distinct British influence. Francophile thinking remained in its infancy; al-'Aqqad had even criticized Arabic poetry and literature for their French inspiration. It was Mandur and Husayn who advocated the shift to a more Francophone influence. Brugman, *An Introduction*, 100–101.

95. Jayyusi, *Trends and Movements*, 525.

96. For more on the relationship between Muhammad Mandur and Taha Husayn, see Mandur's biographical sketch in the Appendix, Part I, "Dramatis Personae."

97. Brugman, *An Introduction*, 402: Jayyusi, *Trends and Movements*, 524.

98. Semah, *Four Egyptian Literary Critics*, 132, 147–148, 153, 158, 161; Brugman, *An Introduction*, 404–405.

99. This style exhibited clear-cut romantic features and followed the ideas about poetry of the French historian and literary critic, Gustave Lanson. Mandur was the scholar who translated Lanson's celebrated article, 'La Methode de l'histoire littéraire," into Arabic and made it the primary vehicle for introducing French literary criticism into Egypt. Gustave Lanson, "La Methode de l'histoire littéraire" (Manhaj al-Bahth fi al-Adab wa al-Lugha; Research Methods in Literature and Language) in al-Naqd al-Manhaji 'and al-Arab (Critique of Methodology among the Arabs) (Cairo: Dar Nahdat Misr li al-Taba'a wa al-Nashr [Egyptian Renaissance Company for Printing and Publishing], 1972 [originally published in Beirut in 1946]), 21; Muhammad Mandur, "al-Shi'r al-Katabi" (Written Poetry) in his Fi al-Mizan al-Jadid (New Balance) (Cairo:Maktabit Lagnat al-Ta'lif, 1944b), 69 and 99; Brugman, An Introduction, 406; Jayyusi, Trends and Movements, 523–524; Semah, Four Egyptian Literary Critics, 189.

100. In his discussions of prominent poets, Mandur failed to cite even one successful Egyptian poet, Matran himself being considered a member of Lebanese-Syrian community in exile—the *mahjar* poets—both in Egypt and in America.

101. Jayyusi, *Trends and Movements*, 524 and 789; Semah, *Four Egyptian Literary Critics*, 154.

102. Semah, *Four Egyptian Literary Critics*, 154; Brugman, *An Introduction*, 406; Muhammad Mandur, *Fi al-Adab wa al-Naqd* (Literature and Criticism) (Cairo: Maktabit Lagnat al-Ta'lif, 1949), 31.

103. For more information on these personal and political differences, see Mandur's biographical sketch in the Appendix, Part I, "Dramatis Personae."

104. A partial list of these radical leftist organizations (and their founding year) include the Egyptian Socialist Party (1921), the Egyptian Communist Party (1922), the Union of Peace Supporters (1934), the Democratic Union (1939), *Iskra* (1943), the Egyptian Movement for National Liberation (Curiel) (1943), the Democratic Movement for National Liberation (Hadeto) (1947), the Egyptian Communist Party (1950), the New Dawn, the Popular Vanguard for Liberation, the National Committee of Workers and Students, and the Congress of Union of Egyptian Workers. For more on these different Communist organizations, see Selma Botman, *The Rise of Egyptian Communism, 1939–1970* (Syracuse: Syracuse University Press, 1988).

105. These included the Liberal Constitutionalist Party of Adli Yakan and 'Abd al-Khaliq Tharwat, the Union (*Ittihad*) Party of King Fu'ad and the Palace, the Sha'b Party of Isma'il Sidqi, and later, the breakaway Sa'dist (Ahmad Mahir) and Qutla Bloc (Makram Ubayd) Parties.

106. Musallam, *From Secularism to Jihad*, 10–11.
107. Musallam, *From Secularism to Jihad*, 200. Scholars writing about the two decades that followed Egypt's 1919 revolution seem similarly unsettled about what this dissension meant for the country's political character. As Egyptian intellectuals in the 1930s backed away from an unadulterated nationalism of the 1920s, Nadav Safran concludes that this change of direction was a "crisis of orientation," a phase of "reaction" in Egypt's intellectual life, a "retreat" from "a vigorous rationalist spirit," and a surrender of an earlier "rationalism and Western cultural orientation." Ibrahim Ibrahim argues, however, that no shift had occurred since there had never really been a solid basis of enlightened rationality in the first place. Egypt's literati, he concludes, had always been steeped in their "traditional culture" and "Islamic upbringing." It was only later they became "enlightened" or modernized, though even then, they remained a "product of two worlds." Charles Smith is less prejudiced, essentialist, and Manichean than Safran when he concludes that the shift toward traditionalism in the 1930s was "designed to placate the religious and political opposition of the time and that, rather than seeking Islamic inspired alternatives, the intellectuals were trying to achieve their previous goals [of modernization] by different means because of the resurgence of Islamic sentiment which had occurred." This suggests an opportunism to surreptitiously follow a modernist agenda, to avoid political accusations of atheism, and to manipulate popular support rather than pursue an authentic Islamic perspective. Smith argues that a number of Egyptian writers in the Liberal Constitutionalist Party purposely explored Islamic themes to counter accusations of Godlessness from the Wafd Party and to appeal for political support from the "ignorant" masses "dominated by religion." Similarly, Israel Gershoni and James Jankowski claim that Egyptian writers shifted to Islamic topics in order to defend Islam from its domestic critics (disparaging the "stagnant orthodox establishment") and foreign detractors (Christian missionaries and Orientalists), to reawaken Egypt to its more authentic Islamic heritage, and to appeal to an educated, yet more traditional middle-class public, what the two scholars call the "new effendiyya" who appeared less Westernized than the preceding generation of white-collar employees. Musallam, *From Secularism to Jihad*, 207; Gershoni and Jankowski, *Redefining the Egyptian Nation*, 11 and 65; Nadav Safran, *Egypt in Search of Political Community: An Analysis of the Intellectual and Political Evolution of Egypt, 1804–1952* (Cambridge, MA: Harvard University Press, 1961), 140; Charles D. Smith, "The 'Crisis of Orientation': The Shift of Egyptian Intellectual to Islamic Subjects in the 1930's," *International Journal of Middle East Studies* 4, (1973): 384, 392–393, and 399; Ibrahim Iskandar Ibrahim, "The Egyptian Intellectuals between Tradition and Modernity" (unpublished Ph.D. dissertation, St. Antony's College, Oxford, 1967), 20, 27, and 29.
108. Musallam, *From Secularism to Jihad*, 6–10; Adnan A. Musallam, *Sayyid Qutb: The Emergence of the Islamicist, 1939–1950* (Jerusalem: Palestinian Academic Society for the Study of International Affairs, 1990), 112.
109. This mix itself seems a response to a hybrid Egyptian public, the new *effendiyya* mentioned in note 12 in this chapter.
110. Musallam, *From Secularism to Jihad*, 9; Musallam, *Sayyid Qutb: The Emergence*, 22–23.
111. Elliott Colla remarks:

> It is impossible to overestimate the degree to which the discovery of King Tutankhamen's tomb changed everything about how Egyptian national elites looked at their past. If there was a single event that pushed the largely scholarly interest in the Pharaonic past and its artifacts into the forefront of the mainstream political and expressive cultures of modern Egypt, it was this.... Moreover, the Pharaonist vision of the past converged in many places with the central ideas and slogans of the national liberation movement, led by Saʿd Zaghloul's Wafd Party.... These ideas coincided with the central aspirations and demands of Egyptian nationalists throughout the 1920s.

Elliott Colla, *Conflicted Antiquities: Egyptology, Egyptomania, Egyptian Modernity* (Durham, NC: Duke University Press, 2007), 117.
112. Ibid., 235.

113. Qutb's proposal for a Pharaonist literature was reminiscent of Muhammad Haykal's enthusiastic call 15 years earlier, although it is not clear whether Qutb was actually revisiting the previous debates about Pharaonism of the 1920s or if he was simply responding ebulliently at the time, October 1944, to the Naguib Mahfouz book he was reviewing, *Kifah Tiba* (The Battle of Thebes) because it was an allegory for overthrowing foreign domination. Qutb's regress was not so much anachronistic as it was simply endorsing an attitude with lingering significance (ibid.) Still, by the 1940s, Qutb was aware of the Islamist arguments against the "idol worship" of Pharaonism and nationalism more generally. By this time, Qutb's "enthusiasm for [the] Pharaonist style was already separated from any particular political program." A few years hence, Qutb saw these beliefs as apostasy and a "cause for concern." Colla, *Conflicted Antiquities*, 177, 235, 238 and 240, 260; Sayyid Qutb, "Kifah Tiba" (The Struggle for Thebes), *al-Risala* 12, no. 587 (October 2, 1944): 89–92.

114. Musallam, *Sayyid Qutb: The Emergence*, 20. This perspective appeared in Qutb's debate with Taha Husayn over *The Future of Culture in Egypt* discussed earlier.

115. Sayyid Qutb, *Ma'rakat al-Islam wa al-Ra'smaliyya* (The Battle of Islam and Capitalism) (Cairo: Dar al-Shuruq, 1974 [originally published in Cairo in 1951]), 27, 35, and 5; Calvert, *Sayyid Qutb*, 161–162.

116. For more on this rebellion, see Ted Swedenburg, *Memories of Revolt: The 1936–1939 Rebellion and the Palestinian National Past* (Fayetteville: University of Arkansas Press, 2003).

117. Musallam, *From Secularism to Jihad*, 92.

118. Khatab, *Political Thought*, 80–81.

119. For more details on Sayyid Qutb's ideas about apologetics, see the Appendix, Part IV.

120. Musallam, *From Secularism to Jihad*, 8–10; Khatab, *Political Thought*, 80–81; Abu Rabi', *Intellectual Origins*, 95. The use of biography here was not accidental. It was done in order to resemble the Western stories of Jesus and thus to demonstrate the humaneness, greatness, but above all, the rationalism of these Islamic personalities in an attempt to covertly promote a modernist agenda and redefine Islam in Western terms. The apologetic nature of these efforts was in response to the efforts of Christian missionaries in Egypt and of Orientalists outside the country.

121. Musallam, *From Secularism to Jihad*, 69–70.

Chapter 3

1. Musallam states that this second volume of poetry never appeared, although its December 1937 publication date was announced earlier in the October and November issues of *al-Risala*. Khatab claims that the book was published but no extant copies can be found. It was, however, catalogued in the library at the Higher Institute of Arabic Studies in Cairo, although the actual copy itself has disappeared. This is not surprising since once Qutb became imprisoned and executed, his publications were ordered removed from Egyptian libraries. Adnan A. Musallam, *From Secularism to Jihad: Sayyid Qutb and the Foundations of Radical Islam* (Westport, CT: Praeger, 2005), 42; Sayed Khatab, *The Political Thought of Sayyid Qutb: The Theory of Jahiliyyah* (London: Routledge, 2006), 56.

2. Musallam, *From Secularism to Jihad*, 42.

3. Many scholars have attempted to identify the cause and occasion of Qutb's reorientation. Muhammad Tawfiq Barakat reduces Qutb's commitment to hearing just one of Hasan al-Banna's speeches, although Musallam argues that "such a [simplistic] assertion . . . does not warrant serious consideration since it . . . fail[s] to take into account the various forces that worked to shape Qutb's personality and outlook on life, for example his upbringing, religious training, personal disappointments, and the state of Egyptian life and society in the first half of this century." Khatab claims that Qutb's discontent with secularism, and with secular politics in particular, was evident even before his arrival in Cairo, back when he lived in Musha where there had been an "impasse" between modernity and tradition. At first, Musallam disagrees, claiming that this aversion to modernity never set in until Qutb had reached the capital. Yet later, he, too, claims that Qutb never actually left the world of Islam; raised religiously as a

child, he remained immersed in a rural-like spiritualism that bordered on mystical Sufism. Musallam also argues, in a somewhat Freudian manner, that it was Qutb's mother's death in 1939 and a "shattered love affair" in or around 1942 or 1943, together with his deteriorating health, that, long after he had settled in Cairo, pushed him into adopting a more serious Islamist animosity toward the West. He then maintains that Qutb sought a comfort and a refuge in religion to soothe the pain, alienation, and unhappiness of his personal emotional problems. However, it may be better to employ a cognitivist approach over a Freudian one to more adequately explain this new direction, seeing it as analytical and deliberate rather than instinctual or impulsive.

Calvert finds it "difficult to account for [Qutb's] turn to a political as opposed to a purely cultural understanding" of Islam. Nevertheless, he provides four answers: (1) the "existential need for ideological certainty in a time of political crisis and social agitation"; (2) "an ideological solution to the problems that faced his county"; (3) a previously formulated doctrine that "looked to the wellbeing of the community rather than the individual"; and (4) a "vocabulary, codes and symbols... untouched by Western experience." Calvert warns his readers, however, not to be condescending or misleading by assuming that Islamism "fulfilled... a political need only." There was, he reminds us, a "deep spiritual need" as well. But see note 61 in Chapter 2. Khatab, *Political Thought*, 45; Musallam, *From Secularism to Jihad*, 48 and 64–69; Adnan A. Musallam, *Sayyid Qutb: The Emergence of the Islamicist, 1939–1950* (Jerusalem: Palestinian Academic Society for the Study of International Affairs, 1990), 6–7, 113; Muhammad Tawfiq Barakat, *Sayyid Qutb: Khulasat hayatihi manhajihi fi al-haraka, al-naqd al-muwajjahu ilayhi* (Sayyid Qutb: Summary of His Life, His Approach in the [Islamic] Movement, [and] the Criticism Directed at Him) (Beirut: Dar al-Da'wah, 1970), 17; John Calvert, *Sayyid Qutb and the Origins of Radical Islamism* (New York: Columbia University Press, 2010), 127–128; Ibrahim M. Abu-Rabi', *Intellectual Origins of Islamic Resurgence in the Modern Arab World* (Albany: State University of New York Press, 1996), 92.

4. The Anglo-Egyptian Treaty of August 26, 1936, called for removing all British troops from Egypt except for 10,000 troops and auxiliary personnel stationed to protect the Suez Canal and for relabeling Britain's highest ruling authority from High Commissioner to Ambassador. The Montreux Convention of the spring of 1937 abolished the capitulations (legal privileges for non-Egyptians) except for extending the duration of mixed courts another 12 years that also came to include criminal cases.

5. His expectations were higher than his actual situation, as measured later by his aspirations for a much higher-ranking position in the Ministry—that of the ministership itself. This is discussed in greater detail in Chapter 5.

6. Musallam, *Sayyid Qutb: The Emergence*, 61–62; Musallam, *From Secularism to Jihad*, 66–67.

7. His mentor, al-'Aqqad, had written a similar novel, *Sarah*, published 10 years earlier, in 1937, which was an autobiographical story of his own love affair. And both could have well been modeled on Muhammad Haykal's novel, *Zaynab*, which was published in 1913 and involved an estranged romance.

8. Musallam, *From Secularism to Jihad*, 66–68.

9. Ibid., 66–69.

10. Ibid., 64–69.

11. Martin Riesebrodt derives his definition of religious fundamentalism from Said Arjomand's concept of revolutionary traditionalism as an ideology that "conjures up a mythical [sic] past to mobilize traditionalists politically" who feel attacked by outside enemies. It is this latter aspect of attack-and-defend-and-counterattack that primarily distinguishes nonviolent religious conservatives or traditionalists from militant fundamentalists. I am, however, unconvinced about the "mythical" aspect that suggests a sort of fabrication. Qutb's depiction of the first generation of Muslims need not be untrue—merely edited, fashioned, and politicized. Perhaps using Benedict Anderson's concept of an "imagined" past is more appropriate, since even invented pasts can become hypostatized. The notion of counterattack is also used by Marty and Appleby who offer a similar definition of religious fundamentalists "fighting back" against an Enlightenment-based modernity. See Martin Riesebrodt, *Pious Passion: The Emergence of Modern Fundamentalism in the*

United States and Iran, trans. Don Reneau (Berkeley: University of California Press, 1993 [orig-
inally published in 1990]), 8; Said Arjomand, "Traditionalism in Twentieth-Century Iran" in
his *From Nationalism to Revolutionary Islam* (Albany: SUNY Press, 1984); Benedict Anderson,
Imagined Communities: Reflections on the Origin and Spread of Nationalism (New York: Verso Press,
1983), 6; Martin E. Marty and R. Scott Appleby, *The Glory and the Power: The Fundamentalist
Challenge to the Modern World* (Boston: Beacon Press, 1992), 17.

12. The British were worried lest German and Italian troops would move across North Africa
and attack Egypt and the Suez Canal. They therefore evoked the emergency clause of the
1936 Anglo-Egyptian Treaty which allowed them to station soldiers outside the Canal
Zone. Thus the treaty, already perceived as weak, proved useless in preserving Egyptian
independence.

13. Musallam, *From Secularism to Jihad,* 73–74; Musallam, *Sayyid Qutb: The Emergence,* 71.

14. Sayyid Qutb. "al-Ghina' al-Marid Yanghur al-Khuluq wa al-Mujtama'a al-Misri" (Sick Singing
Strikes at Egypt's Nature and Society), *al-Risala* 8:374. September 1940: 1382–1384.

15. Musallam, *From Secularism to Jihad,* 75.

16. It is not exactly clear when the first radio station appeared in Cairo. It may have been as early
as the 1920s that the first amateur wireless stations started operating. A United States government document reports two commercial stations were broadcasting in Cairo in 1930. These
and the amateur ventures were all closed down by the government in 1931. However, a year
later, in 1932, a newly established Ministry of Communications contracted with the BBC and
the Marconi Company to set up a government broadcast station. This radio station officially
began its operations in May 1934. Douglas A. Boyd, *Broadcasting in the Arab World: A Survey of
Radio and Television in the Middle East* (Philadelphia: Temple University Press, 1982), 14.

17. Ibid., 15.

18. Musallam, *Sayyid Qutb: The Emergence,* 75.

19. Khatab, *Political Thought,* 110; Sayyid Qutb, "Al-Muqaddasat al-Insaniyya wa al-Qawmiyya"
(Humanistic and National Holies), *al-Shu'un al-Ijtima'iyya* (Social Affairs) 11 (1942), 32–36.

20. Musallam, *From Secularism to Jihad,* 76,Sayyid Qutb, "Min Laghwi al-Sayf: Sarasir" (From
the Chitchat of Summer: Cockroaches) *al-Risala* 14, no. 683 (August 6, 1946): 858; Sayyid
Qutb, "Min Laghwi al-Sayf: Suq al-Raqiq" (From the Chitchat of Summer: The Slave Market),
al-Risala 14, no. 685 (August 19, 1946): 912. For more details on Sayyid Qutb's ideas about
women, see the Appendix, Part II, "Sayyid Qutb on Women and the Family."

21. Khatab, *Political Thought,* 113; Sayyid Qutb, "'Udu' ila al-Sharq" (Hostility toward the East),
al-'Alam al-'Arabi (The Arab World) 1, no. 2 (1947), 3–4.

22. Musallam, *From Secularism to Jihad,* 76.

23. Leonard Binder maintains that Qutb appealed to "the new generation of high school and
college students [who] were [being] offered a choice between Western cultural ideals and
a...reaffirmation of...tradition." Leonard Binder, *Islamic Liberalism: A Critique of Development
Ideologies* (Chicago: University of Chicago Press, 1988), 171.

24. Ibid. A biographic sketch of Muhammad Rashid Rida can be found in the Appendix, Part I,
"Dramatis Personae."

25. See the discussion of Qutb's first publications in the section on "Cairo" in Chapter 2.

26. The title of *al-Risala* came from the phrase *al-risala al-muhammadiyya al-khalida* (The Eternal
Message of Muhammad). It was founded in 1932 by Ahmad Hasan al-Zayyat and played a
"leading role in the intellectual formulation as well as the popular spread of the Islamic orientation." *Al-Thaqafa* was established in 1939 by Ahmad Amin. It was "more a product of the recent
strengthening of the popular Islamic trend than a major contributor to it." Its contents "paralleled those of *al-Risala.*" Gershoni and Jankowski, *Redefining the Egyptian Nation,* 63–64.

27. Musallam, *From Secularism to Jihad,* 53–54.

28. Ibid., 54.

29. Khatab, *Political Thought,* 99–102.

30. Haykal's first book on a religious topic was *Hayat Muhammad* (Life of the Prophet Muhammad)
published in 1935. For a list of these Islamic writings, see the section "Hesitations and Doubts"
in Chapter 2.

31. For al-'Aqqad's analytical approach, see his biographic sketch in the Appendix, Part I, "Dramatis Personae."
32. Khatab, *Political Thought*, 101.
33. This seems to reflect—surprisingly!—a begrudging capitulation to Taha Husayn.
34. Musallam, *From Secularism to Jihad*, 54; Khatab, *Political Thought*, 99–100.
35. Musallam, *From Secularism to Jihad*, 56.
36. Ibid., 2 and 42.
37. Ibid., 27 and 55.
38. William Shepard, "The Development of the Thought of Sayyid Qutb as Reflected in Earlier and Later Editions of 'Social Justice in Islam,'" *Die Welt Des Islams* 32, no. 2 (1992): 201. Abu-Rabi' adds that he prefers to replace Shepard's "moderate radical Islamism" with the phrase "Qutb's newly discovered Muslim social commitments to the plight of the poor in society," which might not be so new. Shepard had contrasted this current "moderate radicalism" to Qutb's later "extreme radicalism" expanded once he was sent to prison after 1954. Abu-Rabi', *Intellectual Origins*, 109.

   Such terms as "moderate," "radical," and "extremist" are often used without clear references. They are borrowed from modern, secular, and national politics, but their use in religious politics proves problematic. Here, the terms "liberal" or "moderate" are closely associated with secularism and modernity. Thus, the flexibility or tolerance in accepting modern, secular, Western ideas defines a liberal. The embrace of tradition, on the other hand, characterizes more a conservative outlook; the stronger the embrace, the deeper the conservatism. Fundamentalism, for its part, is more than conservative; it is the aggressive response of conservatives who feel attacked by outside enemies (see note 11 in this chapter). The terms "radical" and "extreme" can apply to either end of the liberal-conservative spectrum, indicating a more zealous commitment and a less tolerant accommodation.

   In Islam, this liberal-conservative spectrum is also traversed by the four schools of Islamic law: Hanafi tends to be the most liberal and Hanbali tends to be the least, with Maliki and Shafi'i lying in between. For more on these schools of Islamic law, see the discussion in the section *"Shari'a* Law" in Chapter 10.
39. Musallam, *From Secularism to Jihad*, 57; Musallam, *Sayyid Qutb: The Emergence*, 47–48; Abu-Rabi', *Intellectual Origins*, 146.
40. For a list of books written by Egypt's greatest writers who embraced this new, but moderate interest in Islamic subjects, see the section "Hesitations and Doubts" in Chapter 2. Taha Husayn's "turn to Islam," embodied in his earlier 1933 book *'Ala Hamish al-Sira* (On the Margin of the Prophet's Biography), however shallow or superficial, was "a deliberate effort to reach out to the broader reading public in emotional rather than intellectual terms." It may have been partly for this reason that Qutb began to explore aesthetic and affective themes in the Qur'an. Gershoni and Jankowski, *Redefining the Egyptian Nation*, 69–70.
41. Musallam, *From Secularism to Jihad*, 58 and 60.
42. Musallam, *From Secularism to Jihad*, 57–58, 69–70, and 202; Musallam, *Sayyid Qutb: The Emergence*, 58.
43. Musallam, *Sayyid Qutb: The Emergence*, 54.
44. This two-part article appeared in the February and March, 1939, issues of "Cairo's leading cultural and scientific monthly review," *al-Muqtataf* (Selections), and was entitled "al-Taswir al-Fanni fi al-Qur'an al-Karim" (Artistic Imagery in the Noble Qur'an) 94, nos. 2 and 3 (February 2 and March 3, 1939). This differed slightly from the title of his later full volume. According to Musallam, this two-part article marked the beginning of Qutb's serious engagement with Islamic issues. Musallam, *From Secularism to Jihad*, 56–57.
45. Musallam, *From Secularism to Jihad*, 58.
46. Sayyid Qutb, *al-Taswir al-Fanni fi al-Qur'an* (Artistic Imagery in the Qur'an) (Cairo: Dar al-Ma'arif, 1963), 23; Leonard Binder, *Islamic Liberalism: A Critique of Development Ideologies* (Chicago: University of Chicago Press, 1988), 191.
47. Musallam, *From Secularism to Jihad*, 58–60; Musallam, *Sayyid Qutb: The Emergence*, 50–52 and 58.

48. Biographical sketches of Jamal al-Din al-Afghani, Muhammad 'Abduh, and Rashid Rida can be found in the Appendix, Part I, "Dramatis Personae."
49. Musallam, *From Secularism to Jihad*, 58.
50. Qutb, *Artistic Imagery*, 29. I wish to thank Marilyn Booth for her patient and painstaking attention to helping me with this difficult translation. As an alternative rendition, Binder translates this passage in more Freudian terms. Binder, *Islamic Liberalism*, 193–194.
51. Musallam, *From Secularism to Jihad*, 61–63.
52. Ibid., 62.
53. Khatab, *Political Thought*, 84.
54. Binder, *Islamic Liberalism*, 195; Musallam, *From Secularism to Jihad*, 61.
55. Binder, *Islamic Liberalism*, 190. This controversy is discussed in note 58 in Chapter 2.
56. Lest we run up against Max Weber's criticism of "magic" as superstition that opposes rationality and modernity, it may be better were Binder to have spoken instead of the "wonder" of the Qur'an. Max Weber, *Protestant Ethic and the Spirit of Capitalism* (New York: Routledge, 2002), 61.
57. Binder, *Islamic Liberalism*, 195; Musallam, *From Secularism to Jihad*, 60.
58. Binder, *Islamic Liberalism*, 180–181 and ch. 5; Olivier Carré, *Mysticism and Politics: A Critical Reading of Fi Zilal al-Qur'an by Sayyid Qutb (1906–1966)* (Leiden: Brill, 2003), 45.
59. Norman Daniel, *Islam and the West: The Making of an Image* (Edinburgh: Edinburgh University Press, 1980), ch. 5.
60. See, for example, E. P. Thompson's superb analysis of the social control and discipline functions of Protestant Methodism. E. P. Thompson, *Making of the English Working Class* (New York: Vintage Books, 1966), ch. 3. Also see notes 59 and 62 in Chapter.
61. Khatab, *Political Thought*, 93.
62. We shall see later that religious struggle, or *jihad*, includes three kinds, the mildest (although some claim the greatest) being *jihad* of the heart, or personal reorientation. For more, see Chapter 7.
63. Musallam, *From Secularism to Jihad*, 65.
64. Khatab, *Political Thought*, 97; Sayyid Qutb, *Mashahid al-Qiyama fi al-Qur'an* (Scenes of Resurrection in the Qur'an) (Cairo: Dar al-Shuruq. 1947 [11th ed. in 1993]), 269–270.
65. Khatab, *Political Thought*, 95.
66. Carré, *Mysticism and Politics*, 29.
67. Musallam, *From Secularism to Jihad*, 70–71. Musallam makes this conclusion because here for the first time, Qutb cited the Qur'an 3:104 which is conventionally understood as a "motto of the Islamic movement":

> And that there might grow out of you a nation [of people] who invite unto all that is good, and enjoin the doing of what is right and forbid the doing of what is wrong: and it is they who shall be successful.

> Muhammad Asad, trans., *The Message of the Qur'an* (Bristol, UK: Book Foundation, 2003), 98, with some slight alterations by this author.

68. Faruq ascended the throne in July 1937, at the age of 18. At first, he was charming, strong willed, and well loved by his people, the first ruler of Egypt since 1811 to be really Egyptian. But on February 4, 1942, the British ambassador, Sir Miles Lampson, forced Faruq to appoint a pro-British war cabinet from among his opponents in the Wafd Party to assure London of continued national stability. This greatly discredited both the Wafd and King Faruq who then went on to repay "the love and trust of his people with treachery." He was further disgraced when, in 1948, he was held responsible for the weapons that malfunctioned in Egypt's battles in Palestine against Israel. But the final straw was his ugly divorce from the wildly popular Queen Farida announced at the height of the 1948 war. They had been married 10 years, but she had produced only (three) daughters. Afterward, Faruq degenerated further into gambling, licentiousness, pornography, gluttony, and obesity. He did marry a second time in 1951 to Queen Narriman, and their four-month honeymoon was one of the longest and most expensive in Europe. Narriman finally provided Faruq with a male heir, Ahmad Fu'ad, who, however,

never ascended the throne. It was on January 25, the very night when angry protesters burned down Cairo, and six months before the republican revolution, that Faruq threw a party for 600 guests to celebrate his son's birth. After he was exiled from Egypt on July 26, he lived in Rome where he died in a restaurant on March 18, 1965, from overconsumption, overweight, and a cerebral hemorrhage. Afaf Lutfi al-Sayyid Marsot, *Egypt's Liberal Experiment: 1922–1936* (Berkeley: University of California Press, 1977), 190; William Stadiem, *Too Rich: The High Life and Tragic Death of King Farouk* (New York: Carroll & Graf, 1991), 22–25, 47, and 378–382.

69. Musallam, *Sayyid Qutb: The Emergence*, 92; Khatab, *Political Thought*, 149.
70. Musallam, *From Secularism to Jihad*, 73–78.
71. Musallam, *From Secularism to Jihad*, 73–74; Musallam, *Sayyid Qutb: The Emergence*, 78; Khatab, *Political Thought*, 64; Sayyid Qutb, "Mantiq al-Dima' al-Bariya' fi Yawm al-Jala'" (The Logic of Innocent Homicide on Evacuation Day), *al-Risala* 14, no. 661 (March 4, 1946): 238.
72. Musallam, *From Secularism to Jihad*, 83–86.
73. Ibid., 84–86. A biographic sketch of Jamal al-Din al-Afghani can be found in the Appendix, Part I, "Dramatis Personae."
74. Ibid., 84; Qutb, "Min Laghwi al-Sayf: Suq al-Raqiq," 912.
75. John Calvert and William Shepard, "Translators' Introduction," Sayyid Qutb, *A Child from the Village* (Syracuse: Syracuse University Press, 2004), xxi–xxii.
76. This is the dedication in the edition translated by John Calvert and William Shepard:

> "To the author of *The Days*, Dr. Taha Husayn Bey.
> These, dear sir, are 'days' like your 'days,' lived by a village child, some are similar to your days and some are different.
> The difference reflects the difference between one generation and another, one village and another, one life and another, indeed the difference between one nature and another, between one attitude and another.
> But they are, when all is said and done, also 'days.'"

"Bey" is an honorific title applied frequently in Egypt to superiors. Taha Husayn lived from 1889 to 1973, so the two intellectuals were not necessarily from different generations in the strict sense. The difference may well lie in each intellectual's worldview.

Al-Ayyam was published in three parts. The first two parts were published together in 1929 under this title in Arabic, but in English, they were separately titled *An Egyptian Childhood* and *The Stream of Days: A Student at the Azhar*. The third volume appeared in 1967 called *Mudhakhirat Taha Husayn* (Memoirs of Taha Husayn) in Arabic, and *A Passage to France* in the English translation that appeared in 1973.

77. Abu-Rabi', *Intellectual Origins*, 99; Musallam, *From Secularism to Jihad*, 28–29. Husayn's powerful statement embracing Europe's modernity and disavowing Egypt's so-called backwardness appeared in his 1938 book, *Mustaqbal al-Thaqafa fi Misr* (The Future of Culture in Egypt) and is analyzed in Chapter 2.
78. James Toth, "Local Islam Gone Global: The Roots of Religious Militancy in Egypt and Its Transnational Transformation," in *Global Social Movements: A Reader*, June Nash, ed. (Oxford: Blackwell, 2004), 125.

Nowhere to my knowledge did Qutb use the strong Arabic word for "superstition"—*kharafa*—that is employed to condemn false belief. Instead he used such words as *ustura* (sing.), *asatir* (pl.) (legends or myths) and *hadith* (sing.), *hawadith* (pl.) (tales or stories). My gratitude to Asmaa Waguih for explaining the nuance of these words for me.

El-Sayed El-Aswad argues eloquently that rural Islam privileges the invisible domain over the visible realm. The unseen consists of "the nature of the soul or spirit, and unseen beings, as well as such concepts as the creation of the world (and man), fate, death, resurrection, afterlife, magic, envy, *baraka* (or blessing), among others." El-Sayed El-Aswad, "The Cosmological Belief System of Egyptian Peasants," *Anthropos* 89 (1994): 359–377: 361. The visible world includes practical and material day-to-day activities as well as legal, political, and economic practices. Thus, the change in religious understanding that is encountered in moving from the countryside to the city and becoming caught up in the tumult of Islamic activism and militancy actually *reverses* this prioritization, if not outright marginalize or even malign the invisible. El-Aswad, "The Cosmological Belief System of Egyptian Peasants," and his more complete ethnography, *Religion and Folk Cosmology: Scenarios of the Visible and Invisible in Rural Egypt* (Westport, CT: Praeger, 2002).

79. Qutb did not use neo-Platonic or mystical beliefs in his thinking and writing. He was, of course, well aware of village cosmologies, but these seemed to have been discarded once he moved to Cairo and were never used seriously in his texts. Later, Qutb did denounce those who criticized the Islamic state as "the rule of shaykhs and dervishes" in his 1951(c) book *Ma'rakat al-Islam wa al-Ra'smaliyya* (The Battle of Islam and Capitalism) but this was more about condemning urban intellectuals and officials and their limited horizons than about disapproving village religiosities. The point of *A Child* seemed to be fondly and nostalgically remembering village Islam, even some of its more supernatural aspects. Surely the adult Qutb did not go along with the village beliefs in the spiritually possessed mystic (*magzub* or *majd-hub*) of Shaykh Naqib, the local village saints or dervishes (*awliya*) of Shaykh Bakr or Shaykh 'Abd al-Fattah, the village demons (*afarit, jinn,* or *muzayyara*) or the village exorcism rites (*zar*). But his attitude was not condemnatory or self-righteous, but rather wistful and reminiscent. He considered these extraordinary moments a part of a unifying village culture that strongly contrasted with the modern, urbane, scientific, but also corrupt and immoral culture of the city. For a contrasting perspective, see Abu-Rabi', *Intellectual Origins*, 96; Khatab, *Political Thought*, 47–48.

80. There is almost an American Second Amendment quality to the chapter.

81. Musallam, *From Secularism to Jihad*, 86–87.

82. Later in his 1951 book, *Ma'rakat al-Islam wa al-Ra'smaliyya* (The Battle of Islam and Capitalism), Qutb argued that labor is the only justifiable means for generating profits. He claimed that "Islam prevents the excessive accumulation of wealth not based on personal effort and work." He then went on to argue that workers deserved 50 percent of business operations. Calvert, *Sayyid Qutb*, 163.

83. Musallam, *From Secularism to Jihad*, 87.

84. Calvert, *Sayyid Qutb*, 159; Musallam, *From Secularism to Jihad*, 89; Musallam, *Sayyid Qutb: The Emergence*, 84. Qutb once even called these Westernized elite "brown English," because they had abandoned their Egyptian identity and started imitating Western lifestyles. Calvert, *Sayyid Qutb*, 160; Sayyid Qutb, *Ma'rakat al-Islam wa al-Ra'smaliyya* (The Battle of Islam and Capitalism) (Cairo: Dar al-Shuruq, 1975 [originally published in Cairo in 1951]), 99. This is similar to the term used in the 1979 Iranian revolution by Jalal Al-e Ahmad and 'Ali Shari'ati, two religious intellectuals. They wrote about *gharbzadegi* or "Westoxication"—intoxication with the West. Roy Mottahedeh, *The Mantle of the Prophet: Religion and Politics in Iran* (New York: Pantheon Books, 1985), 296, 330. Qutb's words also echo the ideas of Frantz Fanon, the Martinique-Algerian doctor who wrote so passionately about colonialism and African inferiority and self-contempt in such major works as *Black Skin, White Masks* (1952) and *The Wretched of the Earth* (1961). Frantz Fanon, *Peau Noire, Masques Blancs* (Paris: Editions du Seuil, 1952). Published in English as *Black Skin, White Masks*, trans. Charles Lam Markmann (New York: Grove Press, 1967); Frantz Fanon, *Les Damnés de la Terre* (Paris: François Maspero, 1961). Published in English as *The Wrteched of the Earth*, trans. Constance Farrington (New York: Grove Press, 1965).

85. Musallam, *From Secularism to Jihad*, 87–88.

86. See, for example, Sayyid Qutb, "Ra'y fi al-Shi'r bi Munasabat Luzumiyat Mukhayma" (My Opinion of Poetry on the Occasions of [Ahmad] Mukhaymar's "Luzumyat" [Irregular Verse]), al-Kitab (The Book) 3:2 (February 1948), 248–249.

87. Musallam, *From Secularism to Jihad*, 88–89; Musallam, *Sayyid Qutb: The Emergence*, 82–85.

Chapter 4

1. Adnan A. Musallam, *From Secularism to Jihad: Sayyid Qutb and the Foundations of Radical Islam* (Westport, CT: Praeger, 2005), 55 and 56; Elliott Colla, *Conflicted Antiquities: Egyptology,*

Egyptomania, Egyptian Modernity (Durham, NC: Duke University Press, 2007), 234–236, and 260; J. Brugman, *An Introduction to the History of Modern Arabic Literature in Egypt* (Leiden: E. J. Brill, 1984), 304.

2. *New Thought* was founded by Qutb, his brother Muhammad, Muhammad al-Ghazali, Naguib Mahfouz, and four others. Sayyid Qutb became its editor-in-chief but could not be registered as its owner since government employees were forbidden by law to be publishers. Its official owner, Muhammad Hilmi al-Miniyawi, was not only the owner of Dar al-Kitab al-Arabi Press and could, therefore, provide technical assistance, but he was also a founding member of the Muslim Brotherhood. Despite this, and despite repeated requests by the Brotherhood for *New Thought* to become its journal, Qutb refused and remained independent of any Islamic association because he thought that no Islamic association could (yet) satisfy his vision of the right spiritual and dynamic leadership needed to revitalize Egyptian society. Qutb's refusal provoked the Brotherhood to boycott the new journal. Musallam, *From Secularism to Jihad*, 94–96; James Heyworth-Dunne, *Religious and Political Trends in Modern Egypt* (Washington, DC, 1950), 57.

3. Sayed Khatab, *The Political Thought of Sayyid Qutb: The Theory of* Jahiliyyah (London: Routledge, 2006), 55–57, and 138.

4. Ibid., 139; William E. Shepard, *Sayyid Qutb and Islamic Activism: A Translation and Critical Analysis of* Social Justice in Islam (Leiden: E. J. Brill, 1996), xvi.

5. Khatab, *Political Thought*, 113; John Calvert, *Sayyid Qutb and the Origins of Radical Islamism* (New York: Columbia University Press, 2010), 158–159.

6. Khatab, *Political Thought*, 113–114 and 13.

7. Musallam, *From Secularism to Jihad*, 95.

8. This was the official justification. However, while the war in Palestine had erupted in May of 1948, and martial law was imposed on May 13, *New Thought* had actually been closed down two months earlier, in March. Khatab, *Political Thought*, 139.

9. Calvert, *Sayyid Qutb*, 124; Sayyid Qutb, "'Adalu Baramijkum" (The Justice of Your Programs) in *al-Risala* 13, no. 627 (July 9, 1945), 723–724.

10. Musallam, *From Secularism to Jihad*, 96–97.

11. Ibid., 112; John Calvert and William Shepard, "Translators' Introduction," Sayyid Qutb, *A Child from the Village* (Syracuse: Syracuse University Press, 2004), xviii.

12. Taha Husayn, *al-Mu'adhdhabun fi al-Ard* (The Tormented on Earth) (Cairo: Dar al-Ma'arif, 1973), 5 and 9. Translated as *The Sufferers: Stories and Polemics*, Mona El-Zayyat, trans. (Cairo: American University in Cairo Press, 1993), 1 and 4; Musallam, *From Secularism to Jihad*, 19.

13. However, the book was immediately confiscated and removed from store bookshelves. Government censors pointed to Qutb's dedication and its contentious meaning as they accused Qutb of dedicating *Social Justice* to the Muslim Brotherhood, although at the time, Qutb remained an independent thinker. William Shepard reconstructed the original dedication in his analysis of all six editions of Social Justice (*Sayyid Qutb and Islamic Activism*, lxi–lxii).

> "To the youth whom I behold in my imagination coming to restore this religion as it was when it began... striving in the way of God, killing and being killed, believing profoundly that glory belongs to God, to His Apostle, and to the believers...
>
> "To those youth in whom, I doubt not for an instant, the strong spirit of Islam will resurrect the spirit of past generations to serve coming generations in a day almost at hand...
>
> "I dedicate this book."

It was replaced by a milder dedication that removed the references to killing:

> "To the youth whom I behold in my imagination approaching... striving for God with their possessions and their lives, believing profoundly that glory belongs to God and to His Apostle and to the believers.
>
> "To those youth who look to the distant future in the eternal spirit of Islam and who see nothing in the present but dwarfs and bubbles...

"To those youth in whom, I doubt not for an instant, the strong spirit of Islam will resurrect the spirit of past generations to serve coming generations in a day almost at hand...

"I dedicate this book."

The "dwarfs" referred to the contemporary leadership in Egypt and the "bubbles" meant short-lived secular political ideologies (ibid., lxii). The dedication was revised yet again in the third and fourth editions to represent a version more oriented toward Qutb's newfound loyalty to the Muslim Brothers.

Once Qutb had modified and tempered the first dedication, the book went back on sale.

14. Musallam, *From Secularism to Jihad*, 100.
15. Sayyid Qutb, *al-'Adala al-Ijtima'iyya fi al-Islam* (Social Justice in Islam) (Cairo: Maktabat Misr, 1949 [reprinted, Oneonta, NY: Islamic Publications International, 2000]), 113.
16. Ibid., 92.
17. Shepard renders the actual Arabic phrase, *taharrur wijdani* as "liberation of the inward soul," although the word "inward" seems a little redundant. I prefer a less literal translation. Shepard, *Sayyid Qutb and Islamic Activism*, 40.
18. For more on *zakat* and *sadaqa*, see Chapter 9.
19. Qutb, *Social Justice*, 64.
20. Ibid.
21. Shepard, *Sayyid Qutb and Islamic Activism*, 59.
22. Ibid., 37–38.
23. Ibid., 42.
24. This is what I am calling a social democracy or welfare capitalism. For the use of this term, see note 20 in Chapter 1.
25. Shepard. *Sayyid Qutb and Islamic Activism*, 57.
26. The Arabic phrase is *al-takaful al-ijtima'i*. Many writers translate *takaful* as "solidarity." Technically, this is correct. However, I prefer to translate *takaful* as "responsibility" or even "mutual responsibility" in the sense of mutual obligation toward one another. "Responsibility" is often translated as *mas'uliyya*, but this contains the idea of "blame" which I wish to avoid.
27. Qutb, *Social Justice*, 80.
28. The action of *hisba*, or the communal declaration of good and bad, has been abused by the zealous and self-righteous in condemning even the smallest deviation from orthodoxy. For more details, see the discussion in the Epilogue.
29. Details of Qutb's historical narrative and analysis are presented in Chapter 11.
30. Qutb, *Social Justice*, 261.
31. Ibid., 274 and 277.
32. Ahmad ibn Taymiyya (1263–1328) was a famous conservative Hanbali scholar from Syria during the years of the Mongol invasion. (Hanbali law is the most conservative of the four schools or codifications of Islamic law.) Many of Ibn Taymiyya's ideas are similar to those found in kharijite doctrines (discussed in the next note). He was exceptionally strict about divine worship, condemning those who venerated what he called false gods, and repudiating intermediaries, saints, and their mausoleums. He rejected Greek-influenced *kalam*, Islamic philosophy, and mystical Sufism, concluding that these fabrications and distortions were brought about by foreign influences. He criticized Shi'ism, Christianity, and Judaism for their false beliefs and practices. He denounced the Mongols for the duplicity of their religion when they claimed to be Muslims but did not administer Islamic law. He became famous, therefore, for insisting that the only true Islamic rulers were those who governed exclusively by *shari'a*. He criticized the *'ulama* for their blind imitation of tradition, rejected the separation of Islamic law into different schools, and repeatedly counseled recourse to the Qur'an, Sunna, and the *salaf* alone. He advocated *jihad* against those who were in error. He was repeatedly persecuted and imprisoned in Damascus for his extreme ideas.
33. Kharijites were those Muslims who condemned both the third caliph, 'Uthman, who was murdered, and 'Ali, the fourth caliph who succeeded him. When Mu'awiyya, the governor of Syria, sought to avenge his cousin 'Uthman's murder, he demanded that 'Ali, the nephew

and son-in-law of the Prophet, bring 'Uthman's assassins—'Ali's own supporters—to justice. These two fought each other at the Battle of Siffin in Syria in 657. When Mu'awiya's forces entered the battlefield with Qur'ans on their swords, 'Ali desisted and sought arbitration. The Kharijites, who had already condemned the fiscal impropriety and nepotism of 'Uthman, and, by extension, Mu'awiyya, then also withdrew their support for 'Ali because of his recourse to arbitration and compromise. Kharijites soon became symbols of intolerance to diversity and rebellion against the established government. Their principles include

1. Rejecting the arbitration at Siffin, and refusing any negotiation or compromise in religion.
2. Denouncing both 'Uthman and 'Ali as illegitimate rulers.
3. Judging or ruling society only by what God has revealed, the *shari'a*.
4. Upholding or applying the Qur'an as the only source of law.
5. Tasking the ruler solely as the administrator of Islamic law.
6. Electing a caliph's successor on the basis of piety alone, without regard to pedigree.
7. Considering the caliph as first among equals, neither divine nor sacred but, rather, expendable.
8. Calling the caliph to account if he deviates from the Straight Path.
9. Rebelling against unjust, corrupt, or unIslamic tyrants as a religious duty if they do not recant.
10. Declaring *jihad* as the sixth pillar, or obligation, of Islam.
11. Restricting orthodoxy and orthopraxy to very narrow limits, and defining sin as transgression outside these limits.
12. Repudiating Muslims who have committed grave sins as unbelievers (*kafr, kufar*) who endanger the entire community.
13. Acknowledging just two communities: true believers, consisting only of Kharijites, and all others, including other Muslims, as unbelievers.
14. Denouncing any Muslim and his family who are not Kharijites as unbelievers, *takfir*, and condemning them to death.
15. Separating or migrating (*hijra*) from society if it is sinful or ruled by a tyrant.

Jeffrey T. Kenney, *Muslim Rebels: Kharijites and the Politics of Extremism in Egypt* (New York: Oxford University Press, 2006), ch. 2.
34. Musallam, *From Secularism to Jihad*, 99.
35. Ibid., 43; Khatab, *Political Thought*, 1, 49, and 139.
36. John Calvert. "Sayyid Qutb in America," *Newsletter of the International Institute for the Study of Islam*, 7 (March 2001), 8, (also at www.isim.nl/) and "'The World Is an Undutiful Boy!': Sayyid Qutb's American Experience," *Islam and Christian—Muslim Relations* 11, no. 1 (March 2000): 95; Paul Berman, "The Philosopher of Islamic Terror," *New York Times Magazine*, March 23, 2003; Paul Berman, *Terrorism and Liberalism* (New York: W.W. Norton, 2003), 61; Zafar Bangash, "Remembering Sayyid Qutb: An Islamic Intellectual and Leader of Rare Insight and Integrity," in *Milestones*, A. B. Al-Mehri, ed., (Birmingham, UK: Maktabah Booksellers and Publishers, 2006), 183. Calvert, Berman, and Bangash are also cited in Musallam, *From Secularism to Jihad*, 112 and 222; Hamid Algar, "Introduction," *Social Justice in Islam*, John B. Hardie, trans. (Oneonta, NY: Islamic Publications International, 2000), 2; M. M. Siddiqui, "An Outline of Sayyed [*sic*] Qutb's Life," in Sayyid Qutb, *Islam and Universal Peace* (Plainfield, NJ: American Trust Publication, 1993), ix.
37. Musallam, *From Secularism to Jihad*, 113; Siddiqui, "An Outline," ix.
38. Gilles Kepel, *Muslim Extremism in Egypt: The Prophet and the Pharaoh* (Berkeley: University of California Press, 1993 [originally *Le Prophète et Pharaon*, Jon Rothschild, trans. (Paris: Editions La Déouverte, 1984)]), 40. This episode is also reported by Khatab, *Political Thought*, 140; Musallam, *From Secularism to Jihad*, 113; Salah 'Abd al-Fattah al-Khalidi, *Sayid Qutb min al-Milad ila al-Istishhad* (Sayid Qutb from His Birth to His Martyrdom) (Damascus: Dar al-Qalam, 1994), 195; Salah 'Abd al-Fattah al-Khalidi, *Amrika min al-Dakhil bi Minzar Sayyid Qutb* (America from Within: The View of Sayyid Qutb) (Jidda: Dar al-Manara, 1985), 20–27.

39. The story goes that an American woman in Greeley told Qutb in a discussion about American social life that "the issue of sexual relations is a purely biological issue. You—the Orientals—complicate this simple issue by introducing the ethical element in it" and went on to compare human sexuality with animal sexuality: "The horse and the mare, the bull and the cow, the ram and the goat, and the rooster and the hen do not think of this story of ethics while they are mating. So their life is easy, simple and comfortable." Earlier, one of the female teachers at the International Center for Teaching Languages at Wilson Teachers' College in Washington, DC, responded favorably when one of her foreign students told her his own observations. He said to her, "I have noticed that young girls who are 14 years old and boys who are 15 years old engage in complete sexual relations . . . and this is a very early age to engage in these relations." The teacher replied to him, "our life on earth is very short. We do not have time to waste more than 14 years." Shortly thereafter, Qutb found himself in a Washington hotel and the African American elevator operator told him about coming upon couples having sex and who did not even stop when he entered their room. Instead, they asked him to bring them a bottle of Coca-Cola while they continued. "Don't they feel ashamed?" Qutb inquired. "Why?" the operator retorted. "They satisfy their private inclinations and enjoy themselves." Apparently the operator felt comfortable telling Qutb these intimate stories since, in Qutb's view, they were both of the same "despised" color. From these and similar episodes, Qutb concluded that America was absolutely licentious and shameless, and that it practiced widespread abnormal sexuality. He wrote back to a friend in Egypt: "American society does not disapprove of any person's satisfying his pleasure in the way that appeals to him as long as there is not coercion." Musallam cites Sayyid Qutb, *al-Islam wa Mushkilat al-Hadara* (Islam and the Problems of Civilization) (Cairo: Dar Ihya' al-Kutub al-'Arabiya 1962).

40. Qutb later described this occasion as follows:

> The dance floor was illuminated with red, blue, yellow and a few white lights. It intensified (convulsed) to the tunes of the gramophone and was full of bounding feet and seductive legs. Arms circled waists, lips met lips, chests met chests, and the atmosphere was full of passion.

Sayyid Qutb, "Amrika allati Ra'ayt fi Mizan al-Qiyam al-Insaniyya" (The America Which I Saw in the Balance [or Scale] of Human Existence), *al-Risala* 19, no. 959 (November 19, 1951), 1304; Calvert, *Sayyid Qutb*, 150.

I first learned about Qutb's discomfort from the BBC documentary film *The Power of Nightmares: The Rise of the Politics of Fear* and how, in the film, it was understood to reflect Qutb's Puritanism, a serious accusation in America against those disapproving of physical pleasure in today's sexualized, post-Freudian culture. The first of the film's three segments is about Qutb and is called "Baby It's Cold Outside," the title of the popular 1944 Frank Loesser song that was played at the church dance in Greeley.

The documentary was written and produced by Adam Curtis and has been called one of the greatest conspiracy theory films ever created. It documents the parallel rise of the militant Islamist movement (hence, Qutb's appearance) and the American Neo-Conservative movement (the University of Chicago professor and neo-con avatar, Leo Strauss). It consists mostly of BBC archive film with Curtis's commentary. The portion that depicts Qutb in Greeley, Colorado, presents the viewer with clips that display frolicsome cheerleaders and harmless church dances that may well have taken place when Qutb visited. But we can't help but laugh in a patronizing fashion at why anyone but the most uptight and ill-tempered would condemn such innocence, thereby confirming the connections between criticizing "good ol' American fun" and "Islamic Puritanism." But this leaves much room for misunderstanding and derision. Qutb was not the first nor the last to disapprove of America's so-called promiscuity, but it is easy to dismiss such comments by calling them "Puritanical." Calvert writes ("The World Is an Undutiful Boy!" 97) that Qutb had arrived in America prejudging the situation and had already condemned such public displays as "open[ing] the door to social disruption and moral degeneracy," citing an article Qutb published earlier in 1940.

A more serious problem is how this judgmental label of stern Puritanism and sexual frustration fits into the larger and more biased theories explaining terrorism. Scholars such as Raphael Patai (1973) and Mark Juergensmeyer (2000) have both explained the explosion of Islamic terrorism as the result of the supposedly immense frustration in young males generated by living in a homosocial (as opposed to Western heterosocial) society, evoking Freudian theories that connect sexuality and aggression, along with their own ethnocentric perspective of what it is like to live in the gender-segregated societies of the Middle East. However, we should be careful to avoid making any serious connections between Qutb's critique of American sexuality, his lifelong bachelorhood, and his anger against anti-Islamic societies. The roots of terrorism are social and political, not sexual.

Perhaps Patai's *The Arab Mind* is simply a marginal piece that is not necessary to mention, for after all, it was originally published in the "dark days" of social science, a remnant of anthropology's earlier fixation on "culture and personality" studies. Easily dismissed, perhaps, except that it was republished in 2002 by Hatherleigh Press and issued to all US military officers assigned to serve in Iraq. It became their handbook on how to handle "those people." I can only wonder how big a role it played in the torture and prisoner abuse at Abu Ghraib prison in 2004. Raphael Patai, *The Arab Mind* (New York: Scribner, 1973; New York: Hatherleigh Press, 2002), 137; Mark Juergensmeyer, *Terror in the Mind of God* (Berkeley: University of California Press, 2000), 195–207, Kate Zernike, "Detainees Describe Abuses by Guard in Iraq Prison" (*New York Times*, January 12, 2005).

41. Khatab, *Political Thought*, 140.
42. Khatab, *Political Thought*, 145; Musallam *Sayyid Qutb: The Emergence*, 105; Salah 'Abd al-Fattah al-Khalidi, *Sayyid Qutb: al-Shahid al-Hayy* (Sayyid Qutb: The Living Martyr) (Amman: Maktabat al-Aqsa, 1981), 135–136; Yusuf al-'Azm, *Ra'id al-Fikr al-Islam al-Mu'asir: al-Shahid Sayyid Qutb* (Pioneer of Modern Islamic Though: The Martyr Sayyid Qutb) (Damascus and Beirut: Dar al-Qalam, 1980), 207 and 210; Ism'il al-Shatti, "Ma' al-Shahid Sayyid Qutb" (With the Martyr, Sayyid Qutb), *al-Mujtama'a* (Society) 215 (August 27, 1974): 17.

    Qutb himself wrote in his own arrest statement:

    > My attention was very much drawn to the extreme interest in the Brothers shown by American newspapers as well as the British newspapers which used to reach America, and their gloating and obvious placidity over dissolving the Muslim Brothers group, hitting it and killing their leader.

    Musallam, *From Secularism to Jihad*, 121–122; Sayyid Qutb, *Limadha A'dammuni* (Why Did They Execute Me?) (Jidda: al-Sharika al-Sa'udiyya li al-Abhath wa al-Taswiq [Saudi Partners for Research and Marketing], 1965), 10–11.

    John Calvert (*Sayyid Qutb and the Origins of Radical Islamism*, 144–145) doubts that Americans even knew who Hasan al-Banna was and cared even less about his assassination. Calvert concludes that Qutb made this assumption about American ignorance based on conversations with the British Arabist John Heyworth-Dunne when both talked in Washington, DC, in the winter of 1948–49.

43. These events also played a large role in compelling Qutb to write *al-Salam al-'Alami wa al-Islam* (Islam and Universal Peace), which is used to discuss Qutb's view of *jihad* in the section "The Path from *Jahiliyya* to *Hakimiyya*: The Specific Tactics of *Jihad*" in Chapter 7.
44. Khatab, *Political Thought*, 145; Hamid Algar, "Introduction," *Social Justice in Islam by Sayyid Qutb* (Oneonta, NY: Islamic Publications International, 2000), 2.
45. Qutb wrote home to a friend that "the church in America is a place for everything except worship." Musallam, *From Secularism to Jihad*, 116.
46. Khatab, *Political Thought*, 141. Qutb claimed that when he was in Denver that "he did not see a human face with a look that radiated the meaning of humanity." Instead, Qutb wrote, "he found harried crowds resembling an excited herd that knew only lust and money." Musallam, *From Secularism to Jihad*, 114.
47. John Calvert, "'The World Is an Undutiful Boy!' Sayyid Qutb's American Experience," *Islam and Christian-Muslim Relations* 11, no. 1 (March 2000): 88.

48. There must have been advanced plans and contacts with those in America before Qutb traveled for him to set up his itinerary, but I have not come across any record of this. When Qutb arrived in New York, he stayed at a hotel with a friend, probably one of the ship passengers and affiliated himself with a number of social clubs found in the other cities he visited and where he resided while on tour. Calvert, *Sayyid Qutb*, 142; Khatab, *Political Thought*, 114.

49. Calvert, "'The World Is an Undutiful Boy,'" 88. Wilson Teachers College was a segregated African American school for women that merged in 1976 with other District colleges to form the University of the District of Columbia.

50. These stories are recounted in note 39 in this chapter.

51. This included the summer school session and the fall quarter. Calvert, "The World Is an Undutiful Boy," 95.

52. Calvert, "'The World Is an Undutiful Boy,'" 96. Qutb strongly criticized Greeley residents for what he called their obsession with lawn care, an indicator, he claimed, of America's materialism, individualism, and detachment. Yet Qutb was not the only observer to disapprove of the myopia of suburbia or small-town America. The premier urban historian Lewis Mumford was similarly critical of suburban sprawl.

> Thus the ultimate effect of the suburban escape [from the city] in our time is, ironically, a low-grade uniform environment from which escape is impossible. What has happened to the suburban exodus in the United States now threatens, through the same mechanical instrumentalities, to take place, at an equally accelerating rate, everywhere else—unless the most vigorous countermeasures are taken" [486].
>
> [The suburb] was a segregated community, set apart from the city, not merely by space but by class stratification: a sort of green ghetto dedicated to the elite. That smug Victorian phrase, 'We keep ourselves to ourselves,' expresses the spirit of the suburban, in contrast to the city; for the city, by its nature, is a multi-form non-segregated environment" [493].
>
> As an attempt to recover what was missing in the city, the suburban exodus could be amply justified, for it was concerned with primary human needs. But there was another side: the temptation to retreat from unpleasant realities, to shirk public duties, and to find the whole meaning of life in the most element social group, the family, or even in the still more isolated and self-centered individual. What was properly a beginning was treated as an end [494].

   Although they were more scholarly, these words could well have been written by Sayyid Qutb. Lewis Mumford, *The City in History: Its Origins, Its Transformations, and Its Prospects* (New York: Harcourt, Brace and World, 1961).

53. Musallam *From Secularism to Jihad*, 116–117; Calvert, *Sayyid Qutb*, 147.

54. Khatab, *Political Thought*, 141.

55. Khatab, *Political Thought*, 141–143; Musallam, *From Secularism to Jihad*, 118; Sayyid Qutb, "Amrika allati Ra'ayt fi Mizan al-Qiyam al-Insaniyya" (The America Which I Saw in the Balance (or Scale) of Human Existence), *al-Risala* 19, no. 959 (November 19, 1951), 1301.

56. Qutb's reporting style has been called "cartoonish," and consisting of "exaggerations and historical reductionisms." Calvert, "The World Is an Undutiful Boy," 101. We should not forget that Qutb's style of simplification was no different from what ethnocentric American tourists do in the Middle East, what most social commentators do in America when writing editorials, or what Orientalists do in depicting the Muslim world. Few people—should I dare say "with the exception of social scientists and scholars"?—care to acknowledge "the nuances of culture and the continuities which bind humanity together," which Calvert claims Qutb ignored. The asymmetries of power make Qutb's prejudices insignificant in comparison to the biases of those in hegemonic positions.

57. Musallam, *Sayyid Qutb: The Emergence*, 103; Khatab, *Political Thought*, 142–143.

58. Sayyid Qutb, *Ma'alim fi al-Tariq* (Signposts on the Road; also translated as Milestones) (Al-Salimiya, Kuwait: Al-Ittihad al-Islami al-'Alami li al-Munazzamat al-Tullabiya [International

59. Qutb explained American culture and practice by its history and environment: the challenge of taming the wilderness and fighting the natural elements, which encouraged American materialism and pragmatism—an explanation not unlike the eugenic theories adopted by his former mentor, 'Abbas al-'Aqqad, from William Hazlitt (see al-'Aqqad's biographic sketch in the Appendix, Part I, "Dramatis Personae"). However, Qutb was much less scientific when it came to understanding his compatriots whose fall into *jahiliyya* did not deserve a sociological explanation, just contempt and condemnation. Calvert, "The World Is an Undutiful Boy," 99.
60. Khatab, *Political Thought*, 143 and 145.
61. Ibid., 140; Abu-Rabi', *Intellectual Origins*, 133–134.
62. Siddiqui, "An Outline," ix.
63. Musallam, *From Secularism to Jihad*, 119; Musallam, *Sayyid Qutb: The Emergence*, 105.
64. Qutb's arrival had been announced earlier by his colleague, 'Abbas Khidr, in *al-Risala*. The Muslim Brothers in particular were drawn to Qutb because of "his experience in the United States, his observation of Western attitudes toward the Brotherhood and Islam, together with the Brotherhood's appreciation of his writings." Khatab, *Political Thought*, 147; 'Abd al-Baqi Muhammad Husayn, *Sayyid Qutb: Hayatuh wa Adabuh* (Sayyid Qutb: His Life and His Literature) (Al-Mansura, Daqahiliyya, Egypt: Dar al-Wafa', 1986), 43.
65. Musallam, *Sayyid Qutb: The Emergence*,105–106; Khatab, *Political Thought*, 49.
66. Biographic sketches of Abu al-A'la Mawdudi and Abu al-Hasan 'Ali Nadwi can be found in the Appendix, Part I, "Dramatis Personae."
67. Musallam, *From Secularism to Jihad*, 151–152; Khatab, *Political Thought*, 59.
68. The book was originally written in Arabic and then translated by Muhammad Asif Kidwai into English and re-titled, *Islam and the World: The Rise and Decline of Muslims and Its Effect on Mankind*. It was published in 1961 by the Academy of Islamic Research and Publications in Lahore.
69. Khatab, *Political Thought*, 149–150.
70. Ibid., 148–150.
71. Most notably, *Manhaj al-Inqilab al-Islami* (A Program of Islamic Revolution), *al-Mustalahat al-Arba'a fi al-Qur'an* (The Four Terms in the Qur'an), *al-Jihad fi al-Islam* (Jihad in Islam), *al-Islam wa al-Jahiliyya* (Islam and *Jahiliyya*), and *Tadwin al-Dustur al-Islami* (Registration of the Islamic Constitution, also translated as The First Principles of the Islamic State). Abu-Rabi', *Intellectual Origins*, 139; Musallam, *From Secularism to Jihad*, 152; Emmanuel Sivan, *Radical Islam: Medieval Theology and Modern Politics* (New Haven: Yale University Press, 1985), 23.
72. Abu-Rabi', *Intellectual Origins*, 195; Musallam, *From Secularism to Jihad*, 151–152; Shepard, *Sayyid Qutb and Islamic Activism*, xxv. While it is true that both Mawdudi and Qutb used the same key Islamic concepts of *jahiliyya*, *hakimiyya*, and *jihad* (see Chapter 7 for a fuller explanation of these terms) and that both saw Europe as a threat and a danger and blamed Britain as the culprit—offering much the same perspective that Jamal al-Din al-Afghani had proposed a century earlier—it is absurd to claim, as Leonard Binder does, that Qutb served merely as a transmitter of Mawdudi's ideas and that without the South Asian, Qutb's message would have amounted to little of importance. Qutb was hardly Mawdudi's microphone, and he wrote much against the corruption, immorality, and sacrilege of his own country. Even so, originality might not have been held at a premium; after all, these expressions were only a means to the end of moving their own societies toward proper Islamic belief and practice, and not an exclusive literary end in of themselves. Besides, although Qutb's use of similar Islamic and anti-colonial tropes may be derived to some extent, this simply points to a convergence in the economic, political, and cultural conditions of their own two countries. See Leonard Binder, *Islamic Liberalism: A Critique of Development Ideologies* (Chicago: University of Chicago Press, 1988), 174–175.
73. For more details about Ibn Taymiyya and his kharijism, see notes 32 and 33 in this chapter.
74. Qur'an 58:22. It was Ibn Taymiyya's ideas about *jihad* that were used as evidence in Qutb's 1954 and 1965 trials for sedition. But since the concept of *jihad* is so common among Muslims (though not applied in the same manner or for the same reasons), it is more probable that it was the narrow-minded, Manichean rigidity that so characterizes Ibn Taymiyya's kharijite

thinking that angered the Egyptian authorities. The strict inflexibility of delineating those few who are considered good and proper Muslims from those *kuffar*, or unbelievers, who fall outside this small circle (who are then liable for *jihad*), constitutes the hallmark of kharijism's harsh intolerance. This severity becomes incorporated and symbolized in the polarized political structuring of Party of God and Party of Satan, although these have become loosely adopted throughout the Muslim world without necessarily indicating a steadfast kharijite approach. Olivier Carré, *Mysticism and Politics: A Critical Reading of* Fi Zilal al-Qur'an *by Sayyid Qutb (1906–1966)* (Leiden: Brill, 2003), 230.

The Egyptian Islamic scholar Hasan Hanafi admirably captures the consequences of kharijite thinking:

> The actual world was a world of disbelief, a *jahiliyya* world which had to be destroyed completely and totally in order to build a new world of belief where everyone could live and practice his own faith. This division of the world into white and black, good and evil, right and wrong, belief and disbelief, pure and impure made the [Muslim] Brethren [and other Islamists] mind highly Manichean.

Hasan Hanafi, "The Relevance of the Islamic Alternative in Egypt," *Arab Studies Quarterly* 41, nos. 1 and 2 (1982): 60–61.

75. In 9th century Baghdad, a debate erupted over the position of grave sinners in Islam and whether sinners remain Muslims. The Kharijites argued that all sinners are unbelievers (*kuffar*) and must be excommunicated (*takfir*) and expelled from the community. This, however, seemed very rigid and intolerant, so dependent on the Kharijites' particularly broad definition of sin. Other Islamic factions, including the Sunnis, Shi'ites, Murji'ites, and Mu'tazilites, rejected this narrow-mindedness. The Murji'ites claimed that all sinners are believers, that they remain community members, and that it is up to God on Judgment Day, not earthly authority, to decide their status. Yet this, too, was rejected, but for the opposite reason: it appeared too lenient by absolving sinners any responsibility for their actions. The Mu'tazilites struck a compromise by contending that a sinner was neither a believer nor an unbeliever but occupied an intermediate position. They proposed a three-category arrangement—good Muslims, bad Muslims, and unbelievers, to be determined on Judgment Day. Although the Mu'tazilite perspective seemed much less rigid, its idea of accountability was questioned. So although the Mu'tazilites lost the specific debate, their more open-minded perspective won the day. In the end, what triumphed was the Sunni position of Abu al-Hasan al-Ash'ari who struck a point midway between the Kharijites and the Mu'tazilites. He kept the more liberal three-category structure and proposed that sinners ("bad Muslims") were not to be considered unbelievers nor expelled, but they were to be held accountable for their transgressions in both this world and the next, which allowed sinners an opportunity for remorse and repentance. Richard C. Martin and Mark R. Woodward, *Defenders of Reason in Islam* (Oxford: Oneworld, 1997), 103–107; Jeffrey T. Kenney, *Muslim Rebels: Kharijites and the Politics of Extremism in Egypt* (New York: Oxford University Press, 2006), 35–36; John L. Esposito, *Islam: The Straight Path*, 3rd ed. (New York: Oxford University Press, 1998), 70–73.

76. Carré. *Mysticism and Politics*, 94–95. Qutb used a phrase which Carré translates as "pseudo-Muslims" and that Rida had classified as "geographic Muslims" but had not yet apostatized them.

77. Sayyid Qutb, *Muqawwimat al-Tasawwur al-Islami* (Basic Principles of the Islamic Worldview), Rami David, trans. (North Halcedon, NJ: Islamic Publications International, 2006), 85.

Chapter 5

1. Ibrahim M. Abu-Rabi', *Intellectual Origins of Islamic Resurgence in the Modern Arab World* (Albany: State University of New York Press, 1996), 125.

2. Sayyid Qutb, *Ma'alim fi al-Tariq* (Signposts on the Road but also translated as Milestones) (Al-Salimiya, Kuwait: Al-Ittihad al-Islami al-'Alami li al-Munazzamat al-Tullabiya [International Islamic Federation of Student Organizations], 1978a), 7–8.

3. Adnan A. Musallam, *From Secularism to Jihad: Sayyid Qutb and the Foundations of Radical Islam* (Westport, CT: Praeger, 2005), ch. 4.

4. Sayed Khatab, *The Political Thought of Sayyid Qutb: The Theory of* Jahiliyyah (London: Routledge. 2006), 109–110; Sayyid Qutb, "al-Qahira al-Khadda'a" (Cairo the Deceiver), *al-Shu'un al-Ijtima'iyya* (Social Affairs) 5 (May 1941): 30. His admonition appears all too similar to his views about his sojourn to the United States described earlier.

5. Abu-Rabi', *Intellectual Origins*, 180.

6. Khatab, *Political Thought*, 108.

7. Khatab, *Political Thought*, 112; Sayyid Qutb, "Qiyadatuna al-Ruhiyya" (Our Spiritual Leadership), *al-Risala* 15, no. 705 (January 6, 1947), 29.

8. In his introduction to Abul Hasan 'Ali Nadwi's book, *What the World Lost as a Result of the Decline of Muslims*, Qutb wrote in length about the issue of leadership:

> Islam is a doctrine for leadership and world welfare.... The age before Islam was steeped in *jahiliyya* in which the mind and spirit of man had become benighted and high standards and values of life debased. It was the age of tyranny and slavery in which the very roots of humanity were being corroded by a criminally luxurious and wasteful life on the one hand, and hopelessness and frustration and despair on the other....
>
> Islam played a significant role in the reconstruction of humanity. When it had the opportunity, Islam liberated the soul of man from superstitions and banalities, emancipated him front the evils of slavery and degradation, and lifted him out of the slough of filth and disease.... All this was achieved when Islam had a controlling hand in the affairs of the world and had an opportunity of fashioning life according to its own special genius.
>
> Since Islam is pre-eminently a faith that inspires leadership, its real mettle is tested and proven only when it assumes responsibility. It can lead the caravan of life. It cannot be a camp follower....
>
> Then came a period in which Islam lost its leadership due mainly to the failure of Muslims to efficiently sustain and discharge the great responsibility of the trusteeship of mankind which Islam enjoined upon them...
>
> In describing what happened to the world when it was deprived of this noble leadership and when it reverted to its previous state of *jahiliyya*, Nadwi points out, in no uncertain terms, the horrible depravity towards which the world is heading today... the depravity that has come because Muslims have failed in their leadership....
>
> This precise expression [of *jahiliyya*] clearly shows the author's understanding of the essential difference between the spirit of Islam, and the spirit of materialism which prevailed before the advent of Islam and which has been prevailing in the world ever since Islam lost its world leadership.... The world is enduring this *jahiliyya* today as it did in the days of the first barbarism.
>
> The supreme importance of the message of Islam today is obvious and easier to appreciate in the present age, in which the *jahiliyya* stands exposed and its hidden evils unmasked. The whole world has become tired of it. It is therefore precisely the time when the world could turn from the leadership of the *jahiliyya* to the leadership of Islam.

Khatab, *Political Thought*, 149–150; Sayyid Qutb, "Introduction," in Sayyed Abul Hasan 'Ali al-Nadwi, *Islam and the World: The Rise and Decline of Muslims and Its Effect on Mankind*, Muhammad Asif Kidwai, trans. (Leicester: UK Islamic Academy, 2005), v–ix.

9. Musallam, *From Secularism to Jihad*, 71–72.

10. Ibid., 134. Qutb's rhetoric resembled Communist principles, appealing to those attracted to this secular, revolutionary doctrine. Calvert observes that in Qutb's 1951 book *The Battle of Islam and Capitalism*, he "rode the wave of the post-war leftist critique" and that he "drew upon economic analysis and populist rhetoric in order to monopolize the ideological space of the left." John Calvert, *Sayyid Qutb and the Origins of Radical Islamism* (New York: Columbia University Press, 2010), 159.

But while Qutb admired communism's heightened sense of justice, freedom, and equality, he also criticized it sharply for dealing with these just as economic and material values. Islam, he claimed, contained similar principles of fairness, yet it also focused on spiritual values of faith and belief as well. Sayyid Qutb, *al-'Adala al-Ijtima'iyya fi al-Islam* (Social Justice in Islam) (Cairo: Maktabat Misr, 1949 [reprint, Oneonta, NY: Islamic Publications International, 2000]), 167.

11. Sayyid Qutb, *Ma'rakat al-Islam wa al-Ra'smaliyya* (The Battle of Islam and Capitalism) (Cairo: Dar al-Shuruq, 1975[originally published in Cairo in 1951c]), 6; Calvert, *Sayyid Qutb*, 159.

12. Khatab, *Political Thought*, 57; Musallam, *From Secularism to Jihad*, 93–94.

13. It is not clear exactly when Qutb joined the Brotherhood. He may have joined as early as 1951, perhaps as soon as the ban against the Muslim Brotherhood was lifted in December of that year, but was exempted from the standard initiation period, and so was appointed immediately to head the Missionary or Propaganda Section in addition to becoming a member of the Guidance Bureau under the Supreme Guide, the head of the organization. His official membership allowed him greater influence on organizational policy and more impact as a formal liaison between the Brotherhood and the Free Officers instead of just being a sympathetic outsider.

   Yet he might have only become an official member of the Muslim Brotherhood as late as February 1953, even though he performed important Brotherhood duties earlier than this.

   > The exact dates of Qutb's formal affiliation with the Brothers are unclear. However, from all available data it appears that his affiliation grew in stages: first, as a contributing writer to the Brothers' publications; second, as an admirer and friend of the movement in the aftermath of the Brothers' guerrilla war against the British in the Suez canal area late in 1951; and third, as a member and then as a leading ideologue of the Brothers in the aftermath of the 1952 Free Officers revolt, in the early months of 1953.

   Qutb himself wrote about his initial relationship to the Brotherhood, in a statement written for Egyptian investigators after his 1965 arrest. He noted:

   > Despite their hospitality as I joined their society, the sphere of work for me in their view was in cultural matters in the propagation division, the Tuesday lesson, the newspaper, *al-Ikhwan al-Muslimun* (The Muslim Brotherhood) whose editor-in-chief I became, and writing some monthly letters for Islamic cultural purposes. As for executive organizational work, I remained remote from it.

   Olivier Carré, *Mysticism and Politics: A Critical Reading of* Fi Zilal al-Qur'an *by Sayyid Qutb (1906–1966)* (Leiden: Brill, 2003), 5–7; Calvert, *Sayyid Qutb*, 5–7; Mohammed Moinuddin Siddiqui, "An Outline of Sayyed [*sic*] Qutb's Life," in Sayyid Qutb, *Islam and Universal Peace* (Plainfield, IN: American Trust Publications, 1993), x; Musallam, *From Secularism to Jihad*, 130 and 142; Sayyid Qutb, *Limadha A'dammuni* (Why Did They Execute Me?) (Jidda: al-Sharika al-Saudiyya li al-Abhath wa al-Taswiq [Saudi Partners for Research and Marketing], 1965), 12 and 31.

14. Musallam, *From Secularism to Jihad*, 23; Joel Gordon, *Nasser's Blessed Movement: Egypt's Free Officers and the July Revolution* (New York: Oxford University Press, 1992), 26–27; Siddiqui, "An Outline," x.

15. Musallam, *From Secularism to Jihad*, 146–147.

16. The Secret Apparatus, *al-jihaz al-sirri*, was an internal, clandestine, paramilitary unit of the Muslim Brotherhood started in late 1942 or early 1943 and dedicated to train, arm, and deploy fighters to carry out combat operations against those declared to be Brotherhood adversaries. It was never clear whether the apparatus was formal and well organized, or just an unofficial collection of zealous members willing to fight and die for the organization. It was also unclear whether the apparatus was merely defensive, to protect the organization and its members, or a unit committed to planned, offensive action. Although it was accused of *jihad*ist activities, this remains ambiguous and dependent on how *jihad* is actually defined (see the section "The Path from *Jahiliyya* to *Hakimiyya*: The Specific Tactics of *Jihad*" in Chapter 7). Nor was it clear

whether those targeted were just the foreign elements in or next to Egypt—British troops in the Canal Zone or Zionist brigades in Palestine—or domestic enemies who might have included the Palace and the civilian government and, therefore, might have involved insurrection. The answers to these questions remain crucial in designating the Muslim Brotherhood either as a moderate, reformist, and parliamentary party or a militant, terrorist, or revolutionary organization. Richard P. Mitchell, *The Society of the Muslim Brothers* (Oxford: Oxford University Press, 1969), 30–32, 54–56, 75–76.

17. Musallam, *From Secularism to Jihad*, 143–145, and 149. The factional infighting between al-Hudaybi and al-'Ashmawi came to a head in October 1953 when al-'Ashmawi and his radicals were voted out of the Guidance Bureau. A month later, al-'Ashmawi turned and rebelled against al-Hudaybi and his moderates, but the rebellion failed. In December 1953, the radicals were permanently banished from the Brotherhood. This turn toward moderation in the Brotherhood disappointed the 'Abd al-Nassir administration and further drove the Brotherhood and the republican government apart.

18. Ibid., 138. With King Faruq's abdication, General Muhammad Naguib, head of the Free Officers, established a Regency Council to protect the rights of Faruq's son, Ahmad Fu'ad, a one-year, intermediate policy before declaring Egypt a full republic. The council consisted of Prince 'Abd al-Mun'im, a cousin of Faruq, Rashad Muhanna, and Bahi al-Din Barakat, a former Speaker of Parliament. It was abolished on June 18, 1953. Anthony Nutting, *Nasser* (New York: E. P. Dutton, 1972), 42.

19. Khatab, *Political Thought*, 53; John Calvert and William Shepard, "Translators' Introduction," Sayyid Qutb, *A Child from the Village* (Syracuse: Syracuse University Press, 2004), xx.

20. Musallam, *From Secularism to Jihad*, 123 and 139.

21. Carré, *Mysticism and Politics*, 7; Calvert, *Sayyid Qutb*, 180–181; Mitchell, *The Society*, 103–104.

22. Musallam, *From Secularism to Jihad*, 140–142; Gordon, *Blessed Movement*, 77.

23. Musallam, *From Secularism to Jihad*, 142; Carré, *Mysticism and Politics*, 10–11.

24. Musallam, *From Secularism to Jihad*, 138; Hamid Algar, "Introduction" *Social Justice in Islam by Sayyid Qutb* (Oneonta, NY: Islamic Publications International, 2000), 5.

25. Qutb demanded a "just dictator" in a letter published in the newspaper *Akhbar al-Yawm*, August 8, 1952. Musallam, *From Secularism to Jihad*, 141; 'Adil Hammuda, *Sayyid Qutb min al-Qarya ila al-Mashnaqa: Sirat al-Ab al-Ruhi li Jama'at al-'Unf* (Sayyid Qutb from the Village to the Gallows: The Biography of the Spiritual Father of Violent Associations) (Cairo: Dar al-Khayyal, 1996), 119–120; 'Abdallah Imam, *'Abd al-Nassir wa al-Ikhwan* (Abd al-Nassir and the Muslim Brotherhood) (Cairo: Dar al-Khayyal, 1997).

26. Calvert, *Sayyid Qutb*, 182; Musallam, *From Secularism to Jihad*, 140–141.

27. Musallam, *From Secularism to Jihad*, 141.

28. Qutb was responsible for writing such pamphlets as "The Brothers in Battle," "This Treaty Will Not Pass" and "Why Do We Struggle?" in the summer of 1954 against the new administration and its pact. Ibid., 149.

29. Ibid.

30. Carré, *Mysticism and Politics*, 7: Musallam, *From Secularism to Jihad*, 147: Siddiqui, "An Outline," x.

31. Musallam, *From Secularism to Jihad*, 149; Algar, "Introduction," 6.

32. A second report states that Qutb was actually arrested six months after this date, in late April or early May 1955, and that he was tortured for seven hours before being consigned to a military hospital. Yet the April date coincides more with Qutb's actual verdict than with his initial arrest. Siddiqui writes of Qutb's detention:

> At the time of his arrest, he [Qutb] was suffering from high fever. He was taken to prison and the prison officials pounced on him, beating him mercilessly. A dog was then set on him, dragging him around the cell; he was subjected to various kinds of tortures for seven hours. This kind of treatment lasted until 3 May 1955, when he was transferred to a military hospital for the treatment of various illnesses caused by the relentless torture to which he had been subjected.

Siddiqui, "An Outline," x.

33. Ibid., xi, Musallam, *From Secularism to Jihad*, 150 and 165; Calvert, *Sayyid Qutb*, 194.

34. Calvert describes the general condition of incarceration for political prisoners without, however, specifically indicating that Qutb was harmed:

> Torture and mistreatment were common, and were meted out especially to new arrivals whose will, confidence and Islamist identity the guards sought to break. Guards suspended prisoners with their arms tied behind their heads, beat them with clubs, or subjected them to the viciousness of attack dogs.

Calvert, *Sayyid Qutb*, 197–198.

35. Musallam, *From Secularism to Jihad*, 151; Calvert and Shepard, "Translators' Introduction," xx; Calvert, *Sayyid Qutb*, 202–203; William E. Shepard, *Sayyid Qutb and Islamic Activism: A Translation and Critical Analysis of Social Justice in Islam* (Leiden: E. J. Brill, 1996), xvii.

36. Musallam, *From Secularism to Jihad*, 132.

37. Ibid.

38. Carré, *Mysticism and Politics*, 12. The analysis here relies considerably on the major scholarly analysis written by Olivier Carré. However, Carré admitted that he was not presenting a complete and objective digest of Qutb's thoughts, but just those aspects that "interest[ed]" him—an honest, but disappointing acknowledgment. A more balanced statement of Qutb's ideas can be achieved by drawing from his other publications as well. Carré, *Mysticism and Politics*, vii.

39. See the discussion in Chapter 4.

40. Carré, *Mysticism and Politics*, 17; Khatab, *Political Thought*, 160–161.

41. Carré, *Mysticism and Politics*, 250. For an explanation of these religious, political terms, see note 38, Chapter 3, and note 33, Chapter 4.

42. Musallam, *From Secularism to Jihad*, 133.

43. Calvert, *Sayyid Qutb*, 173–174. Is *In the Shade* a modern book? Because Qutb attended secular schools and worked with al-'Aqqad's Diwan school, Elliott Colla concludes that Qutb's Qur'anic interpretation "belongs to modern literary criticism and differs significantly from the kinds of commentaries studied and produced in religious institutions like al-Azhar." Yet at the same time, Colla also agrees that when Qutb's Qur'anic exegesis was published, it was "offered, and received, as a repudiation of the secular culture of Nahda modernity" (The Nahda, or the "Awakening" or "Renaissance," was the Arab modernist project of the 19th and early 20th centuries).

Although *Fi Zilal* was certainly contemporary, published in the middle of the 20th century, it was not necessarily modern; that is, not everything written at this time need be modern in the strict sense of valorizing secularism, nationalism, individualism, egalitarianism, humanism, capitalism, democracy, rationality (or utilitarianism), science, positivism, and progress. Indeed, it seems that Qutb repudiated and turned his back on the modernity that he had embraced just a few years earlier, explicitly rejecting those liberal influences from his schooling and his mentor in the Diwan school.

Colla does acknowledge that Qutb's commentary was different because unlike al-Azhar efforts, it was "addressed to a non-specialist audience, which is part of its lasting popularity." Qutb certainly did not carry the scholastic baggage from formal religious training, but the purpose of his Qur'anic explanations was to target a different, non-expert segment of the public. Elliott Colla, *Conflicted Antiquities: Egyptology, Egyptomania, Egyptian Modernity* (Durham, NC: Duke University Press, 2007), 20, 126, 261, and 264.

44. Ibid., 262 and 165.

45. Khatab, *Political Thought*, 161–162; Abu-Rabi', *Intellectual Origins*, 217.

46. Musallam, *From Secularism to Jihad*, 155; Algar, "Introduction," 9.

47. Qutb, *Signposts on the Road*, 34.

48. Ibid., 21–22.

49. For more on the distinction between Dar al-Islam and Dar al-Harb, see the discussion in the section "Social Critique and Salvation History: *Jahiliyya*" in Chapter 7.

50. Qutb, *Signposts on the Road*, 51.

51. Ibid., 145–147.
52. Ibid., 265–266.
53. Ibid., 274–275.
54. Ibid., 286.
55. For a very insightful analysis about this "ultimate sacrifice" for Muslims, see Talal Asad, *On Suicide Bombing* (New York: Columbia University Press, 2007), ch. 2.
56. Khatab, *Political Thought*, 168; Calvert, *Sayyid Qutb*, 235–236.
57. Musallam, *From Secularism to Jihad*, 164.
58. Ibid., 164–165. Ismail ibn Kathir (1301–72) was a famous 14th-century Syrian scholar who wrote a number of widely read commentaries analyzing the Qur'an and the Sunna about which he was particularly knowledgeable. He was a student of Ibn Taymiyya but also claimed to work within the Shafiʻi school of Islamic law.

    Muhammad ibn ʻAbd al-Wahhab (1703–93) was a religious scholar in the Najd of today's Saudi Arabia and founded the Wahhabi school of Islamic interpretation, a branch of Hanbali law. He joined together with Muhammad ibn Saʻud to establish the first Saudi state, 1744–1818, and his descendants have staffed the *ʻulama* of that country ever since.
59. Calvert, *Sayyid Qutb*, 241.
60. Ibid., 241–243.
61. Ibid.; Musallam, *From Secularism to Jihad*, 168. In post-revolution Egypt, the election for the People's Assembly, held from November 28, 2011, to January 3, 2012, resulted in the Islamists winning 70 percent of the ballots cast. The independent and liberal *Wasat* (Center) Party secured 3.7 percent, the conservative *salafiyyun* of the Islamist Bloc (including al-Nur Party and the Building and Development Party, former members of *al-Jamaʻa al-Islamiyya*) won 27.8 percent, and the moderate Democratic Alliance led by the Freedom and Justice Party tied to the Muslim Brotherhood captured 37.5 percent. This overall proportion closely approaches Qutb's threshold of 75 percent and may encourage the Islamists to advocate an Islamic state more fervently. Sherif Tarek. "Islamists Win 70 Percent of Egypt People's Assembly Party List Seats," *al-Ahram Online*, January 21, 2012, http://english.ahram.org.eg/NewsContent/33/100/32287/Elections-/News/Islamists-win—of-Egypt-Peoples-Assembly-party-lis.aspx.
62. Calvert, *Sayyid Qutb*, 243.
63. Musallam, *From Secularism to Jihad*, 168–169; Algar, "Introduction," 9; Siddiqui, "An Outline," xi; Calvert, *Sayyid Qutb*, 230. Siddiqui reports that 20,000 arrests took place in the summer of 1965, according to a report in the London *Daily Telegraph* of October 11, 1965. John Waterbury reports that 27,000 arrests occurred "in a single day," based on material from the Cairo *Akhbar al-Yawm* of March 29, 1975. Both numbers seem unrealistically high. Siddiqui, "An Outline," xi; John Waterbury, *Egypt: Burdens of the Past, Options for the Future* (Bloomington: Indiana University Press and the American Universities Field Staff, 1978), 241 and 255.
64. Algar, "Introduction," 9. The state prosecutor claimed that al-Hudaybi had intentionally ordered Qutb to organize commando activities both inside and outside prison. But because al-Hudaybi was so moderate and nonbelligerent, it is hard to believe that he would have actually ordered Qutb to establish militant groups.

    Al-Hudaybi had been arrested in 1954 along with Qutb. He was released early from prison in 1955 because of his age, but remained under house arrest until 1961. Several of his supporters criticized Qutb for recruiting members, providing spiritual guidance, and undermining the Supreme Guide's authority. Al-Hudaybi was certainly familiar with the study group organized by Ismaʻil and al-Ghazali, for he had approved of its formation but only on the condition that it eschew violence and promote *daʻwa*. His conditional blessings for the study group, therefore, protected Qutb who repeatedly declared his commitment to al-Hudaybi's conditions and his fealty to the Supreme Guide, much as he had done before 1954.

    Yet al-Hudaybi may not have actually been aware of any informal or stealthy departures from the official educational program. He was certainly dismayed at the new militant attitude and intolerant thinking found in Qutb's writings, especially in *Signposts*, and had actually started to challenge them earlier while in prison. He wrote a strong refutation of *Signposts* in his book *Duʻwat La Qudat* (Preachers, Not Judges) by criticizing Abu al-Aʻla Mawdudi's ideas on faith and practice, Ibn Taymiyya's kharijite thinking, and the Manichean polarities that Qutb had proposed, particularly where Qutb accused Egypt of being permanently steeped in religious ignorance. Al-Hudaybi argued that *jahiliyya* was not a persistent condition but instead simply described pre-Islamic Arabia, and so did not warrant the militancy that Qutb's kharijism prescribed. Al-Hudaybi was also alarmed that these ideas about *jahiliyya* society could morph into beliefs about excommunicating individuals, *takfir*. Qutb reassured him, though, that his accusations of religious ignorance were aimed only at societies, not individuals.

    Preachers Not Judges was published in 1969 and, like parts of *Signposts*, was written earlier in prison as a series of letters al-Hudaybi had written while briefly serving time in Liman Tura prison. Al-Hudaybi was well aware of the complaints of several imprisoned Islamists and struck out strongly in support of these inmates who disagreed with Qutb and were "disheartened by the new [government] persecutions yet unable to come up with a cogent answer to the disciples of Qutb." Their objections concurred with those of many moderate Islamists still free outside of prison. Musallam, *From Secularism to Jihad*, 168; Algar, "Introduction," 11; Calvert, *Sayyid Qutb*, 229; Gilles Kepel, *Muslim Extremism in Egypt: The Prophet and the Pharaoh* (Berkeley: University of California Press, 1993 [originally: *Le Prophète et Pharaon*, Jon Rothschild, trans., Paris: Éditions La Déouverte, 1984]), 29, 62; Emmanuel Sivan, *Radical Islam: Medieval Theology and Modern Politics* (New Haven, CT: Yale University Press, 1985), 108–109.
65. Algar, "Introduction," 9; Calvert, *Sayyid Qutb*, 241 and 243.
66. In a 1975 letter published in the Lebanese Muslim Brotherhood journal, *al-Shihab* (The Meteor); Kepel, *Muslim Extremism*, 61–62.
67. Algar, "Introduction," 9–10.
68. Musallam, *From Secularism to Jihad*, 170; Calvert, *Sayyid Qutb*, 258–259.
69. Calvert, *Sayyid Qutb*, 220–262; Khatab, *Political Thought*, 169; Calvert and Shepard, "Translators' Introduction," xxi; Musallam, *From Secularism to Jihad*, 171. Some of his writings were burned as well, and writers who had once included Qutb's material in their own publications later removed them in the next edition. Khatab, *Political Thought*, 54.

Chapter 6

1. Sayyid Qutb, *Ma'alim fi al-Tariq* (Signposts on the Road but also translated as Milestones) (Al-Salimiya, Kuwait: Al-Ittihad al-Islami al-'Alami li al-Munazzamat al-Tullabiya [International Islamic Federation of Student Organizations], 1978a), 200–202; Sayyid Qutb, *Muqawwimat al-Tasawwur al-Islami* (Basic Principles of the Islamic Worldview), Rami David, trans. (North Halcedon, NJ: Islamic Publications International, 2006), 2.
2. Qutb, *Basic Principles*, 6.
3. Olivier Carré, *Mysticism and Politics: A Critical Reading of* Fi Zilal al-Qur'an *by Sayyid Qutb (1906–1966)* (Leiden: Brill, 2003), 77.
4. Qutb, *Basic Principles*, 3.
5. Ibrahim M. Abu-Rabi', *Intellectual Origins of Islamic Resurgence in the Modern Arab World* (Albany: State University of New York Press, 1996), 146–147, 163.
6. • The Mu'tazila interpreted Islam on the basis of reason and logic, advocating the created nature of the Qur'an, Islam, and hanifiyyism (original monotheism).
   • The Khawarij examined the issue of good and bad Muslims, advocating radical justice and equality among true believers, and excommunication and death for those who have sinned or erred.
   • The Murji'a opposed the Khawarij and advocated tolerance, claiming that only God can judge true or false Muslims on Judgment Day, and not before.
7. • Ya'qub ibn Ishaq al-Kindi (801–873) was a renowned medical scientist and mathematician born in Kufa, Iraq, who introduced Aristotelian Neoplatonism and other elements of Greek and Hellenistic philosophy into Islam.
   • Abu Nasr al-Farabi (878–950) was a Muslim philosopher from Turkistan who introduced the neo-Aristotelian approach into Islamic thinking because he felt Islamic thinking was insufficient and that human reasoning was superior to divine revelation.

• Abu ʿAli al-Husayn ibn Sina (980–1037) was a philosopher-scientist from Persia who became famous for his contributions to Aristotelian philosophy and medical science. His treatises on medicine became standard textbooks at medieval universities.

• Abu al-Walid Muhammad ibn Rushd (1126–1198) was born in Andalucía and became an expert in Islamic theology, law, psychology, political science, mathematics, medicine, geography, and astronomy. He wrote commentaries on Greek philosophy and Plato's *Republic* that greatly influenced both the Muslim world and Europe.

8. For more on *fiqh*, see the section *Shariʿa Law* in Chapter 10.

9. Qutb, *Basic Principles*, 7; John L. Esposito, *Islam: The Straight Path*, 3rd ed. (New York: Oxford University Press, 1998), 69–74.

10. Carré, *Mysticism and Politics,* 12–20.

11. On Qutb's style, Calvert comments:

> Combining Hasan al-Banna's down-to-earth coffee house preaching with the prosaic and didactic literary mode of the effendi intelligentsia, Qutb produced an accessible, highly readable and incisive discourse that avoided the complex methodologies, rhetorical devices and flourishes characteristic of the legal writings of the higher *ʿulama*. Instead of engaging the reader in carefully crafted discussions of *fiqh* (jurisprudence), as was the norm among Azhari scholars, Qutb cut to the point, providing his readers with insights and practical advice, gleaned from scripture, which were relevant to their position as colonial subjects.

John Calvert, *Sayyid Qutb and the Origins of Radical Islamism* (New York: Columbia University Press, 2010), 131.

12. The material below is based on the Rami David's 2006 translation of Sayyid Qutb's 1962 book rendered in English as *Basic Principles of the Islamic Worldview*. The copyright page states that its Arabic title is *Muqawwimat al-Tasawwur al-Islami*. However, Hamid Algar, in his own preface to the David translation, states that the Arabic title of the book "offered here" is, instead, *Khasaʾis al-Tasawwur al-Islami wa Muqawwimatuhu* (The Characteristics and Fundamentals of the Islamic Concept) and that the Arabic title on the copyright page, *Muqawwimat al-Tasawwur al-Islami*, is actually the title of a *second* book in a two-part series that Algar then translates into English as *The Fundamentals of the Islamic Concept*, which "Sayyid Qutb spent part of the time left to him in completing." Another translated edition of *Khasaʾis al-Tasawwur al-Islami wa Muqawwamatuhu* was published earlier in 2000, translated by Mohammed Moinuddin Siddiqui, and was entitled in English *The Islamic Concept and Its Characteristics*. (The word "Fundamentals," or *Muqawwimat*, is not kept in the English title.) Since Siddiqui's volume covers the exact same topics as David's translation, I can only conclude that Algar is right and the copyright page for the David translation is wrong. Musallam lists these two parts of the series as two separate entries, with the "Characteristics and Fundamentals" published in 1962 and "Fundamentals" published 20 years after Qutb's 1966 execution, ca. 1986. Hamid Algar, "Introduction," *Social Justice in Islam by Sayyid Qutb* (Oneonta, NY: Islamic Publications International, 2000), viii; Adnan A. Musallam, *From Secularism to Jihad: Sayyid Qutb and the Foundations of Radical Islam* (Westport, CT: Praeger, 2005), 236.

13. The emphasis on unity helped Qutb dispute the trinitarian argument in Christianity and claim the superiority of Islam's unitarianism.

14. Qutb, *Basic Principles*, 73.

15. For more about *ʿibadat* and *muʿamalat*, see the discussion in section "Shariʿa Law" in Chapter 10.

16. Abu-Rabiʾ, *Intellectual Origins*, 152–153.

17. Sayed Khatab, *The Political Thought of Sayyid Qutb: The Theory of Jahiliyyah* (London: Routledge, 2006), 75.

18. Ibid., 72 and 97.

19. Khatab, *Political Thought*, 125; Carré, *Mysticism and Politics*, 81; Sayed Khatab, *The Power of Sovereignty: The Political and Ideological Philosophy of Sayyid Qutb* (London: Routledge, 2006), 72.

20. Khatab, *Political Thought*, 74.

21. Qur'an 9:30 says:

> And the Jews say, "Ezra is God's son," while the Christians say, "The Christ is God's son." Such are the sayings which they utter with their mouths, following in spirit assertions made in earlier times by people who denied the truth! They deserve the imprecation: "May God destroy them!" Muhammad Asad, trans., *The Message of the Qur'an* (Bristol, UK: Book Foundation, 2003), 296.

Ezra instituted the Second Temple of Israel after the Jews returned from the Babylonian Exile in 459 BC. He is viewed as important as Moses and David. He is accepted among the important prophets in Islam, but has been accused of distorting divine texts. Muhammad Asad goes on to explain this verse in a footnote:

> As regards the belief attributed to the Jews that Ezra…was "God's son," it is to be noted that almost all classical commentators of the Qur'an agree in that only the Jews of Arabia, and not *all* Jews, have been thus accused. (According to a Tradition on the authority of Ibn 'Abbas quoted by Tabari in his commentary on this verse—some of the Jews of Medina once said to Muhammad, "How could we follow thee when thou hast forsaken our *qiblah* and dost not consider Ezra a son of God?") On the other hand, Ezra occupies a unique position in the esteem of all Jews, and has always been praised by them in the most extravagant terms. It was he who restored and codified the Torah after it had been lost during the Babylonian Exile, and "edited" it in more or less the form which it has today; and thus "he promoted the establishment of an exclusive, legalistic type of religion that became dominant in later Judaism" (*Encyclopedia Britannica*, 1963, vol. 9, p. 15). Ever since then he has been venerated to such a degree that his verdicts on the Law of Moses have come to be regarded by the Talmudists as being practically equivalent to the Law itself; which, in Qur'anic ideology, amounts to the unforgivable sin of *shirk* [polytheism], inasmuch as it implies the elevation of a human being to the status of a *quasi*-divine law-giver and the blasphemous attribution to him—albeit metaphorically—of the quality of "sonship" in relation to God. Cf. in this connection Exodus iv, 22–23 ("Israel is My son") or Jeremiah xxxi, 9 ("I am a father to Israel"); expressions to which, because of their idolatrous implications, the Qur'an takes strong exception.

For more on Qutb's views on Christianity and Judaism, see "'People of the Book:' Dhimmis" in Part III of the Appendix.

22. Carré, *Mysticism and Politics*, 108.

23. Qutb, *Signposts*, 143–145.

24. Joel Beinin, "Islam, Marxism and the Shubra al-Kayma Textile Workers: Muslim Brothers and Communists in the Egyptian Trade Union Movement," in *Islam, Politics, and Social Movements*, Edmund Burke III, and Ira M. Lapidus, eds. (Berkeley: University of California Press, 1988), 207–227.

25. William E. Shepard, *Sayyid Qutb and Islamic Activism: A Translation and Critical Analysis of Social Justice in Islam* (Leiden: E. J. Brill, 1996), 31.

26. For more information on kharijite doctrines, see note 33 in Chapter 4.

27. Qutb, *Signposts*, 91.

28. Ibid., 166.

29. Abu-Rabi', *Intellectual Origins*, 130; Sayyid Qutb, *Dirasat Islamiyya* (Islamic Studies) (Cairo: Dar al-Fath, 1953 [reprint 1967]), 11.

30. Richard Tawney wryly called Karl Marx the last of the great schoolmen, referring to those monks who were the scholars and faculty of the European Middle Ages whose writings reinforced the integrated and harmonious model of their own pre-Renaissance society. Tawney made this remark because Marx's vision of a post-revolutionary society essentially saw it as a community of small owners and craftsmen, very much like the medieval social order. Revolutions, then, often use the past, however idealized, as templates for the future. Marx

was no exception, and neither was Qutb. While Marx lectured eloquently on the glory of tomorrow's classless and stateless society (a utopia by any account), Qutb wrote persuasively about the magnificence of Islam's first communities in Mecca and then Medina and the pristine harmony of the *salaf* that comprised Islam's glory and that formed principles that were necessary to use now as well. Richard H. Tawney, *Religion and the Rise of Capitalism* (London: Penguin Books, 1926 [reprint 1990]), 48.

31. Qutb, *Basic Principles*, 204.

32. Ibid., 113–114.

33. The universality of comprehensiveness seemingly results in the world's peoples constituting one big family. Indeed, the integration, harmony, and inclusiveness reflects a homogeneity similar to a family or tribe, a prototype of a pre-state society with its classlessness, rule by charismatic authority that lacks a monopoly of force, a low division of labor, and a mechanical solidarity, to use Emile Durkheim's term. Khatab, *The Power of Sovereignty*, 157.

34. This pair of elements was not in Qutb's original list of characteristics of the Islamic concept. I insert it here because it helps to identify a number of his key ideas about Islam.

35. Esposito, *Islam: The Straight Path*, 68.

36. Calling Qutb a fideist is based on the fact that Qutb embraced faith and revelation and rejected an intellectual reasoning in his religious understanding. This is not quite accurate, however, for Qutb did not view the two as opposites but as complements. Carré, *Mysticism and Politics*, 31 and 48.

37. Ibid., 92.

38. Rashid Rida and Muhammad 'Abduh, coming before Qutb, saw the ties to God to be violated, not by links to nonreligious identities, but by ties to stagnant and blind traditionalism. Ibid., 93.

39. These duties are (1) testimony, *shahada*, testifying that "There is no god but God, and Muhammad is His prophet"; (2) prayer, *salat*, five times a day at prescribed times; (3) fast, *sawm*, from sunup to sundown during the Islamic month of Ramadan; (4) pilgrimage, *hajj*, to the birthplace of Islam at least once in a lifetime, if physical and fiscal well-being permit; and (5) tithes, *zakat*, donating roughly 2½ percent of one's wealth to needy causes.

40. Qutb, *Basic Principles*, 159–160.

41. Carré, *Mysticism and Politics*, 63. This perspective follows from the Ash'arite school of theology established by the followers of Abu al-Hasan al-Ash'ari (873–935). Al-Ash'ari was a scholar born in Basra and employed in 'Abbasid Baghdad who, after 40 years, broke from the liberal "free will" Mu'tazilite school, and fathered an approach that while conservative, nevertheless moderated what then was the literalist understanding of Ahmad ibn Hanbal (780–855) and the textualism of the People of the Hadith (*Ahl al-Hadith*). These arch-conservatives sought to use hadith to fill the gaps in regulations left open by the Qur'an. The Ash'arites strongly supported the doctrines of revelation over reason, God's will over human will, Muslims over other monotheists, the uncreatedness of the Qur'an, God's eternal attributes, and predestination. They argued that while reason could be used to explain faith, there was still a limit to its success and beyond this, revelation took over. By the 11th century, this approach came to dominate Sunni Islam. John L. Esposito, *Islam: The Straight Path*, 3rd ed. (New York: Oxford University Press, 1998), 72–74.

42. Ibid., 68.

43. This is similar to the Calvinist argument that man's salvation is predetermined but, since man does not know what that judgment is, he has to continually work to show God's blessings. This, too, then combines divine will and human will.

44. Ibid., 65.

45. Norman Daniel, *Islam and the West: The Making of an Image* (Edinburgh: Edinburgh University Press, 1980), ch. 5.

46. The "hell and damnation" approach to the two worlds, heaven and hell, and to Judgment Day, easily parallels the evangelical sermons, the hell-fire and brimstone tirades, of the Methodists and Baptists who insisted on these images for guiding believers and worshippers into acting the right way. For an example from Protestantism, see E. P. Thompson, *Making of the English Working Class* (New York: Vintage Books, 1966), ch. 3, on the Methodists' use of imagery for

controlling the working class in England. Qutb was no exception. As he saw true Muslims forming a vanguard and acting to establish an Islamic system, discipline and motivation became quite necessary and, therefore, establishing control was not very surprising. For more on Qutb's views about punishment in Islam, see the discussion in the section "Law-Breaking and Punishment" in Chapter 10.

47. Carré, *Mysticism and Politics,* 69.
48. Khatab, *The Power of Sovereignty,* 72–73.
49. Ibid., 169.
50. Caesar Farah writes about miracles:

> The Quraysh's [the Prophet's tribe in Mecca] skepticism of Muhammad's mission man-ifested itself in another way. If Muhammad were truly sent, so they argued, why did he refuse to produce a sign in testimony of his declared mission or perform a miracle like other prophets before him? Why did he insist, as he did time and again, that he was not sent by God to work miracles? Was it sufficient to argue that the only miracle he was capable of was to point to God's power as manifested in His divine word and in His creation round about them?
>
> The only miracle attributed to Muhammad by the believers in him is the Qur'an. That so illiterate an Arab was capable of such rich utterances was truly miraculous in their eyes. And when the outside observer ponders the powerful impact he wrought on pagan Arabia in a decade of work, he is indeed overwhelmed by the miracle Muhammad performed.
>
> When we consider that the Qur'an mirrors the heart and mind of an Arab principally illiterate and unschooled in any formal knowledge, we cannot but admire the faith which moved, and indeed conditioned, the man Muhammad. While he emphatically denied his ability to perform miracles, arguing all along that God alone was the miracle worker; when considering the effects wrought by the Qur'an on Muhammad's people, and when pondering the magnitude of its impact on Arabs and non-Arabs alike, we cannot deny that this was indeed one of the greatest miracles ever performed by one who insisted he was a mortal like everyone else. This was the miracle of the non-miracle worker.

     Caesar E. Farah, *Islam: Beliefs and Observances,* 7th ed. (New York: Barron's Educational Series, 2003), 45–46 and 64–65.
51. Shepard, *Sayyid Qutb and Islamic Activism,* 13–14.
52. Darwinian evolution is the subject of a controversial book written in 1998 by 'Abd al-Sabur Shahin. In the 1990s, Shahin, together with Yusuf al-Badri—both colleagues at al-Azhar's Islamic Research Academy—had condemned Nasr Hamid Abu Zayd, a junior philosophy pro-fessor at Cairo University who had written a book that analyzed the Qur'an using herme-neutical, deconstructionist theory otherwise reserved for mortal texts. This suggested that the Qur'an is humanly authored and for this, he was accused of blasphemy. Yet later, Shahin went on to write the book *Abi Adam: Qissat al-Khaliqa bayna al-Ustura wa al-Haqiqa* (My Father Adam: The Story of Creation between Myth and Truth), which argues for integrating Darwinian evolution into Islam, thereby earning disapproval from his estranged colleague, al-Badri, for contravening what is the standard creationist perspective in Islam.
53. Qutb, *Basic Principles,* 122–123.
54. Ibid., 142.
55. Ibid., 70–71.
56. Khatab, *The Power of Sovereignty,* 105.
57. Ibid.
58. Qutb, *Signposts,* 80–81.
59. A fine example of negativism comes from Jonathan Edwards, a minister in New England's Great Awakening in the 1730s and 1740s. He is famous for his fire-and-brimstone sermon "Sinners in the Hands of an Angry God" delivered in Enfield, Connecticut, on July 8, 1741, that emphasized the wrath of God against sin.

> O sinner! Consider the fearful danger you are in: it is a great furnace of wrath, a wide and bottomless pit, full of the fire of wrath, that you are held over in the hand of that

God, whose wrath is provoked and incensed as much against you, as against many of
the damned in hell. You hang by a slender thread, with the flames of divine wrath flash-
ing about it, and ready every moment to singe it, and burn it asunder; and you have no
interest in any mediator, and nothing to lay hold of to save yourself, nothing to keep
off the flames of wrath, nothing of your own, nothing that you ever have done, nothing
that you can do, to induce God to spare you one moment.

www.iclnet.org/pub/resources/text/history/spurgeon/web/edwards.sinners.html.

60. For more on this Islamic vanguard, see the discussion in the section "The Path from *Jahiliyya*
to *Hakimiyya*: The Specific Tactics of *Jihad*" and its "*Jihad* of the Heart" in Chapter 7.

61. Sayyid Qutb, *al-'Adala al-Ijtima'iyya fi al-Islam* (Social Justice in Islam) (Cairo: Maktabat Misr,
1949 [reprint, Oneonta, NY: Islamic Publications International, 2000]), 215; Qutb, *Basic
Principles*, 166. For more on the rise and fall of Islamic history, see Chapter 11.

62. For more on Jonathan Edwards, see note 59 in this chapter. Both Edwards and Qutb were
charismatic, demagogic rabble-rousers. But there are some important differences, aside from
their personalities. The Puritan, Calvinist preacher Edwards conceived of men and women
as much more fatalistic, unable to avoid hell no matter what. There in Connecticut, God was
a mean and wrathful God, such that many called Calvin's God the Hebrew God of the Old
Testament. Qutb, on the other hand, presented God as merciful, kind, and forgiving, more
the New Testament variety. Edwards saw Hell as punishment after life; Qutb saw *jahiliyya* as
hell on earth for those living an unIslamic life, though few errant Muslims could actually see
their own decadence and depravity. For Edwards, humanity could not avoid hell. For Qutb,
hell could be overthrown by a triumphant vanguard of Islamic believers.

Yet both used this fiery language to attack the status quo and instill a strict morality and
piety as a form of the rigid social control necessary in moments of social breakdown and
revitalization.

Edwards was part of the First Great Awakening (1730–1750) that preceded the American
Revolution and brought a populist Calvinism—Methodism—to the United States from
England. This period of religious fervor was followed shortly by a Second Great Awakening
that took place after the American Revolution, from 1790 to 1840. Yet a third "Awakening"—
though never labeled as such—ushered in the first formal period of Protestant Fundamentalism
of the late 1880s leading up to World War I. Qutb was similarly caught up in a cyclical fundamentalism. The first Egyptian fundamentalism came with Jamal al-Din al-Afghani at the
same time that it appeared in the United States, the 1880s. Qutb's emergence as a charismatic
demagogue coincided with the reappearance of American fundamentalism in the 1950s which
might have earned the label of a Fourth Great Awakening. The point is that so-called religious
fundamentalism has its cycles, and neither Qutb nor Edwards were immune to the forces that
give rise to them. In fact, they were part and parcel of those forces as major contributors to
this type of religious movement.

63. Qutb, *Basic Principles*, 19.

64. Ibid., 199–200.

65. Ibid., 186.

66. Ibid., ch. 1.

Chapter 7

1. Anthony F. C. Wallace, "Revitalization Movements," *American Anthropologist* 57 (1956): 268–
270; Martin Riesebrodt, *Pious Passion: The Emergence of Modern Fundamentalism in the United
States and Iran*, Don Reneau, trans. (Berkeley: University of California Press, 1993; originally
published in 1990), 24.

2. Sayyid Qutb, *Ma'alim fi al-Tariq* (Signposts on the Road but also translated as Milestones)
(Al-Salimiya, Kuwait: Al-Ittihad al-Islami al-'Alami li al-Munazzamat al-Tullabiya [International
Islamic Federation of Student Organizations], 1978a), 16, 12–125, and 190–192. What Qutb
came to call "the Islamic movement" refers to the wide range of tactics included in *jihad*. Qutb
repeatedly said that "the Islamic movement" could not rely just on nonviolent methods of

expansion alone, and thus the term became his own euphemism for militancy and violence, although it also included community preaching and self-purification as well.

3. Ibid., 24–26; Ibrahim M. Abu-Rabi', *Intellectual Origins of Islamic Resurgence in the Modern Arab World* (Albany: State University of New York Press, 1996), 142.

4. *Jahiliyya* characterizes modern lifestyles and policies. Yet Qutb was less concerned about the West itself and much more agitated by its appearance and influence in the East, and in Egypt in particular. He was especially outraged about the *jahiliyya* at home that needed to be destroyed in order to establish God's dominion on earth. Because the modern world is bankrupt, Qutb argued that imitating its ways and habits are not only futile but blasphemous. The West is morally corrupt, and to go along this decadence, as Egypt was doing, is sheer folly. Until Europe, America and other non-Islamic countries stop their expansion, or modernization, and acknowledge God's dominion and His *shari'a*, then *jahiliyya* will continue—remaining a target that must be destroyed by sincere and righteous Muslims.

5. Sayyid Qutb, *Muqawwimat al-Tasawwur al-Islami* (Basic Principles of the Islamic Worldview), Rami David, trans. (North Halcedon, NJ: Islamic Publications International, 2006), 19.

6. Qutb, *Signposts*, 32.

7. Qutb called *jahiliyya* a "rebellion against God's sovereignty [or dominion] on earth" in *Signposts*, 15.

8. Some writers argue (for example, see Leonard Binder, *Islamic Liberalism: A Critique of Development Ideologies* [Chicago: University of Chicago Press, 1988], 174–175, and note 72 in Chapter 4) that Qutb borrowed the term *jahiliyya* wholesale from Abu al-A'la Mawdudi, the South Asian scholar whose writings had been translated into Arabic and popularized in the late 1940s and early 1950s and whose use of the term was razor-sharp and deliberate. Qutb's earlier treatment was more vague and less religious, however, paralleling his more secular position at the time. His first references to *jahiliyya* and related terms were well within the acceptable bounds of literary writers such as his mentor, 'Abbas al-'Aqqad. Yet as Qutb became more political, his use of the term *jahiliyya* converged with the meaning that Mawdudi used. By the 1950s, Qutb's treatment of the term unmistakably showed that he attached a specific religious definition to it—to be ignorant of God's way, to ignore the *shari'a* and God's dominion, to violate Islamic principles and beliefs—and as a blanket indictment of all Muslim societies, not just a few isolated individuals, classes, or communities. It is clear that Qutb borrowed the term's reference to pre-Islamic times to apply powerfully to today's wayward society. Other writers argue that Qutb's use sharpened in prison and the harsh treatment he received there. Indeed, there was all the reason in the world—torture, homicide, barbarity—to accuse prison guards and officials, and government administrators in general, of being steeped in *jahiliyya* despite their nominal Muslim identity.

9. Qutb, *Signposts*, 147–148.

10. It was never certain in the European Middle Ages if usury meant forbidding any interest whatsoever or just exorbitant rates well above market levels. This ambiguity and slippage provided an important means for stealthy transgressions. For Qutb, however, it meant that the charging of any interest at all was prohibited. For more on usury, see both note 1 and the section on "Usury" in Chapter 9.

11. Qutb, *Signposts*, 76.

12. For more on Qutb's view of women and the family, see the Appendix, Part II.

13. Qutb, *Signposts*, 183.

14. Carré, *Mysticism and Politics*, 189.

15. Shepard, *Sayyid Qutb and Islamic Activism*, 526–527; Qutb, *Signposts*, 175 and 183.

16. Carré, *Mysticism and Politics*, 104–105 and 109; Qutb, *Basic Principles*, 21–25.

17. For more on Sayyid Qutb's views on Christianity and Judaism, see "'People of the Book:' Dhimmis" in Part III of the Appendix.

18. Sayed Khatab, *The Power of Sovereignty: The Political and Ideological Philosophy of Sayyid Qutb* (London: Routledge, 2006), 7.

19. Qutb, *Signposts*, 173–174 and 221.

20. Sayyid Qutb, *al-'Adala al-Ijtima'iyya fi al-Islam* (Social Justice in Islam) (Cairo: Maktabat Misr, 1949 [reprint, Oneonta, NY: Islamic Publications International, 2000]), 262. Qutb's tone

became "darker," more severe and pessimistic, in subsequent editions of *Social Justice*, the emerging set of opposites, of Islam versus *jahiliyya*, becoming more rigid and stark throughout the 1950s and into his prison years up to the end of his life, and his kharijite perspective becoming more pronounced as time went by. He moved from a liberal, human will, or "free will," outlook to a more conservative, God's will, point of view. This exhibited an increasingly "theocentric" perspective that focused solely on the divine and reflected a more cynical attitude. Here Qutb's heightened sensitivity to his own culture on the one hand, and to Western culture and Westernized Egyptians on the other, meant that the separation between the two was growing and the bridge connecting the opposites shrinking. There became only Islamic ethics or *jahili* ethics; Islamic values or *jahili* values; subordination to God or subordination to men; Islamic civilization or *jahili* civilization; Dar al-Islam, homeland of Islam, or Dar al-Harb, home of constant conflict. There seemed to be no middle ground. Even those who call themselves Muslim are either righteous Muslims because they follow what Qutb saw as a true Islamic path, or they follow the decadence, immorality, and bankrupt authority of *jahiliyya*. As Qutb grew more intense, he came to consider the "modern *jahiliyya* [a]s more pernicious and deeper than the pre-Islamic one." The later version of Qutb's concept of *jahiliyya* was "more sophisticated and thoroughgoing than the earlier one"; and whereas in his first Islamist use of *jahiliyya*, Qutb is concerned with its symptoms, in his later, more virulent treatment, he considers mostly its root causes. Shepard, *Sayyid Qutb and Islamic Activism*, xlix–l and xxiv–xxxiv; Abu-Rabi', *Intellectual Origins*, 180; William E. Shepard, "Sayyid Qutb's Doctrine of Jahiliyya," *International Journal of Middle East Studies* 35, no. 4 (November 2003): 527, 533.

21. Qutb, *Signposts*, 271.
22. Ibid., 247.
23. Sayed Khatab, *The Political Thought of Sayyid Qutb: The Theory of Jahiliyyah* (London: Routledge, 2006), 26.
24. This disagreement later translated into strategic difference between Tanzim al-Jihad (the Jihad Organization) which only targeted government officials, and al-Jama'a al-Islamiyya (the Islamic Association) which aimed at all ordinary Muslims. This is discussed in greater detail in the Epilogue.
25. Qutb, *Signposts*, 12.
26. Here, the minority Athanasius clique that advocated Jesus's divinity won a rigged election over the majority Arius group that just promoted his basic prophecy.
27. Ibid., 11–12.
28. Ibid., 34.
29. For more on Qutb's interpretation of Islamic history, see Chapter 11.
30. Qutb, *Social Justice*, 169–170.
31. Shepard, *Sayyid Qutb and Islamic Activism*, ch. 8.
32. Ibid., 206 and 211.
33. Ibid., 328–329.
34. This corresponds to the new goal society of a revitalization movement, following Wallace's model.
35. Those who perform *jihad*. The word *mujahid* (singular; *mujahidun*, plural) is derived from the same trilateral Arabic root as *jihad* and refers to those actively engaged in a struggle to achieve a true Islam. They need not, though, simply be "holy warriors," "militants," or "terrorists."
36. Notwithstanding such confusing pledges of allegiance as the one in the United States which, since 1954, pledges allegiance to the nation, but a nation that is "under" God. It is not exactly clear just where allegiance and loyalty actually lie should there be a contradiction between God and nation. But the pledge does go on to mention an "indivisible" nation—*tawhid*—which Qutb would readily accept.
37. Shepard, *Sayyid Qutb and Islamic Activism*, 298.
38. Qutb, *Signposts*, 107.
39. Ibid., 161.
40. Khatab, *The Power of Sovereignty*, 58 and 82.
41. Charles Lindholm, "Quandaries of Command in Egalitarian Societies: Examples from Swat and Morocco," in *Comparing Muslim Societies: Knowledge and the State in a World Civilization*, Juan R. I. Cole, ed. (Ann Arbor: University of Michigan Press, 1992).

42. The George W. Bush administration, in my opinion, subscribed fully to this erroneous stereotype in predicting an easy outcome to its invasion of Iraq in March 2003. The incorrect assumption of passivity and blind obedience to earthly authority was so far off the mark that the United States continues to suffer for its own lack of thinking and foresight.

43. Khatab, *The Power of Sovereignty*, 35 and 49. For more on authentic Islamic authority, see the section, "The Ruler" in Chapter 10.

44. Qutb, *Signposts*, 53.

45. Ibid., 70–72.

46. Ibid., 72; Abu-Rabi', *Intellectual Origins*, 162.

47. Qutb, *Signposts*, 71.

48. Ibid., 104–105, 111, and 127.

49. Ibid., 128–129.

50. Sayyid Qutb, *al-Salam al-'Alami wa al-Islam* (Islam and Universal Peace) (Plainfield, IN: American Trust Publications,1993a [originally published in Cairo: Maktabat Wahbah, 1951b]), 5–9. This book was published in Cairo in October 1951, Qutb's second volume after returning from the United States. It was a response to international postwar political events such as the Marshall Plan and the Korean War that marked the outbreak of the Cold War. It was translated into English by American Trust Publications and published in 1977 and again in 1993.

51. "Just War" theory attempts to justify and sanction war and violence as a moral and philosophical issue. For example, see Talal Asad, *On Suicide Bombing* (New York: Columbia University Press, 2007); Michael W. Brough, John W. Lango, and Harry van der Linden, eds., *Rethinking the Just War Tradition* (Albany: State University of New York Press, 2007); Jean B. Elshtain, ed., *Just War Theory* (New York: New York University Press, 1992); John Kelsay, *Arguing the Just War in Islam* (Cambridge, MA: Harvard University Press, 2007); Douglas Lackey, *The Ethics of War and Peace* (Englewood Cliffs: Prentice-Hall, 1989); Larry May, *War Crimes and Just War* (Cambridge: Cambridge University Press, 2007); Michael Walzer, *Just and Unjust Wars: A Moral Argument with Historical Illustrations* (New York: Basic Books, 1977); Michael Walzer, *Arguing about War* (New Haven: Yale University Press, 2004).

Contemporary (and secular) Just War theory is derived, in part, from medieval Catholic teachings that, for centuries, justified wars such as the Crusades and the Reformation, following the philosophical writings of St. Augustine (354–430), Thomas Aquinas (1225–1274), and Francisco de Vitoria (1492–1546) (Walzer, *Arguing about War*, 4). Wars are no longer categorically rejected; defensive wars are permitted, and even offensive wars can be initiated under certain conditions—all in ways that oddly, and ironically, echo theories of *jihad* in Islam. See, for example, Hasan al-Banna, "On Jihad," *Five Tracts of Hasan al-Banna (1906–1949)*, Charles Wendell, trans. (Berkeley: University of California Press, 1978).

Yet of course, theory is one thing; actual practice is another, and both Christians and Muslims have a sorry record of undertaking war and committing violence.

52. Qutb, *Islam and Universal Peace*, ch. 2: "The Islamic Concept of Peace." Notwithstanding his own eagerness for worldwide victory, Qutb still argued that the purpose of Islamization is not the same as modernization, Westernization, or imperialism, and that militant *jihad* is not the same as war. The basis of war is nationalism, racism, and classism, he argued. Western military campaigns are fought for the purposes of exploiting countries for their resources and enslaving their people, literally or figuratively, for their economic functions. In Islam, there is no equivalent to imperialism, nor can there be forced conversions. For its part, ordinary war seeks booty and plunder or else to defend or expand nationalism and its boundaries. The goal of a *jihad* of the sword, by contrast, is to preserve, defend, and spread Islam. War aims to elevate one nation's lordship over another, to plunder, exploit and extract assets, and to claim territory or partisan victory. *Jihad's* motives, by comparison, are genuine and altruistic, pursued for the benefit of all humanity. War takes prisoners; *jihad* opens minds, but otherwise leaves people alone and "in place." War seeks to dominate people; *jihad* endeavors to establish the dominion of God and His laws, freeing people to decide on their own beliefs. While war becomes a goal in of itself, *jihad* becomes a means of establishing

genuine peace, freedom, and truth so that humanity can live only under the dominion of God and make up its mind and heart about its own religion. *Jihad* strives to expand the true character of Islam as a universal proclamation of humanity's freedom from servitude to those other than God.

Consequently, the administration of religiously conquered countries permits the free flow of information about Islam, and the freedom and autonomy necessary to absorb and reflect upon that information. Europe conquers for economic gain; Islam conquers for spiritual gain, and while conquered lands are taxed, the revenues remain at home. The conquered are permitted to practice their religion freely, and their places of worship and religious institutions are protected. They are allowed to keep their wealth and property as long as they pay the *jizya* tax ordinarily expected from non-Muslims. (But they do not pay *zakat* which Muslims do, so the tax burden actually balances out, nor do they serve in the military.) Only the possessions of those who have actually fought Islam and who adamantly refuse to pay taxes are confiscated. In general, the people conquered by Islam are treated justly, generously, and humanely. There is no "divide and rule" strategy of setting one subnational group or class against another. Shepard, *Sayyid Qutb and Islamic Activism*, 212–214; Qutb, *Social Justice*, 198–199.

53. Qutb, *Islam and Universal Peace*, 2.

54. Lest Western readers gasp at Qutb's hubris, it is important to remember that the Islamic movement appears no different in its scope and ambition than the European-based forces of modernity that sought to modernize the planet and replicate Euro-American institutions and values throughout the world. See both the discussion in the section "Islam versus Secularism and Modernity" and note 15 in Chapter 8 for more on Qutb's perspective on Islamization or universalizing Islam.

55. Qutb, *Social Justice*, 87. This is *hadith* number 34 listed in the *Forty Sayings of* [Abu Zakaria] *al-Nawawi* (1234–1278) who cited his source as Sahih Muslim's well-regarded compilation of hadith. The original *hadith* is attributed to Abu Sa'id al-Khudri (d. ca. 681), a young companion of the Prophet Muhammad who transmitted over a thousand hadith. Al-Nawawi's wording is slightly different . . .

> Whosoever of you sees an evil, let him change it with his hand; and if he is not able to do so, then [let him change it] with his tongue; and if he is not able to do so, then with his heart—and that is the weakest of faith.

which makes the last phrase in Qutb's version—"that is the minimum faith requires"—more comprehensible.

56. Adnan A. Musallam, *From Secularism to Jihad: Sayyid Qutb and the Foundations of Radical Islam* (Westport, CT: Praeger, 2005), 179–180; Majid Khadduri, *War and Peace in the Law of Islam* (Baltimore: Johns Hopkins University Press, 1955), 55. Khadduri, in turn, cites Ibn Hazm, *al-Fasl fi al-Milala wa al-Ahwa wa al-Nihal* (Cairo 1321 AH, Vol. IV), 135; Ibn Rushd, *Kitab al-Muqaddimat al-Mumahhidat* (Cairo 1325 AH, Vol. I), 259; Buhuti, *Kashshaf al-Qina' 'An Matn al-Iqna'* (Cairo, 1366 AH, Vol. III), 28.

57. Ibn Qayyim al-Jawziyya (1292–1350) was a famous Islamic scholar in Damascus, a devoted student under Ahmad ibn Taymiyya (1263–1328) (see note 32, Chapter 4), and a jurist in the conservative Hanbali school of law. Qutb relied heavily on his book, *Zad al-Ma'ad* (Provision of the Hereafter) and particularly on its chapter, "The Prophet's Treatment of the Unbelievers and the Hypocrites from the Beginning of His Prophethood until His Death." See Qutb, *Signposts*, Chapter 4, "Jihad in the Cause of God."

By defining *jihad* as simply "holy war," Western writers restrict the struggle for God's dominion to just one type, that of violence, militancy, and combat. Yet even "*jihad* of the sword," according to Reuven Firestone, is still "not quite equivalent to the common Western understanding of holy war" which remains "a European invention derived from the study of war in its European context." Reuven Firestone, *Jihad: The Origin of Holy War in Islam* (London: Oxford University Press, 1999), 15 and 18.

58. Qutb, *Islam and Universal Peace*, 9–15. The classical trajectory of stages for militant *jihad* evolves from nonconfrontation (supported by Qur'anic verses 15:94–95 and 16:125), to

defensive fighting (verses 22:39–40 and 2:190), to initiating conditional attacks (verses 2:217 and 2:191), and finally to unmitigated or unconditional attacks (2:216, 9:5, and 9:29). The last approach is upheld by the famous "sword verse," sura 9:5, which is considered by some to abrogate all other 124 *jihad* verses found in the Qur'an:

> And so, when the sacred months are over, slay those who ascribe divinity to aught beside God wherever you may come upon them, and take them captive, and besiege them, and lie in wait for them at every conceivable place. Yet if they repent, and take to prayer, and render the purifying dues, let them go their way: for, behold, God is much-forgiving, a dispenser of grace.

and is often coupled with verse 9:29:

> And fight against those who—despite having been vouchsafed revelation afore-time—do not truly believe either in God or the Last Day, and do not consider forbid-den that which God and His Apostle have forbidden, and do not follow the religion of truth which God has enjoined upon them, till they agree to pay the exemption tax with a willing hand, after having been humbled in war.

Here the enemy is seen to be non-Muslims, sometimes including (though not without contro-versy) People of the Book. Even more contentious is the inclusion of those nominal Muslims accused of apostasy, dissent, or deviancy. Firestone, *Jihad: The Origin of Holy War in Islam*, ch. 3. Also see note 62 in this chapter.

59. David Cook, *Understanding Jihad* (Berkeley: University of California Press, 2005), 35.

60. Hasan al-Banna concluded that al-Bayhaqi's *hadith* is not sound, citing both the Shafi'i scholar, Ahmad ibn Hajar al-'Asqalani (1382–1449), who said "It [the hadith] is well known and often repeated, and was a saying of Ibrahim ibn Abi 'Abla" (d. 769) and the Shafi'i scholar, 'Abd al-Rahim al-'Iraqi (1325–1404), who said "al-Bayhaqi transmitted it with a weak chain of guar-antors on the authority of Jabir, and al-Khatib transmitted it in his history on the authority of Jabir" (perhaps Jabir ibn 'Abd Allah al-Ansari [d. 697] who was a companion of the Prophet). It is significant that this *hadith* does not appear in some of the major *hadith* compilations, those by al-Bukhari, Muslim, Abu Dawud, or Tirmidhi. Al-Banna further concluded:

> Even if it were a sound hadith, it would never warrant abandoning *jihad*, or preparing for it in order to rescue the territories of the Muslims and repel the attacks of unbeliev-ers. Its meaning is simply that it is necessary to struggle with the spirit so that it may be sincerely devoted to God in every one of its acts.

Al-Banna, "On Jihad," 155.

61. For more details on Sayyid Qutb's ideas on "People of the Book," or *Dhimmis*, see the Appendix, Part III.

62. Verse 9:5 mentioned in note 58, this chapter, is also known as the "Islam or the Sword" verse which, while a false dichotomy, highlights the fact that the enemy is considered those outside the Muslim community. Yet Ibn Kathir (for a biographical sketch, see note 58 in Chapter 5) used four "sword verses," including 9:5, to identify those whom Muslims are obligated to fight: (1) idolaters (verse 9:5), (2) Scriptuaries, until they pay the poll tax (verse 9:29), (3) those who outwardly appear as Muslims but oppose Islam (verse 9:73 but also verse 9:123), and (4) those Muslims who unjustly oppress other Muslims (verse 49:9). Firestone, *Jihad: The Origin of Holy War in Islam*, 63. Thus while the third category targets faux Muslims, the fourth categories means that those who incorrectly identify this third group also deserve *jihad*.

63. For more on khorijism, see note 33 in Chapter 4.

64. It was the innovation of Qutb's later followers, such as Usama bin Ladin, who believe that lapsed Muslims can only remain in *jahiliyya* because of the indoctrination and power of the West, that turned Europe and America into Islamism's principal targets rather than local offenders, when the Far Enemy began to trump the Near Enemy. Fawaz Gerges, *The Far Enemy: Why Jihad Went Global* (Cambridge: Cambridge University Press, 2005), 49–50.

65. Qutb, *Basic Principles*, 172 and 286; Qutb, *Signposts*, 129–130.

66. Abu-Rabi', *Intellectual Origins*, 180–181.
67. Qutb, *Signposts*, 86.
68. Ibid., 30–31 and 232.
69. Ibid., 66–67.
70. Carré, *Mysticism and Politics*, 230 and 232.
71. Qutb, *Signposts*, 65.
72. Ibid., 17.
73. Ibid., 65.
74. This separation, the hallmark of Qutb's growing kharijism, was evidently the intention of the Shukri Mustafa group, the Society of Muslims (Jama'at al-Muslimin) established in Egypt in the 1970s. They became known to the press and the public as "Takfir wa al-Hijra"—Excommunication and Migration. They had declared society to be unbelievers (*kuffar*) and went to isolate themselves from their *jahili* society, although it was as much or more a spiritual separation than a physical detachment, since many members lived together, commune-like, in urban apartment buildings. Once it had grown stronger, the association would then re-join society and, once spiritually purified, strive to establish an Islamic state. However, it was not allowed to do so by the Egyptian media and government security and by Mustafa's own sense of insult and dishonor. For more on this organization, see the discussion in the Epilogue.
75. Qutb, *Signposts*, 98–99.
76. Qutb, *Social Justice*, 173.
77. Qutb, *Signposts*, 66.
78. Khatab, *The Power of Sovereignty*, 178.
79. Qutb, *Signposts*, 66–67.
80. Hamas is the acronym for *Harakat al-Muqawama al-Islamiyya*, or the Islamic Resistance Movement.
81. James Toth, "Local Islam Gone Global: The Roots of Religious Militancy in Egypt and Its Transnational Transformation," in *Global Social Movements: A Reader*, June Nash, ed. (Oxford: Blackwell, 2004), 126–128; Hesham al-Awadi, *In Pursuit of Legitimacy: The Muslim Brothers and Mubarak, 1982–2000* (London: Tauris, 2004), ch. 4; Denis J. Sullivan, *Private Voluntary Organizations in Egypt: Islamic Development, Private Initiative, and State Control* (Gainesville: University Press of Florida, 1994), ch. 3.
82. Carré, *Mysticism and Politics*, 236.
83. Still, Qutb's ideas about organized violence and militancy remained undeveloped. These topics were considered in greater detail by those who appeared after Qutb's death. His followers have shown much less patience, wishing to reduce the period of *da'wa*, short-circuiting it by compulsion, and forcibly removing obstacles or even violently calling unbelievers to Islam. They have argued for immediate combat aimed at the top, with an expected trickle-down to follow. Qutb's own approach required years; the top-down method is much quicker and more explosive, but it confronts more powerfully entrenched tyrants. Thus, despite Qutb's own reputation, it was actually 'Abd al-Salam Faraj, one of the intellectual leaders who organized the Jihad Organization in the 1970s, who decided that overthrowing an unbelieving ruler was necessary and unavoidable.
84. Qutb pointed out (*Signposts*, 100) that the expansion of Islam out from the Arabian peninsula was not a conversion of the sword—"there is no compulsion in religion," as Qur'an 2:256 proclaims. He wrote:

> Islam does not force people to accept its belief, but it wants to provide a free environment in which they will have the choice of beliefs. What it wants to abolish are those oppressive political systems under which people are prevented from expressing their freedom to choose whatever beliefs they want, and after that it gives them complete freedom to decide whether to accept Islam or not.

Instead this expansion was but a clearing away of obstacles—just "simple" ones, like conquering the entire Byzantine, Persian, and Roman empires—that prevented people from freely understanding Islam. It was not even in the financial interest of the conquerors to compel conversion, since non-Muslims were taxed at a higher rate than Muslims, though of course, at the same time, ordinary people did convert willingly for just this reason. Yet apart from financial considerations, many people converted because Islam basically offered a simple and comprehensible vision of God, society, and humanity. This is evident from the apologetic character of the anti-Islamic discourse in medieval Europe and its derision of the newer religion for fear it would attract many converts. It was in the interest of early Islamophobes to portray a victorious Islam as conversion by the sword rather than to admit to the purity and simplicity of the Prophet's message. Conquest was certainly accomplished by the sword, but conversion was not. John V. Tolan, *Saracens: Islam in the Medieval European Imagination* (New York: Columbia University Press, 2002), 50.

85. Qutb, *Signposts*, 113 and 133.

86. Muslims who consider *jihad* a required duty of Islamic practice include (1) Kharijites (where it is the Sixth Pillar in addition to the regular Five Pillars of Sunni Islam), (2) Isma'ili Shi'ism (where it is the last of its Seven Pillars that add guardianship and unity to, and remove testimony from, the Five Pillars), (3) Twelvers Shi'ism (where its 10 mandatory practices add to the Five Pillars jihad, permitting good, forbidding evil, loving Muhammad's family, and cursing his enemies), and (4) the neo-Hanbalites who follow the teachings of Ibn Taymiyya. Carré, *Mysticism and Politics*, 249 and 251; Michael Bonner, *Jihad in Islamic History: Doctrines and Practices* (Princeton: Princeton University Press, 2006), 126, 134, 143–144.

87. One debate Qutb participated in was whether *jihad* of any type—but usually referring to militant combat—is obligatory for every Muslims (like prayer) or merely a communal duty such that if some perform it, the remainder are released from the obligation. Muslims are required to fight against those attacking Islam, against those who would block the peaceful spread of Islam, *and* against those unjust and tyrannical rulers and *jahili* institutions that are antithetical to Islam. As a collective responsibility, national armies exist to fulfill this obligation. But as an individual obligation, all individuals must enlist in *jihad*.

    Hasan al-Banna, after summarizing the thoughts of a number of legal scholars from the four schools of Islamic *fiqh*, concluded that *jihad* is a collective duty (*fard kifaya*) in "broadcasting the summons" of Islam, in pro-actively promoting Islam, and it is an individual duty (*fard 'ayn*) in "repuls[ing] the attack of unbelievers," in defending Islam against outsiders. Al-Banna, "On Jihad," 150.

    For his part, Qutb omitted (perhaps purposely so) any specific discussion about whether *jihad* is the duty of all Muslims or just individual Muslims. Instead, he argued that all Muslim need to volunteer and that their choice is part of their evaluation on Judgment Day. Every man is obligated to free other men from the slavery, servitude, and injustice of man-made deities and rulers. For more on *jihad* as a sixth duty in Islam, see note 4 in Chapter 8.

88. Qutb, *Signposts*, 117.

89. For more details on Sayyid Qutb's ideas about apologetics, see the Appendix, Part IV.

90. Qutb, *Signposts*, 112–113, and 133. In defending the use of violence as a necessary tactic to overcome the obstacles that hinder the transmission of Islam, Qutb included *all* the institutions of *jahili* society. By assuming a functionalist model, where society is the sum of its interdependent parts, he condemned all related institutions—the state, the civilization, and, in general, the whole social system and human situation—as guilty of inhibiting Islam's diffusion and preventing people from hearing God's true message. He then declared that all these institutions must be destroyed. Carré, *Mysticism and Politics*, 246; Qutb, *Signposts*, 106.

    Yet Qutb made a fine distinction a social scientist might find hard to accept. Qutb argued that the Islamic movement does not force individuals to accept its beliefs, nor does it even attack individuals at all. What it assails, he claimed, are institutions and traditions so as to release individuals from their poisonous influence which distorts human nature and curtails human freedom. Qutb, *Signposts*, 137. Thus *jihad* annihilates *jahili* institutions, but not the *jahili* people who populate those institutions. They are, instead, educated and taught the ways of Islam in a free and just atmosphere; it is then their right to decide whether to follow God's way or the ways of Satan. Their corrupt traditions and practices are thus destroyed, but they, themselves, are allowed to freely choose either to move into Islam or else to remain wallowing in a dying *jahiliyya*.

In Islam, no one can impose beliefs on another by force. But the absence of compulsion does not mean, however, that the environment or context in which people make decisions concerning religion can not be forcibly manipulated by clearing it of the barriers that impede certain particular choices. In order to establish freedom, justice, and equality for all, *jahiliyya* must be overthrown and demolished. After that, people are free to choose their own religion, although, again, all other religions—except, perhaps, for Judaism and Christianity, and here, only if they pay higher taxes and enter into treaties—are considered false religions, deviations from true monotheism, and therefore eligible for destruction.

Qutb was, therefore, at odds with himself. On the one hand, there is no compulsion in religion, and so, even despite establishing a commanding environment, men and women are nonetheless free to choose their own religion. Yet Qutb also argued that any choice *other than* Islam is an error. Perhaps one conclusion might be that while there is no coercion in religion, the forces of persuasion are such that for all intents and purposes, people are strongly urged to adopt Islam. Qutb was not embarrassed over this confusion, because he felt that since Islam is God's message and will, that pushing people in this direction is for their own good.

91. Qutb, *Signposts*, 111.
92. Ibid., 135–136.
93. Thus, for example, when Hasan Nasrallah, the secretary-general of the Shi'ite organization Hizballah in Lebanon, proclaims Islam (without distinction) as holding the solutions to the problems of *any* society, he is echoing (perhaps unintentionally) the sentiments of Sayyid Qutb.
94. For details about Ibn Qayyim al-Jawziyya, see note 57, this chapter.
95. For the Qur'anic justification of these stages, see note 58, this chapter.
96. Ibid., 109–110.
97. Hasan al-Banna, "On Jihod," *Five Tracts of Hasan al-Banna (1906–1949)*, Charles Wendell, trans. (Berkeley: University of California Press, 1978).
98. Qutb adopted the interpretation of Ibn Taymiyya who argued that Muslim rulers were actually heretics if they did not rule by *shari'a* law. Qutb thus concluded that local government leaders were not true believers and therefore should be targeted. The question that followed after Qutb's execution was whether the entire Muslim society is apostate if *shari'a* does not rule their country, or is it just the country's rulers alone who become liable. For Qutb, the approach to lapsed Muslims was through teaching and education—a *jihad* of the tongue—and so labeling the entire community as heretic was not endangering them. When Qutb berated his co-religionists for deviating from the Straight Path, for being false Muslims and hypocrites, his solution was to correct their *jahili* ways through persuasion, not necessarily by coercion.

Chapter 8

1. Sayed Khatab, *The Power of Sovereignty: The Political and Ideological Philosophy of Sayyid Qutb* (London: Routledge, 2006), 13–14.
2. For details about this distortion, see note 21 in Chapter 6. For Qutb's views on People of the Book, or Dhimmis, see Part III in the Appendix.
3. Sayyid Qutb, *Ma'alim fi al-Tariq* (Signposts on the Road but also translated as Milestones) (Al-Salimiya, Kuwait: Al-Ittihad al-Islami al-'Alami li al-Munazzamat al-Tullabiya [International Islamic Federation of Student Organizations], 1978), 182.
4. Khatab, *The Power of Sovereignty*, 41. Qutb concluded that it is this second group of Muslims, those who do not live in a true Islamic society, who either have to participate in one kind of *jihad* or another to achieve such a civilization, or else their community will revert completely to *jahiliyya*. They can reorient their own faith and practice, and they can preach in the mosques and schools. They can fulfill all their religious duties, and even perform them diligently and sincerely. But if they do not actively seek to establish an Islamic society—one that acknowledges God's dominion and submits to God's law—then they are still unbelievers. In this way, Qutb made *jihad* as a sixth obligation for Muslims a very contested perspective. For more on *jihad* as a collective and individual duty, see note 87 in Chapter 7.

5. William E. Shepard, *Sayyid Qutb and Islamic Activism: A Translation and Critical Analysis of Social Justice in Islam* (Leiden: E. J. Brill, 1996), 8; Khatab, *The Power of Sovereignty*, 41.

6. Qutb, *Signposts*, 146–147.

7. Shepard, *Sayyid Qutb and Islamic Activism*, 8–9.

8. Qutb, *Signposts*, 146, 152–153.

9. Ibid., 207–208.

10. To the best of my knowledge, Qutb did not use the words Islamism or Islamist (*Islamiyyun* in Arabic) in discussing Islam as a system and a doctrine, following the syntax of other"-ism's" such as secularism or capitalism. Islamism as it is used in the West refers to a political ideology and system based on Islam, commonly called "political Islam," although this should be designated just plain Islam, without further distinction, since politics was never separated from religion as it was in Europe. For more on the use of the term Islamism, see note 7 in chapter 1. For more on the structure of religion, see note 26 in this chapter.

11. Sayyid Qutb, *al-'Adala al-Ijtima'iyya fi al-Islam* (Social Justice in Islam) (Cairo: Maktabat Misr, 1949 [reprint, Oneonta, NY: Islamic Publications International, 2000]), 317.

12. Qutb, *Signposts*, 110 and 196–197.

13. Bruce Lawrence argues that Islamism—and religious fundamentalism more generally—are, even in their anti-modernity, consequences of modern life, aside from the basic fact of being conjunctural, of co-existing at the same time in the contemporary world. To some extent, this is true. If Qutb did not have modernity to attack, there would be no way of contrasting the Islamic system, but also, there would be no reason to do so. That the two are opposites is certainly true. Yet Qutb did not stake out an anti-modernist position merely to be contrarian or confrontational. Nor was he deterministic. Qutb had a genuine critique of modernity and unless an inevitability is assumed, the characteristics he condemned can be altered, if not in their heartland in the West, then at least among their imitators in Egypt and the Muslim world. Only if modernity's attributes are considered fixed and unavoidable, where no thing or no one can change them, can Islamism be considered just a reflection of modernity. Egyptian Islamism appeared with Jamal al-Din al-Afghani in the late 1870s, coinciding with the development of modernity, secularism, and nationalism. Modernity and Islamism emerged, then, as viable alternatives and rivals contesting for Egypt's future. Qutb felt that the vile and evil aspects of the modern world are, indeed, contingent and can be rejected and destroyed, and that the utopia of his Islamic society can actually be realized and achieved through human effort. Bruce Lawrence, *Defenders of God: The Fundamentalist Revolt against the Modern Age* (Columbia: University of South Carolina Press, 1989), ch. 1.

14. The unity of religion and worldly affairs, when combined with an active faith (as opposed to a contemplative faith) suggests an almost Calvinist perspective: faith requires good deeds, and good deeds are motivated by faith. But of course, there is a notable difference between Islam and Calvinism: good works in Islam is not the accumulation of individual wealth, as in Calvinism, but rather the collective installation of an Islamic system.

15. The act of modernization clearly does not strike the West as at all inappropriate and appears quite rational, liberal, and even desirable. Neither did Islamization seem out of place for Qutb. The 500-year universalization of European-based modernity did not take place without its own violence, yet few people today would deny that not only has modernity covered the world, but that, moreover, it *should* cover the world. Western imperialism can be justified because it spreads a presumably beneficial modernity to all corners of the globe. Many Americans and Europeans would agree that it is acceptable to spread democracy "by the sword" (or the barrel of a gun) because it is so advantageous to all people. Qutb's rival vision for a universalized Islam was nothing less. He felt no less committed to the spread of what he saw as the salvation of the world, no less but no more messianic than staunch modernizers.

Yet even though spreading modernization required a militancy in order to expand worldwide, Islamization need not be done just through violence. After all, Islamic *da'wa* can take place, and does not appear all that different from the Protestant missionary campaigns of the 19th century that, for Europe, comprised one thrust of its colonial project, often euphemized as "White Man's Burden," "*Mission Civilatrice*," or "Manifest Destiny." A similar spreading of Islam—and of course, properly recognizing that "there is no compulsion in religion" [Qur'an 2:256]—has become one of the important duties for good Muslims.

In examining the emergence of Protestant fundamentalism in the United States from the 1880s to the 1920s, George Marsden remarks that many Americans saw modernity as merely a disguise for Protestantism. The Christian fundamentalists, he claims, were more honest in actually keeping God in their religion and in their lives, and thereby accepting the label "Protestant" rather than call themselves "modern." If Marsden's conclusion is correct—that modernity is just a non-deistic camouflage for Protestant Christian social values, as Max Weber once concluded as well—then Qutb and his followers essentially sought to reverse or eliminate this Christianization masquerading as modernization. George Marsden, *Understanding Fundamentalism and Evangelicalism* (Grand Rapids, MI: William B. Eerdmans, 1991), 91–92.

16. Qutb, *Signposts*, 106–107 and 136–138.

17. When I conducted field research on the Islamic movement in southern Egypt, most of the informants I met had migrated from the countryside to provincial towns and capitals. Many felt that now, since they resided in the cosmopolitan city, they would adopt a newer and more modern version of Islam. They turned their backs on the otherworldly Islam of the village that had included Sufism, saint shrines, and miracles. Instead, they embraced the unyielding Islam advocated by Qutb (and others) that consisted of salafiyyism, legalism, and self-righteousness. They chose a modern doctrine, but one that involved a religious, not a secular, modernity. It was one that functioned to integrate ex-village newcomers with long-time urban residents and to try to realize their immediate goals of revitalizing Egyptian society, advancing its impoverished economy, and empowering the country's disenfranchised citizens, along with their longer-term goals of installing an Islamic system. See James Toth, "Local Islam Gone Global: The Roots of Religious Militancy in Egypt and Its Transnational Transformation," in *Global Social Movements: A Reader*, June Nash, ed. (Oxford: Blackwell, 2004), 124–125.

18. For information about the first two scholars, see note 58, Chapter 2. Khalid Muhammad Khalid attempted to bring together Islam and socialism. He followed in the footsteps of 'Ali 'Abd al-Raziq, Taha Husayn, and Ahmad Amin, an Azhar graduate who strongly advocated secularism. In the 1950s, Khalid came under the influence of Jamal 'Abd al-Nassir and his economic nationalism, but later became disenchanted with that administration which drove him closer to the Muslim Brotherhood. His book on Islamic secularism, *Min Huna Nabda'* (From Here We Start) became more famous (or infamous) with the well-known rebuttal by Muhammad al-Ghazali *Min Huna Na'lam* (From Here We Learn), also translated as *Our Beginning in Wisdom* by Isma'il R. el-Faruqi, (Washington, DC: American Council of Learned Societies, 1953).

19. Qutb, *Signposts*, 208–209. Qutb argued that

> The experimental method, which is the dynamic spirit of modern Europe's industrial culture, did not originate in Europe, but originated in the Islamic universities of Andalucía and of the East. The principle of the experimental method was an offshoot of the Islamic concept and its explanations of the physical world, its phenomena, its forces, and its secrets. Later, by adopting this method, Europe entered into the period of scientific revival, which led, step by step, to greater scientific heights. Meanwhile, the Muslim world gradually drifted away from Islam, as a consequence of which the scientific movement first became inert and later ended completely. Some of the causes which led to this state of inertia were internal to the Muslim society and some were external, such as the invasions of the Muslim world by the Christians and Zionists. Europe removed the foundation of Islamic belief from the methodology of the empirical sciences, and finally, when Europe rebelled against the Church, which in the name of God oppressed the common people, it deprived the empirical sciences of their Islamic method of relating them to God's guidance.

20. Among the humanities, Qutb listed the study of religion, history, psychology, sociology, philosophy, and ethics. He did not include my own discipline of anthropology, but he may well have since it so strongly promotes cultural relativity. For Qutb, the concept of culture, or "civilization" as he called it, meant following a fixed, permanent set of values revealed by God. When challenged by the wide variation in culture as "the human heritage," Qutb noted that "this statement about culture is one of the tricks played by world Jewry whose purpose is to eliminate all limitations...imposed by faith and religion." Was he referring specifically to

Franz Boas, the Jewish physicist and geographer who immigrated from Germany to America in 1887 and who almost single-handedly reversed anthropology's dismal racialist dogmas and introduced the concept of cultural relativity that is so widespread today? If so, then Qutb may well have been right. He could also have been referring to Sigmund Freud, Karl Marx, or Emile Durkheim. Qutb, *Signposts*, 207.

21. Ibid., 205–206; Shepard, *Sayyid Qutb and Islamic Activism*, 301.

22. Qutb, *Signposts*, 216. Although Qutb claimed that Islam did not oppose science, as religion did historically in Europe, he may well have just meant Baconian science, in contrast to Kantian science. The first refers to the finding and organizing of facts and discovering the laws of nature. Here, there is a hard, absolute objective evidence with no room for misinterpretation. "In this view, human senses apprehend facts, and reason discerns the underlying order in them. The task of science, then, is to catalog, organize, and derive theories about the true facts of the universe." Qutb would have agreed entirely, for he saw all sciences leading toward God and documenting His dominion.

    By contrast, there is Kantian science, which is much less acceptable to devout believers. Here, "objective truth is always filtered through subjective experience and perception and thus scientific knowledge is always shaped by the cultural and historical context in which it emerges." This is a more slippery, subjective, and relativistic approach to science that argues against an absolute set of known and accepted facts or values. Instead, "truth" depends on a person's social and historical position. Despite his earlier subjectivism when he was in the Diwan school, Qutb came to see this relativism to be "poisonous" and warned Muslims to be on their guard and stay away from the philosophical speculations of these sciences because of their hatred of religion. Qutb, *Signposts*, 217; Nancy T. Ammerman, "North American Protestant Fundamentalism," in *Fundamentalisms Observed*, Martin E. Marty and R. Scott Appleby, eds. (Chicago: University of Chicago Press, 1991), 9–10.

23. Qutb fumed against modern intellectuals and writers, calling them "Orientalists" and seeing them as major enemies of Islam. The Orientalists' view of Islam might well poison the innocent and naive mind of unsuspecting Muslims who study their own religion under Western tutelage. Edward Said similarly warned Muslims about so-called communities of interpretation, or Western institutions—the media, universities, and so-called Middle East experts—that provide simplified, reductive, monochromatic, and prejudiced images of Islam, especially to those otherwise uneducated about the nuanced details and beauty of their own religion. Edward Said, *Covering Islam: How the Media and the Experts Determine How We See the Rest of the World* (New York: Vintage Books, 1997), 47–58, especially 56; Ibrahim M. Abu-Rabi', *Intellectual Origins of Islamic Resurgence in the Modern Arab World* (Albany: State University of New York Press, 1996), 200–201.

24. Qutb, *Signposts*, 210–211. Some years later, while he was in prison, he wrote the following lines describing (in the third person) his years immediately after World War II.

> The person who is writing these lines has spent forty years of his life in reading books and in research in almost all aspects of human knowledge. He specialized in some branches of knowledge and studied others due to personal interest. Then he turned to the fountainhead of his faith. He came to feel that whatever he had read so far was as nothing in comparison to what he found here. He does not regret spending forty years of his life in the pursuit of these sciences because he came to know the nature of *jahiliyya*, its deviations, its errors and its ignorance, as well as its pomp and noise, its arrogant and boastful claims. Finally, he was convinced that a Muslim cannot combine these two sources—the source of divine guidance and the source of *jahiliyya*—for his education. (Ibid.)

25. More specifically, he criticized the Darwinist perspective of Europe's Thomas Huxley and Egypt's Shibli Shumayyil and Salama Musa. Qutb, *Signposts*, 206; Adnan A. Musallam, *Sayyid Qutb: The Emergence of the Islamicist, 1939–1950* (Jerusalem: Palestinian Academic Society for the Study of International Affairs, 1990), 17; Olivier Carré, *Mysticism and Politics: A Critical Reading of* Fi Zilal al-Qur'an *by Sayyid Qutb (1906–1966)* (Leiden: Brill, 2003), 56.

26. Islam's inclusion of both orthopraxy and orthodoxy makes it a different religion from Christianity. Yet some scholars still seem to define religion *in general* as just faith and belief. They then go on to depict Islam as a quaint throwback or, at least, as a deviation from this normative definition since Islam so clearly has a set of divine practices. The well-known anthropologist, Clifford Geertz, for one, characterizes religion by offering the following definition:

> A religion is (1) a system of symbols which acts to (2) establish powerful, pervasive, and long-lasting moods and motivations in men [*sic*] by (3) formulating conceptions of a general order of existence and (4) clothing these conceptions with such an aura of factuality that (5) the moods and motivations seem uniquely realistic. Clifford Geertz, *The Interpretation of Cultures* (New York: Basic Books, 1973), 90.

This definition holds true only insofar as "religion" is defined just as faith and belief, based exclusively on the Christian experience. But were "religion" defined on the basis of Islam, it would contain both correct belief *and* correct practice. This combination makes secularization a much more difficult process in Islam than in Christianity, where laws have never had divine authority.

This difference also makes such a phrase as "religion and politics" redundant, since the first already includes the second. Should we go further and bracket "political Islam" as an *improper* use of religion for political purposes, this not only ignores the redundancy of the phrase for Islam, but more importantly, it improperly and ethnocentrically raises Christianity's architecture as a universal structure. Talal Asad, *Genealogies of Religion: Discipline and Reasons of Power in Christianity and Islam* (Baltimore: Johns Hopkins University Press, 1993), ch. 1. For more on the use of the term Islamism, see note 10 in this chapter and note 7 in chapter 1.

Judaism, the first of the major Middle East monotheisms, was also difficult to secularize in its templar version. It took the violent destruction of the Second Temple by the Romans in 70—and notwithstanding the Bar-Kochba campaign to restore the Jewish state in 132–35—to transform Judaism from a religion with divine laws administered by sovereign government officials to one where these are enforced inside the states of others by little more than rabbinic authority, community pressure, and group solidarity.

Yet before its defeat under Roman occupation, Judaism was both correct practice *and* belief. In fact, Judaism during the Second Temple was primarily law and practice, while faith and belief were less emphasized as private, personal matters. It was just to infuse Judaism with this kind of greater spiritualism that Jesus led one of several humanizing movements within Judaism after the Hellenistic period that aimed for a greater balance of faith and practice. Since his reforms initially relied on Jewish legal codes, there was no need for religious law. Hugh J. Schonfield, *The Passover Plot: New Light on the History of Jesus* (New York: Bantam Books, 1965), ch. 1.

When Christians and Jews were expelled from Israel and their religions separated, Christians obeyed the dominant, but non-divine Roman legal system, and rejected what formerly had been Jewish law, which now lacked official state sanctions. Christianity has never followed divinely revealed laws like Judaism and Islam have, notwithstanding its canonical and ecclesiastical legal codes.

I wish to thank Peter Machinist for his wonderful assistance and perseverance in helping me understand Jewish law and legal codification.

27. Richard H. Tawney, *Religion and the Rise of Capitalism* (London: Penguin Books, 1926 [reprint 1990]), 22.

28. Nationalism appears more easily accommodated in a Christianity that focuses only on the spiritual dimension and that adjusts, chameleon-like, to the legal contours of whatever society it finds itself in. Islam, by contrast, has both spiritual *and* political elements, so that an unsecularized Islam has much less flexibility or adaptability since it insists that both elements must be enforced. Abu-Rabi', *Intellectual Origins*, 13.

29. Khatab, *The Power of Sovereignty*, 120–121. It was once the case that nationalism was the preeminent and most modern way of identifying oneself. Anything else was considered primitive,

perhaps even atavistic. Historians portrayed Europe and America as rationally progressing toward a nationalism, and earlier identities were discarded. Now, however, in the post-modern world, religion and religious identities are surging back in full force as a worldwide phenomenon. Not all these renewed religious identities are Islamic ones—Protestant, Catholic, Jewish, Hindu fundamentalism also exist—but they are all expanding as national identity assumes secondary importance. Perhaps now, we might even conclude that the Age of Nationalism was simply a brief respite between two periods of intense religious identification. Islam is not the only resurgent religion. Qutb may well be a pioneer of a sectarian future.

30. Ibid., 124–125.
31. Ibid., 120.
32. Al-Afghani's successors—'Abduh, Rida, al-Banna, and Qutb—considered the same problem. Neither Europe during the Renaissance of the 15th and 16th centuries nor Egypt and the Muslim world over the last century have had an easy time changing from a primary identity based on religion to a primary identity based on language, ethnicity, culture, and history, however "inevitable" these were thought to be. The extensive life span of the Islamic movement reflects, in part, the long duration of this question of primary identity and loyalty.
33. Qutb, *Signposts*, 238–239; Shepard, *Sayyid Qutb and Islamic Activism*, 326.
34. Qutb, *Signposts*, 43.
35. Carré, *Mysticism and Politics*, 159–161.
36. Qutb, *Signposts*, 52–53.
37. The classical example would be the different practices and understandings of Islam found in Morocco and in Indonesia, as described by Clifford Geertz, *Islam Observed: Religious Development in Morocco and Indonesia* (New Haven: Yale University Press, 1968).
38. For more, see the section on "Usury" in Chapter 9.
39. Khatab, *The Power of Sovereignty*, 137.
40. Maxime Rodinson emphasizes this support for private property so that he could conclude that Islam is not anti-capitalist. This is true; yet Qutb's understanding of Islam was to harshly criticize the morals and polarization found in European capitalism, and it is not clear whether he considered these fundamental to capitalism per se or just abhorrent characteristics of Europe's own version of it. Maxime Rodinson, *Islam and Capitalism*, Brian Pearce, trans. (Austin: University of Texas Press, 1978), 14. Also, see the section on "Capitalism" in Chapter 9.
41. Qutb, *Social Justice*, 130. For more on Islamic punishments, see the section "Law-Breaking and Punishments" in Chapter 10.
42. Khatab, *The Power of Sovereignty*, 142.
43. Ibid., 139, 143–144, 146, and 147.
44. Shepard, *Sayyid Qutb and Islamic Activism*, 129–130.
45. Abu-Rabi', *Intellectual Origins*, 160–161. Qutb opposed capitalist property arrangements; for its Islamic counterpart, for what Islam offers, see Chapter 9.
46. Many of the early converts to Islam were from the impoverished class. Many of those who did have land and wealth converted later.
47. Qutb, *Social Justice*, 86
48. Abu-Rabi', *Intellectual Origins*, 161.
49. This echoes the arguments of the French Marxist, Nicos Poulantzas, who concludes that the modern capitalist state splits people apart, then only brings them back together under its own aegis and control. Nicos Poulantzas, "Introduction," in *Classes in Contemporary Capitalism*, David Fernbach, trans. (London: Verso Press, 1974). Also see the discussion in the section "Rich and Poor" in Chapter 9.
50. Abu-Rabi', *Intellectual Origins*, 160–161.
51. Khatab, *The Power of Sovereignty*, 151.
52. Recall that the Chinese Communist Party under Mao Tse-tung once derisively called the Communism of its rival, the Soviet Union, "state capitalism" for preserving capitalist operations, but centralizing them under one "owner"—the state.
53. For more on income redistribution in Islam, see the section on "Zakat" in Chapter 9.

54. Only later, after the assassination of 'Abd al-Nassir's successor, Anwar al-Sadat, and the trial of his Islamist assassins when al-Azhar was so seriously embarrassed, did members of this grand university reverse their collaboration and move in a different religious direction.

55. Khatab, *The Power of Sovereignty*, 151–153.

56. Ibid., 159.

57. Ibid., 165 and 170.

58. Calling the Qur'an the Islamic "constitution" is a common metaphor. Hasan al-Banna formulated the well-known expression used regularly by the Muslim Brothers: "God is our goal, the Prophet is our leader, the Qur'an is our constitution, struggle is our way, and death in the service to God is the loftiest of our wishes" (*Allah ghayatuna, al-Rasul za'imuna, al-Qur'an dusturuna, al-jihad sabiluna, al-mawt fi sabil Allah asma amanina*). Richard P. Mitchell, *The Society of the Muslim Brothers* (Oxford: Oxford University Press, 1969), 193–194.

59. Khatab, *The Power of Sovereignty*, 171.

60. Malcolm H. Kerr, *Islamic Reform: The Political and Legal Theories of Muhammad 'Abduh and Rashid Rida* (Berkeley: University of California Press, 1966).

Chapter 9

1. Historically, usury referred to "'whatever is added to the principal' on a loan, or simply 'profit from a loan.'" After the medieval period, scholars slowly began to distinguish between *interesse* and *usura* such that usury came to designate *excessive* or even *illegal* interest rates. The slippage is significant as interest payments became morally acceptable in Western Christianity in the 16th century. John T. Noonan, Jr., *The Scholastic Analysis of Usury* (Cambridge, MA: Harvard University Press, 1957), 31–32; Richard H. Tawney, *Religion and the Rise of Capitalism* (London: Penguin Books, 1926), 54; Benjamin Nelson, *The Idea of Usury: From Tribal Brotherhood to Universal Otherhood* (Chicago: University of Chicago Press, 1969), 17 and 24. The Oxford English Dictionary also reflects this ambiguity: "The fact or practice of lending money at interest; esp. in later use, the practice of charging, taking, or contracting to receive, excessive or illegal rates of interest for money on loan." "usury, n.." OED Online, March 2011, Oxford University Press, http://0-www.oed.com.ilsprod.lib.neu.edu/view/Entry/220740?rskey=leuTFo&result=1&isAdvanced=false.

    The concept of *riba* underwent the same confusion. Today, modern banking and interest-bearing loans flourish in Egypt in part as a result of Muhammad 'Abduh who, as Mufti of Egypt, issued a fatwa that permitted interest payments. El-Gamal quotes 'Abduh's approval of *riba* from the Mufti's 1906 article published in Rashid Rida's journal, *al-Manar*. Mahmoud A. El-Gamal, *Islamic Finance: Law, Economics, and Practice* (Cambridge: Cambridge University Press, 2006), 142 and 208.

2. For more on using the term "social democracy," see note 20 in Chapter 1.

3. William E. Shepard, *Sayyid Qutb and Islamic Activism: A Translation and Critical Analysis of Social Justice in Islam* (Leiden: E. J. Brill, 1996), 15.

4. Eric Wolf coined the term "many-stranded" to refer to multi-purpose hierarchical relationships in peasant societies. Eric Wolf, *Peasants* (Englewood Cliffs, NJ: Prentice-Hall, 1966), 81.

5. Unlike the Calvinism of Reformation England where poverty was an individual opportunity to show God's predetermined blessings or (more likely) His damnation.

6. For more on Poulantzas, see note 49 in Chapter 8.

7. Shepard, *Sayyid Qutb and Islamic Activism*, 132.

8. Both managers and workers are expected to be fair and honest toward one another; otherwise, the ensuing corrupt spirit will deaden both the immediate relationship and the larger community climate in which production and work take place. Wages should be paid promptly and directly, and truthfully reflect the amount of work, skills, and incentives involved. If employment does not generate enough income, the worker is eligible for *zakat*, but this depends, obviously, on an accurate assessment of needs and abilities.

9. Ibrahim M. Abu-Rabi', *Intellectual Origins of Islamic Resurgence in the Modern Arab World* (Albany: State University of New York Press, 1996), 116.

10. Sayyid Qutb, *al-'Adala al-Ijtima'iyya fi al-Islam* (Social Justice in Islam) (Cairo: Maktabat Misr, 1949 [reprint, Oneonta, NY: Islamic Publications International, 2000]), 155–157.

11. Ibid., 158–159.

12. Qutb, *Social Justice*, 153–162. Thus, Qutb's *jihad* to abolish this unbalanced and unharmonious system clearly has the outlines of popular revolutions elsewhere in the modern world. Yet unlike Marx, with his emphasis on class relations, Qutb instead focused on relations with the state, leaving class relatively untouched. Based on my reading of Qutb, he did not advocate a classless society by any means. Wealth, legitimately earned according to the *shari'a*, is valuable and good. Poverty is perhaps unfortunate, but the poor should still have a respectable life. It is excess that is detestable, but short of this, ordinary differences between the rich and the poor are acceptable. What is not tolerable, however, is a corrupt, arrogant, and tyrannical government that protects such extremes.

13. Thus the title of Christopher Hill's path-breaking book on the English revolution: *The World Turned Upside Down: Radical Ideas during the English Revolution* (London: Maurice Temple Smith, 1972).

14. Max Weber, *Protestant Ethic and the Spirit of Capitalism* (New York: Routledge, 2002); Richard H. Tawney, *Religion and the Rise of Capitalism* (London: Penguin Books, 1926 [reprint 1990]), 212–213.

15. Shepard, *Sayyid Qutb and Islamic Activism*, 160–161. Abu Ahwas al-Jashimi is spelled Abu al-Akwas al-Jashmi in Qutb 2000, 161.

16. Abu-Rabi', *Intellectual Origins*, 116–117; Shepard, *Sayyid Qutb and Islamic Activism*, 143.

17. Shepard, *Sayyid Qutb and Islamic Activism*, 147.

18. Qutb, *Social Justice*, 163–164.

19. The best-known scholar is Khalid Muhammad Khalid. For a biographical sketch, see note 18 in Chapter 7.

20. The rate of 2½ percent is standard, but the rates actually vary according to the type of asset. Crops from unirrigated agricultural land require a 10 percent donation, but 5 percent for irrigated land. Investment and inventory generate other amounts, depending on the nature of these assets.

21. Shepard, *Sayyid Qutb and Islamic Activism*, 94.

22. Ibid., 99.

23. Tawney, *Religion and the Rise of Capitalism*, 251–270.

24. Shepard, *Sayyid Qutb and Islamic Activism*, 167.

25. Olivier Carré, *Mysticism and Politics: A Critical Reading of Fi Zilal al-Qur'an by Sayyid Qutb (1906–1966)* (Leiden: Brill, 2003), 216.

26. Charles Tripp, *Islam and the Moral Economy: The Challenge of Capitalism* (Cambridge: Cambridge University Press, 2006), 127; Maxime Rodinson, *Islam and Capitalism*, Brian Pearce, trans. (Austin: University of Texas Press, 1978), 36.

27. Shepard, *Sayyid Qutb and Islamic Activism*, 145–147.

28. Qutb, *Social Justice*, 151. Qur'an 2:280 reads in full: "And if the debtor is in straitened circumstances, then let there be postponement to the time of ease; and that ye remit the debt as almsgiving would be better for you if ye did but know."

29. Shepard, *Sayyid Qutb and Islamic Activism*, 148.

30. In pre-modern Europe, high prices and wide price differentials were often condemned for disguising usury and for accomplishing the same result that interest-bearing credit achieved. The difficulty with commercial profit was that merchants were recognized as needing income, but were only allowed a moderate lifestyle. Anything higher, a lavish lifestyle, was noticeable and could spark accusations of excessive profits, or usury. Yet what constituted appropriate and moderate circumstances and how consumption needs could be so precisely determined were never satisfactorily determined. Tawney, *Religion and the Rise of Capitalism*, 48–67.

31. Carré, *Mysticism and Politics*, 217.

32. See Martin Wilmington's case study on traditional, informal banking in northern Sudan where high rates were not uncommon. Wilmington concludes that such rates were justified because of the risk, the alternative uses for capital, and the general volatility of the market. Martin Wilmington, "Aspects of Moneylending in Northern Sudan," *Middle East Journal* 9, no. 2 (Spring 1955): 139–146.

33. Carré, *Mysticism and Politics,* 216–217.
34. For more, see Gamal, *Islamic Finance;* Timur Kuran, *Islam and Mammon: The Economic Predicaments of Islamism* (Princeton: Princeton University Press, 2004); Zamir Iqbal and Abbas Mirakhor, *An Introduction to Islamic Finance: Theory and Practice* (Singapore: John Wiley, 2007).
35. In the early editions of *Social Justice,* Qutb emphasized community ownership, but in the later editions, while he was in prison, the perspective turned to seeing it as the property of God and then delegated first to the community and later to individual owners. Shepard, *Sayyid Qutb and Islamic Activism.*
36. Qutb, *Social Justice,* 134 and 137–138. I imagine the enclosure laws that privatized the medieval commons and so enraged Renaissance Europe would be proscribed here.
37. Today, the Hamas organization considers all of Palestine a *waqf* from God that cannot be separated into a two-state solution. Its charter states:

    The Islamic Resistance Movement believes that the land of Palestine is an Islamic *waqf* consecrated for future Muslim generations until Judgment Day. It, or any part of it, should not be squandered: it, or any part of it, should not be given up.

38. Located structurally between the peasant and the ruler came various state-sponsored intermediaries, who collected rents or taxes. Charles Issawi, *An Economic History of the Middle East and North Africa* (London: Methuen, 1982), 134–135.
39. Nicholas S. Hopkins, "Land Tenure," in *The Oxford Encyclopedia of the Modern Islamic World,* John L. Esposito, ed. (New York: Oxford University Press, 1995), 446–450. Kenneth Cuno presents the most detailed description of land tenure before the adoption of the European concepts of absolute private ownership in the 19th century. He points out that the fine "distinction between ownership of the land and the possession of its usufruct" tended to be disregarded by rural folk. This ambiguity perfectly mirrors Qutb's conclusion: that God is the owner of land, and that peasants, farmers, and others use land as its stewards. Or rather, they use the *usufruct rights* of the land as its guardians, treating these use rights pretty much like absolute ownership. Yet while they can use this resource, they are not allowed to abuse it, since it is a collective trust, not an absolute, individual right.

    In reviewing the position of the four different schools of Islamic jurisprudence, Cuno also points out that the debate over the true locus of actual ownership—the state or the peasant—was a significant one among legal scholars. Were the state the owner, then peasant inheritance was null and void. But were the peasant the owner (or usufruct holder), and if inheritance operated according to Islamic principles, then the state was denied many of the rights it otherwise claimed. Kenneth M. Cuno, *The Pasha's Peasants: Land, Society, and Economy in Lower Egypt, 1740–1858* (New York: Cambridge University Press, 1992), 64–84.
40. See the discussion in the section, "Islam versus Capitalism" in Chapter 8.
41. Sisters receive one half the portion their brothers inherit. Such unequal inheritance is a major element in the West's condemnation of unequal gender relations in the Muslim world. The common justification is that males are heads of families and therefore must support them. Females, on the other hand, need not be income-earners, although, of course, many are and many have to be. But even when they do earn an income, that income need not strictly go to support the family. Women can inherit, but often do not, with the property remaining with a brother as social security should the woman's marriage break up or should her marital relations require an ally. She can then depend on that brother without being faulted.
42. Impartible inheritance in Europe has weakened under pressure from both the landed aristocracy and the commercial real estate market. As early as the French Revolution, laws began to change so that minimal amounts were bequeathed to each heir. But in England, it was not until 1925 that primogeniture was legally abolished, and even then, parents frequently singled out one heir with testate inheritance or preliminary sales. Many countries continue the tradition by discouraging the division of land in order to maintain a viable agrarian economy and many property owners simply resist and evade the new laws. "Primogeniture," *International Encyclopedia of Marriage and Family,* 2003, *Encyclopedia.com* (February 11, 2012), www.encyclopedia.com/doc/1G2-3406900341.html.

43. Impartibility is not just the evidence of material pursuit; it also reflects ecological variations, economies of scale, and rational land management.

In their study of both patterns of inheritance found in close proximity in northern Italy, Eric Wolf and John Cole conclude that the impartible inheritance system helped contribute to the rise of capitalism since it discarded disinherited siblings who then moved to the cities to fuel the engines of a nascent industrial capitalism and its "dark, Satanic mills." By contrast, they argued, the system of partible inheritance (shared with Islamic societies) led to under-development, poverty, and backwardness since more and more heirs over the generations divided up a fixed amount of land.

What is ignored here, however, is that Islamic partible inheritance does not fragment infinitesimally since even before commercial markets, land was recombined through strategic marriages, either within the family (endogamy: cousin marriages) or outside (exogamy: ficti-tious cousin marriages). Frederik Barth, "Father's Brother's Daughter Marriage in Kurdistan," *Southwestern Journal of Anthropology* 10, no. 2 (Summer 1954): 64–171; Robert Murphy and Leonard Kasdan, "The Structure of Parallel Cousin Marriage," *American Anthropologist*, 61 (1959): 117–129.

Nor does partibility limit occupational diversity, since some brothers can remain in agriculture yet others can go work elsewhere even while their land is managed by those staying at home. This also provides a safety net should industrialization or the urban economy more generally decline. It creates a greater adaptability since all brothers do have a source of income, yet all brothers—but one—can just as well work elsewhere and then leave the single, designated brother back home to manage their shared property. Thus, far from one system being "modern" and the other system being "backward," both systems can generate urban migration from the countryside.

Although Europe's system of primogeniture and impartibility had weakened, as indicated in the previous note, Wolf and Cole felt justified in continuing to treat the two different sys-tems as they were traditionally structured because even as recently as the 1950s, "the past mechanics of the inheritance process are still at work."

Eric Wolf, *Peasants* (Englewood Cliffs, NJ: Prentice-Hall, 1966), 73–77; John W. Cole and Eric R. Wolf, *The Hidden Frontier: Ecology and Ethnicity in an Alpine Village* (New York: Academic Press, 1974), 42–49, 77–83, 189, and ch. 8.

Chapter 10

1. Sayed Khatab, *The Power of Sovereignty: The Political and Ideological Philosophy of Sayyid Qutb* (London: Routledge, 2006), 7.
2. A ruler in Islam who claims holiness, inviolability, and infallibility, as priests and popes do in Catholicism, is claiming co-equality with God, an associationalism or polytheism that is strictly forbidden.
3. Khatab, *The Power of Sovereignty*, 8.
4. This is really not much different from the halls of Western government being filled with grad-uates from law schools and business colleges. In Islam, highly educated and knowledgeable religious figures, graduates of al-Azhar University in Egypt or the Qum theological seminary in Iran (among others), are those who are deeply familiar with Islamic law, making them per-fectly qualified for office.

Ruhullah Khomeini, for example, was a leading Islamic scholar in Iran and published sev-eral books on Islamic thought, law, and ethics. He seems to have had the equivalent of two PhDs or the German *habilitation*. For this, he received the title of *ayatollah*, the highest reli-gious office in Iran. When the 1979 Islamic revolution instituted the new Shi'ite doctrine of *wilayat al-faqih*, or clerical guardianship, he was highly qualified for the nation's highest political office. His policies were highly controversial, of course, but his credentials do seem impeccable. Certainly he was much more qualified for the highest office in Iran than many politicians in the West, notwithstanding their JD or MBA degrees.

The Iranian situation certainly makes the Islamic state a theocracy, though without a con-secrated priesthood. But then we also need to reevaluate whether this "proscription" is nec-essarily such a terrible thing. In Islam, of course, where religion and government co-exist, the repugnance against a theocracy does not exist. Its religious leaders, therefore, should prove no more incapable than Western leaders in soundly guiding their communities.

5. Khatab, *The Power of Sovereignty*, 29.

6. Legislation in the strict sense does not exist since laws were created once and for all by God Who has the only right to prescribe a program for human life. Of course, Islamic law does change, like medieval "natural law" did in Europe. In Islam, the law is adapted to new circumstances through the process of interpretation. When there is no specific law, then instead of legislation, there is *ijtihad*, interpretation. The interpreters of *shari'a*, the *mujtahidun*, fashion new clarifications which makes the *mujtahid* a top figure of state, yet, by and large, mostly an office that provides input to the judicial branch. *Muftis* (legal scholars) and *qadis* (judges) issue *fatawi* (sing., *fatwa*) that provide people with an understanding of how Islamic law currently comprehends and resolves specific issues. Under no circumstance does the *mufti* or *qadi* actually legislate in an Islamic state nor should there be any parliament or congress to pass man-made laws.

   Thus, laws already exist, or can exist through practical interpretation. But a democratic parliament entails the possibility of annulling God's law and thus is prohibited as a flagrant blasphemy and disobedience of God and His power. However, some liberal Islamic thinkers, such as Egypt's Hasan Hanafi, claim that a public debate between rival interpretations, each with slightly different priorities in how they reach their new understanding, might act as a parliament of sorts. But Qutb would not have agreed with this view.

   Among the variations in modern, secular democracies worldwide, the government system is either strongly unified around a president or else mildly centralized around a parliament or congress. The French have the first, the British have the second, and the United States oscillates between the two. In the Middle East, however, both of these branches today are suspected or accused outright of corruption and malfeasance. There is, however, the third branch, the judiciary—somewhat downplayed in the West—which appears the most effective, honest, and trustworthy, and the most publicly visible. It is the one branch most ordinary Middle East people respect, engage with, or confront. It is then followed (in terms of importance) by the executive who should "merely" administer the law and the outcome of judicial proceeding but who, in actuality, commandeers and consolidates much power—often too much—in his own hands, legitimately or otherwise. The last branch—the Parliament or National Assembly—trails in this regard, often appearing more or less as an ineffective debate club or an executive rubber stamp.

7. Khatab, *The Power of Sovereignty*, 38.

8. Sayyid Qutb, *al-'Adala al-Ijtima'iyya fi al-Islam* (Social Justice in Islam) (Cairo: Maktabat Misr, 1949 [reprint, Oneonta, NY: Islamic Publications International, 2000]), 120–121.

9. Parallels with the attitudes toward the constitution in the United States are instructive. Both documents are considered relatively permanent, one is divinely written, the other is not, but is often considered sacred and is difficult to amend, particularly by strict constructionists, federalists (the "Hanbalis" of American politics), and originalists (the "Salafis" of the US judiciary).

   Strict constructionism refers to a conservative legal philosophy that restricts judicial interpretation. It requires a judge to apply the text only as it is literally written. Once the court has a clear meaning of the wording, no further considerations are required. The doctrine is also used as an umbrella term for conservative legal philosophies such as originalism and textualism.

   Originalism is a set of theories that holds that the US constitution has a fixed and knowable meaning, which was established at the time of its original drafting. The interpretation of the constitution should be consistent with what was intended by those who drafted and ratified it or else should be based on what reasonable persons living at the time of its adoption (the "*salaf*") would have declared the ordinary meaning of the text to be.

   Textualism is a theory of legal interpretation that assumes that a law's ordinary meaning should govern its interpretation, as opposed to legislative intent, the initiating problem, or questions of justice and truth. It is a formalist theory that separates legal reasoning from normative or policy considerations.

Rulings issued by the US Supreme Court seem comparable to the *fatwa/fatawi*, or legal pronouncements and decision, emanating from the Islamic *muftis* and *qadis*. Both represent strict interpretations of their respective charters.

10. Qutb, *Social Justice*, 124.

11. Qutb's emphasis noticeably shifted as time went by, from stressing less the bottom-up obedience to authority to focusing more on top-down justice owed the people, with the expectations of the citizens trumping those of the ruler. This was a reflection of his own transformations and his increasing antagonism to Egypt's ruling government, either the king of old or the president in Egypt's new republican system. Shepard, *Sayyid Qutb and Islamic Activism*, xxxvii.

12. Olivier Carré, *Mysticism and Politics: A Critical Reading of* Fi Zilal al-Qur'an *by Sayyid Qutb (1906–1966)* (Leiden: Brill, 2003), 175.

13. Khatab, *Political Thought*, 34; Carré, *Mysticism and Politics*, 180–181; Shepard, *Sayyid Qutb and Islamic Activism*, 112.

14. Carré, *Mysticism and Politics*, 81.

15. Ibid., 178–179.

16. Denise Aigle, "The Mongol Invasions of Bilad al-Sham by Ghazan Khan and Ibn Taymiyah's Three 'Anti-Mongol' Fatwas," *Mamluk Studies Review* 11, no. 2 (2007): 118.

17. The title of sultan was first applied to the Sunni Saljuq ruler, Tughril (r: 1055–63), in 1056, a year after his Turkish nomads from Uzbekistan and Turkestan had conquered Baghdad and abolished the rule of the Shi'ite Persian Buwayhids who themselves had defeated the Abbasid dynasty in 934. Tughril did not depose the incumbent caliph al-Qa'im (r: 1031–75)—because, since Tughril lacked any religious authority, he needed al-Qa'im's legitimacy—but he assumed the real power with al-Qa'im's official recognition. This separated political power from religious authority and reduced the caliphate to puppet status. The Saljuq dynasty of Turkish sultans continued to rule until 1194 and thereafter by Khwarizm Turks until they were conquered by Hulagu Khan, grandson of Genghis Khan, and his Mongol tribes who destroyed Baghdad and the caliphate in 1258. The two offices continued to operate in tandem. Philip K. Hitti, *History of the Arabs* (London: Macmillan, 1970), 474, 476, 482.

18. The first year, 1922, the office was eviscerated and made into a symbolic office. Two years later, the office was abolished altogether.

19. Currently there are two monarchs and royal dynasties ruling in the Arab world who claim a noble pedigree. The king of Jordan, 'Abdullah II, is descended from the Hashim clan of the Quraysh which also furnished kings to Syria and Iraq, imposed after World War I by the British but since abolished. The Alaouite dynasty of King Muhammad VI in Morocco claims descent from the Prophet, his daughter Fatima, and his nephew, 'Ali. Other royalty in the region include the kings of Saudi Arabia and Bahrain, along with rulers in the United Arab Emirates, Kuwait, and Qatar (amirs or princes) and Oman (sultan) but these do not claim descent from the Prophet's family. Historically, there were kings in Egypt and Libya who were not from the Prophet's family. The Imam of Yemen, a member of Zaidi Shi'ite Islam, did claim descent from the Prophet, but was overthrown in 1962.

20. Qutb, *Social Justice*, 208.

21. Despite the practical limits on restoring a worldwide Islamic caliphate, Qutb nevertheless maintained that the Islamic state should be universal. Yet Qutb rejected the idea, first raised by Muhammad Husayn Haykal in the 1930s, that this would create an "Islamic Empire." To Qutb, this phrase suggested the exploitation and oppression practiced by European imperialists. Islam, he concluded, would never be such an imperial power. The Islamic state would, in his mind, be constituted by a number of provinces or existing countries with widely different temperaments, but that they would unite voluntarily and through their common faith. These provinces or countries would not be exploited for their resources or oppressed in order to dominate. There would be a bureaucracy of provincial governors leading up to the imamate, but the local governor would be a smaller version of the *imam* and not a colonial ruler. William E. Shepard, *Sayyid Qutb and Islamic Activism: A Translation and Critical Analysis of* Social Justice in Islam (Leiden: E. J. Brill, 1996), 106.

22. Khatab, *The Power of Sovereignty*, 22–24.

23. This, it seems to me, explains why the common people in Baghdad stood steadfast with Ahmad ibn Hanbal, the founder of the conservative Hanbali school of *fiqh*, in 833, and protested when he was imprisoned by the liberal Mu'tazilite caliph, Abu Ja'far al-Ma'mun. The situation is far too complex and deserves more than just a simple note. But, based on contemporary experiences, I would have guessed the opposite—that the lower classes would have supported the liberals and rejected the conservatives. The paradox is resolved when it becomes clear that a strict adherence to Islamic law benefits the underclasses by keeping the reins tight on the ruling elite. Richard C. Martin and Mark R. Woodward, *Defenders of Reason in Islam* (Oxford: Oneworld, 1997), 18.

24. Sayyid Qutb, *al-Salam al-'Alami wa al-Islam* (Islam and Universal Peace) (Plainfield, IN: American Trust Publications, 1993 [originally published in Cairo: Maktabat Wahbah, 1951]), 53–67, especially page 61.

25. Khatab, *The Power of Sovereignty*, 8.

26. This overview of Egyptian law is drawn from Enid Hill, *al-Sanhuri and Islamic Law* (Cairo: AUC Press, Cairo Papers in the Social Science, vol. 10, monograph 1, Spring, 1987).

27. The *tanzimat*, or reorganization, was a program of modernization in the Ottoman empire from 1839 to 1876 based on European models. It included economic, financial, political, legal, technological, educational, military, and industrial reforms.

28. The longer title is *Murshid al-Hayran ila Ma'rifat Ahwal al-Insan*, Guide of the Confused about Knowledge of the Human Condition. Despite the intriguing and unconventional title, the book was essentially a codification of Hanafi law in Egypt.

29. He claimed that *shari'a* is the best system even for non-Muslims as well, and is the basis, therefore, for including them in the Islamic state. His model of multi-confessionalism basically followed the millet system of the Ottoman Empire with its special taxes and laws for People of the Book.

30. The truth that Qutb endorsed transcends the material truth determined by science. The Qur'an, therefore, cannot be held up to scientific proof, for this implies the possibility of its negation. Nor can the Qur'an be considered "scientifically accurate" (or inaccurate for that matter) for the same reason of denying its divine character. It is a priori irrefutable, no matter what science itself can demonstrate. Finally, this truth cannot be compared to the conclusions of secular theories of human and social behavior. The Qur'an is not a theory, but serves as a guide to theory; it comes prior to theory, not as a consequence. It can demonstrate a certain fact of reality, but that reality cannot determine the authenticity of the Qur'an. Science, Qutb argued, deals only with that which is empirical. It cannot, by definition, examine matters that constitute intangible realities, and this is what the Qur'an includes: truths and wisdoms that go beyond empirical verification. Carré, *Mysticism and Politics*, 46–47. Regarding the "truth" to Islamic history, see both the discussion and note 6 in Chapter 11, this volume.

31. Muhammad Iqbal (1877–1938) was a modern poet and scholar of what is today Pakistan. He was one of the founding fathers of the country, along with Muhammad Jinnah. He was born in Lahore and studied in Britain and later Germany where he earned a law degree. He wrote numerous volumes on religion, philosophy, politics, economics, and history—exactly the same topics found in Sayyid Qutb's Islamic concept. He established and promoted the Muslim League and advanced the creation of Pakistan as a distinct Muslim nation, in contrast to Hindu India. He agitated for Islamic revival, advocated greater unity among Muslim nations, supported preserving Islamic law, and questioned the dominance of secularism in Islam and of foreign influences in general. He participated in the Khilafa Movement of South Asia after World War I which had the twofold purpose of preserving the caliphate and seeking Indian independence. His modernist approach to Islam was quite similar to that of Muhammad 'Abduh in Egypt.

32. Sayyid Qutb, *Muqawwimat al-Tasawwur al-Islami* (Basic Principles of the Islamic Worldview), Rami David, trans. (North Halcedon, NJ: Islamic Publications International, 2006), 11; Ibrahim M. Abu-Rabi', *Intellectual Origins of Islamic Resurgence in the Modern Arab World* (Albany: State University of New York Press, 1996), 173; Leonard Binder, *Islamic Liberalism: A Critique of Development Ideologies* (Chicago: University of Chicago Press, 1988), 184 and 197; Carré, *Mysticism and Politics*, 40.

33. Mu'ammar Qadhdhafi of Libya also distinguished himself by abandoning the Sunna and the Traditions and relying, instead, solely on the Qur'an as the only source for Islamic law. François Burgat, *The Islamic Movement in North Africa,* William Dowell, trans. (Austin: University of Texas Press, 1997), ch. 8, and especially page 155.

34. Adnan A. Musallam, *From Secularism to Jihad: Sayyid Qutb and the Foundations of Radical Islam* (Westport, CT: Praeger, 2005), 176–178.

35. Ibid.; Abd al-Ghani Imad, *Hakimmiyyat Allah wa Sultan al-Faqih: Qira'a fi Khitab al-Harakat al-Islamiyya al-Mu'asira* (The Dominion of God and the Rule of [Religious] Law: [Qur'anic] Recitation in the Discourse of the Contemporary Islamic Movement) (Beirut: Dar al-Tali'a li al-Tiba'a wa al-Nashr, 1997).

36. Shepard, *Sayyid Qutb and Islamic Activism,* xiii. Mainstream scholars of Sunni Islam consider the "door to *ijtihad*" closed by the end of the 9th century. A consensus had formed in answering all outstanding religious questions so that no further interpretation was needed and no further legal changes took place. This stagnation continued until the last third of the 19th century when Jamal al-Din al-Afghani "re-opened" the door by introducing the liberal notion of interpretation that had remained alive in his native Shi'ite Iran. In more recent years, this conventional conclusion of closure has been criticized as inaccurate, and the claim made that interpretations and legal changes had more or less continued throughout the centuries, resulting in an eclectic set of legal codes in the Muslim world. For the orthodox view, see Joseph Schacht, *An Introduction to Islamic Law* (Oxford: Clarendon Press, 1964), 70–71. For a critical view, see Wael B. Hallaq, "Was the Gate of Ijtihad Closed?" *International Journal of Middle East Studies* 16, no. 1 (March 1984): 3–41.

37. Ibid.

38. Carré, *Mysticism and Politics,* 187.

39. Khatab, *The Power of Sovereignty,* 38.

40. Sayyid Qutb, *Ma'alim fi al-Tariq* (Signposts on the Road but also translated as Milestones) (Al-Salimiya, Kuwait: Al-Ittihad al-Islami al-'Alami li al-Munazzamat al-Tullabiya [International Islamic Federation of Student Organizations], 1978), 58 and 62.

41. Caesar E. Farah, *Islam: Beliefs and Observances,* 7th ed. (New York: Barron's Educational Series, 2003), 159–161; John L. Esposito, *Islam: The Straight Path,* 3rd ed. (New York: Oxford University Press, 1998), 178.

42. Khatab, *The Power of Sovereignty,* 38–39.

43. Carré, *Mysticism and Politics,* 93 and 184–188; Abu-Rabi', *Intellectual Origins,* 216.

44. See the discussion in Chapter 6 for more about the schools of *kalam.*

45. Abu-Rabi', *Intellectual Origins,* 175.

46. Carré, *Mysticism and Politics,* 185–187; Qutb, *Basic Principles,* 295–303; Shepard, *Sayyid Qutb and Islamic Activism,* 172 and 337.

47. Qutb, *Social Justice,* 300–301.

48. That is, it is limited by the Qur'an.

49. Qutb, *Signposts,* 157–158.

50. Mohammad Hashim Kamali, *Shari'ah Law: An Introduction* (Oxford: Oneworld Book, 2008), 190–194.

51. Carré, *Mysticism and Politics,* 180.

52. For more details on Qutb's attitude about apologetics, see the Appendix, Part IV.

53. Khatab, *The Power of Sovereignty,* 56.

54. Religion, however, is not an equalizer, not even monotheism. Qutb viewed Islam as superior to Judaism and Christianity because Islam corrected the mistakes Jews and Christians made in their faith and practice. See the discussion in the section "Unity (al-tawhid)" and note 21 in Chapter 6 for more on the "mistakes" that both these religions made.

55. Ibid., 137–138; Qutb, *Basic Principles,* 142. If communal prayer is a metaphor for social equality, it should be noted that there are separate men's and women's sections for prayer. Qutb did not list gender as one identity whose inequality should be eliminated.

56. Khatab, *The Power of Sovereignty,* 61.

57. Qutb, *Signposts,* 176–177.

58. Qutb also agreed that these freedoms should be applied to non-Muslims as well. I assume, then, that if people are free from the obstacles that restrict their thinking but still remain affiliated with Christianity, Judaism, or any other religion, then this should be acceptable and agreeable. Qutb maintained that Islam allows every individual the freedom to think about his religion, although he considered the outcome—conversion—obvious. Khatab, *The Power of Sovereignty*, 85.

59. Khatab, *The Power of Sovereignty*, 97. For more on Qutb's ideas about sexuality, discipline, and control, see the Appendix, Part II on "Women and the Family."

60. Shepard, *Sayyid Qutb and Islamic Activism*, xxx. Interestingly, Lila Abu Lughod also concludes that among the Bedouin of northwest Egypt, the freedom to choose requires autonomy, or freedom from subordination. Only if people are truly free can they voluntarily choose to embrace conventional social values. In religion, this means that individual freedom permits people to freely choose to submit to God. Subordination to all others requires negotiations and bargaining. Lila Abu Lughod, *Veiled Sentiments: Honor and Poetry in a Bedouin Society* (Berkeley: University of California Press, 1986), 244–246.

    Charles Lindholm similarly maintains that the Moroccans and the Pathans of Swat Valley, Pakistan he studied claim to follow a strict egalitarianism and a fervent independence. Submission to a higher state authority must either be through coercion exercised by an allegedly (and perhaps exaggerated) brutal strongman or else to a divinely inspired holy man. It is the latter that permits autonomous men to voluntary restrict their freedom and subscribe to God's correct path, the *shari'a*. Charles Lindholm, "Quandaries of Command in Egalitarian Societies: Examples from Swat and Morocco," in *Comparing Muslim Societies: Knowledge and the State in a World Civilization*, Juan R. I. Cole, ed. (Ann Arbor: University of Michigan Press, 1992), 63–94.

61. Qutb, *Signposts*, 180–182. For the distinction between absolutism and relativism, between Baconian and Kantian science, see note 22 in Chapter 8.

62. In his compelling 2007 article on "fun and fundamentalism," Asef Bayat regrets the disappearance of enjoyment and amusement from the discourse of religious fundamentalism in both Iran and Egypt. His article about the contemporary 20th century is suggestive of the stern admonishments of John Calvin, which, in 16th- and 17th-century England, led to the emergence of the Puritans and Pilgrims of New England and elsewhere, and to the Protestant Reform Church. Yet in writing about early modern Europe, Richard Tawney avoids using such words as "Puritanism" or even "asceticism" and calls it "discipline" instead. This kind of discipline is often required at times when people feel under attack from outside their group—a common condition in religious fundamentalism and other social movements. The demand for self-control—but ultimately, a control exercised by a more dominant and higher authority—appears as a reaction against the economic decline, political subordination, and cultural marginalization that is part and parcel of revitalization movements that involve "picking oneself up by one's bootstraps" and forging ahead. Asef Bayat, "Islamism and the Politics of Fun," *Public Culture* 19, no. 3 (Fall 2007), 433–459; Richard H. Tawney, *Religion and the Rise of Capitalism* (London: Penguin Books, 1926 [reprint 1990]), 213–215; Martin E. Marty and R. Scott Appleby, *The Glory and the Power: The Fundamentalist Challenge to the Modern World* (Boston: Beacon Press, 1992), 24–27.

    Islamists like Qutb are often accused of being Puritanical (see note 40 above in Chapter 4). However, Egypt and the Arab world lack some of the critical ingredients for Puritanism. For one, there is no history of original sin which is carried on generation after generation through (immoral) sexual intercourse. Furthermore, there is no tradition claiming that women are inferior (misogyny) for their (more obvious) role in the procreation that transmits this original sin. Both attitudes permeated Europe, but have not affected the Middle East. The issue for Qutb is more about the public display of sexuality instead of its private enjoyment, which, of course, is morally acceptable.

    Rashid Rida (1865–1935) is often credited for introducing Wahhabi morality into Egyptian salafiyyism and Islamism through the pages of his famous journal, *al-Manar*.

63. Musallam, *From Secularism to Jihad*, 28–29 and 73–74.

Chapter 11

1. For the details about the distortion of Christianity and Judaism, see note 21 in Chapter 6. For Qutb's views on People of the Book, or Dhimmis, see Part III in the Appendix.
2. Olivier Carré, *Mysticism and Politics: A Critical Reading of* Fi Zilal al-Qur'an *by Sayyid Qutb (1906–1966)* (Leiden: Brill, 2003), 39.
3. Adnan A. Musallam, *From Secularism to Jihad: Sayyid Qutb and the Foundations of Radical Islam* (Westport, CT: Praeger, 2005), 71; Ibrahim M. Abu-Rabi', *Intellectual Origins of Islamic Resurgence in the Modern Arab World* (Albany: State University of New York Press, 1996), 142.
4. Carré, *Mysticism and Politics,* 160.
5. Despite the pretense of a Rankean objectivism, Western history since the early 20th century has been by and large value laden, constituting forms of a triumphalist "Whig history"—where "the past is an inevitable progression towards greater liberty and enlightenment, culminating in modern forms of liberal democracy, constitutionalism, personal freedom, and scientific progress"—and a *telos*-dominated "presentism"—the present-day uses of history that influence the depictions or interpretations of the past. In the 1970s, however, this subterfuge of neutrality and impartiality became outmoded under pressure from the anti-war movement, the counterculture, particularist histories (black and feminist history), post-modernism, and skepticism about progress. Since the 1990s, post-colonial and subaltern studies in particular have begun to raise significant critiques against, and revisions of, what had exemplified Max Weber's "iron cage" of history's inescapable rationalization.

   For more, see Yemima Ben-Menahem, "Historical Necessity and Contingency" in *A Companion to the Philosophy of History and Historiography,* Aliezer Tucker, ed. (Oxford: Blackwell, 2009), 120–130; Herbert Butterfield, *The Whig Interpretation of History* (London: G. Bell & Sons, 1951 [originally published in 1931]); Dipesh Chakrabarty, "The Muddle of Modernity," *American Historical Review* 116, no. 3 (June 2011): 663–675; Dipesh Chakrabarty, "Postcoloniality and the Artifice of History: Who Speaks for 'Indian' Pasts," *Representations* 37 (Winter 1992): 1–26; Vinayak Chaturvedi, ed., *Mapping Subaltern Studies and the Postcolonial* (New York: Verso Press, 2000); Nicholas B. Dirks, "History as a Sign of the Modern," *Public Culture* 2, no. 2 (Spring 1990): 25–32; Richard Drayton, "Where Does the World Historian Write From? Objectivity, Moral Conscience and the Past and Present of Imperialism," *Journal of Contemporary History* 46 (2011): 671–685; Jeroen Duindam, "Early Modern Europe: Beyond the Strictures of Modernization and National Historiography," *European History Quarterly* 40, no. 4 (2010): 606–623; Kieran Egan, "Progress in Historiography," *Clio* 8, no. 2 (1979): 195–228; Dilip Parameshwar Gaonkar, "On Alternative Modernities," *Public Culture* 11, no. 1 (1999): 1–18; Thomas Gil, "Leopold Ranke," in *A Companion to the Philosophy of History and Historiography,* Aliezer Tucker, ed. (Oxford: Blackwell, 2009), 383–392; Ranajit Guha and Gayatri Chakravorty Spivak, eds., *Selected Subaltern Studies* (New York: Oxford University Press, 1988); Edward Harrison. "Whigs, Prigs, and Historians of Science," *Nature* 329 (September 17, 1987): 213–214; David L. Hull. "In Defense of Presentism," *History and Theory* 18 (1979): 1–15; Sudipta Kaviraj, "An Outline of a Revisionist Theory of Modernity," *European Journal of Sociology* 46, no. 3 (2005): 497–526; Paul Newall, "Historiographic Objectivity," in *A Companion to the Philosophy of History and Historiography,* Aliezer Tucker, ed. (Oxford: Blackwell, 2009), 172–180; Peter Novick, *That Noble Dream: The "Objectivity Question" and the American Historical Profession* (Cambridge: Cambridge University Press, 1988), especially ch. 15 about the crisis in objectivity and truth beginning in the 1980s; Gyan Prakash, "Writing Post-Orientalist Histories of the Third World: Perspectives from Indian Historiography," *Comparative Study of Society and History* 32, no. 2 (April 1990): 383–408; Beverley Southgate, "Postmodernism," in *A Companion to the Philosophy of History and Historiography,* Aliezer Tucker, ed. (Oxford: Blackwell, 2009), 540–549; Hayden White, *Metahistory: The Historical Imagination of 19th Century Europe* (Baltimore: Johns Hopkins University Press), 1973; "Early Modernities," *Daedalus,* special issue, 127, no. 3 (Summer 1998); and "AHR Roundtable: Historians and the Question of 'Modernity,'" *American History Review,* special issue, 116, no. 3 (June 2011). For more about Weber's "iron cage," see his *Protestant Ethic and the Spirit of Capitalism* (New York: Routledge, 2002), 181; Edward A. Tiryakian, "The Sociological Import of a Metaphor: Tracking the Source of Max Weber's 'Iron Cage,'" *Sociological Inquiry* 51, no. 1 (January 1981): 27–33.

6. Virginia Danielson had such a problem in her research about the famous singer, Umm Kalthum, when she tried to find the exact birth date of the Egyptian diva. Egyptian biographers were much more intent on showing the moral goodness of Umm Kalthum's life, and small matters of exact dating were not important to them. Danielson, however, was operating with a different method whereby the true date, time, and place were of the utmost significance. Her method reinforced the "rightness" of science; their method reinforced the "rightness" of their moral system, culturally connected to and derived from the Qur'an.

7. The Bible Criticism School arose out of 18th- and 19th-century rationalism in Tübingen, Germany, and other European universities. Its scholars examined the factual validity of biblical texts, the historical authenticity of Jesus and his divinity, and the accuracy of the mysteries and miracles of the Old and New Testaments. But unlike Christianity, which so critically relies on faith in its miracles as a cornerstone of its religion, Islam has few miracles that can be proven as "unscientific." Still, cases do occur. Taha Husayn's blasphemous suggestion in 1926 that the Qur'an was not divinely authored but instead written by human poets (for more on Husayn's blasphemy, see note 58 in Chapter 2) was replayed in the 1990s in the case of Nasr Abu Zayd (mentioned in note 52 in Chapter 6) who challenged the miraculous origin of the sacred book. In both cases, their transgressions were the same as those of the Tübingen scholars who sought to secularize religion. For more on the "scientific truth" of the Qur'an, see both the discussion in the section "*Shari'a* Law" and note 30 in Chapter 10 about Qur'anic interpretation.

8. Abu-Rabi', *Intellectual Origins*, 206; William E. Shepard, *Sayyid Qutb and Islamic Activism: A Translation and Critical Analysis of* Social Justice in Islam (Leiden: E. J. Brill, 1996), 314.

9. Abu-Rabi', *Intellectual Origins*, 195. Calvert advances this view when he writes:

> As an educator, he [Qutb] was inclined to believe that Egypt's modernizing school system was the primary conduit of Islam's distorted image. This was by design, and he traced it to the British educational advisers and native disciples who propagated "a general mentality that scorns the Islamic elements in life." Qutb writes that Muslims must win back their Islamic identity from the imperialists. Teachers must replace Eurocentric accounts of history with ones that privilege Islam as the driving force of history.

John Calvert, *Sayyid Qutb and the Origins of Radical Islamism* (New York: Columbia University Press, 2010), 167.

10. Shepard, *Sayyid Qutb and Islamic Activism*, 319 and 321.

11. Musallam, *From Secularism to Jihad*, 104–105; Sayyid Qutb, *al-'Adala al-Ijtima'iyya fi al-Islam* (Social Justice in Islam) (Cairo: Maktabat Misr, 1949 [reprint, Oneonta, NY: Islamic Publications International, 2000]), 207.

12. Sayed Khatab, *The Political Thought of Sayyid Qutb: The Theory of* Jahiliyyah (London: Routledge, 2006), 11. Other sources claim that both Qahtan and Adnan were descended solely from Ibrahim and Isma'il. By giving Qahtan a more ancient pedigree, Qutb anchored him in a history going back to humanity's founder, Adam and Eve.

13. Carré, *Mysticism and Politics*, 35–36.

14. Ibid., 36, Qutb, *Signposts*, 42; Eric R. Wolf, "The Social Organization of Mecca and the Origins of Islam," *Southwest Journal of Anthropology* 7 (Winter 1951): 338–339 and 344–348.

15. Khatab, *Political Thought*, 116.

16. Carré, *Mysticism and Politics*, 29–31 and 36–37; Reuven Firestone, *Jihad: The Origin of Holy War in Islam* (London: Oxford University Press, 1999), 48–50.

17. Qutb, *Signposts*, 24 and 26.

18. Abu-Rabi', *Intellectual Origins*, 173.

19. Ibid.; Qutb, *Signposts*, 27.

20. Qutb, *Signposts*, 21.

21. Ibid., 66–67 and 70.

22. Ibid., 45–46.

23. Ibid., 49–51.

24. Ibid., 54.

25. Abu-Rabi', *Intellectual Origins*, 174.
26. Qutb, *Signposts*, 53.
27. Abu-Rabi', *Intellectual Origins*, 142; Khatab, *Political Thought*, 158; Sayyid Qutb, *al-Salam al-'Alami wa al-Islam* (Islam and Universal Peace) (Plainfield, IN: American Trust Publications, 1993 [originally published in Cairo: Maktabat Wahbah, 1951]), 75.
28. Shepard, *Sayyid Qutb and Islamic Activism*, xlviii.
29. Carré, *Mysticism and Politics*, 160–161.
30. Abu-Rabi', *Intellectual Origins*, 176–178.
31. Carré, *Mysticism and Politics*, 38.
32. Ibid.
33. Qutb, *Social Justice*, 225–226.
34. Drinking alcoholic beverages is forbidden in Islam.
35. Qutb, *Social Justice*, 241.
36. Ibid., 242.
37. Ibid., 244.
38. Ibid., 241 and 246.
39. Ibid., 246; Shepard, *Sayyid Qutb and Islamic Activism*, 253.
40. Qutb, *Social Justice*, 215.
41. 'Amr ibn al-'As (573–664) was the general who conquered Egypt in 640, during the administration of 'Umar ibn al-Khattab, the second caliph, and who brought Islam to the country. He was a close adviser and kinsman to Mu'awiyya. There was no special case that incriminated al-'As, but he displayed the same unIslamic traits as Mu'awiyya. As governor of Egypt, Qutb claimed, he profited from his rule and treated his subjects unfairly.
42. Qutb, *Social Justice*, 222–225. 'Uthman was assassinated in 656 during an armed revolt by enemies from Egypt, Basra, and Kufa who had laid siege to his house in Medina. Few men outside his paid retinue tried to protect him.
43. Ibid., 226.
44. Ibid., 227–229.
45. Ibid., 230.
46. 'Ali's assassin, 'Abd al-Rahman ibn Muljam al-Muradi, was coaxed by his fiancée into avenging 'Ali's attack on the Kharijite camp at Nahrawan (near the future site of Baghdad) that killed her father. Ibn Muljam used a poison sword which took several days to take effect, allowing him to escape. He was eventually caught and killed by 'Ali's kinfolk, precluding his coveted marriage. David Cook, *Martyrdom in Islam*, (Cambridge: Cambridge University Press, 2007), 54. For more on kharijism, see note 33 in Chapter 4.
47. Qutb, *Social Justice*, 231.
48. Ibid., 231 and 236.
49. Shepard, *Sayyid Qutb and Islamic Activism*, xlviii.
50. Ibid., 322; Qutb, *Social Justice*, 265–266.
51. For more about these schools of *kalam*, see the discussion in Chapter 6.
52. Qutb, *Social Justice*, 269.
53. Shepard, *Sayyid Qutb and Islamic Activism*, 282–283.
54. This conquest provoked the Islamists in the 20th century to counter by proclaiming "from Ghana to Ferghana" as the territorial goal of their movement, from the west coast of Africa to the valley just east of Afghanistan.
55. Ibid.
56. Qutb, *Social Justice*, 270–271.
57. Qutb claimed that for centuries, Islam's enemies displayed deceit, wickedness, and hostility, and that the 20th century proved no better. The best way I have come to understand Qutb's allegation of continuous animosity is to read Norman Daniel's 1980 volume, *Islam and the West: The Making of an Image* and Edward Said's 1979 book, *Orientalism*. The first describes the antagonism between Europe and the Islamic world prior to the Renaissance, and the second emphasizes this relationship throughout the modern period. Qutb's belligerence, then, seems to me to be an understandable response to the centuries of European Orientalism, Islamophobia, and prejudice.

58. For more on the Arab contribution to European development, see Jim al-Khalili, *The House of Wisdom: How Arabic Science Saved Ancient Knowledge and Gave Us the Renaissance* (New York: Penguin Press, 2011).

59. Ibid. Qutb, *Social Justice*, 270–271.

60. Shepard, *Sayyid Qutb and Islamic Activism*, li.

Epilogue

1. There are three leadership groups in the Islamic Association: those in exile, those in prison, and those still in the field. There is not always unanimity among them. The proclamation for a cease-fire came from the prison leadership.

2. Shaykh 'Umar was arrested on June 24, 1993, and convicted a year and a half later, on October 1, 1995. He was sentenced to life in prison in 1996 and is currently serving his time in a medical prison in Butner, North Carolina.

3. The four books are (1) *Mubadarat Waqf al-'Unf: Ru'ya Waqi'iyya wa Nazra Shar'iyya* (An Initiative to Stop the Violence: A Pragmatic Perspective and a Legal Study), (2) *Hirmat al-Ghuluw fi al-Din wa Takfir al-Muslimin* (The Unlawfulness of Excess in Religion and Declaring Muslim Unbelievers), (3) *Taslit al-Adwa' 'ala ma Waqa' fi al-Jihad min Akhta'* (Shining the Spotlight on the Mistakes Made in Jihad), and (4) *al-Nasih wa al-Tabyin fi Taslih Mafahim al-Muhtasibin* (Advice and Clarification in Correcting the Concepts of Hisba Agents). All four were published in Cairo by the Islamic Heritage Library in 2002. Diaa Rashwan et al., "The Intellectual Revisionism of al-Jama'a al-Islamiyya 'Revised Concepts' Series," section II, ch. 5, in *The Spectrum of Islamist Movements*, Diaa Rashwan, ed. (Cairo: Al-Ahram Center for Political and Strategic Studies, 2006 [Berlin: Verlag Hans Schiler, 2007]), 315–317.

4. Usama bin Ladin was the founder, organizer, and leader of al-Qa'ida that perpetrated the 9/11 attacks in New York and Washington, DC. He was born on March 10, 1957, in Riyadh, the capital of Saudi Arabia. His family had its roots in the eastern Yemeni region of the Hadramawt, and his father had profited handsomely from building the infrastructure of the modern Saudi state. Young Usama majored in economics and business administration at King 'Abd al-'Aziz University in the more liberal city of Jeddah. After graduation, he was employed in his father's company and in 1979 was its business agent in Peshawar, Pakistan. He partnered with 'Abd Allah Yusuf 'Azam, a Palestinian *'alim* and Muslim Brotherhood recruiter, to help the *mujahidun* of Jami'at Islami (the Islamic Society) in neighboring Afghanistan fight the Soviet troops invited into the country to support the ruling Khalq faction of the Marxist People's Democratic Party of Afghanistan. The 1986 battle in the village of Jaji that defeated the Russian troops strongly enhanced Bin Ladin's reputation. After the Soviet withdrawal in 1989, he returned to Saudi Arabia a hero.

   In 1990, when Saddam Husayn's Iraqi Army threatened to invade the Kingdom after it had occupied Kuwait, Bin Ladin offered military assistance, but the king rejected his proposal and advice, and invited the Americans to fight instead. In response, Bin Ladin left his homeland, moved to Sudan in 1992, and set up an agricultural company. Harassed by Sudanese officials pressured by the American government, he left Sudan in 1996 and returned to Afghanistan. Here, seven years after the Soviets' departure, the Taliban had succeeded in taking over the government. They consisted primarily of those recruited from Wahhabi-financed and -inspired refugee camp schools in Pakistan. Bin Ladin's alliance with the Taliban and his support for their administration earned the condemnation of the United States. He accepted the *bay'a* of Ayman al-Zawahiri; their relationship was reciprocal: al-Zawahiri's faction of Tanzim al-Jihad was insolvent and Bin Ladin adopted its militant ideology inspired by Sayyid Qutb. After September 11, 2001, he and the Taliban officials went into hiding in Pakistan. On May 2, 2011, a commando unit of US Navy Seals and CIA agents attacked his hideaway in Abbottabad, Pakistan, and Bin Ladin was killed in the ensuing gun fight. Lawrence Wright, *The Looming Tower: Al-Qaeda and the Road to 9/11* (New York: Knopf, 2006) and Steve Coll, *The Bin Ladens* [sic]: *An Arabian Family in the American Century* (New York: Penguin Press, 2008).

5. Shortly thereafter, on February 23, 1998, the World Islamic Front for Combat against Jews and Crusaders (al-Jabha al-Islamiyya al-'Alamiyya li-Jihad al-Yahud wa al-Salibiyyin) was established.

The Front included independent Jihad members under al-Zawahiri's leadership along with other groups of jihadists led by Rifa'i Ahmad Taha (al-Jama'a al-Islamiyya, the Islamic Association, Egypt), Fazlur Rahman Khalil (Harakat al-Ansar, the Ansar Movement, Pakistan), Mir Hamza, (Jami'at al-'Ulama, the 'Ulama Association, Pakistan) and 'Abd al-Salam Muhammad, (Harakat al-Jihad, the Jihad Movement, Bangladesh). Al-Zawahiri was independent and therefore was able to sign the founding documents. Rifa'i Taha was repudiated by the Association's home office for his participation. Fazlur Rahman's organization was later renamed Harakat al-Mujahidin (Jihadist Movement). The *Ansar* were originally the helpers of the Prophet Muhammad from the city of Medina who welcomed him when he arrived from Mecca.

The World Front began referring to itself informally as "the base of *jihad*"; this name's abbreviated form, al-Qa'ida in Arabic, was not formally adopted until after the events of September 11. Diaa Rashwan et al., "Qaedat al-Jihad," section I, ch. 1, in *The Spectrum of Islamist Movements*, Diaa Rashwan, ed. (Cairo: Al-Ahram Center for Political and Strategic Studies, 2006 [Berlin: Verlag Hans Schiler, 2007]), 33–34 and 38–39.

6. In writing his book *Preachers, Not Judges*, Hasan Hudaybi directed Qutb and his followers to reject *takfir*, worried that accusations of *jahiliyya*, ignorance, could easily turn into charges of *takfir*, disbelief, followed by the kharijite practice of excommunicating and even executing such unbelievers. Qutb vigorously denied sanctioning such accusations and disparaged the act of declaring and convicting individuals as *kuffar*. However, the distinction between the two concepts is a fine one, so it is not surprising that Qutb's followers easily slipped across the line dividing castigating a society from censuring individuals. *Jahiliyya* applies to entire societies, Qutb argued, not to individuals within those societies. He acknowledged the traditional Sunni interpretation that since God alone knows what exists in a person's heart, the mere declaration of the *shahada*, or Testimony, suffices for confirming one's religion. Yet Qutb repeatedly denounced those who were lapsed Muslims, who declared the *shahada* without sincerity and reverence. The difference, it seems, lies in the intent of the believer: purposeful ignorance could well prove to be disbelief or apostasy; accidental deviation (the more common explanation) merely reflects momentary carelessness; evil intentions versus temporary negligence. Yet thereafter, the intolerance of Qutb's followers in *takfir*'ing the slightest deviation from piety irritated many Egyptians. This rigidity also reflected the growing influence of Wahhabi Islam.

7. Most Muslims view *hisba* as a collective duty, performed by the government. Revising it to mean an individual duty allows private citizens to bypass government authority and unilaterally determine the good and the bad themselves.

8. Following the January 25, 2011, revolution, 'Abbud and Tariq al-Zumar were released on March 10 after 30 years in Tora prison. Both were considered among the masterminds who planned the assassination of Egypt's president, Anwar al-Sadat, on October 6, 1981. But they were convicted in 1982 of just belonging to a terrorist organization, Tanzim al-Jihad, and so received 18-year sentences. However, in 2001, after their sentences were completed, they remained in prison for security reasons, despite dozens of court rulings in their favor and even though the al-Zumar cousins were among the first to back the proscription on violence. Mona El-Nahhas, "Three Decades On," *al-Ahram Weekly*, no. 1039, March 17–23, 2001.

9. Many scholars consider the appearance of the more general Islamic movement at this time to be a response to the disastrous defeat Egypt suffered in the Six-Day war of June 1967 against Israel and to the subsequent delegitimization of nationalism.

10. James Toth, "Local Islam Gone Global: The Roots of Religious Militancy in Egypt and Its Transnational Transformation," in *Global Social Movements: A Reader*, June Nash, ed. (Oxford: Blackwell, 2004), 126–128.

11. The May 15 "Corrective Revolution" came nine months after al-Sadat assumed the office of presidency when 'Abd al-Nassir died of a heart attack on September 28, 1970. More like a purge, it was intended to thwart a plot instigated by the leftist 'Ali Sabri, 'Abd al-Nassir's former vice-president, head of the Arab Socialist Union, and al-Sadat's rival, and to eliminate other threats from the government. In releasing Muslim Brothers, al-Sadat hoped to offset 'Abd al-Nassir's socialism by veering off to the right. This initiated a six-year honeymoon of supporting moderate and anti-Marxist Islamists that ended in 1977.

12. Adnan A. Musallam, *From Secularism to Jihad: Sayyid Qutb and the Foundations of Radical Islam* (Westport, CT: Praeger, 2005), 184–185; Gilles Kepel, *Muslim Extremism in Egypt: The Prophet and the Pharaoh,* Jon Rothschild, trans. (Berkeley: University of California Press, 1993 [originally *Le Prophète et Pharaon* (Paris: Editions La Déouverte, 1984)]), ch. 3.

13. Robin Wright, *Dreams and Shadows: The Future of the Middle East* (London: Penguin Press, 2008), 247; Brynjar Lia, *The Society of the Muslim Brothers in Egypt: The Rise of an Islamic Mass Movement, 1928–1942* (Reading, UK: Ithaca Press, 1998), 241.

14. Many *'ulama* were government employees because al-Azhar had been nationalized in 1961, and the system of religious endowments *(awqaf)* that financed mosque activities had been taken over by the government in the previous century. Thus the distinction in targets—government versus non-government—was not very clear.

15. Saad Eddin Ibrahim, "Anatomy of Egypt's Militant Islamic Groups: Methodological Notes and Preliminary Findings," in his *Egypt, Islam, and Democracy: Twelve Critical Essays* (Cairo: AUC Press, 1996 [reprinted from the original essay in *International Journal of Middle East Studies* 12 (1980)]), 19.

16. Ibid.; Musallam, *From Secularism to Jihad,* 183–184.

17. Toth, "Local Islam Gone Global," 126; Hasan Bakr, *al-'Unf al-Siyyasi fi Misr: Asyut: Bu'rat al-Tawattur: al-Asbab wa al-Dawafi'. 1977–1994* (Political Violence in Egypt: Asyut as a Site of Tension. The Reasons and the Motives. 1977–1994) (Cairo: Markaz al-Mahrusa li al-Bahuth wa al-Tadrib wa al-Nashr, 1994), 49.

18. The ability of the Egyptian government to provide critical social services was severely circumscribed by its adoption of Economic Reform and Structural Adjustment Programs (ERSAPs) as the price it paid for economic and financial assistance from the International Monetary Fund (IMF). This neoliberal program involved guaranteeing fiscal discipline, curbing budget deficits, reducing public expenditures, promoting foreign investment, reforming taxation, deregulation, privatization, and free market trade liberalization. Although officially initiated in 1991, similar neoliberal agreements with the IMF pre-date this time, going back as early as 1977—resulting in the infamous Bread Riots of January 1977—and a debt rescheduling agreement in May 1987 to resolve the country's balance of payments deficit.

19. This seems to be a pseudonym used to protect his family who still lived in Bani Swayf. His real name is Sayyid Imam 'Abd al-'Aziz al-Sharif. Diaa Rashwan et al., "'Abd al-Qadir ibn 'Abd al-'Aziz: The Writings of a Leader of the *Jihadi* School," section III, ch. 2, in *The Spectrum of Islamist Movements,* Diaa Rashwan, ed. (Cairo: Al-Ahram Center for Political and Strategic Studies, 2006 [Berlin: Verlag Hans Schiler, 2007]), 403.

20. For details about the founding of the World Front and its leadership, see note 5 in this chapter.

21. Diaa Rashwan et al., "What Remains of the Egyptian Jihad?" section I, ch. 2, in *The Spectrum of Islamist Movements,* Diaa Rashwan, ed. (Cairo: Al-Ahram Center for Political and Strategic Studies, 2006 [Berlin: Verlag Hans Schiler, 2007]), 65.

22. Geneive Abdo, *No God but God: Egypt and the Triumph of Islam* (Oxford: Oxford University Press, 2000), 20. It is impossible to verify government reports that there was a single, over-arching organization such as the Islamic Association in Imbaba rather than a multitude of small independent organizations. But it is also clear that *al-Jama'a al-Islamiyya* played a significant role in Imbaba's community welfare, although perhaps not alone.

23. Abdo, *No God but God,* 24. Abdo cites a March 1993 report of the Egyptian Organization of Human Rights.

24. Mary Anne Weaver, *A Portrait of Egypt: A Journey through the World of Militant Islam* (New York: Farrar, Straus and Giroux, 2000), 149. Weaver quotes a November 1994 interview with the Islamist lawyer 'Ali Isma'il.

25. Rashwan et al., "What Remains of the Egyptian Jihad?" 63.

26. John Calvert, *Sayyid Qutb and the Origins of Radical Islamism* (New York: Columbia University Press, 2010), 22; Gamal Essam El-Din, "Muslim Brotherhood's Coming Task," *al-Ahram Weekly,* no. 982, January 21–27, 2010, 3; (no author) "Mohamed Badei: Hardliner Lives Up to His Image," *al-Ahram Weekly,* no. 1029, December 30, 2010–January 3, 2011.

27. He received 66 percent of the vote in winning his office.
28. Amira Howeidy, "Hard Days Ahead for the Muslim Brotherhood," *al-Ahram Weekly*, no. 985, February 11–17, 2010, 3; Amira Howeidy, "Double Negatives," *al-Ahram Weekly*, no. 991, March 25–31, 2010, 3; Hossam Tammam, "Not Your Average Crackdown," *al-Ahram Weekly*, no. 986, February 18–24, 2010, 3; Khalil El-Anani, "Opposite Effects," *al-Ahram Weekly*, no. 987, February 25–March 3, 2010, 3.
29. Their tactics were based on the nonviolent methods developed by Gene Sharp and applied earlier by the Otpor! movement to bring down the government of Slobodan Milošević in Serbia. Sharp is a political science professor emeritus at the University of Massachusetts at North Dartmouth. See Gene Sharp, *From Dictatorship to Democracy: A Conceptual Framework for Liberation* (East Boston: Albert Einstein Institution, 2002); David D. Kirkpatrick and David E. Sanger, "A Tunisian-Egyptian Link That Shook Arab History," *New York Times*, February 14, 2011.
30. Ahmed Maher was born in 1980 in Cairo and is a civil engineer who works for a construction company in New Cairo, northeast of the old city. Earlier, he participated in the presidential campaign of Muhammad al-Barada'i, the former director of the International Atomic Energy Agency. Waleed Rashed was born in 1983 in Sharqiyya province and has degrees in commerce and political science. He works as a banker and is a member of Kifaya (Enough), the Egyptian Movement for Change.
31. The Misr Spinning and Weaving Company in al-Mahalla al-Kubra employs 27,000 workers and is the largest textile factory in Egypt. The demonstrations there on April 6, 2008, erupted against a backdrop of deteriorating living conditions for Egypt's working class. Thousands of demonstrators came out on the streets, hurling rocks, chanting anti-government slogans, and confronting the riot police's truncheons, tear gas, and bullets. The demonstration was organized by what came to be called the April 6th Coalition. In al-Mahalla, this coalition included the Islamist Labor Party, the Kifaya Movement for Change, the Karama (Dignity) Party, and the Lawyers' Syndicate. In sympathy and support, a national general strike was announced in Cairo, sponsored by Kifaya, the Muslim Brotherhood, and informal networks created by mobile phone texting, Facebook, and word of mouth. Both local and national demonstrations sought to protest the growing economic hardship and in particular, the spiraling cost of living. The strikes, though, went beyond specific worker demands to address a whole range of national grievances. Thus the April 6th Manifesto reads:

> We want decent wages, education for our kids, a humane system of transportation, a functional system of health and medicine for our children, a functional and independent judiciary, safety and security. We want freedom and dignity, and housing for newly-weds. We don't want price increases, we don't want to be tortured in police stations, we don't want corruption, bribery, arbitrary detentions and manipulation of the judiciary.

At least two people in al-Mahalla were killed in the clashes with security police and hundreds were wounded, nine critically. Ironically, although the Misr workers initiated the April 6th strike, and the April 6th Coalition was formed in solidarity with their action, the workers themselves had pulled out a day earlier when the holding company announced that it would comply with its unfulfilled promises to increase salaries. Two days later, on April 8, government officials visited al-Mahalla, including the prime minister, the ministers of Labor and Immigration, Investment, and Health, and the head of the Egyptian Federation of Trade Unions. The prime minister promised Misr workers an extra one-month bonus and all Egyptian textile workers a half-month bonus. But while the workers had been bought off, the larger grievances remained unresolved. Dina Ezzat, "No Ordinary Sunday," *al-Ahram Weekly*, no. 892, April 10–16, 2008; Faiza Rady, "A Victory for the Workers," *al-Ahram Weekly*, no. 892, April 10–16, 2008.

32. Mike Giglio, "Is Egypt Next?" *Newsweek*, January 23, 2011. Wael Ghonim is the marketing representative for Google based in Dubai, in the United Arab Emirates. He was born in 1980 and lived in Saudi Arabia for 13 years before his family returned to Egypt. He received a

computer engineering degree from Cairo University and a business degree from the American
University in Cairo.

33. On June 6, 2010, Khalid Sa'id was sitting in a cybercafé in Sidi Gabr, a district of central
Alexandria known for its corrupt and harsh police, when two security officers arrested him
and took him away, but not to jail. Instead they dragged him to the lobby of a nearby building and began bashing his head against the tile floor. After 20 minutes, they threw the body
into a police car, drove to police headquarters, only to return 10 minutes later and dump
the corpse in front of the café. Family and friends were extremely outraged. Photographs of
Sa'id's mangled body, smashed face, and broken ribs promptly appeared on the Internet and a
Facebook page was created with 159,000 members.

The Interior Ministry, responsible for the security police, claimed repeatedly that Sa'id,
who they alleged was a known drug dealer and user, had choked on a bag of hashish he had
swallowed to hide evidence and had died on route to the hospital. Despite the graphic evidence
and eyewitnesses, official autopsies repeatedly reported the cause of death to be asphyxiation,
claiming that it was the ambulance attendants who had broken Khalid's ribs as they transferred his body to the morgue and that it was the morgue that had broken Sai'id's jaw in its
attempt to remove the plastic bag from his throat.

Sa'id's family claims that the real reason behind the fatal beating was that Khalid had mobile
phone video footage showing officers sharing the rewards of a drug bust and had planned to
post the clips on YouTube. When he was killed, 200,000 viewers had already downloaded the
evidence of police corruption.

Protest demonstrations immediately erupted in Alexandria and Cairo as marchers accused
Interior Minister Habib al-'Adli of outright murder and demanded an immediate investigation. The case was referred to further autopsy and to the docket of the Alexandria Appeals
Court. After exhuming the body, the three-member committee of forensic experts concurred
with the original report, and at the court hearing, three witnesses testified that Sa'id had died
from swallowing the hashish packet. However, seven other witnesses confirmed that death
had occurred by beatings and blows. The Interior Ministry published the details of Sa'id's
criminal record, which Khalid's mother called "slander." She spoke further, saying the corrupt
Emergency Laws gave police unrestricted power.

Additional protests and candlelight vigils took place. The case was brought up in Egypt's
Parliament as well as with the European Parliament, the United States State Department,
Human Rights Watch, and Amnesty International. It soon entered the realm of presidential
politics as presidential candidates Muhammad al-Barada'i and Ayman Nur adopted the Khalid
Sa'id case as their own. It became a major cause among the Muslim Brotherhood, which spon-
sored a petition campaign demanding reforms.

After many months of protests, vigils, demonstrations, and foreign criticism, the two guilty
security officers were referred to the Alexandria Criminal Court on July 3, 2010. Government
officials continued to downplay the extrajudicial brutality by asking for patience and assumptions of innocence as the notorious case wound its way through the halls of government.
The courts have not yet rendered a verdict. Mohamed El-Sayed, "Unanswered Questions,"
al-Ahram Weekly, no. 1003, June 17–23, 2010; Mohamed El-Sayed, "The Fallout," *al-Ahram
Weekly*, no. 1004, June 24–30, 2010; Gamal Essam El-Din, "In Support of Khaled Said," *al-Ahram Weekly*, no. 1002, July 1–7, 2010; Mohamed El-Sayed, "The Cost of Torture," *al-Ahram
Weekly*, no. 1006, July 8–14, 2010.

34. Hossam Tammam and Patrick Haenni, "Islam in the Insurrection,?" *al-Ahram Weekly*, no.
1037, March 3–9, 2011.

35. Ibid.; Dina Ezzat, "Tactical Gains," *al-Ahram Weekly*, no. 1034, February 10–16, 2011.

36. Shaima el-Karanshawi, "Egypt Court Approves Moderate Islamic Party," *al-Masri al-Yawm*,
February 19, 2011; Tom Perry and Sarah Mikhail, "New Party Shows Deep Political Change in
New Egypt," *Reuters*, February 19, 2011.

37. Both the Egyptian and Turkish parties have adopted platforms of moderate Islamism. The
Turkish party evolved from the Virtue Party which in turn evolved from the Welfare Party.
Its two predecessors, however, were legally banned because of their nonsecular character and

their stress on Turkey's Islamic identity. The Justice and Development Party, by contrast, professes to be secular, nationalist, and supportive of Turkey's bid to join the European Union. It claims to be nonsectarian, democratic, and free-market-oriented, but opponents accuse it of harboring a hidden Islamist agenda, including the adoption of *shari'a* law. Its position on individual freedom and human rights, for example, may well mask the legalization of religious symbols and dress in public venues which are currently prohibited in Turkey. In its diluted form, the Justice and Development Party seems equivalent to the idea of Christian Democracy in Europe where religious values and beliefs, but not practices and actions, are adopted as politically significant and presented as a conservative outlook.

38. Amani Maged, "Not without Squabbles," *al-Ahram Weekly*, no. 1046, May 5–11, 2011.

39. Ibid.; Dina Ezzat, "Squaring the Circle," *al-Ahram Weekly*, no. 1036, February 24–March 2, 2011.

40. David B. Kirkpatrick, "Egypt Elections Expose Division in Muslim Brotherhood," *New York Times*, June 30, 2011; (no author) "Egypt: Muslim Brotherhood Expulsion," *New York Times*, June 22, 2011.

41. (No author) "In Egypt, Youth Wing Breaks from Muslim Brotherhood," *New York Times*, June 23, 2011.

42. Clearly the Brotherhood in Egypt chose a pattern of two separate organizations: the Brotherhood itself, as a social movement, and one or more political parties, separate from the parent organization. Thus the former can continue to subordinate women to men, and non-Muslims to Muslims, even while the spin-off parties participate in modern civil society and, therefore, treat these heretofore lesser identities as equals. The Brotherhood can promote *shari'a* as the only possible legal system; the parties, on the other hand, must participate in the *sturm und drang* of national politics, voting laws in or out according to majority rule where the majority need not be Islamist, but can be secular, nationalist, or socialist. But this organizational structure is not always the case, as Hossam Tammam points out.

The Egyptian example is somewhat similar to the situation seen in Morocco. In Morocco, the Movement for Unity and Reform (*Harakat al-Islah wa al-Tawhid*) constitutes the second largest parliamentary block. It does not officially belong to the regional Muslim Brotherhood federation that includes the Brotherhood in Egypt and Syria, the Islamic Salvation Front in Algeria, the Islah Party in Yemen, and the Islamic Action Front in Jordan. The Movement's political wing is the Justice and Development party (PJD is its French acronym)—the same name as the party in Turkey (see note 37, this chapter)—that appeared as the merger of the Moroccan Popular Democratic Party and the Constitutional Movement in 1996. In 1998, the Movement moved into *da'wa* and religious education and left policy, public affairs, and legislation to the PJD. After a number of so-called terrorist bombings, the two organizations became even more differentiated. The Movement's preachers and proselytizers do not stand as PJD candidates for Parliament and political office. Likewise, the PJD refrains from moralizing and from narrowly defining its constituency. Instead, it claims to appeal to all Moroccans regardless of religion.

By contrast, the Muslim Brotherhood in Algeria and Yemen transformed themselves wholly into political parties, such that the leaders of the Brotherhood became the leaders of political parties, with a few businessmen and tribal leaders added for the sake of appearances. Problems arose, however, when the parties were forced to adjust and compromise with other parties and particularly with the secular government.

In Jordan, a middle course is pursued. The Islamic Action Front, the political party, is a subordinate wing of the Muslim Brotherhood. There remains little daylight between the two. Yet the compromises and concessions the Front is forced to make often embarrass or even anger the Brotherhood, forcing a number of unnecessary debates that detract from the Brotherhood's larger, more religious objectives. This is particularly true when it comes to the uneasy peace treaty between Jordan and Israel; here, compromise can be tantamount to heresy.

Egypt is adopting both the Moroccan model—the Wasat and Current Parties seem to be quite separate—as well as the Jordanian model—the FJP appears as an offshoot of the Brotherhood, although its officers did officially resign from the Brotherhood. In both cases, however, the results leave the parent organization more uniformly radical and distinct from its more moderate and pragmatic political associates. See Hossam Tammam, "Models for an Islamist Political Party," *al-Ahram Weekly*, no. 1039, March 17–23, 2011.

43. Galal Nassar, "Down the Salafi Road," *al-Ahram Weekly*, no. 1027, December 16–22, 2010.

44. Amani Maged, "Salafism [*sic*]: The Unknown Quantity," *al-Ahram Weekly*, no. 1047, May 12–18, 2011.

45. Nassar, "Down the Salafi Road," and Ammar Ali Hassan "Who Attacked the Coptic Church?," *al-Ahram Weekly*, no. 1031, January 13–19, 2011.

46. Hassan "Who Attacked the Coptic Church?" Hassan points out that the large size of *jihadi* organizations like Tanzim al-Jihad and al-Jama'a al-Islamiyya made them easy targets for state security forces. After the defeat of these militants, sympathetic individuals began to join smaller fringe groups, but these were more difficult to investigate. Although all these Islamic groups actually consisted of small, personal cells, the Salafis did not develop any higher structures of command like the two large ones. In addition, since funding had become more difficult as the larger organizations were infiltrated and disrupted, the small Salafi groups became self-financed and harder to trace.

47. The Egyptian media often call these independent "televangelical" preachers—Egypt's answer to Billy Graham and his son, Franklin, Oral Roberts, Pat Robertson, Joel and Victoria Osteen, Jerry Falwell, Jim and Tammy Bakker, Rod Parsley, and Jimmy Swaggart. They include Shaykh Muhammad Hassan, Shaykh Muhammad Husayn Ya'qub, Shaykh Abu Ishaq al-Huwayni, Usama 'Abd al-'Azim, Shaykh Mustafa al-'Adawi, Mahmud al-Masri, and Mahmud 'Amr, and appear on such television networks as al-Nas (People) and al-Rahma (Compassion).

The Shubra mosques include such sermonizers as Fawzi al-Sa'id, Muhammad 'Abd al-Maqsud, Sayyid al-'Arabi, and Shaykh Nashat Ibrahim. The Alexandrian mosques include Muhammad Isma'il al-Muqaddam, Muhammad 'Abd al-Fattah, Ahmad Farid, Sa'id 'Abd al-'Azim, Yassir Brahimi, Ahmad Hatiba, 'Abd al-Mun'im al-Shahat, and Mahmud 'Abd al-Hamid. Maged, "Salafism (*sic*): The Unknown Quantity;" Tammam and Haenni, "Islam in the Insurrection?"

48. Maged, "Salafism (*sic*): The Unknown Quantity." Although it is not entirely correct to equate the Salafis with the Wahhabis since many Wahhabi preachers in Saudi Arabia have moderated their religious discourse, those Egyptians influenced by the Saudis have come to label themselves Salafis, and so the equation has stuck. Also see David Commins, *The Wahhabi Mission and Saudi Arabia* (New York: I. B. Tauris, 2006).

49. Tammam and Haenni, "Islam in the Insurrection?"

50. See, for example, Hassan, "Who Attacked the Coptic Church?"; Gamal Nkrumah, "Copts On the Beat," *al-Ahram Weekly*, no. 1047, May 12–18, 2011; Sameh Fawzi, "In Search of Religious Unity," *al-Ahram Weekly*, no. 1047, May 12–18, 2011; Ammar Ali Hassan, "Counter-revolution and Sectarian Strife," *al-Ahram Weekly*, no. 1047, May 12–18, 2011; Ayman El-Amir, "The Islamist Challenge," *al-Ahram Weekly*, no. 1042, April 7–13, 2011; Injy El-Kashef, "The Shrine Affair," *al-Ahram Weekly*, no. 1042, April 7–13, 2011.

Dramatis Personae

1. Albert Hourani, *Arabic Thought*, 130–131; Elie Kedourie, *Afghani and 'Abduh: An Essay on Religious Unbelief and Political Activism in Modern Islam* (London: Frank Cass, 1966), 8.

2. Hourani, *Arabic Thought*, 132.

3. Kedourie, *Afghani and 'Abduh*, 33; Donald M. Reid, "The 'Urabi Revolution and the British Conquest, 1879–1882," in *Cambridge History of Egypt*, M.W. Daly, ed., vol. 2: *Modern Egypt, from 1517 to the End of the Twentieth Century* (New York: Cambridge University Press, 1998), 223.

4. Ahmad 'Urabi (1839–1911) led an army officers revolt in 1881 protesting the discrimination against native Egyptians in the highest military ranks. Even as he was appointed minister of war, he led another revolt a year later striving for independence from distant British and French fiscal controls. Worried, Khedive Tawfiq requested immediate foreign intervention which provoked popular riots. 'Urabi organized resistance to the British in Alexandria, but

the English instead landed at Isma'iliyya, marched toward Cairo, and defeated 'Urabi at Tal al-Kabir in September, 1882. He was court-martialed and sentenced to death, but instead exiled to Sri Lanka. He quietly returned to Egypt in 1901.

5. Zaki Badawi, *The Reformers of Egypt*, 31.
6. Hourani, *Arabic Thought*, 134; Badawi, *The Reformers of Egypt*, 32.
7. Kedourie, *Afghani and 'Abduh*, 37; Robert L. Tignor, *Modernization and British Colonial Rule in Egypt, 1882–1914* (Princeton: Princeton University Press, 1966), 153–154.
8. Tignor, *Modernization and British Colonial Rule*, 179.
9. Kedourie, *Afghani and 'Abduh*, 5 and 38.
10. J. Brugman, *An Introduction to the History of Modern Arabic Literature*, 158–164.
11. Ibid., 158 and 160.
12. Ibid., 106–112, 151.
13. Jayyusi, *Trends and Movements*, 372.
14. Brugman, *An Introduction to the History of Modern Arabic Literature*, 158–164.
15. Jayyusi, *Trends and Movements*, 373.
16. Brugman, *An Introduction to the History of Modern Arabic Literature*, 190.
17. Jayyusi, *Trends and Movements*, 387.
18. Ibid., 157–158.
19. Fawaz Gerges, *The Far Enemy: Why Jihad Went Global* (Cambridge: Cambridge University Press, 2005), 1.
20. David Held, Anthony McGrew, David Goldblatt, and Jonathan Perraton, *Global Transformations: Politics, Economics and Culture* (Stanford: Stanford University Press, 1999), 195–197, 421–424, and 335–336.
21. Rifa'a al-Tahtawi was one of the first Egyptians to visit Europe and write about its science, history, and civilization. He was born in Sohag, in southern Egypt, graduated from al-Azhar, and participated as a religious teacher in the 1826 student mission khedive Muhammad 'Ali sent to Paris. He returned to Egypt in 1831 and was appointed director of the School of Languages in 1835 to translate European texts into Arabic. His translations covered such topics as philosophy, politics, military affairs, the Enlightenment, and secularism. He essentially saw Egypt and Europe, Christianity and Islam, as both equal and compatible, and was in the forefront of modernizing Islam. He emphasized national unity and patriotic citizenship as the chief means of adapting to modern society.
22. Zaki Badawi, *The Reformers of Egypt: A Critique of al-Afghani, 'Abduh, and Ridha* (Sough Berks, UK: Muslim Institute and Open Press, 1976), 3 and 8.
23. Nikki R. Keddie, *Sayyid Jamal ad-Din* [sic] *"al-Afghani": A Political Biography* (Berkeley: University of California Press, 1972), 2 and 10; Albert Hourani, *Arabic Thought in the Liberal Age, 1798–1939* (Cambridge: Cambridge University Press, 1962), 118.
24. Keddie, *Sayyid Jamal ad-Din* [sic] *"al-Afghani,"* 11, 25–26, 58, and 81.
25. Hourani, *Arabic Thought*, 119–120.
26. Keddie, *Sayyid Jamal ad-Din* [sic] *"al-Afghani,"* ch. 5.
27. Ibid., 92–101; Nadav Safran, *Egypt in Search of Political Community: An Analysis of the Intellectual and Political Evolution of Egypt, 1804–1952* (Cambridge, MA: Harvard University Press, 1961), 46.
28. Keddie, *Sayyid Jamal ad-Din* [sic] *"al-Afghani,"* 153–154 and 171–181.
29. Ibid., 214–228; Badawi, *The Reformers of Egypt*, 6; Hourani, *Arabic Thought*, 109–110, 123, and 128.
30. Keddie, *Sayyid Jamal ad-Din* [sic] *"al-Afghani,"* 225–226.
31. Ibid., 250–268 and ch. 10 and 11.
32. Hourani, *Arabic Thought*, 103, 114–115, and 120; Safran, *Egypt in Search of Political Community*, 44–45.
33. J. Brugman, *An Introduction to the History of Modern Arabic Literature*, 121–133.
34. David Semah, *Four Egyptian Literary Critics* (Leiden: E. J. Brill, 1974), 63.
35. Ibid., 3.
36. Brugman, *An Introduction to the History of Modern Arabic Literature*, 104.
37. Ibid.

38. For more on apologetics, see part IV in the Appendix.

39. Salma Khadra Jayyusi, *Trends and Movements in Modern Arabic Poetry*, 2 vols. (Leiden: E. J. Brill, 1977), 163–164.

40. Richard P. Mitchell, *The Society of the Muslim Brothers* (Oxford: Oxford University Press, 1969), 1–2; Ishak Musa Husaini, *The Moslem Brethren* (Beirut: Khayat's College Book Cooperative, 1956), 1–2 and 9–10.

41. Thameem Ushama, *Hasan al-Banna: Vision and Mission* (Kuala Lumpur: A. S. Noordeen, 1995), 38–39.

42. Brynjar Lia, *The Society of the Muslim Brothers in Egypt: The Rise of an Islamic Mass Movement, 1928–1942* (Reading, UK: Ithaca Press, 1998), 94–95, 151–154, and 256.

43. Ibid., 109–112.

44. Ibid., 235–247.

45. Mitchell, *The Society of the Muslim Brothers*, 17–18 and 30–32; Lia, *The Rise of an Islamic Mass Movement*, 245 and 247–251.

46. Mitchell, *The Society of the Muslim Brothers*, 26–29.

47. Ibid., 64–67.

48. Ushama, *Hasan al-Banna*, 76–79.

49. Arthur Goldschmidt Jr. and Robert Johnston, *Historical Dictionary of Egypt*, 3rd ed. (Lanham, MD: Scarecrow Press, 2003), 193.

50. Ibid., 193; Pierre Cachia, *Taha Husayn: His Place in the Egyptian Literary Renaissance* (Piscataway, NJ: Gorgias Press, 2005), 45.

51. J. Brugman, *An Introduction to the History of Modern Arabic Literature in Egypt* (Leiden: E. J. Brill, 1984), 361.

52. Ibid., 361–362.

53. For more about this controversy, see note 58 in Chapter 2.

54. Ibid., 363–364; Donald Reid, *Cairo University and the Making of Modern Egypt* (Cambridge: Cambridge University Press, 1990), 121.

55. J. Brugman, *An Introduction to the History of Modern Arabic Literature*, 402–404.

56. Ibid.

57. Ibid., 405.

58. Semah, *Four Egyptian Critics*, 153; Jayyusi, *Trends and Movements*, 525.

59. Brugman, *An Introduction to the History of Modern Arabic Literature*, 403.

60. Semah, *Four Egyptian Critics*, 154; Brugman, *An Introduction to the History of Modern Arabic Literature*, 155.

61. Semah, *Four Egyptian Critics*, 158 and 160.

62. Jayyusi, *Trends and Movements*, 525; Muhammad Mandur, "Pygmalion wa al-Asatir fi al-Adab" (Pygmalion and Myths in Literature), in his *Fi al-Mizan al-Jadid* (New Balance) (Cairo: Maktabit Lagnat al-Ta'lif, 1944), 16.

63. Semah, *Four Egyptian Critics*, 160–163.

64. Ibid., 155; Muhammad Mandur, *Fi al-Adab wa al-Naqd* (Literature and Criticism) (Cairo: Maktabit Lagnat al-Ta'lif, 1949), 31.

65. Semah, *Four Egyptian Critics*, 155; Brugman, *An Introduction to the History of Modern Arabic Literature*, 406–407.

66. Semah, *Four Egyptian Critics*, 189; Brugman, *An Introduction to the History of Modern Arabic Literature*, 403–404.

67. Seyyed Vali Reza Nasr, "Sayyid Abu al-A'la Mawdudi," in *The Oxford Encyclopedia of the Modern Islamic World*, John L. Esposito, ed. (New York: Oxford University Press, 1995), 72.

68. Ibid., 73.

69. Ibid., 74–75.

70. Muhammad Qasim Zaman, "Arabic, the Arab Middle East, and the Definitions of Muslim Identity in Twentieth Century India," *Journal of the Royal Asiatic Society* 8, no. 1 (April 1988): 64.

71. Ibid., 66–67.

72. Ibid., 68.

73. Zaki Badawi, *The Reformers of Egypt*, 47; Nayel Musa al-Omran, "Rashid Rida's Efforts in Calling for Muslim Unity and Political Reform," *Journal of Islam in Asia* 6, no. 1 (July 2009): 150.

74. For more on Ibn Hanbal, see note 23 in Chapter 10; for more on Ibn Taymiyya, see note 32 in Chapter 4, and for more on Ibn 'Abd al-Wahhab, see note 58 in Chapter 5.

75. Albert Hourani, *Arabic Thought*, 231.

76. Emad Eldin Shahin, *Through Muslim Eyes: M. Rashid Rida and the West* (Herndon, VA: International Institute of Islamic Thought, 1993), 7; Badawi, *The Reformers of Egypt*, 48.

77. Shahin, *Through Muslim Eyes*, 9; Malcolm H. Kerr, *Islamic Reform: The Political and Legal Theories of Muhammad 'Abduh and Rashid Rida* (Berkeley: University of California Press, 1966), 155.

78. Badawi, *The Reformers of Egypt*, 69.

79. Nadav Safran, *Egypt in Search of Political Community: An Analysis of the Intellectual and Political Evolution of Egypt, 1804–1952* (Cambridge, MA: Harvard University Press, 1961), 78.

80. Shahin, *Through Muslim Eyes*, 84; Assad Nimer Busool, "Rashid Rida's Struggle to Establish a Modern Islamic State," *American Journal of Islamic Studies* 1 (1984): 86.

81. Al-Omran, "Rashid Rida's Efforts," 165.

82. Shahin, *Through Muslim Eyes*, 3.

83. Hourani, *Arabic Thought*, 189; Badawi, *The Reformers of Egypt*, 68; Peter Cachia, *Taha Husayn: His Place in the Egyptian Literary Renaissance* (Piscatawy, NJ: Gorgias Press, 2005), 60. For more on these two literary controversies, see note 58 in Chapter 2.

84. Al-Omran, "Rashid Rida's Efforts," 154–155; Ana Belén Soage, "Rashid Rida's Legacy," *Muslim World* 98 (January 2008): 2 and 16–17.

85. Soage, "Rashid Rida's Legacy," 2 and 10.

On Women and the Family

1. Olivier Carré, *Mysticism and Politics: A Critical Reading of* Fi Zilal al-Qur'an *by Sayyid Qutb (1906–1966)* (Leiden: Brill, 2003), 132.

2. Sayyid Qutb, *Ma'alim fi al-Tariq* (Signposts on the Road but also translated as Milestones) (Al-Salimiya, Kuwait: Al-Ittihad al-Islami al-'Alami li al-Munazzamat al-Tullabiya [International Islamic Federation of Student Organizations], 1978), 183–184.

3. Carré, *Mysticism and Politics*, 133, 146–147.

4. Ibid., 139–140, and 145; William E. Shepard, *Sayyid Qutb and Islamic Activism: A Translation and Critical Analysis of* Social Justice in Islam (Leiden: E. J. Brill, 1996), 71.

5. Shepard, *Sayyid Qutb and Islamic Activism*, 61; Carré, *Mysticism and Politics*, 128.

6. Sayyid Qutb, *Al-'Adala al-Ijtima'iyya fi al-Islam* (Social Justice in Islam) (Cairo: Maktabat Misr, 1949 [reprint, Oneonta, NY: Islamic Publications International, 2000]), 72.

7. Larry Rosen, "The Negotiation of Reality: Male-Female Relations in Sefrou, Morocco," in *Women in the Muslim World*, Lois Beck and Nikki Keddie, eds. (Cambridge, MA: Harvard University Press, 1978), 570; Homa Hoodfar, "Survival Strategies and the Political Economy of Low-Income Households in Cairo," in *Development, Change, and Gender in Cairo: A View from the Household*, Diane Singerman and Homa Hoodfar, eds. (Bloomington: Indiana University Press, 1996), 13.

8. Carré, *Mysticism and Politics*, 128.

9. Carolyn Fluehr-Lobban, *Islamic Society in Practice* (Gainesville: University Press of Florida, 1994), 125; John Calvert, *Sayyid Qutb and the Origins of Radical Islamism* (New York: Columbia University Press, 2010), 108.

10. Qutb, *Social Justice*, 76.

11. For a similar but non-Islamic perspective on women in and out of the workforce, see Karen Sacks, "Engels Revisited: Women, the Organization of Production and Private Property," in *Toward an Anthropology of Women*, Rayna Reiter, ed. (New York: Monthly Review Press, 1975).

12. Sayyid Qutb, *Ma'alim fi al-Tariq* (Signposts on the Road but also translated as Milestones) (Al-Salimiya, Kuwait: Al-Ittihad al-Islami al-'Alami li al-Munazzamat al-Tullabiya [International Islamic Federation of Student Organizations], 1978), 183.

13. For more on Middle East women, see Judith K. Brown, "Note on the Division of Labor by Sex," *American Anthropologist* 72, no. 5 (October 1970): 837–853; James Toth, "Pride, Purdah

or Paychecks: What Maintains the Gender Division of Labor in Rural Egypt," *International Journal of Middle East Studies* 23, no. 2 (May 1991): 213–236; Anne Meneley, *Tournaments of Value: Sociability and Hierarchy in a Yemeni Town* (Toronto: University of Toronto Press, 1996); Judith Tucker, *Women in Nineteenth Century Egypt* (Cambridge: Cambridge University Press, 1985).

On "People of the Book," Dhimmis

1. Mark R. Cohen, *Under the Crescent and Cross: The Jews in the Middle Ages,* (Princeton: Princeton University Press, 1994), 38–40, 54–58, and 73–74.
2. Edward Said, *Orientalism* (New York: Vintage Books, 1979), 286, 293, and 307.
3. Cohen, *Under the Crescent and Cross*, ch. 1.
4. Sayyid Qutb, *Ma'rakatna ma' al-Yahud* (Our Battle with the Jews), in *Past Trials and Present Tribulations: A Muslim Fundamentalist View of the Jews*, Ronald Nettler, ed. (Oxford: Pergamon Press, 1987), 72–85.
5. Named for Israel's defense minister, this sabotage operation was organized by Israeli military intelligence who recruited 13 Egyptian Jews to detonate bombs in Cairo and Alexandria so that they could be blamed on the Muslim Brotherhood. David Hirst, *The Gun and the Olive Branch: The Roots of Violence in the Middle East* (London: Futura Macdonald, 1978), 164–170.
6. Cohen, *Under the Crescent and Cross*, 6.

On Apologetics

1. John V. Tolan, *Saracens: Islam in the Medieval European Imagination* (New York: Columbia University Press, 2002), 50–55.
2. Qutb, *Social Justice in Islam*, 114–115.
3. Ibid., 115–117.
4. Shepard, *Sayyid Qutb and Islamic Activism*, xlii–xliii.
5. Ibid., 105.
6. Qutb, *Signposts on the Road*, 246–247.
7. Ibid., 259.

BIBLIOGRAPHY

Abdo, Geneive. *No God but God: Egypt and the Triumph of Islam*. Oxford: Oxford University Press. 2000.

Abu Lughod, Lila. *Veiled Sentiments: Honor and Poetry in a Bedouin Society*. Berkeley: University of California Press. 1986.

Abu-Rabi', Ibrahim M. *Intellectual Origins of Islamic Resurgence in the Modern Arab World*. Albany: State University of New York Press. 1996.

Adams, Charles C. *Islam and Modernism in Egypt*. Oxford: Oxford University Press. 1933.

Aigle, Denise. "The Mongol Invasions of Bilad al-Sham by Ghazan Khan and Ibn Taymiyah's Three 'Anti-Mongol' Fatwas." *Mamluk Studies Review* 11:2. 2007, 89–120.

Algar, Hamid. "Introduction." *Social Justice in Islam by Sayyid Qutb*. Oneonta, NY: Islamic Publications International. 2000.

Algar, Hamid. "Preface." Sayyid Qutb. *Muqawwimat al-Tasawwur al-Islami* (Basic Principles of the Islamic Worldview). Rami David, trans. North Halcedon, NJ: Islamic Publications International. 2006.

El-Amir, Ayman. "The Islamist Challenge." *Al-Ahram Weekly*. No. 1042. April 7–13, 2011.

Ammerman, Nancy T. "North American Protestant Fundamentalism." In *Fundamentalisms Observed*. Martin E. Marty and R. Scott Appleby, eds. Chicago: University of Chicago Press. 1991.

El-Anani, Khalil. "Opposite Effects." *Al-Ahram Weekly*. No. 987. February 25–March 3, 2010.

Anderson, Benedict. *Imagined Communities: Reflections on the Origin and Spread of Nationalism*. New York: Verso Press. 1983.

Arjomand, Said. "Traditionalism in Twentieth-Century Iran." In his *From Nationalism to Revolutionary Islam*. Albany: State University of New York Press. 1984.

Aroian, Lois A. *The Nationalization of Arabic and Islamic Education in Egypt: Dar al-'Ulum and al-Azhar*. Cairo Papers in the Social Sciences 6:4. Cairo: American University in Cairo Press. 1983.

al-'Aqqad, 'Abbas Mahmud. *Shu'ara Misr wa Bi'atuhum fi al-Jil al-Madi'*. (Poets of Egypt and Their Milieu in the Past Generation). Cairo: Maktabit Higazi. 1937.

Asad, Muhammad., transl. *The Message of the Qur'an*. Bristol, UK: Book Foundation. 2003.

Asad, Talal. *Genealogies of Religion: Discipline and Reasons of Power in Christianity and Islam*. Baltimore: Johns Hopkins University Press. 1993.

Asad, Talal. *On Suicide Bombing*. New York: Columbia University Press. 2007.

El-Aswad, El-Sayed. "The Cosmological Belief System of Egyptian Peasants." *Anthropos* 89. 1994: 359–377.

El-Aswad, El-Sayed. *Religion and Folk Cosmology: Scenarios of the Visible and Invisible in Rural Egypt*. Westport, CT: Praeger. 2002.

Al-Awadi, Hesham. *In Pursuit of Legitimacy: The Muslim Brothers and Mubarak, 1982–2000*. London: Tauris. 2004.

Al-'Azm, Yusuf. *Ra'id al-Fikr al-Islam al-Mu'asir al-Shahid Sayyid Qutb* (Pioneer of Modern Islamic Thought: The Martyr Sayyid Qutb). Damascus and Beirut: Dar al-Qalam. 1980.

Badawi, Zaki. *The Reformers of Egypt: A Critique of al-Afghani, 'Abduh, and Ridha.* Sough Berks UK: Muslim Institute and Open Press. 1976.

Al-Bahr, Sahar. "A Lifetime of Islamic Call—An Interview with Gamal al-Banna." *Al-Ahram Weekly.* No. 941. April 2–8, 2009.

Bakr, Hasan. *Al-'Unf al-Siyyasi fi Misr: Asyut: Bu'rat al-Tawattur: al-Asbab wa al-Dawafi', 1977–1994* (Political Violence in Egypt: Asyut as a Site of Tension. The Reasons and the Motives. 1977–1994). Cairo: Markaz al-Mahrusa li al-Bahuth wa al-Tadrib wa al-Nashr. 1994.

Bangash, Zafar. "Remembering Sayyid Qutb: An Islamic Intellectual and Leader of Rare Insight and Integrity." In *Milestones.* A. B. Al-Mehri, ed. Birmingham, UK: Maktabah Booksellers and Publishers, 2006, 183–185.

Al-Banna, Hasan. "On Jihad." In *Five Tracts of Hasan al-Banna (1906–1949).* Charles Wendell, trans. Berkeley: University of California Press. 1978.

Barakat, Muhammad Tawfiq. *Sayyid Qutb: Khulasat Hayatihi Manhajihi fi al-Haraka, al-Naqd al-Muwajjahu ilayhi* (Sayyid Qutb: Summary of His Life, His Approach in the [Islamic] Movement, [and] the Criticism directed at Him). Beirut: Dar al-Da'wah. 1970.

Barth, Frederik. "Father's Brother's Daughter Marriage in Kurdistan." *Southwestern Journal of Anthropology* 10:2. Summer 1954: 64–171.

Bayat, Asef. "Islamism and the Politics of Fun." *Public Culture* 19:3. Fall 2007. 433–459.

Beinin, Joel. "Islam, Marxism and the Shubra al-Kayma Textile Workers: Muslim Brothers and Communists in the Egyptian Trade Union Movement." In *Islam, Politics, and Social Movements.* Edmund Burke, III, and Ira M. Lapidus, eds. Berkeley: University of California Press. 1988.

Ben-Menahem, Yemima. "Historical Necessity and Contingency." In *A Companion to the Philosophy of History and Historiography.* Aliezer Tucker, ed. Oxford: Blackwell. 2009. 120–130.

Berman, Paul. "The Philosopher of Islamic Terror." *New York Times Magazine.* March 23, 2003a.

Berman, Paul. *Terrorism and Liberalism.* New York: W.W. Norton. 2003b.

Bernal, Martin. *Black Athena: The Afro-Asiatic Roots of Classical Civilization.* New Brunswick: Rutgers University Press. 1987.

Binder, Leonard. *Islamic Liberalism: A Critique of Development Ideologies.* Chicago: University of Chicago Press. 1988.

Booth, Marilyn. "On Gender, History…and Fiction." In *Middle East Historiographies: Narrating the Twentieth Century.* Israel Gershoni, Amy Singer, and Y. Hakan Erdem, eds. Seattle: University of Washington Press. 2006a.

Booth, Marilyn. "Fiction's Imaginative Archive and the Newspaper's Local Scandals: The Case of Nineteenth-Century Egypt." In *Archive Stories: Facts, Fictions, and the Writing of History.* Antoinette Burton, ed. Durham, NC: Duke University Press, 2006b.

Bonner, Michael. *Jihad in Islamic History: Doctrines and Practices.* Princeton: Princeton University Press. 2006.

Botman, Selma. *The Rise of Egyptian Communism, 1939–1970.* Syracuse: Syracuse University Press. 1988.

Boyd, Douglas A. *Broadcasting in the Arab World: A Survey of Radio and Television in the Middle East.* Philadelphia: Temple University Press. 1982.

Brockelmann, Carl. *History of the Islamic Peoples.* Joel Carmichael and Moshe Perlmann, trans. New York: Capricorn Books. 1960.

Brough, Michael W., John W. Lango, and Harry van der Linden, eds. *Rethinking the Just War Tradition.* Albany: State University of New York Press. 2007.

Brown, Judith K. "Note on the Division of Labor by Sex." *American Anthropologist* 72:5. October 1970: 1073–1078.

Brugman, J. *An Introduction to the History of Modern Arabic Literature in Egypt.* Leiden: E. J. Brill. 1984.

Burgat, François. *The Islamic Movement in North Africa.* William Dowell, trans. Austin: University of Texas Press. 1997.

Busool, Assad Nimer. "Rashid Rida's Struggle to Establish a Modern Islamic State." *American Journal of Islamic Studies* 1. 1984: 83–99.

Butterfield, Herbert. *The Whig Interpretation of History*. London: G. Bell. 1951. Originally published in 1931.

Cachia, Pierre. *Taha Husayn: His Place in the Egyptian Literary Renaissance*. Piscataway, NJ: Gorgias Press. 2005. Originally published London: Luzac. 1956.

Calvert, John. "'The World Is an Undutiful Boy!': Sayyid Qutb's American Experience." *Islam and Christian-Muslim Relations* 11:1. March 2000: 87–103.

Calvert, John. "Sayyid Qutb in America." *Newsletter of the International Institute for the Study of Islam* 7. March 2001:8. http://hdl.handle.net/1887/17485.

Calvert, John. *Sayyid Qutb and the Origins of Radical Islamism*. New York: Columbia University Press. 2010.

Calvert, John and William Shepard. "Translators' Introduction." Sayyid Qutb. *A Child from the Village*. Syracuse: Syracuse University Press. 2004.

Carré, Olivier. *Mysticism and Politics: A Critical Reading of Fi Zilal al-Qur'an by Sayyid Qutb (1906–1966)*. Leiden: Brill. 2003.

Chakrabarty, Dipesh. "Postcoloniality and the Artifice of History: Who Speaks for 'Indian' Pasts." *Representations* 37. Winter 1992: 1–26.

Chakrabarty, Dipesh. "The Muddle of Modernity." *American Historical Review* 116:3. June 2011: 663–675.

Chaturvedi, Vinayak, ed. *Mapping Subaltern Studies and the Postcolonial*. New York: Verso Press. 2000.

Cohen, Mark R. *Under the Crescent and Cross: The Jews in the Middle Ages*. Princeton: Princeton University Press. 1994.

Cole, John W. and Eric R. Wolf. *The Hidden Frontier: Ecology and Ethnicity in an Alpine Village*. New York: Academic Press. 1974.

Coll, Steve. *The Bin Ladens [sic]: An Arabian Family in the American Century*. New York: Penguin Press. 2008.

Colla, Elliott. *Conflicted Antiquities: Egyptology, Egyptomania, Egyptian Modernity*. Durham: Duke University Press. 2007.

Commins, David. *The Wahhabi Mission and Saudi Arabia*. New York: I. B. Tauris. 2006.

Cook, David. *Understanding Jihad*. Berkeley: University of California Press. 2005.

Cook, David. *Martyrdom in Islam*. Cambridge: Cambridge University Press. 2007.

Cuno, Kenneth M. *The Pasha's Peasants: Land, Society, and Economy in Lower Egypt, 1740–1858*. New York: Cambridge University Press. 1992.

Daniel, Norman. *Islam and the West: The Making of an Image*. Edinburgh: Edinburgh University Press. 1980.

Danielson, Virginia. *The Voice of Egypt: Umm Kulthum, Arabic Song, and Egyptian Society in the Twentieth Century*. Chicago: University of Chicago Press. 1997.

El-Din, Gamal Essam. "Muslim Brotherhood's Coming Task." *Al-Ahram Weekly*. No. 982. January 21–27, 2010.

El-Din, Gamal Essam. "In Support of Khaled Said." *Al-Ahram Weekly*. No. 1002. July 1–7, 2010.

Dirks, Nicholas B. "History as a Sign of the Modern." *Public Culture* 2:2. Spring 1990: 25–32.

Drayton, Richard. "Where Does the World Historian Write From? Objectivity, Moral Conscience and the Past and Present of Imperialism." *Journal of Contemporary History* 46. 2011: 671–685.

Duindam, Jeroen. "Early Modern Europe: Beyond the Strictures of Modernization and National Historiography." *European History Quarterly* 40:4. 2010: 606–623.

Egan, Kieran. "Progress in Historiography." *Clio* 8:2 1979: 195–228.

"Egypt: Muslim Brotherhood Expulsion." *New York Times*. June 22, 2011.

Eikmeier, Dale C. "Qutbism: An Ideology of Islamic-Fascism." *Parameters* Spring 2007: 85–98.

Elshtain, Jean B., ed. *Just War Theory*. New York: New York University Press. 1992.

Erikson, Marc. "Islamism, Fascism and Terrorism." *Asia Times Online*. Part 1, November 5, 2002; Part 2, November 8, 2002.

Esposito, John L. *Islam: The Straight Path*. 3rd ed. New York: Oxford University Press. 1998.

Ezzat, Dina. "Tactical Gains." *Al-Ahram Weekly*. No. 1034. February 10–16, 2011.

Ezzat, Dina. "Squaring the Circle." *Al-Ahram Weekly*. No. 1036. February 24–March 2, 2011.

Ezzat, Dina. "No Ordinary Sunday." *Al-Ahram Weekly*. No. 892. April 10–16, 2008.

Ezzat, Dina. "'A Terrifying Scene.'" *Al-Ahram Weekly*. No. 1047. May 12–18, 2011.

Fanon, Frantz. *Peau Noire, Masques Blancs*. Paris: Editions du Seuil, 1952. (Published in English as *Black Skin, White Masks*, trans. Charles Lam Markmann [New York: Grove Press, 1967]).

Fanon, Frantz. *Les Damnés de la Terre*. Paris: François Maspero, 1961. (Published in English as *The Wretched of the Earth*, trans. Constance Farrington [New York: Grove Press, 1965]).

Farah, Caesar E. *Islam: Beliefs and Observances*. 7th ed. New York: Barron's Educational Series. 2003.

Fawzi, Sameh. "In Search of Religious Unity." *Al-Ahram Weekly*. No. 1047. May 12–18, 2011.

Firestone, Reuven. *Jihad: The Origin of Holy War in Islam*. London: Oxford University Press. 1999.

Fluehr-Lobban, Carolyn. *Islamic Society in Practice*. Gainesville: University Press of Florida. 1994.

El-Gamal, Mahmoud A. *Islamic Finance: Law, Economics, and Practice*. Cambridge: Cambridge University Press. 2006.

Gaonkar, Dilip Parameshwar. "On Alternative Modernities." *Public Culture* 11:1. 1999: 1–18.

Geertz, Clifford. *Islam Observed: Religious Development in Morocco and Indonesia*. New Haven: Yale University Press. 1968.

Geertz, Clifford. *The Interpretation of Cultures*. New York: Basic Books. 1973.

Gellner, Ernest. *Nations and Nationalism*. Ithaca: Cornell University Press. 1983.

Gerges, Fawaz. *The Far Enemy: Why Jihad Went Global*. Cambridge: Cambridge University Press. 2005.

Gershoni, Israel. "The Evolution of National Culture in Modern Egypt: Intellectual Formation and Social Diffusion, 1892–1945." *Poetics Today* 13:2. Summer 1992: 325–350.

Gershoni, Israel. "The Reader—'Another Production': The Reception of Haykal's Biography of Muhammad and the Shift of Egyptian Intellectual to Islamic Subjects in the 1930s." *Poetics Today* 15:2. Summer 1994: 241–277.

Gershoni, Israel and James P. Jankowski. *Egypt, Islam, and the Arabs: The Search for Egyptian Nationhood, 1900–1930*. Oxford: Oxford University Press. 1986.

Gershoni, Israel and James P. Jankowski. *Redefining the Egyptian Nation, 1930–1945*. Cambridge: Cambridge University Press. 1995.

Gershoni, Israel and James Jankowski. "Print Culture, Social Change, and the Process of Redefining Imagined Communities in Egypt; Response to the Review by Charles D. Smith of Redefining the Egyptian National (IJMES 29, 4 [1997]; 607–622)." *International Journal of Middle East Studies* 31. 1999: 81–94.

Al-Ghazzali, Muhammad (sic). *Our Beginning in Wisdom*. Isma'il R. el-Faruqi, trans. Washington, DC: American Council of Learned Societies. 1953.

Giglio, Mike. "Is Egypt Next?" *Newsweek*. January 23, 2011.

Gil, Thomas. "Leopold Ranke." In *A Companion to the Philosophy of History and Historiography*. Aliezer Tucker, ed. Oxford: Blackwell. 2009. 383–392.

Goldschmidt, Arthur Jr. and Robert Johnston. *Historical Dictionary of Egypt*. 3rd ed. Lanham, MD: Scarecrow Press. 2003.

Gordon, Joel. *Nasser's Blessed Movement: Egypt's Free Officers and the July Revolution*. New York: Oxford University Press. 1992.

Guha, Ranajit, and Gayatri Chakravorty Spivak, eds. *Selected Subaltern Studies*. New York: Oxford University Press. 1988.

Habib, Nader. "Ablaze with Tension." *Al-Ahram Weekly*. No. 1038. March 10–16, 2011.

Haddad, Yvonne. "The Qur'anic Justification of an Islamic Revolution: The View of Sayyid Qutb." *Middle East Journal* 37:1. 1983: 14–29.

Hallaq, Wael B. "Was the Gate of Ijtihad Closed?" *International Journal of Middle East Studies* 16:1. March 1984: 3–41.

El-Hamamsy, Laila Shukry. "The Assertion of Egyptian Identity." In *Ethnic Identity: Cultural Continuities and Change*. George DeVos and Lola Romanucci-Ross, eds. Palo Alto, CA: Mayfield. 1975. 276–306.

Hammuda, 'Adil. *Sayyid Qutb min al-Qarya ila al-Mashnaqa: Sirat al-Ab al-Ruhi li Jama'at al-'Unf* (Sayyid Qutb from the Village to the Gallows: The Biography of the Spiritual Father of Violent Associations). Cairo: Dar al-Khayyal. 1996.

Hanafi, Hasan. "The Relevance of the Islamic Alternative in Egypt." *Arab Studies Quarterly* 4:1–2. 1982: 54–74.

Harrison, Edward. "Whigs, Prigs and Historians of Science." *Nature* 329. September 17, 1987: 213–214.

Hassan, Ammar 'Ali. "Who Attacked the Coptic Church?" *Al-Ahram Weekly*. No. 1031. January 13–19, 2011.

Hassan, Ammar 'Ali. "Counter-revolution and Sectarian Strife." *Al-Ahram Weekly*. No. 1047. May 12–18, 2011.

Held, David, Anthony McGrew, David Goldblatt, and Jonathan Perraton. *Global Transformations: Politics, Economics and Culture*. Stanford: Stanford University Press. 1999.

Herf, Jeffrey. *Nazi Propaganda for the Arab World*. New Haven: Yale University Press. 2009.

Heyworth-Dunne, James. *Religious and Political Trends in Modern Egypt*. Washington, DC: McGregor and Werner. 1950.

Hill, Christopher. *The World Turned Upside Down: Radical Ideas during the English Revolution*. London: Maurice Temple Smith. 1972.

Hill, Enid. *Al-Sanhuri and Islamic Law*. Cairo Papers in the Social Science 10:1. Cairo: AUC Press. Spring 1987.

Hirst, David. *The Gun and the Olive Branch: The Roots of Violence in the Middle East*. London: Futura Macdonald. 1978.

Hitchens, Christopher. "Minority Report" columns. *The Nation*. October 8, 2001; December 17, 2001; and May 13, 2002.

Hitchens, Christopher. "Holy Writ." *Atlantic Monthly*. April 2003.

Hitchens, Christopher. "Stranger in a Strange Land." *Atlantic Monthly*. April 2003.

Hitchens, Christopher. "Where the Twain Should Have Met." *Atlantic Monthly*. September 2003.

Hitchens, Christopher. *God Is Not Great: How Religion Poisons Everything*. New York: Twelve Books. 2007.

Hitchens, Christopher. "Londistan Calling."*Vanity Fair*. June 2007.

Hitti, Philip K. *History of the Arabs*. London: Macmillan. 1970.

Hoffman-Ladd, Valerie J. "Devotion to the Prophet and His Family in Egyptian Sufism." *International Journal of Middle East Studies* 24:4. November 1992: 615–637.

Hoodfar, Homa. "Survival Strategies and the Political Economy of Low-Income Households in Cairo." In *Development, Change, and Gender in Cairo: A View from the Household*. Diane Singerman and Homa Hoodfar, eds. Bloomington: Indiana University Press. 1996. 1–26.

Hopkins, Nicholas S. *Agrarian Transformation in Egypt*. Boulder, CO: Westview Press. 1987.

Hopkins, Nicholas S. "Land Tenure." In *The Oxford Encyclopedia of the Modern Islamic World*. John L. Esposito, ed. New York: Oxford University Press. 1995. 446–450.

Hourani, Albert. *Arabic Thought in the Liberal Age, 1798–1939*. Cambridge: Cambridge University Press. 1962.

Howeidy, Amira. "Hard Days Ahead for the Muslim Brotherhood." *Al-Ahram Weekly*. No. 985. February 11–17, 2010a.

Howeidy, Amira. "Double Negatives." *Al-Ahram Weekly*. No. 991. March 25–31, 2010b.

Howeidy, Amira. "Sectarianism Rears Its Ugly Face." *Al-Ahram Weekly*. No. 1047. May 12–18, 2011.

Al-Hudaybi, Hasan Isma'il. *Du'wat La Qudat: Abhath fi al-'Aqida al-Islamiyya wa Manhaj al-Da'wa ila Allah* (Preachers Not Judges: Research into the Islamic Creed and a Missionary Program for God). Cairo: Dar al-Taba'a wa al-Nashr al-Islamiyya. 1977.

Hull, David L. "In Defense of Presentism." *History and Theory* 18. 1979:1–15.

Hulsman, Cornelis. "Christian Life." In *Upper Egypt: Life along the Nile*. Hojbjerg, Denmark: Moesgard Museum. 2003.

Husaini, Ishak Musa. *The Moslem Brethren*. Beirut: Khayat's College Book Cooperative. 1956.

Husayn, 'Abd al-Baqi Muhammad. *Sayyid Qutb: Hayatuh wa Adabuh* (Sayyid Qutb: His Life and His Literature). Al-Mansura, Daqahiliyya, Egypt: Dar al-Wafa'. 1986.

Husayn, Taha. *The Future of Culture in Egypt*. Sidney Glazer, trans. Washington, DC: American Council of Learned Societies. 1954.

Husayn, Taha. *Al-Mu'adhdhabun fi al-Ard* (The Tormented on Earth). Cairo: Dar al-Ma'arif. 1973. Translated as *The Sufferers: Stories and Polemics*. Mona El-Zayyat, trans. Cairo: American University in Cairo Press. 1993.

Ibrahim, Ibrahim Iskandar. "The Egyptian Intellectuals between Tradition and Modernity." Ph.D. dissertation, St. Antony's College, Oxford, 1967.

Ibrahim, Saad Eddin. "Anatomy of Egypt's Militant Islamic Groups: Methodological Notes and Preliminary Findings." In *Egypt, Islam, and Democracy: Twelve Critical Essays*. Cairo: AUC Press. 1996. Reprinted from the original essay in *International Journal of Middle East Studies* 12:4: 423–453. 1980.

'Imad, 'Abd al-Ghani. *Hakimmiyat Allah wa Sultan al-Faqih: Qira'a fi Khitab al-Harakat al-Islamiyya al-Mu'asira* (The Dominion of God and the Rule of [Religious] Law: [Qur'anic] Recitation in the Discourse of the Contemporary Islamic Movement). Beirut: Dar al-Tali'a li al-Tiba'a wa al-Nashr. 1997.

Imam, 'Abdallah. *'Abd al-Nassir wa al-Ikhwan* (Abd al-Nassir and the Muslim Brotherhood). Cairo: Dar al-Khayyal. 1997.

"In Egypt, Youth Wing Breaks from Muslim Brotherhood." *New York Times*. June 23, 2011.

Iqbal, Zamir and Abbas Mirakhor. *An Introduction to Islamic Finance: Theory and Practice*. Singapore: John Wiley. 2007.

Issawi, Charles. *An Economic History of the Middle East and North Africa*. London: Methuen. 1982.

Jayyusi, Salma Khadra. *Trends and Movements in Modern Arabic Poetry*. 2 vols. Leiden: E. J. Brill. 1977.

Johansen, Baber. *Muhammad Husain Haikal: Europa und der Orient im Weitbildeines Agyptischen Liberalen*. Wiesbaden: Franz Steiner Verlag. 1967.

Juergensmeyer, Mark. *Terror in the Mind of God*. Berkeley: University of California Press. 2000.

Kamali, Mohammad Hashim. *Shari'ah Law: An Introduction*. Oxford: Oneworld Book. 2008.

El-Karanshawi, Shaima. "Egypt Court Approves Moderate Islamic Party." *Al-Masri al-Yawm*. February 19, 2011.

El-Kashef, Injy. "The Shrine Affair." *Al-Ahram Weekly*. No. 1042. April 7–13, 2011.

Kaviraj, Sudipta. "An Outline of a Revisionist Theory of Modernity." *European Journal of Sociology* 46:3. 2005:497–526.

Keddie, Nikki R. *Sayyid Jamal ad-Din* [sic] *"al-Afghani": A Political Biography*. Berkeley: University of California Press. 1972.

Kedourie, Elie *Afghani and 'Abduh: An Essay on Religious Unbelief and Political Activism in Modern Islam*. London: Frank Cass. 1966.

Kelsay, John. *Arguing the Just War in Islam*. Cambridge, MA: Harvard University Press. 2007.

Kenney, Jeffrey T. *Muslim Rebels: Kharijites and the Politics of Extremism in Egypt*. New York: Oxford University Press. 2006.

Kepel, Gilles. *Muslim Extremism in Egypt: The Prophet and the Pharaoh*. Jon Rothschild, trans. Originally *Le Prophète et Pharaon*. Paris: Editions La Déouverte. 1984. Berkeley: University of California Press. 1993.

Kerr, Malcolm H. *Islamic Reform: The Political and Legal Theories of Muhammad 'Abduh and Rashid Rida*. Berkeley, University of California Press. 1966.

Khadduri, Majid. *War and Peace in the Law of Islam*. Baltimore: Johns Hopkins University Press. 1955.

Al-Khalili, Jim. *The House of Wisdom: How Arabic Science Saved Ancient Knowledge and Gave Us the Renaissance*. New York: Penguin Press. 2011.

Al-Khalidi, Salah 'Abd al-Fattah. *Sayyid Qutb al-Shahid al-Hayy* (Sayyid Qutb: The Living Martyr). Amman: Maktabat al-Aqsa. 1981.

Al-Khalidi, Salah 'Abd al-Fattah. *Amrika min al-Dakhil bi Manzar Sayyid Qutb* (America from Within: The View of Sayyid Qutb). Jidda: Dar al-Manara. 1985.

Al-Khalidi, Salah 'Abd al-Fattah. *Sayid Qutb min al-Milad ila al-Istishhad*. (Sayid Qutb from His Birth to His Martyrdom). Damascus: Dar al-Qalam. 1994.

Khatab, Sayed. *The Political Thought of Sayyid Qutb: The Theory of* Jahiliyyah. London: Routledge. 2006.

Khatab, Sayed. *The Power of Sovereignty: The Political and Ideological Philosophy of Sayyid Qutb.* London: Routledge. 2006.

Khouri, Mounah Abdallah. *Poetry and the Making of Modern Egypt (1882–1922)*. Leiden. E. J. Brill. 1971.

Kirkpatrick, David B. "Egypt Elections Expose Division in Muslim Brotherhood." *New York Times*. June 30, 2011.

Kirkpatrick, David D. and David E. Sanger. "A Tunisian-Egyptian Link That Shook Arab History." *New York Times*. February 14, 2011.

Kuran, Timur. *Islam and Mammon: The Economic Predicaments of Islamism*. Princeton: Princeton University Press. 2004.

Lackey, Douglas. *The Ethics of War and Peace*. Englewood Cliffs: Prentice-Hall. 1989.

Lanson, Gustave. "La Methode de l'histoire littéraire" (Manhaj al-Bahth fi al-Adab wa al-Lugha; Research Methods in Literature and Language). In *al-Naqd al-Manhaji 'and al-Arab* (Critique of Methodology among the Arabs). Cairo: Dar Nahdat Misr li al-Taba'a wa al-Nashr (Egyptian Renaissance Company for Printing and Publishing). 1972. Originally published Beirut: 1946.

Lawrence, Bruce. *Defenders of God: The Fundamentalist Revolt against the Modern Age*. Columbia: University of South Carolina Press. 1989.

Lia, Brynjar. *The Society of the Muslim Brothers in Egypt: The Rise of an Islamic Mass Movement, 1928–1942*. Reading, UK: Ithaca Press. 1998.

Lindholm, Charles. "Quandaries of Command in Egalitarian Societies: Examples from Swat and Morocco." In Juan R. I. Cole, ed. *Comparing Muslim Societies: Knowledge and the State in a World Civilization*. Ann Arbor: University of Michigan Press. 1992.

Maged, Amani. "Not without Squabbles." *Al-Ahram Weekly*. No. 1046. May 5–11, 2011a.

Maged, Amani. "Salafism (*sic*): The Unknown Quantity." *Al-Ahram Weekly*. No. 1047. May 12–18, 2011b.

Mandur, Muhammad. "Pygmalion wa al-Asatir fi al-Adab" (Pygmalion and Myths in Literature). In *Fi al-Mizan al-Jadid* (New Balance). Cairo: Maktabit Lagnat al-Ta'lif. 1944a.

Mandur, Muhammad. "Al-Shi'r al-Katabi" (Written Poetry). In *Fi al-Mizan al-Jadid* (New Balance). Cairo: Maktabit Lagnat al-Ta'lif. 1944b.

Mandur, Muhammad. *Fi al-Adab wa al-Naqd* (Literature and Criticism). Cairo: Maktabit Lagnat al-Ta'lif. 1949.

Marsden, George. *Understanding Fundamentalism and Evangelicalism*. Grand Rapids, MI: William B. Eerdmans. 1991.

Marsot, Afaf Lutfi al-Sayyid. *Egypt's Liberal Experiment: 1922–1936*. Berkeley: University of California Press. 1972.

Martin, Richard C. and Mark R. Woodward. *Defenders of Reason in Islam*. Oxford: Oneworld. 1997.

Marty, Martin E. and R. Scott Appleby. *The Glory and the Power: The Fundamentalist Challenge to the Modern World*. Boston: Beacon Press. 1992.

May, Larry. *War Crimes and Just War*. Cambridge: Cambridge University Press. 2007.

Mayers, Kenneth S. "Apollo: Arab-language Literary Magazine, 1932–1934." *Encyclopedia of the Modern Middle East*. Vol. 1. Reeva S. Simon, Philip Mattar, Richard W. Bulliet, eds. New York: Macmillan Reference; Simon & Schuster Macmillan. 1996.

Meneley, Anne. *Tournaments of Value: Sociability and Hierarchy in a Yemeni Town*. Toronto: University of Toronto Press. 1996.

El-Messiri, Sawsan. *Ibn al-Balad: A Concept of Egyptian Identity*. Leiden: E. J. Brill. 1978,

Mitchell, Richard P. *The Society of the Muslim Brothers*. Oxford: Oxford University Press. 1969.

"Mohamed Badei: Hardliner Lives Up to His Image." *Al-Ahram Weekly*. No. 1029. December 30–January 3, 2010–2011.

Mottahedeh, Roy. *The Mantle of the Prophet: Religion and Politics in Iran*. New York: Pantheon Books. 1985.

Mumford, Lewis. *The City in History: Its Origins, Its Transformations, and Its Prospects*. New York: Harcourt, Brace and World. 1961.

Murphy, Robert and Leonard Kasdan. "The Structure of Parallel Cousin Marriage." *American Anthropologist* 61. 1959: 117–129.

Musallam, Adnan A. *Sayyid Qutb: The Emergence of the Islamicist, 1939–1950*. Jerusalem: Palestinian Academic Society for the Study of International Affairs. 1990.

Musallam, Adnan A. *From Secularism to Jihad: Sayyid Qutb and the Foundations of Radical Islam*. Westport, CT: Praeger. 2005.

El-Nahhas, Mona. "Three Decades On." *Al-Ahram Weekly*. No. 1039. March 17–23, 2001.

Nasr, Seyyed Vali Reza. "Sayyid Abu al-A'la Mawdudi." In *Oxford Encyclopedia of the Modern Islamic World*. Vol. 3. John L. Esposito, ed. New York: Oxford University Press. 1995: 71–75.

Nassar, Galal. "Down the Salafi Road." *Al-Ahram Weekly*. No. 1027. December 16–22, 2010.

Nelson, Benjamin. *The Idea of Usury: From Tribal Brotherhood to Universal Otherhood*. Chicago: University of Chicago Press. 1969.

Newall, Paul. "Historiographic Objectivity." In *A Companion to the Philosophy of History and Historiography*. Aliezer Tucker, ed. Oxford: Blackwell. 2009. 172–180.

Nkrumah, Gamal. "Copts on the Beat." *Al-Ahram Weekly*. No. 1047. May 12–18, 2011.

Noonan, John T. Jr. *The Scholastic Analysis of Usury*. Cambridge, MA: Harvard University Press. 1957.

Novick, Peter. *That Noble Dream: The "Objectivity Question" and the American Historical Profession*. Cambridge: Cambridge University Press. 1988.

Nutting, Anthony. *Nasser*. New York: E. P. Dutton. 1972.

al-Omran, Nayel Musa. "Rashid Rida's Efforts in Calling for Muslim Unity and Political Reform." *Journal of Islam in Asia* 6:1. July 2009. 149–166.

Ostle, R. C. "Iliya Abu Madi and Arabic Poetry in the Inter-war Period." In *Studies in Modern Arabic Literature*. R. C. Ostle, ed. London: Aris and Phillips. 1975.

Patai, Raphael. *The Arab Mind*. New York: Scribner. 1973; New York: Hatherleigh Press. 2002.

Perry, Tom and Sarah Mikhail. "New Party Shows Deep Political Change in New Egypt." *Reuters*. February 19, 2011.

Poulantzas, Nicos. "Introduction." In *Classes in Contemporary Capitalism*. David Fernbach, trans. London: Verso Press. 1974.

Prakash, Gyan. "Writing Post-Orientalist Histories of the Third World: Perspectives from Indian Historiography." *Comparative Study of Society and History* 32:2. April 1990: 383–408.

Qutb, Sayyid. "Al-Dalala al-Nafsiyya li al-Alfaz wa al-Tarakib al-'Arabiyya" (The Psychological Indication of Arabic Expressions and Structures). *Sahifat Dar al-'Ulum* 4:3. January 1938a: 23–36.

Qutb, Sayyid. "Bayna al-'Aqqad wa al-Rafi'i" (Between al-'Aqqad and al-Rafi'i). *Al-Risala* 6:201. April 25, 1938b: 692–694.

Qutb, Sayyid. "Al-Ghina' al-Marid Yanghur al-Khuluq wa al-Mujtama'a al-Misri" (Sick Singing Strikes at Egypt's Nature and Society). *Al-Risala* 8: 374. September 1940: 1382–1384.

Qutb, Sayyid. "Al-Qahira al-Khadda'a" (Cairo the Deceiver). *Al-Shu'un al-Ijtima'iyya* (Social Affairs) 5. May 1941: 30–33.

Qutb, Sayyid. "Al-Muqaddasat al-Insaniyya wa al-Qawmiyya" (Humanistic and National Holies). *Al-Shu'un al-Ijtima'iyya* (Social Affairs) 11. 1942: 32–36.

Qutb, Sayyid. "Kifah Tiba" (The Struggle for Thebes). *Al-Risala* 12:587. October 2, 1944: 89–92.

Qutb, Sayyid. "'Adalu Baramijkum." (The Justice of Your Programs). *Al-Risala* 13: 627. July 9, 1945: 723–724.

Qutb, Sayyid. "Mantiq al-Dima' al-Bariya' fi Yawm al-Jala'" (The Logic of Innocent Homicide on Evacuation Day). *Al-Risala* 14:661. March 4, 1946a: 238–239.

Qutb, Sayyid. "Min Laghwi al-Sayf: Sarasir." (From the Chitchat of Summer: Cockroaches). *Al-Risala* 14:683. August 5, 1946b: 856–868

Qutb, Sayyid. "Min Laghwi al-Sayf: Suq al-Raqiq." (From the Chitchat of Summer: The Slave Market). *Al-Risala* 14:685. August 19, 1946c: 911–912.

Qutb, Sayyid. "Qiyadatuna al-Ruhiyya" (Our Spiritual Leadership). *Al-Risala* 15:705. January 6, 1947a: 27–29.

Qutb, Sayyid. "'Udu' ila al-Sharq" (Hostility toward the East). *Al-'Alam al-'Arabi* (The Arab World) 1: 2. 1947a: 3–4.

Qutb, Sayyid. "Ra'y fi al-Shi'r bi Munasabat Luzumiyat Mukhaymar" (My Opinion of Poetry on the Occasions of [Ahmad] Mukhaymar's "Luzumyat" [Irregular Verse]). *Al-Kitab* (The Book) 3:2. February 1948: 248–249.

Qutb, Sayyid. "Amrika allati Ra'ayt fi Mizan al-Qiyam al-Insaniyya" (The America Which I Saw in the Balance [or Scale] of Human Existence). *Al-Risala* 19:959. November 19, 1951: 1301–1306.

Qutb, Sayyid. *Al-Islam wa Mushkilat al-Hadara* (Islam and the Problems of Civilization). Cairo: Dar Ihya' al-Kutub al-'Arabiya. 1962.

Qutb, Sayyid. *Al-Taswir al-Fanni fi al-Qur'an* (Artistic Imagery in the Qur'an). Cairo: Dar al-Ma'arif. 1963. Originally published Cairo: Dar al-Shuruq. 1945.

Qutb, Sayyid. *Limadha A'dummuni* (Why Did They Execute Me?). Jidda: al-Sharika al-Sa'udiyya li al-Abhath wa al-Taswiq (Saudi Partners for Research and Marketing). 1965.

Qutb, Sayyid. *Dirasat Islamiyya* (Islamic Studies). Cairo: Dar al-Fath. 1953. Reprinted 1967.

Qutb, Sayyid. *Ma'rakat al-Islam wa al-Ra'smaliyya* (The Battle of Islam and Capitalism). Originally published Cairo: 1951c. Cairo: Dar al-Shuruq. 1975.

Qutb, Sayyid. *Ma'alim fi al-Tariq* (Signposts on the Road, but also translated as Milestones). Al-Salimiya, Kuwait: Al-Ittihad al-Islami al-'Alami li al-Munazzamat al-Tullabiya (International Islamic Federation of Student Organizations). 1978a.

Qutb, Sayyid. *Fi Zilal al-Qur'an*. 7th ed. Cairo: Dar al-Shuruq. 1978b.

Qutb, Sayyid. *Ma'rakatna ma'a al-Yahud* (Our Battle with the Jews). In *Past Trials and Present Tribulations: A Muslim Fundamentalist View of the Jews*. Ronald Nettler, ed. (ca. early 1950s). Oxford: Pergamon Press. 1987. 72–89.

Qutb, Sayyid. *Al-Salam al-'Alami wa al-Islam* (Islam and Universal Peace). Plainfield, IN: American Trust Publications. 1993a. Originally published in Cairo: Maktabat Wahbah. 1951.

Qutb, Sayyid. *Mashahid al-Qiyama fi al-Qur'an* (Scenes of Resurrection in the Qur'an). Cairo: Dar al-Shuruq. Originally published: 1947b. 11th ed. published in 1993b.

Qutb, Sayyid, *Islamic Lessons*. Cairo: Dar al-Shuruq. 1993c.

Qutb, Sayyid. *Al-'Adala al-Ijtima'iyya fi al-Islam* (Social Justice in Islam). Cairo: Maktabat Misr. 1949. Reprint, Oneonta, NY: Islamic Publications International. 2000.

Qutb, Sayyid. *Tifl min al-Qarya* (A Child from the Village). John Calvert and William Shepard, trans. Syracuse: Syracuse University Press. 2004. Originally published 1946.

Qutb, Sayyid. "Introduction." Sayyed Abul Hasan 'Ali al-Nadwi [sic]. *Islam and the World: The Rise and Decline of Muslims and Its Effect on Mankind*. (Originally entitled *Madha Khasira al-'Alam bi Inhitat al-Muslims* and in English: What the World Lost as a Result of the Decline of Muslims). Muhammad Asif Kidwai, trans. Leicestser, UK: UK Islamic Academy. 2005.

Qutb, Sayyid. *Muqawwimat al-Tasawwur al-Islami* (Basic Principles of the Islamic Worldview). Rami David, trans. North Halcedon, NJ: Islamic Publications International. 2006.

Rady, Faiza. "A Victory for the Workers." *Al-Ahram Weekly*. No. 892. April 10–16, 2008.

Rashwan, Diaa et al. "'Abd al-Qadir ibn 'Abd al-'Aziz: The Writings of a Leader of the Jihadi School." In *The Spectrum of Islamist Movements*, section III, ch. 2. Diaa Rashwan, ed. Al-Ahram Center for Political and Strategic Studies. Cairo: 2006. Berlin: Verlag Hans Schiler. 2007. 403–448.

Rashwan, Diaa et al. "The Intellectual Revisionism of the Jama'a al-Islamiyya's 'Revised Concepts' Series." In *The Spectrum of Islamist Movements*, section II, ch. 5. Diaa Rashwan, ed. Al-Ahram Center for Political and Strategic Studies. Cairo: 2006. Berlin: Verlag Hans Schiler. 2007. 313–370.

Rashwan, Diaa, et al. "Qaedat al-Jihad." In *The Spectrum of Islamist Movements*, section I, ch. 1. Diaa Rashwan, ed. Al-Ahram Center for Political and Strategic Studies. Cairo: 2006. Berlin: Verlag Hans Schiler. 2007. 25–55.

Rashwan, Diaa et al. "What Remains of the Egyptian Jihad?" In *The Spectrum of Islamist Movements*, section I, ch. 2. Diaa Rashwan, ed. Al-Ahram Center for Political and Strategic Studies. Cairo: 2006. Berlin: Verlag Hans Schiler. 2007. 57–75.

Reid, Donald M. *Cairo University and the Making of Modern Egypt*. Cambridge: Cambridge University Press. 1990.

Reid, Donald M. "The 'Urabi Revolution and the British Conquest, 1879–1882." *The Cambridge History of Egypt*. M. W. Daly, ed. Vol. 2: *Modern Egypt, from 1517 to the End of the Twentieth Century*. New York: Cambridge University Press. 1998.

Riesebrodt, Martin. *Pious Passion: The Emergence of Modern Fundamentalism in the United States and Iran*. Don Reneau, trans. Berkeley: University of California Press. 1993 [1990].

Rodinson, Maxime. *Islam and Capitalism*. Brian Pearce, trans. Austin: University of Texas Press. 1978.

Rosen, Larry. "The Negotiation of Reality: Male-Female Relations in Sefrou, Morocco." In *Women in the Muslim World*. Lois Beck and Nikki Keddie, eds. Cambridge, MA: Harvard University Press. 1978. 561–584.

Sacks, Karen. "Engels Revisited: Women, the Organization of Production and Private Property." In *Toward an Anthropology of Women*. Rayna Reiter, ed. New York: Monthly Review Press. 1975.

Safran, Nadav. *Egypt in Search of Political Community: An Analysis of the Intellectual and Political Evolution of Egypt, 1804–1952*. Cambridge, MA: Harvard University Press. 1961.

Said, Edward. *Orientalism*. New York: Vintage Books. 1979.

Said, Edward. *Covering Islam: How the Media and the Experts Determine How We See the Rest of the World*. New York: Vintage Books. 1997.

Sallam, Muhammad Zaghlul. *Al-Naqd al-`Arabi al-Hadith: Usuluhu, Qadayahu, Manhijuhu* (Modern Arabic Criticism: Its Origins, Issues, and Methods). Cairo: Maktabat al-Anjlu al-Misriyah (Anglo-Egyptian Bookstore). 1964.

El-Sayed, Mohamed. "Unanswered Questions." *Al-Ahram Weekly*. No. 1003. June 17–23, 2010.

El-Sayed, Mohamed. "The Fallout." *Al-Ahram Weekly*. No. 1004. June 24–30, 2010.

El-Sayed, Mohamed. "The Cost of Torture." *Al-Ahram Weekly*. No. 1006. July 8–14, 2010.

Schacht, Joseph. *An Introduction to Islamic Law*. Oxford: Clarendon Press. 1964.

Schonfield, Hugh J. *The Passover Plot: New Light on the History of Jesus*. New York: Bantam Books. 1965.

Semah, David. *Four Egyptian Literary Critics*. Leiden: E. J. Brill. 1974.

Shahin, Emad Eldin. *Through Muslim Eyes: M. Rashid Rida and the West*. Herndon, Va.:International Institute of Islamic Thought. 1993.

Al-Shatti, Isma'il. "Ma' al-Shahid Sayyid Qutb" (With the Martyr, Sayyid Qutb). *Al-Mujtama'a* (Society). Kuwait: No. 215. August 27, 1974.

Shepard, William E. "The Development of the Thought of Sayyid Qutb as Reflected in Earlier and Later Editions of 'Social Justice in Islam.'" *Die Welt Des Islams* 32: 2. 1992.

Shepard, William E. *Sayyid Qutb and Islamic Activism: A Translation and Critical Analysis of Social Justice in Islam*. Leiden: E. J. Brill. 1996.

Shepard, William E. "Sayyid Qutb's Doctrine of Jahiliyya." *International Journal of Middle East Studies* 35:4. November 2003.

Shukrallah, Salma. "Muslim Brotherhood Dismisses Two of Its Members, Interrogates Others." *Al-Ahram Online*. July 17, 2011.

Siddiqui, Mohammed Moinuddin. "An Outline of Sayyed [sic] Qutb's Life." In Sayyid Qutb. *Islam and Universal Peace*. Plainfield, IN: American Trust Publications. 1993.

Sivan, Emmanuel. *Radical Islam: Medieval Theology and Modern Politics*. New Haven: Yale University Press. 1985.

Smith, Charles D. "The 'Crisis of Orientation': The Shift of Egyptian Intellectual to Islamic Subjects in the 1930's." *International Journal of Middle East Studies* 4. 1973: 382–410.

Smith, Charles D. *Islam and the Search for Social Order in Modern Egypt: A Biography of Muhammad Husayn Haykal*. Albany: State University of New York Press. 1983.

Smith, Charles D. "'Imagined Identities, Imagined Nationalisms: Print Culture and Egyptian nationalism in Light of Recent Scholarship.' A Review Essay of Israel Gershoni and James

P. Jankowski. *Redefining the Egyptian Nation*, 1930–1945. Cambridge Middle East Studies (New York: Cambridge University Press, 1995). 297." *International Journal of Middle East Studies* 29. 1997: 607–622.

Smith, Charles D. "'Cultural Constructs' and Other Fantasies: Imagined Narratives in *Imagined Communities*; Surrejoinder to Gershoni and Jankowski's 'Print Culture, Social Change, and the Process of Redefining Imagined Communities in Egypt.'" *International Journal of Middle East Studies* 31. 1999: 95–102.

Soage, Ana Belén. "Rashid Rida's Legacy." *The Muslim World* 98. January 2008: 1–23.

Southgate, Beverley. "Postmodernism." In *A Companion to the Philosophy of History and Historiography*. Aliezer Tucker, ed. Oxford: Blackwell. 2009. 540–549.

Stadiem, William. *Too Rich: The High Life and Tragic Death of King Farouk*. New York: Carroll and Graf. 1991.

Sullivan, Denis J. *Private Voluntary Organizations in Egypt: Islamic Development, Private Initiative, and State Control*. Gainesville: University Press of Florida. 1994.

Swedenburg, Ted. *Memories of Revolt: The 1936–1939 Rebellion and the Palestinian National Past*. Fayetteville: University of Arkansas Press. 2003.

Tammam, Hossam. "Not Your Average Crackdown." *Al-Ahram Weekly*. No. 986. February 18–24, 2010.

Tammam, Hossam. "Models for an Islamist Political Party." *Al-Ahram Weekly*. No. 1039. March 17–23, 2011.

Tammam, Hossam and Patrick Haenni. "Islam in the Insurrection?" *Al-Ahram Weekly*. No. 1037. March 3–9, 2011.

Tarek, Sherif. "Islamists Win 70 Percent of Egypt People's Assembly Party List Seats." *Al-Ahram Online*, January 21, 2012. http://english.ahram.org.eg/NewsContent/33/100/32287/Elections-/News/Islamists-win—of-Egypt-Peoples-Assembly-party-lis.aspx.

Tawney, Richard H. *Religion and the Rise of Capitalism*. London: John Murray. 1926. Reprinted London: Hesperides Press, 2008.

Thompson, Edward P. *Making of the English Working Class*. New York: Vintage Books. 1966.

Tignor, Robert L. *Modernization and British Colonial Rule in Egypt, 1882–1914*. Princeton: Princeton University Press. 1966.

Tilly, Charles. "Chapter 2: Theories and Descriptions of Collective Action." In *From Mobilization to Revolution*. Reading, MA: Addison-Wesley. 1978.

Tiryakian, Edward A. "The Sociological Import of a Metaphor: Tracking the Source of Max Weber's 'Iron Cage.'" *Sociological Inquiry* 51:1. January 1981: 27–33.

Tolan, John V. *Saracens: Islam in the Medieval European Imagination*. New York: Columbia University Press. 2002.

Toth, James. "Pride, Purdah or Paychecks: What Maintains the Gender Division of Labor in Rural Egypt." *International Journal of Middle East Studies* 23:2. May 1991: 213–236.

Toth, James. "Local Islam Gone Global: The Roots of Religious Militancy in Egypt and Its Transnational Transformation." In *Global Social Movements: A Reader*. June Nash, ed. Oxford: Blackwell. 2004.

Tripp, Charles. *Islam and the Moral Economy: The Challenge of Capitalism*. Cambridge: Cambridge University Press. 2006.

Tucker, Judith. *Women in Nineteenth Century Egypt*. Cambridge: Cambridge University Press. 1985.

Ushama, Thameem. *Hasan al-Banna: Vision and Mission*. Kuala Lumpur: A.S. Noordeen. 1995.

Wallace, Anthony F.C. "Revitalization Movements." *American Anthropologist* 58:2. 1956: 264–281.

Walzer, Michael. *Just and Unjust Wars: A Moral Argument with Historical Illustrations*. New York: Basic Books. 1977.

Walzer, Michael. *Arguing about War*. New Haven: Yale University Press. 2004.

Waterbury, John. *Egypt: Burdens of the Past, Options for the Future*. Bloomington: Indiana University Press and the American Universities Field Staff. 1978.

Weaver, Mary Anne. *A Portrait of Egypt: A Journey through the World of Militant Islam*. New York: Farrar, Straus and Giroux. 2000.

Weber, Max. *Protestant Ethic and the Spirit of Capitalism.* New York: Routledge. 2002.

White, Hayden. *Metahistory: The Historical Imagination of 19th Century Europe.* Baltimore: Johns Hopkins University Press. 1973.

Wilmington, Martin. "Aspects of Moneylending in Northern Sudan." *Middle East Journal* 9:2. Spring 1955: 139–146.

Wolf, Eric R. "The Social Organization of Mecca and the Origins of Islam." *Southwest Journal of Anthropology* 7. Winter 1951:329–356.

Wolf, Eric R. *Peasants.* Englewood Cliffs, NJ: Prentice-Hall. 1966.

Wright, Lawrence. *The Looming Tower: Al-Qaeda and the Road to 9/11.* New York: Knopf. 2006.

Wright, Robin. *Dreams and Shadows: The Future of the Middle East.* London: Penguin Press. 2008.

Zaman, Muhammad Qasim. "Arabic, the Arab Middle East, and the Definitions of Muslim Identity in Twentieth Century India." *Journal of the Royal Asiatic Society* 8:1. April 1988: 59–81.

Zernike, Kate. "Detainees Describe Abuses by Guard in Iraq Prison." *New York Times.* January 12, 2005.

INDEX

'Abbasids, 228, 229

'Abd al-Nassir, Jamal, 63, 74, 76–80, 87–90, 139, 174–75

'Abd al-Rahman, 'Umar, 233, 240

'Abd al-Raziq, 'Ali, 6, 21, 165, 273, **293**, 333

'Abduh, Muhammad, 45, 71, 91, 99, 110, 164, 168, 187, 199, 203, 244–45, **251–53**, 256, 257, 259, 261, 270–73, 276. *See also* Grandfathers of Islamism

Abraham (prophet), 131, 161, 194, 216

Abu Bakr, al-Siddiq, **223–27**

Abu Shadi, Ahmad Zaki, 23–24, 30, **254–55**. *See also* Apollo School of Poetry

Al-Afghani, Jamal al-Din, 45, 51, 71, 73, 91, 99, 164, 169, 203, 244, 251–53, **256–58**, 261, 271–73. *See also* Grandfathers of Islamism

Akif, Mahdi, 240–41

Alexandria, 40, 79, 237, 241, 245, 252, 254–55, 353, 355, 359

Alexandria University, 255, 265, 266

America, 3, 7, 8, 11, 13, 50, 99, 102, 114, 133, 138, 164, 165, 167, 185, 193, 207, 209, 233, 242, 277, 285, 256

    criticism of, 50–51, 65–69, 73, 75, 87, 99, 102, 114, 126, 185, 209, 231, 256, 280

    Greeley, Colorado, 65–68, 308, 310

    New York City, 213, 35, 58, 64, 66, 68, 233, 254, 294, 310, 349

    return from, 16, 58, 63, 65, 69, 72, 206

    trip to, 13, 16, 38, 44, 50, 58, 63, **64–69**, 75, 280

    Washington, D.C., 65–68, 308–9, 349

Apollo School of Poetry, 20, 23–24, 30, 36, **254–55,** 291, 294, 296

Apologetics, 4, 5, 7, 11, 33, 54, 68, 86, 153–55, 207–8, 212, 260, **282–84**

Apostasy, 6, 10, 14, 71, 84, 102, 108, 116, 125, 127, 146, 150, 157, 168, 178, 193, 202–3, 219, 233, 235, 273, 293, 312, 328, 391, 331, 350

April 6th Movement, 241, 247, 352

Al-'Aqqad, 'Abbas, 16–25, 28–30, 33–34, 36, 41–44, 49, 55, 254–55, **258–61**, 267, 290–94, 296,

299, 311, 316, 324. *See also* Diwan School of Poetry

Arabism, 28, 31–33, 35, 37, 219

Artistic Imagery in the Qur'an (Qutb), 6, **45–48**, 49, 62, 301

Asceticism, 60, 100, 117, 182–83, 227, 345

Ash'arism, 110, 112, 312, 321

Atheism and godlessness, 30, 68, 86, 96, 114, 125, 128, 130, 146, 167, 176, 209, 230, 297

Al-Ayyam (Days), 52–53, 288, 303

Al-Azhar, 12–13, 15, 27, 28, 120, 174–75, 208, 251, 253, 257, 262, 264–65, 272, **287**, 289, 316, 319, 337, 340, 351

Badi'a, Muhammad, 240–42, 245, 247

Al-Banna, Hasan, 9, 13, 31, 32, 34, 44, 65, 71, 74, 75, 76, 91, 99, 157, 164, 203, 245, 246, 256, **261–64**, 298, 304, 319, 328, 330. *See also* Grandfathers of Islamism

The Battle of Islam and Capitalism (Qutb), 57, 304, 313

Bay'a (Oath of Allegiance), 140, 141, 195–96, 349

Beacon. *See Al-Manar*

Berman, Paul, 3–4

Bin Ladin, Usama, 233, 328, **349**

Blocking of the means (*Sadd al-Dhara'i*). *See* Dynamic law

Britain, 16, 44, 165, 185, 254, 258

    collaboration and, 44, 54, 73

    colonialism and, 16, 17, 31, 37, 39, 43, 50–51, 56, 69, 74, 78, 169, 198–99, 212, 246, 252–53, 256–58, 262–63, 268–69, 272–74, 280

    treaties and, 16, 37, 74, 77–79, 199, 263

Cairo, 10–25, 33–41, 43, 53, 56, 69, 73–76, 89–90, 211, 236–41, 245, 251–56, 261–65, 268, 270–72

Cairo University, 27, 237, 253, 264–66, 289, 290, 293, 295, 322, 353

Caliphs and the caliphate, 32, 133, 135, 137, 169, 193–97, 199, 212, 217, 222–29, 268–69, 273, 306–7, 342–43, 348